MW00612772

Investment Risk Management

Investment Risk Management

EDITED BY H. KENT BAKER

and

GREG FILBECK

OXFORD
UNIVERSITY PRESS

Oxford University Press is a department of the University of Oxford.
It furthers the University's objective of excellence in research, scholarship,
and education by publishing worldwide.

Oxford   New York
Auckland   Cape Town   Dar es Salaam   Hong Kong   Karachi
Kuala Lumpur   Madrid   Melbourne   Mexico City   Nairobi
New Delhi   Shanghai   Taipei   Toronto

With offices in
Argentina   Austria   Brazil   Chile   Czech Republic   France   Greece
Guatemala   Hungary   Italy   Japan   Poland   Portugal   Singapore
South Korea   Switzerland   Thailand   Turkey   Ukraine   Vietnam

Oxford is a registered trade mark of Oxford University Press
in the UK and certain other countries.

Published in the United States of America by
Oxford University Press
198 Madison Avenue, New York, NY 10016

© Oxford University Press 2015

Library of Congress Cataloging-in-Publication Data
Investment risk management / edited by H. Kent Baker and Greg Filbeck.
    p.   cm. — (Financial markets and investments series)
  Includes bibliographical references and index.
  ISBN 978–0–19–933196–3 (alk. paper)
1. Investments. 2. Risk. 3. Financial risk. 4. Portfolio management. I. Baker, H. Kent (Harold Kent),
1944– II. Filbeck, Greg.
  HG4521.I4229 2015
  332.6—dc23
                        2014024764

9   8   7   6   5   4   3   2   1

Printed in the United States of America on acid-free paper

Contents

Part One   FOUNDATIONS OF RISK MANAGEMENT

Part Two   TYPES OF RISK

Part Four   RISK MANAGEMENT AND ASSET CLASSES

Part Five   HEDGING RISK

Part Six   GOING FORWARD

List of Figures

List of Tables

Acknowledgments

We are reminded of the following quote by the British author Peter Mayle: "Best advice on writing I've ever received. Finish." Finishing *Investment Risk Analysis* involved the collaboration of many people. As Helen Keller, once said, "Alone we can do so little; together we can do so much." We owe special gratitude to our many collaborators, especially our chapter authors. Without their willingness to share their considerable expertise and knowledge, this book would not have been possible. We greatly appreciate the assistance provided by Scott Parris, Cathryn Vaulman, and the highly professional team at Oxford University Press. We also thank Cherline Daniel, Senior Project Manager, Integra Software Services Pvt Ltd, and Claudie Peterfreund, Cover-to-Cover Indexing Services, for their excellent work. The Kogod School of Business at American University and Penn State Erie, the Behrend College also provided support. Linda and Rory Baker as well as Janis, Aaron, Kyle, and Grant Filbeck deserve special thanks for their encouragement. The authors dedicate this book to Linda Baker and Janis Filbeck.

About the Editors

H. KENT BAKER is a University Professor of Finance in the Kogod School of Business at American University. Professor Baker is an author or editor of 23 books including *Investor Behavior—The Psychology of Financial Planning and Investing, Market Microstructure of Emerging and Developed Markets, Behavioral Finance—Investors, Corporations, and Markets, Portfolio Theory and Management,* and *Survey Research in Corporate Finance.* As one of the most prolific finance academics, he has published more than 150 refereed articles in such journals as the *Journal of Finance, Journal of Financial and Quantitative Analysis, Financial Management, Financial Analysts Journal,* and *Journal of Portfolio Management.* He has consulting and training experience with more than 100 organizations. Professor Baker holds a BSBA from Georgetown University; M.Ed., MBA, and DBA degrees from the University of Maryland; and an MA, MS, and two PhDs from American University. He also holds CFA and CMA designations.

GREG FILBECK holds the Samuel P. Black III Professor of Finance and Risk Management at Penn State Erie, the Behrend College and serves as Associate Director for the Black School of Business and Department Chair for Finance & Business Economics. He formerly served as Senior Vice-President of Kaplan Schweser and held academic appointments at Miami University (Ohio) and the University of Toledo, where he served as the Associate Director of the Center for Family Business. Professor Filbeck is an author or editor of four books and has published more than 75 refereed academic journal articles that have appeared in journals such as *Financial Analysts Journal, Financial Review,* and *Journal of Business, Finance, and Accounting.* Professor Filbeck conducts consulting and training worldwide for candidates for the Chartered Financial Analyst (CFA), Financial Risk Manager (FRM™), and Chartered Alternative Investment Adviser (CAIA®) designations as well as holding all three designations. Professor Filbeck holds a BS from Murray State University, an MS from Penn State University, and a DBA from the University of Kentucky.

About the Contributors

DAVID E. ALLEN is an Adjunct Professor in the Centre for Applied Financial Studies at the University of South Australia and a Visiting Professor in the School of Mathematics and Statistics at the University of Sydney. He was previously Professor of Finance at Edith Cowan University. Professor Allen is the author of three monographs and more than 90 refereed publications on a diverse range of topics covering corporate financial policy decisions, asset pricing, business economics, funds management and performance benchmarking, volatility modeling and hedging, and market microstructure and liquidity. He has an M.Phil in the history of economic thought from the University of Leicester, an MA in economics from the University of St. Andrews, and a PhD in finance from the University of Western Australia.

HAROLD C. BARNETT is a Chicago-based economist consulting on legal and economic issues related to mortgages and mortgage markets and an adjunct professor in the Marshall Bennett Real Estate Institute at Roosevelt University. He has written on equitable mortgages and provided expert testimony on lender and securitizer responsibility for underwriting and funding fraudulent loans. He is actively involved in professional discussion of foreclosures, neighborhood impacts, and mortgage fraud in Chicago. His Building Chicago blog examines the growth and transformation of the urban core. Dr. Barnett worked in Tucson, Arizona as a mortgage broker. For most of his professional career, he was Professor of Economics at the University of Rhode Island where he published on corporate, environmental, and white-collar violations of law. He received his PhD in economics from MIT. Additional information is available at http://www.mortgagemarketconsultant.com.

PHILIPPE BERTRAND is Professor of Finance at IAE of Aix-en-Provence (Aix-Marseille University), a member of CERGAM, and adjunct professor of Finance at KEDGE Business School. Previously, he was a faculty member at the University of Montpellier 1 and head of financial engineering at CCF Capital Management. He is currently president and secretary-general of the French Finance Association (AFFI). Professor Bertrand is a frequent speaker at both academic and professional conferences such as PRMIA Risk Management Seminar. His research focuses on portfolio management, dynamic investment strategies, and performance measurement. He has published several well-known papers in the field of portfolio insurance strategies in such journals as the *Journal of Banking and Finance, Financial Analysts Journal, Geneva Risk and Insurance Review*, and *Journal of Asset Management*.

Professor Bertrand received a PhD from the University of Paris-Dauphine and a diploma in economics and econometrics from the École des Hautes Études en Sciences Sociales (EHESS).

ELIAS BOUKRAMI is a Senior Lecturer in Banking and Finance at Regent's University London. After being the Development Team Leader, he is currently the Programme Director of the MSc Oil and Gas Trade Management. He is also an invited Professor at University Jean Moulin, Lyon 3 IAE, France. Professor Boukrami is an elected member of the Regent's University Senate and an active member of the Regent's Centre for Transnational Studies. He acts as an external member of validation panels and external examiner of various U.K. higher education institutions and is a Fellow member of the Higher Education Academy and member of the Chartered Management Institute. His core area of research includes financial derivatives and particularly swaps contracts, energy, and investment risk issues. He has published *The History of the Algerian Banking and Financial System, from 1830 to 2012*. Professor Boukrami holds a PhD in empirical finance from the Manchester Metropolitan Business School, United Kingdom.

OTHMANE BOUKRAMI is a Senior Vice President at The Currency Exchange Fund (TCX Fund) and is responsible for pricing and valuating exchange and interest rates derivatives in emerging and frontier markets. He previously worked as a Senior Risk Officer at the African Development Bank Group from 2005 to 2009 and as Treasury Marketing Head at Citigroup from 2003 to 2005. Dr. Boukrami holds a master's degree in finance from the ICMA Centre (University of Reading) and a master's degree in banking and finance as well as a PhD in management from the University of Lyon.

M. MARTIN BOYER is the CEFA Professor of Finance and Insurance at HEC Montréal (Université de Montréal). He is the past Chairman of the Finance Department at HEC Montréal and the past editor of *Insurance and Risk Management*. He currently is an associate editor of the *Journal of Risk and Insurance* and of the *Canadian Journal of Administrative Science*. Professor Boyer has received research awards from the Casualty Actuarial Society, Bank of Canada, and American Risk and Insurance Association. He has published on a wide array of research topics in the *Journal of Risk and Insurance*, *Journal of Corporate Finance*, *Journal of Forensic Accounting*, *British Journal of Political Science*, and *Energy Economics*. He holds an MSc in economics from the Université de Montréal and an MA and a PhD from the Wharton School of the University of Pennsylvania.

MARK BRADSHAW is Associate Professor of Accounting in the Carroll School of Management at Boston College. He previously taught at the Booth School of Business, University of Chicago, and Harvard Business School. Professor Bradshaw was also an auditor at Arthur Andersen & Co. His research has been published in *The Accounting Review, Journal of Accounting and Economics, Journal of Accounting Research,* and *Review of Accounting Studies* among others. He is co-author of two books: *Financial Reporting, Financial Statement Analysis, and Valuation: A Strategic Perspective*, 7th edition, published by South-Western Cengage Learning, and *Analysts, Lies, and Statistics: Cutting through the Hype in Corporate Earnings Announcements* published by Institutional Investor Books. Professor Bradshaw received a BBA in accounting and an M.Acc. in financial accounting from University of Georgia and a PhD in accounting from the University of Michigan. He holds the Chartered Public Accountant (CPA) designation.

UDO BROLL is Professor of International Economics Emeritus at the Technische Universität Dresden, Germany, and Visiting Professor of Economics at the University of Augsburg, Germany. He held temporary professorships at the University of Munich, University of Bonn, and University of Saarbrücken before assuming his chair at Dresden. He has published numerous papers in the fields of international economics and the theory of risk management of exporting firms and financial intermediaries. His most recent papers include work on regional investment under uncertain cost of location, exchange rate hedging in a duopoly, and the impact of market transparency in risky loan markets on bank decisions. Professor Broll holds a diploma, a doctoral, and a post-doctoral (habilitation) degree from the University of Konstanz, Germany.

NICOLAS BÜRKLER is Managing Partner at SIM Research Institute Inc., a private research institute specializing in long-term maintenance of value and socioeconomic processes. He also is a researcher at the Lucerne University of Applied Sciences and Arts in the School of Business. Earlier in his career, he worked at a wealth management company where he was responsible for investment strategies. Mr. Bürkler has a master's degree in mechanical engineering from the Swiss Federal Institute of Technology (ETHZ), focusing on financial markets and complex systems. He also assisted the chair for systems design at ETHZ.

PILAR GRAU CARLES is Senior Lecturer in Economics at the Rey Juan Carlos University in Madrid, Spain, where she currently heads the Applied Economics Department at the School of Legal and Social Sciences. She teaches financial and monetary economics both at undergraduate and graduate level. Previously, she held appointments at Universidad Complutense of Madrid and in the financial industry. Professor Grau has published extensively in the areas of financial time series, long-memory, mutual fund performance, and bootstrap methodology. She has also applied similar quantitative methods in public policy settings such as immigration and education. Much of her research is empirical and published in journals such as *Computational Economics, Quantitative Finance, Physica A, Applied Economics,* and *International Migration.* She received her PhD in economics with emphasis on nonlinear financial time series from the Universidad Complutense of Madrid.

LUDWIG B. CHINCARINI is Professor of Finance in the School of Management at the University of San Francisco. He is on the academic council of IndexIQ where he helped launch the first alternative ETFs and is a special consultant to NERA, an economic consulting firm. Other positions held include the Head of Research at Rydex Global Advisors (now Guggenheim Investments) and the Head of Research and New Products at Foliofn. He also worked for the Bank for International Settlements. Professor Chincarini has consulted for hedge funds such as Templeton Capital Advisors and separate account managed platforms such as Curian Capital. He is the author of *Quantitative Equity Portfolio Management* and *The Crisis of Crowding,* a book explaining the causes of the financial crisis of 2007–2008. His articles appear in numerous finance and economics journals. He obtained a BA summa cum laude from the University of California – Berkeley and a PhD from the Massachusetts Institute of Technology.

MARTIN ČIHÁK is Advisor at the International Monetary Fund (IMF) in Washington, DC. In 2011-2013, he was at the World Bank Group, leading the World Bank's inaugural Global Financial Development Report 2013, on the role of the state in finance, and Global Financial Development Report 2014 on financial inclusion (http://www.worldbank.org/financialdevelopment). Before that, he worked at the IMF on financial sector regulation and supervision, financial stability, and financial system reforms. Dr. Čihák has covered these topics in numerous IMF/World Bank missions and a range of publications. He was one of the editors of the IMF-World Bank Financial Sector Assessment Handbook. Before joining the IMF in 2000, Dr. Čihák was a chief analyst in a commercial bank, a university lecturer, and an advisor to a minister. He has MAs in economics and law and received a PhD in economics from the Center for Economic Research and Graduate Education, Charles University, Prague. For some of his recent work, see http://www.ssrn.com/author=735014.

DIDIER COSSIN is the Director of the IMD Global Board Center, Switzerland, and Professor of Finance and Governance at IMD. He works with senior leaders and boards to provide the latest thinking on best-in-class governance, risk and opportunity optimization, investment selection, and strategy design. Professor Cossin has been an advisor to the United Nations and other international organizations, European Central Bank and other central banks, and boards or executive committees of many multinational corporations, financial institutions, and funds. His latest research focuses on uncovering and stimulating best governance practices, notably on board leadership, board strategic involvement, and active chairmanship. He has authored books as well as articles appearing in *Management Science* and other leading journals. He holds a PhD from Harvard University, is former Fulbright Scholar at MIT, and is a graduate of ENS rue d'Ulm, Sorbonne University and EHESS (France).

ASWATH DAMODARAN is a professor of finance at the Stern School of Business at New York University (NYU), where he has taught corporate finance and valuation since 1986. Before joining NYU, he taught at the University of California–Berkeley. His research interests are in corporate finance, valuation, and portfolio management. Practitioners widely use his books on valuation. He received an MBA and PhD from the University of California – Los Angeles (UCLA).

RAMON P. DEGENNARO is the CBA Professor in Banking and Finance at the University of Tennessee. He previously served as a Visiting Scholar at the Federal Reserve Banks of Atlanta and Cleveland. His current research involves financial markets, entrepreneurship, and investments. Professor DeGennaro has published more than 40 refereed articles on financial market volatility, small firm finance, the term structure of interest rates, financial institutions, and investments. His other publications include research reports, book chapters, book reviews, and several Federal Reserve publications. His research has been featured in the *Wall Street Journal*. Professor DeGennaro has been nominated for five university teaching awards. He also consults in the areas of business valuation, investments, and financial management, and has advised the U.S. House of Representatives' Science and Technology Subcommittee on the regulation of the U.S. financial system. Professor DeGennaro holds a PhD in finance from The Ohio State University.

CHANAKA P. EDIRISINGHE is the Kay and Jackson Tai '72 Chair Professor of Finance at Lally School of Management, Rensselaer Polytechnic Institute, NY. Before that he was the Heath Fellow in Business at the University of Tennessee, Knoxville. He has held visiting positions at Chinese University in Beijing, University of Canterbury, New Zealand, and Kansai University, Japan. He has published extensively in operations research and finance focusing on portfolio optimization, risk management, arbitrage pricing of derivatives, and firm strength analysis. He received the prestigious Citation of Excellence Award by Emerald Management Reviews in 2009 for his work on relative firm strength using data envelopment analysis. Professor Edirisinghe also received the 2010 Sarah Alice and Tommy Bronson Outstanding Researcher Award at College of Business, University of Tennessee. He is the former Vice Chair of Financial Services Section of INFORMS. He serves as a consultant to several organizations and he developed the financial trading strategy optimizer and simulator software, Mi$OFT. Professor Edirisinghe holds a PhD in management science from University of British Columbia, Canada.

GREGG FISHER, CFA, CFP, is the Founder and Chief Investment Officer of Gerstein Fisher, an independent investment management and advisory firm in New York City that he founded in 1993. He was a pioneer in introducing fee-based planning and asset class investing to individuals. Mr. Fisher was named to Barron's list of Top 100 Financial Advisors in both 2011 and 2012 and to the Top 1,000 Financial Advisors list in 2011. He is a member of Vistage International, which specializes in executive leadership development and CEO coaching, and also the Young Presidents' Organization. Mr. Fisher holds a degree in finance from the State University of New York at Buffalo and obtained a certificate in financial planning from New York University and also studied at the University of Pittsburgh's Center for Fiduciary Studies.

FELIX GASSER, MFTA, is a Portfolio Manager at FRM/Man Group in Switzerland and manages $2 billion in client portfolios for managed futures and global macro portfolios. He previously served as Head of Managed Futures HF Research at RMF and was in charge of manager selection and due diligence. Mr. Gasser started his career as a futures and physical cocoa and sugar trader and joined the CTA AHL as a trader during their pioneer years in the early 1990s. He also served as a Quantitative Hedge Fund Analyst at Credit Suisse Private Banking and a Product Manager of TradeStation at Dow Jones Switzerland and a Principal in a venture to set up Atree Capital, a start-up systematic CTA. Mr. Gasser studied economics at the University of Zurich.

FRANCA GLENZER is a PhD candidate in finance at Goethe University Frankfurt. Her research interests include behavioral insurance and decision processes in finance. She holds an M.Sc. in insurance and risk management from Humboldt University Berlin.

HUNTER M. HOLZHAUER is an Assistant Professor of Finance at the University of Tennessee at Chattanooga, and has taught both graduate and undergraduate courses in corporate finance, portfolio management, and derivatives. His financial industry experience includes positions as a credit analyst with Colonial Bank and a financial planner and fixed-income portfolio manager with AmSouth Bank. Professor Holzhauer's research interests primarily focus on new and alternative strategies involving investment risk management. He received a BS in business administration and bio-psychology from Birmingham-Southern College, an MBA from Mississippi State University, and a PhD from the University of Alabama.

CLAUS HUBER, CEFA, CFA, FRM, has been running Rodex Risk Advisers, a risk management consultancy since June 2010. Some topics covered by the firm include tail risk insurance, inflation and deflation protection, and market and operational risk. The Rodex Purchasing Power Protection Indices, an investment solution to protect against inflation and deflation, won the Swiss Derivative Award 2012. Dr. Huber's previous roles include Head of Alternative Investment Risk Management at Swiss Re in Zurich, Chief Risk Officer at Credaris Portfolio Management in London, and Credit Strategist at Deutsche Bank in Frankfurt/Main. He holds a PhD in applied financial econometrics from the University of Bremen.

NORBERT J. JOBST is Head of Portfolio Analytics in Lloyds Banking Group's Commercial Banking business where he is responsible for the development of methodologies and models for pricing, client profitability analysis, portfolio risk measurement, and product structuring. Before joining Lloyds TSB in 2008, Dr. Jobst held positions at Standard & Poor's and DBRS where he led research and development of structured rating methodologies. Before that, he conducted research funded by Fidelity Investments. Dr. Jobst has taught at Brunel University, Imperial College, and the European School of Management. He has published in leading journals and also co-authored *The Handbook of Structured Finance*. He holds a degree in mathematics from the University of Applied Sciences in Regensburg, Germany, and a PhD from Brunel University in the United Kingdom.

KOSE JOHN is the Charles William Gerstenberg Professor of Banking and Finance at New York University's Stern School of Business where he teaches corporate finance. His recent areas of research include corporate governance, corporate bankruptcy, executive compensation, and corporate disclosure. He has also conducted research in financial markets and financial theory. He has published more than 100 articles in several top journals including the *American Economic Review*, *Journal of Financial Economics*, *Journal of Finance*, *Review of Financial Studies*, and *Financial Management*. He was awarded the prestigious Jensen Prize for the best paper published in *Journal of Financial Economics* in 2000. Besides his research, Professor John has been recognized for his excellence in teaching and received the Citibank Excellence in Teaching Award in 1996. He holds a PhD in management science from the University of Florida.

BJORN JORGENSEN is Professor of Accounting at the Leeds School of Business at the University of Colorado at Boulder. He previously taught at Columbia Business School, Harvard Business School, and London School of Economics and Political Science. He also served as a visiting academic fellow at the U.S. Securities and Exchange Commission. Professor Jorgensen's research has been published in *The Accounting Review*, *Contemporary Accounting Research*, *Journal of Accounting and Economics*, *Journal of Econometrics*, and *Review of Accounting Studies*. He received an M.S. in mathematical economics from the University of Aarhus and a PhD in accounting and information systems from the Kellogg School of Management at Northwestern University.

RAIMUND M. KOVACEVIC is an Assistant Professor at the Department of Statistics and Operations Research at the University of Vienna. He previously worked as a consultant, project manager, and risk manager in insurance, banking, and energy management for Siemens AG Austria, Feilmeier & Junker GmbH, and Financial Soft Computing GmbH. His main research interests involve stochastic modeling and optimization with applications in risk management for finance, insurance, and energy production and trading. He has published in the *International Journal of Theoretical and Applied Finance, Journal of Risk and Insurance, IMA Journal of Management Mathematics, Statistics and Risk Modeling, Operations Research Spectrum,* and *IIE Transactions.* Professor Kovacevic holds a PhD in economic sciences (statistics) from the University of Vienna,

ANDREAS KRAUSE is an Assistant Professor in the Department of Economics at the University of Bath, United Kingdom. For more than 10 years he has conducted research in financial markets, often using agent-based models, and more recently on systemic risk. He has presented his research at many international conferences and published in a wide variety of journals including the *Journal of Economic Behavior and Organization, IEEE Transactions on Systems, Man, and Cybernetics,* and *Quarterly Review of Economics and Finance.* He holds a PhD in finance from the University of Fribourg (Switzerland), where he also received a master's degree.

MARKUS LEIPPOLD is the Hans Vontobel Professor of Financial Engineering at the University of Zurich. Before joining the University of Zurich faculty, he was an associate professor at Imperial College Business School in London and a visiting professor at the Federal Reserve Bank in New York. Professor Leippold's research has been published in the *Journal of Financial Economics, Review of Financial Studies, Review of Finance, Management Science, Journal of Financial and Quantitative Analysis,* and *Annals of Statistics* among others. His research won several prizes such as the best paper award from the German Finance Association, European Financial Management Association, INQUIRE Europe, and the Sir Clive Granger Memorial Best Paper Prize from the *Applied Financial Economics.* Professor Leippold received a PhD in financial economics from the University of St. Gallen in Switzerland. During his PhD studies, he was a research fellow at the Stern School of Business in New York.

MONICA MARIN is a Lecturer at University of Washington Bothell. She was previously a faculty member at HEC Montreal. Her research interests include corporate risk management, financial distress, and cash holdings. She has published in the *Quarterly Journal of Finance* and has presented papers at numerous finance conferences. Professor Marin holds a PhD in finance from the University of South Carolina.

SUMIT MATHUR is a Product Manager–Risk Solutions at the SAS Institute, Inc. and is responsible for managing requirements and product strategy. He has worked extensively in the area of risk management in leadership roles with banks internationally. Mr. Mathur has a patent in the area of capital optimization. He has published papers in the area of counterparty credit risk, liquidity risk, capital management, and risk aggregation. He received a bachelor's degree in physics from the University of Delhi and an MBA from Birla Institute of Management (India). Mr. Mathur is also a Financial Risk Manager (FRM) certified by the Global Association of Risk Professionals (GARP).

JAMES T. MOSER is an Executive in Residence at American University's Kogod School of Business where he directs the Masters in Finance (MSF) program. Previously, he was the Deputy Chief Economist at the Commodity Futures Trading Commission, a Senior Director at the Chicago Mercantile Exchange, and an Economic Adviser and Research Officer at the Federal Reserve Bank of Chicago. His academic positions have been at the University of Kentucky, Michigan State University, University of Illinois, and the Louisiana Tech. His research focuses on three questions: What is the contribution of derivatives to the real economy? What arrangements do private markets make to resolve problems arising from using derivatives? What is the proper role of government in regulating derivatives activity? As an undergraduate, he majored in economics at Virginia Commonwealth University and received a PhD in finance from The Ohio State University.

TIM NGUYEN is the Director of Alternative Investments at the University of Connecticut Foundation, adjunct professor at Brown University, and teaches investments at several top U.S. universities. He is also a social entrepreneur, having co-founded a nonprofit organization called the Global Association of Alternative Investors, consisting of endowments, foundations, public funds, corporate pensions, sovereign wealth funds, central banks, and major single family offices. To date, the organization has more than 400 members with membership assets totaling more than $17 trillion. In 2009, *The Wall Street* and *Euromoney* recognized him as a "Rising Star of the Endowment & Foundation" universe. Mr. Nguyen holds undergraduate degrees (*magna cum laude*) in psychology and political science from the University of Houston, an MA in religion studies from Yale University, an MPA in economics and public policy from Columbia University, and an MA in Development Studies from Brown University.

SAMUEL OUZAN is a PhD candidate in finance at HEC Montréal (Université de Montréal). Before joining HEC Montréal, he held various research positions at McGill University and Tel Aviv University. His main research interests include behavioral finance and topics in theoretical and empirical asset pricing. He holds an M.A.Sc. in electrical engineering from École Polytechnique de Montréal (Université de Montréal).

RAZVAN PASCALAU is Associate Professor of Economics in the School of Business and Economics at SUNY Plattsburgh. His past work experience includes a position at the Ministry of Finance in Romania as Counselor of European Integration and as a hedge fund consultant. His research interests include empirical asset pricing, applied time series econometrics, and microeconometrics. Dr. Pascalau has published in the *Review of Asset Pricing Studies, Geneva Risk and Insurance Review,* and *International Journal of the Economics and Business*. He holds an MSc degree in finance and a PhD in economics from the University of Alabama.

GEORG CH. PFLUG is a Professor of Statistics and Operations Research at the University of Vienna and a part-time research scholar at the International Institute of Applied Systems Analysis in Laxenburg, Austria. He previously was a professor at the University of Giessen (Germany) and held visiting positions at several institutions including Michigan State University, University of California at Davis, and Princeton University. Professor Pflug's interests include stochastic modeling, stochastic optimization, measuring and managing of risks, and applications in finance, energy, pension funds, and insurance. He is currently editor-in-chief of *Statistics and Decisions* and associate editor at several other journals. He is the author or editor of 10 books. Professor Pflug has more than 70 publications in such journals as the *Annals of Statistics, Journal of Applied Probability, Journal of Banking and Finance,* and many others. He holds a PhD in mathematical statistics from the University of Vienna.

ALOIS PICHLER is a researcher at the Norwegian University of Science and Technology who focuses on risk in electricity networks. He previously worked in the insurance and banking industry. His research focuses on mathematical properties of risk measures with a particular focus on their relation to insurance and to optimization under uncertainty. He holds master's degrees in mathematics and physics from Johannes Kepler University of Linz, Austria, and a PhD in economic sciences from the University of Vienna.

ROBERT J. POWELL is an Associate Professor at the School of Business, Edith Cowan University. He has 20 years of banking experience in South Africa, New Zealand, and Australia. He has been involved in developing and implementing several credit and financial analysis models in banks. Professor Powell has published several journal articles and book chapters on VAR, CVAR, credit risk, and hedge fund regulation. He has an honors degree in commerce from Rhodes University, an M.Com from the University of South Africa, and a PhD in finance from Edith Cowan University.

SIMONE RAAB is a Postdoctoral Researcher in Economics at the University of Augsburg, Germany. She focuses on theoretical research on financial intermediaries, risk management, and cooperative banks. She has published a book on the industrial economics of cooperative banks and a paper on the impact of regional demarcation on conduct and performance in banking markets. In 2013, Dr. Raab won the annual research award of IGA in Innsbruck, Austria. She holds a diploma in business administration and a doctoral degree from the University of Augsburg.

SAMIR SAADI is an Assistant Professor of Finance at the University of Ottawa. He was a Visiting Scholar at the Stern School of Business, New York University, and also a Visiting Researcher at INSEAD (Fontainebleau campus). His research interests include market efficiency, mergers and acquisitions, and corporate payout policy. Along with several book chapters, Professor Saadi has published in such journals as *Financial Management, Contemporary Accounting Research, Journal of International Financial Markets, Institutions and Money, Journal of Business Finance and Accounting, Journal of Business Ethics,* and *Journal of Applied Finance.* He is the recipient of several conference best paper awards and numerous prestigious awards and scholarships from, among others, Queen's University, Social Sciences and Humanities Research Council of Canada, Europlace Institute of Finance (EIF), and the American Finance Association. He has served as a consultant for several companies, mainly on value-based management and export financing. He holds a PhD in finance from Queen's University.

GABRIELE SABATO is an experienced risk management professional who has worked and researched in this field for more than 12 years. Currently, he is a Senior Manager in RBS Group Risk Management responsible for setting and overseeing risk appetite policies and strategies across the Group. Before joining RBS, Dr. Sabato worked for three years in the ABN AMRO Group Risk Management heading up the Group Retail analytics team. He led several Basel II Accord projects including models independent validation, Pillar I compliance, stress testing, and internal capital adequacy assessment process (ICAAP). He spent four years at Experian as a business consultant developing and implementing credit risk models and strategies for several financial institutions across Europe. He has published several articles on risk management in such academic journals as the *Journal of Banking and Finance, Journal of Financial Services Research,* and *ABACUS*. Dr. Sabato holds a PhD in finance from the University of Rome "La Sapienza."

PAVEL V. SHEVCHENKO is a Senior Principal Research Scientist in the Division of Computational Informatics of Commonwealth Scientific and Industrial Research Organisation (CSIRO) of Australia. He joined CSIRO in 1999 to work in the area of financial risk. He leads research and commercial projects on modeling of operational and credit risks, option pricing, insurance, modeling commodities and foreign exchange, and the development of relevant numerical methods and software. He is currently an Adjunct professor at the School of Mathematics and Statistics in the University of New South Wales and the University of Technology Sydney, and associate editor of the *Journal of Operational Risk*. Professor Shevchenko has published extensively in academic journals, consults for major financial institutions, and is a frequent presenter at industry and academic conferences. He is the author of the monograph *Modelling Operational Risk Using Bayesian Inference* published by Springer in 2011. He received an MSc from Moscow Institute of Physics and Technology and Kapitza Institute for Physical Problems and a PhD in theoretical physics from the University of New South Wales.

ABHAY K. SINGH is a Postdoctoral Research Fellow at the School of Business, Edith Cowan University. He has published several book chapters and refereed journal publications on modeling and forecasting risk including VAR, CVAR, and multivariate dependence using extreme value theory and vine copula. He has a B.Tech in information technology, an MBA in finance from the Indian Institute of Information Technology and Management, and a PhD in finance from Edith Cowan University.

CRISTIAN I. TIU is an Associate Professor of Finance in the SUNY system at the University at Buffalo. His research focuses on investments with an emphasis on determinants of performance for institutional investors such as endowment funds and hedge funds. He has published in the *Review of Financial Studies, Mathematical Finance,* and *Journal of Investment Management* and presented his work at numerous conferences. Professor Tiu is a member of the Investment Committee of the University at Buffalo Foundation and several associations including the American Finance Association and the Association of Governing Boards of Universities and Colleges. He has PhDs from the University of Texas at Austin in finance and mathematics.

DIMITRIS TSOUKNIDIS is a Lecturer in Finance at Regent's University London and the Department Research Leader for the Department of Accounting, Finance, and Economics. He has also taught at the ICMA Centre at University of Reading and ALBA Graduate Business School on Risk Management, Quantitative Methods and Shipping Finance. Professor Tsouknidis has provided consultancy to financial institutions on credit risk control and Basel II implementation issues. His research interests focus on asset pricing and credit risk in financial and shipping markets. He has presented his research in international conferences and professional seminar series and serves as a referee to academic journals. Professor Tsouknidis holds a BSc in economics from the University of Thessaly, Greece, an MSc in computational finance from University of Essex, United Kingdom, and an MBA and PhD from Athens University of Economics and Business, Greece.

BERT VAN LIER is the Deputy CEO and Chief Investment Officer of the Currency Exchange Fund and Head of Trading. Before joining TCX in 2007, Mr. van Lier worked for ING Financial Markets in ALM, Fixed Income, Structured Products and, most recently as Managing Director and Global Head Equity Derivatives Sales and Structuring. His main focus is pricing, trading, and liquidity investments. Mr. van Lier holds a master's degree in finance from Tilburg University and an executive master's degree in finance and control from VU University in Amsterdam.

PETER WELZEL is Professor of Economic Policy and Industrial Economics at the University of Augsburg, Germany. Previously, Professor Welzel held a temporary professorship at the University of Munich and a tenured professorship in empirical methods of economics at the University of Jena. He has been visiting professor at the University of Rennes I, France since 1998. Professor Welzel was a scholar of the German National Merit Foundation and John J. McCloy scholar of the Volkswagen Foundation. He currently serves as dean of his faculty and academic director of its MBA program. One focus of his research and publications is on the industrial economics of financial intermediaries, specifically in the theory of risk management. He holds a diploma, a doctoral, and a postdoctoral (habilitation) degree from the University of Augsburg and an MPA from Harvard University's Kennedy School of Government.

KIT PONG WONG is a Professor of Finance and the Director of the School of Economics and Finance at the University of Hong Kong. His research is mainly theoretical and involves corporate finance, real options, and risk management. He is interested in studying how risk-averse firms should hedge their risk exposure to various sources of uncertainty and the optimality of using options as a hedging instrument. His research appears in the *Journal of Banking and Finance, Journal of Business, Journal of Financial and Quantitative Analysis, Journal of Futures Markets,* and *Management Science*. He holds an undergraduate degree in economics from the Chinese University of Hong Kong, a master's degree in economics from the University of Western Ontario, and a PhD in finance from the University of British Columbia.

HUI ZHU is an Assistant Professor of Finance at the University of Ontario Institute of Technology (UOIT). Before joining UOIT, she was an assistant professor at Cape Breton University and also worked as a Postdoctoral Fellow in Finance at the University of Calgary. She has five years' experience teaching advanced and fundamental finance courses. Professor Zhu's current research interests encompass corporate, international, and behavioral finance. Her research has been presented at many conferences and seminars across North America, Europe, and Asia. She has several published papers in journals such as the *Journal of Financial Research, Quarterly Review of Economics and Finance, Journal of Multinational Financial Management,* and *Applied Financial Economics*. Professor Zhu has an MA in economics from University of Victoria and a PhD in economics from Queen's University.

Abbreviations

ABO	accumulated benefit obligation
ABS	asset-backed securities
ADRs	American depository receipts
ADX	average directional index
AFS	available-for-sale
AIFMD	Alternative Investment Fund Managers Directive
ALM	asset liability management
AMA	advanced measurement approach
AMEX	American Stock Exchange
APRA	Australian Prudential Regulation Authority
APT	arbitrage pricing theory
ARMA	autoregressive moving average
ARMs	adjustable rate mortgages
ART	average recovery time
AS	absolute bid-ask spread
ASR	adjusted Sharpe ratio
ASRF	asymptotic single risk factor
AUM	assets under management
AVR	automatic variance ratio
BCBS	Basel Committee on Banking Supervision
BEICFs	business environment and internal control factors
BIA	basic indicator approach
BIS	Bank for International Settlements
B/M	book-to-market
BRIC	Brazil, Russia, India, and China
CAL	capital allocation line
CAP	cumulative accuracy profile
CAPM	capital asset pricing model
CAR	capital adequacy ratio
CARA	constant absolute risk aversion
CBOE	Chicago Board Options Exchange
CBOT	Chicago Board of Trade

CCAR	comprehensive capital analysis and review
CCPs	central counterparties
CDD	cooling degree days
CDF	cumulative distribution function
CDS	credit default swap
CDO	collateralized debt obligation
CEO	chief executive officer
CFMA	Commodity Futures Modernization Act
CFPB	Consumer Financial Protection Bureau
CFTC	Commodity Futures Trading Commission
CIO	chief investment officer
CME	Chicago Mercantile Exchange
CPI	consumer price index
CRAR	capital to risk adequacy ratio
CRAs	credit rating agencies
CRD IV	Capital Requirements Directive IV
CRO	chief risk officer
CRPs	country risk premiums
CTAs	commodity trading advisors
CTE	conditional tail expectation
CVA	credit value adjustment
CVaR	conditional value-at-risk
DARA	decreasing absolute risk aversion
DCF	discounted cash flow
DEA	data envelopment analysis
DFAST	Dodd-Frank Act stress test
DI	diversification index
DJIA	Dow Jones Industrial Average
DOJ	Department of Justice
DR	downside risk
DTI	debt-to-income ratio
DVA	debit value adjustment
DVaR	daily value-at-risk
EAD	exposure at default
EAD	expected amount at default
EBIT	earnings before interest and taxes
EBITDA	earnings before interest depreciation and amortization
EC	economic capital
ECAP	economic capital
ED	external data
EEA	exchange equalization account
EH	expectations hypothesis
EL	expected losses
EMH	efficient market hypothesis
EMIR	European Market Infrastructure Regulation
ERM	enterprise risk management

ERP	equity risk premium
ES	expected shortfall
ETF	exchange-traded fund
Eurex	European Exchange
EVT	extreme value theory
EWMA	exponentially weighted mean averages
FASB	Financial Accounting Standards Board
FATCA	Foreign Account Tax Compliance Act
FCA	Financial Conduct Authority
FCFE	free cash flow to equity
FCOJ	frozen concentrated orange juice
FERMA	Federation of European Risk Management Associations
FHA	Federal Housing Administration
FHFA	Federal Housing Finance Agency
FOMC	Federal Open Market Committee
FRM	financial risk manager
FRR	Financial Reporting Release
FSOC	Financial Stability Oversight Council
FTP	funds transfer pricing
FX	foreign exchange
GAAP	generally accepted accounting principles
GAM	generalized additive models
GAMLSS	generalized additive models for location scale and shape
GAMM	generalized additive mixed models
GARCH	generalized autoregressive conditional heteroskedasticity
GARP	Global Association of Risk Professionals
GDP	gross domestic product
GFC	global financial crisis
GLB	Gramm-Leach-Bliley
GLM	generalized linear model
GLMM	generalized linear mixed models
GMM	generalized method of moments
GPD	generalized Pareto distribution
GSAMP	Goldman Sachs alternative mortgage products
GSCI	Goldman Sachs Commodities Index
GSEs	government sponsored enterprises
G-SIBS	global systemically important banks
GTM	growth-to-momentum
HDD	heating degree days
HE	hedging effectiveness
HH	Hui and Heubel
HP	Hewlett-Packard
HTM	held-to-maturity
IARA	increasing absolute risk aversion
IBRD	International Bank for Reconstruction and Development
ICAAP	internal capital adequacy assessment process

ICBC	Industrial and Commercial Bank of China Limited
ICE	Intercontinental Exchange
ICGN	International Corporate Governance Network
IFRS	International Financial Reporting Standards
i.i.d.	independent and identically distributed
ILD	internal loss data
IMA	internal measurement approach
IMA	internal models approach
IMF	International Monetary Fund
IPO	initial public offering
IRB	internal ratings based
IRR	internal rate of return
IRRBB	interest rate risk in banking book
ISDA	International Swap Dealers' Association
IT	information technology
I-VaR	intraday value-at-risk
JOBS	jumpstart our business startups
JPD	joint probability of default
KYC	know your customer/client
LDA	loss distribution approach
LDCE	loss data collection exercises
LEAPs	long-term equity anticipatory security
LGD	loss given default
LIBOR	London interbank offered rate
LIFFE	London International Financial Futures Exchange
LOT	Lesmond, Ogden, and Trzcinka
LPMs	lower partial moments
LR	liquidity ratio
LTCM	long-term capital management
LTV	loan-to-value
MA	moving averages
MAR	minimum acceptable return
MBS	mortgage-backed securities
MEC	market-efficiency coefficient
MiFID I	Market in Financial Instruments Directive I
ML	Martin liquidity
MLE	maximum likelihood estimation
MLIL	Merrill Lynch Inflation Linked
MPT	modern portfolio theory
MSCI	Morgan Stanley Capital Index
NAV	net asset value
NEO	neuroticism-extroversion-openness
NII	net interest income
NIM	net interest margin
NPLs	nonperforming loans
NPV	net present value

NRSRO	nationally recognized statistical rating organizations
NYMEX	New York Mercantile Exchange
NYSE	New York Stock Exchange
OCC	Options Clearing Corporation
OECD	Organization for Economic Co-operation and Development
OIS	overnight indexed swap
OLS	ordinary least squares
OOI	other operational income
OTC	over-the-counter
OTD	originate-to-distribute
P&L	profit and loss
PBO	projected benefit obligations
PCTR	price change to the turnover ratio
PD	probability of default
pdf	probability density function
PE	price/earnings
PIT	point-in-time
POT	peak-over-threshold
PPE	property, plant, and equipment
PRC	portfolio credit risk
PRMIA	Professional Risk Managers' International Association
PRS	political risk services
PS	percentage spread
QAT	qualitative asset transformation
QE	quantitative easing
QM	qualified mortgage
QRM	qualified residential mortgages
RAPMs	risk-adjusted performance measures
RAROC	risk-adjusted return on capital
RC	regulatory capital
RCAP	regulatory capital
RDR	retail distribution review
RFS	relative firm strength
RGD	recovery given default
ROA	return on assets
ROR	rate of return
RTC	Resolution Trust Corporation
RWAs	risk-weighted assets
SA	standardized approach
S&Ls	savings and loans associations
S&P's	Standard and Poor's
SBA	scenario-based analysis
SCR	solvency capital requirement
SEC	Securities and Exchange Commission
SFA	stochastic frontier analysis
SFE	Sydney Futures Exchange

SIA	Securities Industry Association
SIBs	systemically important banks
SIFIs	systemically important financial institutions
SMEs	small medium enterprises
SML	security market line
SOX	Sarbanes-Oxley Act
SPV	special purpose vehicle
SR	Sharpe ratio
TARP	Troubled Asset Relief Program
TBTF	too big to fail
TEV	tracking-error variance
TIPS	Treasury inflation-protected securities
TQM	total quality management
TR	turnover ratio
TR	Treynor ratio
UEH	unbiased expectation hypothesis
UL	unexpected losses
UPM	upper partial moment
UPR	upside potential ratio
VAMI	Value-Added Monthly Index
VaR	value-at-risk
VIX	Volatility Index
VR	variance ratio
WTI	West Texas Intermediate

Investment Risk Management

Part One

FOUNDATIONS OF RISK MANAGEMENT

1

Investment Risk Management:
An Overview

H. KENT BAKER

University Professor of Finance, Kogod School of Business, American University

GREG FILBECK

Samuel P. Black III Professor of Finance and Risk Management, Black School of Business,
Penn State Erie, The Behrend College

Introduction

> "All courses of action are risky, so prudence is not in avoiding danger
> (it's impossible), but calculating risk and acting decisively."
> Niccolo Machiavelli, *The Prince*

All investments carry with them some degree of risk. In the financial world, individuals, professional money managers, financial institutions, and many others encounter and must deal with risk. Investors can either accept or try to mitigate the risk in investment decision-making. If they choose inaction and engage in inadequate risk management, they are likely to experience severe consequences. If investors take appropriate actions given their investment objectives and risk tolerances, they may lessen the potential for investment losses. Thus, risk management should be proactive as opposed to reactive.

Managing risk has become increasingly difficult due to the multiple aspects of risk. As Bender and Nielsen (2009, p. 57) conclude:

> Recent events have put into stark relief the inadequacy of the current state of risk management. Much has been said about the need for better risk management and a greater degree of risk awareness in the broader investment community. Risk management is a dynamic area, and any set of best practices is bound to evolve over time.

What is risk management in an investment context? Investopedia (2014) describes risk management as a two-step process of determining what risks exist in an investment and then handling those risks in a way best-suited to an investor's investment.

According to Bender and Nielsen (2009), investors should have a risk management framework aligned with their investment objectives and time horizon. Developing an effective framework requires measuring, monitoring, and managing exposures to both economic and fundamental drivers of risk and return across asset classes to avoid overexposures to any one risk factor. Although these three pillars of risk management (measurement, monitoring, and management) encompass different aspects of risk, they are interdependent and should be fully integrated with the investment process. The risk management framework should also enable dealing with risk during both normal times and extreme events.

Starting with Markowitz (1952), researchers have attempted to better understand the relationship between risk and return in a portfolio context. Markowitz's modern portfolio theory (MPT) focuses on the dynamics of total or investment risk as a basis for evaluating risk-return trade-offs. Total risk consists of two major components: market risk and specific risk. *Market risk*, also called *systematic risk*, is the possibility that investors may experience losses due to factors that affect the overall performance of the financial markets. Market risk cannot be eliminated through diversification. Examples of market risk include major natural disasters, recessions, changes in interest rates, and political turmoil. *Specific risk*, also referred to as *unsystematic risk*, is tied directly to the performance of a particular security. An example of specific risk is the risk of a company declaring bankruptcy, which would negatively affect the price of its common stock.

Some contend that investors should only consider a portion of total risk, namely, systematic risk. This component of risk, called *beta*, indicates that highly-diversified investors are not rewarded for total risk, but rather for the level of systematic risk they take. Sharpe (1964), Lintner (1965), and others develop the capital asset pricing model (CAPM) as a one-factor model to investigate risk-return trade-offs using beta. Ross (1976) is among the first to extend the analysis into multiple systematic factors through his arbitrage pricing theory (APT). Fama and French (1993) contend that factors besides market risk influence returns. They include independent variables for market capitalization (size) and the book-to-market ratio as other important contributors to explain the risk-return framework. Carhart (1997) adds momentum as another important factor to explain returns.

Other researchers attempt to focus on downside risk measures such as value-at-risk or risks associated with nonlinear portfolio strategies. *Value-at-risk* (VaR) is defined as the maximum loss over a defined period of time at a stated level of confidence, given normal market conditions. VaR corresponds to the loss in the tail of the return distribution. VaR is a risk measure first used by banks, but increasingly is used in portfolio management. Among other influential measures are the Sortino ratio (Sortino and Price 1994) and the Sterling ratio.

A discussion of risk and its management in a financial and investment context is not restricted to market risk alone. Jorion (2007) identifies credit risk, operational risk, and liquidity risk as other major considerations for investors. *Credit risk* involves the possible default by a counterparty in a financial transaction. *Operational risk* is the risk of loss due to inadequate monitoring systems, management failure, defective controls, fraud, and/or human errors. Operational risk is of greater concern to portfolios that incorporate derivative securities. Derivatives are highly levered instruments due to the low equity investment required to control them. Thus, small changes in value of the derivative contract can substantially influence return on investment. *Liquidity risk* is associated with sustaining losses due to the inability to sufficiently liquidate a position at a fair price. Outside of these core financial risks (market, credit, operational, and liquidity) are a plethora of other risks facing both investors and managers such as country risk, systemic risk, behavioral risk, governance risk, and inflation risk.

Readers of *Investment Risk Management* can gain an in-depth understanding of the major types of risks, how to measure them, how to assess them relative to return, and the instruments available to hedge such risks. They will also become aware of what has been learned about risk management from financial disasters such as the financial crisis of 2007–2008 and gain a glimpse of the future of investment risk management.

Purpose and Scope

The main purpose of *Investment Risk Management* is to provide an in-depth discussion of risk management and a synthesis of relevant research evidence. Risk management is important because it can reduce or augment risk depending on the goals of investors and portfolio managers. The book examines ways to alter exposures through measuring and managing those exposures. Readers can also learn about the latest strategies and trends within risk management. The book presents the crux of various research studies in a straightforward manner focusing on the comprehension of study findings, rather than on the details of mathematical frameworks. Given the nature of the subject, however, using mathematical and statistical concepts is necessary.

The scope of the coverage is broad and attempts to encompass the most important aspects of investment risk management. These self-contained chapters are organized into six parts: (1) foundations of risk management, (2) types of risk, (3) quantitative assessment of risk, (4) risk management and asset classes, (5) hedging risk, and (6) going forward. Overall, the book provides a discussion of such topics as the market for the investments, benchmarks and historical performance, specific investment strategies, and issues about performance evaluation and reporting.

As the fourth in the Financial Markets and Investments Series, *Investment Risk Management* makes an important contribution to the literature on risk management. A robust and evolving body of knowledge on risk management is available based on theoretical and empirical research. Additioinally, many well-established academic textbooks and popular press books cover risk management. This book helps to bridge the gap between research findings and general risk management knowledge and practice. In summary, *Investment Risk Management* provides a fresh look at this intriguing but complex subject.

Distinctive Features

Investment Risk Management has several distinguishing features.

- The book provides a detailed discussion of investment risk management. It also offers a synthesis of recent and relevant research studies in a succinct and clear manner and discusses recent trends in risk management.

- The book skillfully blends the contributions of scholars and practitioners from around the globe into a single review of some of the most critical topics in this area. The varied backgrounds of the contributors assure different perspectives and a rich interplay of ideas. While retaining the content and perspectives of the many contributors, the book follows an internally consistent approach in format and style. Similar to a choir that contains many voices, this book has many authors with their own separate voices. A goal of both a choir and this book is to have the many voices sing together harmoniously. Hence, the book is much more than simply a collection of chapters from an array of different authors.
- When discussing the results of empirical studies that link theory and practice, the objective is to distill them to their essential content so that they are understandable and useful to sophisticated readers.
- Each chapter except Chapter 1 contains four to six discussion questions that reinforce the key concepts. Guideline answers are presented at the end of the book. This feature should be especially important to faculty and students using the book in courses.

Intended Audience

The book's distinctive features should be of interest to a broad audience. However, given the rigorous treatment of the subject, our primary target audience consists of sophisticated practitioners, investors, academics, and graduate-level finance students. Experienced practitioners can use this book to navigate through the key areas in investment risk management. Knowledgeable individual and institutional investors can also benefit as they attempt to expand their knowledge base and apply the concepts discussed to manage their portfolios. Academics can use this book not only as part of graduate finance programs but also to comprehend the various strands of research emerging from this area. The book could serve as a useful text or supplement to programs in risk management. For example, the content in this book could assist candidates for the Financial Risk Manager (FRM™) designation sponsored by the Global Association of Risk Professionals (GARP).

Structure of the Book

The remaining 29 chapters of the book consist of six parts. A brief synopsis of each chapter by part follows.

PART ONE FOUNDATIONS OF RISK MANAGEMENT

Besides Chapter 1, the first part contains three other chapters. These chapters involve measuring and managing risk, how risk management adds value, and accounting and risk management.

Chapter 2 Measuring and Managing Risk (Raimund M. Kovacevic, Georg Ch. Pflug, and Alois Pichler)

This chapter provides an overview of statistical and probabilistic approaches in quantitative risk management. The discussion assumes complete knowledge of the profit-and-loss distribution, which is estimated on the basis of historic data, forecasts, and expert opinion. Risk is measured using statistical parameters of the profit-and-loss distribution, which characterize some but not all of its features. Various risk measures are discussed in light of their properties. Some measures are well known and widely used while others are less popular but exhibit useful features. Risk measures are not only used in quantifying risk but also in financial decision-making such as in portfolio and investment planning or asset-liability management. In such situations, risk is either a constraint by fixing a risk budget that cannot be exceeded or an objective to be minimized. Some typical problems in decision-making that are related to risk management are discussed for the purpose of incorporating the available instruments and risk management actions into the formulation of the corresponding optimization problems.

Chapter 3 How Risk Management Adds Value (M. Martin Boyer and Monica Marin)

This chapter reviews the role of risk management in increasing firm value. It covers the incentives to manage risk, the role of hedging in planning investment and financial decisions, and how hedging can help firm managers better anticipate capital requirements and financing needs. The chapter explains how investment risk management and hedging can help in designing a managerial compensation contract that rewards managers for their talent and effort, rather than compensating them for their luck. The role of risk management in attenuating managerial conflict is also treated, especially as risk management can allow better and more effective coordination between division managers. The chapter finishes by discussing the differences between insurance and hedging for the case of non-financial firms.

Chapter 4 Accounting and Risk Management (Mark Bradshaw and Bjorn Jorgensen)

Although risk is forward-looking, accounting is often backward-looking and relies on historical costs from events realized in the past. This chapter discusses situations in which risk is part of the background inputs in preparing financial statement information. The chapter also highlights examples of how accounting information can inform investment decisions through their primary use as predictors of future firm performance, stock market performance, bankruptcy, corporate fraud, and volatility. Finally, financial statements contain many useful disclosures about risk and management estimates of uncertainties and discount rates. The chapter concludes with a brief discussion of the recent debate over the role of accounting in the financial crisis of 2007–2008.

PART TWO TYPES OF RISK

The second part focuses on various types of risk: market, credit, operational, liquidity, country, systemic, behavioral, governance, and inflation. Risk aggregation is also discussed.

Chapter 5 Market Risk (Ramon P. Degennaro and Chanaka P. Edirisinghe)

Market risk, also called systematic risk, represents the possible loss in value of an investment due to co-movement in prices that cannot be eliminated by diversification. Until recently, financial economists generally thought that these price fluctuations traced to changes in expected cash flows. More recent evidence suggests that these systematic movements trace to changes in discount rates and various risk factors. Future research must determine whether apparent opportunities to earn excess returns represent genuine profit opportunities that reflect inefficiencies or whether they result from previously unknown risk factors including those based on relative inefficiencies of firms in the market. Such inefficiencies are likely to vary across different market sectors, possibly leading to a sector-dependent inefficiency risk factor.

Chapter 6 Credit Risk (Norbert J. Jobst)

Credit risk remains one of the major risks that commercial banks face. The ability to run a sustainable business depends to a large extent on how well banks and others can measure and manage their risk. While market, operational, and liquidity risks are also vital to ensure a bank remains a going concern, the focus of this chapter is on the measurement and management of credit risk that arises from a bank's core lending activities. The chapter introduces key tools to measure credit risk at the individual-asset and portfolio level. This subject matter is followed by a discussion of how these tools are used as part of a bank's credit portfolio management activities. The chapter concludes that key applications such as capital measurement, assessment of portfolio concentrations, risk-based pricing, and complex product structuring all benefit from those techniques and are important inputs to the effective management of a commercial bank.

Chapter 7 Operational Risk (Pavel V. Shevchenko)

Operational risk is not a new concept in the banking industry. Risks such as fraud and processing errors have had to be managed since the beginning of banking. The traditional measure for managing these risks involved using insurance and audits. The management of operational risk in the banking industry has undergone explosive changes over the last decade due to substantial changes in the operational environment. Globalization, complex financial products, changes in information technology, and increases in the number of high-profile operational loss events with some resulting in bankruptcies have prompted regulatory requirements for banks to set aside risk capital to cover operational risk losses. This chapter reviews current approaches for operational risk capital calculations.

Chapter 8 Liquidity Risk (Kose John, Samir Saadi, and Hui Zhu)

The role of market liquidity and its implications on asset prices and financial systems has generated much attention over the past 30 years. This chapter provides an overview of the vast literature on liquidity risk. In the context of this chapter, liquidity risk arises when one party is unable to sell an asset or a security because no one is willing to buy it. The chapter examines the properties and sources of illiquidity and presents the main proxies proposed by the empirical literature to capture liquidity. It also reviews the theoretical and empirical literature that examine whether liquidity risk is a priced risk factor.

Chapter 9 Country Risk (Aswath Damodaran)

Do differences in risk exist across countries? If the answer is yes, judgment is needed in determining how best to reflect those risks in investment analysis. This chapter examines the drivers of country risk, why it varies across countries and across time, and how rating agencies and markets measure country risk. The chapter extends the assessment to estimate equity risk premiums for different countries and looks at how to incorporate this risk into the hurdle rates of companies that may have operations in these countries, even if incorporated.

Chapter 10 Systemic Risk (Andreas Krause)

Systemic risk is the threat to the proper functioning of the financial system. Its origins can be very different, ranging from banks being forced to sell assets in times of market stress, being unable to rollover their debt, or being affected by rumors about their solvency, to direct exposure to other banks that fail. No overall risk measure currently addresses all of these aspects adequately. In response to the credit crisis of 2007–2008, banking regulation seeks to capture some of the aspects of systemic risk and include them in the regulation of banks rather than focusing solely on the solvency of an individual bank. Systemic risk is relevant for banks and investors need to be aware of the threat.

Chapter 11 Behavioral Risk (M. Martin Boyer, Franca Glenzer,
and Samuel Ouzan)

This chapter examines how behavioral factors influence financial decision processes. It takes a behavioral perspective to explain phenomena in financial markets that the neoclassical view of rationally acting agents has trouble explaining. Among these puzzles are the equity premium puzzle and excess volatility. Starting from theoretical challenges to the neoclassical view of thinking including prospect theory, the chapter discusses the most important heuristics and biases in decision-making that help to explain empirically observed asset prices including the role of overconfidence and noise traders on financial markets. The chapter also discusses collective behavior such as herding.

Chapter 12 Governance Risk (Didier Cossin)

Governance has emerged as a clear investment risk. Governance failures affect specific companies and sometimes whole industries with dramatic effects on investment performance. Historically, investors did not consider governance in the investment risk profile but now doing so is necessary. Governance constitutes more than just tail risk (extreme downfalls in difficult cases). Effective boards add value to the organization while ineffective ones destroy value. This chapter focuses on how to decipher good governance from bad governance and effective boards from ineffective ones. The chapter relies on a model of four pillars of effectiveness: (1) people (i.e., board member individual characteristics), (2) information architecture, (3) structures and processes, and (4) group dynamics or culture. These four pillars establish a framework that allows investors to assess the governance risk of their investments.

Chapter 13 Inflation Risk (Claus Huber, Felix Gasser, and Nicolas Bürkler)

This chapter discusses how high inflation has appeared in history, how it could re-emerge, and the means of protection investors have at their disposal to handle inflation.

After reviewing the primary reasons for inflation in the 1970s, which was the last period of high inflation, this chapter explains some differences between the 1970s and the 2010s and how high inflation could re-emerge. The chapter discusses potential sources of inflation, such as low interest rate levels, supply of credit to banks, emerging markets, and the high debt levels of the Western industrialized countries. Standard instruments for inflation protection such as equities, inflation-indexed bonds, gold, commodity futures, timber and real estate, and their specifics are examined. If the next larger scale inflation materializes as a longer-term trend, the chapter also introduces characteristics of trend-following investment strategies such as commodity trading advisors and their suitability for inflation protection.

Chapter 14 Risk Aggregation and Capital Management (Sumit Mathur)
This chapter provides an analysis of the risk aggregation process in banks in both a regulatory and a non-regulatory context. It starts with a brief introduction defining risk aggregation and explains that understanding total risk can lead to improved decision-making. Risk aggregation is then explained at an individual asset risk level involving credit and market risk. Because risk aggregation involves a choice for banks in terms of the risk metric used such as VaR and expected shortfall, the chapter compares these metrics and discusses their relative strengths and limitations. The risk aggregation process offers different ways to aggregate risks, which are broadly classified into the top-down approach and the bottom-up approach. The chapter also reviews the literature on risk aggregation approaches and their pros and cons. Finally, it provides a perspective into new stress testing regulations such as the Dodd-Frank Act that require banks to aggregate risk (capital) and returns (profit/losses) over a longer period of time.

PART THREE QUANTITATIVE ASSESSMENT OF RISK

The third part emphasizes topics associated with measuring risk and examines downside risk and other risk-adjusted performance measures. It also includes a discussion of risk measures including VaR, stress testing, risk management and regulation, risk budgeting, risk-adjusted performance measures, and attribution analysis.

Chapter 15 Value-at-Risk and Other Risk Measures (Markus Lieppold)
Risk is a central theme in financial market theory. Because risk is an abstract concept, its measurement is not a priori clear as with return. This chapter focuses on the most important risk measures in today's financial industry, namely VaR and expected shortfall. To comprehend their origins involves understanding the origin of modern finance. Under the mean-variance paradigm of Markowitz's portfolio theory, risk is defined as the variance of an investment. However, this symmetric measure can be an inappropriate concept to serve as a risk measure. The chapter provides a discussion of the different suggestions presented in the academic literature including the concepts of modern risk measures. These risk measures also have deficiencies, not only when managers use them to control for specific portfolios but also when regulators use them as a tool to safeguard financial markets against systemic risks.

Chapter 16 Stress Testing (Martin Čihák)

Stress testing is a useful and popular but sometimes misunderstood method of analyzing the resilience of financial institutions to adverse events. This chapter aims to further demystify stress tests by illustrating their strengths and weaknesses. It discusses the stress testing process, emphasizing the importance of quality input data for stress tests. The chapter presents basic stress testing techniques including calculations of credit risk, interest rate risk, foreign exchange risk, liquidity risk, and interbank contagion risk. It also discusses the design of stress testing scenarios and linkages between stress testing and early warning systems. The chapter highlights the challenges of stress testing including its data intensity, dependence on simplifying assumptions, and the difficulties of capturing rare but extreme events. To address these challenges, stress test assumptions should be more transparent and stress test results should be presented consistently over time.

Chapter 17 Risk Management and Regulation (David E. Allen, Robert J. Powell, and Abhay K. Singh)

This chapter considers the management and regulation of risk for financial institutions within market settings, and the manner in which the regulatory authorities have responded to economic development and financial innovation. It examines the links between economic circumstances and regulation and the impact of the Great Depression and the aftermath of World War II. The relationship between financial innovation and regulatory changes is explored involving the concepts of the regulatory dialectic and the functional view of regulation embodied by the successive Basel Accords. The discussion also considers risk metrics such as VaR and the regulatory response to the recent financial crisis of 2007–2008.

Chapter 18 Risk Budgeting (Gregg Fisher, Tim Nguyen, and Cristian I. Tiu)

This chapter outlines risk budgeting procedures that allow investors to decompose portfolio risk across market exposures and risk caused by active investment decisions. This portfolio decomposition is especially useful to managers of decentralized institutional investors such as a pension plan or a university endowment fund. The decomposition is also useful to individual investors interested in taking a certain amount of active risk in order to enhance their portfolio overall performance. The chapter further contends that asset allocation and risk management should be compatible with each other. It illustrates a few common errors that may occur when inappropriately using traditional risk measures.

Chapter 19 Risk-Adjusted Performance Measurement (Pilar Grau Carles)

The financial crisis of 2007–2008 reopened the debate about the need for identifying a correct risk measurement in financial time series. Different risk measurements give rise to different risk-adjusted performance values. The most used and best known measurement is the Sharpe ratio, although other risk-reward ratio specifications attempt to correct for its shortcomings. This chapter describes the most popular ratios in the academic literature beyond the mean-variance approach and discusses their advantages and disadvantages. It also provides an analysis of results when calculating risk ratio-based rankings.

Chapter 20 Risk Attribution Analysis (Philippe Bertrand)

A common practice in the financial management industry is to combine portfolio risk attribution with performance attribution. Performance attribution considered alone is insufficient and can be misleading. Tracking-error attribution is only consistent with some types of efficient portfolios. The next step in the portfolio evaluation process combines performance attribution and risk attribution in a single measure of risk-adjusted performance attribution. Given three levels in the analysis of information ratio attribution that can possibly lead to conflicting results, analysts must exercise care in interpretation. Component information ratios are particularly useful in assessing whether equilibrium between expected returns and relative risk has been reached.

PART FOUR RISK MANAGEMENT AND ASSET CLASSES

The fourth part examines risk management practices and issues related to mortgage-backed securities and hedge funds.

Chapter 21 Risk and Mortgage-Backed Securities in a Time of Transition (Harold C. Barnett)

The residential mortgage-backed securities (MBS) market expanded and collapsed as securitizers packaged increasingly toxic loans into private label MBS. New affordability products and expectation of continuously rising home prices replaced underwriting based on the ability to repay. Securitizers and credit rating agencies misrepresented the risk of default. As a result of the financial crisis of 2007–2008, taxpayers now insure or guarantee 90 percent of loan originations. Public and private investors are seeking compensation through litigation. The Dodd-Frank Act of 2010 produced a rigorous ability to repay qualifying standard as well as liability for non-compliance. A lender "skin in the game" or borrower down payment requirement might also be forthcoming. The new rules could substantially reduce the risk of default while excluding many borrowers and first-time homeowners from the mortgage market. An inclusive private label MBS market has not yet emerged.

Chapter 22 Credit Value Adjustment (James T. Moser)

Credit value adjustment (CVA) is a valuation exercise that values the credit exposure an entity has to its contract counterparties. This valuation explicitly recognizes the cost incurred when taking on a credit exposure. Ideally, CVA expresses the price an entity should expect to pay when seeking to hedge the credit risk it incurs by taking on a contract. The chapter reviews the development of both methods to deal with credit exposures in the derivatives markets valuation models. The substantial losses realized during the financial crisis of 2007–2008 prompted financial regulators, especially the Bank of International Settlements, to look more closely at credit risk. Consequently, CVA figures prominently in the Basel III Accord. The chapter reviews its implementation under that Accord.

Chapter 23 Risk Management and Hedge Funds (Razvan Pascalau)

This chapter reviews the most important tools at the disposal of investors to measure the performance and the risks of hedge funds. It considers some well-established risk measures such as the Sharpe, Sortino, and Sterling ratios that are part of hedge fund risk management and practice. The chapter demonstrates these measures empirically using some recent hedge fund data. However, recent hedge fund studies show that hedge fund failure often results from operational issues and not from financial issues. Therefore, the chapter stresses the importance of due diligence and operational risk measures as the more important risk management tools and advocates including them in the hedge fund risk management arsenal.

PART FIVE HEDGING RISK

Investors have numerous ways to hedge risk. The fifth part focuses on hedging risk using options, futures, swaps, credit derivatives, and foreign exchange derivatives.

Chapter 24 Options (Kit Pong Wong, Greg Filbeck, and H. Kent Baker)

This chapter provides an overview of option markets and contracts as well as basic valuation of options. Its primary purpose is to examine the behavior of the competitive firm that faces not only output price uncertainty but also a multiplicative revenue shock. The firm can trade fairly priced commodity futures and option contracts for hedging purposes. This chapter shows that neither the separation theorem nor the full-hedging theorem holds when the revenue shock prevails. The correlation between the random output price and the revenue shock plays a pivotal role in determining the firm's optimal production and hedging decisions. If the correlation is non-positive, the firm optimally produces less than the benchmark level in the absence of the revenue shock. Furthermore, the firm's optimal hedge position includes both the commodity futures and option contracts. However, if the correlation is sufficiently positive, a canonical example is constructed under which the firm optimally produces more, not less, than the benchmark level. The firm as such uses operational and financial hedging as complements to better cope with the multiple sources of uncertainty.

Chapter 25 Futures (Ludwig B. Chincarini)

This chapter discusses the concepts related to using futures to hedge different business risks. Hedging can be useful in reducing business risks in various markets. The chapter provides detailed examples of useful techniques to hedge risks for an equity portfolio manager, a bond manager, a coffee retailer, an airline company, an orange producer, a utility company, and a global portfolio manager. In each example, the method of how to compute the appropriate hedge is discussed and a simple measurement of the effectiveness of the hedge is examined using historical data. The chapter also discusses the basics about how to trade futures contracts, how they should theoretically be valued, and the available contracts for hedging.

Chapter 26 Swaps (Dimitris Tsouknidis and Elias Boukrami)

This chapter analyzes swap contracts and their uses as hedging instruments. It also introduces the basic types and properties of swap contracts and highlights their importance for the financial industry. By using swap contracts, a firm can effectively hedge various risks faced in today's business environment. A series of practical examples is used to exhibit the hedging function of swap contracts for managing risks related to interest rates and foreign exchange rates. The chapter also focuses on using swaps as off-balance sheet activities to hedge risks and to maximize firm value. In the final section, the chapter provides a primer on measuring swap hedging effectiveness that builds upon contemporary banking theory.

Chapter 27 Credit Derivatives (Udo Broll, Simone Raab, and Peter Welzel)

Since the 1990s, credit derivatives allowing the transfer of credit risk without transferring the underlying loan have become an important form of financial contracts. This chapter outlines basic stylized facts of credit derivatives markets. Focusing on the economics of credit derivatives, the chapter introduces the industrial organization approach to banking for an analysis of credit risk transfer. It also presents the optimal extent of hedging with and without basis risk as well as insights into hedging effectiveness and hedging under state-dependent preferences such as over the business cycle. In an extended model of hedging credit risk, higher market transparency in the sense of a more reliable information system in the loan market always raises expected bank profits but may lead to higher or lower expected credit volume. Finally, the chapter reviews other topics and insights from the literature on credit derivatives.

Chapter 28 Foreign Exchange Derivatives in Frontier Markets (Othmane Boukrami and Bert van Lier)

The development of financial markets, including foreign exchange (FX) forwards markets, is an important factor in driving economic development in frontier economies. However, various identified factors exist creating barriers to growth and deepening of local financial markets in these countries including capital controls. This situation leaves FX derivative traders without efficient mechanisms to absorb exposures in the same way they do in established markets. Prospective market makers could jump-start the market development process by building exposures on their own without external hedging options. The lack of market activity leaves them without appropriate pricing benchmarks on which to start trading. This chapter explores the status of local and offshore frontier markets and examines two possible proxies for pricing FX forwards to aid in breaking the deadlock.

PART SIX GOING FORWARD

The sixth and final part deals with lessons learned from past financial disasters, especially the financial crisis of 2007–2008 and focuses on the future of investment risk management.

Chapter 29 Risk Management and Financial Disasters (Gabriele Sabato)

Financial markets have experienced many financial crises across time. Although each boom and crisis has some distinctive features, several recurring themes and common patterns emerge. While the technologies and methodologies to measure risks have reached impressive levels of sophistication and complexity, the financial crisis of 2007–2008 clearly demonstrates that substantial improvements in the way financial institutions measure and manage risks are still urgently needed. This chapter provides an analysis and discussion of recurring themes and patterns that increase the likelihood of financial crises and disasters. It also proposes how the financial industry should evolve to mitigate their impact on the world economy. In particular, financial institutions play a fundamental role in mitigating systemic risk. To increase the soundness of financial institutions, regulatory and supervisory oversight are essential in defining new rules that can lead to improving capital allocation strategies by defining a clear risk-appetite framework, implementing a true enterprise risk management program, which measures and aggregates all risk types, and redefining the role of the risk function within the governance of financial organizations. Improving methods used to measure risks and implementing the proposed changes in risk management would allow financial institutions to reduce the systemic risk and restore the trust of markets and customers to mitigate the impact of the next financial crises.

Chapter 30 *The Future of Risk Management (Hunter M. Holzhauer)*
The previous chapters examine known risk factors that threaten the value of investments and portfolios. This chapter focuses on new trends in risk management. The chapter begins by creating a context for the current perception and state of risk management. It then discusses several topics that will affect the future of risk management. Next, the chapter investigates professional organizations that are helping evolve risk management. The chapter develops a case for regulatory risk as a future concern for risk managers and then investigates multi-asset investing as a popular trend among risk managers. Following a comparison of risk measures currently in use, the chapter explores how innovations in products and technology are changing risk management. The penultimate section discusses risk manager preferences for the future of risk management. The final section concludes with a summary of the purpose and growing importance of risk management within the firm.

Summary and Conclusions

Investment risk management is a complex but intriguing subject. Recent events such as the financial crisis of 2007–2008 dramatically illustrate the inadequacy of the current state of risk management. Not surprisingly, much has been written about the need for both better risk management and increased risk awareness within the investment community. Best practices are evolving within the dynamic area of risk management.

Having a better understanding of investment risk management offers considerable advantages to investors, managers, regulators, and institutions. Before developing a risk management strategy, each group must recognize how to identify sources of risk and understand how to measure them. Risk is commonly classified into various groups including market, credit, operational, and liquidity. Other types of risk are also important. For example, beyond fundamental analysis, investor behavior also plays a role in market dynamics. Corporate governance is important in assessing firm-specific risk, while country risk assessment is important on a macro level. Interested parties also need to understand how the cumulative effect of each risk category affects total portfolio risk.

Investors tend to be more concerned about the threat of extreme losses than extreme gains. Various risk measures such as VaR have emerged to allow for measuring downside risk. Within the left tail of the return distribution, investors are concerned with how bad losses will be if they encounter large losses. Both on a micro (firm) level through risk budgeting and on a macro level through regulatory frameworks, risk management processes play an important role in assessing such concerns. On an ex-post basis, investors need to understand the impact of risk-return trade-offs through risk-adjusted performance measures and attribution analysis.

Risk management can be accomplished through diversification using asset allocation including alternative investments (e.g., hedge funds and mortgage-backed securities) and through derivative securities (e.g., options, futures, and swaps). Risk management is an evolving process. Through lessons learned as a result of the financial crisis of 2007–2008 and other financial disasters, investors can gain access to more effective and sophisticated ways to achieve their return objectives through appropriate risk management. Throughout this book, readers can expect to gain a better understanding not only of the various types of risk and how to measure them, but also of how to hedge these risks. As Warren Buffet once remarked, "Risk comes from not knowing what you're doing."

References

Bender, Jennifer, and Frank Nielsen. 2009. "Best Practices for Investment Risk Management." *The Markit Magazine*, August, 55–57. Available at http://www.markit.com/assets/en/docs/markit-magazine/issue-5/MM05_Kit%20&%20Caboodle.pdf.

Carhart, Mark M. 1997. "On Persistence in Mutual Fund Performance." *Journal of Finance* 52:1, 57–82.

Fama, Eugene F., and Kenneth R. French. 1993. "Common Risk Factors in the Returns on Stocks and Bonds." *Journal of Financial Economics* 33:1, 3–56.

Investopedia. 2014. "Risk Management." Available at http://www.investopedia.com/terms/r/riskmanagement.asp.

Jorion, Philippe. 2007. *Value-at-Risk: The New Benchmark for Managing Financial Risk*, 3rd Edition. New York: McGraw-Hill.

Lintner, John. 1965. "The Valuation of Risky Assets and the Selection of Risky Investments in Stock Portfolios and Capital Budgets." *Review of Economics and Statistics* 47:1, 13–37.

Markowitz, Harry. 1952. "Portfolio Selection." *Journal of Finance* 7:1, 77–91.

Ross, Stephen. 1976. "The Arbitrage Theory of Capital Asset Pricing." *Journal of Economic Theory* 13:3, 341–360.

Sharpe, William F. 1964. "Capital Asset Prices: A Theory of Market Equilibrium under Conditions of Risk." *Journal of Finance* 19:3, 425–442.

Sortino, Frank A., and Lee N. Price. 1994. "Performance Measurement in a Downside Risk Framework." *Journal of Investing* 3:3, 54–69.

2

Measuring and Managing Risk

RAIMUND M. KOVACEVIC

Assistant Professor, Institute for Statistics and Operations Research, University of Vienna

GEORG CH. PFLUG

Professor of Statistics and Operations Research, Institute for Statistics and Operations Research, University of Vienna

ALOIS PICHLER

Researcher, Norwegian University of Science and Technology

Introduction

Risk management is important in many sectors especially in banking, insurance, and finance. In fact, from a societal point of view, a smooth, steady development of economic activities is preferable over quick movements with a high risk of potential large drawdowns. This societal risk aversion is the underlying reason for the development of the Basel framework for banking and its adoption by governments and international associations of states, especially by the European Union. The same is true for the solvency standards for insurance. Conversely, managers often contend that risk management might not be relevant for leading a business. Some question why they should care about risk when a firm's shareholders can take their preferred amount of risk by mixing shares of different firms. In fact, this argument seems reasonable from a theoretical standpoint because it relates to the main point of the famous Modigliani-Miller theorems (Modigliani and Miller 1958). It also relates to risk management (Hommel 2005; McNeil, Frey, and Embrechts 2005). If rational investors have unrestricted access to perfect capital markets, they can replicate any hedging strategy available to a corporation by neglecting any frictions such as transaction costs including taxes and bankruptcy costs.

However, the assumptions for the Modigliani-Miller theorems show that the argument cannot be applied to practical decisions. Access to certain parts of capital markets is easier or at least cheaper for corporations than for private investors. Also, various frictions such as taxes and bankruptcy costs are omnipresent and clearly can change a firm's risk profile. Private investors cannot hedge risk in the same way as specialized firms. Hence, risk management is an important part of corporate management.

Before the financial crisis of 2007–2008, Alan Greenspan, then chairman of the Federal Reserve, stated in a speech at the American Bankers Association Annual Convention in New York on October 5, 2004 (Federal Reserve Board 2004): "It would be a mistake to conclude that the only way to succeed in banking is through ever-greater size and diversity. Indeed, better risk management may be the only truly necessary element of success in banking."

This chapter provides a discussion of the foundations of quantitative risk management from a principled point of view. Economic success cannot be planned without taking uncertainties into account. *Risk* is the danger that unwanted events may happen or that developments go in an unintended direction. Quantifiable risk is described by profit-and-loss distributions arising from risk factors and formed by the actions of a firm. Risk measures such as volatility or value-at-risk (VaR) summarize favorable or unfavorable properties of such distributions. Risk management starts with a given portfolio of financial instruments, real properties, equipment, storage, projects, or other assets or liabilities relevant for business. Given potential actions such as buying or selling hedging instruments or insurance, risk management aims at reshaping the potentially unfavorable, original profit-and-loss distribution such that the return distribution of the resulting portfolio is acceptable. The actions taken should come at minimal costs. This aspect of controlling risk at minimal costs is called "managing" risk.

The three main components, which can be called the "three Ms" of risk analysis, are:

- *Modeling risk.* This includes identifying economically dangerous uncertainties and the risk factors associated with them. Modeling risk also includes the method of observing data and estimating probabilities to quantify and control the risk.
- *Measuring risk.* This relates to a quantitative assessment of the amount of risk caused by the methodology used to measure risk.
- *Managing risk.* This consists of all actions needed to mitigate the risk and/or to alleviate the consequences of unwanted events. It involves selecting appropriate risk-management techniques, making optimal decisions, and implementing and reviewing the risk management process.

Although all three components are discussed, the chapter focuses on managing risk.

This view clearly neglects some aspects of risk management that are often more concerned with regulatory and internal reporting issues than with prospective decision-making. Furthermore, differences exist between asset and liability classes with respect to typical loss models, available instruments, and actions. Some of these "nuts and bolts" of risk management are discussed in detail throughout this book, but the analysis in this chapter deals with the basic aspects.

Finally, the chapter focuses on quantifiable risk, also called *aleatoric risk*, which allows basing risk management on a well-identified statistical model. Aleatoric risk is described by random distributions. It has to be distinguished from *epistemic risk*, which is the risk of using an incorrect statistical model. Although model risk, which is often called *model ambiguity*, is an important issue that is susceptible to mathematical methods (Pflug and Wozabal 2009; Kovacevic 2011; Pflug, Pichler, and Wozabal 2012), such risk goes beyond the scope of this chapter. This chapter also does not discuss Knightian uncertainty (Knight 1964), which refers to completely unquantifiable risk.

The remainder of the chapter is organized as follows. The next section examines the classification of risk and analyzes the foundations of the distributional approach to risk management, in particular risk factors and the resulting profit-and-loss function. The following section discusses deviation-type risk measures and examines both general properties and properties of individual measures. The final section gives an overview of the most important risk management technologies and their use for optimal risk management. The chapter closes with a summary and conclusions.

Classification of Risk

Risk may arise from many sources. In fact, any business activity or contract is subject to an uncertain final outcome. In banking, a widely used classification, which is based on the Basel framework, can be summarized as follows (McNeil et al. 2005).

- *Market risk* is the risk that market prices (e.g., interest rates, foreign exchange, and stock and option prices) change in an unfavorable way or that a market does not function as desired resulting in market liquidity risk or the risk that advantageous transactions cannot be executed. Market risk also includes the price risk for input factors and products, if a firm produces physical goods. Market risk is caused by the universe of all economic agents in the relevant markets.
- *Credit risk* is the risk that a debtor cannot meet all obligations. Credit risk is a counterparty risk (i.e., a risk caused by another economic agent).
- *Liquidity risk* is the risk that the bank cannot satisfy the demand of cash money. This risk is related to the behavior of the customers as a risk factor.
- *Operational risk* is the risk that unwanted events occur in a bank's operational and administrative procedures. The Basel II Accord distinguishes several types of events that fall into the category of operational risks: internal and external fraud, employment practices, clients, products and business practices, damage to physical assets, business disruption and system failures, execution, delivery, and process management. Operational risk is caused by the bank itself as an economic agent.

Most of these core financial risks may also occur in other types of business. For instance, production risk (e.g., machine breakdown and failures of the supply chain) is a form of operational risk. Other important types of risk are:

- *Strategic risk* evolves from new technologies, overall (societal) changes in supply and demand, and effects of corporate strategy (e.g., mergers and acquisitions) among others.
- *Compliance risk* involves various risks related to regulatory and governmental requirements.

Depending on the business under consideration, other risks may also be relevant such as natural disaster, war, and other kinds of political risk.

The order of this enumeration broadly goes from better quantifiable to less quantifiable types of risk. Long-term technological or political risks clearly tend to be more on the side of Knightian uncertainty than of quantifiable risk. Their assessment is typically done by expert opinion. Risk management can be done at the unit level. This practice is common especially given that many firms have separate business units. However, the *integrated risk management approach* looks at the interplay between the different sources of risk and their effect on the overall business. The key to modern risk management is using probabilistic models (i.e., the risk quantification by estimation of the profit-and-loss distributions and their probability densities).

Other ways and methods are available for describing and specifying risk that do not build on the concept of profit-and-loss distribution. For example, McNeil et al. (2005) outline the following alternatives:

- *Scenario based approaches* (also known as *stress tests*) define adverse scenarios. The risk measurement consists in calculating the portfolio value under these scenarios in a "what-if" analysis.
- The *notional approach* defines risk as proportional to the notional amount of a position with constants of proportionality defined to reflect the riskiness of the actual position.
- *Factor sensitivities* measure the change in the value of a position or portfolio, depending on a change in each of the underlying risk factors separately.

Any of these approaches has its merits in a specific situation, but basing risk measurement on the profit-and-loss distribution is most natural, given that a reasonable model can be estimated. Further, the resulting risk figures can be compared across different types of portfolios.

PROFIT-AND-LOSS DISTRIBUTIONS

Single period planning considers only the beginning and the end of the period $[0, T]$, where 0 represents the time now and T the final time. Let Y_T denote the value of the portfolio under consideration, which contains all assets and liabilities relevant for the business under consideration. The profit-and-loss variable Y at the end of the planning horizon is given by Equation 2.1:

$$Y = Y_T - Y_0. \tag{2.1}$$

Here Y_T contains all capital gains, as well as all payouts (as dividends or coupon interest payments) accumulated up to time T, while Y_0 denotes today's value of the portfolio. Assume that Y_0 is known with certainty. In a risky environment, the value of the portfolio at time T is unknown in advance and is modeled as a random variable with distribution function F_{Y_T}. As a result, the profit-and-loss Y is also a random variable with the distribution function shown in Equation 2.2:

$$F_Y(y) = F_{Y_T}(y + Y_0). \tag{2.2}$$

Estimates are often visualized as densities, rather than distribution functions. *Densities* are the derivatives of the distribution functions. Typically, a certain shortfall below the expected value can be absorbed by tapping into the risk capital, which was put aside

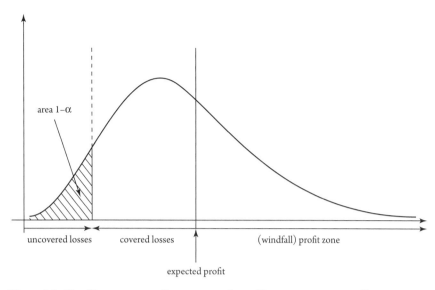

Figure 2.1 THE DENSITY OF A PROFIT-AND-LOSS DISTRIBUTION AND COVERAGE OF LOSSES. This figure shows the expected profit as well as the area of covered and uncovered losses. Uncovered losses occur with a probability of $1 - \alpha$.

for risk coverage, whereas higher shortfalls, which exceed the budget for risk below are uncovered. The probability of occurrence of uncovered losses is $1 - \alpha$, where α is the *risk margin*. Figure 2.1 illustrates this approach. It shows the expected profit as well as the area of covered and uncovered losses in a schematic way. Uncovered losses occur with a probability of $1 - \alpha$.

Depending on the purpose, especially for insurance applications, the pure loss distribution is estimated instead of the profit-and-loss distribution. Generally speaking, loss L is just the negative of profit-and-loss (i.e., $L = Y_0 - Y_T$). Often, when dealing with stock markets, analyzing the distribution of relative returns is useful as shown in Equation 2.3:

$$R_T = \frac{Y_T}{Y_0} - 1, \tag{2.3}$$

or of continuously compounded returns shown in Equation 2.4:

$$r_T = \log(1 + R_T), \tag{2.4}$$

rather than the distribution of the absolute loss or profit-and-loss (i.e., the absolute return).

RISK FACTORS

Although the overall profit-and-loss distribution is the object of primary interest in risk management, typical approaches do not model the portfolio profit-and-loss in a direct way. Overall risk is usually traced to more elementary risk constituents or risk factors. In a stock portfolio, for example, the individual securities may be considered as the relevant risk factors. However, the whole universe of securities is often modeled as dependent on one or several risk factors such as a market index as included in the capital asset pricing model (CAPM) (Sharpe 1964) and its successors. The risk factors for option portfolios are the prices of the underlying securities and the risk factors in insurance are given by variables such as water levels, wind strength, or health condition of individuals.

The broad types of risk previously discussed can be considered as risk factors for overall business risk, but also can be analyzed in greater detail, which leads to the identification of finer risk factors. For example, credit risk contains more detailed risk determinants such as capital structure, credit history, credit rating, industry sectors, and firm size. Market risk may be related to interest rate risk, asset values, asset volatility, foreign exchange, liquidity, or customer behavior.

In this chapter, risk factors are random variables $X_T^{(k)}$ that influence the value of a portfolio under consideration. The influence may be direct as in the case of a stock portfolio or indirect. For a plain vanilla call option on a stock with strike price K, the related profit-and-loss Y. depends on the value of the underlying X_T (the basic risk factor) and the call price c_0 by $Y = \max\{X_T - K, 0\} - c_0$. Generally, profit-and-loss is modeled by applying a profit-and-loss function g to all relevant risk factors as shown in Equation 2.5:

$$Y = g(X_T^{(1)}, \ldots, X_T^{(M)}). \tag{2.5}$$

For a stock portfolio with security prices $X_T^{(i)}$ and portfolio weights w_i this representation takes the simple form shown in Equation 2.6:

$$Y = \sum_{i=1}^{n} w_i X_T^{(i)}. \tag{2.6}$$

Assuming that the risk factors have a joint distribution function f_X, the distribution function of the loss is given by Equation 2.7:

$$F_Y(z) = \int_{g(x_1,\ldots,x_n)\leq z} f_X(x_1, \ldots, x_M)dx_1 \ldots dx_M. \tag{2.7}$$

In practical risk management, the distributions of loss functions and/or risk factors are unknown and must be estimated. Depending on the type of risks, a multitude of statistical and econometric methods can be used to fit reasonable models to available data. Campbell, Lo, and MacKinley (1997) provide an overview. Alexander (2009) discusses market risk modeling while James and Webber (2000) examine for econometric methods applied to interest rates and Gourieroux and Jasiak (2007) review statistical methods in insurance and credit management.

Deviation-Type Risk Measures and Their Properties

The approach used in this chapter focuses on describing risk as a quantity derived from random variables or probability distributions. The random variable approach models the potential outcomes. In finance, potential outcomes are the possible value of at a certain portfolio of assets and liabilities. In insurance, potential outcomes may represent claims, which are relevant because of the terms of the insurance contract.

In principle, risk can be analyzed by the profit-and-loss random variable, as its distribution fully describes the adverse outcomes and their likelihood. However, managers are used to communicating in terms of figures, not in terms of distributions. Therefore, risk measures have been designed to aggregate and express in a single number what is associated with risk of the respective random variable. From a mathematical point of view, risk measures are considered as "functionals" (i.e., mappings from some probability space or a space of distribution functions to a numerical value).

The main purpose of risk measures is twofold. First, risk measures allow a comparison of two different profit-and-loss variables with respect to the inherent risk. Second, risk measures may be used as thresholds. A management decision that results in a profit-and-loss variable with a measured risk larger than a given threshold appears unacceptable and infeasible.

Many risk measures build solely on the distribution irrespective of the version of the random variable considered. These risk measures are called *version independent* and also called *distribution based* or *law invariant*. This chapter focuses on independent risk measures (i.e., statistical parameters). In some cases, the risk of a profit-and-loss variable Y may depend on a second variable Z, for instance, if the risk is defined as the probability of not reaching the same return as with the investment Z as shown in Equation 2.8:

$$R(Y) = P\{Y < Z\}. \tag{2.8}$$

Similar risk measures do not depend solely on the distribution of the random variable Y, and therefore are not version independent in the strict sense of the word. However, the joint distribution of Y and Z determines the risk and by extending the notion of version independence to multivariate distributions, this example is also covered.

Different classifications of risk measures are in use. For example, Pflug and Römisch (2007) provide a broad overview and Rockafellar and Uryasev (2013) offer a detailed analysis of the connections between deviation-type measures, measures of error, and associated statistics and risk aversion. The following discusses natural properties of an important class of risk measures, the *deviation-type* risk measures R. Deviation risk measures are related to acceptability or utility measures U by the relationships shown in Equations 2.9 and 2.10

$$U[Y] = E[Y] - R[Y] \tag{2.9}$$

or

$$R[Y] = E[Y] - U[Y], \tag{2.10}$$

where $E[Y]$ denotes the expectation of the random variable Y. Properties of R translate to properties of U and vice versa.

- Deviation-type functionals are *cash invariant* (i.e., adding a fixed cash amount, which is a constant, does not change the risk profile), and thus the valuation of a random variable in Equation 2.11:

$$R[Y + a] = R[Y]. \tag{2.11}$$

- This property is also called *translation invariance*.
- The property illustrated in Equation 2.12

$$X \leq Y \text{ implies } U[X] \leq U[Y], \text{ i.e. } E[X] - R[X] \leq E[Y] - R[Y] \tag{2.12}$$

- is called *monotonicity*. A monotone utility functional generally assigns higher values to higher financial positions.
- A deviation risk measures is called *convex*, if the property shown in Equation 2.13

$$R[\lambda X + (1 - \lambda) Y] \leq \lambda R[X] + (1 - \lambda) R[Y] \tag{2.13}$$

- holds for $0 \leq \lambda \leq 1$. The natural interpretation of convexity is the well-established thinking that mixing two financial positions reduces the risk in total. The corresponding property for utility measures is concavity.
- Furthermore, a deviation-type measure is *positively homogeneous* if it satisfies
- $\mathcal{R}[\lambda Y] = \lambda \mathcal{R}[Y]$ for positive $\lambda > 0$. This formulation tacitly assumes that the financial position λY is available for any $\lambda > 0$. This means in turn that there are no restrictions on liquidity. The lack of positive homogeneity indicates limitations on liquidity.
- A deviation risk measure $\mathcal{R}$ finally is called *strict*, if it is not negative if applied to any random variable (i.e., $\mathcal{R}[Y] \geq 0$).

In this context, another class of risk measures, closely related to deviation-type measures, is important: *coherent* risk measures (Artzner, Delbaen, Eber, and Heath 1999). Such functionals ρ are translation antivariant (i.e., $\rho[Y + a] = \rho[Y] - a$), point wise antimonotone (i.e., $X \leq Y$ implies that $\rho[X] \leq \rho[Y]$), convex (i.e., $\rho[\lambda X + (1 - \lambda)Y] \leq \lambda\rho[X] + (1 - \lambda)\rho[Y]$ for $0 \leq \lambda \leq 1$) and positive homogeneous. Note that in the original version, they were defined as subadditive (i.e., $\rho[X + Y] \leq \rho[X] + \rho[Y]$), from which—together with positive homogeneity—convexity follows. Coherent risk measures can be interpreted as the amount of capital required to make a profit-and-loss distribution acceptable. $\mathcal{R}$ is a deviation risk measure if and only if $\rho[Y] = \mathcal{R}[Y] - E[Y]$ is a coherent risk measure. This allows constructing coherent risk measures from deviation measures and vice versa. Deviation risk is important because typical financial measures such as volatility and the Basel II VaR fall under this category.

EXAMPLES OF RISK MEASURES

This section presents several important risk measures and their main theoretical properties. The final section then analyzes their behavior in the context of a simple practical portfolio optimization problem.

Variance and Standard Deviation

In his seminal paper, Markowitz (1952) provides the earliest attempt to quantify risk. This work laid the basis for the mean-variance (or mean-standard deviation) approach to financial modeling, which appeared for the first time in the safety first criterion (Roy 1952) and later in the CAPM (Treynor 1962; Sharpe 1964) as well as in the Sharpe ratio (Sharpe 1966), the Black-Scholes option price formula (Black and Scholes 1973) among others. Recall that the variance of a random variable Y is defined in Equation 2.14:

$$Var(Y) = E[(Y - EY)^2], \tag{2.14}$$

and the standard deviation is its square root shown in Equation 2.15:

$$Std(Y) = \sqrt{E[(Y - EY)^2]}. \tag{2.15}$$

The standard deviation of log-returns is called volatility and is typically given in percent of the expectation. Both the variance and the standard deviation are cash-invariant, convex, and strict, but not monotonic. The standard deviation is also (positively) homogeneous. Due to the lack of monotonicity, both the variance and standard deviation are only deviation-type measures, but not deviation measures in the strict sense of the word. A major disadvantage of the variance and the standard deviation is that both measures value deviations in the positive directions and deviations in the negative direction as equal. Evidence suggests that windfall profits should be treated differently from unexpected losses (Acerbi 2004). Markowitz (1952) calls the mean-variance approach "modern portfolio theory," but more modern theoretical frameworks disregard the variance and dwell on asymmetric deviation measures such as the lower semideviation. Furthermore, the widespread mean-variance approach to portfolio management is not consistent with utility theory. A mean-variance efficient portfolio may be unacceptable by decision makers who maximize monotonic, concave expected utility. This drawback does not exist for the lower semideviation, which is discussed in the next section.

Lower Semivariance and Semideviation

Motivated by the idea that negative deviations constitute a real risk, the lower semivariance is defined in Equation 2.16:

$$Var^-(Y) = E[(\min (Y - EY, 0))^2] \tag{2.16}$$

and the lower semideviation is shown in Equation 2.17:

$$Std^-(Y) = \sqrt{E[(\min (Y - EY, 0))^2]}. \tag{2.17}$$

The restriction to only negative deviations implies that the lower semideviation exhibits appropriate properties of a deviation measure: it is cash-invariant, convex, monotonic, and strict.

Lower Mean Absolute Deviation

The variance uses the square function for weighting the deviation from the expectation. Using the absolute value results in the mean absolute deviation in Equation 2.18:

$$Mad\,(Y) = E\,[|Y - EY|].\tag{2.18}$$

Half of this value illustrated in Equation 2.19 is called the *lower mean absolute deviation*:

$$Mad^{-}(Y) = \frac{1}{2}E\,[|Y - EY|].\tag{2.19}$$

Similarly to the lower semideviation, the lower mean absolute deviation exhibits all appropriate properties: it is cash-invariant, convex, monotonic, and strict. Related to the lower mean absolute deviation is the *Dutch premium principle* as a utility measure, which has its initial applications in insurance (van Heerwaarden and Kaas 1992). Its formula is given in Equation 2.20:

$$EY - \lambda E\big[\min\,(Y - EY, 0)\big] = EY - \lambda Mad^{-}(Y)\tag{2.20}$$

for some $0 < \lambda < 1$. Evidently, it averages the deviation from the expected value (the lump sum premium according the equivalence principle).

Value-at-Risk

The most prominent risk measure is the value-at-risk. By definition, the VaR at level α specifies the deviation from the expectation, such that the probability of events exceeding it is the prescribed level α as illustrated in Equation 2.21:

$$P\big\{Y > EY - VaR_{\alpha}(Y)\big\} = \alpha.\tag{2.21}$$

Using the notion of quantiles, the VaR equals the expectation minus the $(1 - \alpha)$ quantile in Equation 2.22:

$$VaR_{\alpha}(Y) = EY - Q_{(1-\alpha)}(Y)\tag{2.22}$$

where the quantile is defined as in Equation 2.23:

$$P\big\{Y < Q_{\beta}\,(Y)\big\} = \beta.\tag{2.23}$$

In the banking industry, the VaR is related to certain target period (e.g., one day, 10 days, one month, or one year). For instance $VaR_{0.90}{}^{10\,\text{days}}$ expresses the fact that the target period is 10 days and the confidence level is 90 percent. With a probability of α, the value of the portfolio at the target time will not fall $VaR_{g}{}^{\text{time period}}$ units below the expected value. Figure 2.2 shows a schematic profit-and-loss density. The shaded area represents the probability of getting an outcome larger than expectation minus $VaR_{0.9}$, which is 90 percent. The uncovered losses occur in 10 percent of the cases: with a VaR at a confidence level of 90 percent, 10 percent of the potential returns fall more than 200 units below the expected return (ER), which here is 1,000.

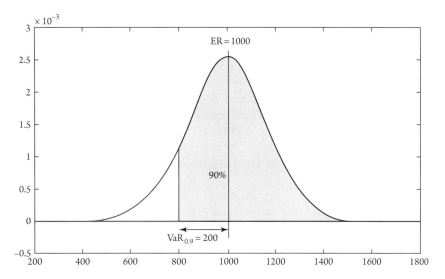

Figure 2.2 THE VAR AT A CONFIDENCE LEVEL OF 90 PERCENT.   This figure shows that with a VaR at a confidence level of 90 percent, 10 percent of the potential returns fall more than 200 units below the expected return, which here is 1,000.

The advantage of the VaR as a risk measure lies in the fact that it is a monetary value, which is easy to interpret and is defined for every return or value distribution. VaR can be used both in theoretical models and in simulations, and it can be explained to non-experts without difficulty. However, some caveats are associated with the VaR. While it is cash-invariant, monotonic, and strict, VaR is not convex and therefore difficult to use within optimization problems.

Also, VaR does not contain any information about those $(1 - \alpha)100$ percent cases, in which the value lies below the expectation minus the VaR. This means that two different distributions, which are equal in their positive tails, but very different in the negative tails, are treated equally by the VaR. Further, knowing the VaR of every individual position of a portfolio does not allow any conclusion for the VaR of the entire portfolio. Indeed, this is the reason banks have to report on credit risk, market risk, and operational risk separately in an extensive and comprehensive risk report within the Basel framework. Further, knowing the VaR for a certain period of time does not say anything about the VaR for a different period of time. Finally, the VaR might be subject to confusion with the variance of a random variable, although these are clearly very distinct concepts.

The Average Value-at-Risk and Its Associated Deviation

The average value-at-risk (AVaR) avoids some drawbacks of the VaR. It is defined for a parameter α, which again is called level. The AVaR averages the bad scenarios (how bad is bad?), which as well explains its name and is shown in Equation 2.24:

$$AVaR_\alpha (Y) = E\left[Y|Y \leq Q_\alpha (Y)\right]. \tag{2.24}$$

The latter formula justifies the alternative name conditional value-at-risk (CVaR), which is frequently used particularly in finance. In insurance, the AVaR is known as conditional tail expectation and it is important in multiple perspectives. Above all, the conditional tail expectation is important to evaluate the potential deviation of a portfolio's loss from its expected mean and thus is important for insurance industry regulations (Ko, Russo, and Shyamalkumar 2009). The conditional tail expectation can be employed as a premium principle generalizing the equivalence principle, such that loadings to the insurance premium are naturally incorporated (Pichler 2013). These loadings can represent the degree of uncertainty, as the insurance does not ultimately know the distribution function of the loss distribution, but it may relate to avoidance of ruin risk equally well.

While the AVaR is a utility measure, the associated deviation measure is the average value-at-risk deviation (AVaRD) is illustrated in Equation 2.25:

$$AVaRD_\alpha(Y) = EY - AVaR_\alpha(Y). \tag{2.25}$$

The AVaRD is a cash-invariant, convex, monotonic, and strict deviation risk measure. The AVaRD is a very general risk measure. In fact, as Kusuoka (2001) notes, any risk measure satisfying the essential axioms introduced above can be built from combinations of AVaRD measures at different levels.

The Entropic Deviation
This entopic deviation (EntD) measure is defined in Equation 2.26:

$$EntD_\gamma(Y) = EY + \frac{1}{\gamma} logE\left[\exp\left(-\gamma Y\right)\right]. \tag{2.26}$$

It is related to the monotonic and concave exponential utility function $y \to -\exp(-\gamma y)$. The parameter γ determines the risk aversion. The EntD is cash-invariant, convex, strict, and monotonic, but not positively homogeneous.

The Linear-Quadratic Error Measure
The variance is the minimal value of the following "prediction problem" is shown in Equation 2.27:

$$min_a E\left[\left(Y - a\right)^2\right]. \tag{2.27}$$

But as stated previously, the symmetric weighting of profits above and below expectation is not appropriate. By considering the asymmetric function in Equation 2.28,

$$h(y) = \begin{cases} y & if\ y \geq 0 \\ y^2 & if\ y < 0 \end{cases} \tag{2.28}$$

one may define the linear-quadratic error measure as shown in Equation 2.29:

$$LQE(Y) = min_a E\left[h\left(Y - a\right)\right]. \tag{2.29}$$

This measure is cash-invariant, convex, monotonic, and strict.

Special Properties of the Normal Distribution and Applications

The normal distribution is of particular importance in finance because the returns on a stock market series are often considered normally distributed. For this reason, some relationships for the VaR and the AVaR for the normal distribution are shown.

- If Y is normally distributed with mean μ and variance σ^2, then $VaR_\alpha(Y) = \sigma\Phi^{-1}(\alpha)$,
  where Φ is the standard normal distribution function.
- If the volatility is given as $v = \sigma\mu$ (typically in percent), then $VaR_\alpha(Y) = \mu v\Phi^{-1}(\alpha)$.
- If the one-day volatility is v, then the t-day volatility is $\sqrt{t}v$ and hence for normal distributions (and only for normal distributions) $VaR_\alpha^{t\ days} = \sqrt{t}VaR_\alpha^{1\ day}$.
  The formula is often referred to as the *square root of time formula* and applied to estimate the VaR even for data that are known not to be normally distributed.
- If all data are multivariate normal, then the portfolio VaR can be calculated on the basis of the VaRs of the individual components and their covariance matrix as well.

The Basel II Accord requires holding risk capital for credit, market, and operational risk.

- The required risk capital for credit risk is calculated according to the so-called Basel formula. It estimates the $VaR_{99.9\%}^{1\ year}$ taking into account the correlation among the debtors,
- Risk capital for market risk: $VaR_{99\%}^{10\ days}$.
- Risk capital for operational risk: $VaR_{99.9\%}^{1\ year}$, meaning that with a probability of 99.9 percent, the one-year losses caused by events in the bank's operations are covered by the corresponding risk capital.
- The required risk capital for credit risk is calculated according to the so-called Basel formula. It estimates the $VaR_{99.9\%}^{1\ year}$ taking into account the correlation among the debtors.

RISK MEASURES IN APPLICATIONS

To illustrate typical differences between individual measures requires using each measure for optimal portfolio selection. The portfolio will consist of positions in the following assets.

- Citigroup Bond Index World Government Bond Index All maturities (1BO).
- Morgan Stanley Capital International (MSCI) World Information Technology Index
  (2IT).
- MSCI World Utilities Index (3UT).
- MSC World Financials Index (4FI).
- Dow Jones Composite REIT Index (5RE).
- DJ UBS Commodity Index (6CO).

For each risk measure $\mathcal{R}$, the general portfolio optimization problem can be formulated as shown in Equation 2.30:

$$\min_w \mathcal{R}(Y_w)$$
$$s.t. \ E[Y_w] = \mu,$$

(2.30)

where the risk factors X_i are the returns of the individual securities i and $Y_w = \sum_{i=1}^{K} w_i X_i$ is the portfolio return with portfolio weights w_i. The optimal portfolio compositions and the minimal achievable risk depend on the return level μ. The curve relating the return levels to the minimal risk levels is called the *efficient frontier*. Note that both the one fund and the two fund theorem, originally formulated for the mean-variance case (Merton 1972), also hold for generalized portfolio optimization problems (Rockafellar, Uryasev, and Zabarankin 2006).

The following pictures show the efficient frontiers and the optimal portfolio compositions for the portfolio optimization problems with different risk measures $\mathcal{R}$ using empirical weekly return data from the years 2007 through 2011. The upper part of each figure shows the efficient frontier and the risk/return of each individual asset: the vertical axis depicts the expected portfolio return μ and the horizontal axis of the upper part relates to the respective risk measure analyzed. The lower part of each figure shows the portfolio composition, dependent on the respective risk. Because both parts share the horizontal axis, one can see the optimal (efficient) portfolio composition in terms of a percentage using a different shade for each asset type. Typically, the portfolio is diversified and assets with smaller risk enter the composition for low values of risk. When the risk increases, a tendency exists for fewer assets entering the

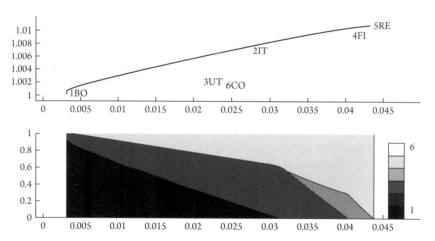

Figure 2.3 STANDARD DEVIATION, EFFICIENT FRONTIER, AND PORTFOLIO COMPOSITION.   For the upper figure, the risk dimension (horizontal axis) is the standard deviation. Asset 1 (1BO), which has the smallest risk, is selected for 100 percent at the lower end of the risk scale, while asset 5 (5RE), with highest risk and return, is selected for 100 percent at the upper end of the risk scale. The assets 3 (3UT) and 6 (6CO) are never picked.

optimal portfolios and assets with higher risk are gradually preferred at the cost of less risky assets. At the endpoint of maximal return only one asset (the one with maximal return and risk, in this case 5RE, the REIT index) is picked for 100 percent and all other assets are neglected. Although this structure is common to all figures, it differs in the compositions of the optimal portfolio. The choice of the method on how risk is quantified affects the final allocation decision, because each individual risk measure leads to a different trade-off between risk and expectation. If an asset does not enter the composition, this means that any portfolio containing this asset is dominated by some portfolio without the asset in terms of both, expectation and in risk.

The effects of the different risk measures are discussed in Figures 2.3–2.9. In Figure 2.3, the risk dimension (horizontal axis) shows the standard deviation. Asset 1 (1BO), which has the smallest risk, is selected for 100 percent at the lower end of the risk scale, while asset 5 (5RE), with highest risk and return, is selected for 100 percent at the upper end of the risk scale. The assets 3 (3UT) and 6 (6CO) are never picked.

Figure 2.4 is similar to Figure 2.3 but with the lower standard deviation as risk dimension (horizontal axis). Because this risk measure is convex, the efficient frontier is concave. The selected assets are similar to the case with standard deviation (Figure 2.3) but asset 4 (4FI) is initially picked.

In Figure 2.5, the risk dimension (horizontal axis) is the mean absolute deviation. Because this risk measure is also convex, the efficient frontier is concave. Asset 4 (4FI), asset 3 (3UT), and asset 6 (6CO) are never picked.

In Figure 2.6, risk is given by the VaR. The efficient frontier is not concave because the VaR is not convex. Asset 2 (2IT) is only picked for low risk portfolios and at the high risk end, not only asset 5 (5RE), but also assets 1 (1BO) and 4 (4FI) are in the portfolio.

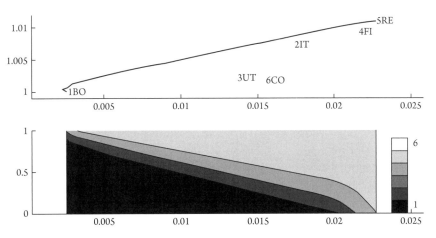

Figure 2.4 LOWER STANDARD DEVIATION, EFFICIENT FRONTIER, AND PORTFOLIO COMPOSITION.   This illustration is similar to Figure 2.3 but with the lower standard deviation as risk dimension (horizontal axis). Because this risk measure is convex, the efficient frontier is concave. The selected assets are similar to the case with standard deviation (Figure 2.3) but asset 4 (4FI) is initially picked.

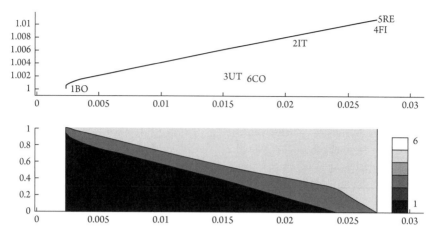

Figure 2.5 MEAN ABSOLUTE DEVIATION, EFFICIENT FRONTIER, AND PORTFOLIO COMPOSITION.   In this figure, the risk dimension (horizontal axis) is the mean absolute deviation. Because this risk measure is convex, the efficient frontier is concave. Asset 4 (4FI), asset 3 (3UT), and asset 6 (6CO) are never picked.

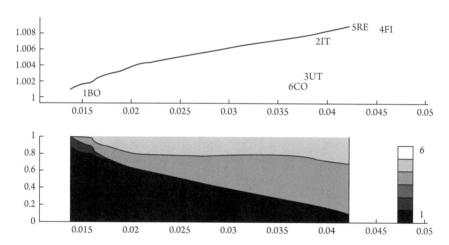

Figure 2.6 VALUE-AT-RISK, EFFICIENT FRONTIER, AND PORTFOLIO COMPOSITION. In this figure, the risk dimension (horizontal axis) is the VaR. The efficient frontier is not concave because the VaR is not convex. Asset 2 (2IT) is only picked for low risk portfolios and at the high risk end, not only asset 5 (5RE), but also assets 1 (1BO) and 4 (4FI) are in the portfolio.

AVaRD depicts risk in Figure 2.7. Because this risk measure is convex again, the efficient frontier is concave. The picked assets are similar to the ones picked by VaR but at the high risk end, only asset 5 (5RE) remains in the portfolio.

In Figure 2.8, the risk dimension (horizontal axis) is given by the entropic deviation. Because this risk measure is convex, the efficient frontier is concave. Unlike other

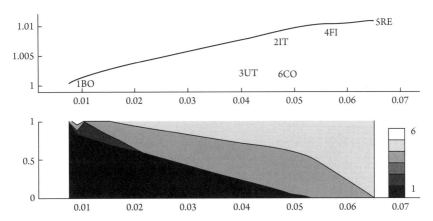

Figure 2.7 AVERAGE VALUE-AT-RISK DEVIATION, EFFICIENT FRONTIER, AND PORTFOLIO COMPOSITION.   In this figure, the risk dimension (horizontal axis) is the AVaRD. Because this risk measure is convex, the efficient frontier is concave. The picked assets are similar to the ones picked by VaR but at the high risk end, only asset 5 (5RE) remains in the portfolio.

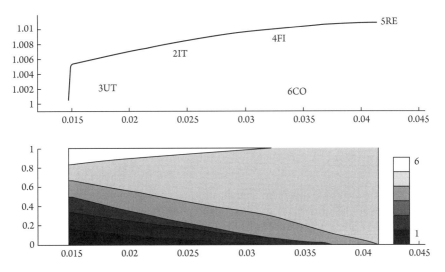

Figure 2.8 ENTROPIC DEVIATION, EFFICIENT FRONTIER, AND PORTFOLIO COMPOSITION.   In this figure, the risk dimension (horizontal axis) is the entropic deviation. Because this risk measure is convex, the efficient frontier is concave. Unlike other deviation risk measures, all assets are chosen for low risk. At the high risk end, only asset 5 (5RE) remains in the portfolio.

deviation risk measures, all assets are chosen for low risk. At the high risk end, only assets 5 (5RE) remains in the portfolio.

Risk in Figure 2.9 is the linear-quadratic error measure. This risk measure penalizes deviations from the expectation differently. Lower values (losses) are penalized with quadratic weights while higher values (windfall profits) are penalized with linear

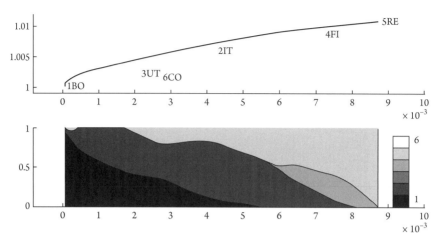

Figure 2.9 LINEAR-QUADRATIC ERROR MEASURE, EFFICIENT FRONTIER, AND PORTFOLIO COMPOSITION.   In this figure, the risk dimension (horizontal axis) is the linear-quadratic error measure. This risk measure penalizes deviations from the expectation differently. Lower values (losses) are penalized with quadratic weights while higher values (windfall profits) are penalized with linear weights. Because this risk measure is convex, the efficient frontier is concave. The optimal portfolios have a more irregular structure than with other risk measures.

weights. Because this risk measure is convex, the efficient frontier is concave. The optimal portfolios have a more irregular structure than with other risk measures.

Managing Risk

Once risks are identified and quantified, the ultimate goal is to set appropriate actions. Four basic types of actions are available for risk reduction (Bodie and Merton 2000; Dorfman and Cather 2012).

- *Risk avoidance* or *preventive risk management*. A firm may avoid completely certain activities or business lines in order to avoid the induced risk.
- *Risk retention*. A firm may take no special action to prevent or reduce a certain risk and just take it and use the firm's own resources to deal with the consequences if a loss occurs.
- *Loss prevention*. A firm takes all actions to systematically reduce the likelihood or severity of potential losses. The firm may aim at the distribution of a risk factor or at the profit-and-loss function. Typical actions involve risk-based pricing, diversification, and portfolio optimization but also organizational measures such as risk limits and early warning systems, or training of staff.
- *Risk transfer*. This involves transferring the risk to other market participants. Insurance and hedging are the main types of action.

Loss prevention and risk transfer are often referred to as *risk mitigation*. From a financial point of view, the most important methods are insurance, hedging, and diversification. Using insurance, a firm (the insured) pays a fixed premium (or a fixed stream of premiums) to reduce potential (random) future losses. The insurer receives the premium and has to pay the insured sum if the insured event occurs. Both classical insurance products as well as options fall under this category. By contrast, hedging is an action that reduces the risk exposure but also reduces the possibilities of gains. Various delivery contracts with fixed prices or forward, futures, and swaps are typical instruments to achieve this effect. Finally, diversification consists in spreading the invested sum among different securities, instead of investing in a single security. Ideally, the alternative securities should be uncorrelated, but it is a typical application of portfolio optimization to find a well-diversified portfolio in the presence of some correlation between the individual securities. Financial optimization can also be an important tool to build an integrated risk management strategy.

Unfortunately, completely eliminating risk by risk mitigation is impossible in finance. Given that risk avoidance is an option only for individual lines of business, some amount of risk must be taken (risk retention). For the remaining risks, a certain amount of capital, called *risk capital*, has to be allocated to cover possible losses. Usually, a distinction exists between regulatory and economic risk capital. The most important regulatory approach (the Basel Accords) developed from the Basel I Accord (Basel Committee on Banking Supervision 1988), formulating the necessity of holding a certain percentage of the notional amount as risk capital; the Basel II Accord (Basel Committee on Banking Supervision 2006), which builds the minimum capital requirements on the VaR and the Basel III Accord (Basel Committee on Banking Supervision 2011), bringing in long-term aspects and adaption for cyclical effects.

OPTIMIZATION IN RISK MANAGEMENT

As already pointed out in the distribution-based approach, risk management is the process of using the methods (avoidance, retention, prevention, and transfer) to change at minimum cost the profit-and-loss distribution of a portfolio of assets and liabilities (e.g., securities, projects, or business lines) such that the resulting risk is acceptable. More formally, let $w^0 = (w_1{}^0, \ldots, w_k{}^0)$ denote the investments into the individual assets and liabilities (instruments). Basically, w^0 is the number of units of individual instruments (e.g., the number of contracts of a certain type). For some purposes, however, calculating in terms of money invested is easier. The second convention is used in the following, which also avoids the necessity to formulate mixed integer optimization problems. Each instrument i is influenced by risk factors with random end value $X_1, \ldots, X_n$, which leads to a profit-and-loss $Y_i = f_i(X_1, \ldots, X_n)$ (including the market value and accumulated cash-flows) per unit of investment into instrument i. Typically, assets lead to positive and liabilities to negative profit-and-loss, or at least have the probability mass centered at the positive, respectively negative side. The overall profit-and-loss of the initial portfolio then is given by $Y_{w_0} = \sum_{i=1}^{k} w_i{}^0 \cdot Y_i$.

If its overall risk is larger than some risk budget γ (i.e., $\mathcal{R}(Y_w) > \gamma$), then the portfolio must be reallocated. In practical risk management, several risk measures $\mathcal{R}_j$, related to internal and regulatory requirements and describing the riskiness of individual asset and liability classes, can be relevant. In this case, several risk constraints $R_j(Y_w) > \gamma_j$ have to be considered. The new allocation is denoted by $w = (w_1, \ldots, w_k)$ and the resulting profit-and-loss is shown in Equation 2.31

$$Y_w = \sum_{i=1}^{k} w_i Y_i. \tag{2.31}$$

The reallocation of the portfolio leads to costs: if $c_i(w - w^0)$ denotes the transaction costs (Scherer 2004) for the reallocation of instrument i with cost function $c_i(\cdot)$, then the overall costs d are defined by Equation 2.32:

$$\sum_{i=1}^{k} w_i^0 + d = \sum_{i=1}^{k} w_i + \sum_{i=1}^{k} c(w_i - w_i^0). \tag{2.32}$$

If some w_i represents the number of instruments of type i (instead of the sum invested) and p_i represents the price or value of instrument i at the beginning, then w_i and w_i^0 have to be replaced by $p_i \cdot w_i$ and $p_i w_i^0$ in the first and second sum in Equation 2.32.

So far the assumption is that all weights w_i are nonnegative and an instrument i is an asset or a liability that is reflected by the distribution of its profit-and-loss Y_i. For some instruments, in particular assets such as stocks or futures that are traded at liquid exchanges, shorting them may also be possible. Thus, the assumption is made that assets and liabilities are ordered such that the first l assets are restricted to be nonnegative, while the rest is not bounded below.

Based on this setup the pure risk management problem of reaching a favorable distribution at lowest costs can be written as shown in Equation 2.33:

$$\begin{aligned}
\min_{d,w} \quad & d \\
\text{s.t.} \quad & R_j(Y_w) \leq \gamma_j \quad, \quad j \in \{1, \cdots, J\} \\
& \sum_{i=1}^{k} w_i^0 + d = \sum_{i=1}^{k} w_i + \sum_{i=1}^{k} c(w_i - w_i^0) \\
& w_i \geq 0, \qquad i \in \{1, \cdots, l\}.
\end{aligned} \tag{2.33}$$

Pure risk management sometimes may lead to business plans that observe given risk budget constraints but lead to poor results in term of expected profit-and-loss. To overcome this problem, a slightly extended optimization problem, which maximizes the expected net present value (NPV), can be solved.

Such an approach leads to an additional issue. In the pure problem as shown in Equation 2.33, the budget d used for financing the reallocation can be completely determined by optimization. Usually its value is zero or positive, but it might be also negative in some cases. If d is higher than the available budget, then reaching a favorable profit-and-loss distribution is impossible and emergency steps have to be taken. In the extended risk management problem, the expectation compensates for initial reallocation costs. For the optimal allocation, both the expectation and reallocation budget might be high, leading to a favorable distribution that is not financeable by the available budget. To obtain a favorable distribution with available budget δ requires adding the restriction $d \geq \delta$. If $\delta = 0$, this relationship is called a *self-financing reallocation*. With continuously compounded interest rate ρ, the extended optimization problem can be formulated as shown in Equation 2.34:

$$
\begin{aligned}
\max_{d,w} \quad & e^{-\rho \cdot T} E[Y_w] - d \\
\text{s.t.} \quad & \mathcal{R}_j(Y_w) \leq \gamma_j \quad , \quad j \in \{1, \cdots, J\} \\
& \sum_{i=1}^{k} w_i^0 + d = \sum_{i=1}^{k} w_i + \sum_{i=1}^{k} c(w_i - w_i^0) \\
& w_i \geq 0, \qquad \quad i \in \{1, \cdots, l\} \\
& d \leq \delta.
\end{aligned}
\tag{2.34}
$$

This chapter describes the optimization problems in a direct way, using the expectation and risk functional just as functions of the decision variables w. However, calculating analytic expressions for those that are functional and directly using them within an optimization problem, as the joint risk factor distribution, as well as the profit-and-loss function, may be quite complex. Therefore, the typical approach consists of approximating the risk factor distribution by a discrete, finite dimensional distribution (i.e., in representing it by some kind of scenarios). Cornuejols and Tütüncü (2007) provide many examples of scenario-based formulations.

Different approaches for scenario generation exist such as sample average approximation or Monte Carlo sampling (Kleywegt, Shapiro, and Homen-de-Mello 2001; Pagnocelli, Ahmed, and Shapiro 2009), the quasi Monte Carlo approach (Drew and Homem-de- Mello 2006), moment matching (Høyland and Wallace 2001), and approximation by minimizing some probability distance between the true and the discrete distribution (Dupacova, Gröwe-Kuska, and Römisch 2003). Usually, discretization leads to over-optimistic results in terms of the objective function. The latter approach has the advantage that for some distances (Kovacevic and Pichler 2012; Pflug and Pichler 2012) calculating bounds for the error in optimal value, resulting from the discretization, is possible.

In both optimization problems, Equations 2.33 and 2.34, the objective and constraints, except the risk budget constraints, are linear. The class of nonlinearity, and therefore speed, accuracy, and validity of the calculations largely depend on the risk measures used. For the AVaRD, the problem can easily be reformulated as a linear one (Rockafellar and Uryasev 2000). Variance and standard deviation, as well as all kinds of semi-variances and semi-deviations, finally lead to second order cone programming (still in the framework of convex optimization), where good algorithms exist. Unfortunately, the VaR is non-convex and is difficult to treat in an optimization problem. Danielsson, Embrechts, Goodhart, Keating, Muennich, Renault, and Shin (2001) discuss this problem and other pros and cons of the VaR methodology. Replacing the VaR with the AVaRD is usually a good idea because this leads to a tractable problem and the VaR constraint will still be satisfied. As Rockafellar and Uryasev (2000) show, the AVaRD gives an upper bound on the VaR.

RISK MANAGEMENT TECHNOLOGIES AND OPTIMIZATION

Having discussed the main types of actions in risk management, the focus now turns to analyzing how these technologies fit into the general optimization framework. When formulating Equations 2.33 and 2.34, a risk budgeting approach is used that considers the amount of final risk to handle as a constraint. Risk retention is inherent and the risk budgets together with the available budget are the most important parameters to be clarified before starting optimization.

Optimization automatically takes diversification into account. This is true in the independent case, but optimization can also deal with dependent random variables in an appropriate way. The optimal decision may also lead to zero weights in some instruments, which is risk avoidance.

Other risk management technologies usually involve some additional modeling, either extending the class of assets and liabilities or introducing additional constraints. Insurance contracts are handled by appropriate profit-and-loss and cost functions. The profit-and-loss function models the insured loss, while the cost function represents the present value of premium payments. Although the losses can be directly related to the risk factors, one may also want to insure instruments with profit-and-loss Y_i, instead of risk factors. In this case, additional securities with profit-and-loss as shown in Equation 2.35:

$$Y_j = g_j(X_1, \ldots, X_n) = h_j(Y_1, \ldots, Y_k) \tag{2.35}$$

can be introduced, where the function h models the profit-and-loss of the insurance instrument depending on the values of the asset and liabilities.

For classical insurance contracts, profit-and-loss of an insurance instrument j often depends on the weight w_i of the insured asset i For example, consider proportional insurance for an instrument I, where typically profit-and-loss per unit Y_i is a nonpositive valued random variable. The profit-and-loss of an uninsured position is given by $Y_j = w_i \cdot Y_i$. Hence the profit-and-loss of the insurance contract (per insured unit) is given by Equation 2.36:

$$Y_j = -w_i Y_i. \tag{2.36}$$

The weight $0 \le w_j \le 1$ related to the insurance contract models the percentage of the loss insured by the contract. Profit-and-loss is difficult to handle numerically in an optimization program because of its bilinear (nonconvex) structure. However, considering fixed positions w_i (some property) that have to be insured often makes sense. Costs $c(w_j)$ are the present value of premium payment and are calculated by actuarial methods. The simple proportional insurance can easily be extended to other types of insurance and reinsurance. Daykin, Pentikäinen, and Pesonen (1994) discuss such an approach for frequently used contract specifications and (Straub 1997) and Gerber (1997) on pricing of insurance contracts.

From the viewpoint of the optimization, framework options with maturity T are just another type of insurance contract. A plain vanilla put can be used to insure against a *drawdown* (e.g., the event of some spot price falling below the options strike-price K). Given a position w_i of some instrument I, the option here has profit-and-loss $w_i \max\{K - Y_i, 0\}$ and the costs are given by the price of a put option plus transaction costs.

In a similar manner, hedging instruments such as swaps and futures can be modeled by using their end cash flows as the related profit-and-loss. For exchange traded hedging instruments (with margin accounting), no initial price has to be considered. For over-the-counter (OTC) contracts without margin accounting, the value of the contract has to be considered. Transaction costs may be present in both cases.

In practice, an important part of risk management deals with constraints on the portfolio weights. Such restrictions can be easily implemented within an optimization formulation. Typical constraints are lower and upper bounds on individual positions, the accumulated weights over investment classes (e.g., stocks, bonds, and alternatives assets) and restrictions on the overall risk exposure to short or long positions. This exposure can be modeled by introducing additional nonnegative variables w^+ (the long exposure) and w^- (the short exposure), and defining $\sum w_i = w^+ - w^-$ within the relevant investment class.

Other actions in risk reduction are more difficult to model. The influence of each action has to be translated into some change of the shape of the loss curve. In operational risk, for instance, some changes in an organization may change the loss distribution (Loehndorf, Petzel, and Portmann 2007). Another example is retrofitting activities to reduce the risk of building collapse in earthquakes (Kunreuther, Deodatis, and Smyth 2004).

Summary and Conclusions

The first step in risk management of investments and/or liabilities is identifying the risk factors and estimating the profit-and-loss distribution. Not only the mean and variance but also the full distribution is needed to assess risk, in particular (extreme) downside risk. The literature contains many risk measures. Regulators require some of them such as the variance and the VaR. Some have better properties but are just used for internal purposes. Different risk measures can lead to quite different optimal decisions and the choice of the appropriate measure has to be done with care.

The main importance of the optimization approach lies in the integrated view on risk management and the related decisions. Even the modeling needs deep insight into the interplay among all relevant risk factors, the resulting profit-and-loss distributions, and the effect of the different types of actions. This already forms the basis of successful risk management. Optimization goes further: it fulfills all regulatory and internal risk budget targets and leads to an optimally balanced portfolio that takes into account the trade-offs in terms of risk (and potentially expected profit) and costs for all modeled actions.

Discussion Questions

1. Discuss the uses and limitations of the standard deviation (volatility) as risk measure.
2. Discuss the advantages and disadvantages of VaR as risk measure.
3. Explain why basing risk management on the profit-and-loss distribution is reasonable.
4. Discuss the different roles of a risk measure in the context of financial optimization.
5. Identify the drawbacks of the described profit-and-loss distributional approach.

References

Acerbi, Carlo. 2004. "Coherent Representations of Subjective Risk Aversion." In Giorgio Szegoe, ed., *Risk Measures for the 21st Century*, 147–208 . Hoboken, NJ: John Wiley & Sons.

Alexander, Carol. 2009. *Market Risk Analysis*. 4 Volume Boxset: *Quantitative Methods in Finance; Practical Financial Econometrics; Pricing, Hedging and Trading Financial Instruments; Value-at-Risk Models*. Chichester: John Wiley & Sons.

Artzner, Philippe, Freddy Delbaen, Jean-Marc Eber, and David Heath. 1999. "Coherent Measures of Risk." *Mathematical Finance* 9:3, 203–228.

Basel Committee on Banking Supervision. 1988. *International Convergence of Capital Measurement and Capital Standards*. Available at http://www.bis.org/publ/bcbs04a.htm.

Basel Committee on Banking Supervision. 2006 . *International Convergence of Capital Measurement and Capital Standards*. Available at http://www.bis.org/publ/bcbs128.htm.

Basel Committee on Banking Supervision. 2011. *Basel III: A Global Regulatory Framework for More Resilient Banks and Banking Systems*. Available at http://www.bis.org/publ/bcbs189.htm.

Black, Fischer, and Myron Scholes. 1973. "The Pricing of Options and Corporate Liabilities."*Journal of Political Economy* 81:3, 637–654.

Bodie, Zvi, and Robert C. Merton. 2000. *Finance*. Upper Saddle River, NJ: Prentice Hall International.

Campbell, John Y., Andrew W. Lo, and A. Craig MacKinley. 1997. *The Econometric of Financial Markets*. Princeton, NJ: Princeton University Press.

Cornuejols, Gerard, and Reha Tütüncü. 2007. *Optimization Methods in Finance*. Cambridge: Cambridge University Press.

Danielsson, Jon, Paul Embrechts, Charles Goodhart, Con Keating, Felix Muennich, Olivier Renault, and Hyun Song Shin. 2001. "An Academic Response to Basel II." Financial Markets Group, London School of Economics. Available at http://www.bis.org.

Daykin, Chris D., Teivo Pentikäinen, and Martti Pesonen. 1994. *Practical Risk Theory for Actuaries*. London: Chapman & Hall.

Dorfman, Mark S., and David Cather. 2012. *Introduction to Risk Management and Insurance*. Upper Saddle River, NJ: Pearson.

Drew, Shane S., and Tito Homem-de-Mello. 2006. "Quasi-Monte Carlo Strategies for Stochastic Optimization." *Proceedings of the 38th Conference on Winter Simulation*, 774–782.

Dupacova, Jitka, Nicole Gröwe-Kuska, and Werner Römisch. 2003. "Scenario Reduction in Stochastic Programming: An Approach Using Probability Metrics." *Mathematical Programming*, Series A, 95:3, 493–511.

Federal Reserve Board. 2004. *Remark by Chairman Alan Greenspan—Banking*. Available at http://www.federalreserve.gov/BOARDDOCS/Speeches/2004/20041005/.

Gerber, Hans U. 1997. *Life Insurance Mathematics*. Berlin: Springer.

Gourieroux, Christian, and Joann Jasiak. 2007. *The Econometrics of Individual Risk: Credit, Insurance, and Marketing*. Princeton, NJ: Princeton University Press.

Hommel, Ulrich. 2005. "Value-Based Motives for Corporate Risk Management." In Michael Frenkel, Ulrich Hommel, and Markus Rudolf, eds., *Risk Management—Challenge and Opportunity*, 455–478. Berlin: Springer.

Høyland, Kjetil, and Stein W. Wallace. 2001. "Generating Scenario Trees for Multistage." *Quantitative Finance* 47:2, 295–307.

James, Jessica, and Nick Webber. 2000. *Interest Rate Modelling*. Chichester: John Wiley & Sons.

Kleywegt, Anton J., Alexander Shapiro, and Tito Homem-de-Mello 2001. "The Sample Average Approximation Method for Stochastic Discrete Optimization." *SIAM Journal of Optimization* 12:2, 479–502.

Knight, Frank H. 1964. *Risk, Uncertainty and Profit*. New York: Sentry Press.

Ko, Bangwon, Ralph P. Russo, and Nariankadu D. Shyamalkumar. 2009. "A Note on the Nonparametric Estimation of the CTE." *ASTIN Bulletin* 39:2, 717–734.

Kovacevic, Raimund. 2011. "Maximum-Loss, Minimum-Win and the Esscher Pricing Principle." *IMA Journal of Management Mathematics* 23:4, 325–340.

Kovacevic, Raimund, and Alois Pichler. 2012. "Stochastic Trees—A Process Distance Approach." Available at http://www.speps.org.

Kunreuther, Howard, George Deodatis, and Andrew Smyth. 2004. "Integrating Mitigation with Risk Transfer Instruments." In Eugen N. Gurenko, ed., *Catastrophe Risk and Reinsurance—A Country Risk Management Perspective*, 117–134. London: Incisive Financial Publishing.

Kusuoka, Shigeo. 2001. "On Law Invariant Coherent Risk Measures." *Advances in Mathematical Economics* 3, 83–95.

Loehndorf, Nils, Erhard Petzel, and Thomas Portmann. 2007. "Effective Enterprise Risk Management—Quantifying Operational Risks and Selecting Efficient Risk Mitigation Measures." Available at http://www.ermsymposium.org/2007/pdf/papers/Loehndorf.pdf.

Markowitz, Harry. 1952. "Portfolio Selection." *Journal of Finance* 7:1, 77–91.

McNeil, Alexander J., Rüdiger Frey, and Paul Embrechts. 2005. *Quantitative Risk Management—Concepts, Techniques, Tools.* Princeton, NJ: Princeton University Press.

Merton, Robert C. 1972. "An Analytic Derivation of the Efficient Portfolio Frontier." *Journal of Financial and Quantitative Analysis* 7:4, 1851–1872.

Modigliani, Franco, and Merton Miller. 1958. "The Cost of Capital, Corporation Finance and the Theory of Investment." *American Economic Review* 48:3, 261–297.

Pagnocelli, Bernardo, Shabbir Ahmed, and Alexander Shapiro. 2009. "Sample Average Approximation Method for Chance Constrained Programming: Theory and Applications." *Journal of Optimization Theory and Applications* 142:2, 389–416.

Pflug, Georg Ch., and Alois Pichler. 2012. "A Distance for Multistage Stochastic Optimization Models." *SIAM Journal on Optimization* 22:1, 1–23.

Pflug, Georg Ch., and Werner Römisch. 2007. *Modeling, Measuring and Managing Risk.* Singapore: World Scientific.

Pflug, Georg.Ch., and David Wozabal. 2009. "Ambiguity in Portfolio Selection." In M. A. H. Dempster, Gautam Mitra, and Georg Ch. Pflug, eds., *Quantitative Fund Management*, 377–392. Boca Raton, FL: Chapman & Hall.

Pflug, Georg Ch., Alois Pichler, and David Wozabal. 2012. "The 1/N Investment Strategy Is Optimal under High Model Ambiguity." *Journal of Banking and Finance* 36:2, 410–417.

Pichler, Alois. 2013. "Premiums and Reserve, Adjusted by Distortions." *Scandinavian Actuarial Journal.* DOI:10.1080/03461238.2013.830228 l.

Rockafellar, R. Tyrrell, and Stanislav Uryasev. 2000. "Optimization of Conditional Value-at-Risk" *.Journal of Risk* 2:3, 21–41.

Rockafellar, R. Tyrrell, and Stanislav Uryasev. 2013. "The Fundamental Risk Quadrangle in Risk Management, Optimization and Statistical Estimation." *Surveys in Operations Research and Management Science* 18:1-2, 33–53.

Rockafellar, R. Tyrrell, Stanislav Uryasev, and Michael Zabarankin. 2006. *"Master funds in portfolio analysis with general deviation measures." Journal of Banking and Finance* 30: 2, 743–778.

Roy, Arthur D. 1952. "Safety First and the Holding of Assets." *Econometrica* 20:3, 431–450.

Scherer, Bernd. 2004. *Portfolio Construction and Risk Budgeting.* London: Risk Books.

Sharpe, William F. 1964. "Capital Asset Prices—A Theory of Market Equilibrium under Conditions of Risk." *Journal of Finance* 19:3, 425–442.

Sharpe, William F. 1966. "Mutual Fund Performance." *Journal of Business* 39:1, 119–138.

Straub, Erwin. 1997. *Non-life Insurance Mathematics.* Berlin: Springer.

Treynor, Jack L. 1966. "Toward a Theory of Market Value of Risky Assets." In Robert A. Korjczyk, ed. 1999, *Asset Pricing and Portfolio Performance: Models, Strategy, and Performance Metrics.* London: Risk Publications.

van Heerwaarden, Antonius, and Rob Kaas. 1992. "The Dutch Premium Principle." *Insurance: Mathematics and Economics* 11:2, 129–133.

3

How Risk Management Adds Value

M. MARTIN BOYER

CEFA Professor of Finance and Insurance, HEC Montréal

MONICA MARIN

Lecturer, University of Washington Bothell

Introduction

In the past few decades, financial risk management has gained greater popularity as corporations became increasingly conscious of the possibility of unexpected and harmful events negatively affecting their cash flows and resources. The objective of financial risk management is to assess and manage the corporation's exposure to various sources of risk by using financial derivatives, insurance, and other operations.

Financial risk management can reduce or even completely eliminate some specific risks that have a negative impact on a firm's value (Das and Teng 1999). Corporations purchase insurance to manage firm-specific risk and take offsetting positions in financial derivatives to deal with market risk. The latter activity, also called *hedging*, aims to alter exposure to interest rate, commodity, and foreign exchange risk using derivatives (MacKay and Moeller 2007). Hedging can reduce a firm's cash flow volatility (Froot, Scharfstein, and Stein 1993), which in turn can increase expected cash flows, minimize future underinvestment and default probability, and create value. Risk management specialists must have a proper understanding of derivative securities and the risks that should be hedged. They also have to find the balance between different risk management activities and the firm's goals, which can be as diverse as increasing capital efficiency, decreasing earnings volatility, reducing the cost of external capital, and increasing shareholder value (Chew 2008).

This chapter aims to highlight the ways in which financial risk management has become a critical aspect of value maximization. It shows how risk management increases a firm's value by reducing its cash flow volatility, probability of default, and underinvestment. The remainder of the chapter is organized as follows. The first two sections discuss stakeholders' incentives to manage risk, as well as the theories and empirical predictions on the impact of hedging on a firm's cash flow volatility, probability of financial distress, debt capacity, underinvestment, and ultimately on firm value. The third section focuses on how optimal hedging is determined based on different investment and financing needs, and on hedging as a way to minimize agency problems. The chapter closes by discussing insurance as a method to manage the firm's pure risks.

Incentives to Manage Risk for Stakeholders

Unexpected events can have harmful consequences for the firm's shareholders, debt holders, managers, employees, clients, and suppliers. Therefore, a firm's choice to hedge has inevitable consequences on all stakeholders. Moreover, due to the high transaction costs, firms are usually in a better position to hedge risk than individual investors. The impact on the different stakeholders is highlighted below.

SHAREHOLDERS

Since shareholders already have the possibility to eliminate firm-specific risk through asset diversification, corporate risk management may not seem important to them. However, if the probability of bankruptcy increases substantially without risk management, shareholders run the risk of losing their initial investment. To the extent that hedging decreases a firm's probability of financial distress and increases expected cash flows and value, hedging can benefit the shareholders. As Lin, Pantzalis, and Park (2010) show, financial derivatives reduce the risk that a firm's stock will be mispriced. They attribute this result to the notion that hedging improves firm transparency and predictability of firm cash flows.

Conversely, as shareholders see their position as that of a call option on the firm's assets, their wealth will decrease when volatility is decreased by using a hedging position. Consequently, if hedging reduces cash flow volatility without increasing expected cash flows, then hedging only becomes a transfer of wealth from equity holders to debt holders who become the real beneficiaries of the hedging position.

A firm that is closely held, or whose ownership is concentrated in the hands of a limited number of shareholders, or whose shareholders do not own fully diversified portfolios, will have a higher incentive to manage risk. For example, Mayers and Smith (1982) find that closely held property-casualty insurance companies buy more reinsurance.

DEBT HOLDERS

A decrease in cash flow volatility and in a firm's overall risk due to hedging benefits the debt holders because they are more likely to get their investment back. Due to their priority claim on a firm's assets, debt holders would like the firm to hedge even if expected cash flows and firm value do not increase (Campello, Lin, Ma, and Zou 2011).

MANAGERS

Given the separation between ownership and control, important conflicts between a firm's managers and its shareholders are likely (Jensen and Mekling 1976). Optimally designing executive compensation contracts is critical in order to minimize this agency problem. Managerial compensation packages are often tied to company performance measures. For example, compensation via stock ownership provides managers with an incentive to create value but also exposes them to market risk. Assuming that managers are risk averse and that their individual portfolios are not completely diversified, they will be more likely to manage firm risk. Along these lines, Smith and Stulz (1985) argue that the more wealth managers have invested in the company, the more incentive they will have to hedge. If they own a substantial fraction of the firm, their risk aversion will likely lead them to hedge more (Nam, Wang, and Zhang 2008).

By contrast, option-based compensation provides managers with less incentive to hedge than stock ownership because they are not constrained to exercise the option if stock prices go down. Tufano (1996) shows that compensation contracts that are linear or concave in firm value provide managers with an incentive to hedge. Consistent with this argument, he finds that managers of gold mining firms hedge less if their compensation is based on stock options as opposed to shares of common stock. Rogers (2002) shows that managerial incentives are important when making the hedging decision and option holdings represent a determinant of the risk management choice.

Allegedly, stock- or option- based compensation exposes managers to risks that they cannot control. Hedging reduces or eliminates this risk exposure, thus allowing shareholders to evaluate managers based solely on the latter's performance. As a result, hedging aligns managers' incentives with the interests of the shareholders, and thus increases their responsibilities and self-consciousness. Ashley and Yang (2004) find that hedging improves executive compensation contracts and performance evaluation, and that the increase in firm value associated with hedging is even greater for the firms that have a management team that is more difficult to monitor and to evaluate.

A similar argument can be made with respect to the managers' reputation as hedging helps reduce the information asymmetry between managers and shareholders about the source and magnitude of the risks the firm faces. If the labor market revises its opinion about the manager quality based on firm performance, then some managers will tend to undertake hedging activities to influence the market perception (Demarzo and Duffie 1995).

EMPLOYEES

Firm employees benefit from their firm's hedging practices because their job security is directly linked to the firm's risk of bankruptcy. Riskier and highly levered firms are more likely to lay workers off in response to a short-term reduction in the demand for their product. Employees may also lose career advancement opportunities and substantial benefits if the firm does not perform well. Therefore, firms who care about their employees (or who ask their employees to invest in firm-specific human capital) would then have greater incentives to hedge.

CLIENTS/SUPPLIERS

Firm clients and suppliers care about whether the firm uses hedging strategies. When these stakeholders expect the firm to honor its commitments and warranties, they also expect it to remain solvent, offer additional products, and increase the value of existing products. By reducing the probability of default and underinvestment, risk management helps firms to make choices that benefit their clients/suppliers. Additionally, hedging can make corporate disclosures, such as earnings and cash flows, more informative, so it gives a more accurate view of firm performance to clients and suppliers as well as to outside investors (Demarzo and Duffie 1995).

While stakeholders' incentives are very important in determining a firm's hedging policy, the firm's characteristics, industry specifics, capital structure, available investment opportunities, and exposure to different types of risk are equally important. For example, Petersen and Thiagarajan (2000) explore firms' reasons to manage gold price risk, Brown (2001) provides evidence on why and how firms manage foreign exchange risk, and Faulkender (2005) examines the use of interest rate swaps.

Theory and Empirical Predictions on the Impact of Hedging

In a seminal paper, Froot et al. (1993) show how hedging can reduce the impact of costly external capital. By hedging, a firm stabilizes its cash flows and ensures that sufficient internal funds will be available when it needs them. By lowering cash flow volatility, hedging allows a better planning of future capital needs, lower expected tax liabilities, higher expected after-tax cash flows, lower need to access external capital markets, lower cost of financial distress, and higher debt capacity. Thus, risk management indirectly improves the quality of investment and operation decisions (Smith and Stulz 1985), which helps create value.

A few empirical studies investigate the direct impact of risk management activity on firm value and find mixed results. Allayannis and Weston (2001) and Carter, Rogers, and Simkins (2006) find a positive relationship between the use of foreign currency risk management instruments and firm value. Boyer and Marin (2013) find a negative relationship between the use of foreign exchange hedging instruments and the risk of bankruptcy. In a framework in which revenues and costs are nonlinearly related to prices, Mackay and Moeller (2007) contend that risk management adds value to the firm. By contrast, Jin and Jorion (2006) examine the extent of hedging for gas and oil producers and find that it has no impact on firm market value, evidence which is consistent with Tufano (1996).

HEDGING AND TAX EFFECTS

Following Modigliani and Miller (1958), hedging policy is irrelevant in the absence of transaction costs and taxes. All else equal, the value of a firm that chooses to hedge will not change as investors can change their holdings to offset any change in the firm's hedging policy and leave the distribution of their future wealth unaffected. However, when taxes and/or bankruptcy costs are present, reducing cash flow volatility through hedging affects a firm's investment decisions (Hållsten 1966). Given the progressive tax structure in most countries (i.e., it varies with the companies' income), corporate tax liabilities increase nonlinearly with pre-tax cash flows, such that post-tax cash flows become a concave function of pre-tax cash flows (Graham and Smith 1999). If hedging reduces the volatility of firms' earnings, it will also reduce expected tax payments and increase after-tax cash flows and value (Mayers and Smith 1982; Smith and Stulz 1985). Studies by Nance, Smith, and Smithson (1993), Mian (1996), and Geczy, Minton, and Schrand (1997) find that the more likely a firm is to hedge, the greater is the likelihood that a pre-tax income falls in the progressive region of the tax schedule. Graham and Rogers (2002) find no evidence to support the idea that firms hedge in response to tax convexity. They rather find that firms hedge in response to expected financial distress costs and firm size, and to increase their debt capacity.

Interestingly, the cost of many hedging positions is tax-deductible so that hedging reduces the volatility of the firm's taxable cash flows using pre-tax dollars. Consequently the firm's expected after-tax profit would usually be higher after the hedge (Mintz 1990). Consider the following simple example that shows the difference between a hedging firm's and a non-hedging firm's expected after-tax profit.

Baker's Pains and Gains Inc. sells a large fraction of its arthritis drugs in Canada for which it receives payments in Canadian dollars. Given that its costs are denominated in U.S. dollars, the firm's taxable earnings are subject to currency risk. Currency fluctuations are the firm's only source of risk, so the firm's pre-tax hedged and unhedged positions in two equally likely exchange rate scenarios can be described in Panel A of Table 3.1 . The firm achieves a higher average pre-tax profit if it chooses not to hedge. Assume, however, a 40 percent profit tax but no tax deduction on losses. Thus, the expected after-tax profits will be higher if the firm chooses to hedge as shown in Panel B of Table 3.1.

HEDGING AND EXTERNAL CAPITAL MARKETS

Hedging preserves internal funds by covering losses caused by risky events and avoids the need for external financing (Gay and Nam 1998). Similarly, Adam (2002) shows that hedging reduces a firm's dependence on external capital markets.

Table 3.1 **An Example of the Value of Hedging Using After-Tax Income**

	Weak USD	*Strong USD*	*Average*
Panel A. Pre-tax Income for Two Equally Likely Scenarios (in USD Millions)			
Unhedged	100	−20	40
Hedged	35	35	35
Panel B. Post-Tax Income for Two Equally Likely Scenarios (in USD Millions)			
Unhedged	60	−20	20
Hedged	21	21	21

Note: Panel A presents the two possible pre-tax vectors of cash flows (unhedged versus hedged) obtainable from a firm's operations in the events of a weak USD and a strong USD. Panel B shows the same vectors post-tax.

HEDGING AND FINANCIAL DISTRESS

Mayers and Smith (1982) recognize that transaction costs of bankruptcy can induce public corporations to use derivatives. In particular, hedging with derivatives reduces cash flow volatility (Stulz 1984), which in turn reduces the probability of incurring direct and indirect bankruptcy costs. According to Bhabra and Yao (2011), the latter amounts to between 6 and 18 percent of the firm's pre-bankruptcy value. Therefore, firms that are more likely subject to financial distress have greater incentives to hedge in order to reduce their probability of going bankrupt. Smith and Stulz (1985), Froot et al. (1993), Nance et al. (1993), and Tufano (1996) predict a more extensive risk management activity for firms that are more likely to face financial distress. These firms are generally smaller and have high leverage and high operating costs. For such firms, a decrease in the probability of bankruptcy and underinvestment is highly desirable. Thus, their shareholders will be interested in hedging even if they have well-diversified portfolios. Leland (1998) shows that high bankruptcy costs can be associated with large hedging benefits.

More recent studies have different findings regarding the influence of financial distress on firms' hedging decisions. The transaction costs of entering a hedging position may be substantial and thus prohibitive for financially constrained firms. Using dynamic models, Mello and Parsons (2000), Rampini and Viswanathan (2010, 2013), and Bolton, Chen, and Wang (2011) show that financially constrained firms tend to hedge less or not at all due to collateral costs associated with hedging. Rampini, Sufi, and Viswanathan (2014) provide empirical evidence on how airlines vary their jet fuel hedging based on their proximity to financial distress.

Assuming that smaller firms are more likely to be financially constrained than larger ones so that larger firms have the ability to set a comprehensive hedging program, larger firms should therefore be more likely to use derivatives than smaller firms (Booth, Smith, and Stolz 1984; Block and Gallagher 1986; Nance et al. 1993; Mian 1996; Tufano 1996; Geczy et al. 1997; Chelst and Bodily 2000; Graham and Rogers 2002). This difference is mainly due to high transaction costs and therefore economies of scale.

HEDGING AND UNDERINVESTMENT

The prospect of financial distress imposes important indirect costs to the company including underinvesting in profitable projects (Myers 1977). Because firms in financial distress tend to focus their resources on meeting their financial obligations, they are less likely to make capital investments. Hedging reduces a firm's probability of financial distress and thus underinvestment. According to Smith and Stulz (1985), hedging reduces the need to access the outside capital markets, which in turn also reduces underinvestment. External capital is usually more costly than firms' internal capital. In many cases, a project may have a positive net present value (NPV) if financed with internal capital, but becomes unattractive if using external capital. This is a consequence of the agency conflict between equity holders and debt holders, a situation also called the "debt over-hang" problem. Assuming that management's incentives are aligned with those of the shareholders and that the firm is highly leveraged, management may pass up valuable investment opportunities in order to avoid a wealth transfer from the shareholders to the debt holders. Hedging alleviates this problem by ensuring enough internal funds are available for future investment needs.

Empirical research generally finds that firms with more investment opportunities are more likely to hedge (Nance et al. 1993; Berkman and Bradbury 1996; Gay and Nam 1998), in contrast, Geczy et al. (1997) do not find a significant relationship between hedging and investment opportunities, while Mian (1996) finds conflicting evidence when using different measures for investment opportunities.

Asset tangibility is also related to a firm's hedging activities (Froot et al. 1993). Empirical evidence shows that firms with high capital expenditures are more likely to hedge (Fok, Carroll, and Chiou 1997; Adam 2009). Moreover, Deshmukh and Vogt (2005) find that investment spending sensitivity to cash flow is lower when the extent of hedging is higher, conditional on the firm hedging.

HEDGING AND DEBT CAPACITY

Risk management can increase a firm's debt capacity in order to take advantage of the interest tax shield (Graham and Smith 1999). Because creditors recognize that shareholders have an incentive to increase risk after raising debt, creditors thus require a higher rate of return (cost of debt). To avoid this, firms need to credibly show that they will not engage in riskier activities that would increase the probability of default. Hedging risk enables firms to issue more debt (Leland 1998) to take advantage of the interest tax shield while limiting their probability of financial distress. Although equity holders recognize that hedging benefits debt holders, they will still pre-commit to hedge due to the tax advantages of debt. Graham and Rogers (2002) provide empirical evidence that firms engage in hedging to increase their debt capacity.

The access to external capital also benefits firms by allowing them to invest in projects that have a positive NPV. The empirical literature is mixed with respect to the relationship between firm leverage and its hedging activity, a relationship plagued by endogeneity (Leland 1998; Cooper and Mello 1999; Fehle and Tsyplakov 2005). While Block and Gallagher (1986) and Geczy et al. (1997) find no relationship between the two, Leland (1998), Cooper and Mello (1999), and Haushalter (2000) show that highly levered firms have more incentives to hedge their risks.

Optimal Hedging with Investment and Financing Opportunities

Raising money from outside sources puts a potential strain on a firm's current cash flows, which makes raising future outside capital even more difficult and costly (Myers and Majluf 1984). According to Gay and Nam (1998), hedging can reduce that strain if it allows firms to avoid unnecessary cash flows associated with the need to raise capital from outside investors. Firms with increasing marginal costs of external finance should hedge their cash flows to decrease the cost of debt and increase their debt capacity. This action also allows the firm to fund its investments while having to rely less on costly external funds in bad economic times.

The firm's optimal hedging strategy also depends on the nature of its investment and financing opportunities. Including the randomness of investment and financing opportunities as a factor of optimal hedging strategy leads to a bigger range of optimal hedge ratio. Thus, what is the optimal hedge ratio of changing investment opportunities? If a positive correlation exists between investment opportunities and the risks wanted to be hedged, the firm will not want to hedge that much in order to not eliminate those investment opportunities. More precisely, if the risks represent a source of uncertainty, then the more sensitive investment opportunities are to this source of uncertainty, the smaller should be the hedge ratio. Thus, firms should adjust their hedging strategies as a function of the different investment opportunities' sensitivities to risks. The following example illustrates this correlation between investment opportunities and the risk to be hedged.

Monty Algold (MA) is a gold mining company that mostly operates mature mines. It currently produces 100 units of gold per period at zero marginal cost (equivalently, the price of each unit of gold is superior by 100 to the extraction cost). MA's periodic cash flows are therefore $100p_g$, where p_g is the random price of gold. MA can also invest in exploration activities today. Exploration costs I, which allows MA to discover a vein that contains $f_g(I)$ units of gold for the next period. The per unit extraction cost of this new vein is cg and must be paid in period 2. The value of gold exploration is thus $(p_g - c_g)f_g(I) - I$.

Now suppose Bakken Oil (BO) is a company similar to Monty Algold: It produces 100 units of oil per period worth $100p_o$, where p_o is the random price of oil (same distribution as p_g). As for MA, BO can invest today an amount I in new wells, but its marginal cost of extracting the new oil in Period 2 is $c_o > c_g$. The value of oil exploration is thus $(p_o - c_o)f_o(I) - I$. Finally, suppose that in expectation oil and gold exploration have the same value so that $E((p_g - c_g)f_g(I) - I) = E((p_o - c_o)f_o(I) - I)$ This means that $f_o(I)/f_g(I) = (E(p_g) - c_g)/(E(p_o) - c_o)$, with $E(p_g) = E(p_o)$.

The only difference between the two companies lies in the higher cost of development by BO. In other words, BO's investment opportunities are more leveraged with respect to its commodity price. Suppose for instance that $c_g = 0$ and $c_o = 50$, then MA's cash flows drop by 10 percent when the price of gold drops from 100 to 90, whereas BO's cash flows drop by 20 percent when the price of oil drops from 100 to 90. The consequence is that MA and BO should have different hedging strategies because the value of BO is more exposed to the price of oil than is the value of MA exposed to the price of gold. BO should use more hedging instruments than MA.

An optimal hedging strategy does not imply complete insulation of a firm's value from all sources of risk. Firms are less likely to hedge and hedge less often if their investment opportunities are closely correlated with the source of uncertainty. However, they hedge more if their investment opportunities are correlated with the collateral they need to put up in order to raise external funds (Stulz 1984). In general, the hedging strategies of large firms depend on a number of additional considerations that may not be at all related to their core operations such as exchange rate exposure (Bolton et al. 2011).

Nonlinear hedging instruments, such as options, usually allow firms to coordinate investment and financing plans more precisely than linear hedging instruments such as forwards, futures, and swaps. In particular, using futures involves a difficult trade-off between insulating the present value of all cash flows versus insulating the level of cash at each point in time. Finally, the nature of product market competition and the hedging strategies adopted by a firm's competitor also affects a firm's decision on its hedging strategy (Bolton et al. 2011).

HEDGING TO HELP FIRMS PLAN THEIR CAPITAL NEEDS

Determining the optimal capital structure is critical to finance a firm's assets and increase its value. Corporate risk management and hedging in particular can help a firm determine its optimal debt-to-equity ratio. Corporate risk management can also solve both the over-investment problem and the underinvestment problem in planning a firm's capital needs.

In the first case, a firm usually has considerable liquidity and managers want to increase a firm's growth rate because it increases the value of equity. They may take more risk and over-invest by accepting negative NPV projects in order to diversify a firm's activities and increase its size (Devine 1987). To do so, managers increase a firm's bankruptcy risk and cost even if they might use less than the value maximizing level of debt financing. Hedging can help break this circle by lowering both a firm's bankruptcy and debt cost and allowing it to get additional external capital to grow.

As discussed earlier, managers might underinvest and thereby forego positive NPV projects. This situation occurs because a firm's existing debt captures most of the projects' benefits and management cannot obtain any additional external capital. Hedging helps firms reduce the extent of this problem by reducing the probability of financial distress. It, therefore, decreases the cost of debt and allows the firm to issue more debt without exceeding its optimal debt-to-equity ratio (Gay and Nam 1998).

STAKEHOLDER CONFLICTS AND AGENCY PROBLEMS

Shareholders are mainly interested in increasing stock prices, debt holders in lowering a firm's probability of default, and managers in maintaining and improving a certain job security and reputation. Although these goals do not necessarily exclude each other, situations often arise when managers' actions are in conflict with either the shareholders' or the debt holders' desires. These 'agency problems' are likely to be attenuated through risk management.

Managing Conflicts between Managers and Shareholders

Managers and shareholders sometimes have different incentives. Thus, conflicts may arise from the managers' potential loyalty deficit toward the firm's stakeholders, or more generally from the managers' goal to further their own interest to the detriment of the shareholders (Felo 2001). This type of agency problem is likely more severe if a firm's shares are more widely held because gaining agreement from shareholders on the choice of a firm's executive management is more difficult (Felo 2001). Despite having the proper interest alignment, managers may still prefer to invest in assets that reduce too much the risk. The managers are, therefore, more likely to invest in larger, more diversified projects and prefer investments that pay off earlier and quicker. Giving managers investment freedom has both benefits and costs. The benefits will be greater in a more uncertain economic environment, whereas the costs will be greater when the interests of managers and shareholders diverge.

Corporate risk management can be used to partially attenuate the agency problem between shareholders and managers in the same way as financial leverage. In some cases, shareholders prefer higher leverage because larger debt obligations limit the managers' ability to use excess cash and resources in ways that do not benefit the firm as whole. When this is the case, managers are more concerned about meeting their debt obligations before investing in projects that would further their own interest.

The agency problem between firm's shareholders and its managers arises especially because managers usually have more information about the firm than its shareholders, especially the ones with smaller share ownership. The costs associated with agency problems can thus be reduced by improving information efficiency through a reduction in earnings volatility. Thus, compensation contracts should not depend on risks that managers cannot control, or any risk that is unrelated to the managers' effort; corporate risk management and hedging can help achieve this goal (Ashley and Yang 2004).

Suppose a simple model where firm value depends on three random factors: (1) the fundamental idiosyncratic value of the assets (F), (2) the manager's effort (e), and (3) some random hedgeable component (ε). In other words, $V = F + e + \varepsilon$. Although managers have control over e only, it is not observable by shareholders. Yet, shareholders can observe V. If shareholders want to reward managers for their efforts, shareholders need to reduce the variability in what they observe in terms of firm value. That comes from using hedging instruments to eliminate the ϵ contribution to total firm value.

In designing an optimal compensation contract, identifying and defining the factors used to reward managers are important. In particular, this involves designing the contract based on the firm's performance compared to some benchmark (Waddock and Graves 1997). So-called relative performance contracts that reward managers for performing better than a market or an industry benchmark have both advantages and disadvantages. One advantage is that the contracts eliminate the effect of some risks, such as systematic risks, that are beyond the manager's control. Yet, a disadvantage is that the contracts may cause firms to compete too aggressively with others such as reducing products' price as low as possible, which results ultimately in reducing the industry's overall profitability.

Alleviating Coordination Problems through Financial Risk Management

Consider as in Boyer, Boyer, and Garcia (2013) a firm as a portfolio of projects giving rise to a transformation possibility frontier for cash flows as in Figure 3.1. This frontier considers all possible vectors of cash flows obtainable from a firm's operations. The firm's distribution of cash flows can only be changed by altering its portfolio of projects. Point A_0 in Figure 3.1 represents the firm's combination of projects that maximizes its market value. This point is found by finding where the *iso-value line* is tangent to the firm's transformation possibility frontier. The slope of the iso-value line is the market price of risk.

Adjusting a firm's portfolio of projects is neither easy nor costless. It involves division managers who must agree and coordinate their effort to alter the mix. Some division managers have to make concessions, thus creating conflicts if managers do not share the same information and objectives. Suppose as in Boyer, Boyer, and Garcia (2013)

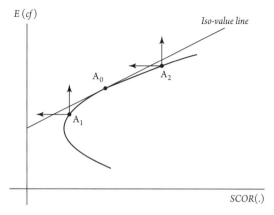

Figure 3.1 Transformation Possibility Frontier and Optimal Firm Value.
This figure represents a firm's transformation possibility frontier between risk on the
horizontal axis and expected cash flows on the vertical axis. Arrows indicate the directions
in which each manager can increase firm value. The slope of the iso-value line is the market
price of risk. Firm value is maximized at point A_0, where the slope of the firm's
transformation possibility frontier is equal to the market price of risk.

a separation between managing operational risk, which they define as the management of the riskiness of cash flows, represented by the horizontal axis in Figure 3.1,
and managing production, which they define as the management of expected cash
flows, represented by the vertical axis. Conflicts appear as the operational risk manager
will tend to oppose projects that increase cash flow risk while the production manager will tend to resist projects that reduce expected cash flows. This "coordination
problem" illustrates the difficulty in getting managers to make concessions that appear
detrimental but are necessary to maximize firm value.

To illustrate the cost of altering the portfolio of projects, suppose the firm is currently
at point A_1 in Figure 3.1 but firm value would be maximized at point A_0. Movement
toward point A_0 requires that the operational risk manager destroy firm value in the
short run by letting risk increase above its current level so that the production manager
has the flexibility to increase the expected cash flows. Coordination is obviously difficult
because one manager must assume career risk in destroying value in the short run.

Implementing new projects and abandoning existing ones can generate conflicts
within a firm. This is why firms often use steering committees that involve senior executives from different functions and business units to make decisions about major strategic
activities. A consensus must be reached before implementing the reviewed changes
in activities. Clearly, managing and solving these coordination problems can be both
expensive and time-consuming. As Boyer et al. (2013) show, financial risk management
can mitigate coordination problems by reducing the impact of disagreements between
divisional managers. This occurs even though the financial risk manager is only trading
financial assets at their market value, so that he does not create (or destroy) value.

Because trading financial assets at their market value does not create value, this
action will help the firm only if it reduces the cost of implementing necessary changes
in a firm's activities resulting from a change in the market price of risk. Firms that are

more reactive to changes in the market price of risk and that are therefore more subject to coordination problems are more likely to use hedging.

Figure 3.2 illustrates the role of the financial risk manager. Suppose a firm's initial mix is at A_2, although its optimal mix should be A_0. Unfortunately, the production manager is only willing to invest in projects that increase expected cash flows, whereas the operational risk manager only wants to invest in projects that reduce risk. Consider the iso-value line that goes through A_2. When capital markets are perfect, the financial risk manager can enter into open market financial transactions to move the firm's risk-return profile from A_2 to any point on the same iso-value line. This means that a movement to point B does not change the firm's value because financial transactions occur at market prices. By doing so, the financial risk manager is creating room for the production manager and the operational risk manager to move from B to A_0.

A financial risk manager increases a firm's value by creating the possibility of a change in the firm's product mix from which both managers can agree. Because of the presence of the financial risk manager, the move from A_2 to A_0 has been achieved at a lower coordination cost because none of the managers is asked to destroy value in the short run.

What type of firm is more likely to use financial risk instruments? The answer is a firm that has a flatter or less concave possibility frontier. Observe Figure 3.3 where two firms have currently the same optimal risk-reward relationship (point A). The difference between the two firms comes in the shape of the possibility frontier as one frontier is more concave than the other. Following a change in the market price of risk, moving from the point A to B_{low}—the firm's new optimal point that has a more concave production function—requires little in the way of changes in the portfolio of projects.

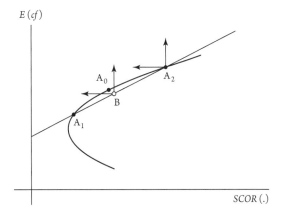

Figure 3.2 THE ROLE OF FINANCIAL RISK MANAGEMENT IN CREATING ROOM FOR VALUE CREATION. Using a firm's transformation possibility frontier between risk on the horizontal axis and expected cash flows on the vertical axis, this figures illustrates the situation of a firm that has a suboptimal combination of projects at A_2, and that is unable to convince its managers to go against their nature (e.g., not trying to move left by reducing risk or moving by increasing expected cash flows) so that firm value is not maximized. By allowing movement along the firm's iso-value line, to point B, financial risk management gives two other managers maneuvering space that allows them to increase firm value to A_0.

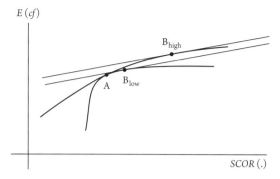

Figure 3.3 THE IMPACT OF THE CONCAVITY OF THE FIRM'S TRANSFORMATION POSSIBILITY FRONTIER AFTER A CHANGE IN THE MARKET PRICE OF RISK. Assuming the existence of two firms each having their own transformation possibility frontier between risk on the horizontal axis and expected cash flows on the vertical axis, this figure illustrates that the more concave the frontier of a firm, the lower is the need for financial risk management because moving from A to B_{low} creates less value moving from A to B_{high}.

By contrast, a firm whose possibility frontier is flatter will see its optimal projects mix change more, from the point A to B_{high}.

The role of the financial risk manager is not to create wealth directly, but to engage in zero-cost/zero-profit transactions that reduce managerial conflicts and coordination problems. The facilitating role of financial risk management becomes even more critical when the market price of risk is volatile, and when small fluctuations in the market price of risk generate important changes in the optimal set of projects and activities.

Insurance versus Hedging

Firms face three categories of business risk, but they can eliminate only one of them by using insurance. One category of business risk is price risk including output price risk, input price risk, commodity price risk, exchange rate risk, and interest rate risk. Previous sections have addressed the hedging of most of these risks. The second category is credit risk, which is related to the possibility of a loss arising from a debtor being unable to pay its credit obligation to the firm (e.g., a borrower who defaults on its interest payment, or a customer who cannot pay for the products or services it previously purchased). Finally, the third category of business risk is pure risk, which is also the one that can be reduced or eliminated by using insurance. Examples of risks in this category include damage to assets, worker injury, employee benefits, legal liability, and reputational loss.

Only some of a firm's pure risk events are insurable such as product liability suits, toxic torts, and physical damage to corporate assets. The traditional view of insurance is that large public firms often purchase insurance to hedge against large potential losses while self-insuring against smaller ones. Doherty and Smith (2005), however, provide a counter example. For such corporations or even the medium-sized ones, the costs of small losses are easily predictable because they occur with regularity. By contrast, larger losses are rarer and much less predictable so even large corporations need to have insurance in order to hedge these events. Using insurance allows firms to take advantage of insurance companies' efficiency. Insurance companies also provide firms with risk-assessment, risk monitoring, and loss-settlement services (Mayers and Smith 1990). However, insurance companies have a limited capacity to underwrite very large or highly specialized exposures such as catastrophic loss. Thus, they use reinsurance, which is provided by companies that insure insurance companies, in order to distribute those large and specialized risks on a secondary market. Insurance companies can also employ other methods such as dispersing coverage over a large geographic area or using catastrophe bonds in order to manage exposures to catastrophic loss.

The rationale for taking insurance differs between individuals and corporations. Individuals choose to purchase insurance if the insurer has a comparative advantage in bearing the risks, such as the ability to pool risks and to access capital markets. Consequently, individuals transfer risk to insurance companies to reduce their personal risks while paying a risk premium to the insurer. Similar reasons drive the decision of smaller corporations to buy insurance because they have a more limited ability to bear certain risks. Firms self-insure against some risks because they have specialized expertise in assuming that risk or they have a comparative advantage (Vercammen and van Kooten 1994). Purchasing insurance reduces the expected standard deviation of a firm's cash flows, but not a firm's cost of capital (Santomero and Babbel 1997). Thus, why do large corporations buy insurance?

Some real benefits result when large corporations buy insurance. These benefits include reducing not only the potential conflicts between shareholders and bondholders in companies with substantial amounts of debt but also the expected cost of financing losses, the cost of new investment opportunities, and the firm's expected tax liability. What insurance provides in addition to the benefits from hedging is the benefit for large corporations of using insurers' claims handling and measuring services.

Insurance companies provide both services and advantages to non-financial firms (Mayers and Smith 1987). These services include the processing and the settling of claims, the assessment of loss exposures, the design, administration, and auditing of safety and other loss-control programs, and risk pooling. The insurers' comparative advantage occurs because of a high frequency of events. In general, insurance policy's loading is less costly than the firms' costs of obtaining comparable services. Moreover, bundling claims processing and loss control services with the financial responsibility of paying losses are significantly efficient with insurance companies to insist corporations to insure their risks. Large corporations may also be required to purchase insurance to satisfy regulatory requirements.

Summary and Conclusions

Corporate risk management has gradually become an important part of corporate activities. The goal of this chapter has been to explain how corporate risk management increases firm value by reducing a firm's cash flow volatility and by lowering the probability of underinvestment and the probability of default. Corporations invest in activities that reduce their corporate risk even if shareholders can diversify away the company-specific risk themselves by holding a large portfolio with shares of many companies. Even if corporate risk management does not necessarily reduce all shareholders' risk, it allows firms to increase their market value from many different aspects.

The first section of this chapter focused on the incentives to manage risks. The second section presented the main theoretical reasons risk management adds value to the firm. These reasons include reducing cash flow volatility, increasing access to external capital, increasing debt capacity, reducing the probability of financial distress, taking advantage of corporate taxes, and crowding out of investment to avoid underinvestment problems. Hedging improves a firm's value if it reduces the volatility of its future cash flows and increases its expected cash flows by decreasing a firm's expected tax payments, reducing its expected cost of financial distress, allowing for a better planning of the firm's future capital needs, and reducing a firm's need to access external capital markets.

The third section examines the relationship between hedging and changing investment and financing opportunities, and shows that an optimal hedging strategy does not always imply complete insulation of a firm's value from all sources of risk. A firm will have less incentive to hedge if its investment opportunities are correlated with the source of uncertainty, and more incentive if its investment opportunities are correlated with the value of its assets it puts up as collateral to raise external funds more. However, a firm will be more likely to hedge if agency problems are substantial. Hedging alleviates agency problems not only between shareholders and managers, similarly to the use of financial leverage or the design of an optimal executive compensation contract, but also between shareholders and bondholders.

The final section of this chapter examined the use of insurance to cover firms' pure risks. As an important risk management method, insurance improves firms' value by reducing underinvestment and its likelihood of financial distress, by improving contractual terms, taking advantage of insurers' service efficiencies or of tax benefits, and satisfying regulatory requirements of some countries.

Discussion Questions

1. How does hedging differ from insurance?
2. Why does hedging create value only if the firm's cost structure is convex in the hedgeable risk?
3. Explain whether financial risk management allows a better assessment of managerial quality.
4. Discuss the following assertion. Entering into a financial derivative position creates no value directly and destroys value in the short run. Thus, the only reason that non-financial firms use such instruments is to speculate.

References

Adam, Tim R. 2002. "Risk Management and the Credit Risk Premium." *Journal of Banking and Finance* 26:2, 243–269.

Adam, Tim R. 2009. "Capital Expenditures, Financial Constraints, and the Use of Options." *Journal of Financial Economics* 92:2, 238–251.

Allayannis, George, and James P. Weston 2001. "The Use of Foreign Currency Derivatives and Firm Market Value." *Review of Financial Studies* 14:1, 243–275.

Ashley, Allan S., and Simon M. Yang. 2004. "Executive Compensation and Earnings Persistence." *Journal of Business Ethics* 50:4, 369–382.

Berkman, Henk, and Michael E. Bradbury. 1996. "Empirical Evidence on the Corporate Use of Derivatives." *Financial Management* 25:2, 5–13.

Bhabra, Gurmeet S., and Yuan Yao. 2011. "Is Bankruptcy Costly? Recent Evidence on the Magnitude and Determinants of Indirect Bankruptcy Costs." *Journal of Applied Finance & Banking* 1:2, 39–68.

Block, Stanley B., and Timothy J. Gallagher. 1986. "The Use of Interest Rate Futures and Options by Corporate Financial Managers." *Financial Management* 5:3, 73–78.

Bolton, Patrick, Hui Chen, and Neng Wang. 2011. "A Unified Theory of Tobin's Q, Corporate Investment, Financing, and Risk Management." *Journal of Finance* 66:5, 1545–1578.

Booth, James R., Richard L,Smith, and Richard W. Stolz, 1984. "The Use of Interest Rate Futures by Financial Institutions." *Journal of Bank Research* 15:1, 15–20.

Boyer, Marcel, M. Martin Boyer, and René Garcia. 2013. "Alleviating Coordination Problems and Regulatory Constraints through Financial Risk Management." *Quarterly Journal of Finance* 3:2, 1350009-1-1350009-39.

Boyer, M. Martin, and Monica Marin. 2013. "Financial Distress Risk and the Managing of Foreign Currency Exposure." *Quarterly Journal of Finance* 3:1, 1350002-1-1350002-36 2.

Brown, Gregory W. 2001. "Managing Foreign Exchange Risk with Derivatives." *Journal of Financial Economics* 60:2-3, 401–448.

Campello, Murillo, Chen Lin, Yue Ma, and Hong Zou. 2011. "The Real and Financial Implications of Corporate Hedging." *Journal of Finance* 66:5, 1615–1647.

Carter, David A., Daniel A. Rogers, and Betty J. Simkins. 2006. "Does Hedging Affect Firm Value? Evidence from the US Airline Industry." *Financial Management* 35:1, 53–86.

Chelst, Kenneth, and Samuel E. Bodily. 2000. "Structured Risk Management: Filling a Gap in Decision Analysis Education." *Journal of the Operational Research Society* 51:12, 1420–1432.

Chew, Donald H. 2008. *Corporate Risk Management*. New York: Columbia University Press.

Cooper, Ian A., and Antonio S. Mello. 1999. "Corporate Hedging: The Relevance of Contract Specifications and Banking Relationships." *European Finance Review* 2:2, 195–223.

Das, T. K., and Bing-Sheng Teng.1999. "Managing Risks in Strategic Alliances." *Academy of Management Executive* 13:4, 50–62.

DeMarzo, Peter M., and Darrell Duffie. 1995. "Corporate Incentives for Hedging and Hedge Accounting." *Review of Financial Studies* 8:3, 743–715.

Deshmukh, Sanjay, and Stephen C. Vogt. 2005. "Investment, Cash Flow and Corporate Hedging." *Journal of Corporate Finance* 11:4, 628–644.

Devine, James N. 1987. "Cyclical Over-Investment and Crisis in a Labor-Scarce Economy." *Eastern Economic Journal* 13:3, 271–280.

Doherty, Neil A., and Clifford W. Smith, Jr. 2005. "Corporate Insurance Strategy: The Case of British Petroleum." *Journal of Applied Corporate Finance* 6:3, 4–15.

Faulkender, Michael. 2005. "Hedging or Market Timing? Selecting the Interest Rate Exposure of Corporate Debt." *Journal of Finance* 60:2, 931–962.

Fehle, Frank, and Sergey Tsyplakov. 2005. "Dynamic Risk Management: Theory and Evidence." *Journal of Financial Economics* 78:1, 3–47.

Felo, Andrew J. 2001. "Ethics Programs, Board Involvement, and Potential Conflicts of Interest in Corporate Governance." *Journal of Business Ethics* 32:3, 205–218.

Fok, Robert C. W., Carolyn Carroll, and Ming C. Chiou. 1997. "Determinants of Corporate Hedging and Derivatives: A Revisit." *Journal of Economics and Business* 49:6, 569–585.

Froot, Kenneth A., David A. Scharfstein, and Jeremy C. Stein. 1993. "Risk Management: Coordinating Corporate Investment and Financing Policies." *Journal of Finance* 48:5, 1629–1658.

Gay, Gerald D., and Jouahn Nam. 1998. "The Underinvestment Problem and Corporate Derivatives Use." *Financial Management* 27:4, 53–69.

Geczy, Christopher C., Bernadette A. Minton, and Catherine Schrand. 1997. "Why Firms Use Currency Derivatives." *Journal of Finance* 52:4, 1323–1354.

Graham, John R., and Daniel Rogers, 2002. "Do Firms Hedge in Response to Tax Incentives?" *Journal of Finance* 57:2, 815–840.

Graham, John R., and Clifford W. Smith, Jr. 1999. "Tax Incentive to Hedge." *Journal of Finance* 54:6, 2241–2262.

Hållsten, Bertil. 1966. "Note on Modigliani and Miller's Extension of the Theory of Investment and Financing." *Swedish Journal of Economics* 68:2, 74–88.

Haushalter, G. David 2000. "Financing Policy, Basis Risk, and Corporate Hedging: Evidence from Oil and Gas Producers." *Journal of Finance* 55:1, 107–152.

Jensen, Michael C., and William H. Mekling. 1976. "Theory of the Firm: Managerial Behavior, Agency Costs and Ownership Structure." *Journal of Financial Economics* 3:4, 305–360.

Jin, Yanbo, and Philippe Jorion. 2006. "Firm Value and Hedging: Evidence from U.S. Oil and Gas Producers." *Journal of Finance* 61:2, 893–919.

Leland, Hayne E. 1998. "Agency Costs, Risk Management, and Capital Structure." *Journal of Finance* 53:4, 1213–1243.

Lin, J. Barry, Christos Pantzalis, and Jung Chul Park. 2010. "Corporate Hedging Policy and Equity Mispricing." *Financial Review* 45:3, 803–824.

MacKay, Peter, and Sara B. Moeller. 2007. "The Value of Corporate Risk Management." *Journal of Finance* 52:3, 1379–1418.

Mayers, David, and Clifford W. Smith, Jr. 1982. "On the Corporate Demand for Insurance." *Journal of Business* 55:2, 281–296.

Mayers, David, and Clifford W. Smith, Jr. 1987. "Corporate Insurance and the Under Investment Problem." *Journal of Risk and Insurance* 54:1, 45–54.

Mayers, David, and Clifford W. Smith, Jr. 1990. "On the Corporate Demand for Insurance: Evidence from the Reinsurance Market." *Journal of Business* 63:1, 19–40.

Mello, Antonio, and John Parsons. 2000. "Hedging and Liquidity." *Review of Financial Studies* 13:1, 127–153.

Mian, Shehzad. 1996. "Evidence on Corporate Hedging Policy." *Journal of Financial and Quantitative Analysis* 11:3, 419–439.

Mintz, Jack M. 1990. "Corporate Tax Holidays and Investment." *The World Bank Economic Review* 4:1, 81–102.

Modigliani, Franco, and Merton H. Miller. 1958. "The Cost of Capital, Corporation Finance and the Theory of Investment." *American Economic Review* 48:3, 261–297.

Myers, Stewart C. 1977. "Determinants of Corporate Borrowing." *Journal of Financial Economics* 5:2, 147–175.

Myers, Stewart C., and Nicholas S. Majluf. 1984. "Corporate Financing and Investment Decisions When Firms Have Information That Investors Do Not Have." *Journal of Financial Economics* 13:2, 187–221.

Nam, Jouahn, Jun Wang, and Ge Zhang. 2008. "Managerial Career Concerns and Risk Management." *Journal of Risk and Insurance* 75:3, 785–809.

Nance, Deana, Clifford W. Smith, Jr., and Charles Smithson. 1993. "Determinants of Corporate Hedging." *Journal of Finance* 48:1, 267–284.

Petersen, Mitchell A., and S. Ramu Thiagarajan. 2000. "Risk Management and Hedging: With and Without Derivatives." *Financial Management* 29:4, 5–29.

Rampini, Adriano, and S. Viswanathan. 2010. "Collateral, Risk Management, and the Distribution of Debt Capacity." *Journal of Finance* 65:6, 2293–2322.

Rampini, Adriano, and S. Viswanathan. 2013. "Collateral and Capital Structure." *Journal of Financial Economics* 109:2, 466–492.

Rampini, Adriano, Amir Sufi, and S. Viswanathan. 2014. "Dynamic Risk Management." *Journal of Financial Economics* 111:2, 271–296.

Rogers, Daniel A. 2002. "Does Executive Portfolio Structure Affect Risk Management? CEO Risk-taking Incentives and Corporate Derivative Usage." *Journal of Banking and Finance* 26:2-3, 271–295.

Santomero, Anthony M., and David F. Babbel. 1997. "Financial Risk Management by Insurers: An Analysis of the Process." *Journal of Risk and Insurance* 64:2, 231–270.

Smith, Clifford W., and René M. Stulz. 1985. "The Determinants of Firms' Hedging Policies." *Journal of Financial and Quantitative Analysis* 20:4, 391–405.

Stulz, René M. 1984. "Optimal Hedging Policies." *Journal of Financial and Quantitative Analysis* 19:2, 127–140.

Tufano, Peter. 1996. "Who Manages Risk? An Empirical Examination of Risk Management Practices in the Gold Mining Industry." *Journal of Finance* 51:4, 1097–1137.

Vercammen, James, and G. Cornelis van Kooten. 1994. "Moral Hazard Cycles in Individual-Coverage Crop Insurance." *American Journal of Agricultural Economics* 76:2, 250–261.

Waddock, Sandra A., and Samuel B. Graves. 1997. "The Corporate Social Performance-Financial Performance Link." *Strategic Management Journal* 18:4, 303–319.

4

Accounting and Risk Management

MARK BRADSHAW

Associate Professor of Accounting, Carroll School of Management, Boston College

BJORN JORGENSEN

Professor of Accounting and Financial Management, London School of Economics

Introduction

Risk assessment is a forward-looking activity. In contrast, a prevailing sentiment among investors is that financial statements are "backwards-looking." External auditors, who provide a level of certification of financial statements, have even been condescendingly described as those who go in after battle and bayonet the wounded. Thus, a natural question is whether any value exists in using financial statements as part of a risk management program.

Indeed, in many jurisdictions around the world, financial reports filed annually include income statements and statements of cash flows for the three most recently completed fiscal years and balance sheets for the end of the two most recent years. Although this information pertains to the past, the primary purpose of financial statements is exactly the opposite. For example, in the United States, the Financial Accounting Standards Board (FASB) has been granted authority by the Securities Exchange Commission (SEC) to establish financial reporting standards. The Financial Accounting Standards Board (2008, para. 37) clarifies the purpose of financial reporting in *Statement of Financial Accounting Concepts No. 2*, "Qualitative Characteristics of Accounting Information." That purpose is summarized as follows:

> [F]inancial reporting should provide information to help investors, creditors, and others assess the amounts, timing, and uncertainty of *prospective* net cash inflows to the related enterprise. (Emphasis added)

Obviously, this objective emphasizes the future, rather than the past. Yet, financial statements certainly capture the recent past. Aware of this surface contradiction, the Financial Accounting Standards Board (2008, para. 42) further emphasized:

> Investors and creditors often use information about the past to help in assessing the prospects of an enterprise. Thus, although investment and credit

decisions reflect investors' and creditors' expectations about future enterprise performance, those expectations are commonly based at least partly on
evaluations of past enterprise performance.

In addition to this notion of using the past as a guide to the future, recognizing that
"financial reports" does not narrowly refer to just the financial statements is important
because the term crucially incorporates a wide spectrum of information conveyed in the
footnotes to the financial statements.

This chapter provides a discussion of various ways in which information in the financial statements captures or is useful in providing signals about various risks. As a prelude
to that discussion, establishing the importance of summary financial statements relative
to alternative measures of performance, namely cash flows-based information, is necessary. Dechow (1994) studies the historical relationship between current earnings and
future cash flows as well as current cash flows and future cash flows. She finds that if
investors need expectations of future cash flows, they are better off with historical information about earnings than cash flows. The superior ability of earnings as a predictor
of future cash flows arises from the use of "accruals," which are the basis of accounting.
Accruals are judgments about the economics of transactions and events. They include
decisions such as recognizing revenues before cash has actually been collected or defer-
ring revenues when cash has been collected up front. Similarly, accruals also recognize
expenses such as pensions before they have been paid or capitalizing cash expenditures for long-lived assets and periodically expensing them as the asset is used up (i.e.,
depreciation). Dechow (p. 35) concludes that:

> [O]ne role of accounting accruals is to provide a measure of short-term per-
> formance that more closely reflects expected cash flows than do realized cash
> flows. . . . [O]ver short measurement intervals earnings are more strongly
> associated with stock returns than are realized cash flows.

The prior FASB quote is theoretical and the empirical study by Dechow (1994)
is based on thousands of observations, so both are somewhat removed from practical financial reporting in a firm-specific user-friendly context. However, practice also
confirms the usefulness of accounting information in providing valuable information
for investors and creditors. For example, a quarterly earnings announcement season
occurs, but not a cash flows announcement season. Earnings announcements are part of
a closely followed quarterly ceremony in developed capital markets around the world.
The timing of the announcement of quarterly earnings is typically coordinated around
meetings of boards of directors and conference calls with analysts, the press, and shareholders. Headlines in the financial press inevitably highlight earnings, not cash flows.

Second, investors closely examine occasional failures in financial reporting. Such
failures have immediate and substantial impacts on securities prices and inevitably pertain to management attempts to manipulate accounting information, not cash flows.
A criticism of accruals-based financial statements relative to cash flows is that financial
statements can be manipulated by managers. Ironically, the opposite is true: cash flows
are much more easily manipulated than earnings. For example, at the end of a quarter, a
manager could simply push back the payment of trade liabilities by two weeks, thereby
increasing operating cash flows. No auditor, analyst, or regulator would express concern

over this decision, but an attempt to similarly pump up reported earnings would likely be identified by one of these external watchdogs.

Finally, numerous successful investors emphasize the analysis of financial statements as part of their fortune. For example, Lynch (1989), who discusses this strategy extensively in his best-selling book, *One Up on Wall Street*, provides anecdotes about when he identifies a stock for purchase or sale, which are supported by numerous charts such as those in Figure 4.1. The premise for analyzing the concurrent trend in earnings and stock prices, which are unarguably forward looking, is that they track each other reasonably well. However, when prices either lag or lead earnings, then some phenomenon exists that warrants further attention. In Figure 4.1, earnings are increasing but price is not, so either the market has identified some important factor that has not yet made its way into reported earnings or the market is overlooking valuable information.

A rich history of empirical evidence shows how the market systematically misinterprets accounting information, collectively known as stock price anomalies (Basu 2004). A well-known example is post-earnings announcement drift, demonstrated convincingly by Bernard and Thomas (1989, 1990). *Post-earnings announcement drift* is the tendency for quarterly earnings increases to persist for three more quarters. Bernard and Thomas show that the market did not understand this relationship, which resulted in a relatively risk-free trading strategy that persisted for over a decade after publication. Similar anomalies based on accounting signals include the earnings-to-price anomaly (Basu 1977), accruals anomaly (Sloan 1996), bankruptcy risk anomaly (Dichev 1998), and F-score anomaly (Piotroski 2000).

The chapter is organized around the theme that accounting captures information useful for predicting future outcomes, especially future cash flows. The exposition relies partly on evidence from relevant empirical research studies, but the discussion is framed within the context of external financial statement users concerned with compiling information helpful to practical risk assessment. The first section explains how accounting actually incorporates forward-looking measures of risk into various elements of financial statements. The second summarizes various elements of risk that are conveyed through required or voluntary disclosures. The third section describes how risk disclosures and financial statement information can be combined to forecast several risk-related outcomes. The fourth section assesses the role of the accounting system in the financial crisis of 2007–2008. The final section concludes.

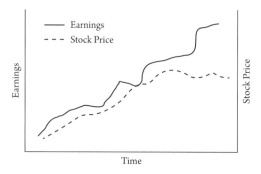

Figure 4.1 THE RELATIONSHIP BETWEEN EARNINGS AND STOCK PRICES. This figure shows a hypothetical time-series for earnings and stock prices for a typical firm.

Measures of Risk as Inputs into Elements of Financial Statements

Financial statements are based on qualitative or quantitative inputs that represent direct measurements of risk. In these circumstances, measures of risk determine elements in the financial statements. This relationship is in contrast to the more prevailing view of how accounting might capture risk, which is that the financial statements are used to determine quantified or qualitative assessments of contemporaneous or future risk. This latter role is discussed in the next section. This section illustrates several important financial statement line items that are based on forward-looking measures of risk. These include the accounting for loss contingencies, executive stock options, and defined benefit plans.

LOSS CONTINGENCIES

Loss contingencies reflect quantification of future losses that might occur upon some triggering event and they are recognized if certain criteria are met. Thus, loss contingencies directly capture a future risk faced by a firm. Current U.S. generally accepted accounting principles (GAAP) recognizes loss contingencies on the balance sheet as a liability, provided that a loss has occurred that is both probable and estimable. If both these conditions are met, then firms recognize the most likely loss under US GAAP or, if all losses are equally likely, then firms recognize the smallest loss. Regulators express concerns that some managers might overstate a recognized loss contingency to create a "cookie jar reserve" for future years. An excess liability is a "cookie jar" in the sense that it can be reversed in future years, and the reversal would be recognized as some sort of gain that could presumably be used strategically to offset other, as of yet known losses or expenses. A second expressed concern is that managers might avoid or delay recognition of losses merely by assessing that a loss contingency is not reliably estimable. In that case, if the loss contingency is probable, then the range of possible losses must be disclosed in the footnotes to the financial statements. Inevitably, the liabilities section of a balance sheet includes a line item with a title such as "commitments and contingencies." Although no balance will be presented, a reference to a footnote will provide a discussion of such contingencies.

As should be evident, the accounting for loss contingencies does not naturally map into a strictly financial view of contingencies, which would be based on discounted present value calculations. Not surprisingly, Michels (2013) documents that loss contingencies have a larger effect on stock market returns if they are recognized rather than simply footnoted as supplemental disclosure.

Turning to the "probable" criterion for recognition, U.S. accountants and auditors often perceive this condition to mean "more likely than 80 percent." International Financial Reporting Standards (IFRS), which are the authoritative accounting standards used in more than 100 countries, interpret "probably" to mean "more likely than not" or "more likely than 50 percent." This difference in probability thresholds, 80 percent versus 50 percent, across the two primary sets of accounting standards in the world creates a large wedge for differences in interpretation. Two otherwise similar companies, where one company reports under IFRS and the other reports under

U.S. GAAP, are likely to have fundamentally different reported liabilities. Companies reporting under IFRS are much more likely to report a loss and associated contingent liability than a firm reporting under U.S. GAAP.

EXECUTIVE STOCK OPTIONS

U.S. accounting standards require that employee stock options granted with a fixed strike price at or out of the money be accounted for using grant date fair value accounting. *Fair value accounting* means that on the date that the options are granted, accountants record a fair value estimate, typically using the Black-Scholes or a binomial option pricing model. The inputs into the option pricing models include estimates of future volatility, discount rates, future dividend payout ratios, and estimated date to exercise. Equity compensation expense is thus an attempt by accountants to measure the value of options granted, which is largely driven by estimates of underlying riskiness of the equity claim.

Hodder, Mayew, McAnally, and Weaver (2006), Johnston (2006), and Bartov, Mohanram, and Nissim (2007) provide evidence that managers use future volatility estimates that are biased downwards relative to two benchmarks: the ex post volatility and the implied volatility from traded equity options. A lower estimate of future volatility leads to a lower grant date fair value of the stock options, which in turn results in higher reported earnings. From a regulatory perspective, Spatt, Alexander, Nimalendran, and Oldfield (2005) suggest that the U.S. SEC permits firms to develop alternate other market-based estimates of fair value. In response, Zions Bancorporation developed an auction market for its executive stock options producing market-clearing prices that the SEC deemed could be used as fair value estimates for accounting purposes.

DEFINED BENEFIT PENSION PLANS

Defined benefit pension plans are promises to pay a retirement benefit to employees upon retirement, often based on the length of an employee's service, age, earnings history, and other factors. The accounting standards for such plans use direct measures of risk in determining associated liabilities and assets, and also require such forward-looking risk-related estimates as including future investment rate of returns on pension plan assets, projected future salary growth rates, mortality risk, and discount rates. Bergstresser, Desai, and Rauh (2006) suggest that managers can manipulate firm earnings through the assumed future rates of return on the firm's pension assets and, further, that firms change their asset allocation toward more risky assets to justify the higher expected rates of return. However, the expected rate of return on pension plan assets cannot be used for last minute earnings management for two reasons. First, the underlying expected returns used to determine the current year pension expense have to be decided and disclosed in the annual report of the prior fiscal year (Picconi 2006). Second, pension plan asset return estimates represent long-run performance and hence are sticky over time.

Projected salary growth rates are an accounting estimate that can be used in a similar way. Past U.S. accounting standards required only the Accumulated Benefit

Obligation (ABO) to be recognized on the balance sheet, but ABO excludes future salary increases. In contrast, current U.S. GAAP requires recognition of Projected Benefit Obligations (PBO), which also includes the present value of future salary increases. This is important when employees' pension benefits are computed based on some percentage of final or career-average salary. Because salary increases have not yet occurred (e.g., employees might get fired), PBO did not previously fit the conceptual framework's description of a liability. Starting in 2006, the difference between PBO and ABO for pension liabilities and the present value of healthcare benefits and other post-retirement benefits promised to retirees became recognized on the balance sheet. Chang (2009) and Fried (2013) provide evidence consistent with stronger incentives for earnings management after 2009.

Assumed mortality rates may be manipulated. In the United States, assumed mortality rates are available on regulatory filings that defined benefit plans make with the Department of Labor. Kisser, Kiff, Oppers, and Soto (2012) find evidence that mortality rate assumptions imply that people die too quickly. As a consequence, these biased mortality rate assumptions lead to a lower PBO and lower reported pension expense. Further, Kisser et al. estimate that an additional year of life expectancy can increase average pension obligations 3 to 4 percent, corresponding in aggregate to 1.5 percent of 2007 U.S. gross domestic product (GDP).

Discount rates are another accounting estimate that reflects risk. If the discount rate estimate is managed upwards, the reported pension obligation decreases, improving the perceived funding status of the pension plan based on the firm's balance sheet. Anantharaman (2013) documents that the size of the actuarial firms hired as external assessors matters, noting that larger actuarial firms tend to be conservative and recommend lower discount rate assumptions that result in higher liabilities and expense.

A viable argument is that an accounting benefit arises from investing in more risky pension plan assets. Pension plan assets' returns on the income statement rely mainly on expected rate of return, providing credit from the risk premium without the downside of volatility, which affects the funding status on the balance sheet. Put differently, the expected return appears on the income statement, while actual returns appear on the balance sheet (the difference categorized within a section called "other comprehensive income" that some investors seem to dismiss). Bloomfield, Nelson, and Smith (2006) investigate feedback loops between stock prices and reported accounting performance. In a pension plan setting, such feedback loops may arise when a firm invests its own equity in its defined benefit pension plan although the Employee Retirement Income Security Act of 1974 caps such investments at 10 percent.

Risk Disclosures in Required Notes and Voluntary Disclosures

This section highlights the disclosures of risk in financial statements. Two types of risk measures exist. Two-sided measures consider both upside gain and downside loss, such as standard deviation or variance. In contrast, one-sided risk measures consider either gains or losses (but not both) such as value-at-risk (VaR). *VaR* measures, for a given time horizon, the difference in the value at the mean outcome relative to say the 95 percent or 99 percent worst outcome.

Jorion (2002) studies eight U.S. commercial banks with the largest derivatives positions and finds that quarterly disclosures of VaR predict the variability of future unexpected trading revenues. Thus, these risk disclosures would seem to be a valuable tool for the assessment and management of firm-specific risks.

Financial firms have long faced risk-based regulation, but some non-financial firms also face mandatory risk disclosure requirements since January 1997, when the Securities and Exchange Commission (1997) issued *Financial Reporting Release (FRR) No. 48*. It required the disclosure of information about risks in one of three formats: VaR, sensitivity, or tabular. If firms choose the sensitivity format, then *FRR No. 48* requires disclosure of the sensitivity to various market risk factors of future cash flows related only to financial instruments and derivatives. The economic magnitudes of different sensitivities are not immediately comparable across different factors without knowing the likelihood of a 10 percent change in interest rates relative to the likelihood of a 10 percent change in exchange rates.

The last risk disclosure format allowed under *FRR No. 48* is the tabular format that provides a table with narrative information. This tabular format requires notional amounts for individual exposures for different time horizons, similar to operating and capital lease disclosures in notes to the financial statements. Hodder and McAnally (2001) show how financial statement users can convert risk disclosures from the tabular format into the sensitivity format, whereas the reverse conversion is not possible.

The disclosure requirements regarding risk continue to evolve. For example, the Securities and Exchange Commission (2001) issued *FRR No. 60* ("Cautionary Advice Regarding Disclosure about Critical Accounting Policies"), which requires that managers discuss what they perceive to be the critical accounting choices, methods, and estimates as well as their sensitivity. Additionally, firms supplement with voluntary disclosure practices such as earnings preannouncement warnings (Soffer, Thiagarajan, and Walther 2000).

Risk Forecasting Using Financial Statements and Footnotes

This section explores the use of financial statement information in predicting future risk outcomes, most often stock price drops. As mentioned previously, the search for accounting signals that are predictive of future outcomes not anticipated by the market is a fruitful area for researchers and practitioners. The search for profitable trading strategies fueled the growth in the number and total investments deployed by hedge funds in the late 1990s and early 2000s, and a decline in profitable trading opportunities (Green, Hand, and Soliman 2011).

In the same spirit, a rich history exists of identifying accounting signals useful for predicting events such as bankruptcy and financial reporting fraud that might trigger large stock price drops. Understanding factors that are predictive of large stock price drops is useful to portfolio and risk-management applications. Further, due to the increasing ease of trading options to capitalize perceived mispricing of stock market risk, more recent efforts have identified predictors of future stock price volatility, which is often an antecedent to stock price drops for some firms. This section highlights methodologies for predicting bankruptcy, financial reporting fraud, stock price volatility, and crash risk, and ends with a brief discussion of whether professional analysts convey useful information about future firm-specific risk.

CORPORATE BANKRUPTCY

One of the oldest uses of accounting information for risk assessment is the prediction of corporate bankruptcy. Beaver (1966) and Altman (1968) develop parsimonious models incorporating various accounting and market signals into bankruptcy prediction models. Practitioners around the world use Altman's Z-score model, which has performed remarkably well in predicting firm bankruptcies since its inception. As Bellovary, Giacomino, and Akers (2007) discuss, attempts to formally predict bankruptcy actually go back to at least the 1930s. Equation 4.1 shows the original Altman Z-score model.

$$
\begin{aligned}
\text{Z-score} = \; & 1.2 \, (\text{Net working capital/Total assets}) \\
& + 1.4 \, (\text{Retained earnings/Total assets}) \\
& + 3.3 \, (\text{Earnings before interest and taxes/Total assets}) \\
& + 0.6 \, (\text{Market value of equity/Book value of liabilities}) \\
& + 1.0 \, (\text{Sales/Total assets})
\end{aligned}
\tag{4.1}
$$

The individual factors in the model are intuitive. With the exception of the ratio of market value of equity to book value of liabilities, all factors are scaled by total assets; the scaling permits the cross-sectional estimation and application of the model. The first factor captures short-term liquidity risk. The second factor proxies for the accumulated profitability in the past. In contrast, the third factor measures current profitability. The fourth factor uses the market value of equity and when compared with the book value of liabilities, this factor is useful in capturing long-term solvency risk and to some extent the market's pricing of that risk. The final factor is a measure of the efficiency with which a firm generates sales from its assets in place.

Depending on the specification of Type I versus Type II error costs, the general cutoffs for discriminating firms likely to go bankrupt is a Z-score somewhere below 2.0. The inputs are specified such that lower values are more likely associated with the risk of bankruptcy. For example, the factor that carries the largest coefficient in the model is earnings before interest and taxes (EBIT) scaled by total assets, which is a version of return on assets (ROA). Firms that generate higher profitability in terms of ROA are clearly less likely to be subject to bankruptcy.

Altman (1968) developed his model based on only 66 manufacturing firms. Several refinements are available to improve shortcomings of the Altman bankruptcy risk prediction model. For example, extensions or revisions to the model are available for private and non-manufacturing firms (Altman 2000), small businesses (Edmister 1972), banks (Sinkey 1975), Internet firms (Wang 2004), and non-U.S. firms (Bellovary et al. 2007). Researchers have also developed and used alternative statistical methods including logit models (Ohlson 1980), neural network modeling

(Boritz and Kennedy 1995), hazard models (Shumway 2001), and judgment-based approaches (Zimmer 1980).

These models owe much of their popularity to their ease of implementation and reasonable performance in statistical holdout tests. However, most bankruptcy prediction models exhibit superior performance over relatively short horizons such as one-year ahead, but by this time, most investors have already recognized liquidity and solvency issues. For example, in Altman's original analysis, the accuracy of the model was only 36 percent five years before a bankruptcy filing, but 95 percent in the year before filing. Thus, relying on accounting-based bankruptcy prediction scores is not very timely, but recognizing patterns across time is quite useful.

A substitute for this type of risk analysis is the credit rating agencies such as Moody's and Standard and Poor's. However, Altman and Saunders (1997) tabulate Z-scores and credit agency bond ratings, which are perfectly monotonic, which suggests that the basis for the credit rating agencies' ratings incorporates the Z-scores or very similar information. As seen in the financial crisis of 2007–2008, the credit rating agencies did not provide very timely rating information. Thus, despite the advances in using financial statements to predict corporate bankruptcy, the predictive ability of accounting-based models is limited to near-term horizons.

FINANCIAL REPORTING FRAUD

Recent years have witnessed many major financial reporting manipulations associated with large, globally well-known firms such as Satyam, Xerox, Sunbeam, Parmalat, Lernout & Hauspie, and Sanyo. Although the Sarbanes-Oxley Act was implemented in the United States in 2002, no evidence exists that the incidence of corporate accounting manipulation has declined as a consequence. Financial reporting manipulation ranges from small massaging or smoothing of reported figures up to large-scale fraud aimed at deceiving investors over long periods. Beasley, Carcello, Hermanson, and Neal (2010) examine fraudulent financial reporting from 1998 to 2007 and report an increase in the number of frauds relative to the prior 10-year period (i.e., 347 versus 294). More importantly, they estimate the cumulative amount of misstatements during this period to be $120 billion. Given the previous discussion about the strong link between reported profits and stock prices, the effect of these frauds is a major misallocation of resources in the economy.

Because the impacts of financial misreporting on the economy can be so large, another long-standing use of accounting information in assessing risk is identifying financial misreporting risk. Practitioners routinely scour financial statements for evidence of accounting manipulation. Large brokerages such as Morgan Stanley and Credit Suisse, as well as boutique research firms like RiskMetrics, Algorithmics (acquired by Fitch Services), and Vision Research Associates perform professional accounting analysis. Parsing firms' reported profits into "expected" and "unexpected" components provides a platform for individual analysis into a firm's financial reporting choices and operations to better understand the 'unexpected' part of their reported profits. These analyses generally focus on small-scale attempts to affect reported financial numbers by small amounts. Attention here is restricted, however, to quantitative modeling that is aimed at picking up larger-scale financial manipulations because, like bankruptcy, the revelation of these types of manipulation typically triggers large price drops that can torpedo an investors' portfolio return.

Beneish (1999) provide a multi-variable discriminate analysis approach to predicting large corporate fraud that parallels the bankruptcy prediction modeling of Altman (1968). He examines a sample of firms busted by the SEC for accounting manipulation. The most common types of manipulation include overstatement of revenue, overstatement of inventory, and for growing firms capitalizing rather than expensing certain costs. All three have the effect of increasing earnings relative to what they would be otherwise. Like Altman's bankruptcy model that incorporates factors associated with bankruptcy, Beneish employs factors associated with financial misreporting typically through overstatement of reported earnings or assets, and understatement of liabilities. He also includes factors associated with preconditions that might generate incentives for corporate managers to overstate profits or net assets. Among his sample of manipulators, Beneish finds that manipulators show (1) increasing accounts receivable relative to sales, (2) deteriorating gross margins, (3) deteriorating asset quality, (4) high sales growth, (5) increasing leverage, and (6) high total accruals. Accordingly, Equation 4.2 shows the full model:

$$Y = -4.84 + 0.92\text{DSRI} + 0.528\text{GMI} + 0.404\text{AQI} + 0.892\text{SGI} + 0.115\text{DEPI} \atop -0.172\text{SGAI} - 0.327\text{LVGI} + 4.679\text{TATA}. \qquad (4.2)$$

Table 4.1 provides the descriptions of individual factors. In the model, Y is a weighted average statistical score, akin to the Altman Z-score, but the factors are specified such that higher values are associated with a greater probability of the firm being a manipulator.

As with any statistical attempt to identify rare events, this model suffers from several shortcomings. First, three of the eight factors (DEPI, SGAI, and LVGI) are not significantly associated with fraud risk in Beneish's test sample. He retains these factors in the model based on the ex ante arguments for including them, and any underlying correlation structure among these and the other factors that are significant in his analysis. Second, the probability equivalents of the model output are economically small. For example, when applying this fraud prediction model to Sunbeam in 1997, which later had to be restated for substantial fraud, the probability estimate of manipulation is only about 3.5 percent. Thus, practical use of the model relies on benchmarks that are close to zero. Finally, because some factors are evidence of manipulation and others are preconditions that might trigger manipulation, whether a firm classified as a manipulator has done so or is at risk for doing so is indeterminate. Nevertheless, as Beneish (1999, p. 24) states, "Because companies that are discovered manipulating earnings see their stocks plummet in value, the model can be a useful screening device for investment professionals."

STOCK PRICE CRASHES

The risk implicitly being addressed by these bankruptcy and fraud prediction models is the risk of a large stock price decline. Large price drops or crashes can occur for numerous reasons other than bankruptcy or fraud. Features of the options pricing market

Table 4.1 **Beneish Model Factor Definitions**

Factor	Description	Rationale
DSRI	Days sales receivable index	Increasing accounts receivable as a percentage of sales is consistent with overstatement of sales
GMI	Gross margin index	Decreasing gross margins intensify incentives to manipulate earnings
AQI	Asset quality index	Increasing fractions of "other" assets are consistent with capitalization of expenses
SGI	Sales growth index	High sales growth intensifies incentives to manipulate earnings
DEPI	Depreciation index	Decreasing depreciation rates are consistent with underreporting of expenses
SGAI	Sales, general, and administrative expense index	Increasing SG&A expenses intensifies incentives to manipulate earnings
LVGI	Leverage index	High leverage intensifies incentives to manipulate earnings
TATA	Total accruals to total assets index	High accruals are consistent with discretionary accounting decisions that increase reported earnings

Source: Beneish (1991).

are useful in predicting future stock price crashes. Among other inputs into a standard Black-Scholes pricing model, arguably the most important factor is stock price volatility, which should be constant across any chain of options on a particular stock. However, the implied volatilities for options on the same stock reveal a pattern whereby deep out-of-the-money options have higher implied volatilities, as sketched in Figure 4.2.

In other words, out-of-the-money put options are more expensive than similar out-of-the-money call options, which is consistent with a climate of negative expectations. More importantly, those expectations reflect beliefs in large stock price drops. By plotting implied volatilities for a chain of option prices with strikes around the current trading price, the plot reveals a downward sloping "smirk." Recently, Credit Suisse used information in implied volatilities of the S&P 500 index to construct a "fear barometer" that is meant to predict large, downward market-wide moves.

Duan and Wei (2009) show that the downward slopes of smirk curves are associated with systematic risk, suggesting that some knowledge of firm-specific fundamentals might also be helpful in forecasting large firm-specific stock price drops. Lyle (2012) contends that accounting quality can affect option pricing and returns even if it is completely idiosyncratic and unassociated with equity returns. Hutton, Marcus, and Tehranian (2009) demonstrate that a measure of financial reporting opacity is associated with stock price crashes, defined as three standard deviation drops in stock price. Their arguments rely on a theoretical model by Jin and Myers (2006) that characterized

Figure 4.2 Option Smirk Curve. This figure shows a stylized plot of implied
volatilities across a range of out-of-the-money and in-the-money stock options.

firms as having a tendency to stockpile bad news through various channels such as
accounting. The stockpile accumulates to a point where hiding the news is either cost
ineffective or impossible to continue, at which time its revelation to the market triggers a
stock price crash. In a follow-up to the Hutton et al. (2009) analysis, Bradshaw, Hutton,
Marcus, and Tehranian (2013) show that several financial constructs are incrementally informative of future stock price crashes, which is consistent with some degree of
inefficiency in option prices.

FORECASTING FIRM-SPECIFIC VOLATILITY

Along the lines of the previous link between volatilities implied in stock option prices
and financial accounting information, recent efforts examine whether information in
financial statements can be useful in predicting future volatility of firm-specific prices.
An ability to predict future volatility has immediate benefits for creditors and portfolio managers who attempt to manage risk by balancing expected returns against risk
reflected in future volatility. In theory, such idiosyncratic risk should not be priced
because investors can diversify such risk away through a portfolio of holdings. However,
if frictions prevent theoretical diversification, then idiosyncratic risk may be priced.

Sridharan (2013) examines whether accounting fundamentals are informative about
future equity volatility. Given the link between historic and future volatility, she first
measures expectations of future volatility using implied option volatility. Sridharan then
decomposes equity return volatility into earnings yield variance, market risk premium
variance, and the covariance of the first two factors. Accounting-based fundamentals
include a measure of firm size, growth in sales, and volatility of earnings. Together, these
three factors explain one-fifth of future equity. Similar to the preceding discussion about
financial information being informative of future stock price crashes incremental to the
information available in the implied volatility curve, Sridharan finds that accounting-
based fundamental information is indeed associated with future volatility, but is not
fully impounded in the implied volatility from option prices. Again, this finding points
to a role of financial reporting in the management of firm-specific and portfolio risk.

ANALYST FORECASTS OF RISK

A final example of the use of financial reporting information to predict future risk captured by large stock price drops or volatility in general involves how sell-side analysts

quantify such risks. Analysts presumably analyze publicly available signals and generate private information through financial statement analysis and valuation. They then convey their research through various channels, which contribute to the overall efficient functioning of capital markets. One argument is that analysts simply piggyback on information already publicly available, so are merely megaphones within the capital markets (Altinkilic and Hansen 2009). An alternative is that analysts' private processing of information and distribution of their research convey new information previously not widely available (Asquith, Mikhail, and Au 2005).

Lui, Markov, and Tamayo (2007) examine risk ratings issued by Salomon Smith Barney during 1997–2003. The measure of risk being forecasted by these analysts is said to be price volatility and the predictability of future financial results. Like stock recommendations, the brokerage uses five categories of risk: low, medium, high, speculative, and venture. The most interesting part of their analysis is not necessarily whether analysts are capable at forecasting firm-specific risk, but what factors are correlated with analysts' risk assessments. The authors not only examine accounting-based measures of risk such as debt-to-equity, book-to-market, and market capitalization but also other measures such as whether the firm recently had an initial public offering. They also examine whether analysts' risk ratings capture classic measures of risk including market beta, idiosyncratic risk, and a measure of illiquidity.

Analysts assign higher risk ratings to small firms, high book-to-market firms, and firms with high leverage; idiosyncratic risk is also correlated with analysts' assessments of risk. When examining the association between analysts' risk ratings and future volatility, Lui et al. (2007) document that analysts' risk ratings are incrementally informative even after controlling for this underlying variation in fundamental predictors of future risk. In a follow-up analysis, Lui et al. (2012) examine changes in analysts' risk ratings. As a benchmark of the informativeness of changes in risk ratings, they simultaneously examine changes in credit rating changes. Perhaps surprisingly, risk rating changes have a much larger impact than credit rating changes, which are ubiquitous measures of forward-looking firm-specific risk. Overall, analysts apparently can provide incremental information to the market through their process of deriving risk ratings based on factors like those examined, as well as other proprietary analyses.

The Role of Accounting in the Financial Crisis of 2007–2008

This section briefly addresses two possible roles accounting had in the financial crisis of 2007–2008. One role involves whether accounting contributed to the depth of the financial crisis and the other shows how risk measurements changed in response to the financial crisis.

Accounting regulation has gravitated toward a higher emphasis on fair value or mark-to-market accounting in recent years and less emphasis on the alternative, historical cost accounting. A long-standing debate exists among investors about the role that fair value accounting had in the crisis (Laux and Leuz 2010). Critics of fair value accounting argue that writing assets "up" enables banks to ratchet up leverage, which deepens the impact of crashes. By contrast, others note that the writing "down" of assets is timely and serves as a barometer of impending crashes that provides valuable early warning signals. The role of accounting in the crisis centers on the role of fair value accounting but is also affected to a lesser extent by forward-looking disclosures such as VaR.

In an earlier paper on fair value accounting for regulation of financial institutions, Bernard, Merton, and Palepu (1995) address how financial regulation might be affected by or can affect the usefulness of fair value versus historical cost accounting. They conclude that fair value accounting is timelier than historical cost accounting but may contain more noise and provoke contagion, which was alarming and foreshadowed the recent financial crisis. Notwithstanding these concerns about fair value, Desai, Rajgopal, and Yu (2013) document an association between banks' financial statement indicators before the financial crisis and the subsequent financial distress of these banks. Reinforcing the beneficial role of fair value accounting, Laux and Leuz (2009, 2010) conclude that fair value was far from being the primary impetus of the financial crisis.

Accounting rules have changed markedly in response to the financial crisis of 2007–2008. During this crisis, banks lobbied to change the classification of marketable securities (between levels 1 through 3) and to change the presentation of unrealized holding gains or losses on certain securities. Further, to illustrate the evolution of risk disclosures and their underlying assumptions around the financial crisis, consider the case of Barclays PLC. As the latest financial crisis hit, Barclays PLC (2008, p. 120) reported in its financial statements reported that:

> Daily Value at Risk is an estimate of the potential loss arising from unfavourable market movements, if the current positions were to be held unchanged for one business day. Barclays Capital uses the historical simulation method with a two year unweighted historical period.
>
> In 2008, the confidence level was changed to 95% from 98% as an increasing incidence of significant market movements made the existing measure more volatile and less effective for risk management purposes. Switching to 95% made DVaR more stable and consequently improved management, transparency and control of the market risk profile.

The reported nominal risk exposure using daily value-at-risk (DVaR) based on a 95 percent confidence level is mechanically lower than that based on a 98 percent level, but Barclays PLC reported DVaR for both confidence levels in 2008. In its 2009 financial statements, however, Barclays PLC reported DVaR at 95 percent only. It supplemented this disclosure with expected shortfall, which is measured as the average DVaR over all outcomes below the confidence level, and a "3W" disclosure, which is the average of the three largest one-day losses. While the Financial Services Authority in England requires that back-testing be done using 99 percent confidence levels, the VaR reported in Barclays PLC 2012 financial statements uses a 95 percent confidence level. Thus, variation between regulation and practice persists.

Overall, the recent financial crisis was the outcome of many market forces and fair value accounting is at best only a minor player in this ecosystem. Incentives of originating banks, loan aggregators, rating agencies, asset managers, and numerous other financial institutions exhibited non-surprising behavior based on their incentives. Although overstated, blaming the crisis on the fair value accounting is akin to "killing the messenger."

Summary and Conclusions

Despite accounting being backwards looking in the sense that it records historical transactions, the manner in which accruals are entered into financial statements allows accounting earnings to better predict future operating performance than cash flows. Put differently, if the objective is measuring the timing, amount, and variability of future cash flows, earnings is king and cash is not. In preparing financial statements, management makes estimates that reveal its private information about the future, including forward-looking estimates and future risks associated with business strategy. Because investors are naturally skeptical about management estimates, the appropriate use of financial statements and accounting information about the preparation of the numbers continues to be a challenge. One stream of accounting research reveals price anomalies that once documented eventually disappear, suggesting that these anomalies did not involve investment strategies with uncompensated systematic risks.

Researchers and investors alike can use financial statement information to predict bankruptcy, large corporate frauds, and future firm-specific stock return volatility or stock option volatility. Although early research focused on how accounting information predicts stock return behavior, one current frontier of accounting research investigates how accounting information predicts the return on derivatives positions such as options.

Financial statements also provide some direct disclosure of risk information that can predict future risks. For example, VaR disclosures are informative of future risks. Similar to earnings management through accrual choices and accounting estimates, managers' choice of accounting estimates can affect risk disclosures in the financial statements. The choice of volatility used affects the accounting cost of stock options granted to employees. Although management prepares information in the financial statements that provides information about risks, financial intermediaries also collect, process, and disclose information that provides information about risks. Specifically, analysts produce and disclose information related to future realizations such as target prices and forecasts of future dividends and future earnings, but they also provide forecasts of risk. Such risk forecasts appear informative of price volatility and the predictability of future financial results.

Discussion Questions

1. Given that accounting is backwards looking, explain why accounting accruals are informative about the future.
2. Given that investors appear to process accounting information imperfectly, discuss one price anomaly and how investors may profit from using this anomaly.
3. List several useful variables in predicting large corporate frauds and discuss the implications for investment decisions.

4. Identify the conditions under which forecasting of firm-specific volatility may or may not be valuable for investment decisions.
5. Practitioners have used and disclosed VaR since the 1990s. The Basel Committee on Banking Supervision has proposed replacing VaR with a different one-sided risk measure called expected shortfall, which represents the average VaR among all sufficiently unfavorable outcomes. Discuss how this will change the reporting of risks under *FRR No. 48*.
6. Before January 1, 2005, Norwegian Telenor ASA prepared its financial statements according to Norwegian Generally Accepted Accounting Principles (N GAAP). Starting in 2005, Telenor ASA used International Financial Reporting Standards (IFRS). Telenor also provided reconciliation to U.S. GAAP. Telenor has a defined benefit pension plan and therefore needs to assume a discount rate to determine its pension benefit obligations.

   At the end of 2005, the same discount rate is used for both IFRS and US GAAP. At the end of 2004, a lower discount rate is used under IFRS than for US GAAP. For US GAAP the discount rate included an assumed risk premium for corporate rate bonds over the Norwegian government bond rate. At the end of 2005, assume that the more conservative government bond rate could also be used as the discount rate for US GAAP. Application of a more conservative approach to determining the US GAAP discount rate is regarded as a change in estimate (Telenor 2005).

Year	Accounting Standard	Discount Rate Assumed to Determine Pension Obligations
2002	N GAAP	6.5
2003	N GAAP	5.7
2004	N GAAP	5.0
2004	US GAAP	5.0
2004	IFRS	4.5*
2005	IFRS	3.9
2005	*US GAAP*	3.9

   *As stated in the 2005 financial statements.

   Discuss the effect of lower assumed discount rates on the pension obligations and whether Telenor should apply different discount rates when reporting 2004 fiscal year performance under IFRS and U.S. GAAP.

References

Altinkilic, Oya, and Robert S. Hansen. 2009. "On the Information Role of Stock Recommendation Revisions." *Journal of Accounting and Economics* 48:1, 17–36.
Altman, Edward I. 1968. "Financial Ratios, Discriminant Analysis and the Prediction of Corporate Bankruptcy." *Journal of Finance* 23:4, 589–609.

Altman, Edward I. 2000. "Predicting Financial Distress of Companies: Revisiting the Z-Score and ZETA® Models." Working Paper, New York University.

Altman, Edward I., and Anthony Saunders. 1997. "Credit Risk Measurement: Developments over the Last 20 Years." *Journal of Banking & Finance* 21:11–12, 1721–1742.

Anantharaman, Divya. 2013. "Actuarial Independence, Client Importance and Pension Assumptions." Working Paper, Rutgers University.

Asquith, Paul, Michael B. Mikhail, and Andrea S. Au. 2005. "Information Content of Equity Analyst Reports." *Journal of Financial Economics* 75:2, 245–282.

Barclays PLC. Annual Report. 2008. Available at http://group.barclays.com/Satellite?blobcol= urldata&blobheader=application%2Fpdf&blobheadername1=Content-Disposition& blobheadername2=MDT-Type&blobheadervalue1=inline%3B+filename%3D2008- Barclays-Bank-PLC-Annual-Report-PDF.pdf&blobheadervalue2=abinary%3B+charset% 3DUTF-8&blobkey=id&blobtable=MungoBlobs&blobwhere=1330686340598&ssbinary= true.

Bartov, Eli, Partha Mohanram, and Doron Nissim. 2007. "Managerial Discretion and the Economic Determinants of the Disclosed Volatility Parameter for Valuing ESOs." *Review of Accounting Studies* 12:1, 155–179.

Basu, Sanjoi. 1977. "Investment Performance of Common Stocks in Relation to Their Price-Earnings Ratios: A Test of the Efficient Market Hypothesis." *Journal of Finance* 32:3, 663–682.

Basu, Sudipta. 2004. "What Do We Learn from Two New Accounting-based Stock Market Anomalies?" *Journal of Accounting and Economics* 38:1, 333–348.

Beasley, Mark S., Joseph V. Carcello, Dana R. Hermanson, and Terry L. Neal. 2010. "Fraudulent Financial Reporting 1998–2007: An Analysis of U.S. Public Companies." Committee of Sponsoring Organizations of the Threadway Commission.

Beaver, William H. 1966. "Financial Ratios as Predictors of Failure." *Journal of Accounting Research* 4:Supplement, 71–111.

Bellovary, Jodi, Don Giacomino, and Michael Akers. 2007. "A Review of Bankruptcy Prediction Studies: 1930 to Present." *Journal of Financial Education* 33:1, 1–42.

Beneish, Messod D. 1999. "The Detection of Earnings Manipulation." *Financial Analysts Journal* 55:5, 24–36.

Beneish, Messod D. 1999. "Incentives and Penalties Related to Earnings Overstatements that Violate GAAP." *Accounting Review* 74:4, 425–457.

Bergstresser, Daniel, Mihir Desai, and Joshua Rauh. 2006. "Earnings Manipulation, Pension Assumptions and Managerial Investment Decisions." *Quarterly Journal of Economics* 121:1, 157–195.

Bernard, Victor L., and Jacob K. Thomas. 1989. "Post-Earnings Announcement Drift: Delayed Price Response or Risk Premium?" *Journal of Accounting Research* (Supplement) 27, 1–36.

Bernard, Victor L., and Jacob K. Thomas. 1990. "Evidence That Stock Prices Do Not Fully Reflect the Implications of Current Earnings for Future Earnings." *Journal of Accounting and Economics* 13:4, 305–340.

Bernard, Victor L., Robert C. Merton, and Krishna G. Palepu. 1995. "Mark-to-market Accounting for Banks and Thrifts: Lessons from the Danish Experience." *Journal of Accounting Research* 33:1, 1–32.

Bloomfield, Robert J., Mark W. Nelson, and Steven Smith. 2006. "Feedback Loops, Fair Value and Correlated Investments." *Review of Accounting Studies* 11:2–3, 377–416.

Boritz, J. Efrim, and Duane B. Kennedy. 1995. "Effectiveness of Neural Network Types for Prediction of Business Failure." *Expert Systems with Applications* 9:4, 503–512.

Bradshaw, Mark T., Amy P. Hutton, and Alan J. Marcus, and Hassan Tehranian. 2013. "Opacity, Crash Risk, and the Option Smirk Curve." Working Paper, Boston College.

Chang, Woo-Jin. 2009. "Economic Consequences of the Transition from Disclosure to Recognition of Pension Funded Status Following SFAS 158." Working Paper, INSEAD.

Dechow, Patricia M. 1994. "Accounting Earnings and Cash Flows as Measures of Firm Performance: The Role of Accounting Accruals." *Journal of Accounting and Economics* 18:1, 3–42.

Desai, Hemang, Shiva Rajgopal, and Jeff Jiewei Yu. 2013. "Did Information Intermediaries See the Warning Signals of the Banking Crisis from Leading Indicators in Banks' Financial Statements?" Working Paper, Southern Methodist University.

Dichev, Ilia D. 1998. "Is the Risk of Bankruptcy a Systematic Risk?" *Journal of Finance* 53:3, 1131–1147.

Duan, Jin-Chuan, and Jason Wei. 2009. "Systematic Risk and the Price Structure of Individual Equity Options." *Review of Financial Studies* 22:5, 1981–2006.

Edmister, Robert O. 1972. "An Empirical Test of Financial Ratio Analysis for Small Business Failure Prediction." *Journal of Financial and Quantitative Analysis* 7:2, 1477–1493.

Financial Accounting Standards Board. 2008. *Statement of Financial Accounting Concepts No. 2* [as amended], "Qualitative Characteristics of Accounting Information."

Fried, Abraham N. 2013. "An Event Study Analysis of Statement of Financial Accounting Standards No. 158." *Accounting and Finance Research* 2:2, 45–58.

Green, Jeremiah, John R. M. Hand, and Mark T. Soliman. 2011. "Going, Going, Gone? The Apparent Demise of the Accruals Anomaly." *Management Science* 57:5, 797–816.

Hodder, Leslie, and Mary Lea McAnally. 2001. "SEC Market Risk Disclosures: Enhancing Comparability." *Financial Analysts Journal* 57:2, 62–78.

Hodder, Leslie, William J. Mayew, Mary Lea McAnally, and Connie D. Weaver. 2006. "Employee Stock Option Fair-value Estimates: Do Managerial Discretion and Incentives Explain Accuracy?" *Contemporary Accounting Research* 23:4, 933–975.

Hutton, Amy P., Alan J. Marcus, and Hassan Tehranian. 2009. "Opaque Financial Reports, R-square, and Crash Risk." *Journal of Financial Economics* 94:1, 67–86.

Jin, Li, and Stewart C. Myers. 2006. "R^2 around the World: New Theory and New Tests." *Journal of Financial Economics* 79:2, 257–292.

Johnston, Derek M. 2006. "Managing Stock Option Expense: The Manipulation of Option-pricing Model Assumptions." *Contemporary Accounting Research* 23:2, 395–425.

Jorion, Phillippe. 2002. "How Informative Are Value-at-Risk Disclosures?" *Accounting Review* 77:4, 911–931.

Kisser, Michael, John Kiff, Stefan Erik Oppers, and Mauricio Soto. 2012. "The Impact of Longevity Improvements on U.S. Corporate Defined Benefit Pension Plans." IMF Working Paper.

Laux, Christian, and Christian Leuz. 2009. "The Crisis of Fair-value Accounting: Making Sense of the Recent Debate." *Accounting, Organizations and Society* 34:6–7, 826–834.

Laux, Christian, and Christian Leuz. 2010. "Did Fair-value Accounting Contribute to the Financial Crisis?" *Journal of Economic Perspectives* 24:1, 93–118.

Lui, Daphne, Stanimir Markov, and Ane Tamayo. 2007. "What Makes a Stock Risky? Evidence from Sell-side Analysts' Risk Ratings." *Journal of Accounting Research* 45:3, 629–665.

Lui, Daphne, Stanimir Markov, and Ane Tamayo. 2012. "Equity Analysts and the Market's Assessment of Risk." *Journal of Accounting Research* 50:5, 1287–1317.

Lyle, Matthew. 2012. "How Does Accounting Quality Affect Option Returns?" PhD dissertation, University of Toronto.

Lynch, Peter. 1989. *One Up on Wall Street*. New York: Simon and Shuster.

Michels, Jeremy. 2013. "Disclosure versus Recognition: Inferences from Subsequent Events." Working Paper, University of Pennsylvania.

Ohlson, James A. 1980. "Financial Ratios and the Probabilistic Prediction of Bankruptcy." *Journal of Accounting Research* 18:1, 109–131.

Picconi, Marc. 2006. "The Perils of Pensions: Does Pension Accounting Lead Investors and Analysts Astray?" *Accounting Review* 81:4, 925–955.

Piotroski, Joseph D. 2000. "Value Investing: The Use of Historical Financial Statement Information to Separate Winners from Losers." *Journal of Accounting Research* 38:Supplement, 1–41.

Securities and Exchange Commission. 1997. *Financial Reporting Release No. 48*. "Disclosure of Accounting Policies for Derivative Financial Instruments and Derivative Commodity Instruments and Disclosure of Quantitative Information about Market Risk Inherent in Derivative Financial Instruments, Other Financial Instruments and Derivative Commodity Instruments." Washington, DC: Securities and Exchange Commission.

Securities and Exchange Commission. 2001. *Financial Reporting Release No. 60.* "Cautionary Advice Regarding Disclosure about Critical Accounting Policies." Washington, DC: Securities and Exchange Commission.

Shumway, Tyler. 2001. "Forecasting Bankruptcy More Accurately: A Simple Hazard Model." *Journal of Business* 74:1, 101–124.

Sinkey, Jr., Joseph F. 1975. "A Multivariate Statistical Analysis of the Characteristics of Problem Banks." *Journal of Finance* 30:1, 21–36.

Sloan, Richard G. 1996. "Do Stock Prices Fully Reflect Information in Accruals and Cash Flows about Future Earnings?" *Accounting Review* 71:3, 289–315.

Soffer, Leonard C., S. Ramu Thiagarajan, and Beverly R. Walther. 2000. "Earnings Preannouncement Strategies." *Review of Accounting Studies* 5:1, 5–26.

Spatt, Chester S., Cindy R. Alexander, M. Nimalendran, and George Oldfield. 2005. "Economic Evaluation of Alternative Market Instrument Designs: Toward a Market-Based Approach to Estimating the Fair Value of Employee Stock Options." U.S. Securities and Exchange Commission, Office of Economic Analysis, August 31. Available at http://www.sec.gov/news/extra/memo083105.htm.

Sridharan, Suhas. 2013. "Volatility Forecasting Using Financial Statement Information." Working Paper, UCLA. Available at http://papers.ssrn.com/sol3/papers.cfm?abstract_id=1984324.

Telenor. *Annual Report.* 2005. Available at http://www.telenor.com/wp-content/uploads/2012/03/report2005_v1.pdf.

Wang, Bin. 2004. "Strategy Changes and Internet Firm Survival." PhD dissertation,University of Minnesota.

Zimmer, Ian. 1980. "A Lens Study of the Prediction of Corporate Failure by Bank Loan Officers." *Journal of Accounting Research* 18:2, 629–636.

Part Two

TYPES OF RISK

5

Market Risk

RAMON P. DEGENNARO

CBA Professor of Banking and Finance, The University of Tennessee

CHANAKA P. EDIRISINGHE

Kay and Jackson Tai Chair Professor of Finance, Rensselaer Polytechnic Institute

Introduction

According to NASDAQ (2014), market risk results from the fluctuating prices of investments as they trade in the global markets. Investopedia (2014) uses similar language, viewing *market risk* as the possibility that investors might experience losses due to factors affecting the overall performance of the financial markets.

MANAGING MARKET RISK

Although diversifying away uncorrelated asset-specific risks is possible with a sufficiently large number of assets in a portfolio, the remaining systematic risk in the portfolio is associated with the overall risk factors of the economy. Asset allocation can then protect against market risk because different portions of the market tend to underperform relative to the market at different times. The practice of dividing financial resources among different asset categories such as stocks, bonds, mutual funds, investment partnerships, real estate, cash equivalents, and private equity is likely to lessen risk exposure because each asset class has a less than perfect correlation to each of the others. For example, when stock prices rise, bond prices often fall. At a time when the stock market begins to fall, real estate may begin generating above average returns.

An important model expressing the idea of market risk is the capital asset pricing model (CAPM) shown in Equation 5.1,

$$E(R_i) = R_f + \beta_i(E(R_m) - R_f),\qquad(5.1)$$

where $E(R_i)$ is the expected return on asset i; R_f is the risk-free rate of interest; β_i is a measure of the correspondence between asset i's return and the market's return less the riskless rate; and $E(R_m)$ is the expected return of the market. More precisely, β_i is $Cov(R_i, R_m)/Var(R_m)$.

This model, which traces to Sharpe (1964), expresses the expected return on capital assets as a function of the expected excess return on the market above the risk-free rate. The term β_i represents the sensitivity of the asset to the market. When beta equals one, the asset tends to move in the same direction as the market and by the same percentage amount. A beta greater than unity indicates that the asset tends to move more than the market; a positive beta less than one means that the asset tends to move less than the market; and an asset with a negative beta tends to move in the opposite direction of the market. The key insight of the CAPM is that beta measures the type of risk that cannot be eliminated by diversification. Because this type of risk is inherent in the market system, it also is called *systematic risk*.

When applying Equation 5.1 to a portfolio, the resulting beta, referred to as the *portfolio beta*, measures the sensitivity of portfolio return to the market risk. By choosing the constituent assets in the portfolio, investors can construct portfolios of the desired sensitivity to market risk. That is, a well-diversified portfolio consisting of positive and negative asset betas may be designed to achieve a portfolio beta of a specified value, say β_P. Then, the value of β_P is determined by the mixing proportions of the individual assets, say x_i for asset i. This relationship is linear with n assets in the portfolio as shown in Equation 5.2,

$$\beta_P = \beta_1 x_1 + \beta_2 x_2 + \cdots + \beta_n x_n. \tag{5.2}$$

Thus, fund managers may adopt different asset allocation styles to make portfolios become more or less risky, relative to the market risk, for a chosen universe of assets, in which an allocation such that $\beta_P = 0$ corresponds to a market risk-neutral portfolio. Furthermore, a dynamic asset allocation style may be considered in which the portfolio beta is temporally adjusted via portfolio rebalancing, say every month or quarter, to align the portfolio with evolving market or economic conditions. In such a scenario, a positive portfolio beta may be desired when the asset manager believes that the overall market is in an "up" mode, negative β_P when the overall market is in a "down" mode, and relative beta is close to zero when the market is in "congestion."

The remainder of the chapter is organized as follows. The next section describes factor models of asset returns and discounted cash flow (DCF) models of asset valuation. Next, the important topic of determining discount rates is addressed to establish its connection to market risk. Then, relative firm strength analysis models are discussed in the context of firm financial statements. These strengths are shown to vary across different economic states, leading to the notion of state-dependent risk of firm inefficiency. The last two sections offer directions for future research and a summary and conclusions.

Risk Factors and Valuation

Factors affecting risk in asset returns have been under intense discussion since the development of the CAPM. This section examines those factors, beyond the beta risk, leading to the concept of a risk premium. This is extended in a later section to include a factor related to firm inefficiencies. Also, this section introduces the basic firm valuation model and identifies discount rates as a critical ingredient in cash flow valuation.

THE FAMA-FRENCH THREE-FACTOR MODEL

The CAPM has been tested extensively using historical data (Reinganum 1981; Ang and Chen 2007). While beta risk can explain a substantial portion of the return of diversified portfolios, the results vary depending on the data period and the fund universe. For example, for 10 portfolios from the Athens Stock Exchange, the adjusted R^2 varied from 47 to 68 percent indicating the percentage of variability in the portfolio explained by beta (Theriou, Aggelidis, Maditinos, and Ševic 2010). Fama and French (1995) propose two additional risk factors to explain the variation of portfolio return: the size of the stocks as measured by market capitalization and the book-to-market (B/M) value of the stocks in a portfolio. Adding these two factors of risk in the economy can explain as much as 95 percent of the portfolio returns. For example, using data from the United Kingdom, portfolios formed according to B/M and size resulted in R^2 values from 87 to 94 percent (Bhatnagar and Ramlogan 2012).

Small companies logically should be more return sensitive than large firms as a result of their relatively less diversified nature and their reduced ability to absorb negative financial events. This sensitivity is termed *size risk*. Investors accepting this risk are compensated in the market in the form of a size premium. The annual size premium exhibited a historical average of about 3.3 percent from 1926 to 2002, with more recent data suggesting a range of 1.5 to 2 percent (Womack and Zhang 2003). In contrast, the value risk proposition hinges on the notion that a high B/M value usually indicates that the firm's public market value has fallen due to doubt about future earnings, perhaps arising from the firm's adverse positioning in the current or future market climate or to changes in the applicable discount rate. Therefore, such companies are expected to be exposed to greater risk of bankruptcy or other financial troubles. Empirical studies show that shares with high B/M have outperformed low B/M shares resulting in a value premium (Fama and French 1993; Lakonishok, Shleifer, and Vishny 1994; Haugen 1997). Womack and Zhang (2003) report that the annual value premium had a historical average of about 5.1 percent from 1926 to 2002, with more recent data suggesting a range of 3 to 5.4 percent.

THE DISCOUNTED DIVIDEND MODEL

Rather than determine expected returns, the discounted dividend model in Equation provides a way to value assets:

$$V_t = \sum_{t=0}^{\infty} \frac{E(D_{t+1})}{1 + k_{t+1}}, \tag{5.3}$$

where V_t is the value of the share at time t; $E(D_{t+1})$ is the expected dividends per share; k_{t+1} is the cost of equity or the expected return on equity both at time $t + 1$. This model expresses the value of an asset as the present value of expected future cash flows, discounted at the rate appropriate to the asset's risk.

Given a constant growth rate in the dividend D and the cost of equity k, the model collapses to the familiar Gordon constant growth model (Gordon and Shapiro 1956):

$$V_t = \frac{D_1}{k - g},$$
(5.4)

where g = the dividend growth rate and the other terms are as defined above. The discount rate k in the Gordon model essentially corresponds to $E(R_i)$, the expected return on the asset in the CAPM.

Cochrane (2011) reports that financial economists used to think that asset prices changed because the expected cash flows in Equation 5.3 changed. Recently and notwithstanding some evidence to the contrary (Hirschey 2003), financial economists' beliefs have shifted. Cochran notes that financial economists now hold the view that changes in discount rates account for the majority and perhaps the vast majority of price changes.

Factors Affecting Discount Rates across Securities

According to traditional risk measures, including the CAPM's beta and other recognized pricing factors such as value and size, achieving excess returns, commonly called *alpha*, seems possible. This assumption forms the basis for trading strategies that lead to what appear to be higher expected returns than they deserve, at least based on traditional measures of risk (Cochrane 2011).

The apparent excess returns probably trace to undocumented sources of risk. This opportunity seems to exist with value stocks (Cochrane 2011). Value stocks appear to offer higher expected returns than their betas would suggest. Because price changes in value stocks tend to be correlated, a portfolio of value stocks cannot be fully diversified no matter how many value stocks an investor adds to the portfolio. Whatever is the source of higher expected returns for value stocks, it seems to trace to a risk factor that researchers had not previously recognized.

This finding should prove to be the case for other investment strategies built to capture excess returns. Jegadeesh and Titman (1993), for example, show that momentum strategies seem to offer excess returns. Fama and French (2008) show that strategies built around certain accounting variables also tend to produce returns that exceed those that traditional risk profiles suggest. One interpretation of these findings is that the market is simply inefficient. Another possibility is that researchers have yet to uncover a priced factor.

WHY DO DISCOUNT RATES CHANGE?

Given the evidence that changes in discount rates cause price changes in stocks more than changes in expected cash flows do, the question becomes, "Why do discount rates change?" The taxonomy structuring the following discussion has its roots in Cochrane (2011).

Theories Built on Fundamental Factors
Macroeconomic explanations for changes in discount rates link expected returns, and hence discount rates, to macro or microeconomic data such as consumption.

Essentially, investors bid up the prices of assets that perform well when consumption is high. Because prices are high, expected returns are low. Conversely, investors shun assets that provide a considerable pay off when few assets are available to buy and consumption is low.

Researchers use many different approaches to explore the links between consumption and asset prices. For example, Eichenbaum, Hansen, and Singleton (1988) use a generalized method of moments (GMM) approach to study nonseparability across durable and nondurable goods. Barro (2006), building on the work of Rietz (1988), contends that rare economic disasters can explain otherwise puzzling phenomena, including the large premium on equities and high stock volatility. Such disasters can affect measured covariances as well as the means of economic data, particularly over relatively short sample periods.

Hedging Other Income

Financial professionals often advise their clients to avoid investing in their employers' stock because doing so exposes them to potentially sharp declines in values of their asset portfolios at the very time they lose their jobs. This logic makes sense. If a critical mass of investors shuns a given class of stocks for similar reasons, then the affected stocks' prices fall enough to offer a larger expected return than traditional risk measures would imply. Conversely, these investors would bid up the prices of stocks that pay off handsomely when their employment prospects are dim, so that their expected returns would appear to be too low according to traditional risk measures.

Because this return differential depends on investors' desire to hedge against uncertain wage income, it need not rely on irrationality or bias. The return differential need not be constant across securities or through time. Because the return differential traces to hedging needs, the amount of income requiring hedging would vary based on the amount of other assets.

Behavioral Theories

Behavioral theories of asset prices and returns draw on the psychology literature showing that investors sometimes form biased expectations (Barberis and Thaler 2003). Behavioral models do not differ from rational models in that they tie prices to expected cash flows and discount rates. The difference between models is that the expectations of the cash flows or risk, which affects the discount rates, are biased in behavioral models.

Recently, interest within the field of behavioral finance has broadened regarding the impact of affect (mood) on risk aversion. Kamstra, Kramer, and Levi (2000, 2002) consider how daylight-saving time changes influence international stock-index returns. They build on the notion that the loss or gain of an hour interrupts the sleep habits of market participants, causing what is called *sleep desynchronosis*. This condition has a negative impact on mood in the populations of countries that adhere to daylight-saving time changes. Psychologists show that sleep desynchronosis can cause anxiety and depression (Coren 1996; Costa 1997). In fact, Kamstra et al. (2000) find economically meaningful consequences in several markets around the world. These findings include a $30 billion loss in stock market value, on average, immediately following the spring and fall clock adjustments in the United States alone.

Related work investigates the impact of seasonal depression, known as *seasonal affective disorder* or SAD in its most severe form, on equity and bond markets around the world. Kamstra, Kramer, and Levi (2003) study equity market return seasonality in the United States, Canada, Sweden, Germany, the United Kingdom, Japan, New Zealand, Australia, and South Africa. They find that as the night lengthens in the fall, equity market prices tend to decline. This price decline leads to higher expected returns for investors who hold risky stock through the winter and into the spring when the length of daylight rebounds. The authors also find the seasonal effect in stock returns is stronger at higher latitudes, where the fluctuation in daylight is more extreme, and the effect is offset by six months in southern hemisphere countries, as are the seasons. This seasonal pattern in equity returns is roughly consistent with the old market adage "sell in May and go away." The authors frame their findings in the context of research showing SAD arises primarily due to seasonal fluctuations in daylight and studies such as Kramer and Weber (2012) finding depressed people are more averse to financial risk.

Building on the connection between seasonal swings in daylight and time-varying risk aversion, Kamstra, Kramer, and Levi (2014) study the opposite end of the risk spectrum relative to risky stock, specifically, safe government bonds, and find a reverse seasonality. During the seasons when investors seem to be reluctant to hold risky equities, they tend to prefer holding safe U.S. Treasury securities. Kamstra, Kramer, Levi, and Wermers (2013) study the flow of funds between safe and risky categories of mutual fund flows and find similarly supportive evidence. In the fall a net flow of funds tends to occur from risky mutual fund categories to safer ones and the net flows reverse in the winter and spring.

This seasonal pattern in flows survives a battery of controls for other possible seasonal influences including capital gains overhang, end-of-tax year effects, liquidity, and performance chasing. Kamstra, Kramer, Levi, and Wang (2013) consider whether reasonable seasonal variation in investor risk preferences is capable of generating the observed seasonal variation in equity and risk-free returns. They consider an Epstein and Zin (1989) model modified to incorporate seasonally varying risk aversion and seasonally varying elasticity of intertemporal substitution. Kamstra et al. find seasonal variation in both sets of parameters is required to match the observed seasonal variation in returns.

Researchers continue to explore seasonally varying risk aversion in other contexts. Dowling and Lucey (2008) expand the Kamstra et al. (2003) study to a broader class of 37 countries. DeGennaro, Kamstra, and Kramer (2008) find a pattern in equity bid-ask spreads that is consistent with seasonal changes in risk aversion associated with seasonal patterns in daylight. Researchers find that SAD affects initial public offering (IPO) returns (Dolvin and Pyles 2007; Kliger, Gurevich, and Haim 2012), analyst earnings forecasts (Lo and Wu 2008; Dolvin, Pyles, and Wu 2009), and real estate investment trust (REIT) returns (Pyles 2009).

A key feature of pricing effects traced to SAD is that no reason exists for it to vanish, even if clever traders become aware of this effect. This is because SAD has its roots in the variation in the supply of risk-bearing services rather than some market inefficiency. As the supply of risk-bearing services decreases, the price of those services and thus the discount rate attached to risky assets increases. This relationship, in turn, causes asset prices to fall.

Theories Based on Frictions

Intermediated markets can also produce discount rate changes. Investors, acting as principals, give their money to agents, such as mutual funds and hedge funds, some of which use leverage. In normal times, this arrangement works fine. If markets decline sharply, fund managers need to sell assets to meet redemptions and debt constraints. If enough assets are subject to such sales, prices could decrease at least until well-capitalized investors and intermediaries arrive to take advantage of the lower prices.

How long prices remain low and expected returns remain high can vary across asset classes. Mitchell, Pedersen, and Pulvino (2007) describe a case in which months passed before generalized funds became available to replace specialized funds that had abandoned a market. In contrast, flash crashes almost by definition attract buyers in a matter of minutes.

MEAN REVERSION

Changes in discount rates do not mean that prices are mean-reverting in the long run. For example, SAD suggests that the prices of risky assets tend to fall as winter approaches and rise as it recedes. Yet, stock prices are still essentially uncorrelated through time so thinking that the longer an investor is in the market, the safer he will be is incorrect. The range of observed rates of return narrows as the holding period increases. For example, over the period 1926–2012, one-year returns vary from a loss of about 44 percent to a gain of about 58 percent. For 75-year holding periods within this interval the range for the rate of return is only from 9.4 to 11.7 percent.

These results do not translate into a narrower range of dollar payoffs. As the investment horizon increases so do the potential losses and gains in dollar terms. For example, an investor starting with $10,000 would have just under $15,800 after the best year during the sample period. He would have only about $5,600 after the worst year. The 102-percentage-point difference between the best and the worst year's returns results in a $10,200 difference, or a little more than the original investment. For a 75-year horizon, the best period from 1926 to 2012 yielded an 11.7 percent annual return. Even the worst 75-year period is close behind at 9.4 percent or just over two percentage points from best to worst. The range of realized rates of return has indeed narrowed dramatically. Over 75 years, even a small difference in rates of return translates into an enormous change in dollars of almost $33 million. Although two percentage points is not a large difference, 75 years is a very long time.

Fundamental Analysis and Firm Efficiency

Fundamental valuation of a firm is sensitive to the discount rate, which in turn is influenced by such factors as behavior or frictions. Why a single metric such as B/M would entirely encompass the notion of firm value is not obvious. The question of firm valuation and its connection to the stock market return has been addressed in the context of fundamental analysis, dating back to Graham and Dodd (1934), who analyze information from a firm's financial statements to evaluate its investment worthiness. For this purpose, analysts often use DCF models of firm valuation such as the dividend discount model, free cash flow to equity model, and residual income valuation model (Stowe, Robinson, Pinto, and McLeavey 2002). These valuation models determine a firm's intrinsic value by forecasting such factors as future dividends, cash flows, and growth rates and then discounting them using a specific cost of capital.

Based on such a valuation framework, analysts can determine if the shares are trading at a discount to the market or are over-valued. Ohlson (1995) develops a model of a firm's market value as it relates to future earnings, book values, and dividends. Growing evidence suggests that financial and accounting variables have predictive power of stock returns (Campbell and Shiller 1988; Fama and French 1999). Hirschey (2003) concludes that in the long run, trends in stock prices mirror real changes in business prospects as measured by such factors as revenues, earnings, and dividends. Kim and Lee (2006) find that by analyzing the fundamental financial ratios of firms, buying underpriced firms and selling overpriced firms in Korea was an effective strategy up to at least five years. The underlying premise of such analysis is that capital markets are informationally efficient and the economic fundamentals of firms are strongly correlated with their stock returns. This premise is often referred to as the *semi-strong efficient market hypothesis* (EMH), which states that a firm's current market prices fully reflects all publicly available information consisting of past prices and data reported in a company's financial statements.

FROM FIRM VALUATION TO RELATIVE FIRM STRENGTH

Using a single accounting metric such as B/M in the Fama-French three-factor model (Fama and French 1993) or the absolute intrinsic valuation of a single firm in DCF analysis fails to capture investment risks that are more fundamental to the competitive business landscape. That is, they do not directly incorporate relative effects due to managerial, operational, or competitive forces. A firm's income statements and balance sheets exhibit its financial performance relative to competition in a general context—acceptance of its goods and services by the market. However, a firm's fundamental business strength is much more than that because it reflects how well the firm is managing its business relative to its competition in a number of perspectives: profitability, asset utilization, liquidity, leverage, valuation, and growth. Thus, the aim should be to measure a firm's strength on a relative basis comparing it to financial statements of other firms. This comparison, or benchmarking, must be based on firms within the same market segment or industry that compete for supply and demand and account for economies of scale of production and internal productivities.

Much discussion focuses on the merits of incorporating a firm's relative operating efficiencies, or lack thereof, as a basis for being exposed to additional investment risks, especially during bad economic times. Edirisinghe and Zhang (2007, 2008) propose using 18 accounting ratios to benchmark a given firm relative to many other firms in the same sector or industry to evaluate the *relative firm strength* (RFS), or efficiency, using *data envelopment analysis* (DEA) methodology from production economics. DEA is a non-parametric method for measuring the relative efficiencies of a set of firms (say, in a given market sector) by relating output metrics to input metrics and categorizing the firms as efficient or inefficient (Charnes, Cooper, and Rhodes 1978). The RFS metric

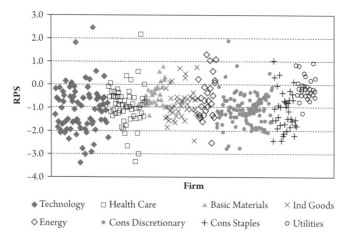

Figure 5.1 Relative Firm Strengths for Firms in Each Sector for 2011Q1.
This figure shows the variation of firm strengths for Q1 of 2011 for each firm in each
market sector.

is used to identify relatively strong and weak firms, which can then be used to form long
and short stock portfolios for enhanced portfolio performance (i.e., reduced portfolio
risks or improved portfolio returns relative to the market).

Figure 5.1 depicts DEA-based RFS scores for 416 firms for each sector excluding
financials using quarterly financial statement data of Q1 of 2011. The input variables
are accounts receivables, long-term debt, capital expenditures, and cost of goods sold;
the output variables are revenue, earnings per share, price/book ratio, and net income
growth. Specifying an RFS of over ln (0.70) = −0.36 for identifying strong stocks resulted in 97 stocks in a long portfolio. A short threshold RFS of ln (0.20) = −1.61 resulted
in a short portfolio of 77 stocks. Identifying strong and weak stocks of each sector with a
relative analysis within the sector helps to mitigate certain sectorial risks that adversely
affect firms and hence portfolios.

This work is not necessarily geared toward identifying another risk factor for returns
of diversified portfolios. Instead, it attempts to guide asset selections to form portfolios
so as to reduce risk exposure due to managerial efficiencies. Using the Fama-French
three-factor model to forecast individual stock returns results in fairly weak predictions. As Figure 5.2 shows, the R^2 of the regressions of stock returns on the specific
factor model is presented using quarterly data from 1980 to 2009 for a sample of S&P
100 index firms. The regressions improve somewhat using the Carhart (1997) model,
which adds a fourth factor that captures "momentum" returns to the Fama-French
three-factor model. When adding RFS to the factor regression, a statistically significant
improvement occurs in the predictive power of individual asset returns, which is the
basic idea that is captured in stock selections.

Avkiran and Morita (2010) propose applying the above DEA-based methodology
in the context of the Japanese banking sector as a new investment tool. Nguyen and
Swanson (2009) offer another use of the above relative firm efficiency concept and use
a stochastic frontier analysis (SFA) approach to evaluate firm efficiency. While SFA is a

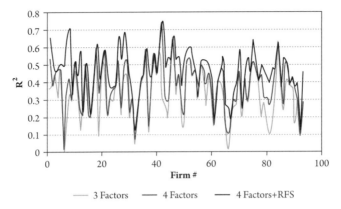

Figure 5.2 R^2 OF FACTOR REGRESSIONS OF STOCK RETURNS.   This figure shows R^2 of the risk factor models for each firm's quarterly return from 1980 to 2009 for a sample of the S&P 100 index firms.

parametric method for efficiency evaluation, its advantage is that it measures efficiency in the presence of statistical noise. Using a Cobb-Douglas production functional form, the logarithm of a firm's market equity is related to logarithms of book equity, long-term debt/total assets, capital expenditure/sales, research and development (R&D)/sales, advertising/sales, and property, plant, and equipment (PPE)/total assets, and earnings before interest and taxes, depreciation and amortization (EBITDA)/total assets. They show that portfolios composed of highly efficient firms significantly underperform the portfolios composed of inefficient firms even after adjusting for firm characteristics and risk factors, suggesting a required premium for the inefficient firms.

Market Risk and Regime Changes
The time-variation in stock returns embeds changes in expected returns arising from cyclical changes of economic states (Campbell and Cochrane 1999; Campbell 2000). Moreover, changes in economic states also affect the relative performance or productivity of firms that are challenged by supply and demand competition. As inefficient firms are subject to adverse business conditions with changes in market regimes, the risk premiums required by the market for investments in such firms also change. Consequently, RFS analysis for portfolio risk-return allocation needs to consider the additional risks presented due to changes in the market states.

In the absence of any change in the market state, stock returns have a constant mean and volatility. Under market regime switching, the average level of returns can be modeled as random switching from one mean level to another as the stock market switches states in response to underlying changes such as a shift in the required risk premium or economic states. Each return regime can be associated with a different mean and volatility. Several multi-regime models of stock returns are available (Brooks and Katsaris 2005; Powell, Roa, Shi, and Xayavong 2007).

Edirisinghe and Zhang (2013) use S&P 500 index returns to identify market regimes based on quarterly periods from 1971 to 2010. Given that the states of the economy are not directly observable, they use a hidden Markov model based on a mixture

Table 5.1 **Quarterly State Probabilities for the Three Market Regime Model**

Market Regime	Weak	Normal	Strong	Probability
Weak	0.1667	0.5833	0.2500	0.0813
Normal	0.0750	0.8000	0.1250	0.7437
Strong	0.0371	0.6296	0.3333	0.1750

Note: This table shows regime switching transition probabilities for the market using the S&P 500 index quarterly data from 1971 to 2010 and the probability for each market state.

(weighted) normal distribution and using the 160 quarters of data. As Table 5.1 shows, the authors identify three regimes, which they label strong, normal, and weak, along with quarterly state transitional probabilities. These probabilities indicate that quarters with returns that are largely from either strong or weak regimes are not highly persistent. The normal regime is dominant with about 75 percent of the quarters having a positive mean return of 2.9 percent. The weak regime is less frequent with about 8 percent of the quarters characterized by a negative average return of –10.6 percent, while the strong regime pertains to about 17 percent of quarters with an average return of 8.9 percent.

The particular state of the market economy has a significant impact on the relative strength of a given firm compared to its competition, and all market sectors exhibit this state-dependent performance variation. When conducting the unconditional analysis depicted in Figure 5.1 under a market state dependent setting, the number of stocks in a long portfolio increases for strong market regimes, while the number of stocks in a short portfolio increases under a weak regime. Moreover, contributions to these portfolios from a given market sector also change due to the economic state. In summary, risks to a portfolio arising from a particular group of assets such as a sector must be examined in the context of evolving market states. Such a sector-based risk can be asymmetric across different economic states.

The Future

A key task for the finance profession going forward is determining whether known pricing anomalies are evidence of inefficiency or whether they trace to unknown sources of risk. If researchers find an anomaly, does a proxy variable for the anomaly produce correctly signed and statistically significant coefficients in a multivariate regression that controls for other known sources of risk? Lustig, Roussanov, and Verdelhan (2011) show that a carry-trade factor explains reported carry-trade profits, for example.

Given the large number of apparent sources of abnormal returns, the typical approach of sorting portfolios according to selected traits and then comparing returns based on portfolio betas that control for some factor is too cumbersome. Researchers simply cannot sort assets into that many portfolios based on that many characteristics. Instead, they probably need to build a new approach around multivariate regression analysis.

Summary and Conclusions

Market risk, sometimes called systematic risk, is the co-movement in prices that cannot be eliminated by diversification. Market risk in a simplistic sense is beta risk, which is in comparison to the market portfolio. Because anomalies exist in trying to explain stock returns solely using market returns, additional risk factors have been introduced, most notably value and size risks. The particular discount rate used for firm valuation highly influences the value risk factor. A case can also be made for risks based on relative inefficiencies of firms in the market as an added dimension of unexplained risk.

Until recently, financial economists generally believed that these fluctuations traced to changes in expected cash flows. The evidence now suggests that these systematic movements trace mostly to changes in discount rates and risk. Future research will likely strive to determine whether apparent opportunities to earn excess returns represent genuine inefficiencies or whether they result from previously unknown risk factors.

Acknowledgments

Professor DeGennaro thanks Mark Kamstra and Lisa Kramer for helpful discussions. The authors adapted portions of this chapter with permission from *How the Stock Market Works* (2014). The Teaching Company is available at www. thegreatcourses.com.

Discussion Questions

1. Explain how demographic shifts might change the aggregate supply of the willingness to bear risk and affect asset prices.
2. Identify the tasks that gain importance for investment advisors and portfolio managers if apparent excess returns turn out to have their origin in previously unknown systematic risk factors.
3. Discuss whether constructing a well-diversified portfolio is possible that completely hedges all market risks including beta, value, and size risks. Indicate whether such portfolios would be characterized by a zero alpha.
4. Explain how the state of the economy might affect market risk and what caution an investment advisor might give to a potential client on the risk exposure of a portfolio.

References

Ang, Andrew, and Joseph Chen. 2007. "CAPM Over the Long Run: 1926–2001." *Journal of Empirical Finance* 14:1, 1–40.

Avkiran, Necmi K., and Hiroshi Morita. 2010. "Predicting Japanese Bank Stock Performance with a Composite Relative Efficiency Metric: A New Investment Tool." *Pacific-Basin Finance Journal* 18:3, 254–271.

Barberis, Nicholas, and Richard Thaler. 2003. "A Survey of Behavioral Finance." In George Constantinides, René Stulz, and Milton Harris, eds., *Handbook of the Economics of Finance*, 1053–1128. Amsterdam: North Holland.

Barro, Robert J. 2006. "Rare Disasters and Asset Markets in the Twentieth Century." *Quarterly Journal of Economics* 121:3, 823–866.

Bhatnagar, Chandra Shekhar, and Riad Ramlogan. 2012. "The Capital Asset Pricing Model versus the Three Factor Model: A United Kingdom Perspective." *International Journal of Business and Social Research* 2:1, 51–65.

Brooks, Chris, and Apostolos Katsaris. 2005. "A Three-Regime Model of Speculative Behavior: Modelling the Evolution of the S&P 500 Composite Index." *Economic Journal* 115:505, 767–797.

Campbell, John Y. 2000. "Asset Pricing at the Millennium." *Journal of Finance* 55:4, 1515-1567.

Campbell, John Y., and John H Cochrane. 1999. "By Force of Habit: A Consumption-based Explanation of Aggregate Stock Market Behavior." *Journal of Political Economy* 107:2, 205–251.

Campbell, John Y., and Robert J. Shiller. 1988. "Stock Prices, Earnings, and Expected Dividends." *Journal of Finance* 43:3, 661–676.

Carhart, Mark M. 1997. "On Persistence in Mutual Fund Performance." *Journal of Finance* 52:1, 57–82.

Charnes, A., W. Cooper, and E. Rhodes. 1978. "Measuring the Efficiency of Decision-making Units." *European Journal of Operational Research* 2:6, 429–444.

Cochrane, John H. 2011. "Presidential Address: Discount Rates." *Journal of Finance* 66:4, 1047–1108.

Coren, Stanley. 1996. *Sleep Thieves*. New York: Free Press Paperbacks.

Costa, Giovanni. 1997. "The Problem: Shiftwork." *Chronobiology International* 14:2, 89–98.

DeGennaro, Ramon P., Mark J. Kamstra, and Lisa A Kramer. 2008. "Does Risk Aversion Vary during the Year? Evidence from Bid-Ask Spreads." Working Paper, University of Toronto.

Dolvin, Steven D., and Mark K. Pyles. 2007. "Seasonal Affective Disorder and the Pricing of IPOs." *Review of Accounting and Finance* 6:2, 214–228.

Dolvin, Steven D., Mark K. Pyles, and Qun Wu. 2009. "Analysts Get SAD Too: The Effect of Seasonal Affective Disorder on Stock Analysts' Earnings Estimates." *Journal of Behavioral Finance* 10:4, 214–225.

Dowling, Michael, and Brian M. Lucey. 2008. "Robust Global Mood Influences in Equity Pricing." *Journal of Multinational Financial Management* 18:2, 145–164.

Edirisinghe, Nalin C.P., and Xin Zhang. 2007. "Generalized DEA Model of Fundamental Analysis and Its Application to Portfolio Optimization." *Journal of Banking and Finance* 31:11, 3311–3335.

Edirisinghe, Nalin C.P. and Xin Zhang. 2008. "Portfolio Selection under DEA-based Relative Financial Strength Indicators: Case of US industries." *Journal of the Operational Research Society* 59:6, 842–856.

Edirisinghe, Nalin C.P., and Xin Zhang. 2013. "Dynamic Portfolio Optimization under Regime-based Firm Strength." In Horand I. Gassmann and William T. Ziemba, eds., *Stochastic Programming: Applications in Finance, Energy and Logistics*, 129–165. Singapore: World Scientific Publishing.

Eichenbaum, Martin S., Lars Peter Hansen, and Kenneth J. Singleton. 1988. "A Time Series Analysis of Representative Agent Models of Consumption and Leisure Choice under Uncertainty." *Quarterly Journal of Economics* 103:1, 51–78.

Epstein, Larry G., and Stanley E. Zin. 1989. "Substitution, Risk Aversion, and the Temporal Behavior of Consumption and Asset Returns: A Theoretical Framework." *Econometrica* 57:4, 937–969.

Fama, Eugene F., and Kenneth R. French. 1993. "Common Risk Factors in the Returns on Stock and Bonds." *Journal of Financial Economics* 33:1, 3–56.

Fama, Eugene F., and Kenneth R. French. 1995. "Size and Book-to-market Factors in Earnings and Stock Returns." *Journal of Finance* 50:1, 131–155.

Fama, Eugene F., and Kenneth R. French. 1999. "Business Conditions and Expected Returns on Stocks and Bonds." *Journal of Financial Economics* 25:1, 23–49.

Fama, Eugene F., and Kenneth R. French. 2008. "Dissecting Anomalies." *Journal of Finance* 63:4, 1653–1678.

Gordon, Myron J., and Eli Shapiro. 1956. "Capital Equipment Analysis: The Required Rate of Profit." *Management Science* 3:1, 102–110.

Graham, Benjamin, and David Dodd. 1934. *Security Analysis.* New York: McGraw-Hill.

Haugen, Robert A. 1997. "The Race between Value and Growth." *Journal of Investing* 6:1, 23–31.

Hirschey, Mark. 2003. "Extreme Return Reversal in the Stock Market." *Journal of Portfolio Management* 29:3, 78–90.

Investopedia. 2014. "Market Risk." Available at http://www.investopedia.com/terms/m/marketrisk.asp.

Jegadeesh, Narasimhan, and Sheridan Titman. 1993. "Returns to Buying Winners and Selling Losers: Implications for Stock Market ¬ Efficiency." *Journal of Finance* 48:1, 65–91.

Kamstra, Mark J., Lisa A. Kramer, and Maurice D Levi 2000. "Losing Sleep at the Market: The Daylight Saving Anomaly." *American Economic Review* 90:4, 1005–1011.

Kamstra, Mark J., Lisa A Kramer, and Maurice D. Levi 2002. "Losing Sleep at the Market: The Daylight Saving Anomaly: Reply." *American Economic Review* 92:4, 1257–1263.

Kamstra, Mark J., Lisa A Kramer, and Maurice D. Levi 2003. "Winter Blues: A SAD Stock Market Cycle." *American Economic Review* 93:1, 324–343.

Kamstra, Mark J, Lisa A. Kramer, and Maurice D. Levi. 2014. "Seasonal Variation in Treasury Returns." *Critical Finance Review*, forthcoming.

Kamstra, Mark J., Lisa A. Kramer, Maurice D. Levi, and Tan Wang. 2013. "Seasonally Varying Preferences: Foundations for an Empirical Regularity." Working Paper, University of Toronto.

Kamstra, Mark J., Lisa A. Kramer, Maurice D Levi, and Russell Wermers. 2013. "Seasonal Asset Allocation: Evidence from Mutual Fund Flows." Working Paper, University of Maryland.

Kim, Byoung Joon, and Phil Sang Lee. 2006. "An Analysis on the Long-term Performance of Value Investment Strategy in Korea." *Asia-Pacific Journal of Financial Studies* 35, 1–39.

Kliger, Doron, Gregory Gurevich, and Abraham Haim. 2012. "When Chronobiology Met Economics: Seasonal Affective Disorder and the Demand for Initial Public Offerings." *Journal of Neuroscience, Psychology, and Economics* 5:3, 131–151.

Kramer, Lisa A., and J. Mark Weber. 2012. "This Is Your Portfolio on Winter: Seasonal Affective Disorder and Risk Aversion in Financial Decision Making." *Social Psychological and Personality Science* 3:2, 193–199.

Lakonishok, Josef, Andrei Shleifer, and Robert W. Vishny. 1994. "Contrarian Investment, Extrapolation, and Risk." *Journal of Finance* 49:5, 1541–1578.

Lo, Kin, and Serena Shuo Wu. 2008. "The Impact of Seasonal Affective Disorder on Financial Analysts and Equity Market Returns." Working Paper, University of British Columbia.

Lustig, Hanno N., Nikolai Roussanov, and Adrien Verdelhan. 2011. "Common Risk Factors in Currency Markets." *Review of Financial Studies* 24:11, 3731–3777.

Mitchell, Mark, Lasse Heje Pedersen, and Todd Pulvino. 2007. "Slow-moving Capital." *American Economic Review* 97:2, 215–220.

NASDAQ. 2014. "Market Risk." Available at http://www.nasdaq.com/investing/risk/market-risk.aspx.

Nguyen, Giao, and Peggy Swanson. 2009. "Firm Characteristics, Relative Efficiency, and Equity Returns." *Journal of Financial and Quantitative Analysis* 44:1, 213–236.

Ohlson, James A. 1995. "Earnings, Book Values, and Dividends in Security Valuation." *Contemporary Accounting Research* 11:2, 661–687.

Powell, John, Rubén Roa, Jing Shi, and Viliphonh Xayavong. 2007. "A Test for Long-Term Cyclical Clustering of Stock Market Regimes." *Australian Journal of Management* 32:2, 205–221.

Pyles, Mark K. 2009. "The Influence of Seasonal Depression on Equity Returns: Further Evidence from Real Estate Investment Trusts." *Quarterly Journal of Finance and Accounting* 48:2, 63–83.

Reinganum, Marc R. 1981. "A New Empirical Perspective on the CAPM." *Journal of Financial and Quantitative Analysis* 16:4, 439–462.

Rietz, Thomas A. 1988. "The Equity Risk Premium: A Solution." *Journal of Monetary Economics* 22:1, 117–131.

Sharpe, William F. 1964. "Capital Asset Prices: A Theory of Market Equilibrium under Conditions of Risk." *Journal of Finance* 19:3, 425–442.

Stowe, John D., Thomas R. Robinson, Jerald E. Pinto, and Dennis W. McLeavey. 2002. *Analysis of Equity Investments: Valuation*. Baltimore, MD: United Book Press.

Theriou, Nikolaos G., Vassilios P. Aggelidis, Dimitrios I. Maditinos, and Željko Ševic. 2010. "Testing the Relation between Beta and Returns in the Athens Stock Exchange." *Managerial Finance* 36:12, 1043–1056.

Womack, Kent L., and Ying Zhang. 2003. "Understanding Risk and Return, the CAPM, and the Fama-French Three-Factor Model." Working Paper, Rotman School of Management, University of Toronto.

6

Credit Risk

NORBERT J. JOBST

Head of Portfolio Analytics, Lloyds Banking Group, Commercial Banking

Introduction

Credit risk is an important risk facing banks and other businesses. The purpose of this chapter is to provide an overview of commonly used methods and tools when measuring and managing credit risk. A more exhaustive discussion is available in Duffie and Singleton (2003), Schönbucher (2003), de Servigny and Renault (2004), de Servigny and Jobst (2007), and Benvegnu, Bluhm, and Müller (2008).

This chapter discusses various methods that are used to estimate the credit risk associated with a single credit risky instrument such as a loan. This risk can be decomposed into two components: *default risk* and *recovery risk*. The former estimates the likelihood of default, while the latter measures the recovery in the event of default. Credit rating agencies (CRAs) such as Standard & Poor's Corporation (S&P) Moody's Investors Service, Inc., or Fitch Ratings assign a credit rating that market participants use as an indicator of credit quality and default risk.

Another widely used approach to quantify credit risk is the application of statistical techniques, also known as *credit scoring*. Using historical data, analysts use statistical tools to generate a credit score or a probability of default for an obligor. This chapter discusses the most commonly used statistical approaches.

Black and Scholes (1973) and Merton (1974) consider a more fundamental approach to measure default risk. Default can be viewed as the exercise of an option by a firm's shareholders. Therefore, default probabilities can be derived, at least in principle, based on the Black-Scholes option pricing framework. This framework leads to the so-called structural or Merton models, which are also discussed in this chapter.

Although a vast literature exists on the modeling of default risk, recovery risk is not as well understood. In part driven by the Basel II Accord requirements, efforts to measure recovery have increased over the last decade and are briefly discussed in this chapter. This discussion is followed by a section on joint defaults, correlation, and credit portfolio models that are used to measure and manage portfolio risk.

Equipped with tools to measure risk of single exposures and of portfolios of exposures, the final section discusses their practical application within the context of a bank's active credit portfolio management activities. Portfolio reporting, capital requirements, risk-based pricing, and securitization are specific applications of such models and are briefly discussed.

Credit Risk Measurement

This section provides an overview of tools for measuring the risk of individual credit exposures, namely credit ratings, probability of default, and recovery rates. These are all important measures that market participants actively use when pricing assets or when determining the amount of capital one needs to hold against credit risk exposures.

CREDIT RATING APPROACH

A *credit rating* represents a CRA's opinion about the creditworthiness of an obligor usually with respect to a particular debt security or other financial obligation. It also applies to an issuer's general creditworthiness. Ratings from various agencies do not convey the same information. S&P perceives its ratings primarily as an opinion on the likelihood of default of an issuer, while Moody's ratings tend to reflect the agency's opinion on the expected loss (probability of default times loss severity) on a facility.

Table 6.1 reports S&P's and Moody's rating scales. Although these scales are not directly comparable, most market participants make such a comparison in practice. The rating universe consists of two very broad categories: investment grade and non-investment grade (or speculative grade). Investment grade issues are relatively stable with moderate default risk while bonds in the non-investment grade category are much more likely to default. The coarse grid AAA, AA, A to CCC can be supplemented with plusses and minuses in order to provide a finer indication of risk.

A CRA's opinion relies on various analyses based on a defined analytical framework. For industrial companies, the analysis is typically split between business reviews (e.g., firm competitiveness, quality of the management and of its policies, business fundamentals, regulatory actions, markets, operations, and cost control) and quantitative analyses (e.g., financial ratios). Some typical financial ratios include earnings before interest, taxes, depreciation, and amortization (EBITDA), operating income/sales, or total debt/capital.

After a CRA assigns a rating, it monitors the rating on an ongoing basis. As a result of the surveillance process, the CRA may decide to initiate a review and change an existing rating. An important fact that CRAs persistently emphasize, particularly after the financial crises of 2007–2008, is that their ratings are opinions. They do not constitute any recommendation to purchase, sell, or hold any type of security. CRAs regularly publish tables reporting observed default rates for each rating category, year, industry, and region. These tables reflect the empirical average default frequencies of firms within the rated universe.

Table 6.1 **Standard & Poor's and Moody's Rating Scales**

Credit Rating Agency	**Investment Grade**			**Non-Investment Grade**			
Standard & Poor's	AAA	AA	A	BBB	BB	B	CCC
Moody's	AAA	Aa	A	Baa	Ba	B	Caa

Table 6.2 displays cumulative default rates from Standard & Poor's and Moody's. A striking difference exists in default patterns between investment grade and speculative grade categories. This difference holds for both data sets. The clear link between observed default rates and rating categories is the best support for agencies' claim that their grades are appropriate measures of creditworthiness. Rating agencies also *calculate transition matrices*, which are tables reporting probabilities of migrations from one rating category to another.

ESTIMATING CUMULATIVE DEFAULT RATES AND TRANSITION MATRICES

Although many studies estimate transition matrices and default curves, the most common approach is the so-called *cohort analysis*. The cohort approach derives historic average default or rating transition probabilities by observing the performance of groups of companies—frequently called *cohorts*—with identical credit ratings. These estimates are particularly suitable in the context of long-term "through-the-cycle" risk management, which attempts to dampen fluctuations due to business cycle and other economic effects.

Start by considering all companies at a specific point in time t. The total number of companies in the kth cohort at time t is denoted by $N_k(t)$, and the total number of observed defaults in period T (i.e., between time $t + T - 1$ and time $t + T$) is denoted by $D_k(t, T)$. Next, Equation 6.1 provides an estimate for the (marginal) probability of default in year T (as seen from time t):

$$P_k(t, T) = \frac{D_k(t, T)}{N_k(t)}. \tag{6.1}$$

Repeating this analysis for cohorts created at M different points in time (e.g., annually) allows obtaining an estimate for the unconditional probability of default in period T in Equation 6.2:

$$\overline{P}_k(T) = \sum_{t=1}^{M} w_k(t) P_k(t). \tag{6.2}$$

These unconditional probabilities are simply weighted averages of the estimates obtained for cohorts considered in different periods. Typically, $w_k(t) = \frac{1}{M}$ (each period is equally weighted), or $w_k(t) = \frac{N_k(t)}{\sum_{m=1}^{M} N_k(m)}$ (weighted according to the number of observations in different periods).

Cumulative (multi-year) probabilities $\overline{P}_k^{cum}(T)$ can be derived from the unconditional marginal probabilities $\overline{P}_k(T)$ by means of using Equation 6.3:

$$\overline{P}_k^{cum}(1) = \overline{P}_k(1),$$
$$\overline{P}_k^{cum}(T) = \overline{P}_k^{cum}(T-1) + \left(1 - \overline{P}_k^{cum}(T-1)\right)\overline{P}_k(T). \tag{6.3}$$

This approach has been used to calculate the default curves shown in Panel A of Table 6.2.

Table 6.2 **Cumulative Default Rates by Rating Category**

Panel A. S&P's Global Corporate Average Default Rates: 1981–2010

Rating/Year	1	2	3	4	5	6	7	8	9	10
AAA	0.000%	0.030%	0.140%	0.260%	0.380%	0.500%	0.560%	0.660%	0.720%	0.790%
AA	0.020	0.070	0.150	0.260	0.370	0.490	0.580	0.670	0.740	0.820
A	0.080	0.190	0.330	0.500	0.680	0.890	1.150	1.370	1.600	1.840
BBB	0.250	0.700	1.190	1.800	2.430	3.050	3.590	4.140	4.680	5.220
BB	0.950	2.830	5.030	7.140	9.040	10.870	12.480	13.970	15.350	16.540
B	4.700	10.400	15.220	18.980	21.760	23.990	25.820	27.320	28.640	29.940
CCC-C	27.390	36.790	42.120	45.210	47.640	48.720	49.720	50.610	51.880	52.880

Panel B. Moody's Global Corporate Average Cumulative Default Rates: 1983–2010

Rating/Year	1	2	3	4	5	6	7	8	9	10
Aaa	0.000%	0.016%	0.016%	0.048%	0.086%	0.132%	0.182%	0.186%	0.186%	0.186%
Aa	0.023	0.066	0.116	0.202	0.291	0.351	0.388	0.419	0.447	0.501
A	0.062	0.200	0.414	0.623	0.853	1.099	1.371	1.677	1.969	2.216
Bbb	0.202	0.561	0.998	1.501	2.060	2.636	3.175	3.710	4.260	4.890
Bb	1.197	3.437	6.183	9.067	11.510	13.757	15.760	17.679	19.526	21.337
B	4.466	10.524	16.526	21.774	26.524	31.034	35.301	39.032	42.312	45.194
Caa-C	22.492	34.488	43.976	51.508	57.758	61.398	64.238	67.597	70.705	74.790

Source: Standard & Poor's and Moody's.

The cohort approach is also frequently employed in calculating ratings transition probabilities, or transition matrices. Instead of counting the number of defaults, $D_k(t, T)$, the number of rating migrations from rating class k to a different class l, $N_{kl}(t, T)$ can be used. Although matrices can be obtained for different horizons T, a common approach is to focus on the average one-year transition matrix, denoted by $\overline{Q}$. Assuming that rating transitions follow a time homogeneous Markov process, the T-period matrix $\overline{Q}(T)$ is given by $\overline{Q}(T) = \overline{Q}^T$. Jafry and Schuermann (2003) provide an overview of more advanced approaches to estimate transition matrices.

STATISTICAL MODELING AND CREDIT SCORING

Banks may not desire to or cannot rely on the assessments of the CRAs. Therefore, banks develop internal methods to estimate the credit risk of their clients. In order to quantify this credit risk, practitioners often build models that provide the probability of default (PD) of specific obligors over a given period, or models that assign a so-called *credit score* to an obligor. For example, a number between 1 and 10 with 1 corresponding to low risk and 10 corresponding to high risk of default.

Two fundamentally different approaches are available to model default probabilities or to assign credit scores: (1) a statistical approach and (2) a structural approach, which is also called the Merton model. Both approaches, along with many hybrids, are commonly used in practice. Although many approaches are available from classical statistics that can be successfully used to estimate default probabilities, the most common approach—logistic regression—is discussed next.

Logistic regression provides conditional probabilities of default given the values of risk factors. Consider a vector X of risk factors, with $X \in R^d$. In a logistic regression, the probability of a default (symbolized by a "1") in a given period (e.g., one year), conditional on the information X, is written as the logit transformation of a linear combination X. The simplest choice, which is frequently used, is the so-called *linear logit model*, as shown in Equation 6.4:

$$P(1|X) = \frac{1}{1 + e^{-\left(\beta_0 + \sum_{i=1}^{d} \beta_i x_i\right)}}. \tag{6.4}$$

Another approach uses all first and second order combinations of risk factors resulting in Equation 6.5:

$$P(1|X) = \frac{1}{1 + e^{-\left(\beta_0 + \sum_{i=1}^{d} \beta_i x_i + \sum_{j=1}^{p} \sum_{k=j}^{p} \delta_{jk} x_j x_k\right)}}. \tag{6.5}$$

Specifying a model of any of the above types requires estimating the model parameters (i.e., the β_j). The standard approach for doing so is to maximize, with respect to the β_j, the log-likelihood function in Equation 6.6:

$$L(\beta) = \sum_{i=1}^{N} \left\{ Y_i \log P(1|X_i) + (1 - Y_i) \log(1 - P(1|X_i)) \right\}, \tag{6.6}$$

where $(X_i, Y_i), i = 1 \dots N$ are observed pairs of risk factors and default indicators (1 for default and 0 for no default). This approach is often called *logistic regression*.

In practice, the variables X can contain firm-specific financial ratios, macroeconomic variables, or other product/firm-specific indicators, which allows the estimation of probabilities of default that are more responsive or dependent on the current state of a company or economy. Such measures are often called *point-in-time* (PIT) *estimates* that perform well over short prediction horizons (e.g., one to three years). This also marks one of the key differences to the stable, historic average probabilities provided by the CRAs.

STRUCTURAL MODELS OF CREDIT RISK

In their original option pricing paper, Black and Scholes (1973) suggest that their methodology could be used to price corporate securities. Merton (1974) subsequently uses their suggestion. Since then, multiple model extensions have been proposed and some commercial products have been successfully placed.

Using simplifying assumptions about the firm value dynamics and capital structure, Merton (1974) is able to give pricing formulas for corporate bonds and equities in the familiar Black and Scholes (1973) paradigm. In the Merton model, a firm with value V is assumed to be financed through equity (with value S) and pure discount bonds with value P and maturity T. The principal of the debt is K. The value of the firm is the sum of the values of its securities: $V_t = S_t + P_t$. At the maturity date T, the firm is considered solvent if its value is sufficient to repay the principal of the debt. Otherwise, the firm defaults.

The value of the firm V is assumed to follow a geometric Brownian motion such that $dV = \mu V dt + \sigma_V V dZ$. Default occurs if the value of the firm is insufficient to repay the debt principal: $V_T < K$. In that case, bondholders have priority over shareholders and seize the entire value of the firm V_T. Otherwise (if $V_T \geq K$), bondholders receive what they are due: the principal K. Thus, their payoff is $P(T, T) = \min(K, V_T) = K - \max(K - V_T, 0)$.

Equity holders receive nothing if the firm defaults but profit from all the upside when the firm is solvent (i.e., the entire value of the firm net of the repayment of the debt $(V_T - K)$ falls in the hands of shareholders). The payoff to equity holders is therefore $\max(V_T - K, 0)$. Merton (1974) makes the same assumptions as Black and Scholes (1973) and the calls and the puts can be priced using Black-Scholes option prices.

Although the Merton model relies on fairly strong assumptions, it has been successfully commercialized, particularly by Moody's KMB Credit Monitor® (Crosbie and Bohn 2003). The probability of default is given by Equation 6.7:

$$PD_t = N(-DD), \text{ where}$$

$$DD = \frac{\ln(V_t) - \ln(K) + (\mu - \sigma_V^2/2)(T - t)}{\sigma_V \sqrt{T - t}}, \tag{6.7}$$

where DD is the so-called distance to default, using the following notation, $N(.)$ is the cumulative Gaussian distribution; V_t is the value of the firm at t; K is the default threshold; σ_V is the asset volatility of the firm; and μ is the expected return on the assets. Moody's KMV departs from the classic Merton model and assumes that the capital structure of an issuer consists of long-term debt (i.e., with maturity longer than the chosen horizon) denoted LT and short-term debt (maturing before the chosen horizon) denoted ST. The practical convention for choosing the default value, K, is $K = ST + 0.5\,LT$.

Finally, different ways of solving for σ_V are available and for V_t as this is normally unobservable. A straightforward approach to the estimation of V_t and σ_V is the iterative scheme of Vassalou and Xing (2004). According to this approach, a time series of asset values is computed from a times series of equity values by means of the Black-Scholes formula for call options, and σ_V is subsequently estimated from this time series.

Although the Merton model proves popular, one disadvantage is that its application is limited to asset classes for which liquid (equity) pricing data are available. The outputs of the model can be classified as *point-in-time* due to the model's dependence on current market information. As such, Merton models also tend to perform better over shorter horizons.

PERFORMANCE ANALYSIS FOR PROBABILITY OF DEFAULT MODELS

A commonly used measure of classification performance is the Gini curve or cumulative accuracy profile (CAP). This curve assesses the consistency of the predictions of a scoring model (in terms of the ranking of firms by order of default probability) to the ranking of observed defaults. Firms are first sorted in descending order of default probability as produced by the model and then compared to the fraction of firms that have actually defaulted. A perfect model assigns the D highest default probabilities to the D firms out of a sample of N that actually default.

RECOVERY RISK

The previous sections reviewed various approaches to assessing default risk. However, the credit risk to which an investor is exposed consists of both default risk and recovery risk. To date, much less research effort focuses on modeling recovery risk than on understanding default risk. Consequently, the literature on this topic is smaller. Asarnow and Edwards (1995) and Altman and Kishore (1996) publish perhaps the earliest works on recoveries. Altman (2008) provides a comprehensive overview.

The quantity that characterizes recovery risk is *recovery given default* (RGD) or equivalently *loss given default* (LGD). RGD is usually defined as the ratio of the recovery value from a defaulted debt instrument and the invested par amount, and LGD = 1 − RGD. Various ways are available to define the recovery value. For example, some define it as the traded value of the defaulted security immediately after default, while others define recovery value as the payout to the debt holder at the time of emergence from bankruptcy, which is often called *ultimate recovery*. Which definition is appropriate depends on the purpose of the analysis. For example, investors such as mutual bond funds who sell debt securities immediately after they have defaulted should be interested in the first type of recovery value. By contrast, investors such as banks that work out defaulted loans should care about the second type of recovery.

A prominent feature of RGD is its high uncertainty given the information a typical investor can obtain at a time before default. For this reason, modeling the uncertainty associated with recovery and not just its expected value given relevant factors is desirable.

Perhaps the most commonly used approach to modeling RGD is the *beta distribution*. Here one assumes that RGD has the following conditional probability density function (pdf) as shown in Equation 6.8:

$$p(r|D, x) = \frac{1}{B(\alpha(x), \beta(x))} \left(\frac{r - r_{\min}}{r_{\max}} \right)^{\beta(x)-1} \left(1 - \frac{r - r_{\min}}{r_{\max}} \right)^{\alpha(x)-1}, \qquad (6.8)$$

where $r_{\max}$ is the largest and $r_{\min}$ the smallest possible value of RGD; B denotes the beta function; and α and β are parameterized functions of the risk factors x. The D in the above notation indicates the need to condition all probabilities on default having happened. Often the assumption is that α and β are linear in the risk factors x. Estimating the model parameters using the maximum-likelihood method is then straightforward.

Credit Portfolio Risk and Modeling

Following the introduction of commonly used approaches to measure PD and LGD, the chapter now introduces the tools enabling the analysis of portfolios. Portfolios of credits have the potential of suffering large losses with small, but non-negligible probabilities. If a severe downturn in the overall economy occurs, the likelihood of multiple defaults will increase because many of the assets in the portfolio will decline simultaneously in quality.

Figure 6.1 illustrates this relationship in more detail. It shows that macroeconomic and sector-specific shocks lead to increases in the default rates of entire segments of the economy and push up correlations.

In general, the default or insolvency rates appear to be almost a mirror image of the growth rate implying that defaults tend to be correlated as they depend on a common factor. This dependence or correlation is the cause for the so-called fat-tailed nature of loss distributions.

FACTOR MODELS OF CREDIT RISK

The purpose of a portfolio model is to analyze the risk characteristics of a portfolio by estimating its loss distribution at a future time horizon. The risk contribution of individual exposures within the portfolio can be derived and will be discussed later in this section.

Typically, portfolio models such as MKMV RiskFrontier or RiskMetrics® Credit Manager apply Monte Carlo simulation to calculate the portfolio loss distribution by

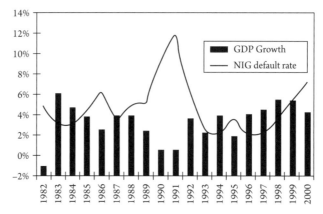

Figure 6.1 US GDP GROWTH AND AGGREGATE DEFAULT RATES. This figure illustrates the relationship between macroeconomic indicators and observed default rates. Source: de Servigny and Renault (2004).

sampling from the joint distribution of obligor asset values in a portfolio. The underlying assumptions are based on the standard Merton framework previously discussed:

- An obligor's default at the horizon depends on whether its asset value is greater than its liabilities.
- The asset value of an obligor at the horizon follows a normal distribution.
- The default barrier (level of liabilities) is calibrated to an obligor's probability of default.

Asset Value Process
The basic algorithm is based on the market standard Merton (or Gaussian copula) approach widely used in the industry. The future (change in) asset value V_i of an obligor is unknown and given by Equation 6.9:

$$V_i = \beta_{ik}F_k + \sqrt{1 - \beta_{ik}^2}\, \varepsilon_i, \tag{6.9}$$

where F_k denotes the systematic component (factor); ε_i is the idiosyncratic factor; and β_{ik} denotes the sensitivity of obligor i to risk factor k, which is commonly known as the square root of the obligor's R^2 parameter (i.e., $\beta_{ik} = \sqrt{R^2(i)}$). Both F_k and ε_i are standard normal random variables (RVs).

Default Threshold
An obligor is assumed to default at the horizon if the value of its underlying assets falls below its total liabilities (default threshold). The rationale for the assumption is that a company would not default if assets are left over after fulfilling its liabilities. In practice, the default probability PD_i is considered to be known, which allows deriving the default threshold Z_i directly (without referencing the firm's actual liabilities), that is

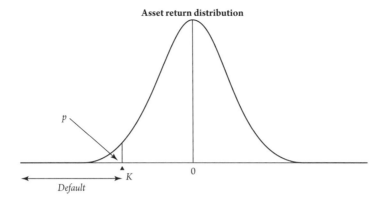

Figure 6.2 THE ASSET RETURN SET-UP.   This figure illustrates the calibration of the default threshold in asset value driven credit portfolio simulation models.

$$Z_i = N^{-1}(PD_i). \tag{6.10}$$

Figure 6.2 provides a graphical representation of this approach.

Conditional Default Probabilities
Within the above framework, the probability of default of an obligor, conditional on the factor F_k is given by Equation 6.11:

$$p_j^F = \Phi\left(\frac{Z_j - \beta_{jk}F_k}{\sqrt{1 - \beta_{jk}^2}}\right). \tag{6.11}$$

Correlation Framework
In practice, the systematic risk is constructed using a multifactor model, which leads to using Monte Carlo simulation as the approach to estimate a portfolio loss distribution. Frequently, each factor F_k represents either an industry sector or a country. The correlation structures of the factors are specified in a correlation matrix $\sum_K$. As a result, the correlation $\hat{\rho}_{ij}$ between the asset values of two different obligors, i and j, in industries, k and l, respectively, is given by $\hat{\rho}_{ij} = \beta_{ik}\beta_{jl}\rho_{kl}$.

Simulating Correlated Defaults
In each scenario, a set of correlated systematic factor realizations and independent (idiosyncratic) risk factors are drawn from relevant normal distributions. A standard algorithm to sample multivariate normal RV based on Cholesky decomposition of the correlation matrix $\sum_K$ is used for the systematic factors, and the idiosyncratic risk of each obligor is drawn independently from a standard normal distribution. Given the realizations of these random variables, the asset value given in Equation 6.9 is computed and compared to the default threshold (Equation 6.10) for each obligor.

One generalization of the approach outlined in the previous section is to simulate not just the event of default, but the exact time of default. Li (2000) introduces this approach, usually called the "Gaussian Copula" default time approach, which has become a market standard for the pricing of collateralized debt obligations (CDOs) and baskets of credit derivatives. Once a default situation (i.e., time or event) has been identified, the fractional loss of a loan in default at horizon is frequently assumed to be known (expected LGD) or drawn randomly from a beta distribution with a mean equal to the LGD and a given variance.

Homogeneous Pools of Assets

For large portfolios, aggregation of loans of similar characteristics into so-called *loan pools* facilitates more efficient computation. The loans in a loan pool are assumed to be homogeneous (i.e., have identical PD, LGD, exposure at default (EAD), and factor loading/industry sector).

A loan's EAD in a loan pool can be obtained by dividing the total exposures of the loan pool by the total number of loans. The fractional loss of a loan pool can be calculated from the number of defaulted loans at horizon and from the loan pool's LGD assumption. The LGD is assumed to be identical and constant across all underlying loans. While this neglects any uncertainty on the recovery value, LGD serves as a good approximation for any loan pools backed by at least 50 loans. In practice, the approximation works for a loan pool with an even smaller number of loans. Because the loans in a loan pool are homogeneous, the number of defaults in a pool follows a binominal distribution. The distribution is characterized by two parameters: default probability conditional on the systematic risk of a scenario and the total number of loans in a pool. The conditional PD is given by Equation 6.11 and for a total of N exposures in the portfolio, the probability of n defaults (out of N exposures) is given by Equation 6.12:

$$p_j^F(k) = \binom{N}{n} \left(p_j^F\right)^n \left(1 - p_j^F\right)^{N_j - n}. \tag{6.12}$$

Within the Monte-Carlo simulation, for a given draw of the systematic factor F_k, the number of defaults in the portfolio is drawn randomly from this distribution.

Computationally, this approach is relatively involved and in order to improve the performance a normal approximation can be employed. Essentially, conditional on the outcome of F_k, its mean is given by Equation 6.11 and the standard deviation is given by Equation 6.13:

$$\sigma_j^F = \sqrt{p_j^F} \sqrt{\left(1 - p_j^F\right)}. \tag{6.13}$$

Monte-Carlo Simulation, Loss Distribution, and Risk Contributions

Given the framework outlined above, the simulation of losses within a large credit portfolio proceeds as follows:

- Draw a set of correlated standard normal factor realizations, F_k, using a standard Cholesky decomposition-based algorithm.
- Draw a specific risk, ε_i, for each obligor i. The obligor-specific risks are independently and identically distributed standard normal variables.

- Determine whether an obligor defaults at the horizon by comparing the asset value, V_i, to the obligor's default point, Z_i, implied from its default probability to the horizon.
- Draw a set of recovery values from a beta distribution for the defaulted exposures.
- Compute the loss of each exposure in a portfolio and sum the values for the exposures into a loss for the portfolio.
- For every loan pool j, given F_k, draw a random variable $N(p_j^F, \sigma_j^F)$ – the percentage of the pool that defaults in this scenario.
- Add the loan pool losses to the single credit losses to get portfolio loss.

Replicating this simulation exercise many times allows generating the portfolio loss distribution.

The resulting loss distribution and simulation outcomes hold much good information for risk measurement. Portfolio risk is typically measured through metrics such as portfolio volatility, value-at-risk (VaR), or expected shortfall (ES). For example, ES is a so-called coherent risk measure and defined as Equation 6.14:

$$ES_\alpha(L) = E\left(L | L > VaR_\alpha(L)\right), \qquad (6.14)$$

where $VaR_\alpha(L) = \min(P(L \leq l) \geq \alpha)$ is the *VaR* and α denotes the required confidence level (e.g., $\alpha = 99.9$ percent).

This conditional expected value can be calculated as the mean over those scenarios that have a loss exceeding the minimum loss value at a certain confidence level (i.e., VaR) at that quantile. Thus, the calculation of ES uses only a small number of scenarios generated in a Monte Carlo simulation. For example, in a Monte Carlo simulation of 100,000 scenarios, the calculation of the ES at the confidence level of 99 percent uses only 1,000 of those scenarios. The concern in credit risk management often focuses on extreme losses in excess of a portfolio's expected loss (i.e., $PCR_\alpha(L) = VaR_\alpha(L) - EL$, where *PCR* denotes portfolio credit risk).

In order to compute marginal risk contributions (i.e., the contribution of a single exposure to the overall portfolio risk), ES contributions are commonly used. In practice, the average losses for an exposure over all those scenarios for which portfolio losses exceed the portfolios VaR are computed (i.e., $ESC_{i,\alpha}(L) = E\left(L_i | L \geq VaR_\alpha(L)\right)$, where L_i denotes losses from asset i). For ES, the following relationship holds: $ES_\alpha(L) = \sum_i ESC_{i,\alpha}(L)$.

CORRELATIONS: EMPIRICAL ESTIMATION

As previously indicated, key inputs to portfolio models are PDs and LGDs. The correlation between obligors and, therefore, their joint default behavior also heavily influence portfolio risk. The two most common approaches to estimate correlations for factor models are: (1) extracting asset correlation from empirical default observations and (2) estimating correlations from equity returns/asset values.

Default-Based Correlations

Consider two firms originally rated i and j, respectively, and let D denote the default category. The marginal probabilities of default are p_i^D and p_j^D while $p_{i,j}^{D,D}$ denotes the joint probability of the two firms defaulting over a chosen horizon. The default correlation can then be shown to be given by Equation 6.15:

$$\rho_{i,j}^{D,D} = \frac{p_{i,j}^{D,D} - p_i^D p_j^D}{\sqrt{p_i^D (1 - p_i^D) p_j^D (1 - p_j^D)}}.$$ (6.15)

Obtaining individual probabilities of default per rating class is straightforward. These statistics can be read from transition matrices. The only unknown term that has to be estimated in (Equation 6.16) is the joint probability $p_{i,j}^{D,D}$.

Consider the joint migration of two obligors from the same class i (say a BB rating) to default D. Assume N_i^t firms rated at the beginning of a year t. From a given set with N_i^t elements, $N_i^t(N_i^t - 1)/2$ different pairs can be created. Denoting by $T_{i,D}^t$ the number of bonds migrating from this group to default D, $T_{i,D}^t (T_{i,D}^t - 1)/2$ defaulting pairs can be created. Taking the ratio of the number of pairs that defaulted to the number of pairs that could have defaulted results in a natural estimator of the joint probability. Considering n years of data instead of just one year, the estimator is shown in Equation 6.16:

$$p_{i,i}^{D,D} = \sum_{t=1}^n w_i^t \frac{T_{i,D}^t (T_{i,D}^t - 1)}{N_i^t (N_i^t - 1)},$$ (6.16)

where w are weights representing the relative importance of a given year as discussed previously.

The estimated joint default probabilities can be used to back out the latent variable correlation $\sum = [\rho_{ij}]$ within the factor model set-up described in the previous part. Consider two companies or two industries i and j. Their joint default probability P_{ij} is given by Equation 6.17:

$$P_{ij} = \Phi \left(Z_i, Z_j, \rho_{ij} \right)$$ (6.17)

where Z_i and Z_j correspond to the default thresholds, for each of these companies or the average default threshold for each industrial sector.

The asset correlation between the two companies or between the two sectors can be derived by solving Equation 6.18:

$$\rho_{ij} = \Phi^{-1}(P_{ij}, Z_i, Z_j).$$ (6.18)

In this particular context, computing pairwise industry default correlation enables generating the corresponding pairwise industry asset correlation. This approach is typically called the joint probability of default (JPD) approach.

Alternatively, the asset correlation can also be extracted directly through a maximum likelihood estimation (MLE), as described originally in Gordy and Heitfield (2002). Demey, Jouanin, Roget, and Roncalli (2004) suggest a simplified version of the previous estimation technique in which all inter-industry correlation parameters are assumed to be equal. Thanks to this additional constraint, the number of parameters to estimate is limited to two for each company or sector.

Empirical Results of JPD and MLE Techniques
Jobst and de Servigny (2006) use the S&P Credit Pro 6.60 database over the period 1981 to 2003. The database contains 66,536 annual observations and 1,170 default events. On a yearly basis and for each of 13 industrial sectors, the authors compare the value of the asset-implied correlation estimated under the JPD and the MLE techniques and find a close match between the two approaches.

Equity-Based Models
An alternative to default-based correlation estimates is to use equity price data, which can be motivated by the relationship established by Merton (1974) among a firm's asset value, equity value, and ultimately default. In equity-based correlation models, each asset is typically regressed on a composite factor. This results in an estimate of the firm's sensitivity to that factor (i.e., the wider economy). Individual assets undergo correlation analysis through the dependence of each asset on these composite factors that take sector and country/region characteristics into consideration.

Different ways are available to construct the composite factors that vary in their degree of complexity and the equity returns data available. For example, one approach is to use observed value weighted factors such as the publicly quoted equity indices. Alternatively, individual stock returns can be used and aggregated into unobservable factors that are used for model calibration.

Once the index returns are constructed, the R^2 values are computed from two inputs: stock returns and index returns. Each stock is mapped to its associated sector and region indices. This mapping can be based on the stock's country of origin and sector information available in the data. The model in Equation 6.19 can then be estimated:

$$r_{it} = \alpha_i + \beta_i \Phi_{it} + \mu_{it}, \tag{6.19}$$

where r_{it} is the $T \times 1$ vector of time series returns for security i in quarter t; T is the total number of observations; Φ_{it} is the $T \times 1$ composite index (systematic factor) applicable to this firm; α_i is the intercept of the model; and μ_{it} is the $T \times 1$ matrix of residual return. The estimation follows a standard linear regression where β_i is the factor loading, that describes the linear relationship between r_{it} and Φ_{it}.

Using β_i also called *factor loading*, R_i^2 is given by Equation 6.20:

$$\Rightarrow R_i^2 = \frac{\beta_i^2 \cdot \sigma^2(\Phi_{it})}{\sigma^2(r_{it})}, \tag{6.20}$$

where $\sigma^2(\Phi_{it})$ is the variance of the index and $\sigma^2(r_{it})$ the variance of the individual stock.

Asset correlation between two firms can be written as a product of correlation between the factor indices, ρ_{Φ_j, Φ_k}, and the square root of the R^2 of these firms, leading to Equation 6.21:

$$\Rightarrow \rho_{j,k} = \sqrt{R_j^2} \sqrt{R_k^2} \cdot \rho_{\Phi_j, \Phi_k}. \tag{6.21}$$

If two companies are in the same region and sector, the correlation is equal to the product of its R^2 values. Typically, equity- and default-based correlations compare reasonably well on average, but large differences can be observed at a more granular (e.g., sector) level.

Application: Active Credit Portfolio Management

The tools described throughout the previous sections are widely used within banks and other financial institutions to measure and manage the risks in their portfolios. Key applications include portfolio reporting (credit risk capital and concentrations), risk-adjusted return measurement, and risk transfer/securitization.

PORTFOLIO REPORTING: CREDIT RISK CAPITAL AND CONCENTRATIONS

Before the financial crisis of 2007–2008, most banks measured the amount of capital they needed to remain a going concern internally. This capital was frequently denoted as economic capital (EC) and typically computed using portfolio models such as the one outlined in previous sections. The portfolio model uses internal PDs, LGDs, and correlations and a confidence level set based on the target rating that the bank wanted to maintain or achieve.

In line with Basel II regulation, a common assumption was that the regulatory confidence level (99.9 percent) equates to a BBB target debt rating and that a bank desiring a higher rating should set capital at a higher level (e.g., AA = 99.97 percent). Figure 6.3 provides a graphical representation.

Technically, EC could be defined as shown in Equation 6.22:

$$EC_\alpha(L) = VaR_\alpha(L) - EL, \tag{6.22}$$

where $VaR_\alpha(L) = \min_l (P(L \leq l) \geq \alpha)$ is the portfolio VaR; $EL = PD(LGD)(EAD)$ is the portfolio expected loss; L is the portfolio loss; PD is the probability of default; LGD is the loss given default; and EAD denotes the exposure at default.

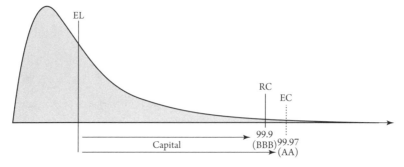

Figure 6.3 THE LINK BETWEEN LOSS DISTRIBUTION AND CAPITAL. This figure shows how portfolio capital requirements can be estimated from a bank portfolio loss distribution.

In practice, the loss distribution is derived from simulating the bank's entire portfolio using portfolio models such as the ones discussed previously. With the introduction of a firmer regulatory framework and throughout the financial crises, regulators have defined capital requirements more stringently and regulatory capital (RC) has become a more important and binding constraint for most institutions.

Although different regulatory regimes exist, the internal ratings based (IRB) approach is frequently adopted and further discussed next. This framework has been chosen for illustrative purposes due to its close link with the portfolio modeling framework introduced earlier in the chapter. Hence, the following section does not provide an exhaustive overview or RC calculations and regimes.

The foundation IRB approach requires the bank to have an internal rating model validated by the regulatory body for that purpose but the regulator provides the LGD. In the advanced IRB, the bank can also use its internal LGD and EAD models, subject to regulatory approval.

Under the IRB framework including advanced IRB and foundation IRB approaches, the capital requirement (K) is computed using a simplified version of the portfolio models introduced earlier. The asymptotic single risk factor (ASRF) model assumes that a single systemic risk factor drives all firms and that the portfolio is infinitely divisible. Under this assumption, no Monte Carlo simulation is required and the capital requirement (K) can be computed as Equation 6.23:

$$K = \left[N \left(\frac{1}{\sqrt{(1-R)}} N^{-1}(PD) + \frac{\sqrt{R}}{\sqrt{(1-R)}} N^{-1}(0.999) \right) LGD - PD\,LGD \right] \underbrace{\frac{(1 + (M-2.5)\,b(PD))}{1 - 1.5\,b(PD)}}_{\text{Maturity Adjustment}},$$

$$(6.23)$$

where

$$R = 0.12 \cdot \frac{1 - e^{-50.PD}}{1 - e^{-50}} + 0.24 \cdot \left(1 - \frac{1 - e^{-50.PD}}{1 - e^{-50}} \right) - 0.04. \overbrace{\left(1 - \frac{\min\{\max\{5, S\}, 50\} - 5}{45} \right)}^{\text{Additional factor for SMEs}},$$

where $S =$ group turnover in EUR millions and $b(PD) = (0.11852 - 0.05478\,In(PD))^2$, where the values are defined by the regulatory authorities. The additional adjustment factor for small medium enterprises (SMEs) applies to companies with a consolidated group turnover (S) lower than EUR50m have R (correlation) reduced linearly by up to 4 percent for EUR5m turnover. S substitutes total assets of the consolidated group for total annual sales when total assets are a more meaningful indicator of size (e.g., financials).

The capital requirement is expressed as a percentage of the exposure. In order to derive the risk-weighted assets (RWA), K is multiplied by EAD and the inverse of the minimum capital ratio of 8 percent (defined by the Basel framework) (i.e., by a factor of 12.5) and is shown in Equation 6:24:

$$RWA = 12.5K(EAD) = RW(EAD). \tag{6.24}$$

For retail exposures, a firm provides its own estimates of PD and LGD. No concept is available for foundation and advanced under IRB for retail exposures and a maturity adjustment also does not apply. For retail exposures secured by real estate collateral, the correlation R is 0.15. For all other retail exposures, the correlation R is shown in Equation 6.25:

$$R = 0.03 \frac{\left(1 - e^{-35\,PD}\right)}{\left(1 - e^{-35}\right)} + 0.16 \left[1 - \frac{1 - e^{-35\,PD}}{\left(1 - e^{-35}\right)}\right]. \tag{6.25}$$

RC has clearly become a critical measure for banks but some features of pre-financial crisis of 2007–2008 EC frameworks may still be desired. Therefore, portfolio models and EC technology can be used to adjust RC for internal purposes such as pricing and internal capital adequacy assessments. This situation could result in internal capital (adjusted RC) that:

- Increases capital for highly cyclical sectors or sectors to which the bank has already has a large exposure;
- Reduces capital for low risk lending;
- Requires additional capital for large exposures (name concentration); and
- Adjusts capital in recognition of the banks internal view of LGD (i.e., less reliance on regulatory LGD for F-IRB banks).

Figure 6.4 shows how industrial sector and credit rating (Rating 4 = low risk, Rating 18 = high risk) could influence the amount of capital allocated to hold against a credit exposure assuming 11 percent of RWA would have to be held on average. For lower risk exposures, the capital could fall below 11 percent of RWA and highly cyclical sectors could require additional capital. Such a system can be calibrated to be neutral at total portfolio level, while influencing capital allocation at an exposure level to drive desired behaviors.

CONCENTRATION REPORTING

The previous discussion has already introduced the concept of concentration. In practice, understanding the sector and name concentrations that are prevalent in a large bank portfolio are important and different measures are used to quantify this risk. Tasche (2008) introduces the so-called *diversification index* (DI). At a portfolio level (L denotes the overall portfolio), $DI_\zeta(L) = \frac{\zeta_\alpha(L)}{\sum_i \zeta_\alpha(L_i)}$, where $\zeta_\alpha(L_i)$ denotes the risk (VaR, ES, or loss volatility) of sub-portfolio i on a "stand-alone" basis (i.e., when the risk is estimated for each sub-portfolio separately). This gives an indication of how well the portfolio is diversified. For example, a value close to 1 indicates that the portfolio is not very diversified, whereas a value below 1 indicates diversification.

The marginal diversification index, $DI_{i,\zeta}(L) = DI_\zeta(L_i|L) = \frac{\zeta_\alpha(L_i|L)}{\zeta_\alpha(L_i)}$, provides similar information but at a sub-portfolio level. The numerator denotes the risk contribution of

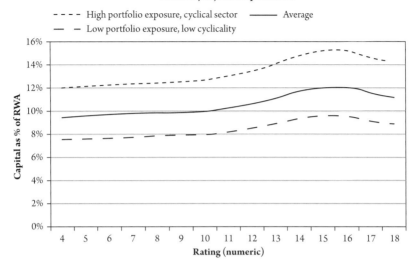

Figure 6.4 Sᴇᴄᴛᴏʀ Oᴠᴇʀʟᴀʏ ᴛᴏ Rᴇɢᴜʟᴀᴛᴏʀʏ Cᴀᴘɪᴛᴀʟ Dᴇʀɪᴠᴇᴅ ғʀᴏᴍ Eᴄᴏɴᴏᴍɪᴄ Cᴀᴘɪᴛᴀʟ Mᴏᴅᴇʟɪɴɢ. This figure illustrates how capital requirements, expressed as a percentage of risk-weighted assets (RWA), could be made more risk-sensitive and reflect credit rating, sector cyclicality, and existing portfolio compositions.

sub-portfolio *i* in the context of the overall portfolio, which is divided by the risk of this sub-portfolio when analyzed on its own. For example, a value close to 1 would indicate that sub-portfolio *i* is not benefiting from/contributing to diversification with the wider portfolio.

Alternatively, simple ratios such as $\zeta_\alpha(L_i)/EL_i$ or $\zeta_\alpha(L_i)/EAD_i$ or the percentage share of those measures (e.g., $\frac{\zeta_\alpha(L_i)}{\sum_i \zeta_\alpha(L_i)} / \frac{EAD_i}{\sum_i EAD_i}$) are used to provide insight into portfolio segments that provide diversification or add concentration.

RISK-ADJUSTED RETURNS

Another important application of credit risk modeling is *risk-based pricing* (i.e., the calculation of risk-adjusted returns and profitability measures that allow comparison of profitability of different business portfolios or transactions). Banks typically try to achieve a desirable amount of return for a given level of risk. As with any portfolio, some assets deliver larger returns when compared to the level of risk they are consuming, while others consume too much risk for the level of return they are generating. An asset that appears "cheap" is not necessarily mispriced in the market but could result from its unique position within the existing portfolio. Similarly, an asset could appear "expensive" as a result of the concentration of similar assets in the portfolio.

Risk-adjusted return on capital (RAROC) and similar measures are frequently used to monitor and manage profitability. RAROC is commonly defined as shown in Equation 6.26:

$$RAROC_P = \frac{EP}{C_\alpha(L)} + r = \frac{T(I - Co - EL)}{C_\alpha(L)} + r, \tag{6.26}$$

where EP is economic profit; C is economic capital or regulatory capital; T denotes $1 -$ tax rate; I is income; Co is cost including funding costs; EL is expected loss; and r is the risk-free rate.

Income is often separated into net interest income (NII) and other operational income (OOI). The risk-free rate, r, could be eliminated from the definition above to simplify notation and computation.

RAROC enables the comparison of transactions or portfolios with different risk profiles as it highlights the return per unit of risk. Naturally, one would chose the less risky investment if the RAROCs are identical.

Although RAROC and similar metrics are conceptually well established, practical computation is not always trivial in the context of the availability and reliability of good quality information on individual investments. One simplification is to eliminate the need of cost information. However, due to the importance of funding costs, these costs are typically considered but other costs (e.g., staffing and premises) may be excluded.

To steer a bank's origination activities (i.e., build its portfolio), transactions are frequently benchmarked against a required or aspired hurdle rate. This hurdle rate is typically aligned with a bank's cost of capital. Yet, it could be above or below and could be adjusted for some business areas if, for example, the focus for that area is on balance sheet or franchise growth.

RISK TRANSFER AND SECURITIZATION

Portfolio management involves not only reporting and return measurement to steer portfolio building (origination) but also the disposal of assets from an existing portfolio. The aim is often to free up resources (capital or funding) and also to improve portfolio characteristic (enhance return or reduce concentrations).

In addition to asset sales, securitization is a popular tool to transfer risks. Although securitizations typically differ in detail with respect to their exact cash flow mechanics, a good first indication of the level of risk transfer can be obtained by modeling them as synthetic securitization tranches assuming losses are passed through sequentially.

Figure 6.5 shows that each transaction is characterized by a level of subordination (the attachment point A). Unless losses in the transaction's reference portfolio exceed A, the note holder (protection seller) will not suffer a loss.

To assess the risk on the securitization, several useful *tranche* risk measures, such as the tranche default probability, expected loss, and the LGD need to be understood. Assuming a pass-through securitization, these risks can all be computed by "overlaying" the tranche on the portfolio loss distribution as shown schematically in Figure 6.6. Here, the tranche has an attachment point equal to 4 percent of the total notional amount of the portfolio, and a thickness also equal to 4 percent. This means that the tranche will no longer suffer losses above 8 percent of the portfolio notional amount. For this reason, this upper loss level is referred to as the *detachment point*.

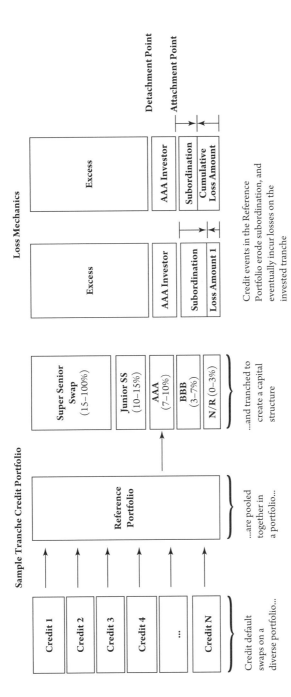

Figure 6.5 SYNTHETIC SECURITIZATION STRUCTURE AND LOSS MECHANICS. This figure shows how a portfolio of assets can be pooled and transformed into capital notes (the tranches) for investors. The right panel also shows how the loss mechanics work and influence subordination levels.

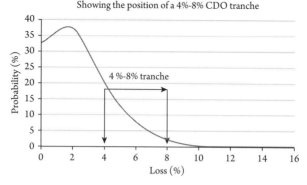

Figure 6.6 Hypothetical CDO Portfolio Loss Distribution and Tranche (4 to 8 Percent) Overlay. This table shows how tranche risk measures are different for different tranches as determined by their attachment point and detachment point. For example, 6 to 12 percent indicates a tranche with a 6 percent attachment point, also called subordination, and 12 percent detachment point.

From now onwards, the assumption is that correlated defaults and the portfolio loss distribution are simulated efficiently and available. A few typical risk measures can be computed using those default simulations.

TRANCHE DEFAULT PROBABILITY

Given an attachment point A and detachment point D (i.e., a tranche thickness equal to $D - A$), the *tranche default probability* is the probability that portfolio losses at maturity T exceeds A. This is given by Equation 6.27:

$$PD^{Tj} = P(L(T) \geq A) = E[1_{\{L(T)\geq A\}}], \qquad (6.27)$$

where $L(t)$ is the cumulative portfolio loss up to time t; 1 is the indicator function; and $E[\ ]$ denotes the expectation that is determined by averaging the overall simulation paths. This forms the basis for assigning a rating to a synthetic CDO tranche for a PD-based rating.

EXPECTED TRANCHE LOSS

Instead of only focusing on the likelihood of losses, the actual size of all losses may also be of interest. The cumulative loss on tranche j at time t, $L^{Tj}(t)$, is given by Equation 6.28:

$$L^{Tj}(t) = (L(t) - A)1_{\{A\leq L(t)\leq D\}} + (D - A)1_{\{L(t)\geq D\}}. \qquad (6.28)$$

The expected tranche loss is therefore given by Equation 6.29:

$$E\left[L^{Tj}(t)\right] = E\left[(L(t) - A)1_{\{A\leq L(t)\leq D\}} + (D - A)1_{\{L(t)\geq D\}}\right]. \qquad (6.29)$$

Table 6.3 **Four CDO Tranches for an Underlying Portfolio of 100 "BBB" Exposures**

This table shows the tranche default probabilities (PD), expected losses (EL), and loss-given-default (LGD) for four CDO tranches referencing a portfolio of 100 "BBB" companies.

Tranche	0% – 6%	6% – 12%	12% – 18%	36% – 42%
PD	70.00%	6.98%	0.95%	0.00%
EL	27.13%	2.68%	0.40%	0.00%
LGD	38.76%	38.40%	42.59%	–

which can be computed by simulation analysis. An expected loss rating assigned by rating agencies such as Moody's is partly based on this measure of tranche risk.

TRANCHE LOSS GIVEN DEFAULT

From the expected tranche loss and the tranche PD, the tranche LGD is simply given by $LGD^{Tj} = \frac{E\left(L^{Tj}(t)\right)}{PD^{Tj}}$ under the assumption of independence between tranche PD and LGD. Table 6.3 shows the results obtained from a typical portfolio model for four CDO tranches and an underlying portfolio of 100 "BBB" exposures and highlights the effect of tranching.

Summary and Conclusions

This chapter introduced various techniques used for measuring and managing credit risk. Starting with single asset risks such as PD and LGD for an obligor, the focus shifted to portfolio credit risk and correlation. Dependency between defaults and firm behaviors is crucial for understanding portfolio risk. Not surprisingly, regulatory capital as well as internal capital frameworks is often defined based on credit portfolio modeling approaches that explicitly use correlation. Banks and other financial institutions widely use those techniques. The chapter describes some of these applications. Capital measurement, portfolio concentrations, risk-based pricing, and complex product structuring, all benefit from those techniques and will do so for the foreseeable future. Changes in regulation, mostly involving capital and liquidity requirements, require those applications and models to constantly evolve. Bank internal models and methodologies often supplement pure regulatory models/frameworks to derive an economic view about its business and clients that will drive bank portfolio composition and staff behavior.

Disclaimer

The opinions expressed in this chapter are those of the author and do not necessarily reflect views of his employer.

Discussion Questions

1. Explain the difference between "point-in-time" and "through-the-cycle" credit risk indicators.
2. Explain a methodology that can be used to build a transition matrix from a history of 25 years of rating information and whether this matrix can be used to derive default probabilities for longer horizons.
3. Define VaR and discuss how this measure is used in practice.
4. Identify the key inputs to a credit portfolio simulation model and three practical areas of usage for such models.
5. Explain one main difference between the Merton model and a statistical credit-scoring model such as the linear logit model for estimating probabilities of default.

References

Altman, Edward. 2008. "Default Recovery Rates and LGD in Credit Risk Modelling and Practice: An Updated Review of the Literature and Empirical Evidence." In Steward Jones and David A. Hensher, eds., *Advances in Credit Risk Modelling and Corporate Bankruptcy Prediction*, 175–206. Cambridge: Cambridge University Press.

Altman, Edward, and Vellore Kishore. 1996. "Almost Everything You Wanted to Know about Recoveries on Defaulted Bonds." *Financial Analysts Journal* 52:6, 57–64.

Asarnow, Elliot, and David Edwards. 1995. "Measuring Loss on Defaulted Bank Loans: A 24 Year Study." *Journal of Commercial Bank Lending* 77:7, 11–23.

Benvegnu, Stephan, Christian Bluhm, and Cristoph Müller, eds. 2008. *A Guide to Active Credit Portfolio Management: Spotlight on Illiquid Credit Risks.* London: Risk Books.

Black, Fisher, and Myron Scholes. 1973. "The Pricing of Options and Corporate Liabilities." *Journal of Political Economy* 81:3, 637–659.

Crosbie, Peter, and Jeffrey Bohn. 2003. "Modeling Default Risk." Working Paper, Moody's KMV.

Demey, Paul, Jean-Frédéric Jouanin, Céline Roget, and Thierry Roncalli. 2004. "Maximum Likelihood Estimate of Default Correlations." *Risk*, November, 104–108.

de Servigny, Arnaud, and Norbert Jobst. 2007. *The Handbook of Structured Finance.* New York: McGraw-Hill.

de Servigny, Arnaud, and Olivier Renault. 2004. *Measuring and Managing Credit Risk.* New York. McGraw-Hill.

Duffie, Darrel, and Kenneth Singleton. 2003. *Credit Risk.* Princeton, NJ: Princeton University Press.

Gordy, Michael, and Erik Heitfield. 2002. "Estimating Default Correlations from Short Panels of Credit Rating Performance Data." Working Paper, Federal Reserve Board.

Jafry, Yusuf, and Til Schuermann. 2003. "Measurement and Estimation of Credit Migration Matrices." Working Paper, Federal Reserve Board of New York.

Jobst, Norbert, and Arnaud de Servigny. 2006. "An Empirical Assessment of Equity Default Swaps II: Multivariate Insights." *Risk*, January, 97–99.

Li, David. 2000. "On Default Correlation: A Copula Function Approach." *Journal of Fixed Income* 9:4, 43–54.

Merton, Robert. 1974. "On the Pricing of Corporate Debt: The Risk Structure of Interest Rates." *Journal of Finance* 29:2, 449–470.

Schönbucher, Philipp. 2003. *Credit Derivative Pricing Models.* Chichester, UK: John Wiley & Sons.

Tasche, Dirk. 2008. "Capital Allocation to Business Units and Sub-Portfolios: The Euler Principle." Working Paper, Lloyds TSB Bank.

Vassalou, Maria, and Yuhang Xing. 2004. "Default Risk in Equity Returns." *Journal of Finance* 54:2, 831–868.

7

Operational Risk

PAVEL V. SHEVCHENKO

Senior Principal Research Scientist, CSIRO Computational Informatics, Sydney

Introduction

The management of operational risk in the banking industry has undergone dramatic changes over the last decade due to substantial changes in the operational risk environment. Globalization, deregulation, the use of complex financial products, and changes in information technology have resulted in exposure to new risks very different from market and credit risks. In response, the Basel Committee on Banking Supervision (BCBS) has developed a regulatory framework, referred to as the Basel II Accord (BCBS 2006), that introduced the operational risk category and corresponding capital requirements against operational risk losses. The Basel II Accord (BCBS 2006, p. 144) defines *operational risk* as: "the risk of loss resulting from inadequate or failed internal processes, people and systems or from external events. This definition includes legal risk, but excludes strategic and reputational risk." The Basel III Accord, which will be implemented piecemeal until 2019, has no explicit changes to the operational risk framework but focuses on comprehensive and dynamic capital, risk, and liquidity management that cannot be achieved if operational risk is not well managed. The International Actuarial Association has adopted the same definition of operational risk in the capital requirements for insurance companies referred to as Solvency II. Similar developments also took place in the pension fund industry. For example, the Australian Prudential Regulation Authority (APRA) Prudential Standard 114 introduced operational risk capital requirements for pension funds starting from July 2013.

Operational risk was the third major risk category coming under the Basel Accord framework following market and credit risks. A conceptual difference between operational risk and market or credit risk is that operational risk represents a downside risk with no upside potential. The term "operational risk" started to be used within financial institutions after the Barings Bank event in 1995, when a rogue trader caused the collapse of the institution by placing bets in the Asian markets and keeping these contracts out of management's sights. At that time, these losses could not be classified as either market or credit risk and the term "operational risk" started to be used in the industry to define situations where such losses could arise.

Operational risk is important in many financial institutions. Examples of extremely large operational risk losses are Barings Bank in 1995, when the actions of one rogue trader caused a bankruptcy as a result of GBP 1.3 billion derivative trading loss; Enron's bankruptcy in 2001, as a result of actions of its executives with USD 2.2 billion loss; Société Générale losses of EUR 4.9 billion in 2008 due to unauthorized trades; and Knight Capital Corporation's losses of USD 450 million within 30 minutes in 2012 due to a software glitch after installing new high-frequency trading software.

The Basel Committee does not possess any formal supervisory authority and its conclusions do not have legal force. It formulates broad supervisory standards and guidelines and recommends statements of best practice in the expectation that individual authorities will take steps to implement them through detailed arrangements that are best suited to their own national systems. In this way, the Committee encourages convergence toward both common approaches and standards without attempting detailed standardization of supervisory techniques in member countries. In Australia, all major banks have already received advanced measurement approach (AMA) accreditation for operational risk starting from 2008. In 2012, a capital against operational risk in major Australian banks ranged from AUD 1.8 to 2.5 billion (8 to 10 percent of the total capital). Rapid progress in the development of quantitative methodology for estimating operational risk capital under the AMA within major banks in Australia can be attributed to the choice by APRA to link AMA in operational risk to the Internal Ratings-Based Approach in credit risk (APRA 2008). In other countries, the progression of operational risk systems has lagged behind the Australian example. However, modeling operational risk in large banks in other countries is now becoming increasingly prominent.

During the late 1990s and early 2000s, the progress in operational risk was very slow. Some very large global banks such as Lehman Brothers did not have an operational risk department until 2004. Over the past five years, many major banks adopted the loss distribution approach (LDA), based on statistical modeling of frequency and severity of operational risk events, for AMA accreditation to quantify operational risk capital despite the presence of unresolved methodological challenges in its implementation. Different approaches and methods are still under debate. This chapter provides a review of quantitative methods proposed in the literature for the LDA as well as their pitfalls and challenges.

The remainder of the chapter is organized as follows. It examines regulatory approaches for operational risk followed by a discussion of the loss distribution approach and the four data elements of operational risk AMA. Next, the chapter focuses on the topics of modeling severity tail, modeling dependence, and multifactor modeling. The next to last section reviews operational risk in other industries. The chapter ends with a summary and conclusions.

Regulatory Approaches for Operational Risk

The Basel II/Basel III Accord framework is based on a three conceptual pillars.

- *Pillar I. Minimum capital requirements*. This pillar requires an explicit minimum capital allocated for operational risk that can be calculated using different approaches.
- *Pillar II. Supervisory review process*. This pillar focuses on the supervision of a bank's systems and capital adequacy by regulatory authorities.

- *Pillar III. Market discipline.* The objective of this pillar is to establish market discipline through public disclosure of risk measures and other relevant information on risk management.

This chapter focuses on Pillar I and reviews some probabilistic models for operational risk. Many models have been suggested for modeling operational risk under Basel II. In brief, two conceptual approaches are the so-called *top-down* (e.g., multifactor equity pricing models, the capital asset pricing model (CAPM), and income- or expense-based models) and *bottom-up approach* (process-based models such as causal networks, multifactor causal models, reliability models, and loss distribution approach models). Under the top-down approach, estimating the risk for a firm is based on macro data such as gross income or analyzing overall company losses. Under the bottom-up approach, the risks are quantified at the local level (e.g., process level, event types, business units, or business line/event type risk cells) and aggregated to find the risk for the whole firm. Under the Basel II Accord framework, three approaches can be used to quantify the operational risk annual capital charge (BCBS 2006): the basic indicator approach (BIA), standardized approach (SA), and advanced measurement approach (AMA). Internationally active banks and banks with substantial operational risk exposures (e.g., specialized processing banks) are expected to use the AMA.

THE BASIC INDICATOR APPROACH

The BIA is the simplest method under the Basel II Accord framework to calculate the capital against operational risk where the capital is calculated as shown in Equation 7.1:

$$C = \alpha \frac{1}{n} \sum_{j=1}^{3} \max(GI(j), 0), \quad n = \sum_{j=1}^{3} 1_{\{GI(j)>0\}}, \qquad (7.1)$$

where $GI(j)$ is the annual gross incomes of a bank for each of the previous three years; n is the number of years with positive gross income; and $1_{\{\cdot\}}$ is an indicator function equal to 1 if condition in $\{\cdot\}$ is true and zero otherwise. The regulators not only introduced capital charges for operational risk but also established that these figures would be significant at a minimum 15 percent of the firm's gross income. This method is the top-down approach.

THE STANDARDIZED APPROACH

In the SA, bank's activities are divided into eight business lines: (1) corporate finance, (2) trading and sales, (3) retail banking, (4) commercial banking, (5) payment and settlements, (6) agency services, (7) asset management, and (8) retail brokerage. The capital is calculated for each business line using its gross income and a special factor assigned for this business line. The total capital is the summation of capital charges across the business lines. The actual Basel II Accord formula, given by Equation 7.2, allows offsetting positive capital charges if gross income in some business lines is negative

$$C = \frac{1}{3} \sum_{j=1}^{3} \max \left[\sum_{i=1}^{8} \beta_i GI_i(j), 0 \right], \tag{7.2}$$

where β_i are the factors for eight business lines listed in Table 7.1 and $GI_i(j)$, $j = 1, 2, 3$ is the annual gross income of the i-th business line in each the previous three years. Within each business line, gross income is a broad indicator that serves as a proxy for the scale of business operations and thus the likely scale of operational risk exposure within each of these business lines. Beta factors β_i serve as a proxy for the industry-wide relationship between the operational risk loss experience for a given business line and the aggregate level of gross income for that business line. The SA also belongs to the top-down method category.

THE ADVANCED MEASUREMENT APPROACH

Under the AMA, a bank can calculate the capital charge using an internally developed model subject to regulatory approval. Under this approach, a bank should demonstrate the accuracy of the internal models within matrix of the Basel II Accord risk cells (i.e., eight business lines by seven event types listed in Table 7.1) relevant to the bank and satisfy various criteria such as using internal data, relevant external data, scenario analysis, and factors reflecting the business environment and internal control systems. The risk measure should correspond to the 99.9 percent confidence level for one-year period.

Table 7.1 **The Basel II Accord Business Lines and Event Types for Operational Risk**

i	Business Line, BL(i)	β_i(%)	j	Event Type, ET(j)
1	Corporate finance	18	1	Internal fraud
2	Trading and sales	18	2	External fraud
3	Retail banking	12	3	Employment practices and workplace safety
4	Commercial banking	15	4	Clients, products, and business practices
5	Payment and settlements	18	5	Damage to physical assets
6	Agency services	15	6	Business disruption and system failures
7	Asset management	12	7	Execution, delivery, and process management
8	Retail brokerage	12		

Note: This table shows the Basel II Accord's eight business lines and seven event types $\beta_1, \ldots, \beta_8$ are the business line factors used in the Basel II standardized approach.

Source: BCBS 2006, 147, 302, 305–307.

The intention of the AMA is to provide an incentive to a bank to invest into development of a sound operational risk practices and risk management. When compared to other approaches, the capital reserves under the AMA will be more relevant to the actual risk profile of a bank. The capital from the AMA is expected to be lower than the capital calculated under the SA. The regulatory accreditation for the AMA indicates to a market that a bank has developed a sound risk management practice.

Under the AMA, banks could use their own internal models to estimate capital. As imagined, given the early stages of banks' frameworks, the range of practice was quite broad. The methodological focus of most banks in Europe was on using scenario analysis. By contrast, the focus in the United States was on internal and external loss data. The initial Basel II Accord proposal (BCBS 2001, Annex 4) suggests three approaches for the AMA: the Internal Measurement Approach (IMA), Score Card Approach, and Loss Distribution Approach (LDA). A more recent Basel II Accord document (BCBS 2006) does not give any guidance for the AMA approach and allows flexibility. Regulators and industry practitioners consider the LDA to be the most comprehensive approach. As a bottom-up method, LDA is the most common practice in the industry and is a focus of this chapter.

RISK ORGANIZATION AND GOVERNANCE

Organization and structure within any large business are critical for business success and essential for a sound operational risk management framework. Although this chapter focuses on measurement models that often involve complex mathematics and statistics, the final success of operational risk management lies in having an appropriate and efficient organizational design and good governance closely monitored by the regulators. The common industry practice for operational risk governance relies on business line management, an independent corporate operational risk management function, and an independent review (e.g., internal audit). Depending on the business nature, size, and complexity, the implementation of the governance and organizational structure will vary. In all cases, however, the operational risk governance function should be fully integrated into the bank's overall risk management governance structure. Although this topic is not discussed in this chapter, a useful reference is Hoffman (2002).

Loss Distribution Approach

The LDA approach for operational risk is based on modeling the annual frequency (number of events per annum) N_j and severity (amount) $X_1^{(j)}, X_2^{(j)}, \ldots$ of operational risk losses for each risk cell $j = 1, 2, \ldots, J$. Basel II categorization includes 56 risk cells (eight business lines times seven event types in Table 7.1), but it may differ across banks. The annual loss in the risk cell is the aggregation of severities over one-year horizon presented in Equation 7.3:

$$Z_j = X_1^{(j)} + X_2^{(j)} + \cdots + X_{N_j}^{(j)}. \tag{7.3}$$

Then, as shown in Equation 7.4, the total loss over all risk cells is the sum of annual losses across the cells

$$Z = \sum_{j=1}^{J} Z_j. \tag{7.4}$$

The regulatory capital is defined by Equation 7.5 as the 0.999 value-at-risk (VaR) over the next year, which is the quantile of the distribution of the total loss Z

$$VaR_q[Z] = \inf\{z : \Pr[Z > z] \le 1 - q\}, \; q = 0.999. \tag{7.5}$$

That is, the 0.999 VaR is the smallest value such that the probability that the annual loss Z exceeds this value is no larger than 0.001. Thus, VaR measures the worst loss that is only exceeded with a small probability $1 - q$. For example, a value of $q = 0.999$ implies that a bank will have a capital sufficient, on average, to cover losses in 999 out of 1,000 years. The wisdom of the choice of the 0.999 VaR as a risk measure for capital is highly contested (Danielsson, Embrechts, Goodhart, Keating, Muennich, Renault, and Shil 2001). However, a formal Basel II Accord requirement for operational risk capital charge refers to VaR.

Another popular risk measure is the so-called *expected shortfall* (ES), formally defined in Equation 7.6, which represents the expected value of losses that have exceeded the corresponding VaR

$$ES_q[Z] = \frac{1}{1 - q} \int_q^1 VaR_p[Z] dp, \tag{7.6}$$

which is just $ES_q[Z] = E[Z|Z \ge VaR_q[Z]]$ if distribution of Z is continuous at $VaR_q[Z]$. ES is considered a better risk measure because it satisfies the diversification property that can fail for VaR (i.e., the VaR of the sum of risks may appear to be larger than the sum of VaRs of these risks). However, ES is not the best measure of operational risk because some operational risks exhibit such heavy tails that even the mean (expected loss) may not exist. These outcomes are the so-called infinite mean distributions reported in the literature for operational risk.

Debate exists in the literature over the most appropriate choice of a risk measure. For example, BCBS (2012) asks for a possible transition from VaR to ES as the underlying risk measure. VaR generally does not have the diversification property whereas ES does. However, Gneiting (2011) implies that VaR generally is statistically back testable but ES is not. Furthermore, VaR typically has certain robustness properties that ES does not (Cont, Deguest, and Scandolo 2010). Thus, despite its shortcomings, VaR is likely to remain in force.

The frequency N is modeled by discrete random variable with some frequency distribution $p_n = \Pr[N = n]$. A Poisson distribution, defined in Equation 7.7, is typically used in practice:

$$p_n = \frac{\lambda^k}{k!} e^{-\lambda}, \quad \lambda > 0, \; k = 0, 1, 2, \ldots. \tag{7.7}$$

Severity X_i is modeled by continuous random variable with severity distribution $F(x)$, such as using lognormal, Weibull, and Pareto as discussed in the following sections.

For a single risk cell, a common assumption is that frequency and severities are independent and severities $X_1, X_2, \ldots$ are independent and identically distributed. Knowing frequency and severity distributions, the distribution $H(z)$ for the annual loss in a single risk cell (Equation 7.3) can be calculated numerically using Monte Carlo or convolution techniques such as Panjer recursion or FFT (Shevchenko 2010). Given that operational risk distributions are typically heavy tailed (i.e., distribution tail $1 - F(x)$ decays to 0 slower than any exponential $\exp(-\varepsilon x)$, $\varepsilon > 0$), the approximation in Equation 7.8 may work very well

$$1 - H(z) \approx E[N](1 - F(z)), \quad \text{as} \quad z \to \infty. \tag{7.8}$$

This result is valid for heavy tailed severity distributions and frequency distributions with $\sum_{n=0}^{\infty} (1 + \varepsilon)^n \Pr[N = n] < \infty$ for some $\varepsilon > 0$ such as Poisson, binomial, and negative binomial. Consistent with Böcker and Klüppelberg (2005), this asymptotic result can be used to estimate the quantile of the annual loss using Equation 7.9:

$$VaR_q[Z] \approx F^{-1}\left(1 - \frac{1 - q}{E[N]}\right), \quad \text{as} \quad q \to 1. \tag{7.9}$$

Given that only $E[N]$ contributes to the high quantile of the compound distribution, using different frequency distributions such as Poisson or negative binomial will have a small impact on the capital in the case of heavy tailed severities. In this case, using a simplest distribution (i.e., Poisson) is justified. Equation 7.9 is asymptotic result for the quantile level $q \to 1$. Degen (2010) derives the first correction to this approximation that in the case of a Poisson frequency adds the term $E[X]E[N]$ to the right side of Equation 7.9.

Estimation of the annual loss distribution by modeling frequency and severity of losses is a well-known actuarial technique (Klugman, Panjer, and Willmot 1998). The technique is also used to model solvency requirements for the insurance industry (Sandström 2006). Numerous books discuss different quantitative aspects of the LDA modeling (King 2001; Cruz 2002; Panjer 2006; Chernobai, Rachev, and Fabozzi 2007; Shevchenko 2011; Cruz, Peters, and Shevchenko 2014; Peters and Shevchenko 2014).

The rationale to model frequency and severity separately is because some factors may affect frequency only while other factors may affect severity only. Below are several examples.

- As the business grows (e.g., volume of the transactions grows), the expected number of losses changes and this should be accounted for in forecasting the number of losses over the next year.
- The general economic inflation affects the loss sizes (severity).
- The insurance for operational risk losses is more easily incorporated because insurance policies typically apply per event and affect the severity.

The initial Basel II Accord proposal suggested that the capital charge should cover unexpected losses (UL), while expected losses (EL) should be covered by the bank through internal provisions. The reasoning was that many bank activities have regular losses such as credit card fraud. However, the accounting rules for provisions may not

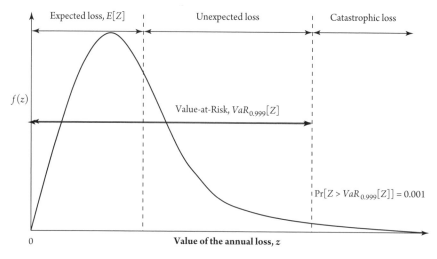

Figure 7.1 OPERATIONAL RISK CAPITAL REQUIREMENTS.   This figure illustrates the expected and unexpected losses in the operational risk capital requirements at the 99.9 percent confidence level for a one-year horizon. $f(z)$ is the probability density function of the total annual loss Z across all risk cells in a firm.

reflect the true EL. As a result, the final Basel II version proposed calculating *regulatory capital* as the sum of EL and UL, unless the bank can demonstrate an adequate capture of EL through its internal business practices (BCBS 2006). Hereinafter, for simplicity, capital is a sum of the EL and UL, which is the 99.9 percent VaR. The loss exceeding the 99.9 percent VaR does not require a capital charge. This is a so-called *catastrophic loss* or *stress loss*, also often called a one in 1,000 year event. Figure 7.1 illustrates the EL, UL, and VaR quantities.

The main purpose of the capital charge required by banking industry regulators is to protect a bank against potential losses; it can be viewed as a form of self-insurance. Although regulatory capital for operational risk is based on the 99.9 percent confidence level over a one-year holding period, *economic capital*, which is quantified and allocated by a bank internally, is often higher. For example, some banks use the 99.95 to 99.98 percent confidence levels for economic capital. Economic capital can be viewed as the amount that market forces imply for the risk and determined from bank credit rating.

Four Data Elements of Operational Risk AMA

The Basel II Accord specifies the requirement for the data that should be collected and used for the AMA. Basel II AMA requires (BCBS 2006, p. 152) that:

> Any operational risk measurement system must have certain key features to meet the supervisory soundness standard set out in this section. These elements must include the use of internal data, relevant external data, scenario analysis and factors reflecting the business environment and internal control systems.

Combining these different data sources for model estimation is one of the main challenges in operational risk. The intention of using several data sources is to develop a model based on the largest possible data set to increase the accuracy and stability of the capital estimate. Some of the main features of the required data sources are summarized as follows.

INTERNAL DATA

The internal data should be collected over a minimum five-year period to be used for capital charge calculations. When a bank initially starts using the AMA framework, a three-year period is acceptable. Due to a short observation period, the internal data for many risk cells typically contain few if any high-impact/low-frequency losses. A bank must be able to map its historical internal loss data into the relevant Basel II risk cells. The data must capture all material activities and exposures from all appropriate subsystems and geographic locations. A bank can have an appropriate reporting threshold for internal data collection, typically of the order of EUR 10,000. Aside from information on gross loss amounts, a bank should collect information about the date of the event, any recoveries of gross loss amounts, as well as some descriptive information about the drivers of the loss event. Generally speaking, omitting data increases uncertainty in modeling but having a reporting threshold helps to avoid difficulties with collecting too many small losses. Often, the analysis simply ignores data below a reported level, arguing that the capital is mainly determined by the low-frequency/heavy-tailed severity risks. However, the impact of data truncation for other risks can be significant. Recent studies addressing this problem include Mignola and Ugoccioni (2006) and Shevchenko and Temnov (2009).

EXTERNAL DATA

A bank's operational risk measurement system must use relevant external data. These data should include actual loss amounts, information on the scale of business operations where the event occurred, and information on the causes and circumstances of the loss events. Industry data are available through external databases from vendors (e.g., Algo OpData provides publicly reported operational risk losses above USD 1 million) and consortia of banks (e.g., ORX provides operational risk losses above EUR 20,000 reported by ORX members). The external data are difficult to use directly due to different volumes and other factors. Moreover, the data have a survival bias as typically the data of all collapsed companies are unavailable. Several authors report no strong evidence of a relationship between operational risk and bank factors such as total assets and number of employees. Ganegoda and Evans (2013) identify dependence on a bank size for some risk cells by fitting distributions where both scale and shape distribution parameters are considered functions of the factors. Cope, Piche, and Walter (2012) investigate the dependence on various regulatory, legal, geographical, and economic indicators and report some relationships.

The literature includes several loss data collection exercises (LDCE) for historical operational risk losses over many institutions. Two important papers are Moscadelli

(2004), who analyzes the 2002 LDCE, and Dutta and Perry (2006), who examine the 2004 LDCE where the data are mainly above EUR 10,000 and USD 10,000, respectively. BCBS (2009) contains the results for the 2008 LDCE. To show the severity and frequency of operational risk in the banking industry, Data summary from trading and sales and corporate finance business lines has been presented in Table 7.2.

Table 7.2 **Operational Risk Frequency and Severity**

Event Type	Frequency	% Total Frequency	Amount	% Total Amount
Trading and Sales				
Internal fraud	32.2	1.0	145.8	11.0
External fraud	31.7	1.0	4.5	0.3
Employment practices and workplace safety	96.9	3.1	30.3	2.3
Clients, products, and business practices	398.6	12.7	384.7	29.0
Damage to physical assets	12.2	0.4	2.7	0.2
Business disruption and system failures	157.6	5.0	23.8	1.8
Execution, delivery, and process management	2, 400.6	76.7	732.6	55.3
Corporate Finance				
Internal fraud	3.5	1.6	6.6	0.24
External fraud	11.5	5.4	3.2	0.12
Employment practices and workplace safety	21.6	10.1	16.2	0.59
Clients, products, and business practices	100.2	47.1	2, 565.1	93.67
Damage to physical assets	2.4	1.1	0.1	0.004
Business disruption and system failures	4.6	2.2	0.6	0.02
Execution, delivery, and process management	69.1	32.5	146.7	5.36

Note: This table shows the trading and sales and corporate finance business lines. The results show annualized loss frequency and annualized loss amount (EUR million) from the 2008 Loss Data Collection Exercise for Operational Risk (BCBS 2009). The % total frequency and amount is in percent with respect to the total (across event types) frequency and amount, respectively.

BCBS also provides results for other business lines. As Table 7.2 shows, the frequencies and severities of losses can differ substantially across risk cells.

SCENARIO ANALYSIS

A bank must use scenario analysis in conjunction with external data to evaluate its exposure to high-severity events. *Scenario analysis* is a process undertaken by experienced business managers and risk management experts to identify risks, analyze past internal/external events, and consider current and planned controls in the banks. The process may involve workshops to identify weaknesses, strengths, and other factors; opinions on the impact and likelihood of losses; and opinions on sample characteristics or distribution parameters of the potential losses. As a result, some rough quantitative assessment of risk frequency and severity distributions can be obtained.

When assigning loss severities to scenarios, the range of practice varies substantially. Some institutions assign loss ranges with lower and upper bounds, while other institutions assign just lower bounds, or point estimates of the anticipated loss amounts. For example, an expert may estimate the expected number of events for a risk and then can estimate that if the loss occurs, the probabilities of the loss exceeding $L_1, L_2, \ldots, L_n$ are $p_1, p_2, \ldots, p_n$. An analyst can use this information to fit frequency and severity distributions.

Scenario analysis is very subjective and should be combined with the actual loss data. It should also be used for stress testing (e.g., to assess the impact of potential losses arising from multiple simultaneous loss events). A vast literature exists on expert elicitation published by statisticians, especially in areas such as security and ecology. O'Hagan, Buck, Daneshkhah, Eiser, Garthwaite, Jenkinson, Oakley, and Rakow (2006) provide a good review but published studies on using expert elicitation for operational risk LDA are scarce and include Frachot, Moudoulaud, and Roncalli (2005), Alderweireld, Garcia, and Léonard (2006), Steinhoff and Baule (2006), and Peters and Hübner (2009). These studies suggest that operational risk experts understand questions on how often the loss exceeding some level may occur. Here, experts express the opinion that a loss of amount L or higher is expected to occur every k years. Ergashev (2012) proposes a framework incorporating scenario analysis into operational risk modeling. The basis for the framework is that only worst-case scenarios contain valuable information about the tail behavior of operational losses. One of the current problems with combining scenario analysis and historical data is that the data are collected for the Basel II Accord risk cells but scenario analysis is done at the loss process level.

BUSINESS ENVIRONMENT AND INTERNAL CONTROL FACTORS

A bank's methodology must capture the key business environment and internal control factors affecting operational risk. These factors should help to make forward-looking estimation, account for the quality of the controls and operating environments, and align capital assessments with risk management objectives. In practice, accounting for factors reflecting the business environment and internal control systems is often achieved via ad hoc scaling of data. However, this task can also be accomplished using statistically sound methods as discussed in the section on multifactor modeling.

COMBINING DATA SOURCES

Many approaches are available to combine different data sources of information including ad hoc procedures, parametric and nonparametric Bayesian methods, and general non-probabilistic methods such as Dempster-Shafer theory. Shevchenko and Wüthrich (2010) provide a review of the methods.

Numerical ad hoc procedures include estimation of severity distribution $F(x)$ as a mixture as illustrated in Equation 7.10:

$$F(x) = w_1 F_{SA}(x) + w_2 F_I(x) + (1 - w_1 - w_2)F_E(x) \qquad (7.10)$$

where $F_{SA}(x), F_I(x)$, and $F_E(x)$ are the distributions identified by scenario analysis, internal data, and external data, respectively, using expert specified weights w_1 and w_2. Another example is the minimum variance principle where the combined estimator is a linear combination of the individual estimators obtained from internal data, external data, and scenario analysis separately with weights chosen to minimize the variance of the combined estimator.

Under the Bayesian approach, both data and parameters are considered random. Consider a vector of data $\mathbf{Y} = (Y_1, \ldots, Y_n)$ whose density for a given parameter $\boldsymbol{\theta}$ is $\ell(\mathbf{y}|\boldsymbol{\theta})$. A convenient way is to think that parameter is a random variable with some distribution and the true value, which is deterministic but unknown, of the parameter is a realization of this random variable. Then, the joint density of the data and parameters is $\ell(\mathbf{y}|\boldsymbol{\theta})\pi(\boldsymbol{\theta}) = \pi(\boldsymbol{\theta}|\mathbf{y})f(\mathbf{y})$, where $\pi(\boldsymbol{\theta})$ is the so-called *prior density* of the parameters and $\pi(\boldsymbol{\theta}|\mathbf{y})$ is the *posterior density* (density of parameter given data), and Bayes's rule is given by Equation 7.11:

$$\pi(\boldsymbol{\theta}|\mathbf{y}) \propto \ell(\mathbf{y}|\boldsymbol{\theta})\pi(\boldsymbol{\theta}). \qquad (7.11)$$

Thus, the posterior is basically a product of the prior density, which can be estimated using expert opinions or external data, and the likelihood of the data $\ell(\mathbf{y}|\boldsymbol{\theta})$. Shevchenko and Wüthrich (2006) consider applying Bayesian methods to combine two data sources (expert opinions and internal data; or external data and internal data) in operational risk. Lambrigger, Shevchenko, and Wüthrich (2007) combine three data sources (internal data, external data, and expert opinions). Bühlmann, Shevchenko, and Wüthrich (2007) discuss closely related methods of credibility theory in operational risk.

Another approach is the use of nonparametric Bayesian methods. The nonparametric approach does not assume that the underlying loss process generating distribution is parametric. Instead, the prior on the distribution is determined directly followed by finding the posterior of the distribution given data, which combines the prior with an empirical data distribution. One of the most popular Bayesian nonparametric models is based on the Dirichlet process. Cope (2012) uses this approach to combine an empirical data distribution with expert opinion, where the Dirichlet process is used as a prior and specified via expert opinions.

Neil, Häger, and Andersen (2009) apply *Bayesian networks* for operational risk. Bayesian networks are directed acyclical graphs accounting for causal links between the events. The underlying theory of Bayesian networks combines Bayesian probability theory and uses conditional independence to represent dependencies between variables. The ability of Bayesian networks to account for causal dependencies enables risk analysts to link the operational conditions of the bank, including control environment, directly to the probability of losses occurring, as well as the severity of the losses. Bayesian networks are certainly suitable as a tool for risk management but their use for calculating economic capital is still to be developed.

Dempster (1968) and Shafer (1976) suggest Dempster's rule for combining evidence in the Dempster-Shafer theory of evidence. A central object in the theory is the so-called Dempster-Shafer structure, which is similar to a discrete distribution except that the locations where the probability mass resides are sets of real values (focal elements) rather than points. Unlike a discrete probability distribution on the real line, where the mass is concentrated at distinct points, the focal elements of a Dempster-Shafer structure may overlap, and this is the fundamental difference that distinguishes Dempster-Shafer theory from traditional probability theory. The central method in the Dempster-Shafer theory is Dempster's rule to combine independent Dempster-Shafer structures that produce another Dempster-Shafer structure. It is often referred to as a generalization of the Bayesian method. Closely related are probability boxes (also referred to as *p-boxes*) that attempt to model uncertainty by constructing the bounds on cumulative distribution functions. Ferson, Kreinovich, Ginzburg, Myers, and Sentz (2003) provide a good summary on the methods for obtaining Dempster-Shafer structures and p-boxes, and aggregation methods handling a conflict between the objects from different sources. Berger (1985) considers this approach as an unnecessary elaboration that can be handled within the Bayesian paradigm through Baysian robustness. These methods are attractive for operational risk and Sakalo and Delasey (2011) apply them for operational risk. However, applying this method to combine p-box for historical losses with statistically uncertain bounds with the expert specified p-box with certain bounds is questionable.

Overall, the Bayesian methods can be well suited for modeling operational risk. In particular, a Bayesian framework is a convenient way to combine different data sources (e.g., internal data, external data, and expert opinions). It is also well suited to account for the parameter uncertainties that can be very large due to small data sets and may lead to a significant capital increase (Shevchenko 2008).

Modeling Severity Tail

Due to simple fitting procedure, one of the popular distributions to model severity X is lognormal (i.e., $\ln X$ is modeled by normal distribution). It is a heavy tailed distribution in which the tail decays more slowly than any exponential tail. A lognormal distribution often provides a reasonable overall statistical fit. For example, BCBS (2001) suggests using a lognormal distribution for operational risk at the beginning of Basel II development. However, due to the high quantile level requirement for operational risk capital, accurate modeling of extremely high losses is critical. Also, finding a standard two-parameter distribution that would provide a good fit to operational risk severity both in the main body of losses and in the tail is difficult. Typically, the modelers introduce the high threshold u and model losses below and above the threshold using different distributions. Formally, this means that the severity density is modeled as presented in Equation 7.12:

$$f(x) = w_1 f_1(x) + w_2 f_2(x), \quad w_1 + w_2 = 1; \ w_1 \geq 0; \ w_2 \geq 0, \qquad (7.12)$$

where $f_1(x)$ and $f_2(x)$ are proper densities defined on $x < u$ and $x \geq u$, respectively. A popular choice for $f_1(x)$ corresponds to an empirical distribution of data below the threshold. Regarding $f_2(x)$, the modeler can try shifted or truncated lognormal or some other standard distributions. The modeler can also rely on asymptotic extreme value theory (EVT) that essentially states that under general conditions as the threshold u increases, the distribution of loss exceedance $Y = X - u$ over u converges to a generalized Pareto distribution (GPD) shown in Equation 7.13:

$$G(y; \xi, \beta) = \begin{cases} 1 - (1 + \xi y/\beta)^{-1/\xi}; & \xi \neq 0 \\ 1 - \exp(-y/\beta); & \xi = 0 \end{cases} \qquad (7.13)$$

with $y \geq 0$ if $\xi \geq 0$ and $0 \leq y \leq -\beta/\xi$ when $\xi < 0$ (McNeil, Frey, and Embrechts 2005). The case $\xi = 0$ corresponds to exponential distribution. If $\xi > 0$, the GPD is heavy tailed and some moments do not exist (if $\xi \geq 1/m$, then the m-th moment and higher moments do not exist). The study of operational risk data in Moscadelli (2004), analyzing the 2002 LDCE using EVT and several standard two-parameter distributions, reports even the cases of $\xi \geq 1$ for some risk cells that correspond to infinite mean distributions (Nešlehová, Embrechts, and Chavez-Demoulin 2006). The case $\xi < 0$ seemingly appears irrelevant to modeling operational risk as all reported results indicate non-negative shape parameter. However, one could think of a risk control mechanism restricting the losses by an upper level and then the case of $\xi < 0$ might be relevant.

For a random variable X, whose distribution is $\Pr[X \leq x] = F(x)$, the distribution of exceedance of X over u is given by Equation 7.14:

$$F_u(y) = \Pr[X - u \leq y | X > u] = \frac{F(y + u) - F(u)}{1 - F(u)} \qquad (7.14)$$

that converges to GPD as u increases. Then the overall severity distribution can be modeled as shown in Equation 7.15:

$$F(x) = \begin{cases} G(x - u; \xi, \beta) \times (1 - F_n(u)) + F_n(u); & x \geq u \\ F_n(x) = \frac{1}{K} \sum_{k=1}^{K} 1_{X_k \leq x}; & x < u \end{cases} \qquad (7.15)$$

that corresponds to the empirical distribution for $x < u$ and GPD for $x \geq u$. It can be used to extrapolate to the quantiles beyond maximum historically observed loss. Figure 7.2 provides an illustration.

Because EVT is a limiting (asymptotic) result, it should be used with caution. In particular, a standard distribution fitting can work better than EVT in some situations. The analysis of the 2004 LDCE in Dutta and Perry (2006) tests the four-parameter g-and-h

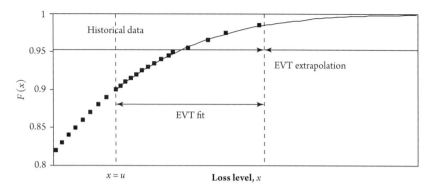

Figure 7.2 EXTREME VALUE THEORY TO FIT SEVERITY DISTRIBUTION.   This figure illustrates the use of extreme value theory (EVT) to fit severity distribution $F(x)$: fitting generalized Pareto distribution (GPD) to the historically observed losses above large threshold u and using GPD to extrapolate to the quantiles beyond historically observed maximum loss.

and GB2 distributions as well as GPD and several two-parameter distributions. Degen, Embrechts, and Lambrigger (2007) compare the g-and-h with GPD. They demonstrate that for the g-and-h distribution, convergence of the excess distribution to the GPD distribution is extremely slow. Therefore, quantile estimation using EVT may lead to inaccurate results if data are well modeled by the g-and-h distribution. Many other types of known and less known distributions are available that might be appropriate for operational risk severity as discussed in books Panjer (2006), Peters and Shevchenko (2014), or Cruz et al. (2014).

Modeling Dependence

The Basel II Accord operational risk framework (BCBS 2006, p.152) requires that:

> Risk measures for different operational risk estimates must be added for purposes of calculating the regulatory minimum capital requirement. However, the bank may be permitted to use internally determined correlations in operational risk losses across individual operational risk estimates, provided it can demonstrate to the satisfaction of the national supervisor that its systems for determining correlations are sound, implemented with integrity, and take into account the uncertainty surrounding any such correlation estimates (particularly in periods of stress). The bank must validate its correlation assumptions using appropriate quantitative and qualitative techniques.

Thus, if dependence is properly quantified between all risk cells $j = 1, \ldots, J$ then, under the LDA model, the capital is calculated using Equation 7.16 as

$$C = VaR_q[Z_1 + Z_2 + \cdots + Z_J]. \tag{7.16}$$

Otherwise the capital should be calculated as shown in Equation 7.17:

$$C = VaR_q[Z_1] + VaR_q[Z_2] + \cdots + VaR_q[Z_J]. \tag{7.17}$$

The latter is equivalent to the assumption of perfect positive dependence between annual losses of the risk cells. In principle, VaR can be estimated at any level of granularity and then the capital is calculated as a sum of resulting VaRs. Often banks quantify VaR for business lines and add up these estimates to get capital, but for simplicity of notations, Equation 7.17 is given at the level of risk cells. The capital under Equation 7.16 is expected to be less than under Equation 7.17. However, in general, the sum of VaRs across risks is not the most conservative estimate of the total VaR. In principle, the upper conservative bound can be larger for some distributions (Artzner, Delbaen, Eber, and Heath 1999; Embrechts, Lambrigger, and Wüthrich 2009; Embrechts, Nešlehová, and Wüthrich 2009). That is, Equation 7.18 is possibly valid in some cases

$$VaR_q[Z] > VaR_q[Z_1] + VaR_q[Z_2] + \cdots VaR_q[Z_J]. \tag{7.18}$$

This outcome is often the case for heavy tailed distributions and large quantiles.

As documented in the literature, the dependence between different operational risks can be introduced by:

- Modeling dependence between the annual counts via a copula (Frachot, Roncalli, and Salomon 2004; Bee 2005; Aue and Klakbrener 2006);
- Using common shock models to introduce events common across different risks and leading to the dependence between frequencies and dependence between severities occurring at the same time (Lindskog and McNeil 2003);
- Modeling dependence between the annual losses of different risks via copulas (Embrechts and Puccetti 2008; Giacometti, Rachev, Chernobai, and Bertocchi 2008);
- Using the multivariate compound Poisson model based on Lévy copulas (Böcker and Klppelberg 2008, 2010); and
- Using structural models with common (systematic) factors that can lead to the dependence between severities and frequencies of different risks and within risk (e.g., using dependence between risk profiles considered in Peters, Shevchenko, and Wüthrich 2009).

The popular current practice is to introduce dependence between frequencies (annual counts) of the risks while severities are assumed independent. Typically, this results in a small increase in the capital (about 10 percent) when compared to the case of independent risks. However, modeling dependence is still an open question and a difficult task with many challenges to be resolved. The main problem here is a lack of data.

Multifactor Modeling

For operational risk measurement and management, understanding the relationship of operational risk losses to explanatory variables such as key control and business environment variables and external macroeconomic variables is important. The standard approach to incorporating these relationships into the model is to assume that model parameters are functions of these explanatory variables. For example, consider a random sample of independent data $Y_1, \ldots, Y_n$; its realization is denoted as $y_1, \ldots, y_n$. Let $f(y_i; \boldsymbol{\theta})$ be the density function of Y_i with parameter vector $\boldsymbol{\theta} = (\theta^{(1)}, \ldots, \theta^{(K)})$. Each parameter $\theta^{(k)}$ can be modeled as a function of explanatory variables as given by Equation 7.19:

$$g_k(\theta_i^k) = \beta_1^{(k)} X_{i,1}^{(k)} + \beta_2^{(k)} X_{i,2}^{(k)} + \cdots + \beta_J^{(k)} X_{i,J}^{(k)}, \tag{7.19}$$

where $X_{i,j}^{(k)}$ is the value of the j-th explanatory variable relating to data point Y_i in the k-th distributional parameter and $g_k(\cdot)$ is the link function specified by the modeler. Then the modeler estimates parameters $\beta_j^{(k)}$ using, for example, the maximum likelihood method by maximizing the model likelihood given by Equation 7.20 with respect to $\beta_j^{(k)}$

$$\prod_{i=1}^{n} f(y_i; \boldsymbol{\theta}_i). \tag{7.20}$$

For example, consider log losses $Y_1, Y_2, \ldots, Y_n$ observed for some risk process and corresponding vectors of explanatory variables $\mathbf{X}_1, \mathbf{X}_2, \ldots, \mathbf{X}_n$ such as system downtime and number of employees, and assume that the density of log-losses is a normal density $f_N(y_i; \mu_i, \sigma)$ with mean parameter μ_i and volatility parameter σ. Next, assume that mean μ_i is related to explanatory variables as shown in Equation 7.21:

$$\mu_i = \beta_1 X_{i,1} + \beta_2 X_{i,2} + \cdots + \beta_J X_{i,J}. \tag{7.21}$$

That is, the link function is $g(\mu) = \mu$ and the volatility parameter σ is constant. This outcome corresponds to the standard linear regression presented in Equation 7.22:

$$Y_i = \beta_1 X_{i,1} + \beta_2 X_{i,2} + \cdots + \beta_J X_{i,J} + \varepsilon_i, \tag{7.22}$$

where ε_i are independent random variables from a normal distribution with zero mean and variance σ^2. In this case, maximization of the likelihood corresponds to the ordinary least square method.

The generalized linear model (GLM) allows for a response variable to have a distribution different from a normal distribution. In particular, GLM considers that given explanatory variables X_i, the response variable Y_i has some distribution with mean μ_i such that $g(\mu_i) = \beta_1 X_{i,1} + \cdots + \beta_J X_{i,J}$, where $g(\cdot)$ is monotonic and differentiable link function. Furthermore, it assumes that response variable belongs to the *exponential family* distribution defined in Equation 7.23:

$$f(y_i; \theta_i, \phi) = \exp\left(\frac{y_i \theta_i - b(\theta_i)}{\phi} + c(y_i, \phi)\right) \tag{7.23}$$

for some parameter θ_i, dispersion parameter ϕ, and functions $b(\cdot)$ and $c(\cdot)$. This family contains many standard distributions including continuous and discrete distributions such as the normal, exponential, gamma, chi-squared, Bernoulli, Poisson, and many others. For example,

- A normal distribution with mean μ and variance σ^2 corresponds to identity link function $g(\mu) = \mu, \theta = \mu$, and $\phi = \sigma^2$.
- A Poisson distribution with intensity parameter λ is obtained by $\theta = \ln \lambda, b(\theta) = \lambda$, $\phi = 1$ and $c(y, \phi) = -\ln y!$ and logarithmic link function $g(\lambda) = \ln \lambda$.

Efficient ways are available to estimate model parameters $\beta_1, \ldots, \beta_J$ via iteratively weighted least square for maximum likelihood and carry out the model/variable selection. McCullagh and Nelder (1989) provide a detailed treatment of GLM.

Generalized additive models for location scale and shape (GAMLSS) have been recently introduced. Rigby and Stasinopoulos (2005) propose a very general class of regression models that incorporates popular generalized linear models (GLM), generalized additive models (GAM), generalized linear mixed models (GLMM), and generalized additive mixed models (GAMM). However, GAMLSS is more general than the previously mentioned models because it relaxes the assumption that the response variable belongs to the natural exponential family. GAMLSS is a convenient framework to test various distributional assumptions such as Gumbel, Weibull, and Student-t in addition to the standard natural exponential family distributions. The second advantage of the GAMLSS framework is that it does not limit the modeling to the location of the distribution as in GLM and the other similar frameworks. The standard GLM setup (similarly to the ordinary least squares method) cannot model distributional parameters other than the location parameter explicitly. In the GAMLSS framework, all distributional parameters can be explicitly modeled using both fixed and random effects. Furthermore, each distributional parameter can be modeled as linear or nonlinear, parametric or smooth nonparametric functions of explanatory variables and random effects.

Operational Risk in Other Industries

Broadly speaking, operational risk is the risk of any operational failure within a company. It has been managed in manufacturing and services industries using total quality management (TQM) and reliability theory for a long time. In the manufacturing, reliability theory and TQM have had a major impact on the design of new products for many decades in efforts to improve the quality and reduce the risk (Bergman 1985). For example, in the design and construction of aircraft, a concept such as optimal redundancy has had a major impact on the design processes for many years. In the manufacturing world of micro-electronics, TQM has received much attention in the daily assembly and manufacturing of the actual products. One advantage that the manufacturing world has is that measurements of products and processes are actually relatively easy. By contrast, the measurements of products and processes are not as easy in the service industries. After many decades, operational risk is still a major concern in many service industries, including transportation (e.g., aviation), medical and health care industries, hospitality including the cruise industry, power generation (e.g., nuclear), and the military.

Some of these service industries have a long history in dealing with operational risk (Cruz and Pinedo 2008) and have developed a good track record. Similar to these industries, the operational risk management framework in financial institutions should deal with the product design phase (e.g., credit cards and derivatives), the process design phase (e.g., using specific facilities and resources to deliver the product), and the process management phase, which deals with how the product is sold and maintained. Xu, Pinedo, and Xue (2013) provide a good overview of operational risk from the operations management perspective.

Summary and Conclusions

Over the past five years, many major banks have received accreditation under the Basel II Accord AMA by adopting LDA despite the presence of unresolved methodological challenges in its implementation. Operational risk is the most difficult risk to quantify when compared to market or credit risk and can be the most devastating. This chapter reviews methods for the LDA implementation as well as their pitfalls and challenges. Many aspects of the LDA may require sophisticated statistical methods and different approaches are hotly debated.

The major problem in operational risk is a lack of quality data that complicates conducting advanced research in the area. In the past, most banks did not collect operational risk data because doing so was not required and collecting such data was costly. Moreover, indirect operational risk losses cannot be measured accurately. The duration of operational risk events can be substantial and evaluation of the impact of the event can take years. Practitioners should be careful with using statistical methods fitting distributions to the risk cell data because operational risk losses within a data set may not be generated by the same loss generating mechanism that statistical models often assume. Finally, statistical modeling is only part of the operational risk management framework that includes organizational and governance structure; policies, procedures, and processes; and systems to identify, measure, monitor, control, and mitigate operational risk.

Discussion Questions

1. List and discuss three pillars of the Basel II Accord framework.
2. List two methods for calculating operational risk capital and discuss the differences.
3. Identify and discuss issues with using VaR and ES for measuring operational risk.
4. Discuss the need to combine internal data with external data and scenario analysis for estimating operational risk.

References

Alderweireld, Thomas, Joao Garcia, and Luc Léonard. 2006. "A Practical Operational Risk Scenario Analysis Quantification." *Risk Magazine* 19:2, 93–95.

APRA. 2008. *Capital Adequacy: Advanced Measurement Approaches to Operational Risk.* Australian Prudential Regulation Authority, Prudential Standard APS 115.

Artzner, Philippe, Freddy Delbaen, Jean-Marc Eber, and David Heath. 1999. "Coherent Measures of Risk." *Mathematical Finance* 9:3, 203–228.

Aue, Falko, and Michael Klakbrener. 2006. "LDA at Work: Deutsche Bank's Approach to Quantify Operational Risk." *Journal of Operational Risk* 1:4, 49–93.

BCBS. 2001. *Working Paper on the Regulatory Treatment of Operational Risk*. Basel Committee on Banking Supervision, Bank for International Settlements, Basel.

BCBS. 2006. *International Convergence of Capital Measurement and Capital Standards: A Revised Framework*. Basel Committee on Banking Supervision, Bank for International Settlements, Basel.

BCBS. 2009. *Results from the 2008 Loss Data Collection Exercise for Operational Risk*. Basel Committee on Banking Supervision, Bank for International Settlements, Basel.

BCBS. 2012. *Fundamental Review of the Trading Book*. Basel Committee on Banking Supervision, Bank for International Settlements, Basel.

Bee, Marco. 2005. *Copula-based Multivariate Models with Applications to Risk Management and Insurance*. Available at http://dx.doi.org/10.2139/ssrn.795964.

Berger, James O. 1985. *Statistical Decision Theory and Bayesian Analysis*, 2nd Edition. New York: Springer.

Bergman, Bo. 1985. "On Reliability Theory and Its Applications." *Scandinavian Journal of Statistics* 12:1, 1–41.

Böcker, Klaus, and Claudia Klüppelberg. 2005. "Operational VAR: A Closed-form Approximation." *Risk Magazine* 8:12, 90–93.

Böcker, Klaus, and Claudia Klüppelberg. 2008. "Modelling and Measuring Multivariate Operational Risk with Lévy Copulas." *Journal of Operational Risk* 3:2, 3–27.

Böcker, Klaus, and Claudia Klüppelberg. 2010. "Multivariate Models for Operational Risk." *Quantitative Finance* 10:8, 855–869.

Bühlmann, Hans, Pavel V. Shevchenko, and Mario V. Wüthrich. 2007. "A 'Toy' Model for Operational Risk Quantification Using Credibility Theory." *Journal of Operational Risk* 2:1, 3–19.

Chernobai, Anna S., Svetlozar T. Rachev, and Frank J. Fabozzi. 2007. *Operational Risk: A Guide to Basel II Capital Requirements, Models and Analysis*. Hoboken, NJ: John Wiley & Sons.

Cont, Rama, Romain Deguest, and Giacomo Scandolo. 2010. "Robustness and Sensitivity Analysis of Risk Measurement Procedures." *Quantitative Finance* 10:6, 593–606.

Cope, Eric W. 2012. "Combining Scenario Analysis with Loss Data in Operational Risk Quantification." *Journal of Operational Risk* 7:1, 39–56.

Cope, Eric W., Mark T. Piche, and John S. Walter. 2012. "Macroenvironmental Determinants of Operational Loss Severity." *Journal of Banking & Finance* 36:5, 1362–1380.

Cruz, Marcelo G. 2002. *Modeling, Measuring and Hedging Operational Risk*. Chichester: John Wiley & Sons.

Cruz, Marcelo G., and Michael Pinedo. 2008. "Total Quality Management and Operational Risk in the Service Industry." In Zhi-Long Chen and S. Raghavan, eds., *Tutorials in Operations Research*, 154–169. Hanover: INFORMS.

Cruz, Marcelo G., Gareth W. Peters, and Pavel V. Shevchenko. 2014. Fundamental Aspects of Operational Risk and Insurance Analytics: a *Handbook of Operational Risk*. Hoboken, NJ: John Wiley & Sons.

Danielsson, Jón, Paul Embrechts, Charles Goodhart, Con Keating, Felix Muennich, Olivier Renault, and Hyun Song Shin. 2001. "An Academic Response to Basel II." Available at ftp://ftp.math.ethz.ch/hg/users/embrecht/Basel2.pdf.

Degen, Matthias. 2010. "The Calculation of Minimum Regulatory Capital Using Single-Loss Approximations." *Journal of Operational Risk* 5:4, 3–17.

Degen, Matthias, Paul Embrechts, and Dominik D. Lambrigger. 2007. "The Quantitative Modeling of Operational Risk: Between g-and-h and EVT." *ASTIN Bulletin* 37:2, 265–291.

Dempster, Arthur P. 1968. "A Generalization of Bayesian Inference." *Journal of the Royal Statistical Society*, Series B, 30:2, 205–247.

Dutta, Kabir, and Jason Perry. 2006. *A Tale of Tails: An Empirical Analysis of Loss Distribution Models for Estimating Operational Risk Capital.* Working Paper No. 06–13, Federal Reserve Bank of Boston.

Embrechts, Paul, and Giovanni Puccetti. 2008. "Aggregation Operational Risk across Matrix Structured Loss Data." *Journal of Operational Risk* 3:2, 29–44.

Embrechts, Paul, Dominik D. Lambrigger, and Mario V. Wüthrich. 2009. "Multivariate Extremes and the Aggregation of Dependent Risks: Examples and Counter-Examples." *Extremes* 12:2, 107–127.

Embrechts, Paul, Johanna Nešlehová, and Mario V. Wüthrich. 2009. "Additivity Properties for Value-at-Risk under Archimedean Dependence and Heavy-tailedness." *Insurance: Mathematics and Economics* 44:2, 164–169.

Ergashev, Bakhodir A. 2012. "A Theoretical Framework for Incorporating Scenarios into Operational Risk Modeling." *Journal of Financial Services Research* 41:3, 145-161.

Ferson, Scott, Vladik Kreinovich, Lev Ginzburg, Davis S. Myers, and Kari Sentz. 2003. *Constructing Probability Boxes and Dempster-Shafer Structures.* SAND report: SAND2002-4015. Albuquerque, NM and Livermore, CA: Sandia National Laboratories.

Frachot, Antoine, Olivier Moudoulaud, and Thierry Roncalli. 2005. "Loss Distribution Approach in Practice." In Michael K. Ong, ed., *The Basel Handbook: A Guide for Financial Practitioners,* 369–396. London: Risk Books.

Frachot, Antoine, Thierry Roncalli, and Eric Salomon. 2004. "The Correlation Problem in Operational Risk." Available at http://ssrn.com/abstract=1032594.

Ganegoda, Amandha, and John Evans. 2013. "A Scaling Model for Severity of Operational Losses Using Generalized Additive Models for Location Scale and Shape (GAMLSS)." *Annals of Actuarial Science* 7:1, 61–100.

Giacometti, Rosella, Svetlozar Rachev, Anna Chernobai, and Marida Bertocchi. 2008. "Aggregation Issues in Operational Risk." *Journal of Operational Risk* 3:3, 3–23.

Gneiting, Tilmann. 2011. "Making and Evaluating Point Forecasts." *Journal of the American Statistical Association* 106:494, 746–762.

Hoffman, Douglas G. 2002. *Managing Operational Risk: 20 Firmwide Best Practice Strategies.* New York: John Wiley & Sons.

King, Jack L. 2001. *Operational Risk: Measurements and Modelling.* Chichester: John Wiley & Sons.

Klugman, Stuart A., Harry H. Panjer, and Gordon E. Willmot. 1998. *Loss Models: From Data to Decisions.* New York: John Wiley & Sons.

Lambrigger, Dominik D., Pavel V. Shevchenko, and Mario V. Wüthrich. 2007. "The Quantification of Operational Risk Using Internal Data, Relevant External Data and Expert Opinions." *Journal of Operational Risk* 2:3, 3–27.

Lindskog, Filip, and Alexander J. McNeil. 2003. "Common Poisson Shock Models: Application to Insurance and Credit Risk Modelling." *ASTIN Bulletin* 33:2, 209–238.

McCullagh, Peter, and James A. Nelder. 1989. *Generalized Linear Models.* London: Chapman & Hall.

McNeil, Alexander J., Rüdiger Frey, and Paul Embrechts. 2005. *Quantitative Risk Management: Concepts, Techniques and Tools.* Princeton, NJ: Princeton University Press.

Mignola, Giulio, and Roberto Ugoccioni. 2006. "Effect of a Data Collection Threshold in the Loss Distribution Approach." *Journal of Operational Risk* 1:4, 35–47.

Moscadelli, Marco. 2004. *The Modelling of Operational Risk: Experiences with the Analysis of the Data Collected by the Basel Committee.* Working Paper No. 517, Bank of Italy.

Neil, Martin, David Häger, and Lasse B. Andersen. 2009. "Modeling Operational Risk in Financial Institutions Using Hybrid Dynamic Bayesian Networks." *Journal of Operational Risk* 4:1, 3–33.

Nešlehová, Johanna, Paul Embrechts, and Valérie Chavez-Demoulin. 2006. "Infinite Mean Models and the LDA for Operational Risk." *Journal of Operational Risk* 1:1, 3–25.

O'Hagan, Anthony, Caitlin E. Buck, Alireza Daneshkhah, J. Richard Eiser, Paul H. Garthwaite, David J. Jenkinson, Jeremy E. Oakley, and Tim Rakow. 2006. *Uncertain Judgements: Eliciting Expert's Probabilities.* Chichester: John Wiley & Sons.

Panjer, Harry H. 2006. *Operational Risks: Modeling Analytics*. New York: John Wiley & Sons.

Peters, Gareth W., and Pavel V. Shevchenko. 2014. Advances in Heavy Tailed Risk Modeling: a *Handbook of Operational Risk*. Hoboken, NJ: John Wiley & Sons.

Peters, Gareth W., Pavel V. Shevchenko, and Mario V. Wüthrich. 2009. "Dynamic Operational Risk: Modeling Dependence and Combining Different Data Sources of Information." *Journal of Operational Risk* 4:2, 69–104.

Peters, Jean-Philippe, and Georges Hübner. 2009. "Modeling Operational Risk Based on Multiple Experts Opinions." In Greg N. Gregoriou, ed., *Operational Risk toward Basel III: Best Practices and Issues in Modeling, Management, and Regulation*, 3-22. Hoboken, NJ: John Wiley & Sons.

Rigby, Robert A., and D. Mikis Stasinopoulos. 2005. "Generalized Additive Models for Location, Scale and Shape." *Journal of the Royal Statistical Society*, Series C (Applied Statistics), 54:3, 507–554.

Sakalo, Tatiana, and Matthew Delasey. 2011. "A Framework for Uncertainty Modeling in Operational Risk." *Journal of Operational Risk* 6:4, 21–57.

Sandström, Arne. 2006. *Solvency: Models, Assessment and Regulation*. Boca Raton, FL: Chapman & Hall/CRC.

Shafer, Glenn. 1976. *A Mathematical Theory of Evidence*. Princeton, NJ: Princeton University Press.

Shevchenko, Pavel V. 2008. "Estimation of Operational Risk Capital Charge under Parameter Uncertainty." *Journal of Operational Risk* 3:1, 51–63.

Shevchenko, Pavel V. 2010. "Calculation of Aggregate Loss Distributions." *Journal of Operational Risk* 5:2, 3–40.

Shevchenko, Pavel V. 2011. *Modelling Operational Risk Using Bayesian Inference*. Berlin: Springer.

Shevchenko, Pavel V., and Grigory Temnov. 2009. "Modeling Operational Risk Data Reported above a Time-varying Threshold." *Journal of Operational Risk* 4:2, 19–42.

Shevchenko, Pavel V., and Mario V. Wüthrich. 2006. "The Structural Modeling of Operational Risk via Bayesian Inference: Combining Loss Data with Expert Opinions." *Journal of Operational Risk* 1:3, 3–26.

Shevchenko, Pavel V., and Mario V. Wüthrich. 2010. "Operational Risk: Combining Internal Data, External Data and Expert Opinions." In Klaus Böcker, ed., *Rethinking Risk Measurement and Reporting*, Volume 2, 401–437. London: Risk Books.

Steinhoff, Carsten, and Rainer Baule. 2006. "How to Validate Operational Risk Distributions." *Operational Risk & Compliance*, August 1, 36–39. Available at http://www.risk.net/operational-risk-and-regulation/feature/1516610/how-validate-op-risk-distributions.

Xu, Yuqian, Michael Pinedo, and Mei Xue. 2013. "Operational Risk in Financial Services: A Tutorial and Review from an Operations Management Perspective." Working Paper, New York University, Stern School of Business.

8

Liquidity Risk

KOSE JOHN

Charles William Gerstenberg Professor of Banking and Finance, New York University

SAMIR SAADI

Assistant Professor of Finance, University of Ottawa

HUI ZHU

Assistant Professor of Finance, University of Ontario Institute of Technology

Introduction

The past few decades have witnessed a growing interest in liquidity among financial market participants, regulators, and academicians. This interest is not surprising given the complex nature of liquidity and its direct consequences on the price of assets, market actors, and the efficiency and stability of financial markets. As Fernandez (1999, p. 1), the former Senior Vice President and Chief Economist of Securities Industry Association (SIA), states:

> Liquidity is the lifeblood of financial markets. Its adequate provision is critical for the smooth operation of an economy. Its sudden erosion in even a single market segment or in an individual instrument can stimulate disruptions that are transmitted through increasingly interdependent and interconnected financial markets worldwide. Despite its importance, problems in measuring and monitoring liquidity risk persist.

Liquidity risk can be divided into two different but related parts: asset/market liquidity and funding liquidity. In the context of this chapter, liquidity risk arises when a seller of an asset or security cannot sell it because no one is willing to buy it.

The primary purpose of this chapter is to provide an overview of the liquidity literature. Given the extensive literature, the chapter concentrates on some of the more important works that examine liquidity characteristics, propose liquidity proxies, and test whether illiquidity is a priced risk factor.

The remainder of the chapter is organized as follows. The first section discusses the properties and sources of illiquidity. The next section focuses on the main proxies contained in the empirical literature to capture liquidity. The third part reviews the theoretical and empirical literature that examines whether a liquidity premium is priced. The fourth section concludes the chapter.

Properties of Liquidity and Sources of Illiquidity

As Baker (1996, p. 1) notes, "there is no single unambiguous theoretically correct or universally accepted definition of liquidity." The challenge of defining liquidity comes from its complexity and multidimensional properties. Liquidity often refers to an asset's market liquidity or funding liquidity. *Market liquidity* is the ease with which investors can trade an asset or a security. *Funding liquidity* denotes the ease with which traders obtain capital. Although this chapter focuses on market liquidity, funding liquidity and market liquidity are actually linked (Brunnermeier and Pedersen 2009). The liquidity provided by traders to the market depends on their ability to get funding, but their capital and margin requirements (i.e., funding) also depend on an asset's market liquidity. Brunnermeier and Pedersen present a model showing that when margins are destabilizing, such as during a financial crisis, market liquidity and funding liquidity can be mutually reinforcing and cause liquidity spirals.

In the context of this chapter, *liquidity risk* is the risk associated with an asset or security that cannot be sold rapidly enough to avoid capital loss. Liquidity risk becomes extremely important to parties who currently hold or are about to hold an asset because it affects their ability to trade. Hence, liquidity risk relates to the degree of the lack of liquidity or simply the degree of illiquidity of an asset or a security.

Kyle (1985), Harris (1990), Baker (1996), and Von Wyss (2004) discuss several dimensions of trading liquidity (depth, resilience, immediacy, and tightness or breadth). These dimensions are equally important but may not exist concurrently. For example, during the financial crisis of 2007–2008, breadth and depth occurred but immediacy and resiliency were missing. Below is a brief discussion of the various dimensions of trading liquidity.

1. *Depth* refers to the presence of a large volume of buy and sell orders without having a substantial impact on prices. Depth can be measured by the possible number of trades (i.e., volume of transactions) that does not lead to a change in the quoted price.
2. *Resilience* can be proxied by the speed required for a trade's price impact to dispel and considers the elasticity of supply and demand.
3. *Immediacy* refers to the speed at which an order can be executed at the prevalent price. It mirrors the efficiency of the trading and settlement systems.
4. *Tightness* or *breadth* can be assessed by the magnitude of the bid-ask spread. According to Hasbrouck (2003), liquidity tightness is associated with the costs of providing liquidity, particularly the cost of immediacy.

Illiquidity is associated with the different factors that impede the ease with which an asset can be traded. The market microstructure literature extensively covers these factors (Kyle 1985; O'Hara 1995; Madhavan 2000; Amihud, Mendelson, and Pedersen

2005; Baker and Kiymaz 2013). Amihud et al. discuss the following factors that can be considered as sources of illiquidity:

1. *Search costs.* When finding a counterparty to execute a trade requires time, an investor may be forced to make price concessions to facilitate and expedite the transaction. Thus, search costs induce the uncertainty about the price needed to complete the trade. Search costs are prevalent especially in over-the-counter (OTC) markets.
2. *Exogenous trading costs.* These costs are associated with executing a trade and include broker commissions, exchange fees, transaction taxes, and remuneration for setting up a trading system.
3. *Inventory risk for the market maker.* When a counterparty is unavailable to complete a sell transaction, an investor may have to sell to a market maker who then needs to carry inventory. Accordingly, the market maker bears inventory risk that is compensated by the bid-ask spread.
4. *Private information.* Uninformed investors face information risk when trading with informed traders. Hence, the informed party requires compensation in the form of the bid-ask spread in the case of the market maker as a protection against potential losses that can occur when trading against an informed counterparty. Easley and O'Hara (2004) develop a rational expectations model with asymmetric information and show that adverse selection generated by private information leads to equilibrium differences in asset returns. Specifically, in a finite economy, uninformed investors demand a premium for holding shares in firms with greater private information and less public information.

Measuring Liquidity Risk

Many measures of liquidity are available. Although this section presents some of the main proxies used in empirical studies, Von Wyss (2004) and Gabrielsen, Marzo, and Zagaglia (2011) provide a more exhaustive list of measures. Von Wyss classifies liquidity measures into one-dimensional measures (i.e., those considering only one variable) and multidimensional measures (i.e., those considering more than one variable). This chapter, however, uses a more common classification that separates liquidity measures into the following four categories: (1) volume-based measures, (2) transaction cost measures, (3) price-based measures, and (4) market-impact measures.

VOLUME-BASED MEASURES

The first liquidity measure involves volume. The basic idea behind volume-based measures is that they link the volume of an asset to its price and try to capture the depth dimension of liquidity. Trade volume is an indirect but widely used liquidity measure. The intuition is that more actively traded assets tend to be more liquid. The main advantage of the trade volume measure is that it is simple and easy to obtain given the widespread availability of volume data. However, volume is also correlated to volatility, which can impede liquidity. Moreover, using trade volume as a proxy for liquidity suffers from a double counting problem. Addressing this issue involves using a scaled measure that divides market capitalization by the trade volume.

The liquidity ratio (LR) is another measure that uses volume and price as key components. The *liquidity ratio* measures the trade volume necessary to make the price change by one percent. Formally, Equation 8.1 presents the liquidity ratio:

$$LR_{it} = \frac{\sum_{t=1}^{T} P_{it} V_{it}}{\sum_{t=1}^{T} |P_{it} - P_{it-1}|}, \tag{8.1}$$

where P_{it} is the price of an asset or security i on time t and V_{it} is the trade volume. The denominator in Equation 8.1 measures the absolute price change of asset i over one period of time, which could be daily but most often is set at a monthly frequency. A relatively high liquidity ratio means that a high volume of trade has a relatively low impact on asset price change, which is indicative of high liquidity.

The Martin (1975) liquidity (ML) index is another liquidity ratio that relates trade volume to asset price. However unlike LR, which is asset-specific, Martin's measure is computed over all the assets available on a market making it a market-specific measure. Formally, Equation 8.2 shows the ML index:

$$ML_t = \sum_{i=1}^{N} \frac{(P_{it} - P_{it-1})^2}{V_{it}}, \tag{8.2}$$

where P_{it} is the closing price of an asset or security i on time t; V_{it} is the trade volume; and N is the total number of assets in the market. ML is better measured on a daily basis. As Equations 8.1 and 8.2 show, ML is inversely related to LR, which indicates that as ML increases, LR decreases.

Hui and Heubel (1984) propose another liquidity index measured at the asset level that captures the liquidity dimension linking trade volume to its impact on asset prices, namely, resiliency. The Hui and Heubel liquidity (HH) index is the ratio of the largest price change of an asset by the trade volume to market capitalization. Equation 8.3 shows the analytical expression of the HH measure:

$$HH_i = \frac{(P_{i\,max} - P_{i\,min})/P_{i\,min}}{V/N \times P_{avg}}, \tag{8.3}$$

where $P_{i\,max}$ is the highest daily price recorded for asset i over a five-day period; $P_{i\,min}$ is the lowest daily price recorder for asset i over a five-day period; V is the total volume of assets traded; N is the total number of assets in the market; and P_{avg} is the average closing price over a five-day period. Similar to ML, the higher the HH index is, the lower the liquidity will be. The HH measure encompasses other volume-based liquidity measures that link trade volume to asset price (Baker 1996). A major shortcoming of the HH index is the fact that a five-day period is long enough to allow for stock prices to adjust to illiquidity problem.

A popular liquidity measure is the turnover ratio (TR), which relates trade volume to the number of asset units outstanding (Datar, Naik, and Radcliffe 1998). Formally, Equation 8.4 shows the TR for an asset i during a period of time t:

$$TR_{it} = \frac{\sum_{i=1}^{N} P_{it} \times Q_{it}}{P_{avg} \times V},$$ (8.4)

where P_{it} is the price of an asset i; Q_{it} is the trade volume; N is the number of transaction over period of time t; and V is the total number of outstanding units of asset units. The TR can be interpreted as the number of times the outstanding volume of an asset i changes hands. The relative popularity of the TR, compared to the liquidity measures proposed by Martin (1975) and Hui and Heubel (1984), is due to its simplicity and the availability of data required to compute the TR. Users of the TR should be mindful of the effect of volatility of turnover on this volume-based liquidity measure as trade volume can shift dramatically due, for instance, to the release of important firm-specific or even market-wide news.

Equation 8.5 below shows a liquidity measure that is inversely related to the TR. It is expressed as the absolute value of the market index average daily price change to the TR (PCTR):

$$PCTR_{it} = \frac{|\%\Delta P|}{TR_{it}}.$$ (8.5)

As PCTR increases, the depth dimension decreases leading to lower asset liquidity.

Amihud (2002) designs a volume-based liquidity ratio called the *Amihud illiquidity ratio* (ILLIQ), which is the ratio of the absolute value of the daily stock return to the corresponding daily dollar volume shown in Equation 8.6:

$$ILLIQ_{it} = \frac{|R_{it}|}{\sum_{i=1}^{N} P_{it} \times Q_{it}},$$ (8.6)

where R_{it} is the return in time t of an asset i expressed in absolute value; P_{it} is the price; Q_{it} is the trade volume; and N is the number of transaction over period of time t. This measure can also be averaged over a month (year) to get the monthly (yearly) liquidity measure. The intuition behind the ILLIQ is that a trade of a given amount has a larger price impact for more illiquid assets. In fact, the ILLIQ is designed to capture the price impact of trades that characterizes liquidity depth and resilience.

TRANSACTION COST MEASURES

Transaction cost measures are liquidity proxies designed to capture transaction costs and the trading frictions related to secondary markets. Although several transaction cost-based measures are available, the bid-ask spread and its variants are the most commonly used. This is because they tend to measure implicit and explicit transaction costs besides their ability to convey insight about information asymmetry in the market. The *bid-ask spread* can be defined as a percentage spread or the absolute difference between the bid and the ask price. Let P_A denote the ask price, P_B the bid price, and P_M the midpoint $P_M = (P_A + P_B)/2$, then Equation 8.7 formally gives the *absolute bid-ask spread* (AS) as:

$$AS = P_A - P_B$$ (8.7)

and Equation 8.8 shows the measure of *percentage spread* (PS):

$$PS = \frac{P_A - P_B}{M}. \tag{8.8}$$

The lower the bid-ask spreads, the more liquid is the security in question. Both the absolute bid-ask spread and the percentage spread are computed using quoted bid and ask prices. The spread measure given by Equation 8.8 is also called the *dealer spread*. When the highest bid and lowest ask prices in the market for the same stock at the same time are used, the spread is called the *market spread*. Other measures of spread can be generated using, for instance, the weighted averages of completed trades over a period of time, hence the name *realized spread*. Alternative versions of spread are the half of spread (given by AS/2) and the log absolute spread. Roll (1984) offers the most popular spread measure known as the *effective spread*, which is constructed using a model that attempts to depict market prices and/or returns. The effective spread can be calculated as the square root of the negative covariance between adjacent price changes. Because Roll's model is based on the assumption that information is homogenous across traders, it does not elaborate on the possible components of the spread.

PRICE-BASED MEASURES

The basic idea behind price-based liquidity measures is that liquidity can be measured through asset price or market index behavior. To distinguish between short-term and long-term volatility, Hasbrouck and Schwartz (1988) propose the market-efficiency coefficient (MEC), also known as the variance ratio (VR), which Equation 8.9 defines as:

$$VR_i = \frac{VAR(R_{it})}{K \times VAR(r_{it})}, \tag{8.9}$$

where $VAR(R_{it})$ is the return variance of a longer period; $VAR(r_{it})$ is the return variance of a short period; and K is the number of short periods in the longer period. VAR is not the same as value-at-risk (VaR). With high execution cost, the volatility of realized prices is larger than the volatility of the equilibrium price. Thus, a variance ratio larger than one indicates liquidity. Ito, Lyons, and Melvin (1998) use a variant version of the variance ratio defined as $1 - VR_i$, where liquid market is characterized by $1 - VR_i > 0$.

The VR is also widely used to test for the efficient market hypothesis (EHM) and more specifically the random walk hypothesis. The gist of VR tests is that if a stock's return is purely random, the variance of K-period return is K times the variance of the one-period return. Hence, the VR, defined as the ratio of $1/K$ times the variance of the K-period return to the variance of the one-period return, should be equal to one for all values of K. That is, if the return series follows a random walk, then the VR should be equal to one. A potential limitation of the VR tests is that they are asymptotic tests, so their sampling distributions in finite samples are approximated by their limiting distributions. An assumption underlying the VR tests is that stock returns are at least identically, if not normally, distributed and that the variance of the random walk increments in a finite sample is linear in the sampling interval. Even though the VR test is quite powerful against homoskedastic or heteroskedastic, and independent and identically distributed (*i.i.d.*) null hypotheses (Smith and Ryoo 2003), the sampling distribution of the VR statistic can be far from normal in finite samples, showing severe bias and right skewness. More powerful VR tests are available such as the automatic variance ratio (AVR) test developed by Choi (1999), sub-sampling test of Whang and Kim (2003), and the power transformed joint variance ratio test proposed by Chen and Deo (2006).

The Marsh and Rock (1986) liquidity (MR) ratio is expressed in Equation 8.10:

$$MR_i = \frac{1}{K} \sum\nolimits_{k=1}^{K} \left| \frac{P_{ik} - P_{ik-1}}{P_{ik}} \right| \times 100, \tag{8.10}$$

where K is the number of transactions for asset i over a certain period. Compared to the aforementioned volume-based liquidity ratios, the MR ratio considers the relationship between the absolutely value of the price change and the number of transactions rather than the trade volume.

Another price-based yet simple measure of liquidity is the number of zero-return days, which is computed as the fraction of days with no price change in an asset, hence days with zero volume. This measure captures the trading intensity of an asset. It is also used in international studies where volume data are typically unavailable. For example, Bekaert, Harvey, and Lundblad (2007) in a cross-country study use the fraction of days with zero returns within a month to measure illiquidity.

Lesmond, Ogden, and Trzcinka (1999) develop a model-based measure using Tobin's (1958) limited dependent variable procedure to infer the cost of trade from the occurrence of zero returns. This measure, known as the Lesmond, Ogden, and Trzcinka (LOT) measure, is easy to implement because only the time series of daily security returns is needed to estimate the transaction costs for a stock. Another important advantage associated with using the LOT measure is that it captures the direct costs of trade (e.g., commissions) and also trading costs due to price impact and opportunity costs. Lesmond et al. report an 85 percent cross-sectional correlation between their estimates and realized spread plus commission estimates within New York Stock Exchange (NYSE) and American Stock Exchange (AMEX) stocks. A disadvantage of the LOT measure is that it is based on the unrealistic assumption that returns are normally distributed.

MARKET-IMPACT MEASURES

Market-impact measures are designed to address one of the shortcomings of the previously mentioned liquidity ratios, such as the ML and the HH, which do not differentiate between price changes due to anticipated versus unanticipated trade volume. The latter typically arise following firm- or market-specific new information. One way to address this issue is to estimate the intrinsic liquidity of an asset based on market-adjusted liquidity. To estimate market-adjusted liquidity requires first running the following ordinary least squares (OLS) regression of the asset's return on the return of the market as shown in Equation 8.11:

$$R_i = \alpha + \beta_i R_m + u_i, \tag{8.11}$$

where R_i is the daily return on a security i; β_i is the beta of the security; R_m is the daily return on the market index (e.g., S&P 500); and u_i are the residuals.

Next, the regression residuals from Equation 8.11 are used to estimate another OLS regression of residuals' variance on the daily percentage change in dollar volume traded (ΔV_i) in Equation 8.12:

$$\hat{u}_i^2 = \theta + \gamma \Delta u_i + \varepsilon_i. \tag{8.12}$$

The coefficient γ captures the sensitivity of asset price volatility to trade volume. A higher (smaller) γ indicates that the asset is less (more) liquid. Furthermore, the higher (smaller) γ is, the less (more) is the liquidity breadth. Achieving a more accurate estimation of market-adjusted liquidity requires using more appropriate econometric techniques such as autoregressive moving average (ARMA) or generalized autoregressive conditional heteroskedasticity (GARCH) type models (e.g., AR(1)-EGARCH (1,1)). Vector autoregressive models are other commonly used models that can be implemented to measure asset or market liquidity. The empirical macroeconomics literature often uses vector autoregressive models to assess the impact of various shocks on economic structure. Applications to liquidity estimation and market efficiency include Hasbrouck (1991a, 1991b, 1993, 2002) and Chung, Han, and Tse (1996) among others.

Kyle (1985) proposes another market-impact liquidity measure known as Kyle's lambda (λ). Kyle's model is based on asymmetric information where order flow moves prices because uninformed traders anticipate to be trading against informed traders. Kyle's lambda λ can be estimated by running the following regression (preferably using intra-day data) in Equation 8.13:

$$\Delta P_t = \alpha + \lambda V_t + u_t, \tag{8.13}$$

where ΔP_t is a change in an asset's price; V_t is signed trade size (volume); and u_t are the residuals. A buy signal is generated if the sign of V_t is positive (i.e., $\Delta P_t > 0$), and a sell signal is generated if the sign of V_t is negative (i.e., $\Delta P_t < 0$).

For virtually all the proposed measures, liquidity is negatively associated with volatility and positively correlated with size. These relationships raise some challenges when estimating the effect of liquidity. What is the "best" or most recommended proxy of liquidity? Based on recent papers comparing a large numbers of liquidity proxies, the ILLIQ measure seems to be the most appropriate for within-country analysis. In a comprehensive study examining the reliability of the widely used liquidity proxies, Goyenko, Holden, and Trzcinka (2009) demonstrate that ILLIQ is a good proxy for price impact. Dick-Nielsen, Feldhütter, and Lando (2009) reach a similar conclusion involving bonds spreads. For cross-country analysis, Lesmond (2005) finds that price-based liquidity measures proposed by Roll (1984) and Lesmond et al. (1999) outperform volume-based liquidity measures.

Is Liquidity Risk Priced?

The market liquidity literature evolved in the form of waves or streams. An early stream of papers related to market liquidity emphasizes the determinants of liquidity such as trade volume, stock price, firm size, and returns volatility (Demsetz 1968; Tinic 1972; Benston and Hagerman 1974). For instance, Tinic reports a positive association between trading activity and liquidity.

A subsequent stream of literature examines the relationship between returns and liquidity. To do so, empirical papers use different proxies for illiquidity such as bid-ask spreads, probability of informed trading (PIN), and price impacts (Amihud and Mendelson 1986; Brennan and Subrahmanyan 1996; Datar et al. 1998; Easley, Hvidkjaer, and O'Hara 2002). Overall, this stream of literature shows that expected stock returns are positively related to stock illiquidity.

Amihud and Mendelson (1986) propose a microstructure equilibrium model where transaction costs are exogenous and individual traders are risk neutral with exogenous trading horizon. Their model predicts a relationship not only between expected returns and spread but also between expected returns and turnover. They confirm their model predictions using 49 stock portfolios, sorted by their betas and transaction costs estimated using bid-ask spreads.

Eleswarapu (1997) reports a similar conclusion by testing Amihud and Mendelson's (1986) prediction using Nasdaq data over the 1973–1990 period. Moreover, Eleswarapu documents much stronger evidence for Nasdaq than for NYSE, as reported by Chen and Kan (1989) and Eleswarapu and Reinganum (1993). Eleswarapu argues that the stronger evidence on the Nasdaq is because the Nasdaq transaction costs proxy (i.e., dealers' inside spreads) is a better proxy than NYSE's proxy (i.e., quoted spread).

Using turnover as a measure of liquidity, Datar et al. (1998) find that higher turnover is associated with lower expected returns. Using a Kyle-inspired model to estimated illiquidity, Brennan and Subrahmanyam (1996) report that returns increase with the level of illiquidity. Amihud (2002) considers expected illiquidity and unexpected illiquidity. He finds that expected illiquidity is associated with higher expected return while unexpected illiquidity decreases stock prices. Acharya and Pedersen (2005) report a two-way causal relationship between liquidity risk and prices.

A third stream of literature examines the time series properties of aggregate liquidity proxies and documents the existence of predictability and commonality in liquidity (Chordia, Roll and Subrahmanyam 2001; Hasbrouck and Seppi 2001; Huberman and Halka 2001; Amihud 2002; Jones 2002). For instance, Jones shows that liquidity measures based on bid-ask spreads and turnover predict stock returns up to three years. He also documents that these liquidity measures dominate traditional predictor variables such as dividend yields, earnings yields, and riskless rates. In the same vein, Amihud shows that his illiquidity measure, denoted previously as ILLIQ, has a positive and significant effect on ex ante stock excess return.

The fourth and most recent stream of literature investigates whether the systematic, non-diversifiable component of liquidity risk is priced. Although dominated by empirical work, the bulk of this stream of literature supports the proposition that liquidity risk should be priced in financial markets for most classes of assets (Bangia, Diebold, Schuermann, and Stroughair 1999; Holmström and Tirole 2001; Pastor and Stambaugh 2003; Acharya and Pedersen 2005; Sadka 2006; Chordia, Roll, and Subrahmanyam 2005). An exception includes Piqueira (2006), who fails to find a liquidity risk premium.

Similar to the asset pricing literature explaining pricing anomalies, the limited theoretical studies justifying the existence of a liquidity premium consider illiquidity as a market friction for which investors need to be compensated (Amihud and Mendelson 1986; Acharya and Pedersen 2005). Under the assumption that transaction costs vary over time, Acharya and Pedersen propose a liquidity-adjusted capital asset pricing model (CAPM). In particular, they use a four-beta model to explain gross expected returns (i.e., the traditional market beta and three betas capturing illiquidity). Their model outperforms the standard CAPM and most of the estimated annualized premium corresponds to market illiquidity. Acharya and Pedersen also show that because of its persistence, liquidity can predict future returns. Bekaert et al. (2007) use a pricing kernel that generates a multi-factor model in which liquidity is one of the factors.

Korajczyk and Sadka (2008) employ principal components analysis to extract a common component from different proxies of liquidity, which they call "systematic liquidity." Using a Fama-French three-factor framework (Fama and French 1992), they find that systematic liquidity is priced. Other related papers examine how the heterogeneity among investors in terms of investment horizon and liquidity influence asset pricing (i.e., clientele effects). Amihud et al. (2005) and Acerbi and Scandolo (2007) contend that the existence of clientele effects plays a major role in the pricing of liquidity risk and influences the magnitude of liquidity premium. The implications of the pricing of liquidity risk include that liquidity affects portfolio decisions (Longstaff 2001) and transaction costs (Jarrow and Subramanian 1997) and that estimates of liquidity risk can predict future returns (Chordia, Roll, and Subrahmanyam 2001; Acharya and Pedersen 2005; Liu 2006). The empirical literature contains various terms of the estimates of liquidity premium. For instance, Pastor and Stambaugh (2003) document a 7.5 percent annual premium whereas Acharya and Pederson (2005) report an annual premium of 1.1 percent.

The empirical literature also examines the characteristics of the liquidity premium (Amihud 2002; Chordia, Roll, and Subrahmanyam 2000, 2001, 2002; Pastor and Stambaugh 2003; Brunnemeier and Pedersen 2005, 2009; Carlin, Lobo, and Viswanathan 2007). Pastor and Stambaugh show that liquidity risk is mostly low and steady. Studies rarely document high liquidity premiums, which are sporadic. Yet, liquidity risk can have a major impact on the stability of a financial system. In fact, market liquidity risk can cause a financial crisis, which can ultimately damage the real economy.

Studies also examine the behavior of liquidity in developing and emerging markets (Jun, Marathe, and Shawky 2003; Lesmond 2005; Bekaert et al. 2007; Silva and Chávez 2008; Hearn, Piesse, and Strange 2010). For example, Jun et al. report a positive correlation between the stock returns and liquidity premium in 27 emerging equity markets both in cross-sectional and time-series regression analyses. Lesmond examines the liquidity premium in 23 emerging markets and finds that the political regime and law classification of the economy affect it. Hearn et al. show that illiquidity in African equity markets increases during financial crisis and decreases during economic recession.

Besides the stock market, empirical studies also examine liquidity premiums across other financial assets such as covered bonds, government bonds, closed-end funds, interest rate swap contracts, and index-linked bonds (Amihud and Mendelson 1991; Boudoukh and Whitelaw 1991; Warga 1992; Kamara 1994; Elton and Green 1998;

Fleming 2002; Krishnamurthi 2002; Breger and Stovel 2004; Longstaff 2004; Manzler 2004; Koziol and Sauerbier 2007).

Summary and Conclusions

The role of market liquidity and its implications on asset prices and the financial system have generated attention since the 1980s leading to much empirical and theoretical research. Early empirical research emphasized the characteristics of market liquidity and proposed several proxies to capture them. Because of its multidimensional nature, no single measure captures all aspects of liquidity.

More recent research looks at whether liquidity risk is priced. Pricing of liquidity risk is consistent with risk-reward trade-off theory. Thus, all things equal, market participants require a higher expected return as a compensation for added liquidity risk. Asset pricing models support this theory that as an asset's market-liquidity risk increases so should its required return. The bulk of the empirical studies examining the systematic component of liquidity risk support the theoretical prediction that illiquidity is a priced risk factor.

Researchers initially documented the behavior of the liquidity premium in developed stock markets but eventually turned their attention to emerging markets and other financial assets. Although market liquidity risk tends to be low and steady, it can have serious repercussions on the stability of the financial system and can contribute to financial crises. Given its importance, market liquidity risk continues to be a subject of much debate among market participants, academicians, and policy makers.

Discussion Questions

1. Define liquidity as related to finance.
2. Discuss how funding liquidity and market liquidity are linked.
3. Discuss why measuring liquidity is difficult.
4. Identify the most reliable illiquidity measures among those used in empirical studies and justify why this is the case.

References

Acerbi, Carlo, and Giacomo Scandolo. 2007. "Liquidity Risk Theory and Coherent Measures of Risk." Working Paper, University of Verona.

Acharya, Viral V., and Lasse Heje Pedersen. 2005. "Asset Pricing with Liquidity Risk." *Journal of Financial Economics* 77:2, 375–410.

Amihud, Yakov. 2002. "Illiquidity and Stock Returns: Cross-section and Time-series Effects." *Journal of Financial Markets* 5:1, 31–56.

Amihud, Yakov, and Haim Mendelson. 1986. "Asset Pricing and the Bid-ask Spread." *Journal of Financial Economics* 17:2, 223–249.

Amihud, Yakov, and Haim Mendelson. 1991. "Liquidity, Maturity and the Yields on U.S. Government Securities." *Journal of Finance* 46:4, 1411–1426.

Amihud, Yakov, Haim Mendelson, and Lasse Heje Pedersen. 2005. "Liquidity and Asset Prices." *Foundations and Trends in Finance* 1:4, 269–364.

Baker, H. Kent. 1996. "Trading Location and Liquidity: An Analysis of U.S. Dealer and Agency Markets for Common Stocks." *Financial Markets, Institutions & Instruments* 5:4, 1–51.

Baker, H. Kent, and Halil Kiymaz, eds. 2013. *Market Microstructure in Emerging and Developed Markets.* Hoboken, NJ: John Wiley & Sons.

Bangia, Anil, Francis X. Diebold, Til Schuermann, and John D. Stroughair. 1999. "Modeling Liquidity Risk, with Implications for Traditional Market Risk Measurement and Management." Working Paper, The Wharton School, University of Pennsylvania.

Bekaert, Geert, Campbell R. Harvey, and Christian Lundblad. 2007. "Liquidity and Expected Returns: Lessons from Emerging Markets." *Review of Financial Studies* 20:6, 1783–1831.

Benston, George J., and Robert L. Hagerman. 1974. "Determinants of Bid-asked Spreads in the Over-the-Counter Market." *Journal of Financial Economics* 1:4, 353–364.

Boudoukh, Jacob, and Robert F. Whitelaw. 1991. "The Benchmark Effect in the Japanese Government Bond Market." *Journal of Fixed Income* 1:2, 52–59.

Breger, Ludovic, and Darren Stovel. 2004. "Agency Ratings in the Pfandbrief Market." *Journal of Portfolio Management* 30:4, 239–243.

Brennan, Michael J., and Avanidhar Subrahmanyam. 1996. "Market Microstructure and Asset Pricing: On the Compensation for Illiquidity in Stock Returns." *Journal of Financial Economics* 41:3, 441–464.

Brunnermeier, Markus K., and Lasse Heje Pedersen. 2005. "Predatory Trading." *Journal of Finance* 60:4, 1825–1863.

Brunnermeier, Markus K., and Lasse Heje Pedersen. 2009. "Market Liquidity and Funding Liquidity." *Review of Financial Studies* 22:6, 2201–2238.

Carlin, Bruce Ian, Miguel Sousa Lobo, and S. Viswanathan. 2007. "Episodic Liquidity Crises: Cooperative and Predatory Trading." *Journal of Finance* 62:5, 2235–2274.

Chen, Nai-Fu, and Raymond Kan. 1989. "Expected Return and the Bid-ask Spread." Working Paper, University of Chicago.

Chen, Willa W., and Rohit S. Deo. 2006. "The Variance Ratio Statistic at Large Horizons." *Econometric Theory* 22:2, 206–234.

Choi, In. 1999. "Testing the Random Walk Hypothesis for Real Exchange Rates." *Journal of Applied Econometrics* 14:3, 293–308.

Chordia, Tarun, Richard Roll, and Avanidhar Subrahmanyam. 2000. "Commonality in Liquidity." *Journal of Financial Economics* 56:1, 3–28.

Chordia, Tarun, Richard Roll, and Avanidhar Subrahmanyam. 2001. "Market Liquidity and Trading Activity." *Journal of Finance* 56:2, 501–530.

Chordia, Tarun, Richard Roll, and Avanidhar Subrahmanyam. 2002. "Order Imbalance, Liquidity, and Market Returns." *Journal of Financial Economics* 65:1, 111–130.

Chordia, Tarun, Richard Roll, and Avanidhar Subrahmanyam. 2005. "An Empirical Analysis of Stock and Bond Market Liquidity." *Review of Financial Studies* 18:1, 85–129.

Chung, Marcus M.C., K. C. Han, and Maurice K. S. Tse. 1996. "Interrelationship among the Price Indexes of the NYSE, AMEX, and OTC." *International Review of Economics and Finance* 5:1, 63–75.

Datar, Vinay T., Narayan Y. Naik, and Robert Radcliffe. 1998. "Liquidity and Stock Returns: An Alternative Test." *Journal of Financial Markets* 1:2, 205–219.

Demsetz, Harold. 1968. "The Cost of Transacting." *Quarterly Journal of Economics* 82:1, 35–53.

Dick-Nielsen, Jens, Peter Feldhütter, and David Lando. 2009. "Corporate Bond Liquidity before and after the Onset of the Subprime Crisis." *Journal of Financial Economics* 103:3, 471–492.

Easley, David, and Maureen O'Hara 2004. "Information and the Cost of Capital." *Journal of Finance* 59:4, 1553–1583.

Easley, David, Soren Hvidkjaer, and Maureen O'Hara 2002. "Is Information Risk a Determinant of Asset Returns?" *Journal of Finance* 57:5, 2185–2221.

Eleswarapu, Venkat R. 1997. "Cost of Transacting and Expected Returns in the Nasdaq Market." *Journal of Finance* 52:5, 2113–2127.

Eleswarapu, Venkat R., and Marc R. Reinganum. 1993. "The Seasonal Behavior of the Liquidity Premium in Asset Pricing." *Journal of Financial Economics* 34:3, 373–386.

Elton, Edwin J., and Clifton T. Green. 1998. "Tax and Liquidity Effects in Pricing of Government Bonds." *Journal of Finance* 53:5, 1533–1562.

Fama, Eugene F., and Kenneth R. French. 1992. "The Cross-Section of Expected Stock Returns." *Journal of Finance* 47:2, 427–465.

Fernandez, Frank A. 1999. "Liquidity Risk: New Approaches to Measurement and Monitoring." Working Paper, Securities Industry Association, New York.

Fleming, Michael J. 2002. "Are Larger Treasury Issues More Liquid? Evidence from Bill Reopenings." *Journal of Money, Credit and Banking* 34:3, 707–735.

Gabrielsen, Ros, Massimiliano Marzo, and Paolo Zagaglia. 2011. "Measuring Market Liquidity: An Introductory Survey." Working Paper, Rimini Centre for Economic Analysis.

Goyenko, Ruslan Y., Craig W. Holden, and Charles A. Trzcinka. 2009. "Do Liquidity Measures Measure Liquidity?" *Journal of Financial Economics* 92:2, 153–181.

Harris, Lawrence. 1990. "Statistical Properties of the Roll Serial Covariance Bid/Ask Spread Estimator." *Journal of Finance* 45:2, 568–579.

Hasbrouck, Joel. 1991a. "The Summary Informativeness of Stock Trades: An Econometric Analysis." *Review of Financial Studies* 4:3, 571–595.

Hasbrouck, Joel. 1991b. "Measuring the Information Content of Stock Trades." *Journal of Finance* 46:1, 179–207.

Hasbrouck, Joel. 1993. "Assessing the Quality of a Security Market: A New Approach to Transaction-Cost Measurement." *Review of Financial Studies* 6:1,192–212.

Hasbrouck, Joel. 2002. "Stalking the 'Efficient Price' in Market Microstructure Specifications: An Overview." *Journal of Financial Markets* 5:3, 329–339.

Hasbrouck, Joel. 2003. "Intraday Price Formation in U.S. Equity Index Markets." *Journal of Finance* 58:6, 2375–2400.

Hasbrouck, Joel, and Robert A. Schwartz. 1988. "Liquidity and Execution Costs in Equity Markets." *Journal of Portfolio Management* 14:3, 10–16.

Hasbrouck, Joel, and Duane J. Seppi. 2001. "Common Factors in Prices, Order Flows and Liquidity." *Journal of Financial Economics* 59:3, 383–411.

Hearn, Bruce, Jenifer Piesse, and Roger Strange. 2010. "Market Liquidity and Stock Size Premia in Emerging Financial Markets: The Implications for Foreign Investment." *International Business Review* 19:5, 489–501.

Holmström, Bengt, and Jean Tirole. 2001. "LAPM: A Liquidity-Based Asset Pricing Model." *Journal of Finance* 56:5, 1837–1867.

Huberman, Gur, and Dominika Halka. 2001. "Systematic Liquidity." *Journal of Financial Research* 24:2, 161–178.

Hui, Baldwin, and Barbara Heubel. 1984. "Comparative Liquidity Advantages among Major U. S. Stock Markets." Working Paper, DRI Financial Information Group Study Series.

Ito, Takatoshi, Richard K. Lyons, and Michael T. Melvin. 1998. "Is There Private Information in the FX Market? The Tokyo Experiment." *Journal of Finance* 53:3, 1111–1130.

Jarrow, Robert A., and Ajay Subramanian. 1997. "Mopping up Liquidity." *Risk* 10:10, 170–173.

Jones, Charles. 2002. "A Century of Stock Market Liquidity and Trading Costs." Working Paper, Columbia University.

Jun, Sang-Gyung, Achla Marathe, and Hany A. Shawky. 2003. "Liquidity and Stock Returns in Emerging Equity Markets." *Emerging Markets Review* 4:1, 1–24.

Kamara, Avraham. 1994. "Liquidity, Taxes, and Short-term Treasury Yields." *Journal of Financial and Quantitative Analysis* 29:3, 403–416.

Korajczyk, Robert A., and Ronnie Sadka. 2008. "Pricing the Commonality across Alternative Measures of Liquidity." *Journal of Financial Economics* 87:1, 45–72.

Koziol, Christian, and Peter Sauerbier. 2007. "Valuation of Bond Illiquidity: An Option-theoretical Approach." *Journal of Fixed Income* 16:4, 81–107.

Krishnamurthi, Arvind. 2002. "The Bond/old-bond Spread." *Journal of Financial Economics* 66:2, 463–506.

Kyle, Albert S. 1985. "Continuous Auctions and Insider Trading." *Econometrica* 53:6, 1315–1335.

Lesmond, David A. 2005. "Liquidity of Emerging Markets." *Journal of Financial Economics* 77:2, 411–452.

Lesmond, David A., Joseph P. Ogden, and Charles Trzcinka. 1999. "A New Estimate of Transaction Costs." *Review of Financial Studies* 12:5, 1113–1141.

Liu, Weimin. 2006. "A Liquidity-Augmented Capital Asset Pricing Model." *Journal of Financial Economics* 82:3, 631–671.

Longstaff, Francis A. 2001. "Optimal Portfolio Choice and the Valuation of Illiquid Securities." *Review of Financial Studies* 14:2, 407–431.

Longstaff, Francis A. 2004. "The Flight-to-Liquidity Premium in U.S. Treasury Bond Prices." *Journal of Business* 77:3, 511–526.

Madhavan, Ananth. 2000. "Market Microstructure: A Survey." *Journal of Financial Markets* 3:3, 205–258.

Manzler, David. 2004. "Liquidity, Liquidity Risk and the Closed-End Fund Discount." Working Paper, University of Cincinnati.

Marsh, Terry, and Kevin Rock. 1986. "Exchange Listing and Liquidity: A Comparison of the American Stock Exchange with the NASDAQ National Market System." American Stock Exchange Transactions Data Research Project, American Stock Exchange.

Martin, Peter. 1975. "Analysis of the Impact of Competitive Rates on the Liquidity of NYSE Stocks." Economic Staff Paper, Securities and Exchange Commission.

O'Hara, Maureen. 1995. *Market Microstructure Theory.* Cambridge, MA. Blackwell Publishers.

Pastor, Lubos, and Robert F. Stambaugh. 2003. "Liquidity Risk and Expected Stock Returns." *Journal of Political Economy* 111:3, 642–685.

Piqueira, Natalia. 2006. "Trading Activity, Illiquidity Costs and Stock Returns." Working Paper, University of Houston.

Roll, Richard. 1984. "A Simple Implicit Measure of the Effective Bid-Ask Spread in an Efficient Market." *Journal of Finance* 39:4, 1127–1139.

Sadka, Ronnie. 2006. "Momentum and Post-Earnings-Announcement Drift Anomalies: The Role of Liquidity Risk." *Journal of Financial Economics* 80:2, 309–349.

Silva, Ana Cristina, and Gonzalo A. Chávez. 2008. "Cross-Listing and Liquidity in Emerging Market Stocks." *Journal of Banking and Finance* 32:3, 420–433.

Smith, Graham, and Hyun-Jung Ryoo. 2003. "Variance Ratio Tests of the Random Walk Hypothesis for European Emerging Stock Markets." *European Journal of Finance* 9:3, 290–300.

Tinic, Seha M. 1972. "The Economics of Liquidity Services." *Quarterly Journal of Economics* 86:1, 79–93.

Tobin, James. 1958. "Estimation of Relationships for Limited Dependent Variables." *Econometrica* 26:1, 24–36.

Von Wyss, Rico. 2004. "Measuring and Predicting Liquidity in the Stock Market." Doctoral Dissertation, St. Gallen University.

Warga, Arthur. 1992. "Bond Returns, Liquidity, and Missing Data." *Journal of Financial and Quantitative Analysis* 27:4, 605–617.

Whang, Yoon-Jae, and Jinho Kim. 2003. "A Multiple Variance Ratio Test Using Subsampling." *Economics Letters* 79:2, 225–230.

9

Country Risk

ASWATH DAMODARAN

Professor of Finance, Stern School of Business, New York University

Introduction

With globalization, investors and companies are facing questions as they shift from the local markets to foreign ones. Are investments in different countries exposed to different amounts of risk? Is this risk diversifiable in global portfolios? Should companies demand higher returns in some countries, for similar investments, than in others? This chapter proposes to answer all three questions. The first part begins by taking a big picture view of country risk, its sources, and its consequences for investors, companies, and governments. It then moves on to assess the history of government defaults over time and evaluates sovereign ratings and credit default swaps (CDSs) as measures of sovereign default risk. The third part extends the analysis to investigate investing in equities in different countries by exploring whether equity risk premiums (ERPs) should vary across countries, and if they do, how best to estimate these premiums. The final part examines the implications of differences in ERPs across countries for the valuation of companies.

As companies and investors globalize, they are increasingly faced with risk estimation questions associated with this globalization. This chapter begins with an overview of overall country risk, its sources, and measures. It continues with a discussion of sovereign default risk and examines sovereign ratings and CDSs as measures of that risk. The chapter extends that discussion to country risk from the perspective of equity investors, by exploring ERPs for different countries and consequences for valuation. The final section contends that a company's exposure to country risk should not be determined by where it is incorporated but by where the company operates.

Country Risk

Are investors exposed to more risk when they invest in some countries than in others? The answer is obviously affirmative, but analyzing this risk requires a closer look at why risk varies across countries. This section breaks down country risk into its constituent parts and looks at services that try to measure this risk.

SOURCES OF COUNTRY RISK

Accepting the proposition that risk exposure can vary across countries, the next step is to investigate the sources that causes variation.

- *Life cycle.* In company valuation, where a company is in its life cycle can affect its exposure to risk. Young, growth companies are more exposed to risk because they have limited resources to overcome setbacks and are far more dependent on the macro environment staying stable to succeed. The same factors affect countries in the life cycle, with countries that are in early growth, with few established business and small markets being more exposed to risk than larger, more mature countries. Global market and economic shocks create much more damage in emerging markets than in developed markets.
- *Political risk.* Differences in political risk, a category including everything from how the government is structured to how smoothly political power is transferred in the country, can affect the risk of investments in that country. Thus, investments in countries that are more exposed to corruption, physical violence, or nationalization/expropriation by governments will also have more risk.
- *Legal system.* Some variation can be traced to the legal system in a country in terms of both structure (the protection of property rights) and efficiency (the speed with which legal disputes are resolved). The weaker the protection for property rights and the less efficient the legal system in enforcing those rights, the greater is the risk in investments in that country.
- *Economic structure.* Some countries are dependent upon a specific commodity, product, or service for their economic success. Such dependencies can create additional risk for investors and businesses because a drop in the commodity's price or demand for the product/service can create severe economic pain that spreads well beyond the companies that produce that product.

MEASURING COUNTRY RISK

As the discussion in the previous section indicates, country risk can come from many different sources. Although risk measures are available on each dimension, having composite measures of risk that incorporate all types of country risk would be useful. These composite measures should incorporate all dimensions of risk and allow for easy comparisons across countries.

Several services attempt to measure country risk but not always from the same perspective or for the same audience. For instance, Political Risk Services (PRS) provides numerical measures of country risk for more than a 100 countries. The service is commercial and PRS makes the scores available only to paying members. PRS uses 22 variables to measure risk in countries on three dimensions: political, financial, and economic. It provides country risk scores on each dimension separately as well as a composite score for the country. The scores range from 0 to 100, with higher scores (80 to 100) indicating lower risk and lower scores (0 to 20) indicating higher risk. Besides providing current assessments, PRS provides forecasts of country risk scores for the countries that it follows.

Alternatively, the World Bank provides a collected resource base that draws together risk measures from different services into one database of governance indicators (see http://data.worldbank.org/data-catalog/worldwide-governance-indicators). The World Bank provides six indicators for 215 countries measuring corruption, government effectiveness, political stability, regulatory quality, rule of law, and voice/accountability, with a scaling around zero, with negative numbers indicating more risk and positive numbers less risk.

The services that measure country risk with scores provide some valuable information about risk variations across countries, but how useful these measures are for investors and businesses interested in investing in emerging markets is unclear for three reasons. First, many of the entities that develop the methodologies and convert them into scores are not business entities and consider risks that may have little relevance for businesses. Second, the scores are not standardized and each service uses its own protocol. Thus, higher scores go with lower risk with the PRS risk measure but the World Bank's measures of risk are scaled around zero, with more negative numbers indicating higher risk. Third, even using the numbers from one service, the country risk scores are more useful for ranking the countries than for measuring relative risk.

Sovereign Default Risk

The most direct measure of country risk is an assessment of default risk when lending to the government of that country. This risk, termed *sovereign default risk*, has a long measurement history going back in history. This section begins by examining the history of sovereign defaults, both in foreign currency and local currency terms, and follows up by looking at measures of sovereign default risk, ranging from sovereign ratings to market-based measures.

A HISTORY OF SOVEREIGN DEFAULTS

Across time, many governments have been dependent on debt borrowed from other countries or banks in those countries, usually denominated in a foreign currency. A large proportion of sovereign defaults have occurred with this type of sovereign borrowing, when the borrowing country has insufficient amounts of the foreign currency to meet its obligations, without the recourse of being able to print money in that currency. Between 2000 and 2010, sovereign defaults have mostly been on foreign currency debt, starting with a relatively small default by Ukraine in January 2000, followed by the largest sovereign default of the decade with Argentina in November 2001. Going back further in time, sovereign defaults have occurred frequently over the last two centuries, although the defaults have been bunched up in eight sub-periods. Hatchondo, Martinez, and Sapriza (2007) summarize defaults over time for most countries in Europe and Latin America.

Although rationalizing how countries can default on foreign currency debt is easy, explaining why they default on local currency debt is more difficult. Theoretically, countries should be able to print more of the local currency to meet their obligations and thus should never default. Three reasons help to explain why local currency default occurs and will continue to occur. First, before 1971, some countries followed the gold standard, restricting their capacity to print currency. Second, for countries that adopt a shared currency such as the Euro, the trade-off is that they lose the capacity to print currency at will. Third, printing more currency to pay bloated debt obligations has implications. It debases and devalues the currency and causes inflation to increase exponentially, which in turn can cause the real economy to shrink. Investors abandon financial assets and markets and move to real assets such as real estate and gold and firms shift from real investments to financial speculation. Countries therefore have to evaluate the trade-off between which action (default or currency debasement) has lower long-term costs and to pick one. Some choose default as the less costly option.

CONSEQUENCES OF DEFAULT

What happens when a government defaults? In the eighteenth century, shows of military force often followed government defaults. In the twentieth century, sovereign defaults have had both economic and political consequences, besides the obvious implication that lenders to that government lose some or much of what is owed to them.

- *Reputation loss.* A government that defaults is tagged with the "deadbeat" label for years after the event, which increases the difficultly of raising financing in future rounds.
- *Capital market turmoil.* Defaulting on sovereign debt has repercussions for all capital markets in the defaulting country. Investors withdraw from equity and bond markets increasing the difficulty for private enterprises to raise funds for projects.
- *Real output.* The uncertainty created by sovereign default also has ripple effects on real investment and consumption. In general, economic recessions follow sovereign defaults as consumers hold back on spending and firms are reluctant to commit resources to long-term investments.
- *Political instability.* Default can also strike a blow to the national psyche, which in turn can put the leadership class at risk. The wave of defaults that swept through Europe in the 1920s, with Germany, Austria, Hungary, and Italy all falling victim, allowed for the rise of the Nazis and set the stage for World War II. In Latin America, defaults and coups have gone hand in hand for much of the last two centuries.

In summary, default is costly and countries do not and should not take the possibility of default lightly. Default is particularly expensive when it leads to banking crises and currency devaluations. The former have a long-standing impact on the capacity of firms to fund their investments, whereas the latter create political and institutional instability that lasts for long periods.

MEASURING SOVEREIGN DEFAULT RISK

If governments can default, measures of sovereign default risk are needed not only to set interest rates on sovereign bonds and loans but also to price all other assets. This section provides a first look at the determinants and measurements of sovereign default risk.

Factors Determining Sovereign Default Risk

Governments, individuals, and firms default for similar reasons. In good times, they borrow far more than they can afford, given their tax revenues, and then find themselves unable to meet their debt obligations during downturns. The factors determining sovereign default risk are not very different from those that determine corporate default risk.

- *Degree of indebtedness.* The most logical place to start assessing default risk is by investigating how much a sovereign entity owes not only to foreign banks/investors but also to its own citizens in both debt and pension/healthcare claims. Because countries with larger economies can borrow more money, in absolute terms, the debt owed is usually scaled to the gross domestic product (GDP) of the country.
- *Revenues/Inflows to government.* Government revenues usually come from tax receipts, which in turn are a function of both the tax code and the efficiency with which the government collects taxes. Holding all else constant, access to a larger tax base and a more efficient tax system should increase potential tax revenues, which the government can in turn use to meet its debt obligations.
- *Stability of revenues.* Countries with more stable revenue streams should face less default risk, other factors remaining equal, than countries with volatile revenues. But what drives revenue stability? Because revenues come from taxing income and consumption in the nation's economy, countries with more diversified economies should have more stable tax revenues than countries that are dependent on one or a few sectors or on a volatile tax base for their prosperity.
- *Political risk.* Given that sovereign default often exposes the political leadership to pressure, autocracies that worry less about political backlash exists may be more likely to default than democracies. Given that the alternative to default is printing more money, the independence and power of the central bank will also affect assessments of default risk.
- *Implicit backing from other entities.* When Greece, Portugal, and Spain entered the European Union (EU), investors, analysts, and ratings agencies reduced their assessments of default risk in these countries. Implicitly, they were assuming that the stronger EU countries, especially, Germany, France, and the Scandinavian countries, would protect the weaker countries from defaulting.

In summary, a full assessment of default risk in a sovereign entity requires the assessor to go beyond the numbers and understand how the country's economy works, the strength of its tax system, and the trustworthiness of its governing institutions.

Sovereign Ratings

Few investors have the resources or the time to dedicate to understanding foreign countries. Not surprisingly, third parties have stepped into the breach with their assessments of sovereign default risk. Of these third party assessors, credit ratings agencies (CRAs) emerged with the biggest advantages because of their experience in assessing default risk for corporations and the familiarity that investors have with their rating systems. Moody's, Standard and Poor's (S&P's), and Fitch have been rating corporate bond offerings since the early part of the twentieth century. Since 1994, the number of countries with sovereign ratings has surged, just as the market for sovereign bonds has expanded. In 2013, Moody's, S&P's, and Fitch had ratings available for more than a 100 countries apiece.

In addition to more countries being rated, the ratings themselves have become comprehensive. Moody's and S&P's now provide two ratings for each country: a local currency rating for domestic currency debt/bonds and a foreign currency rating for government borrowings in a foreign currency. For the most part, local currency ratings are as high as or higher than the foreign currency rating for the obvious reason that governments have more power to print more of their own currency.

Sovereign ratings can change over time but they do so slowly. The best measure of sovereign ratings changes is a ratings transition matrix, measuring the probability of a ratings change in a time period. Using Fitch's sovereign ratings to illustrate our point, Table 9.1 summarizes the annual probability of ratings transitions, by rating, from 1995 to 2008.

Table 9.1 provides evidence on how little sovereign ratings change on an annual basis, especially for higher rated countries. An AAA rated sovereign has a 99.42 percent chance of remaining AAA rated the next year. By contrast, a BBB rated sovereign has an 8.11 percent chance of being upgraded, an 87.84 percent chance of remaining unchanged, and a 4.06 percent chance of being downgraded. The ratings transition tables at Moody's and S&P's tell the same story of ratings stickiness. As discussed later in this chapter, one critique of sovereign ratings is that sovereign ratings do not change quickly enough to alert investors of imminent danger. Some evidence in S&P's latest update on transition probabilities suggests that sovereign ratings have become more volatile, with BBB rated countries showing only a 57.1 percent likelihood of staying with the same rating from 2010 to 2012 (Standard & Poor's 2013).

The sales pitch from CRAs for sovereign ratings is that they are effective measures of default risk in bonds (or loans) issued by that sovereign. But do they work as advertised? Each CRA goes to great pains to argue that notwithstanding errors on some countries, a high correlation exists between sovereign ratings and sovereign defaults. The CRAs

Table 9.1 **Fitch Sovereign Transition Rates across the Major Rating Categories: 1995 to 2008**

Rating	AAA (%)	AA (%)	B (%)	BB (%)	BB (%)	B (%)	CCC to C (%)	D (%)	Total (%)
AAA	99.42	0.58	0.00	0.00	0.00	0.00	0.00	0.00	100.00
AA	4.12	94.12	1.18	0.00	0.00	0.59	0.00	0.00	100.00
A	0.00	3.55	92.91	3.55	0.00	0.00	0.00	0.00	100.00
BBB	0.00	0.00	8.11	87.84	3.38	0.68	0.00	0.00	100.00
BB	0.00	0.00	0.00	9.04	83.51	5.85	0.00	1.60	100.00
B	0.00	0.00	0.00	0.00	12.12	84.09	3.03	0.76	100.00
CCC to C	0.00	0.00	0.00	0.00	0.00	23.09	53.85	23.09	100.00

Note: This table shows the annual probability of ratings transitions in percent, by rating, from 1995 to 2008 as provided by Fitch. The evidence shows how little sovereign ratings change on an annual basis, especially for higher rated countries.

provide evidence to back up their claims with tables that show higher default rates over time for lower ratings countries.

Notwithstanding this overall track record of success, critics note that CRAs have failed investors on the following counts:

- *Upward biased ratings.* Critics accuse CRAs of being far too optimistic in their assessments of both corporate and sovereign ratings. While some offer the conflict of interest of having issuers pay for the rating as the rationale for the upward bias in corporate ratings, that argument does not hold up for sovereign ratings because the issuing governments do not pay ratings agencies.
- *Herd behavior.* When a CRA lowers or raises a sovereign rating, other CRAs often follow suit. This herd behavior reduces the value of having three separate ratings agencies because their assessments of sovereign risk no longer appear independent.
- *Too little, too late.* To price sovereign bonds or set interest rates on sovereign loans, investors (banks) need assessments of default risk that are updated and timely. Some contend that CRAs take too long to change ratings and that these changes happen too late to protect investors from a crisis.
- *Vicious cycle.* Once a market is in crisis, the perception is that CRAs sometimes over react and lower ratings too much, thus creating a feedback effect that makes the crisis worse.

Overall, some maintain that sovereign ratings provide lagged and sometimes flawed measures of sovereign default risk.

Market Interest Rates

The growth of the sovereign ratings business reflected the growth in the sovereign bond market in the 1980s and 1990s. As more countries have shifted from bank loans to bonds, the market prices commanded by these bonds and the resulting interest rates have yielded an alternate measure of sovereign default risk, continuously updated in financial markets. When a government issues bonds denominated in a foreign currency, the interest rate on the bond can be compared to a rate on a riskless investment in that currency to get a market measure of the default spread for that country.

To illustrate, the Brazilian government had a 10-year dollar denominated bond outstanding in January 2013, with a market interest rate of 2.50 percent. At the same time, the 10-year U.S. Treasury bond rate was 1.76 percent. Assuming that the U.S. Treasury is default free, the difference between the two rates (0.74 percent) can be viewed as the market's assessment of the default spread for Brazil. Table 9.2 summarizes interest rates and default spreads for four Latin American countries in January 2013, using dollar denominated bonds issued by these countries as well as the sovereign foreign currency ratings from Moody's at the time.

Despite a strong correlation between sovereign ratings and market default spreads, several advantages exist to using the default spreads. First, the market differentiation for risk is more granular than the ratings agencies. Thus, Peru and Brazil have the same Moody's rating (Baa2) but the market sees more default risk in Peru. Second, the market-based spreads are more dynamic than ratings with changes occurring as events unfold.

Table 9.2 **Default Spreads on Dollar Denominated Bonds in Latin America in January 2013**

Country	Moody's Rating	Interest Rate on $ Denominated 10-Year Bond (%)	10-Year U.S. Treasury Bond Rate (%)	Default Spread (%)
Mexico	Baa1	2.38	1.76	0.62
Brazil	Baa2	2.50	1.76	0.74
Colombia	Baa3	3.12	1.76	1.36
Peru	Baa2	3.05	1.76	1.29

Note: This table shows current yields to maturity and spreads in percent on 10-year bonds in Mexico, Brazil, Colombia, and Peru.

To use market-based default spreads as a measure of country default risk requires a default free security in the currency in which the bonds are issued. Local currency bonds issued by governments cannot be compared because the differences in rates can be due to differences in expected inflation. Even with dollar-denominated bonds, the assumption that the U.S. Treasury bond rate is default free allows backing out default spreads from the interest rates.

One advantage that market spreads have over ratings is that they can adjust quickly to information. As a consequence, they provide earlier signals of imminent danger and default than ratings agencies do. However, market-based default measures carry their own costs. They tend to be far more volatile than ratings and can be affected by variables that have nothing to do with default. Liquidity and investor demand can sometimes cause shifts in spreads that have little or nothing to do with default risk.

In general, the sovereign bond market leads ratings agencies, with default spreads usually climbing ahead of a rating downgrade and dropping before an upgrade. Notwithstanding the lead-lag relationship, a change in sovereign ratings is still an informational event that creates a price impact at the time that it occurs. In summary, concluding that sovereign ratings are useless would be a mistake because sovereign bond markets seem to draw on ratings and changes in these ratings when pricing bonds.

Credit Default Swaps

The credit default swap (CDS) market allows investors to buy protection against default in a security. The buyer of a CDS on a specific bond makes payments of the "spread" each period to the seller of the CDS. The payment is specified as a percentage (spread) of the notional or face value of the bond being insured. In return, the seller agrees to make the buyer whole if the issuer of the bond (reference entity) fails to pay, restructures, or goes bankrupt (credit event), by either physically delivering the defaulted bond and getting par value for it or by settling or paying the CDS buyer the difference between the par value and the market price. In effect, the buyer of the CDS is protected from losses arising from credit events over the life of the CDS.

Two points are worth emphasizing about a CDS that may undercut the protection against default that it is designed to offer. First, a credit event triggers the protection against failure. If no credit event occurs and the market price of the bond collapses, the buyer will not be compensated. Second, the guarantee is only as good as the credit standing of the seller of the CDS. If the seller defaults, the insurance guarantee will fail. On the other side of the transaction, the buyer may default on the spread payments that he has contractually agreed to make.

Assuming away counterparty risk and liquidity effects, the prices that investors set for credit default swaps should provide updated measures of default risk in the reference entity. In contrast to ratings that get updated infrequently, CDS prices should adjust to reflect current information on default risk. To illustrate this point, a month-by-month analysis of Greece from 2006 to 2010 show stagnant ratings for most of the period before moving late in 2009 and 2010 when Greece was downgraded. However, the CDS spread and default spreads for Greece moved higher much earlier.

CDS spreads are more timely and dynamic than sovereign ratings and reflect changes in the issuing entities. Yet, the basic issue remains. Studies that explore whether changes in CDS spreads are better predictors of future default risk than sovereign ratings find that changes in CDS spreads lead changes in the sovereign bond yields and in sovereign ratings (Ismailescu and Kazemi 2010).

Several inherent limitations exist with using CDS prices as predictors of country default risk. First, the exposure to counterparty and liquidity risk, endemic to the CDS market, can cause changes in CDS prices that have little to do with default risk. Thus, a large portion of the surge in CDS prices during the last quarter of 2008 can be traced to the failure of Lehman Brothers and the subsequent surge in concerns about counterparty risk. Second, the narrowness of the CDS market can make individual CDS susceptible to illiquidity problems, with a concurrent effect on prices. Notwithstanding these limitations, changes in CDS prices supply important information about shifts in default risk in entities. In summary, the current evidence shows that changes in CDS prices provide information, albeit noisy, of changes in default risk. However, little evidence indicates that it is superior to market default spreads obtained from government bonds in assessing this risk.

Country Equity Risk

Sovereign default risk is a relevant measure of risk for those investing in sovereign debt or bonds of a country. But is this true for an investor or a business that is considering investing in equity in the same country? This section begins by examining whether adjustments should be made to the equity risk premium (ERP) in different countries for variations in country risk and then turns to examining measures of country equity risk.

SHOULD THERE BE A COUNTRY ERP?

Is investing in a stock in an emerging market such as Malaysian or Brazilian more risky than investing in the United States? The answer to most seems to be obviously affirmative, with the solution being to use higher ERPs when investing in riskier emerging markets. Critics offer three distinct and different arguments against this practice.

- *Country risk is diversifiable.* Country risk should not be priced if companies and more importantly investors in these companies can diversify it away. This argument is predicated on two assumptions: low or no correlation exists across country returns and marginal investors who hold large positions in a company and trade these positions are globally diversified. Although improved market access, lower transactions costs, and new forms of securities have improved the odds for the latter, those same developments ironically have increased correlation across markets. The evidence indicates that correlation across markets has risen over time (Yang, Tapon, and Sun 2006) and has been higher during periods of extreme stress or high volatility (Ball and Torous 2000).

- *Beta captures country risk.* This statement assumes that all assets, no matter where they are traded, should face the same global ERP, with differences in risk captured by differences in betas. Although the argument is reasonable, it flounders in practice, partly because betas do not seem capable of carrying the weight of measuring country risk. If betas are measured against local indices, as many estimation services do, the average beta within each market has to be one. Thus, having betas capture country risk would be mathematically impossible. If betas are estimated against a global equity index, such as the Morgan Stanley Capital Index (MSCI), a possibility exists that betas could capture country risk, but little evidence supports that they do in practice. Because the global equity indices are market weighted, companies in developed markets often have higher betas, whereas those in small, risky emerging markets report low betas. Using these betas with a global ERP will lead to lower costs of equity for emerging market companies than developed market companies. Although practitioners can use creative fixes to get around this problem, the adjustments seem to be based on little more than the desire to end up with higher expected returns for emerging market companies.

- *Country risk should be reflected in cash flows, not discount rates.* The essence of this argument is that country risk and its consequences are better reflected in the cash flows than in the discount rate. Proponents of this point of view contend that bringing in the likelihood of negative events such as political chaos, nationalization, and economic meltdowns into the expected cash flows effectively adjusts the riskiness of cash flows, thus eliminating the need for adjusting the discount rate. This assumption is false. To illustrate why, consider a simple example in which a company is considering making the same type of investment in two countries. For simplicity, assume that the investment is expected to deliver $90, with certainty in country 1 (a mature market); it is expected to generate $100 with 90 percent probability in country 2 (an emerging market) but with a 10 percent chance that disaster will strike (and the cash flow will be $0). The expected cash flow is $90 on both investments, but only a risk-neutral investor would be indifferent between the two. A risk-averse investor would prefer the investment in the mature market over the emerging market investment and would demand a premium for investing in the emerging market. To adjust cash flows for risk requires computing certainty equivalents for the expected cash flows, which would require exactly the same information and adjustment process needed to adjust discount rates.

Several elements in each of the arguments are persuasive but none of them is persuasive enough. First, investors have become more globally diversified over the last three decades and portions of country risk can therefore be diversified in their portfolios. However, the home bias remaining in investor portfolios exposes investors disproportionately to home country risk, and the increase in correlation across markets has made a portion of country risk into non-diversifiable or market risk. Second, as stocks are traded in multiple markets and in many currencies, estimating global betas becomes more meaningful. Yet, these betas cannot carry the burden of capturing country risk in addition to all other macro risk exposures. Finally, certain types of country risk are better embedded in the cash flows than in the risk premium or discount rates. In particular, risks that are discrete and isolated to individual countries should be incorporated into probabilities and expected cash flows. Good examples would be risks associated with nationalization or related to acts of God such as hurricanes and earthquakes.

After diversifying away the portion of country risk, estimating a meaningful global beta, and incorporating discrete risks into the expected cash flows, investors are still faced with residual country risk that has only one place to go: the ERP. Evidence supports the proposition that investors should incorporate additional country risk into ERP estimates in riskier market. For example, Fernandez, Aguirreamalloa, and Avendano (2013), who survey academics, analysts, and companies in 82 countries on ERPs, report that average premiums vary widely across markets and are higher for riskier emerging markets. Table 9.3 shows the results of this survey. Again, this finding does not conclusively prove that country risk commands a premium, but it does indicate that those who conduct valuations in these countries seem to act as if it does.

Ultimately, the question of whether country risk matters and should affect the ERP is an empirical one, not a theoretical one, and for the moment, at least, the evidence seems to suggest that investors should incorporate country risk into their discount rates. This practice could change with continued movement toward a global economy with globally diversified investors and a global equity market.

Table 9.3 **Survey Estimates of ERP, by Region in 2012**

Area	Number	Average ERP (%)	Median ERP (%)
Africa	9	8.62	8.59
Developed markets	20	6.06	6.01
Eastern Europe	12	7.63	7.96
Emerging Asia	13	7.60	7.42
EU troubled	5	7.16	6.81
Latin America	15	9.67	9.49
Middle East	8	8.43	8.88
Total	82	7.77	7.76

Note: This table presents the results of a 2012 survey of academics, analysts, and companies in 82 countries on ERPs. It shows that average premiums vary widely across markets and are higher for riskier emerging markets.

Source: Fernandez, Aguirreamalloa, and Avendano 2013.

MEASURES OF COUNTRY EQUITY RISK

If country risk is not diversifiable, either because the marginal investor is not globally diversified or because the risk is correlated across markets, investors are left with the task of measuring country risk and estimating country risk premiums (CRPs). How do investors estimate country-specific ERPs? This section provides a discussion of three choices. The first possibility is to use historical data in each market to estimate an ERP for that market. This approach is fraught with statistical and structural problems in most emerging markets. The second choice is to start with an ERP for a mature market such as the United States and to build up to or estimate additional risk premiums for riskier countries. The third option is to use the market pricing of equities within each market to back out estimates of an implied ERP for the market.

Historical Risk Premiums

Most practitioners, when estimating risk premiums in the United States, look at historical measures. Consequently, they look at what they would have earned as investors by investing in equities as opposed to investing in riskless investments. Ibbotson Associates, which is the most widely used estimation service for this purpose, has stock return data and risk-free rates going back to 1926 (Morningstar 2011). Other less widely used databases began as early as 1792 (Siegel 1998; Goetzmann and Ibbotson 2005). The rationale presented by those who use shorter periods is that both the risk aversion of the average investor and equity market risk fundamentals are likely to change over time, and that using a shorter and more recent time period provides a more updated estimate. This logic has to be offset against a cost associated with using shorter time periods, which is the greater noise in the risk premium estimate. In fact, given the annual standard deviation in stock returns between 1926 and 2012 of 19.88 percent, the standard error associated with the risk premium estimate can be estimated in Table 9.4 for different estimation periods, based on a rounded up annualized standard deviation of 20 percent.

Even using the entire period for Ibbotson data (about 85 years) yields a substantial standard error of 2.2 percent. The standard errors from 10-year and 20-year estimates are likely to be almost as large as or larger than the actual risk premium estimated. The cost of using shorter time periods seems to overwhelm any advantages associated with getting a more updated premium.

Table 9.4 **Standard Errors in Historical Risk Premiums**

Estimation Period in Years	Standard Error of Risk Premium Estimate
5	$20\% / \sqrt{5} = 8.94\%$
10	$20\% / \sqrt{10} = 6.32\%$
25	$20\% / \sqrt{25} = 4.00\%$
50	$20\% / \sqrt{50} = 2.83\%$
80	$20\% / \sqrt{80} = 2.23\%$

With emerging markets, investors are unlikely to have access to as much historical data as is available in the United States. By combining this assumption with the high volatility in stock returns in these markets, the conclusion is that historical risk premiums can be computed for these markets but they will be useless because of the large standard errors in the estimates.

Mature Market Plus

If the historical data in emerging markets are too short term or noisy to use in computing ERPs, the solution may be to estimate an ERP for a mature market and then augment that premium for additional country risk (CRP) in a riskier emerging market as shown in Equation 9.1:

$$ERP \ = \ \text{Base premium for a mature equity market} \ + \ CRP. \qquad (9.1)$$

The country risk premium could reflect the extra risk in a specific market. This reduces the estimation to two numbers: an ERP for a mature equity market and the additional risk premium, if any, for country risk.

Mature Market Premium

Between 1928 and 2012, stocks delivered an annual premium, on a compounded basis, of 4.20 percent over the 10-year bond rate. Accepting the premise that the U.S. equity market is a mature market, consistency would then require using this as the ERP, in every other equity market deemed mature. For instance, the ERP in January 2013 would be 4.20 percent in Germany, France, and the United Kingdom. Markets that are not mature, however, require measuring country risk and converting the measure into a CRP, which will augment the mature market premium.

Country Risk Premium

This section reviews three approaches for estimating the risk premium for emerging markets. The first uses default spreads based upon country bonds or ratings, whereas the latter two use equity market volatility as an input in estimating the CRPs.

The simplest and most widely used proxy for the CRP is the sovereign default spread for a country, reflecting the credit risk that lenders observe in that country. The previous section includes measures of this default risk, including the sovereign bond market and market-based measures (sovereign bond spread and CDS). If a market-based measure of the default spread for a country is available, it can be added to the mature market premium as the additional CRP. To estimate the ERP for Brazil, in January 2013, would involve using either the sovereign Brazil U.S. $bond spread at the time (0.74 percent) or the Brazil CDS spread (1.44 percent) as the CRP for Brazil. Adding this value to the mature market premium would have yielded the total ERP for Brazil.

Many emerging market countries do not have government bonds denominated in another currency and some do not have a sovereign rating. For the first group that has sovereign ratings but no foreign currency government bonds, a simple solution is available. Assuming that countries with the similar default risk should have the same sovereign rating, the typical default spread for other countries that have the same rating as the analyzed country can be used and dollar denominated or Euro denominated bonds outstanding. Table 9.5 provides estimates of the typical default spreads for bonds in different sovereign ratings classes in January 2013.

Thus, Bulgaria with a Baa2 rating would have been assigned a default spread of 1.75 percent. The second group offers even more tenuous grounds. Assuming the availability of a country risk score from a service such as PRS for the country, other countries could be identified that are rated and have similar scores, and then the default spreads that these countries face could be assigned. If Cuba and Tanzania have the same country risk score from PRS indicating similar country risk, then Cuba's rating of Caa1 would be assigned to Tanzania, which is not rated, giving it the same default spread (7.00 percent).

Although many analysts use default spreads as proxies for country risk, the evidence to support that usage is still sparse. Abuaf (2011) examines American Depository Receipts (ADRs) from 10 emerging markets and relates the returns on these ADRs to returns on the S&P 500, which yields a conventional beta, and to the CDS spreads for the countries of incorporation. He finds that ADR returns as well as multiples such as

Table 9.5 **Default Spreads by Ratings Class: Sovereign vs. Corporate in January 2013**

Moody's Rating	Sovereign Bonds/CDS (%)	Corporate Bonds (%)
Aaa/AAA	0.00	0.40
Aa1/AA+	0.25	0.57
Aa2/AA	0.50	0.73
Aa3/AA–	0.70	0.78
A1/A+	0.85	0.82
A2/A	1.00	0.95
A3/A–	1.15	1.31
Baa1/BBB+	1.50	1.55
Baa2/BBB	1.75	1.84
Baa3/BBB–	2.00	2.28
Ba1/BB+	2.40	3.12
Ba2/BB	2.75	3.97
Ba3/BB–	3.25	4.81
B1/B+	4.00	5.65
B2/B	5.00	6.49
B3/B–	6.00	7.34
Caa1/ CCC+	7.00	7.75
Caa2/CCC	8.50	8.75
Caa3/ CCC–	10.00	10.00

Source: Damodaran Online (available at http://www.damodaran.com).

price/earnings (PE) ratios are correlated with movement in the CDS spreads over time and argues for the addition of the CDS spread or some multiple of it to the costs of equity and capital to incorporate country risk.

A second approach for estimating the risk premium for emerging markers involves using relative equity market standard deviations. Some analysts believe that the ERPs of markets should reflect the differences in equity risk, as measured by the volatilities of these markets. A conventional measure of equity risk is the standard deviation in stock prices; higher standard deviations are generally associated with more risk. Scaling the standard deviation of one market against another provides a means of obtaining a measure of relative risk. For instance, Equation 9.2 shows the relative standard deviation for country X against the United States:

$$\text{Relative } \sigma_{\text{Country X}} = \frac{\sigma_{\text{Country X}}}{\sigma_{\text{US}}}. \tag{9.2}$$

For example, assuming both a linear relationship between ERPs and equity market standard deviations and that the risk premium for the United States can be computed using historical data, Equation 9.3 shows the ERP for country X:

$$\text{ERP}_{\text{Country X}} = \text{Risk premium}_{\text{US}} \left(\text{Relative } \sigma_{\text{Country X}} \right). \tag{9.3}$$

Assume that an analyst is using an ERP for the United States of 5.80 percent. The annualized standard deviation in the S&P 500 in two years before January 2013, using weekly returns, was 17.67 percent, whereas the standard deviation in the Bovespa (the Brazilian equity index) over the same period was 21.62 percent. If the dependence on historical volatility is troubling, the options market can be used to get implied volatilities for both the U.S. market (18.03 percent) and for the Bovespa (23.56 percent). Using historical volatility values, the estimate of a total risk premium for Brazil would be as follows:

$\text{ERP}_{\text{Brazil}} = 5.80 \text{ percent } (21.62 \text{ percent}/17.67 \text{ percent}) = 7.10 \text{ percent.}$

The CRP for Brazil can be isolated as follows:

$\text{CRP}_{\text{Brazil}} = 7.10 \text{ percent} - 5.80 \text{ percent} = 1.30 \text{ percent.}$

Although this approach has intuitive appeal, problems exist with using standard deviations computed in markets with widely different market structures and liquidity. Given that more liquid markets often show higher volatility, this approach will understate premiums for illiquid markets and overstate the premiums for liquid markets. For instance, the standard deviations for Panama and Costa Rica are lower than the standard deviation in the S&P 500, leading to ERPs for those countries that are lower than the United States. The second problem is related to currencies given that the standard deviations are usually measured in local currency terms. The standard deviation in the U.S. market is a dollar standard deviation, whereas the standard deviation in the Brazilian market is based on nominal Brazilian $R returns. This is a relatively simple problem to fix because the standard deviations can be measured in the same currency. That is, an investor could estimate the standard deviation in dollar returns for the Brazilian market.

In the first approach to computing ERPs, the assumption is that the default spreads (actual or implied) for the country are good measures of the additional risk faced when investing in equity in that country. The second approach contends that the information in equity market volatility can be used to compute the CRP. The third approach melds the first two and tries to use the information in both the country default spread and the equity market volatility.

The country default spreads provide an important first step in measuring country equity risk, but still only measure the premium for default risk. Intuitively, the country ERP is expected to be larger than the country default risk spread. To address the issue of how much higher requires looking at the volatility of the equity market in a country relative to the volatility of the sovereign bond used to estimate the spread. This framework yields Equation 9.4 that is used to estimate the country ERP.

$$\text{Country risk premium} = \text{Country default spread} \left(\frac{\sigma_{\text{Equity}}}{\sigma_{\text{Country bond}}} \right). \quad (9.4)$$

To illustrate, consider again the case of Brazil. As noted earlier, the default spread for Brazil in January 2013, based upon its sovereign rating, was 1.75 percent. The annualized standard deviations were computed, using two years of weekly returns, in both the equity market and the government bond, in early January 2013. The annualized standard deviation in the Brazilian dollar denominated 10-year bond was 10.61 percent, well below the standard deviation in the Brazilian equity index of 21.62 percent. The resulting country ERP for Brazil is as follows:

Brazil CRP = 1.75 percent (21.62 percent/10.61 percent) = 3.57 percent.

Unlike the equity standard deviation approach, this premium is in addition to a mature market ERP. Thus, assuming a 5.8 percent mature market premium, a total ERP for Brazil of 9.37 percent is computed:

Brazil's Total ERP = 5.8 percent + 3.57 percent = 9.37 percent.

This CRP will increase if the country rating drops or if the relative volatility of the equity market increases.

Two potential measurement problems occur with using this approach. The first is that the relative standard deviation of equity is a volatile number, both across countries ranging from 2.70 for Thailand to 0.50 for Greece and across time. Brazil's relative volatility numbers have ranged from close to 1.00 to well above 2.00. The second is that computing the relative volatility requires estimating volatility in the government bond, which, in turn, presupposes that long-term government bonds not only exist but are also traded. One indication that the government bond is not heavily traded is an abnormally low standard deviation on the bond yield.

In countries where these data items are unavailable, three choices are available. One is to fall back on one of the other two approaches. The second is to use a different market measure of default risk, such as the CDS spread, and compute the standard deviation in the spread. This number can be standardized by dividing the level of the spread. The third is to compute a cross-sectional average of the ratio of stock market to bond market volatility across countries, where both items are available, and use that average. In 2013, for instance, there were 27 emerging markets where both the equity market volatility and the government bond volatility numbers were available at least for 100 trading weeks (Damodaran 2013). The median ratio, across these markets, of equity market volatility to bond price volatility was approximately 1.86.

Choosing between the Approaches

The three approaches to estimating CRPs usually give different estimates, with the bond default spread and relative equity standard deviation approaches generally yielding lower CRPs than the melded approach that uses both the country bond default spread and the equity and bond standard deviations. Table 9.6 begins with a CRP of 5.80 percent for the United States and by extension, for mature markets and estimates country equity and total risk premium using the three approaches for Brazil. The melded bond default spread yields a much larger estimate of the ERP than the other approaches. In particular, the melded CDS approach offers more promise going forward, as more countries have CDS traded on them.

Market-Based Erp

The peril of starting with a mature market premium and augmenting it with a CRP is that it is built on two estimates: one reflecting history (the mature market premium) and the other based on judgment (default spreads and volatilities). Thus, equity investors in individual markets may have expected ERPs that are very different from these estimates. This section examines ways in which stock prices can be used to deduce ERPs for markets.

Table 9.6 **Country and Total ERP, Using Different Approaches: Brazil in January 2013**

Approach	*Mature Market Equity Premium (%)*	*Brazil CRP (%)*	*Total ERP (%)*
Sovereign-rating based default spread	5.80	0.75	7.55
Relative equity market standard deviations	5.80	0.30	7.10
Melded approach (Bond default spread) × (Relative standard deviation$_{Bond}$)	5.80	0.75(1.88) = 3.57	9.37
Melded Approach (CDS) × (Relative standard deviation$_{CDS}$)	5.80	1.44(1.08) = 1.55	7.35

Source: Damodaran Online (available at http://www.damodaran.com).

Implied ERP

An alternative is available to estimating risk premiums that does not require historical data or corrections for country risk, but does assume that the overall market is correctly priced. Consider, for instance, Equation 9.5 shows a simple valuation model for stocks:

$$Value = \frac{\text{Expected dividends next period}}{\text{Required return on equity} - \text{Expected growth rate}}. \tag{9.5}$$

This model is essentially the present value of dividends growing at a constant rate. Three of the four inputs in this model can be obtained: the current level of the market (value), the expected dividends next period, and the expected growth rate in earnings and dividends in the long term. The only "unknown" is the required return on equity. Solving for it results in an implied expected return on stocks. Subtracting out the risk-free rate will yield an implied ERP.

The model can be extended to allow for dividends to grow at higher rates at least for short time periods. The model has two limiting assumptions: (1) companies pay out their residual cash flows in dividends, when many companies either use other forms of returning cash (stock buybacks in the United States) or hold on to the cash and (2) companies collectively are in stable growth. Both assumptions can be relaxed with alternate measures of cash flow (dividends plus buybacks or free cash flow to equity) replacing dividends and two-stage models, assuming higher growth for an initial period before stable growth sets in.

Given its long history and wide following, the S&P 500 index is a logical choice to calculate the implied ERP measure. On January 1, 2013, the S&P 500 stood at 1426.19, representing a substantial increase from 1257.60 at the start of 2012. The 10-year U.S. Treasury bond rate (assumed to be risk free) stood at 1.76 percent and the total dividends and buybacks for the trailing 12 months leading into January 2013 climbed to 72.25. Because this number has been volatile over the previous decade, the average yield of 4.87 percent (dividends plus buybacks, as a percent of the index level) from 2003 to 2012 was applied to the index level at the start of 2013 (1426.19) to arrive at a normalized cash flow of 69.46. Analysts continued to be optimistic about earnings growth in the face of signs of a pickup in the U.S. economy, forecasting a compounded annual growth rate of 5.27 percent a year. After 2017, the assumption is that the growth rate will converge to the nominal growth rate of the economy, assumed to be equal to the U.S. Treasury bond rate of 1.76 percent. The expected return on stocks of 7.54 percent is obtained by solving for the discount rate that yields the present value for the expected cash flows that is equal to the index level (1426.19). Subtracting the risk-free rate of 1.76 percent yields an implied ERP of 5.78 percent.

The advantage of the implied premium approach is that it is market-driven, current, and does not require any historical data. Thus, it can be used to estimate implied equity premiums in any market, no matter how short that market's history. The implied premium approach is, however, bounded by whether the model used for the valuation is the right one and the availability and reliability of the inputs to that model. Earlier in this chapter, the CRPs were estimated for Brazil using default spreads and equity market volatility. To provide a contrast, the implied ERP is estimated for the Brazilian equity market in January 2013, from the following inputs.

- The index (Bovespa) was trading at 60,952 on January 1, 2013, and the dividend yield on the index over the previous 12 months was about 3.55 percent. Although stock buybacks represented negligible cash flows, the free cash flow to equity (FCFE) was computed for companies in the index, and the aggregate FCFE yield across the companies was about 4.50 percent. FCFE is the cash flow left over after reinvestment, taxes, and debt payments/inflows. It is a rough measure of potential dividends.
- Earnings in companies in the index are expected to grow 10 percent in U.S. dollar terms over the next five years, and 1.76 percent (set equal to the U.S. Treasury bond rate) thereafter.
- The risk-free rate is the 10-year U.S. Treasury bond rate of 1.76 percent.
- The time line of cash flows is shown below:

$$60,952 = \frac{3,017}{(1+r)} + \frac{3,319}{(1+r)^2} + \frac{3,651}{(1+r)^2} + \frac{4,016}{(1+r)^4} + \frac{4,417(1.0176)}{(r-0.0176)(1+r)^5}.$$

These inputs yield an expected return on equity of 8.25 percent, which when compared to the U.S. Treasury bond rate of 1.76 percent on that day results in an implied equity premium of 6.49 percent. For simplicity, this analysis used nominal dollar expected growth rates and U.S. Treasury bond rates, but it could have been done entirely in the local currency resulting in both higher growth rates and a higher risk-free rate. Compared to the U.S. implied ERP of 5.78 percent on the same day, that would suggest an additional CRP of 0.71 percent for Brazil.

Country Risk Exposure to Country Risk

Accepting the proposition that country risk commands a premium because it is not diversifiable, the follow-up question relates to the exposure of individual companies to that risk. Should all companies in a country with substantial country risk be equally exposed to country risk? While intuition suggests that they should not, the discussion begins by looking at standard approaches that assume that they are. This framework is followed by examining ways in which differences across companies in country risk exposure can be brought into ERPs and cost of equity estimates.

COUNTRY OF INCORPORATION

The easiest assumption to make when dealing with country risk, and the one that is most often made, is that all companies that are incorporated in a country are equally exposed to country risk in that country. The cost of equity for a firm in a market with country risk can then be written as shown in Equation 9.6:

$$\text{Cost of equity} = R_F + \beta \, (\text{Mature market premium}) + \text{CRP}, \qquad (9.6)$$

where R_F is the risk-free rate; β is beta, a measure of systematic risk; and CRP is the country risk premium.

Given that Brazil had an estimated CRP of 3.57 percent from the melded approach, each company in the market will have an additional CRP of 3.57 percent added to its cost of equity. For instance, the cost of equity for Ambev, a Latin American beverage company listed in Brazil, with a beta of 0.80, in U.S. dollar terms would be as follows in 2011, assuming a U.S. Treasury bond rate of 3.25 percent as the risk-free rate and an ERP of 6.00 percent for mature markets:

Cost of equity for Ambev = 3.25 percent + 0.80 (6.00 percent) + 3.57 percent = 11.62 percent.

In some cases, analysts modify this approach to scale the CRP by beta. Using this modification, the estimated cost of equity for Ambev would be:

Cost of equity for Ambev = 3.25 percent + 0.80 (6.00 percent + 3.57 percent) = 10.91 percent.

With both approaches, all Brazilian companies are treated as being exposed to only Brazilian country risk, even though their operations may extend into other markets.

THE OPERATIONS-WEIGHTED ERP

For investors who are uncomfortable with the notion that all companies in a market are equally exposed to country risk or that a company is exposed only to its local market's risk, the alternative is to compute a CRP for each company that reflects its operating exposure. Thus, if a company derives half of its value from Brazil and half from Argentina, the CRP will be an average of the CRPs for the two countries. Given that value is difficult to estimate for individual countries, the weighting has to be based on more observable variables such as revenues or operating income. Table 9.7 provides estimates of the ERP and CRP exposure for Ambev in 2011 with a mature market premium of 6 percent.

Table 9.7 **Revenue-Weighted ERP and CRP for Ambev across Operating Regions in 2011**

Country	Revenues ($)	Revenue Weight (%)	ERP (%)	CRP (%)	Weighted ERP (%)	Weighted CRP (%)
Argentina	19.00	9.31	15.00	9.00	1.40	0.84
Bolivia	4.00	1.96	10.88	4.88	0.21	0.10
Brazil	130.00	63.73	8.63	2.63	5.50	1.67
Canada	23.00	11.27	6.00	0.00	0.68	0.00
Chile	7.00	3.43	7.05	1.05	0.24	0.04
Ecuador	6.00	2.94	18.75	12.75	0.55	0.38
Paraguay	3.00	1.47	12.00	6.00	0.18	0.09
Peru	12.00	5.88	9.00	3.00	0.53	0.18
Total	204.00	100.00			9.28	3.28

Source: Amgen Annual Report and Damodaran Online (available at http://www.damodaran.com).

Although Ambev is incorporated in Brazil, it generates substantial revenues from both other Latin American countries and in Canada. Once the weighted premium has been computed, it can either be added to the standard single-factor model as a constant or scaled, based upon beta. Thus, the estimated cost of equity for Ambev, using the two approaches would have been calculated using a beta of 0.80 for Ambev, a U.S. dollar risk-free rate of 3.25 percent, and a 6.00 percent ERP for mature markets:

The constant approach: 3.25 percent + 0.80 (6.00 percent) + 3.28 percent = 11.33 percent,

The scaled approach: 3.25 percent + 0.80 (6.00 percent + 3.28 percent) = 10.67 percent.

The approaches yield similar values when the beta value is close to one, but can diverge when the beta is much lower or higher than one. When using the latter approach, the assumption is that a company's exposure to country risk is proportional to its exposure to all other market risk, which is measured by the beta.

Using this approach, the exposure to country risk or emerging market risk is not restricted to emerging market companies. Many companies headquartered in developed markets such as the United States, Western Europe, and Japan derive at least some of their revenues from emerging or riskier markets and therefore have higher composite ERPs. For instance, Table 9.8 provides an estimate of the composite ERP for Coca-Cola.

As with Ambev, the weighted ERP for the company could be used to compute its overall cost of equity. For valuing regional divisions, the divisional ERP can be used. Thus, the ERP used to value Coca-Cola's Latin American business would be 9.42 percent. Rather than breaking the revenues down by country, they are broken down by region and attached as an ERP to each region, computed as a GDP-weighted average of the ERPs of the countries in that region. The rationale for this approach is

Table 9.8 **Revenue-Weighted ERP and CRP for Coca Cola across Operating Regions**

Region	Revenues (%)	ERP (%)	CRP (%)
Western Europe	19	6.67	0.67
Eastern Europe and Russia	5	8.60	2.60
Asia	15	7.63	1.63
Latin America	15	9.42	3.42
Australia and New Zealand	4	6.00	0.00
Africa	4	9.82	3.82
North America	38	6.00	0.00
Coca-Cola (Company)	100	7.17	1.17

Source: Coca-Cola Annual Report and Damodaran Online (available at http://www.damodaran.com).

twofold. First, given that Coca-Cola derives its revenues from almost every country in the world, computing the ERPs by region is more tractable than by country. Second, Coca-Cola does not break down its revenues at least for public consumption by country, but it does so by region.

LAMBDAS

The most general approach to a company's exposure to country risk is to allow for each company to have an exposure to country risk that is different from its exposure to all other market risk. For lack of a better term, call the measure lambda (γ). As with beta, lambda is scaled around one, with a lambda of one indicating a company with average exposure to country risk and a lambda above or below one indicating above or below average exposure to country risk. The cost of equity for a firm in an emerging market is expressed as shown in Equation 9.7:

$$\text{Expected return} = R_F + \beta \, (\text{Mature market ERP}) + \gamma \, (\text{CRP}). \qquad (9.7)$$

This approach essentially converts the expected return model to a two-factor model, with the second factor being country risk, with γ measuring exposure to country risk. But what are the determinants of this exposure? The first and most obvious determinant is how much of the revenues a firm derives from the country in question. A company that derives 30 percent of its revenues from Brazil should be less exposed to Brazilian country risk than a company that derives 70 percent of its revenues from Brazil. The second is the location of its operations because a company can be exposed to country risk even if it derives no revenues from that country provided that its production facilities are in that country. Companies that can move their production facilities elsewhere can spread their risk across several countries, but the problem is exaggerated for those companies that cannot move such facilities, as is often the case with natural resource companies. Finally, companies may be able to reduce this exposure by buying insurance against specific unpleasant contingencies and by using derivatives.

The simplest measure of lambda is based entirely on revenues. Given the constraint that the average lambda across all stocks must be one (someone has to bear the country risk), the percentage of revenues that a company gets from a market cannot be lambda. This measure, shown in Equation 9.8, can be scaled by dividing it by the percent of revenues that the average company in the market gets from the country to derive a lambda.

$$\text{Lambda}_j = \frac{\% \text{ of Revenue in the country}_{\text{Company}}}{\% \text{ of Revnue in the country}_{\text{Average company in the market}}}. \qquad (9.8)$$

Applying this approach to Ambev, which derives 64 percent of its revenues in Brazil, when the average company in the Brazilian market was obtaining 75 percent, would have yielded:

$$\text{Lambda}_{\text{Ambev}} = 64 \text{ percent} / 75 \text{ percent} = 0.85.$$

Note that completing the process requires estimating Ambev's lambdas in the other countries in which it operates.

The second measure draws on the stock prices of a company and how they move relative to movements in country risk. Sovereign bonds issued by countries offer a simple and updated measure of country risk. As investor assessments of country risk become more optimistic, sovereign bonds increase in price, just as they decrease when investors become more pessimistic. A regression of the returns on a stock against the returns on a country bond should yield a measure of lambda in the slope coefficient. Applying this approach to the Ambev, monthly stock returns on the stock were regressed against monthly returns on the 10-year dollar denominated Brazilian government bond to derive the following:

$$\text{Return}_{\text{Ambev}} = 0.015 + 0.6551\ \text{Return}_{\text{Brazil \$ Bond}}.$$

Based upon this regression, Ambev has a lambda of 0.66 for its Brazilian operations and its U.S. dollar cost of equity, using a beta of 0.80, a U.S. dollar risk-free rate of 3.25 percent, a mature market ERP of 6 percent, and a country ERP of 3.57 percent for Brazil is:

Cost of Equity for Ambev = 3.25 percent + 0.80 (6.00 percent) + 0.66 (3.57 percent) = 10.41 percent.

What are the limitations of this approach? First, the lambdas estimated from these regressions are likely to have large standard errors. For example, the standard error in the lambda estimate of Ambev is 0.35. Second, the country must have bonds that are liquid and widely traded, preferably in a more stable currency such as the dollar or euro. Third, Ambev's risk exposure is ignored in other emerging markets.

In general, as the number of countries from which a company derives its revenues increases, the lambda approach becomes less practical because investors must estimate lambdas for each market (Damodaran 2003). Thus, investors would not even attempt to use this approach for Coca-Cola because it is designed more for a company that is exposed to risk in only one or two emerging markets with the balance of its revenues coming from developed markets.

Summary and Conclusions

As companies expand operations into emerging markets and investors search for investment opportunities in Asia and Latin America, they are also increasingly exposed to additional risk in these countries. Although globally diversified investors can eliminate some country risk by diversifying across equities in many countries, the increasing correlation across markets suggests that investors cannot entirely diversify away country risk. Estimating the CRP involves considering three measures: (1) the default spread on a government bond issued by that country, (2) a premium obtained by scaling up the ERP in the United States by the volatility of the country equity market relative to the U.S. equity market, and (3) a melded premium where the default spread on the country bond is adjusted for the higher volatility of the equity market. The chapter also discussed how to estimate an implied ERP from stock prices and expected cash flows.

Discussion Questions

1. Analysts often argue that a country cannot default on its local currency bonds because it has the power to print more currency to pay off its debt. Explain why this argument is incorrect.
2. Discuss whether sovereign ratings are good measures of sovereign default risk.
3. The sovereign default spread for a government can be estimated from sovereign bonds in U.S. dollars or the sovereign CDS market. Explain why the two approaches may result in different answers.
4. Given that some country equity risk is diversifiable to global investors, discuss whether it should be included in the price.
5. ERPs in emerging markets converged toward ERPs in developed markets between 2008 and 2012. Explain reasons for this trend.
6. Discuss whether analysts should use models that assume U.S. companies are not exposed to emerging market risk.
7. All companies in an emerging market are not equally exposed to the risk in that emerging market. Identify factors that explain differences in country risk exposure across companies and discuss how to measure that risk exposure.

References

Abuaf, Niso. 2011. "Valuing Emerging Market Equities—The Empirical Evidence." *Journal of Applied Finance* 21:2, 1–19.

Ball, Clifford, and Walter Torous. 2000. "Stochastic Correlation across International Stock Markets." *Journal of Empirical Finance* 7:4, 373–388.

Damodaran, Aswath. 2003. "Estimating Company Exposure to Country Risk." *Journal of Applied Finance* 13:2, 64–78.

Damodaran, Aswath. 2013. "ERPs: Determinants, Estimation and Implications—The 2013 Edition." Available at http://papers.ssrn.com/sol3/papers.cfm?abstract_id=2238064.

Fernandez, Pablo, Javier Aguirreamalloa, and Luis Corres Avendano. 2013. "Market Risk Premium Used in 82 Countries in 2012: A Survey with 82 Answers." Available at http://papers.ssrn.com/sol3/papers.cfm?abstract_id=2084213.

Goetzmann, William, and Roger Ibbotson. 2005. "History and the ERP." Working Paper, Yale University. Available at http://papers.ssrn.com/sol3/papers.cfm?abstract_id=702341.

Hatchondo, Juan Carlos, Leonardo Martinez, and Horacio Sapriza. 2007. "The Economics of Sovereign Default." *Economic Quarterly* 93:2, 163–187.

Ismailescu, Iuliana, and Hossein Kazemi. 2010. "The Reaction of Emerging Markets Credit Default Swap Spreads to Sovereign Credit Rating Changes and Country Fundamentals." *Journal of Banking and Finance* 34:12, 2861–2873.

Morningstar. 2011. *Ibbotson Stocks, Bonds, Bills and Inflation Yearbook (SBBI)*, 2011 Edition. Chicago: Morningstar.

Siegel, Jeremy J. 1998. *Stocks for the Long Run*, 2nd Edition. New York: McGraw Hill.

Standard & Poor's. 2013. *Default Study: Sovereign Defaults and Rating Transition Data, 2012 Update.* Available at http://www.standardandpoors.com/ratings/articles/en/us/?articleType=HTML&assetID=1245350156739.

Yang, Li, Francis Tapon, and Yiguo Sun. 2006. "International Correlations across Stock Markets and Industries: Trends and Patterns 1988-2002." *Applied Financial Economics* 16:16, 1171–1183.

10

Systemic Risk

ANDREAS KRAUSE

Assistant Professor Department of Economics, University of Bath, Great Britain

Introduction

Systemic risk is much more difficult to define than some other concepts in finance. Because no single generally accepted definition is available, different authors use varying definitions of systemic risk. A common element of most definitions is that a usually exogenous event has adverse effects on a large fraction of members of a financial system. In this context, adverse effects usually refer to large losses to or failures of members such as banks. The exogenous event triggering the losses can be a macroeconomic shock, the failure of a financial institution, or simply a large market movement that causes a loss to some market members. Any such initial losses will accumulate as they spread through the financial system and are often referred to as a *domino effect*.

Such a general definition, as given in Schwarcz (2008) and similarly expressed in Kaufmann and Scott (2003), encompasses a wide range of scenarios. Most commonly systemic risk is associated with the banking system and is seen as the threat of banks failing and any such failures spreading to other banks. In this case, the trigger event could be a single bank failing for some exogenous reason such as experiencing a large trading loss, and this initial bank failure then spreads via financial linkages to other banks. Schwarcz refers to this view on systemic risk as *institutional systemic risk* because it affects financial institutions such as banks.

Systemic risk, however, can also affect financial markets and investors directly rather than indirectly via financial institutions. In this context, systemic risk needs to be clearly distinguished from *systematic risk*, which is the undiversifiable risk often referred to as *market risk* to which even well-diversified market participants are exposed. Therefore, systematic risk captures the co-movement of assets in a market. Using this definition, systemic risk goes beyond the aspect by being concerned about the impact a loss in some assets or asset classes will have on other assets and their investors. In reaction to facing losses in an asset, investors might reallocate their portfolios causing prices in other assets to fall or rise. Such movements might cause losses to other investors who in turn will reallocate their portfolios, exacerbating any movements of asset prices. This *market systemic risk* cannot be viewed as isolated from the previously mentioned institutional systemic risk as any losses incurred by financial institutions can lead to their failure and can subsequently spread. Any asset sales in reaction to such failures will affect market prices that can lead to portfolio reallocations as previously outlined.

De Bandt and Hartmann (2000, p. 10) define a systemic event as "an event, where the release of 'bad news' about a financial institution, or even its failure, or the crash of a financial market leads in a sequential fashion to considerable adverse effects on one or several other financial institutions or markets, e.g., their failure or crash" and based on this definition systemic risk then as "the risk of experiencing systemic events." The emphasis of systemic risk in this definition is on the sequential effect an initial shock has on other financial institutions that were financially sound before the initial shock, often referred to as *contagion*.

Financial institutions are commonly meant to be commercial banks, but systemic risk also includes insurance companies, hedge funds, mutual funds, and pension funds. As the credit crisis of 2007–2008 shows with the failure of AIG, insurance companies can be severely affected due to their exposure in financial markets and derivatives positions. Hedge funds experienced a similar situation as the failure of Long Term Capital Management in 1998 caused severe losses and a systemic event could only be averted with the intervention of the Federal Reserve.

The remainder of this chapter mostly focuses on institutional systemic risk, more specifically on banks. To this effect the coming sections, after briefly outlining the costs of systemic events, explore different sources of systemic risk, the measurement of systemic risk, its regulation as well as implications for investments covering aspects of market systemic risk.

Prevalence and Costs of Systemic Events

Banking crises are seemingly rare events that most people will not experience often. Nevertheless, Kaufmann (2000) lists 54 pure banking crises (12 in developed countries) between 1975 and 1997 (i.e., before the credit crisis of 2007-2008), in addition to 32 crises that were a combined banking and currency crisis of which six were in developed countries. In more than 80 percent of cases, these banking crises led to losses from reduced economic growth, averaging cumulative costs of around 15 percent of the gross domestic product (GDP) for pure banking crises and more than 18 percent for combined banking and currency crises. Pure currency crises only resulted in losses averaging 8 percent of GDP, putting the additional costs of a banking crisis in these instances at roughly 10 percent of GDP. Smith (2012) obtains slightly larger losses and estimates the costs of the credit crisis of 2007–2008 at around 25 percent of GDP.

Thus, systemic events can impose large costs on an economy. Some use these costs to justify tight regulation of banks. In order to regulate banks appropriately, a thorough understanding of the causes of systemic risk and potential remedies is important. Such an understanding is also important for those investing not only in banks or similar financial institutions but also in other assets.

Sources of Systemic Risk

The origins of systemic risk can be varied. Although classifying the origins of systemic risk can be difficult in real banking crises as the causes are often not singular, such distinctions are much more straightforward to make in theoretical contributions. Following Acharya (2009), Hellwig (2009), Haldane and May (2011), and Allen and Carletti (2013), five main origins of systemic risk can be distinguished.

First, banks might invest in similar assets such as loans to the same industries. Any losses from such assets might affect other banks and make them vulnerable to failure. Second, a bank's assets might unexpectedly decrease in value such as due to a fire sale by other banks that cannot be absorbed in the market. The losses arising from those situations can cause other banks to fail. Third, banks might find rolling over existing funding of their assets difficult leading to a sale of assets in response. These sales might reduce the price obtained and impose losses on the bank, weakening their capital base. Fourth, if a bank fails, the public might withdraw money from other banks as a precaution, causing bank runs that can bring down other banks. Finally, banks lend money to each other such as in the form of interbank loans. The default of one bank will impose losses on others, which might cause their downfall. The coming sections provide a discussion of these causes of systemic risk.

ASSET CORRELATION

A common observation is that bank behavior is much alike in many ways. Banks tend to grant loans to similar sectors of the economy such as housing loans and invest in similar products such as subprime mortgage derivatives and proprietary trading. If an exogenous shock lowers the value of these assets, all banks could suffer substantial losses and many such banks might fail, causing a systemic event.

With the exception of some private banks, most banks have limited liability. Thus, if they fail, the owners do not have to cover any losses from their private wealth, but the losses are borne by depositors who will not be repaid the full value of their funds. This limited liability would imply an incentive to engage in risk-shifting by the individual bank as is well documented in the corporate finance literature (Jensen and Meckling 1976; Myers 2001). A bank failure results in two effects. It allows the remaining banks to increase their deposits from those being withdrawn from the failed bank and similarly to expand their loans to those the failing bank has withdrawn. Because confidence in the banking system declines, depositors are less willing to use banks for their excess cash, thus reducing the amount of deposits available within the banking system.

Acharya (2009) contends that the second effect dominates. He then argues for the existence of *systemic risk-shifting* in which banks choose an asset structure that increases systemic risk. As banks are not benefitting from the failure of other banks, they seek to ensure that they survive if the other banks survive, thus investing into the same assets. The downside is that if an exogenous shock hits those assets in which banks are invested, all banks are likely to suffer substantial losses and many may fail, causing a systemic event. The reason for this behavior is that some banks fail while others survive. Those surviving would also suffer from the reduced confidence in the banking system.

The incentives to differentiate their holdings ensuring survival if others fail, are limited. Thus, failing as others fail is a better option.

An implication of this finding is that in order to reduce systemic risk-shifting, capital regulation needs to consider the correlation between assets of banks. The higher the correlation of the assets held by a bank with those of other banks, the higher the capital a bank needs to hold. Such a capital requirement has a twofold effect. First, it reduces the incentives to choose assets that are highly correlated with other banks as this would increase capital requirements and thereby costs. Second, in situations where banks are choosing assets that are highly correlated, the higher capital requirements make banks less susceptible to losses and thereby reduce systemic risk.

MARKET RISK

Banks are exposed to the usual market risk in that the value of their assets changes. Given the regulatory structure of the banking industry, any losses arising from changes in asset values can be amplified and cause additional losses to banks and thereby increase the risks to the banking system as a whole.

In times of market stress, the value of assets decreases. As Cifuentes, Shin, and Ferucci (2005) point out, the minimum capital requirements by regulators can cause a cascade effect in sales by banks. The reduced value of bank assets may force banks to decrease their overall risk exposure because they might be unable to fulfill the capital requirements. The way to reduce the risk exposure is to sell assets. Such a sale will further depress market values if markets are not perfectly liquid and thus decrease the value of assets held by banks. This cumulative effect can then lead to bank failures even if the initial shock was not large enough to have such an effect. Even without initial losses, a mere increase in the volatility of markets can necessitate the reduction of assets held to comply with capital regulations that use risk-weighted assets as their basis. Thus, asset reduction can cause a cascading effect leading to bank failures.

As Acharya, Shin, and Yorulmazer (2009) point out, the low values of assets from such fire sales are excellent opportunities for healthy banks to acquire assets below their fundamental values. This scenario, however, necessitates sufficient liquidity to finance such purchases. In times of high returns and booming banking sectors, the likelihood of benefitting from fire sales is low while returns from investing into risky assets is relatively high. Hence, banks hold few funds in cash. In contrast, as a banking crisis unfolds, these relationships are reversed and banks hold more liquid funds. These incentives lead to a situation in which, at the onset of a banking crisis, banks are holding too little cash to be able to fund the purchase of risky assets shed by failing banks. Thus, the incentives for banks are not conducive to limit the impact of fire sales in times of crises.

Evidence summarized in Shleifer and Vishny (2011) points toward the existence of fire sales by banks. Arbitrage that would normally prevent prices of financial assets from dropping does not work sufficiently well to prevent a substantial price impact. An additional complication is that in cases of derivatives and collateralized securities, a drop in asset values requires additional cash to meet margin requirements. This situation is often exacerbated by margins increasing in times of market downturns due to higher volatility.

Another way market risk can affect a bank is when the value of collateral decreases. Whenever a bank has borrowed funds secured by collateral, a reduction in the value of this collateral requires a bank to either add additional collateral to the pool, to bind resources, or to reduce borrowing, which typically requires the sale of assets to finance the reduced borrowing. As Benmelech and Bergman (2011) show, such a situation can spread across banks as the strength of bank balance sheets weaken and thus hamper the raising of funds.

FUNDING LIQUIDITY RISK

One role of banks is to transform short-term deposits into long-term assets (i.e., loans). This process, however, poses what can be referred to as *rollover risk* as the assets need to be refinanced frequently. Acharya, Gale, and Yorulmazer (2011) model this risk.

The value of the assets of a bank must exceed their total liabilities (i.e., in a simplified banking system, these liabilities are the deposits). If these deposits are very short term, not much additional information will be forthcoming to assess the value of the bank's assets between rollovers. When depositing funds with a bank, the depositors want to ensure that at the next possible withdrawal date, the value of the assets at least covers the deposits. If the liquidation of assets is costly, this coverage should be net of any such costs. As the maximum deposits that can be attracted are this net amount, the longer the asset's maturity the smaller is the amount of deposits because, at every intermediate renewal of deposits, an additional discount is added. The more renewals are required until the maturity of assets, the fewer deposits that can be supported. Similarly, a shortening of the length of deposits reduces the amount that the bank can attract for given asset maturities, easily causing a liquidity shortfall with the bank.

He and Xiong (2012) similarly find that frequent rollovers and the associated costs of potentially increasing interest rates in case of an emerging crisis lead to higher default rates. As Acharya and Viswanathan (2011) show, problems in rolling over funding can require banks to reduce leverage by selling assets, causing a further deterioration of funding liquidity. Such a change in the behavior of deposits can cause a squeeze on the liquidity of banks and could lead to a widespread funding squeeze as seen in the credit crisis of 2007-2008, affecting the efficient functioning of the entire banking system.

INFORMATION CONTAGION

Early models of systemic risk addressed the problem of *bank runs*, i.e., the sudden withdrawal of deposits. In a seminal paper, Diamond and Dybvig (1983) show that such a bank run is an equilibrium outcome. Depositors use the bank to store their funds such that they can withdraw them for consumption as needed. Withdrawals due to liquidity needs may exceed the cash reserves of the bank, which will then leave the bank unable to meet these demands. The liquidation of other assets such as loans at short notice will cause losses that result in deposits not being repaid in full. As depositors are paid in the order in which they demand their deposits back, this framework provides an incentive to withdraw deposits early in order to avoid losses. Thus, the fear of withdrawals can lead even those who do not have any liquidity needs to withdraw their deposits, exacerbating withdrawals. This situation can lead to self-fulfilling prophecies:

when depositors think that withdrawals will be high, they will withdraw their deposits and a bank run will emerge.

The reason for such a bank run can be based not only on the withdrawals of others due to liquidity needs but also on doubts related to a bank's solvency. Fearing that a bank may become insolvent (e.g., due to its exposure in loans to certain industries that cause large losses) can also lead to depositors withdrawing their deposits. Other depositors observing such withdrawals would then join to avoid losses. This form of bank run would only affect a single bank and as such is not a systemic event. However, information on the losses made by one bank and the subsequent bank run can easily lead to the belief that other banks have similar problems. Thus, the bank run can spread to other banks as information spreads.

For this mechanism of bank runs to work, no actual losses are required, merely the belief that a specific bank might be unable to repay its deposits in full. Even someone knowing that this is false would act rationally withdrawing his money if he believes that others will do so. Consequently, a bank run on a single bank can easily lead to a systemic event as information spreads.

Diamond and Dybvig (1983) propose two possible solutions to prevent bank runs: suspending convertibility and providing deposit insurance. Suspending convertibility works by setting a limit on how many deposits can be withdrawn in any period. If the number of depositors requiring withdrawal of their deposits due to liquidity needs is known, then the limit can be set at that point and a bank run would not occur. No incentive would exist to withdraw deposits without liquidity needs as the bank would be able to repay all deposits at a later stage. The problem occurs, however, if the amounts withdrawn for liquidity reasons are unknown, as in this case, it might well be that the limit is set too low and not all such depositors would be able to obtain their deposits back as desired, causing inefficiency.

The implementation of deposit insurance also prevents a bank run. If, in the event of the bank being unable to repay all deposits, this insurance covers any losses, then no incentive exists for withdrawing deposits unless liquidity needs dictate it. An alternative to deposit insurance would be a central bank that credibly acts as a lender of last resort (i.e., provides loans to a bank having to repay deposits). In this case, no incentive is present to withdraw deposits early. This outcome only works if depositors believe the bank is financially sound and will not suffer any losses that would limit the amount of deposits repaid at a later time.

Shin (2009) provides a detailed analysis of the bank run on Northern Rock in September 2007 that started the credit crisis of 2007–2008 in the United Kingdom. Bank runs in modern times have been rare. For example, before 2007 the last bank run in the United Kingdom was in 1866 on Overend, Gurney & Co. and in the early 1930s in the United States.

CREDIT RISK CONTAGION

Banks often lend each other money through so-called *interbank loans*. For those banks with excess liquidity, making interbank loans is a convenient way to generate additional returns while providing banks needing liquidity with a convenient source of short-term funds. Such needs for funds can arise if a bank finds itself in a position of a sudden and unexpectedly large withdrawal of deposits while other banks might see an inflow of deposits that cannot be invested sufficiently quickly into loans.

Allen and Gale (2000) show that such arrangements can make a financial system more stable by spreading the liquidity risk across all banks of the financial system. A bank facing a liquidity shortfall can borrow additional funds and can prevent its demise from a bank run or lack of depositor funding. Thus, the financial system can effectively absorb idiosyncratic risks. Interbank lending can reduce systemic risk. Interbank loans, however, might actually increase systemic risk by spreading the failure of one bank to other banks. If a bank faces a deposit withdrawal that exceeds the amount of interbank loans it can obtain to cover the shortage, the bank will fail and subsequently those banks that have granted interbank loans will suffer losses in the liquidation process. Such losses will reduce the amount of equity a bank holds and either lead directly to its failure or weaken its capital base such that any losses from other activities might more easily cause the banks to fail. Therefore, the failure of one bank can spread to other banks, causing a systemic event.

According to Allen and Gale (2000), the more interconnected banks are the less likely this scenario is and systemic risk is lower. Rochet and Tirole (1996) also contend that interbank lending acts as a monitoring device, reducing the propensity of banks to take on too high risks that endanger customer deposits, as other banks are better equipped to detect such behavior and the threat of not granting interbank loans acts as a deterrent.

Although the model in Allen and Gale (2000) is theoretical in nature and only investigated financial systems with four banks, subsequent research investigates larger and more realistic banking systems. For example, Iori, Jafarey, and Padilla (2006) examine banking systems with 400 banks and observe that when banks are all identical, a higher interconnectivity reduces the number of banks failing (i.e., systemic risk is lower). Allowing banks to be heterogeneous, however, can increase systemic risk as the connectivity increases, depending on a range of other parameters. Furfine (2003) conducts an analysis with similar results for the Federal funds market using actual data.

The model used by Iori et al. (2006) makes many unrealistic assumptions (e.g., the distribution of interbank loans is random). In practice, such loans have a wide range of properties that suggest more complex structures such as larger banks having more connections than smaller banks, some banks (mostly large banks) being highly connected with each other, and other (smaller) banks having only very few connections among them.

Krause and Giansante (2012) seek to overcome this limitation by allowing not only for heterogeneous banks in all aspects of their structure but also by providing different network structures of interbank loans. Furthermore, the authors introduce the possibility of both failure due to solvency in the form described previously and liquidity withdrawals of a failing bank from those it has granted interbank loans. They find that the overall structure of the network of interbank lending plays an important role for systemic risk, at least comparable with the influence of capital requirements. Other models coming to similar conclusions are Gai and Kapadia (2010) as well as Haldane and May (2011).

The importance of the network of interbank loans and other comparable bilateral exposures of banks against each other, such as those arising from payment systems or over-the-counter (OTC) derivatives positions, gave rise to the notion of *too-interconnected-to-fail*, which refers to a bank that if failing would cause losses to many other banks and could cause a cascade of subsequent failures. The failing bank does not necessarily have to be large or have the most connections to have this effect, but its ability to spread any losses to many banks contributes to systemic risk. Iyer and Peydro-Alcalde (2011) provide empirical evidence from the Indian banking system for the relevance of such mechanisms as do Cont, Moussa, and Santos (2010) for Brazil.

Measuring Systemic Risk

Systemic risk is not simply the aggregate risk of individual banks. In general, no direct connection exists between the risks of individual banks and the systemic risk of the banking system to which these banks belong. Although the risk of bankruptcy of banks can be high, the structure of the banks might be such that contagion is unlikely to occur. Examples include a situation in which banks serve different parts of the market and hence asset correlation is low, they are not lending much to each other, deposit insurance prevents bank runs, and funding is stable. Yet, banks might show a low risk of bankruptcy but their common exposure to certain industries, high interbank lending, and absence of a viable deposit insurance scheme might make the systemic risk substantially higher.

As the origins of systemic risk can differ, the way systemic risk is measured reflects this variety. Most measures of systemic risk rely on market data. Typically, no access to internal data of banks is available, even for regulators. Similarly, details of funding sources and conditions are unknown and thus any liquidity risk is difficult to assess. In recent years, however, regulators have gained access to more data by banks, such as information on their counterparties, but for confidentiality reasons cannot make this information available for external analysis.

A generally accepted measure of systemic risk is unavailable. Chen, Iyengar, and Moallemi (2013) provide an axiomatic treatment of the desirable properties of such a measure, which does not directly lead to risk measures that cover all aspects of systemic risk discussed above. Three commonly used approaches to assess systemic risk are available: CoVaR, network measures, and stress testing.

COVAR

A feature of all versions of systemic risk is an exogenous event similarly affects losses spread from one bank to another. Stock prices of banks should reflect this event. In times of higher systemic risks, extreme movements that are more likely to be attributed to systemic risk should become more common. Hence, the vulnerability of a bank to systemic risk can be measured by using a measure called CoVaR, introduced in Adrian and Brunnermeier (2009).

Equation 10.1 implicitly defines the value-at-risk (VaR) of bank i (VaR_q^i) as

$$Prob\left(R^i < VaR_q^i\right) = q. \tag{10.1}$$

The CoVaR of bank j is then the VaR of a bank conditional upon the VaR of bank i being breached illustrated in Equation 10.2:

$$Prob\left(R^j < CoVaR_q^{j|i}|R^i < VaR_q^i\right) = q. \qquad (10.2)$$

Thus, the CoVaR measures the size of the losses a bank makes if another banks is in trouble (i.e., it provides a measure for the size of potential losses that can spill over from bank i to bank j). As Equation 10.3 shows, CoVar is

$$\Delta CoVaR_q^{j|i} = CoVaR_q^{j|i} - VaR_q^j. \qquad (10.3)$$

This measure expresses the marginal contribution bank i makes to the risk of bank j. Although this measure does not assess the systemic risk of a banking system in itself, this can be achieved by setting j equal to the banking system. In this case $\Delta CoVaR_q^{system|i}$ denotes the contribution bank i makes to the systemic risk of the banking system, or in other words the risk a failure of bank i poses to the entire banking system. Similarly $\Delta CoVaR_q^{j|system}$ could be obtained to measure the impact a crisis in the banking system would have on bank j.

Whether this measure is suitable to express systemic risk would depend on whether the market from which the data originate can assess these aspects correctly. Given the limited information the market has on both the exposure of a bank to specific industries and direct financial links between banks, whether such a measure could perform adequately is questionable. In the absence of market data such as for mutual banks or non-listed banks, this measure cannot be applied.

Despite these shortcomings, many researchers use this methodology to assess the systemic risk of banks. Acharya, Pedersen, Philippon, and Richardson (2010) modify the CoVaR to use systemic expected shortfall, replacing the VaR with expected shortfall. Straetmans and Chaudhry (2012) use a similar idea by focusing on extreme returns of banks. Gauthier, Lehar, and Souissi (2012) provide an overview of how some of these measures compare in their empirical performance to measure the systemic risk of Canadian banks.

The use of CoVaR and similar measures might be able to detect systemic risks arising from asset correlation and market risks if sufficient information on the assets of banks are available. Assessing the systemic risks arising from the other sources of systemic risk would be much more difficult.

NETWORK MEASURES

During the credit crisis of 2007–2008, direct financial links between banks were an important aspect of the crisis. Such links not only transmitted losses through the banking system but also led to a widespread funding crisis. Hence, the network of such financial links generally plays an important role, and the position of a bank in such a network is an important indicator of its contribution to systemic risk. Battiston, Puliga, Kaushik, Tasca, and Caldarelli (2012) develop a measure, which they call DebtRank, related to PageRank used by Google to present search results. It measures the impact that a bank failure has on all other banks (i.e., how much in losses its failure would cause). Martinez-Jaramillo, Alexandrova-Kabadjova, Bravo-Benitez, and Solorano-Margain (2012) use a range of centrality measures and derive similar results. Thurner and Poledna (2013) show that increasing knowledge about DebtRank of a bank can reduce the overall systemic risk as banks will take this information into account when making their lending decisions.

This measure and similar network measures depend on the availability of data, particularly the bilateral exposure of banks. Such information is unavailable to the general public but regulators and central banks either have access to such data or could easily require banks to disclose it. No proposal by regulators exists that would make use of such information for regulatory measures. Further, the general public has not been given access making its applicability limited.

STRESS TESTING

In many cases, systemic events can be seen as the consequence of an extreme external shock to the banking system. Assessing the vulnerability of the banking system to such shocks would be desirable. *Stress testing* analyses the impact a specific scenario on banks such as how much losses a bank faces if GDP falls by 5 percent. Using such an analysis would allow the identification of banks that cannot withstand these scenarios. The difficulty lies in both identifying relevant scenarios and providing a full and comprehensive evaluation of all consequences. Feedback mechanisms through markets are not well understood and often ignored in such tests.

In response to the credit crisis of 2007–2008, regulators required banks to submit results from such stress tests with normalized scenarios. For example, the U.S. scenario in 2012 was that U.S. unemployment would reach 13 percent, stocks would fall by 50 percent, and house prices would fall by 21 percent (Board of Governors of the Federal Reserve System 2012). Some criticize such scenarios for being unrealistic or not severe enough to be a real test of the banks' exposures. Others criticize the stress test required of European Union banks in 2011 in which a default of Greece was not included as a possibility despite the fact that credit default swaps made such a scenario nearly certain (Bloomberg 2011).

Another shortcoming of such stress tests is that connections between banks are usually ignored. That is, the failure of a bank in such an exercise does not affect other banks by treating them as isolated entities. The Bank of England uses a model that goes beyond this treatment of banks as isolated units by allowing for their interaction in the RAMSI model, overcoming this shortcoming (Burrows, Learmonth, and McKeown 2012). If conducted properly, stress testing allows the impact a certain situation has on individual banks to be assessed, but it does not provide a comprehensive assessment of systemic risk.

Regulation of Systemic Risk

The banking sector is one of the most heavily regulated sectors of the economy. Such regulation has generally been justified as protecting depositors from the failure of banks and ensuring the proper functioning of the banking system for the benefit of the wider economy. To this effect, banks generally require a license to operate, are subject to minimum requirements in term of capital, and enhanced disclosure of financial information. The 1988 Basel Accord harmonized such rules, initially imposed by national regulators unilaterally, and regulators widely adopted these rules as the relevant regulatory framework. It required banks to hold a minimum capital of 8 percent of the risk-weighted assets as a central piece of the regulation. This requirement has been amended to incorporate not only credit risk as initially envisaged but also market risk (1996 amendment) and the inclusion of operational risk (Basel II in 2004). More recently in the aftermath of the financial crisis of the 2007–2008 crisis, a new set of rules has been published in 2011 (Basel III). These rules place more emphasis on the risks banks pose to the banking system as a whole rather than focus only on the risks of an individual bank.

Two general approaches are available for regulating banks. One approach is to regulate banks as independent entities, not taking into account the consequences that a failure would have for other banks (*microprudential regulation*). Another approach is to take into account that banks are not isolated entities and consider the consequences their failure would have on other banks and the financial system as a whole (*macroprudential regulation*). Only the latter actually addresses the problem of systemic risk. Brunnermeier, Crocket, Goodhart, Hellwig, Persaud, and Shin (2009) provide an overview of the principles of microprudential and macroprudential regulation.

MICROPRUDENTIAL REGULATION

The traditional aim of banking regulation has been to ensure the soundness of individual banks, (i.e., limit the risks such banks are taking). To this end, regulation treats banks as if they are isolated institutions and neglects any connections among individual banks.

The original Basel Accord, which laid down international standards on banking supervision, was the central piece of regulation. Although it also included principles of banking supervision and information disclosure, the key aspect of regulation was the establishment of minimum capital requirements for banks. Such capital requirements were based on the risk of the assets in which the banks invested either through an assessment of actual risks or formulaic risk assessments.

The aim of this regulation was to reduce the likelihood of a bank failing, but it focused solely on solvency issues. Liquidity problems and the threat to financial systems as a whole were excluded from these considerations until the revisions for Basel III after the credit crisis of 2007–2008. The Basel Committee on Banking Supervision (2011, 2013a) provides the details of the capital and liquidity regulation in Basel III, respectively.

Thus, microprudential regulation does not consider systemic risk and only affects it by making the failure of a bank less likely. Such regulation does not consider the threat a failing bank poses to the financial system. This is what macroprudential regulation aims to accomplish. However, some microprudential regulation has macroprudential elements that also address various aspects of systemic risk. Thus, drawing a clear distinction between these two types of regulation is not possible.

The main idea behind the Basel regulation is that banks should hold a minimum capital relative to risk-weighted assets. The well-known "8 percent rule" for banks meant that capital must be at least 8 percent of risk weighed assets. In the light of the credit crisis of 2007–2008, adjustments have been made as to what qualifies as capital and how risk weights are calculated. A shift has occurred toward capital being more restricted to common equity and retained earnings with other forms of capital, such as subordinated debts, either not counting toward capital or its use being limited. The introduction of limits on dividends and stock repurchases for banks not fulfilling the minimum standards as well as additional capital buffers have brought the capital requirements to 10.5 percent. Additionally, regulators can impose a countercyclical buffer of up to 2.5 percent if they think that banks are expanding their lending unsustainably. All these measures seek to strengthen the capital base of banks and thereby reduce the likelihood of their failure.

A major concern during the credit crisis of 2007-2008 was that banks, while fulfilling their capital requirements, were building up large positions in what was seen as low-risk assets. Hence, banks were highly leveraged. The supposedly low risk assets caused substantial losses and due to the high leverage led to the failure of some banks. In reaction to this development, Basel III now requires a maximum leverage of 3 percent with the United States imposing a much stricter limit of 6 percent for systemically important banks and 5 percent for other bank holding companies.

Another new development in Basel III was the introduction of liquidity requirements, which aim at ensuring that banks can meet their obligations as money is withdrawn, either through depositors or other banks. Banks need to have sufficient liquid funds to cover 30 days of sustained fund withdrawals (i.e., a liquidity coverage ratio) as defined by national regulators. Additionally, the net stable funding ratio requires banks to match the maturities of their assets and liabilities more closely in that long-term and stable liabilities such as deposits, equity, and long-term interbank loans have to exceed long-term assets such as loans.

The aim of these regulations is to reduce the threat of bank failure and is thus clearly microprudential. The Basel III regulation also includes a strictly macroprudential element that is discussed below.

MACROPRUDENTIAL REGULATION

The aim of macroprudential regulation is to limit systemic risk by taking a more holistic view of the financial system. However, in a free market economy, regulation cannot be of the financial system itself, but only constraints put on the behavior of individual banks. These constraints should be designed such that they minimize systemic risk as a whole and consider the impact the failure of a particular bank has on the stability of the financial system. Hanson, Kashyap, and Stein (2011) provide an overview of issues surrounding macroprudential regulation.

Focusing on the tools of macroprudential regulation as discussed in Galati and Moessner (2013), the emphasis of regulators has shifted toward complementing the existing microprudential regulations with countercyclical capital requirements, capital surcharges, liquidity requirements, and risk concentration limits. Basel III includes these aspects, which should be fully implemented by 2019.

Besides the rules of capital and liquidity requirements applicable to all banks, the rules in Basel III also seek to identify those banks, the so-called *systemically important banks* (SIBs), that are most likely to cause a systemic event if they fail. The focus of the Basel Committee is on the global impact any such failure would have and therefore seek to identify *global systemically important banks* (G-SIBs). According to the Basel Committee on Banking Supervision (2013b, p. 3), the aim is to "reduce the probability of failure of G-SIBs by increasing their going-concern loss absorbency; and reduce the extent or impact of failure of G-SIBs, by improving global recovery and resolution frameworks."

The Bank for International Settlements chose an indicator-based approach to assess whether a bank is systemically important. This approach contains five elements: cross-jurisdictional activity, size, interconnectedness, substitutability and financial institution infrastructure, and complexity. The cross-jurisdictional activity captures all assets and liabilities that lie outside of the country in which the bank has its headquarters, thus explicitly assessing the global nature of a bank. The size of a bank, measured by total assets, takes into account the impact the failure of a large bank will have on the global financial system, the so-called *too-big-to-fail* problem. Its interconnectedness (i.e., assets and liabilities from and to other banks as well as securities issued) measures how much a bank is integrated into the financial network. It thus indicates how exposed a bank is to receive any shocks from other banks as well as how much it can transmit such shocks. This is the problem of *too-interconnected-to-fail*. The more important a bank is in a financial system through the amount of payments it processes, the amount of assets it manages, and the amount of underwriting of debt and equity, the larger the impact of its failure will be on the financial system. Hence, the substitutability and financial institution infrastructure forms the fourth indicator. Finally, a bank engaging in considerable trading and OTC derivatives will have a large potential impact on financial markets that can spread. These aspects are included in an indicator called *complexity*.

The relative importance of a bank in each category is evaluated and aggregated to obtain a global score for the importance of a bank. If this score exceeds a certain threshold, it is classified as G-SIB and has to hold additional capital. Depending on the score, the additional capital to be held is 1, 1.5, 2, 2.5, or 3.5 percent as detailed in Basel Committee on Banking Supervision (2013b). In November 2012 a total of 28 banks were classified as G-SIBs (Financial Stability Board 2012), 14 banks requiring an additional 1 percent of capital, eight banks require 1.5 percent, two banks need 2 percent, four banks require 2.5 percent, and no bank requires 3.5 percent.

These measures seek to address systemic risk explicitly rather than focusing on the prevention of failures of a single bank only. Here some factors contributing to systemic risk as discussed in the previous section are addressed. Thus, only this small part of the Basel regulation is a truly macroprudential regulatory element.

A reasonable argument is that the strengthening of the microprudential element of the regulation in Basel III seeks to reduce the threat of information contagion by reassuring the market that the failure of one bank is not indicative of a wider problem across banks. The more stringent capital requirements should also reduce systemic risk arising from market risk as any losses should be more easily absorbed through the banks' higher capital and the same higher capital buffers would allow banks to abstain from fire sales in the first place. Although funding liquidity risk is not addressed explicitly, it is considered through the various liquidity measures introduced in Basel III. The introduction of a net stable funding ratio seeks to align the maturities of assets and liabilities such that rollover risks are reduced. The liquidity coverage ratio pursues the aim that banks can withstand the withdrawal of funds in times of crisis, thus also reducing the threat of bank runs. Including interconnectedness as one of the indicators for G-SIBs explicitly addresses the credit risk contagion. What remains unaddressed is the problem of asset correlation as none of the measures addresses this problem satisfactorily. Here national regulators have the discretion to set limits on the concentration of exposures for individual banks, although without addressing the problem of similar exposures across banks.

Hence, the Basel III regulation addresses various macroprudential elements in its regulatory framework either through introducing new measures or the strengthening of already existing requirements. Besides these measures, the Dodd-Frank Act of 2010 in the United States required large U.S. banks to provide resolution plans (*living wills*) that consist of information about the structure and practice of banks that allow a quick and orderly liquidation of banks. Similar requirements have been imposed on banks in the United Kingdom and European Union.

Implications for Investment Management

Thus far the evaluation of systemic risk has exclusively focused on banks. Few studies examine the implications for investment management. Because investments can suffer from similar problems, systemic risk is not restricted to banks, insurance companies, and similar organizations. This section provides some results reported in the literature on hedge funds, exchange traded funds (ETFs), and money market funds before briefly evaluating the causes of systemic risk in an investment setting.

HEDGE FUNDS

Hedge funds often have sizeable long and short positions, exposing their counterparties, usually large investment banks, to sizeable risks. Low margin requirements allow hedge funds to be highly leveraged and thus cause large losses on their counterparties if they fail. Using derivatives can aggravate any losses hedge funds incur. These sizeable losses imposed on banks can then trigger a systemic event as a bank acting as counterparty fails.

If hedge funds change positions, they might also cause a run on their prime broker by suddenly withdrawing large amounts of cash positions for investment. In turn, this outcome can cause a systemic event if the bank cannot meet these obligations. Dixon, Clancy, and Kumar (2012) discuss in detail how hedge funds can contribute to systemic risk.

EXCHANGE TRADED FUNDS

ETFs often represent an alternative to mutual funds for investors and allow them to trade throughout the day and take short positions. A sizeable fraction of ETFs do not hold the underlying assets, usually the components of an index, but use derivatives to achieve the desired exposure. The derivatives most commonly used are a total return swaps or equity-linked notes. Collateral is given to cover the counterparty risks.

As Ramaswamy (2011) points out, the existence of ETFs using such replication techniques can affect systemic risk in different ways. First, doubt might arise over the solvency of the counterparty providing the derivative, which can lead to sudden withdrawals of money by investors. In turn, this situation can lead to liquidating positions by the fund and thereby exposing the investment bank hedging their positions to market risk. These liquidations can also increase correlations between assets in the market and as such might spread losses if investors observe widespread withdrawals, causing a systemic event.

Redemptions require paying cash to investors, which can lead to a funding crisis by the ETF as the monies might not be easily available because they are being tied up as long-term deposits. Similarly, banks might be unable to repay those deposits as demanded, leading to fire sales and bank runs. Investors in other ETFs might observe these events and decide to withdraw their investments, causing a run on ETFs with widespread losses that can subsequently spread to banks.

MONEY MARKET FUNDS

Recently, attention has focused on *shadow banks*, which are non-bank financial institutions that in many aspects act similar to banks by providing loans but without taking deposits. One aspect in this field that affects investment management is the proposed regulation of money market funds by requiring them to hold minimum amounts of liquid assets (European Commission 2013; Financial Stability Board 2013). Money market funds serve as a substitute to deposits and commonly can be redeemed instantly at face value. These funds invest in short-term debt issued by governments, banks, and industrial companies, and hold more than a quarter of the instruments issued. Similar to deposits, money market funds are subject to runs and thus could be forced to sell quickly large amounts of debt instruments in a fire sale. Such runs could consequently spread to other funds due to losses arising from the lower value of bonds. This affects not only the value of the funds but also banks that hold large amounts of such debt. Thus, a run on money market funds could affect the wider stability of the financial system. Similarly sales of debt by banks would affect the value of money market funds.

EFFECTS ON INVESTMENT RISKS

An aspect worth considering in investment management is asset correlation. Investment managers often agree on the types of assets in which to invest such as stocks in specific industries, or investors choose funds specializing in certain assets. Most funds, with the notable exception of hedge funds, provide information on such exposures and investors can avoid a too high correlation between their investments. If investment managers, who largely agree on their assessment of future prospects of assets, lower their expectations and start to withdraw investments in some sectors, the large overall exposures might cause prices to fall substantially, resulting in losses on other funds that might not be justified fundamentally.

Although mainly affecting hedge funds, the possibility also exists that some investment managers diversify their holdings into derivatives and securitized assets, exposing them to counterparty risks and the systemic risk in the banking sector from which such assets originate. Finally, investment funds that hold securities for longer periods often engage in securities lending to short sellers, mainly banks and hedge funds, in order to increase returns from their holdings. This arrangement exposes them to counterparty risk and therefore systemic risk. Thus, investment managers are also exposed to systemic risk that investors need to consider in their overall risk assessment, beyond the assessment of investment risks themselves.

Summary and Conclusions

Systemic risk is the threat that exogenous events can have large adverse effects on the entire financial system. Such risk has come to the attention of regulators in the aftermath of the credit crisis of 2007–2008 and has led to much research. This chapter provides an overview of the sources of systemic risk, namely the risks arising from banks investing in similar assets, the risk from fire sales, risks from a mismatch in the maturity of deposits and assets, bank runs, and direct exposures to other banks. Each contributes to the overall systemic risk. Despite its importance, the measures of systemic risk are not easily capable of providing a good indicator of such risk. Regulation has responded to the experience of the credit crisis of 2007–2008 by giving more prominence to macroprudential regulation that seeks to address the threat to the financial system as a whole rather than solely focus on individual banks. Finally, the chapter shows systemic risk can affect investment management.

   Understanding systemic risk is only in its infancy. The fact that systemic events are rare does not provide a large data set to empirically analyze a wide variety of aspects of systemic risk. The complexity of the issues at hand and how they interact are only partly understood and await much more work in the future. At this stage the implications for investment management and how fund managers should take these aspects into account are unclear. What has become increasingly clear is that all aspects are somehow connected and systemic risk can originate at many points in the economy through a wide range of such connections.

Discussion Questions

1. Discuss how systemic risk differs from systematic risk.
2. Give some examples of how sources of systemic risk are connected.
3. Discuss the problem of assessing systemic risk when only the risk of individual banks can be determined.
4. Regulators can only constrain the behavior of individual banks through incentives such as capital and liquidity requirements but they cannot affect systemic risk directly. Identify the problems that such a regulatory approach might cause in effectively regulating systemic risk.

References

Acharya, Viral V. 2009. "A Theory of Systemic Risk and Design of Prudential Bank Regulation." *Journal of Financial Stability* 5:3, 224–255.
Acharya, Viral V., and S. Viswanathan. 2011. "Leverage, Moral Hazard, and Liquidity." *Journal of Finance* 66:1, 99–138.

Acharya, Viral V., Douglas Gale, and Tanju Yorulmazer. 2011. "Rollover Risk and Market Freezes." *Journal of Finance* 66:4, 1177–1209.

Acharya, Viral V., Hyun Song Shin, and Tanju Yorulmazer. 2009. "Endogenous Choice of Bank Liquidity: The Role of Fire Sales." Working Paper No. 376, Bank of England.

Acharya, Viral V., Lasse H. Pedersen, Thomas Philippon, and Matthew Richardson. 2010. "Measuring Systemic Risk." Working Paper 10-02 Federal Reserve Bank of Cleveland.

Adrian, Tobias, and Markus K. Brunnermaier. 2009. "CoVaR." Staff Report Number 348, Federal Reserve Bank of New York.

Allen, Franklin, and Elena Carletti. 2013. "What Is Systemic Risk?" *Journal of Money, Credit and Banking*, Supplement to 45:1, 121–127.

Allen, Franklin, and Douglas Gale. 2000. "Financial Contagion." *Journal of Political Economy* 108:1, 1–33.

Basel Committee on Banking Supervision. 2011. "Basel III: A Global Regulatory Framework for More Resilient Banks and Banking Systems." Bank for International Settlements.

Basel Committee on Banking Supervision. 2013a. "Basel III: The Liquidity Coverage Ratio and Liquidity Risk Monitoring Tools." Bank for International Settlements.

Basel Committee on Banking Supervision. 2013b. "Global Systemically Important Banks: Updated Assessment Methodology and the Higher Loss Absorbency Requirement." Bank for International Settlements.

Battiston, Stefano, Michelangelo Puliga, Rahul Kaushik, Paolo Tasca, and Guido Caldarelli. 2012. "DebtRank: Too Central to Fail? Financial Networks, the FED and Systemic Risk." *Scientific Reports* 2:541, 1–6.

Benmelech, Efraim, and Nittai K. Bergman. 2011. "Bankruptcy and the Collateral Channel." *Journal of Finance* 66:2, 337–378.

Bloomberg. 2011. "European Bank Stress Tests Compromised by Greek Non-Default, German Mutiny." Available at http://www.bloomberg.com/news/2011-07-14/european-bank-stress-tests-compromised-by-greek-non-default-german-mutiny.html.

Board of Governors of the Federal Reserve System. 2012. "Comprehensive Capital Analysis and Review 2012: Methodology and Results for Stress Scenario Projections."

Brunnermeier, Markus, Andrew Crocket, Charles Goodhart, Martin Hellwig, Avanish Persaud, and Hyin Shin. 2009. "The Fundamental Principles of Financial Regulation." Geneva Report on the World Economy 11, CEPR Working Paper.

Burrows, Oliver, David Learmonth, and Jack McKeown. 2012. "RAMSI: A Top-down Stress-Testing Model." Financial Stability Paper 17, Bank of England.

Chen, Chen, Garud Iyengar, and Ciamac C. Moallemi. 2013. "An Axiomatic Approach to Systemic Risk." *Management Science* 59:6, 1373–1388.

Cifuentes, Rodrigo, Hyun Song Shin, and Gianluigi Ferucci. 2005. "Liquidity Risk and Contagion." *Journal of the European Economic Association* 3:2–3, 556–566.

Cont, Rama, Amal Moussa, and Edson Bestos e Santos. 2010. "Network Structure and Systemic Risk in Banking Systems." Working Paper, Columbia University.

De Bandt, Olivier, and Philipp Hartmann. 2000. "Systemic Risk: A Survey." Working Paper No. 35, European Central Bank.

Diamond, Douglas W., and Philip H. Dybvig. 1983. "Bank Runs, Deposit Insurance, and Liquidity." *Journal of Political Economy* 91:3, 401–419.

Dixon, Lloyd, Noreen Clancy, and Krishna B. Kumar. 2012. *Hedge Funds and Systemic Risk*. Rand Corporation, Pittsburgh, PA.

European Commission. 2013. "Proposal for a Regulation of the European Parliament and of the Council on Money Market Funds." COM/2013/0615 final - 2013/0306 (COD)

Financial Stability Board. 2012. "Update of Group of Global Systemically Important Banks (G-SIBs)."

Financial Stability Board. 2013. "Strengthening Oversight and Regulation of Shadow Banking—An Overview of Policy Recommendations."

Furfine, Craig H. 2003. "Interbank Exposures: Quantifying the Risk of Contagion." *Journal of Money, Credit and Banking* 35:1, 111–128.

Gai, Prasanna, and Sujit Kapadia. 2010. "Contagion in Financial Networks." *Proceedings of the Royal Society A* 466, 2401–2423.

Galati, Gabriele, and Richhild Moessner. 2013. "Macroprudential Policy—A Literature Review." *Journal of Economic Surveys* 27:5, 846–878.

Gauthier, Celine, Alfred Lehar, and Moez Souissi. 2012. "Macroprudential Capital Requirements and Systemic Risk." *Journal of Financial Intermediation* 21:4, 594–618.

Haldane, Andrew G., and Robert M. May. 2011. "Systemic Risk in Banking Ecosystems." *Nature* 469, 351–355.

Hanson, Samuel G., Anial K. Kashyap, and Jeremy C. Stein. 2011. "A Macroprudential Approach to Financial Regulation." *Journal of Economic Perspectives* 25:1, 3–28.

He, Zhiguo, and Wei Xiong. 2012. "Rollover Risk and Credit Risk." *Journal of Finance* 67:2, 391–429.

Hellwig, Martin F. 2009. "Systemic Risk in the Financial Sector: An Analysis of the Subprime-Mortgage Financial Crisis." *De Economist* 157:2, 129–207.

Iori, Giulia, Saqib Jafarey, and Francisco G. Padilla. 2006. "Systemic Risk on the Interbank Market." *Journal of Economic Behavior & Organization* 61:4, 525–542.

Iyer, Rajkamal, and Jose L. Peydro-Alcalde. 2011. "Interbank Contagion: Evidence from a Natural Experiment." *Review of Financial Studies* 24:4, 1337–1377.

Jensen, Michael C., and William H. Meckling. 1976. "Theory of the Firm: Managerial Behavior, Agency Costs and Ownership Structure." *Journal of Financial Economics* 3:4, 305–360.

Kaufmann, George G. 2000. "Banking and Currency Crises and Systemic Risk: A Taxonomy and Review." *Financial Markets, Institutions & Instruments* 9:2, 69–131.

Kaufmann, George G., and Kenneth E. Scott. 2003. "What Is Systemic Risk, and Do Bank Regulators Retard or Contribute to It?" *The Independent Review* 7:3, 371–391.

Krause, Andreas, and Simone Giansante. 2012. "Interbank Lending and the Spread of Bank Failures: A Network Model of Systemic Risk." *Journal of Economic Behavior & Organization* 83:3, 583–608.

Martinez-Jaramillo, Serafin, Biliana Alexandrova-Kabadjova, Bernardo Bravo-Benitez, and Juan Pablo Solorzano-Margain. 2012. "An Empirical Study of the Mexican Banking System's Network and Its Implications for Systemic Risk." Working Paper 2012-07, Banco de Mexico.

Myers, Stewart C. 2001. "Capital Structure." *Journal of Economic Perspectives* 15:2, 81–102.

Ramaswamy, Srichander. 2011. "Market Structures and Systemic Risks of Exchange Traded Funds." BIS Working Papers No 343, Bank for International Settlements.

Rochet, Jean-Charles, and Jean Tirole. 1996. "Interbank Lending and Systemic Risk." *Journal of Monet, Credit and Banking* 28:4, 733–762.

Schwarcz, Steven L. 2008. "Systemic Risk." *Georgetown Law Journal* 97:1, 193–249.

Shin, Hyun Song. 2009. "Reflections on Northern Rock: The Bank Run that Heralded the Global Financial Crisis." *Journal of Economic Perspectives* 23:1, 101–119.

Shleifer, Andrei, and Robert Vishny. 2011. "Fire Sales in Finance and Macroeconomics." *Journal of Economic Perspectives* 25:1, 29–48.

Smith, Andrew. 2012. "Measuring the Macroeconomic Costs of Banking Crises." Discussion Papers Economics No. 2012-06, Griffith Business School, Griffith University.

Straetmans, Stefan, and Sajid M. Chaudhry. 2012. "Tail Risks and Systemic Risks for U.S. and Eurozone Financial Institutions in the Wake of the Global Financial Crisis." Working Paper, Maastricht University.

Thurner, Stefan, and Sebastian Poledna. 2013. "DebtRank-Transparency: Controlling Systemic Risk in Financial Networks." *Scientific Reports* 3:1888, 1–7.

11

Behavioral Risk

M. MARTIN BOYER

Professor of Finance and Insurance, HEC Montréal

FRANCA GLENZER

PhD Candidate in Finance, Goethe Universität Frankfurt

SAMUEL OUZAN

PhD Candidate in Finance, HEC Montréal

Introduction

Although a common practice is to differentiate between rational choices as predicted by traditional economics and irrational choices as frequently observed in reality, that distinction is often flawed. Under an experimental laboratory setting, scholars can present clearly defined decision tasks, provide information at no cost, and control for many factors influencing individual behavior. Yet, judging whether decisions in the real world are truly irrational given an individual's objective function, experiences, constraints, and computational abilities is more difficult. For instance Gigerenzer (1991, 2008) and Gigerenzer and Selten (2001) develop models of ecological decision-making in which the notion of an efficient decision accounts for the cognitive and time constraints that individuals face in their decision-making process.

Whether decisions that deviate from classical economic theory are irrational, taking a behavioral approach to finance allows a better understanding of individual investment behavior and of phenomena that appear to be present in financial markets. Baker and Nofsinger (2010) provide an extensive survey of behavioral finance. In fact, many empirically observed phenomena in asset pricing cannot be explained by the classical financial economics approach that posits the existence of an individual (i.e., the *homo economicus*) who knows how to correctly perceive and assess the available information and then make the optimal decision. For example, as the efficient market hypothesis (EMH) is built on the assumption that security prices reflect all available information (Fama 1970), any deviation from a stock's fundamental value should be temporary. Yet, some empirical evidence does not support this assumption (Hirshleifer 2001).

As a response to the inability of traditional finance to explain systematic and persistent stock market anomalies such as the equity premium puzzle (Mehra and Prescott

1985; Kocherlakota 1996; Bouvrette 2013), the closed end fund puzzle (De Long et al. 1990a; Lee, Shleifer, and Thaler 1991; Shleifer 2000) or the market's excess volatility (LeRoy and Porter 1981; Shiller 1981), the field of behavioral finance emerged (Shiller 2003; Baker and Nofsinger 2010). It combines insights from both finance and psychology to arrive at models of human decision processes that better explain and forecast decisions that seem to deviate from what traditional economics dubs a rational choice.

The purpose of this chapter is to provide insights into the impact of behavioral factors on financial decision-making. The biases that arise in the decision-making process can result in costly outcomes both on the individual level and market level. The term *behavioral risk* refers to these adverse developments that stem from individuals deviating from lending and investment behavior as prescribed by economic theory.

This chapter begins by presenting theoretical concepts related to the investors' utility function and then moves to more applied problems such as investor heuristics, overconfidence, noise trader risk, and herding behavior in financial markets. Although these are not the only types of behavioral risks, they are the most prominent in the academic and professional literature. Baker and Nofsinger (2010) provide a more extensive survey.

Loss Aversion and Framing

Loss aversion and framing are two major psychological concepts that play a crucial role in behavioral finance. They form the basis for many models of behavioral decision-making. This chapter addresses two such models. *Loss aversion* represents the tendency of individuals to be more sensitive to decreases in their level of wealth than to increases. By contrast, *framing* refers to how alternatives are presented to individuals. According to Tversky and Kahneman (1992, p. 298), "The rational theory of choice assumes description invariance: equivalent formulations of a choice problem should give rise to the same preference order (Arrow, 2004). Contrary to this assumption, there is much evidence that variations in the framing of options . . . yield systematically different preferences." This chapter discusses several models that incorporate the notions of loss aversion and framing, prospect theory (Kahneman and Tversky 1979; Tversky and Kahneman 1992) and realization utility (Barberis and Xiong 2012).

A related concept is *mental accounting* as explained by Thaler (1980). It describes how individuals keep different mental accounts and assign economic outcomes to these accounts, such as saving for a car and saving for a holiday. This separation of accounts can lead to an inconsistent assessment of the same event, depending on the mental account under consideration. In a sense, by assigning a choice to a particular mental account, individuals influence the framing of that choice.

PROSPECT THEORY

Prospect theory is a descriptive model of choice under uncertainty that aims at capturing observed biases in decision-making that expected utility theory has so far neglected (Altman 2010). In their seminal article, Kahneman and Tversky (1979) conduct several experiments and show that individuals tend to exhibit the following biases: loss aversion, overweighing of small probabilities, and underweighting of medium and high probabilities. Using the expected utility framework, individuals make decisions under risk based on maximizing their expected utility given objective probabilities and known outcomes, Kahneman and Tversky propose that individuals subjectively weigh both the probabilities and the possible outcomes.

The asymmetry between gains and losses and the way individuals code economic outcomes are key ingredients in the theoretical explanation of the equity premium puzzle (Benartzi and Thaler 1995). The *equity premium* states that because stock returns outperform bond returns by such a large margin, then only an abnormally high level of risk aversion could explain why investors hold bonds (Mehra and Prescott 1985). Benartzi and Thaler combine loss aversion and mental accounting to provide a theoretical basis for explaining this phenomenon. They conclude that investors are more inclined to take risks if they evaluate portfolio performance infrequently. In particular, they find that an evaluation period of one year makes investors indifferent between holding stocks or bonds. If the evaluation period increases, stocks become more attractive, suggesting that frequently evaluating a portfolio is not only costly but also affects asset allocation.

The Disposition Effect and Realization Utility

According to Thaler (1999), individuals might derive utility from realized gains and losses rather than terminal wealth because a realized loss is more painful than an unrealized loss. This idea first appears in Shefrin and Statman (1985). They combine prospect theory, mental accounting, tax considerations, regret aversion, and self-control to explain the tendency to sell winning stocks too early and hold losing stocks too long. Shefrin and Statman were the first to call this famous phenomenon the *disposition effect.* Kaustia (2010) provides more discussion on the topic.

Barberis and Xiong (2009) investigate whether prospect theory can predict a disposition effect. They find that framing gains and losses in terms of realizing gains and losses predicts a disposition effect while framing them in terms of annual gains and losses fails to do so. The authors isolate and emphasize the central role of realized transactions on individual investor perception. Barberis and Xiong (2012) develop a more comprehensive analysis on that subject, which they call *realization utility*. This model assumes that investors see the investment process as a series of distinct episodes during each of which they either make or lose money. Investors experience a burst of pleasure when they sell an asset at a gain, but receive a burst of pain when they sell an asset at a loss relative to its purchase price. An important implication of that model is that even if the functional form of realization utility is linear and concave, the investor can be risk-seeking. Indeed, a highly volatile stock may imply a large gain in the future that investors can enjoy realizing. Frydman, Barberis, Camerer, Bossaets, and Rangel (2012) find evidence supporting the realization utility hypothesis using data on brain activity.

Another phenomenon that realization utility can explain is excessive trading behavior. Barber and Odean (2000) report that after transaction costs, the average return of investors in their sample is below the return of multiple benchmarks. This phenomenon is known as *excessive trading behavior* because frequent trading hurts investors' performance. Barberis and Xiong (2012) contend that after a stock has risen in value relative to the purchase price, investors are tempted to sell the stock to receive a burst of positive utility. The transaction costs lead the investors to underperform against the benchmarks. Realization utility also offers an explanation for underperformance before transaction costs (Barber, Lee, Liu, and Odean 2009).

Heuristics in Decision-Making

When faced with a decision task, individuals often lack the ability to carry out the complex optimization expected from them under standard economic theory. Instead, the decision maker may rely on simple cognitive strategies or intuitive heuristics (mental shortcuts) in order to eliminate some dimensions of the decision task. Although these strategies facilitate decision-making, they also induce decisions that deviate from outcomes prescribed by economic theory. Among the most important heuristics are representativeness, anchoring, contamination effect, and familiarity bias.

THE REPRESENTATIVENESS HEURISTIC

The representativeness heuristic can be conceptualized as the tendency to assess the similarity of outcomes based on stereotypes and then to use these assessments of similarity as a basis of judgment. Psychologists observe that individuals often try to interpret random events as the result of a thoughtful and predictable series of events. For instance, society frequently tries to assign blame to some individual when a major accident occurs.

Related to the interpretation of random events are the terms *apophenia* and *pareidolia*, which Powers (2012) defines as a phenomenon in which people believe that systematic patterns exist in entirely random data. Some contend that the Rorschach inkblot test in which a psychologist analyzes a subject's interpretation of inkblots using some sort of interpretation grid falls within the realm of apophenia. According to Chapman and Chapman (1982), the Rorschach inkblot test was once the most widely used test for revealing hidden emotions. The "science" behind such tests is that humans have attitudes and motivations that are hidden from conscious awareness. Hume (1757, p. 11) recognized this human tendency more than 250 years ago when he stated:

> There is a universal tendency among mankind to conceive all beings like themselves, and to transfer to every object those qualities with which they are familiarly acquainted, and of which they are intimately conscious. We find human faces in the moon, armies in the clouds; and by a natural propensity, if not corrected by experience and reflection, ascribe malice and good will to everything that hurts or pleases us.

The human tendency of trying to find a pattern in randomness is a normal human bias. McFadden (1999, p. 93) writes:

Tune (1964) and Kahneman and Tversky (1972) document experimentally that individuals intuitively reject randomness when they see recognizable patterns or streaks, systematically underestimating the probability that these can occur by chance. These biases reinforce the influence of random coincidences on beliefs and behavior.

Sterman (1994) and McFadden (1999) call this search for confirmation of current beliefs a quest for "emotional and spiritual sustenance." This confirmation bias serves as one explanation for the hot-hand fallacy as described by Gilovich, Vallone, and Tversky (1985). They find that people often assume the existence of a "hot hand" in basketball. Although no empirical evidence shows that a basketball player has a higher chance of making a successful shot if the previous shots were successful, many people still assume a positive correlation between events. This phenomenon occurs when people perceive outcomes to depend on abilities. In the case of random events such as a coin toss, individuals will often assume a negative correlation; this is known as the *gambler's fallacy* (Tversky and Kahneman 1971). Assuming a fair coin, the probability of throwing heads after a sequence of tails is still one half, but people often overestimate this probability. As an explanation, Tversky and Kahneman propose the so-called *law of small numbers* by which people expect the large sample properties of a random event to be reflected in a small sample. In other words, because the number of heads should equal the number of tails in an infinite sample of coin tosses, both outcomes are assumed to occur equally often in a sample of say 10 tosses. Both fallacies can be observed in a financial decision setting where individuals exhibit greater trust in human performance when predicting a random sequence than in betting randomly (Huber, Kirchler, and Stöckl 2010).

Another example of apophenia is the quest for predictability of business cycles. Within insurance markets, the property and liability insurance market was in upheaval in the 1970s and 1980s because of the rapid rise of insurance premiums. The cyclicality of insurer profitability was a hot topic and generated a wide body of literature (Boyer, Jacquier, and Van Norden 2012). Despite the lack of accepted econometric evidence of the existence of such cycles, the fascination with assuming such cycles and thus predictability remains.

ANCHORING AND THE CONTAMINATION EFFECT

The *anchoring heuristic* is associated with people's tendency to anchor their thoughts and judgments to a reference point. As irrelevant as past information may be, it still anchors and contaminates people's guesses. According to Tversky and Kahneman (1974), when forming estimates and predictions, people usually start with some initial arbitrary value and make adjustments from that value. An interesting implication from the anchoring heuristic is *overconfidence*. When people are asked to provide an estimate of the 98 percent confidence interval of a stock market index, they tend to anchor on their best estimate of the index and provide a confidence interval that is too small (Tversky and Kahneman 1982). They hence overestimate the precision of their stock market index estimate. The same heuristic applies to the *purchase price fallacy* or *the sunk cost fallacy*, whereby investors anchor their estimate of the minimum value of a security on the purchase price. Anchoring on the purchase price often leads investors to keep securities that have lost value for too long, and sell securities that have gained value too early (Odean 1998).

THE FAMILIARITY BIAS

People dislike ambiguity and tend to invest in what they know. This phenomenon is an important behavioral risk because manifesting a bias toward the familiar suggests a potential lack of diversification. According to French and Poterba (1991), a lack of diversification appears to be the result of investor choices rather than institutional constraints. Familiarity could refer either to a *local bias*, when investors display a preference for local assets, or to a *home bias*, when an individual's portfolio is heavily biased toward domestic equity.

Both institutional and behavioral explanations exist for familiarity bias. Perhaps the most popular rational explanation is asymmetric information. Several studies contend that the local bias may be a rational response to better information about familiar assets (Ivković and Weisbenner 2005; Massa and Simonov 2006). Economic and cultural distance, which represents a barrier to the flow of information, could explain home bias (Hau 2001). However, rational explanations for familiarity can only explain part of the home bias. Among popular behavioral explanations, researchers have analyzed the role of overconfidence, regret, patriotism, and social identification. This relatively new and growing literature finds that investors exhibit overconfidence in predicting returns of familiar assets. They then may prefer to invest in local assets to avoid regret or because of social identification and patriotism (Foad 2010).

Similar to familiarity, the *availability bias* is a cognitive heuristic in which a decision maker relies upon knowledge that is readily available rather than examining other alternatives or procedures. Availability can be viewed as the tendency to disproportionally recall very recent events or events in which the person is emotionally involved. The more salient an event, the more likely it is to drive an individual's investment decision.

Apart from geographical effects, a familiarity bias also exists in the domain of professional disciplines that causes biases in financial decision-making. Legoux, Boyer, Léger, and Robert (2014) test the optimistic and confirmation biases of financial and information technology (IT) experts regarding major IT investments. The interest of focusing on IT investment projects is that they can generate considerable wealth for the investing company and for the service providers, but they can also fail. As a result of the capital needed for such investments, the delay between investment and profits, and the intangibility of IT investments, such projects are highly risky and uncertain. This uncertainty drives the financial market's reaction to major IT investments, which is compounded by the generally limited understanding of the IT industry by financial analysts.

The phenomenon akin to the IT exuberance of the late 1990s is not new (Perez 2002). As Schiller (2000) comments, persistent cognitive biases in investors' behavior (Tversky and Kahneman 1974; Thaler 1993) would be evidence of investors displaying optimistic biases that resulted in the IT exuberance. Such optimistic biases can be defined as an impression of invulnerability (Weinstein and Klein 1995). Because optimistic biases play a role in protecting a person's self-image, they are widespread and hard to dampen (Kreuter and Strecher 1995).

Similar to Madsen (1994), Legoux et al. (2014) partly attribute systematic optimism to a *confirmation bias*, which Klayman (1995) defines as an inclination by individuals to retain a currently favored hypothesis throughout their decision process. Under the confirmation bias framework, analysts investigate each potential investment in a hypothetical-deductive manner. First, they pay attention to a subset of information to generate a focal hypothesis about the market's likely reaction to the announcement of the investment. Analysts then test their focal hypothesis with the remaining information. If the hypothesis cannot be supported, they generate a new hypothesis and repeat the process. Legoux et al. propose that the confirmation bias framework implies that optimism originates in the hypothesis generation phase of the evaluation process so that any optimistic outlook is then theorized to be confirmed by individuals in the hypothesis testing phase of the process. The authors show that competent analysts tend to pay attention initially to their area of expertise and then confirm their focal hypothesis with the information from another source. Their findings support the assertion that analysts attribute more weight to information in which they have some expertise.

Technical Analysis

Technical analysis can be seen as one example of pattern recognition, which is a topic previously addressed. Pring (2002, p. 2) defines *technical analysis* as:

> A reflection of the idea that prices move in trends that are determined by the changing attitudes of investors toward a variety of economic, monetary, political, and psychological forces. The art of technical analysis, for it is an art, is to identify a trend reversal at a relatively early stage and ride on that trend until the weight of the evidence shows or proves that the trend has reversed.

One of these techniques calls for examining charts and requires developing algorithms that recognize patterns in the charts (Dawson and Steeley 2003; Park and Irwin 2007). Technical analysts give various names to patterns that reflect the shapes and other features of past price or volume behavior. For example, names used in bar chart analysis include spikes, tops, and bottoms (and double-tops and double-bottoms), as well as wedges, triangles, flags, head-and-shoulders, candlesticks, Japanese candles, and dead-cat bounce. These images are not very different from the subconscious recognition of animals and faces in Rorschach inkblot tests.

Frankel and Froot (1986, 1990) provide an early example of the impact of technical analysis. They combine a standard monetary model of open economy macroeconomics with a chartist-fundamentalist approach to expectation formation in order to explain excess volatility and bubble formation in asset prices. Their evidence shows that a large deviation of a stock price from its fundamental value can be so large from the fundamentalist's perspective as to trigger a switch of some agents from fundamentalist to chartist behavior. The more the market composition changes in favor of the chartist group, the less pressure exists for prices to revert to their fundamental anchor values thereby creating a long-standing divergence between observed prices and their fundamental value.

A relationship appears to exist between the use of chart patterns by technical analysts and that of ink-blot tests by psychologists to determine the subconscious drivers of an individual's behavior. Similarly, the use and appearance of graphs has an important impact on decision-making (Remus 1984). That is why the format in which financial product information is conveyed to investors influences their beliefs and choices (Kahneman and Tversky 1979; Durbach and Stewart 2011; Glenzer, Gründl, and Wilde 2013).

For instance, an individual's subconscious reaction to patterns occurs when he is asked to give his appreciation on paintings or patterns drawn using fractal mathematics. In this context, fractals display self-similarity so that a small part of the pattern looks much like the pattern as a whole. Mandelbrot (1977, 1982) provides an early contribution on the topic. In contrast to Euclidean geometry, the dimension of a fractal is not an integer. In visual perception and skin conductance tests, Wise and Taylor (2002) find that participants consistently express a preference for fractal dimension values in the range of 1.3 to 1.5. Could it be that asset return patterns with a fractal dimension between 1.3 and 1.5 induce bliss and reduce the risk aversion of market participants? If true, then being able to anticipate such patterns would allow technical traders to anticipate a period of bliss among participants and possibly profit from such trades. Research has not yet shown this link. Taffler and Tuckett (2010) provide further discussion of emotional finance.

Overconfidence

According to Glaser and Weber (2010), a crucial aspect of decision-making and the most prevalent judgment bias is the subjective assessment of probabilities that occurs when individuals are asked to estimate probabilities. In this context, *overconfidence* refers to the tendency to overestimate or exaggerate one's ability to successfully perform a particular task. DeBondt and Thaler (1995) contend that perhaps the most robust finding in the psychology of judgment is that people are overconfident. Plous (1993) notes that overconfidence has been called the most "pervasive and potentially catastrophic" of all the cognitive biases to which humans fall victim. Lichtenstein, Fischhoff, and Phillips (1982) find that overconfidence occurs in most tasks because assessors tend to overestimate how much they know. Also, the degree of overconfidence depends of the difficulty of the task, so that as the difficulty of the task increases so does the level of overconfidence.

One facet of overconfidence is the *better-than-average effect*, which Taylor and Brown (1988) document as individuals having unrealistically positive views of themselves. This behavior is characterized by individuals judging themselves to be better than others with respect to skills or positive character traits. For example, Sevenson (1981) documents a widely cited experiment in which researchers asked students to compare themselves with the drivers they encounter on the road. The results show that 82 percent of the respondents rank themselves among the 30 percent of drivers with the highest driving safety.

Overconfident investors have the tendency to purchase high risk stocks and to under-diversify their portfolio. Nofsingser (2007, p. 10) states that security selection "is precisely this type of task at which people exhibit the greatest overconfidence." For example, Odean (1998) reports a positive correlation between the presence of overconfident traders and the volatility of asset prices. He also demonstrates that over-confident traders hold undiversified portfolios and have lower expected utility than rational traders. Models of investor overconfidence also predict high trading volumes, a phenomenon known as *excessive trading*.

As Daniel, Hirshleifer, and Subrahmanyam (1998) show, the combination of the overreaction and self-attribution biases can reconcile short-run positive autocorrelation with long-run negative autocorrelation. Their theory also provides an explanation for the pattern that stock price reactions, after a public event, have the same sign as post event long-run abnormal returns. Researchers sometimes interpret this phenomenon as market under-reaction. From a behavioral risk perspective, overconfident informed traders lose money on average. Using the notion of *noise trader risk*, as defined by De Long et al. (1990a), Daniel, Hirshleifer, and Subrahmanyam (2001) develop a model in which overconfidence allows risk-averse traders to exploit information more effectively and thus to increase their profits.

Noise Trader Risk

Does the presence of mispricing predict possible profit? In the traditional framework, economic agents are rational, markets are frictionless, and hence markets are efficient. The *efficient market hypothesis* implies that observed asset prices reflect fundamental values and that deviations only occur in the short run. Behavioral finance, however, claims that some characteristics of asset prices are most presumably interpreted as persistent deviations from fundamental value. The principal argument against persist-ent mispricing is that it creates arbitrage opportunities so that rational traders will immediately take advantage of these prices deviation, thereby correcting the mispricing (Shleifer and Summers 1990). By contrast, De Long et al. (1990a) and Shleifer (2000) maintain that correcting the mispricing is not straightforward and could be very risky. This means that some rational individuals could prefer to behave irrationally.

Black (1986) was the first to introduce the notion of noise traders who trade on noise as opposed to information. Shleifer and Vishny (1997) further analyze this phe-nomenon and describe an economy in which rational traders (arbitrageurs) bet against irrational traders—another name for "noise traders." They associate noise trader risk with the risk of mispricing being exploited by arbitrageurs. Shleifer and Vishny show that under certain conditions, arbitrageurs face difficulties in profitably exploiting market inefficiencies even if implementation costs, such as transactions costs and a short-sell constraint, are low. De Long et al. (1990a) show that if noise trader risk is systematic and if arbitrageurs are risk-averse and have a short planning horizon, arbi-trage will be limited even without implementation costs. In a related study, De Long, Shleifer, Summers, and Waldmann (1990b) describe an economy where noise traders follow positive-feedback strategies (i.e., buy when prices rise and sell when prices fall). For this type of economy, the authors show that arbitrageurs may prefer to trade in the same direction as noise traders. Instead of correcting the mispricing, arbitrageurs will therefore exacerbate it.

In theory, any evidence of persistent mispricing will be sufficient to assert that limits exist to an informed trader's ability to benefit from arbitrage opportunities. The presence of mispricing is not testable because any mispricing is inevitably tested jointly with some equilibrium asset-pricing model (Fama 1970). Despite this obvious problem, Barberis and Thaler (2005) note several cases where researchers report financial market anomalies that almost certainly indicate persistent mispricing.

Collective Irrationality and Herding

Herding in financial markets is a common phenomenon used to explain the existence and persistence of asset bubbles. As highlighted in Cipriani and Guarino (2009), much literature tries to identify the mechanisms that lead traders to herd (Gale 1996; Hirshleifer and Teoh 2003; Vives 2010). Herding can only occur when agents play sequentially so that early movers have a disproportionately large impact on prices because future traders will base their trading on the early movers' behavior (Caplin and Leahy 1993, 1994; Bulow and Klemperer 1994; Avery and Zemsky 1998). Informed traders can behave as if they are uninformed because the risk of going against the herd is larger than the potential gain from being right. The best that informed traders can do when faced with herding is to stay away from that market.

According to financial theory, prices often adjust to the order flow (Evans and Lyons 2002; Bjønnes and Rime 2005; Boyer and van Norden 2006). In financial markets, the herding of rational traders is possible because of different sources of market uncertainty (Scharfstein and Stein 1990).

As Avery and Zemsky (1998) show, herding behavior in financial markets cannot occur based on a single source of uncertainty and cannot affect market prices even when two sources of uncertainty are present. In contrast to Banerjee (1992), the model of Avery and Zemsky (1998) does not lead to herd behavior as the result of a single source of uncertainty because Avery and Zemsky assume that all traders are rational and have access to a steady flow of information that leads to prices to converge to the asset's fundamental value. Herding behavior can have an important short-term impact on asset prices when three sources of uncertainty in the market are present: the impact of a shock, existence of a shock, and quality of the trader's information. These three sources of uncertainty are important because for herding to have an economic impact, one needs to have, in a market composed of sophisticated agents, traders who erroneously believe that they have information that is more accurate than reality. This means that agents are incapable of separating a market composed of informed traders from one consisting of traders who are herding. According to Avery and Zemsky, the probability of having a state in which sophisticated agents are mistaken enough to create economically significant herding that leads to bubbles and crashes is very unlikely.

Hong and Stein (1999) propose a theory that unifies the observed under- and over-reaction of capital markets to news. They suggest that by dividing the population of traders between news-watchers (fundamental traders) and momentum traders (chartists), the possibility exists of inferring information from the other traders' trading behavior. In such a model, market prices can be out-of-equilibrium in the sense that past returns can be positively correlated with current returns (i.e., returns display momentum) in the short-run and negatively correlated (i.e., returns display reversal) in the long run. Dasgupta, Prat, and Verardo (2011) report a similar result using the trading behavior of institutional investors.

Summary and Conclusions

The risk associated with individual behavior has become a hot topic in financial research. The efficient market hypothesis is no longer free from attacks from either theoretical or empirical perspectives. This chapter highlights some biases in investor behavior, theories explaining some apparently irrational market behavior, and fields other than finance where behavioral risk is present. After introducing "traditional" approaches to behavioral risk in finance, the chapter focuses on modifications to the neo-classical expected utility paradigm such as loss aversion, framing, realization theory, and prospect theory. These modifications introduce biases in the way that individuals treat gains and losses.

The chapter also covers heuristics in decision-making including representativeness, anchoring, and contamination. The effect of familiarity bias occurs in other markets besides capital markets such as in the field of insurance pricing. Additionally, the chapter considers technical analysis because it has characteristics that are similar to those associated with the familiarity bias and pattern recognition bias. Next, the chapter examines overconfidence because of its economic impact on financial markets. Finally, the risks associated with noise traders and collective irrationality (herding) are examined. The fact that the presence of uninformed traders can throw a market into imbalance is a risk with which informed traders must contend when their wealth is not infinite. Finite wealth limits the informed traders' ability to quickly adjust security prices to their fundamental value. Herding is also a risk that concerns informed traders. When current trades occur because similar trades have occurred in the past, a rational response is for informed traders to trade in the same direction as the herd despite knowing that such trades move the price away from the fundamental value. The impact of behavioral risk is not trivial and permeates many stakeholders in society. For example, individuals are increasingly responsible for accumulating sufficient wealth to provide for their old age with the disappearance of defined benefit pension plans in favor of defined contribution pension plans being the main driver. The risk that different biases, heuristics, and apparent sub-optimal behaviors discussed in this chapter will affect their investment decisions becomes an important concern for financial markets, financial regulators, and public policy makers.

Even if individual investors are not directly responsible for their own accumulation of wealth, ample evidence suggests that professional traders are not impervious to behavioral risk. This means that pension plan managers may be subject to the same biases as the future pensioners. The same challenges can be encountered at the national level if a country has a partially capitalized public pension plan. The ways in which behavioral risk affects financial decisions begets the question of behavioral risk management. The evidence on the impact of behavioral risk highlights the need for portfolio managers to acknowledge the existence of this type of risk and install processes that would identify and manage it. For instance, one may think about the possibility of adopting a systematic review of the firm's investment processes by teams that differ with respect to experience, discipline, sex, and cultural background. Although individuals in the review team are probably no less affected by biases, diversification could possibly mitigate the economic impact of behavioral risk.

Discussion Questions

1. Discuss the importance of framing or mental accounting from a behavioral risk perspective and its relationship to Benartzi and Thaler's explanation of the equity premium puzzle.
2. Explain whether the absence of an arbitrage opportunity necessarily implies that markets are efficient.
3. Explain the implications of familiarity bias for asset allocation.
4. Explain how pareidolia and apophenia can be observed in financial markets.
5. Explain how the anchoring heuristic is related to an agent's overconfident behavior and illustrate how overconfidence affects trading behavior.

References

Altman, Morris. 2010. "Prospect Theory and Behavioral Finance." In H. Kent Baker and John R. Nofsinger, eds., *Behavioral Finance: Investors, Corporations, and Markets*, 191–209. Hoboken, NJ: John Wiley & Sons.

Arrow, Kenneth J. 2004. "Risk Perception in Psychology and Economics." *Economic Inquiries* 201:1, 1–9.

Avery, Christopher, and Peter Zemsky. 1998. "Multidimensional Uncertainty and Herd Behavior in Financial Markets." *American Economic Review* 88:4, 724–748.

Baker, H. Kent, and John R. Nofsinger, eds. 2010. *Behavioral Finance: Investors, Corporations, and Markets*. Hoboken, NJ: John Wiley & Sons.

Banerjee, Abhijit V. 1992. "A Simple Model of Herd Behavior." *Quarterly Journal of Economics* 107:3, 797–817.

Barber, Brad N., Yi-Tsung Lee, Yu-Jane Liu, and Terrance Odean. 2009. "Just How Much Do Investors Lose from Trade?" *Review of Financial Studies* 22:2, 151–186.

Barber, Brad N., and Terrance Odean. 2000. "Trading Is Hazardous to Your Wealth: The Common Stock Performance for Individual Investors." *Journal of Finance* 55:2, 773–806.

Barberis, Nicholas, and Richard H. Thaler. 2005. "A Survey of Behavioral Finance." In Richard H. Thaler, ed., *Advances in Behavioral Finance*, Volume 2, 1–78. New York: Russell Sage Foundation.

Barberis, Nicholas, and Wei Xiong. 2009. "What Drives the Disposition Effect? An Analysis of a Long-Standing Preference-Based Explanation." *Journal of Finance* 64:2, 751–784.

Barberis, Nicholas, and Wei Xiong. 2012. "Realization Utility." *Journal of Financial Economics* 104:2, 251–271.

Benartzi, Shlomo, and Richard H. Thaler. 1995. "Myopic Loss Aversion and the Equity Premium Puzzle." *Quarterly Journal of Economics* 110:1, 75–92.

Bjønnes, Geir H., and Dagfime Rime. 2005. "Dealer Behavior and Trading Systems in Foreign Exchange Markets." *Journal of Financial Economics* 75:3, 571–605.

Black, Fischer. 1986. "Noise." *Journal of Finance* 41:3, 529–544.

Bouvrette, Jean-Charles. 2013. "Tarification des actifs financiers et consommation: Évaluation du risque de composition de la consommation." PhD dissertation, HEC Montréal.

Boyer, M. Martin, Eric Jacquier, and Simon Van Norden. 2012. "Are Underwriting Cycles Real and Forecastable?" *Journal of Risk and Insurance* 79:4, 995–1015.

Boyer, M. Martin, and Simon van Norden. 2006. "Exchange Rates and Order Flow in the Long Run." *Finance Research Letters* 3:4, 235–243.

Bulow, Jeremy, and Paul Klemperer. 1994. "Rational Frenzies and Crashes." *Journal of Political Economy* 102:1, 1–23.

Caplin, Andrew, and John Leahy. 1993. "Sectoral Shocks, Learning and Aggregate Fluctuations." *Review of Economic Studies* 60:4, 777–794.

Caplin, Andrew, and John Leahy. 1994. "Business as Usual, Market Crashes, and Wisdom after the Fact." *American Economic Review* 84:3, 548–565.

Chapman, Loren J., and Jean Chapman. 1982. "Test Results Are What You Think They Are." In Daniel Kahneman, Paul Slovic, and Amos Tversky, eds., *Judgment under Uncertainty: Heuristics and Biases*, 239–248. Cambridge: Cambridge University Press.

Cipriani, Marco, and Antonio Guarino. 2009. "Herd Behavior in Financial Markets: An Experiment with Financial Market Professionals." *Journal of the European Economic Association* 7:1, 206–233.

Daniel, Kent, David Hirshleifer, and Avanidhar Subrahmanyam. 1998. "Investor Psychology and Security Market Under- and Overreactions." *Journal of Finance* 53:6, 1839–1885.

Daniel, Kent, David Hirshleifer, and Avanidhar Subrahmanyam. 2001. "Overconfidence, Arbitrage, and Equilibrium Asset Pricing." *Journal of Finance* 56:3, 921–965.

Dasgupta, Amil, Andrea Prat, and Michela Verardo. 2011. "The Price Impact of Institutional Herding." *Review of Financial Studies* 24:3, 892–925.

Dawson, Edward R., and James M. Steeley. 2003. "On the Existence of Visual Technical Patterns in the UK Stock Market." *Journal of Business Finance & Accounting* 30:1, 263–293.

DeBondt, Werner F. M., and Richard H. Thaler. 1995. "Financial Decision-Making in Markets and Firms: A Behavioral Perspective." In Robert A. Jarrow, Voijslav Maksimovic, and William T. Ziemba, eds., *Finance, Handbooks in Operations Research and Management Science*, 385–410. Amsterdam: North Holland.

De Long, J. Bradford, Andrei Shleifer, Lawrence H. Summers, and Robert J. Waldmann. 1990a. "Noise Trader Risk in Financial Markets." *Journal of Political Economy* 98:4, 703–738.

De Long, J. Bradford, Andrei Shleifer, Lawrence H. Summers, and Robert J. Waldmann. 1990b. "Positive Feedback Investment Strategies and Destabilizing Rational Speculation." *Journal of Finance* 45:2, 375–395.

Durbach, Ian N., and Theodor J. Stewart. 2011. "An Experimental Study of the Effect of Uncertainty Representation on Decision Making." *European Journal of Operational Research* 214:2, 380–392.

Evans, Martin D. D., and Richard K. Lyons. 2002. "*Order Flow and Exchange Rate Dynamics.*" *Journal of Political Economy* 110:1, 170–180.

Fama, Eugene F. 1970. "Efficient Capital Markets: A Review of Theory and Empirical Work." *Journal of Finance* 25:2, 383–417.

Foad, Hisham. 2010. "Familiarity Bias." In H. Kent Backer and John R. Nofsinger, eds., *Behavioral Finance: Investors, Corporations, and Markets*, 277–294. Hoboken, NJ: John Wiley & Sons.

Frankel, Jeffrey A., and Kenneth A. Froot. 1986. "Understanding the US Dollar in the Eighties: The Expectations of Chartists and Fundamentalists." *Economic Record* 1:2, 24–38.

Frankel, Jeffrey A., and Kenneth A. Froot. 1990. "Chartists, Fundamentalists, and Trading in the Foreign Exchange Market." *American Economic Review* 80:2, 181–185.

French, Kenneth R., and James M. Poterba. 1991. "Investor Diversification and International Equity Markets." *American Economic Review* 81:2, 222–226.

Frydman, Cary, Nicholas Barberis, Colin Camerer, Peter Bossaerts, and Antonio Rangel. 2012. "Using Neural Data to Test a Theory of Investor Behavior: An Application to Realization." NBER Working Paper.

Gale, Douglas. 1996. "What Have We Learned from Social Learning?" *European Economic Review* 40:3, 617–628.

Gigerenzer, Gerd. 1991. "From Tools to Theories: A Heuristic of Discovery in Cognitive Psychology." *Psychological Review* 98:2, 254–267.

Gigerenzer, Gerd. 2008. *Rationality for Mortals: How People Cope with Uncertainty*. New York: Oxford University Press.

Gigerenzer, Gerd, and Reinhard Selten. 2001. *Bounded Rationality: The Adaptive Toolbox*. Cambridge, MA: MIT Press.

Gilovich, Thomas, Robert Vallone, and Amos Tversky. 1985. "The Hot Hand in Basketball: On the Misperception of Random Sequences." *Cognitive Psychology* 3:17, 295–314.

Glaser, Markus, and Martin Weber. 2010. "Overconfidence." In H. Kent Baker and John R. Nofsinger, eds., *Behavioral Finance: Investors, Corporations, and Markets*, 241–258. Hoboken, NJ: John Wiley & Sons.

Glenzer, Franca, Helmut Gründl, and Christian Wilde. 2013. "And Lead Us Not into Temptation: Presentation Formats and the Choice of Risky Alternatives." ICIR Working Paper No. 13.

Hau, Harald. 2001. "Location Matter: An Examination of Trading Profits." *Journal of Finance* 56:5, 1959–1983.

Hirshleifer, David. 2001. "Investor Psychology and Asset Pricing." *Journal of Finance* 56:4, 1533–1597.

Hirshleifer, David, and Siew H. Teoh. 2003. "Herd Behaviour and Cascading in Capital Markets: A Review and Synthesis." *European Financial Management* 9:1, 25–66.

Hong, Harrison, and Jeremy C. Stein. 1999. "A Unified Theory of Underreaction, Momentum Trading, and Overreaction in Asset Markets." *Journal of Finance* 54:6, 2143–2184.

Hong, Harrison, and Jeremy C. Stein. 2007. "Disagreement and the Stock Market." *Journal of Economic Perspectives* 21:2, 109–128.

Huber, Jürgen, Michael Kirchler, and Thomas Stöckl. 2010. "The Hot Hand Belief and the Gambler's Fallacy in Investment Decisions under Risk." *Theory and Decision* 68:4, 445–462.

Hume, David. 1757. *The Natural History of Religion*. London: A. and H. Bradlaugh Bonner.

Ivković, Zoran, and Scott Weisbenner. 2005. "Local Does as Local Is: Information Content of the Geography of Individual Investors' Common Stock Investments." *Journal of Finance* 60:1, 267–306.

Kahneman, Daniel, and Amos Tversky. 1972. "Subjective Probability: A Judgment of Representativeness." *Cognitive Psychology* 3:3, 430–451.

Kahneman, Daniel, and Amos Tversky. 1979. "Prospect Theory: An Analysis of Decision under Risk." *Econometrica* 47:2, 263–292.

Kaustia, Markku. 2010. "Disposition Effect." In H. Kent Baker and John R. Nofsinger, eds., *Behavioral Finance: Investors, Corporations, and Markets*, 171–189. Hoboken, NJ: John Wiley & Sons.

Klayman, Joshua. 1995. "Varieties of Confirmation Bias." In Jerome R. Busemeyer, Reid Hastie, and Douglas L. Medin, eds., *Decision Making from a Cognitive Perspective*, 365–418. New York: Academic Press.

Kocherlakota, Narayana R. 1996. "The Equity Premium: It's Still a Puzzle." *Journal of Economic Literature* 34:1, 42–71.

Kreuter, Matthew W., and Victor J. Strecher. 1995. "Changing Inaccurate Perceptions of Health Risk: Results from a Randomized Trial." *Health Psychology* 14:1, 56–63.

Lee, Charles M. C., Andrei Shleifer, and Richard H. Thaler. 1991. "Investor Sentiment and the Closed-End Fund Puzzle." *Journal of Finance* 46:1, 75–109.

Legoux, Renaud, M. Martin Boyer, Pierre-Majorique Léger, and Jaques Robert. 2014. "Confirmation Biases in the Financial Analysis of IT investments." *Journal of the Association for Information Systems* 15:1, Article 1.

Leroy, Stephen F., and Richard D. Porter. 1981. "The Present-Value Relation: Tests Based on Implied Variance Bounds." *Econometrica* 49:3, 555–573.

Lichtenstein, Sarah, Baruch Fischhoff, and Lawrence D. Phillips. 1982. "Calibration of Probabilities: The State of the Art to 1980." In Daniel Kahneman, Paul Slovic, and Amos Tversky, eds., *Judgment under Uncertainty: Heuristics and Biases*, 306–334. Cambridge: Cambridge University Press.

Madsen, Jakob B. 1994. "Tests of Rationality Versus an 'Over Optimist' Bias." *Journal of Economic Psychology* 15:4, 587–599.

Mandelbrot, Benoit B. 1977. *Fractals: Form, Chance and Dimension*. New York: W. H. Freeman and Company.

Mandelbrot, Benoit B. 1982. *The Fractal Geometry of Nature*. New York: W. H. Freeman and Company.

Massa, Massimo, and Andrei Simonov. 2006. "Hedging, Familiarity and Portfolio Choice." *Review of Financial Studies* 19:2, 633–685.

McFadden, Daniel. 1999. "Rationality for Economists?" *Journal of Risk and Uncertainty* 19:1, 73–105.

Mehra, Rajnish, and Edward C. Prescott. 1985. "The Equity Premium: A Puzzle." *Journal of Monetary Economics* 15:2, 145–161.

Nofsinger, John R. 2007. *The Psychology of Investing*, 3rd edition. Upper Saddle River, NJ: Prentice Hall.

Odean, Terrance. 1998. "Volume, Volatility, Price and Profit When All Traders Are Above Average." *Journal of Finance* 53:6, 1887–1934.

Park, Cheol-Ho, and Scott H. Irwin. 2007. "What Do We Know about the Profitability of Technical Analysis?" *Journal of Economic Surveys* 21:4, 786–826.

Perez, Carlota. 2002. *Technological Revolutions and Financial Capital: The Dynamics of Bubbles and Golden Ages*. Cheltenham, UK: Edward Elgar.

Plous, Scott. 1993. *The Psychology of Judgment and Decision Making*. New York: McGraw-Hill.

Powers, Michael. 2012. *Acts of God and Man*. New York: Columbia University Press.

Pring, Martin J. 2002. *Technical Analysis Explained: The Successful Investor's Guide to Spotting Investment Trends and Turning Points*. New York: McGraw-Hill.

Remus, William. 1984. "An Empirical Investigation of the Impact of Graphical and Tabular Data Presentations on Decision Making." *Management Science* 30:5, 533–542.

Scharfstein, David S., and Jeremy C. Stein. 1990. "Herd Behavior and Investment." *American Economic Review* 80:3, 465–479.

Sevenson, Ola. 1981. "Are We All Less Risky and More Skilful Than Our Fellow Drivers?" *Acta Psychologica* 47:2, 143–148.

Shefrin, Hersh, and Meir Statman. 1985. "The Disposition to Sell Winners Too Early and Ride Losers Too Long: Theory and Evidence." *Journal of Finance* 40:3, 777–790.

Shiller, Robert J. 1981. "Do Stock Prices Move Too Much to Be Justified by Subsequent Changes in Dividends?" *American Economic Review* 71:3, 421–436.

Schiller, Robert J. 2000. *Irrational Exuberance*. Princeton, NJ: Princeton University Press.

Shiller, Robert J. 2003. "From Efficient Markets Theory to Behavioral Finance." *Journal of Economic Perspectives* 17:1, 83–104.

Shleifer, Andrei. 2000. *Inefficient Markets: An Introduction to Behavioural Finance*. Clarendon Lectures in Economics. Oxford: Oxford University Press.

Shleifer, Andrei, and Lawrence H. Summers. 1990. "The Noise Trader Approach to Finance." *Journal of Economic Perspectives* 4:2, 19–33.

Shleifer, Andrei, and Robert W. Vishny. 1997. "The Limits of Arbitrage." *Journal of Finance* 52:1, 35–55.

Sterman, John D. 1994. "Learning in and about Complex Systems." *System Dynamics Review* 10:2, 291–330.

Taffler, Richard J., and David A. Tuckett. 2010. "Emotional Finance: The Role of the Unconscious in Financial Decisions." In H. Kent Baker and John R. Nofsinger, eds., *Behavioral Finance: Investors, Corporations, and Markets*, 95–11. Hoboken, NJ: John Wiley & Sons.

Taylor, Shelley E., and Jonathon D. Brown. 1988. "Illusion and Well Being: A Social Psychology Perspective on Mental Health." *Psychological Bulletin* 103:2, 193–210.

Thaler, Richard. H. 1980. "Toward a Positive Theory of Consumer Choice." *Journal of Economic Behavior and Organization* 1:1, 39–60.

Thaler, Richard H. 1993. *Advances in Behavioral Finance.* New York: Russell Sage Foundation.

Thaler, Richard. H. 1999. "Mental Accounting Matters." *Journal of Behavioral Decision Making* 12:3, 183–206.

Tune, G. S. 1964. "Response Preferences: A Review of Some Relevant Literature." *Psychological Bulletin* 61:4, 286–302.

Tversky, Amos, and Daniel Kahneman. 1971. "Belief in the Law of Small Numbers." *Psychological Bulletin* 76:2, 105–110.

Tversky, Amos, and Daniel Kahneman. 1974. "Judgment under Uncertainty: Heuristics and Biases." *Science* 185:4157, 1124–1131.

Tversky, Amos, and Daniel Kahneman. 1982. "Judgment under Uncertainty: Heuristics and Biases." In Daniel Kahneman, Paul Slovic, and Amos Tversky, eds., *Judgment under Uncertainty: Heuristics and Biases*, 3–20. Cambridge: Cambridge University Press.

Tversky, Amos, and Daniel Kahneman. 1992. "Advances in Prospect Theory: Cumulative Representation of Uncertainty." *Journal of Risk and Uncertainty* 5:4, 297–323.

Vives, Xavier. 2010. *Information and Learning in Markets: The Impact of Market Microstructure.* Princeton, NJ: University Press.

Weinstein, Neil D., and William M. Klein. 1995. "Resistance of Personal Risk Perceptions to Debiasing Interventions." *Health Psychology,* 14:2, 132–140.

Wise, James A., and Richard P. Taylor. 2002. "Fractal Design Strategies for Enhancement of Knowledge Work Environments." *Proceedings of the Human Factors and Ergonomics Society Annual Meeting* 46:9, 854–858.

12

Governance Risk

DIDIER COSSIN

Professor of Finance and Governance, UBS Chair in Banking and Finance, and Director of the
IMD Global Board Center, IMD, Switzerland

Introduction

Governance is defined as the ability to make the right decisions at the highest levels of organizations. Governance failures attract the attention and affect the expectations of society at large. Historically, achieving good governance has been challenging for many companies.

While many cultural differences exist in the constitution of boards and governance systems, boards are expected to set the direction and define the objectives of the organization concerned. They are also supposed to select, monitor, and support the team in place to accomplish these objectives and to work constructively with owners and other stakeholders. Unfortunately, achievement has been sparse with some spectacular failures.

The BP Macondo field explosion of April 2010 is such an event because it dramatically affected the investment performance of the BP stock as well as the entire oil and gas industry in terms of investment choices (Cossin and Constantinou 2011). The Tepco example of Fukushima had an impact on nuclear industry investments from suppliers to producers. Banking crises such as in Asia during the 1990s and in the West in 2008 also affected investments. In all cases, governance failures occurred as driving forces of these failures. Several authors point out the responsibility of bank boards during the crisis. Pirson and Turnbull (2011) identify a lack of access to relevant information from the board members and a lack of knowledge and ability to process the right information from the same board members. Bates and Leclere (2009) and Ladd (2010) note the increasing importance of risk oversight. The focus is on the weakness of risk committee structure organization, or lack of direct lines between chief risk officer (CRO) and the board, or simply the poverty of risk thinking on the board. In general, executive teams have been ahead of boards in terms of technical knowledge and abilities. When their leadership role came into conflict with their risk management role and the sustainability of the business, boards did not have the capacity to intervene. The same can be said in many cases, such as the operational issues of British Petroleum (BP) and Tepco, the succession issues at Hewlett-Packard and ABB, the integrity issues at Olympus and Ecobank, and the strategic issues at Kodak and others.

Governance constitutes one of the most impactful risks any organization faces. Governance and the functioning of boards can thus be one of the typical tail risks of investments from actual economic impact as well as from social expectations and reputational effects as in the previous examples. Research shows that governance affects investment performance throughout the performance curve and not just within the lower tail of the return distribution.

While early studies such as Gompers, Ishii, and Metrick (2003) show the overall impact of governance on performance, more recent studies analyze the effect in more depth in the United States (Brown and Caylor 2004; Bhagat and Bolton 2008; Harford, Mansi, and Maxwell 2008), Japan (Bauer, Frijns, Otten, and Tourani-Rad. 2008), Hong Kong (Cheung, Stouraitis, and Tan 2010), Taiwan (Filatotchev, Lien and Piesse 2005), and across emerging markets (Klapper and Love 2004). While more sophisticated results lead to more differentiated answers, the impact on operational performance and operational risks or on valuation is often strong. Bradley (2004) points out these that studies may be weak in identifying the drivers of good governance. Indeed, most empirical studies focus on easy metrics of governance, either linked to the legal system (shareholder protection) or simple board structure issues (e.g., size of board, separation of the chief executive officer (CEO) and board chair) or on combinations (e.g., Governance Metrics International (GMI) metrics measures). Clinical practice shows that governance performance is more complex and requires deeper understanding.

What makes an organization more prone to successful governance cannot be identified as easily from the outside the organization. Institutions with the same structures may differ strongly in governance performance. With strong social pressure on governance, many institutions have organized themselves for "lip service" governance that appears to check all the right boxes but does not achieve real governance performance.

This chapter clarifies the major drivers of governance success and identifies the typical areas of governance failures. It focuses on board activity as a legal framework and other regulatory structural issues. Public information-based due diligence can offer the signals that correspond to what may be obtained with private information (e.g., poor CEO board relationships, weak strategic thinking on the board, unfocused or uncommitted boards, dominating executive or board members, poor information design, weak processes or weak structures, and poor group dynamics).

Governance risk can be better managed at the investment level. A better knowledge of governance risk will not only safeguard portfolios more successfully but will also provide return opportunities. As many activist shareholders demonstrate, governance risk can even be an area of investment by itself.

Risk and Governance: First Principles

As individuals are overstretched by the complexity of risks pervading the world, governance has become essential to organizational success. When experience and knowledge are overstretched in a single individual, a small group of individuals must lead the organization to continued success. Often, however, boards are not strong. In order to be effective, boards need to work in many dimensions. A strong governance system helps to ensure a balance and complementarity of power between key actors such as the CEO and his team, board, and shareholders. Every governance system has its own way of trying to balance this power. This chapter seeks to describe ways to find that balance to ensure effective decision-making at the organizational level.

In its most simple approach, corporate governance is about how a firm is directed and controlled. The numerous corporate governance codes around the world mainly focus on the corporate board of directors as the main vehicle to reach good corporate governance, with some minor attention to the relationship with and the respective role of shareholders and top management. Of lesser importance is other layers of the structure including the internal organization, business units, operating companies, subsidiaries, and joint ventures. The basic rules of corporate governance recommend sufficient checks and balances, segregation of functions, and accountability for delegated decision-making power. However, insufficient attention focuses on the need to apply these rules to all levels of decision-making. The attention placed on compliance with corporate governance codes and regulations is ineffective without a well-developed system of internal governance.

In the United States, the Sarbanes-Oxley Act (SOX) was a first attempt to regulate the internal governance aspects from the perspective of internal control and risk management. From a theoretical perspective, the Enterprise Risk Management (ERM) model encompasses all types of risks. However, the auditors and internal control departments mostly focus on traditional financial and operational risk management, often ignoring governance risk. This omission could have resulted from the fact that governance is a complex domain that is at the intersection of many theoretical fields including law, economy, psychology, and moral philosophy. Thus, identifying the key elements that drive the issues is challenging. Figure 12.1 illustrates the theoretical underpinnings of a comprehensive analysis of governance. Governance analysis levers many different social sciences and is thus complex to comprehend fully.

The Organization for Economic Co-operation and Development (OECD) Steering Group on Corporate Governance identifies the failures in risk management as the most

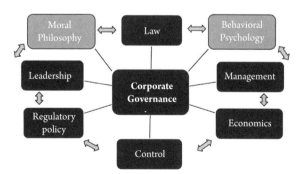

Figure 12.1 AN INTERDISCIPLINARY VIEW OF GOVERNANCE.   The theoretical basis of governance draws from several disciplines of the social sciences. This figure shows such interdisciplinary underpinnings of governance. Source: Cossin 2014.

important diagnosis of the financial crisis of 2007–2008 (OECD 2009). The OECD largely attributes this failure to weaknesses in corporate governance more than to flawed risk models.

The OECD identified the lack of information about exposures not reaching the board and even senior levels of management. These activities are usually board responsibilities. In other cases, boards approved strategies but then failed to establish suitable metrics to monitor their implementation. Organization disclosures about foreseeable risk factors and about the systems in place for monitoring and managing risk proved inadequate. To overcome such issues, new ERM models, such as the ISO 31000, establish clear guidelines. For example, they emphasize that "risk governance" refers to the architecture (principles, framework, and process) for managing risks effectively, while "managing risk" refers to applying that architecture to particular risks.

Management should help the board exercise its responsibility to oversee risk exposure and to decide on the risk appetite of the corporation. The board must ensure that the risk appetite is a coherent reflection of the organization's strategic targets. In making important board decisions on strategic choices, directors should undertake a true audit of the strategic risks involved including different scenarios and their underlying risks and assumptions as well as overall firm-wide risk exposure.

The analysis of the failures in corporate risk management is incomplete without considering behavioral dimensions. Lower prestige and status of risk management staff vis-à-vis traders and sales people play an important role in suppressing the efficient flow of information and discussion of risk. The top or senior risk managers should have a high-ranking status and be allowed to have a direct reporting line with the board of directors comparable to that of an internal auditor. The CRO should have direct access to the board and the audit committee as is already the case for the internal auditor.

Companies should also move toward a culture of shared responsibility and mutual respect. The organization chart should ensure that a culture exists that enables reporting all relevant information on risk exposure and possible issues to the top layers of the organization. This structure encourages a mentality to share information more efficiently and to engage in a more effective dialogue across the firm. "Bad news should travel fast" is the successful recipe of many long-standing family business firms.

Governance Mechanisms

Most academic research focuses on formal aspects of governance. Indeed objective information is available on board size, committee structure, and individual qualifications. Thus, research has typically focused on these aspects. What drives good governance is often more complex. Board culture, group dynamics, and individual psychology may matter as much but they are more difficult to measure.

IN SEARCH OF THE RIGHT ATTITUDE AND BEHAVIOR

The main critique on the effectiveness of governance and the board of directors is that boards fail to understand and manage risk, while tolerating perverse incentive systems.

Some blame shareholders for tolerating inappropriate board behavior while allowing or promoting a high level of leverage and exhibiting a short-term focus.

These deficiencies can be overcome by engaging in appropriate corporate behavior and developing the right governance attitude. Such goals cannot be reached only through regulation or legislation. According to the International Corporate Governance Network (ICGN) (2009), reform is as much about behavior as it is about prescription including improving the focus of the governance codes and on redefining best practices. Historically, governance codes and recommendations focused on structural governance factors such as composition of the board of directors, CEO-Chair duality, independent directors, and presence of board committees. Best practices were defined with reference to input characteristics that are simple to monitor.

Effective governance processes and attitude also drive board effectiveness and governance quality (Association of British Insurers 2012). Yet, assessing corporate attitudes and behaviors does not stop at the board of directors or at the level of top management. The corporate mindset, ethical attitude, and integrity of the entire organization necessitate much more attention in order to guarantee that good structures, principles, and processes are applied in practice. Combining corporate with internal governance is also the broader framework from which analysis should occur. The appropriate tone and culture emerge from the board. The governance attitude reflects the tone toward shareholders, which should not be overly promising or create unrealistic expectations. The management of information disclosure to investors by a management team is a rich signal of governance in terms of both shareholder relations and board–management relationship. Managers must educate their shareholders and try to withstand short-term market pressures. But the dedication from both management and the board to do so are revealing of governance processes beyond the point of the communication itself. Strong managers with good governance have a discrete but influential board support in defending long-term strategies and investments, even if short-term oriented shareholders and share traders pressure them to act otherwise.

IN SEARCH OF THE RIGHT BALANCE IN THE BOARD'S ROLE

Governance codes result in more duties and time commitments for directors. Although the board's role has drastically increased during the last decade, some criticize boards for being too complacent (Kiel and Nicholson 2005).

Given governance failures, determining the right balance of board duties is critical (Bukhvalov and Bukhvalova 2011). This balance requires a reconsideration of the role of boards involving the appropriate board leadership. Historically, the board is responsible for setting a firm's direction and the tone at the top as well as selecting, monitoring, and supporting the CEO and his team in reaching the defined objectives. Bordean, Crișan, and Zenovia (2012) discuss the different conceptualizations of the strategic role of the board. National and institutional differences exist. In some cases, establishing strategy is a board function, while in others it resides with the management team. In some cases, such as in Chinese state-owned enterprises, CEO nomination does not belong to the board (Cossin and Lu 2012a). In other cases, those outside of the board, such as a large family owner, set the tone of the board. Attention should also be given to the personality of the board members. For example, do they have an appropriate attitude, alignment with corporate values, ambitions, corporate strategy, and time horizon? The board should discuss strategic scenarios and alternatives as well as specific risk/performance profiles including the specific risk appetite of the firm. The board's role does not stop with nominating top managers. Non-executive directors should also critically monitor and evaluate management in the light of these principles, including decisions on their remuneration, while being supportive of management. This requires a delicate balance.

The monitoring of corporate performance and reporting should pay attention to financial and non-financial reporting as well as to audit, internal control, and risk management. One of the duties of the board is to have a clear understanding of the final goals of the firm, considering criteria to evaluate the long-term shareholder value as well as the impact on the relevant stakeholders. Such a framework should be applied when making important strategic decisions and monitoring the execution of resulting choices.

IN SEARCH OF THE RIGHT BALANCE IN BOARD COMPOSITION

Although board independence remains an important aspect of corporate governance, independence should not be the only consideration. First, independence cannot come at the detriment of sufficient business insight, expertise, and knowledge of the strategic challenges and risk of the business portfolio. In this regard, an OECD report analyzes the opinion of several headhunters, who emphasize that the focus of SOX on the independence of directors has an "unintended consequence" because "such focus discards from board candidacy many individuals with thorough knowledge of business, in this particular case, of the banking sector" (Guerrera and Thal-Larsen 2008; cited in Kirkpatrick 2009, p. 22).

In its governance analysis, the de Larosière Group (2009) states that the failure of checks and balances aggravated failures in risk assessment and risk management. Many boards and senior managements of financial firms neither understood the characteristics of their new, highly complex financial products nor were aware of the aggregate exposure of their companies, resulting in an underestimation of their risks. Many board members and shareholders did not provide the necessary oversight or control of management. Kirkpatrick (2009) points to the lack of sufficient expertise on the boards and especially on specialist risk and audit committees of failing organizations. Studies such as that of Wang and Hsu (2013) trace changes in board composition which serves to support the correctness of this diagnosis. The large number of non-executive board members may have increased the difficulty for external directors to influence boardroom decision-making.

The greater the percentage of external directors, the more unitary boards tend to limit the number of executive directors to the CEO, often complemented by the CFO. The dominance of the CEO becomes greater, as less scope exists for external directors to develop working relationships with senior members of management. CEOs may have great ability to manage the information flow to the rest of the board. Non-executive directors are at an inherent disadvantage relative to executive management, due to their part-time role and their position outside the organizational structure. They invariably rely on organization insiders for information and expertise. Regardless of their independent stature, they will face an uphill struggle to significantly challenge executive management.

The two areas of the economy that have been subject to volatile cycles of boom and bust over the last decade—financial services and technology—are potentially highly opaque to non-specialist board members. The emphasis placed on independence in corporate governance codes, European directives, and public discourse has created unrealistic expectations of what boards can achieve. Looking forward, the holy grail of boardroom design should not be independence, but boardroom competence and professionalism. Mahadeo, Soobaroyen, and Hanuman (2012) discuss the importance of competence.

Second, the codes have not paid sufficient attention to the importance of personality and attitude issues. Overly stressing independence and the need for critical attitudes and positions can lead to board processes that are at odds with a consensus-driven decision-making in a collegial (one-tier) board. More attention should be paid to the appropriate tone for directors. All should adhere to and apply the principles of integrity and responsible business leadership. The level of dedication and commitment of the board members to the job of the board tends to be a strong driver of governance performance as well (Kirkpatrick 2009). This dedication level becomes a concern when directors are located far away, or have other important and time-consuming responsibilities, or simply have too many board memberships.

For all levels in the organization, the choice of people is essential. Such choices should be based on fitting personality with the corporate values. The strategic goals and challenges must be included into all evaluation and remuneration systems. Evaluation of board effectiveness, as well as the monitoring and remuneration of top managers, should attach much more importance to these "soft" elements; a hard job but all the more rewarding in the long run.

Principles of "Good Governance on the Move"

As part of an effort to avoid future crises, policy makers and regulators are exploring and implementing changes to corporate governance practices. Board structures and practices should be designed to improve:

- Board responsibility for corporate governance transparency,
- Director competency and commitment,
- Board accountability and objectivity,
- Board leadership, integrity, ethics, and responsibility,
- Attention to information, agenda design, and strategy,
- Protection against board entrenchment,
- Shareholder input in director selection, and
- Shareholder communications.

Risk Governance: What Is The Actual Company Status?

In view of this new context, companies are trying to come to grips with these new specific guidelines, such as the board's oversight of risk management practices, linkage of executive compensation with risk, and additional disclosures on risk management. The following questions arise:

- Is the board well equipped to deliver effective risk oversight?
- In what way is the board most challenged in linking risk to strategy?
- Is risk management considered fundamental to achieving the business objectives?
- Is risk management about realizing the upside or is it only about minimizing the downside to which businesses could be exposed?
- Will risk management continue to be equally important when "normalcy" is restored in the developed markets?
- What is needed for directors to embed risk thinking into decision-making?
- Are risk dimensions beyond usual risk lines considered such as complacency in organizational culture or compliance effectiveness?

What Makes an Effective Board?

The question "what makes an effective board?" is a difficult one to answer. What may work within one organization may be unsuitable for another. Board effectiveness varies and company culture may affect board characteristics.

Almost all boards have weaknesses. Overall, the state of governance is not strong. Leadership teams tend to be more effective than boards. Most boards comply with classical corporate governance standards and now follow commonly agreed practices on board size, presence of independent directors, and constitution of committees. But within this framework, how many CEOs consider their boards to be as effective as their executive team? How many rely on their boards for true value creation? In fact, boards are seriously lagging to the point that many board chairs accept having board members who do not add value.

Figure 12.2 illustrates that effective boards are those that lever "excellence" in four dimensions. These dimensions provide a good checklist from which to work to identify board strengths and weaknesses. Although board issues seem well hidden from the public, subtle indicators can be captured from public information, and these indicators get confirmed by more in-depth and typically private information.

THE FIRST PILLAR: PEOPLE—QUALITY, DIVERSITY, FOCUS, AND DEDICATION

Four dimensions are associated with the people pillar. This dimension includes the quality of individuals, board diversity, and the focus and dedication of directors to board work.

Quality
The quality of the individuals selected for board service remains a key driver of governance performance (Kirkpatrick 2009). Boards should be composed of high-quality individuals who are outstanding in their respective fields, such as CEOs, academics, and government officials. However, they could lack the necessary knowledge to perform

Figure 12.2 THE DRIVERS OF GOVERNANCE PERFORMANCE.   This figure presents the four pillars of board effectiveness that ultimately drive governance performance. The first pillar includes the quality (i.e., personal characteristics), diversity, focus, and dedication of directors to the board. The second pillar addresses the board's involvement in the design of the information architecture. The third pillar deals with board structures and processes such as the structure of board committees and the board evaluation process. The fourth pillar focuses on the dynamics that underline board interactions. Source: Cossin 2014.

their tasks as members of a specific board. The case of JP Morgan's 2012 loss and its use of a complex trading system (the credit default swap CDX.NA.IG.9 index) illustrate this point (Farzad 2012). JP Morgan incurred a loss of several billions of dollars as it overlooked the warnings about the risks involved in the trading system. News later emerged that none of the three directors on the board's risk-policy committee had worked as a banker or had any experience in Wall Street in the past 25 years. This illustration clearly underlines the importance of the quality of board committees. Further, members of specific committees are expected to have the necessary and relevant knowledge. Otherwise, limited knowledge affects their ability to perform their functions effectively. To overcome this problem, effective boards establish performance and knowledge standards for individual directors, educate their board members, and conduct evaluation along those standards.

Diversity

Diversity in terms of industry and professional background, as well as gender, personality, and opinion enhances the quality of the board (Mahadeo, Soobaroyen, and Hanuman 2012). Board members should possess a wide range of knowledge, skills, and personal attributes: sound judgment, integrity, and high ethical standards; strong interpersonal skills; and the ability and willingness to challenge and probe. Mahadeo et al. indicate that beyond individual excellence, diversity in the group promotes the presence of task-related expertise on the board such as technology expertise on a bank board as well as creativity toward finding solutions and overcoming blind spots in group dynamics.

In determining board composition, balancing formal qualifications with consideration of personal qualities and relevant experience is important. In general, the board is expected to aim for a diverse composition in terms of gender, age, geography, professional and industry experience, and personality. Different board compositions provide diverse connections with the inside and outside environment (e.g., competitors, suppliers, investors, politicians, the media, and management). Director characteristics could affect their competence and incentives to monitor and to advise managers. As a result, directors could be chosen either to maximize value by making decisions that best fit the interests of shareholders (Marlin and Geiger 2012) or to protect the interests of executives.

Personality differences are a strong driver of board performance overall (Spanberger 2011; Kueppers 2013). Classical psychological assessments are often used such as the Neuroticism-Extroversion-Openness (NEO) test based on five personality traits: need for stability, extraversion, openness to experience, agreeableness, and conscientiousness. Understanding the personality differences and determining a board's ability to bridge them is an important dimension of board assessment. Typical public information warning signals would be a strongly emotional CEO, a highly extraverted board chair, and the combination of the two. Figure 12.3 illustrates a psychological profile of a sample board. In this figure, each board member is represented by one of the lines. In the emotionality panel, the board chair's profile is located at the resilient extreme of the spectrum signaling him as a highly resilient individual, while the CEO's profile is found in the reactive extreme, meaning that he is a highly reactive individual. This combination of personalities created problematic conditions for the board. While this level of information is inaccessible to investors, some patterns can be detected from the outside of the organization that signal what a deeper level of investigation would confirm scientifically.

Diversity creates complexity. Managing a diverse board is more complex than managing a homogeneous one. Diversity raises communication-related barriers with different frames of reference, words and actions mean different things. It can also raise conflicts as well as identity and trust-related barriers making identifying with and deeply trusting people who differ from others more difficult. Thus, a very diverse board may be an unsuccessful board by not managing its diversity well. The fourth pillar on group dynamics/board culture addresses this problem.

Focus and Dedication

The director's focus and dedication to the firm's activities is essential (Kirkpatrick 2009). Focus could be diminished by directors' misunderstanding their roles and functions within the board. To reinforce their focus, boards need to establish a statement of purpose and define their role in a manner that adds value to firm activities. Boards should regularly reflect on their involvement and strive to make efforts that are distinctive from other parts in the organization and to improve decisions made by the firm.

Dealing with ambiguities in decision-making is inevitable and is a sign that the board addresses real issues. Well-focused boards distinguish the adequate context in which to perform a supervisory role and in which to offer support to management. Such boards are not only quick to determine when proactive risk oversight is needed but also efficient in identifying and acting on the need to communicate the firm's strategic objectives in order to manage its reputation during a crisis. Additionally, a successful agenda strengthens the focus of the board. This agenda focuses more on the future than

NEO GROUP FEEDBACK FORM

●━A ●━B ●━C ●━D ●━E ●━F ●━G ●━H ●━I ●━J ●━K ●━L

EMOTIONALITY	Resilient	Responsive	Reactive
N1 Worry	0 — Unworried; calm; unconcerned	33 — 43 — 58 — Usually calm, sometimes worrying	68 — Worrying, tense, apprehensive — 100
N2 Anger	0 — Even-tempered; slow to anger	33 — Seldom angry, but can be provoked	68 — Quick to anger, hot-blooded — 100
N3 Moodiness	0 — Optimistic; contented; no blues	33 — 43 — Sensitive to losing, but recover well	68 — Self-blaming; pessimist; blues — 100
N4 Social concerns	0 — Socially confident, self-assured	33 — 58 — Gets embarrassed, then get over it	68 — Sensitive to embarrassment, shy — 100
N5 Self-indulgence	0 — Resists temptation; stoic	33 — 58 — Sometimes yield to temptation	68 — Easily tempted; self-indulgent — 100
N6 Sensitivity to stress	0 — Resilient to stress and crises	33 — 43 — 58 — Experiences stress, but can cope	68 — Sensitive to stress & pressure — 100

EXTRAVERSION	Introvert	Ambivert	Extravert
E1 Warmth	0 — Reserved; distant; cool	33 — 43 — 58 — Moderately engaged	68 — Attached; affectionate; warm — 100
E2 Outgoingness	0 — Loner; prefer privacy	33 — Mix well, but enjoy privacy	68 — Sociable; prefer company — 100
E3 Assertiveness	0 — Non-assertive; passive	33 — 43 — 58 — Comfortable in foreground	68 — Dominant; speak up; leading — 100
E4 Activity level	0 — Slow-paced; inactive; laid-back	33 — 43 — 58 — Ordinary pace and energy	68 — Active; energetic; fast-paced — 100
E5 Excitement seeking	0 — Conventional; avoid risks	33 — 58 — Enjoy moderate stimulation	68 — Seeking pleasure, thrills, adventures — 100
E6 Positive emotions	0 — Serious, sober, lacking enthusiasm	33 — 43 — Neither serious nor cheery	68 — Cheerful; light-hearted; joyful — 100

OPENNESS	Preserver	Adaptor	Explorer
O1 Imagination	0 — Down to earth; focused; realistic	33 — 43 — 58 — Occasional daydreamer	68 — Imaginative; abstract; creative — 100
O2 Aesthetic sense	0 — Prosaic, unmoved or bored by art	33 — 43 — 58 — Moderate interest in art	68 — Artistic, aesthetic, stylish — 100
O3 Depth of emotions	0 — Discount own and others' feelings	33 — 43 — Accepting of feelings	68 — Interested in own and others feelings — 100
O4 Willingness to experiment	0 — Habitual, like routine & familiar	33 — 43 — Try new things incrementally	68 — Experimental; seeking novelty — 100
O5 Intellectual curiosity	0 — Practical; here and now	33 — 43 — 58 — Moderate interest in abstraction	68 — Inquisitive; theoretical; curious — 100
O6 Tolerance for diversity	0 — Conservative; dogmatic	33 — 43 — 58 — Middle of the road	68 — Liberal; unconventional; tolerant — 100

AGREEABLENESS	Challenger	Negotiator	Conciliator
A1 Trust in others	0 — Cynical; sceptical; suspicious	33 — 43 — 58 — Cautiously trusting	68 — Trusting; forgiving; accepting — 100
A2 Candor	0 — Guarded; cautious; political	33 — 58 — Tactical and open	Frank; open; straight-forward — 100
A3 Consideration for others	0 — Self-absorbed; high self-interest	33 — 43 — 58 — Giving if asked	68 — Considerate; helpful; nurturing — 100
A4 Compliance	0 — Competitive; head-strong; fighter	33 — Can compromise if necessary	68 — Cooperative; compliant; peaceful — 100
A5 Modesty	0 — Self-promoting; seen as arrogant	33 — Feel equal to others	68 — Self-effacing; humble; modest — 100
A6 Sympathy	0 — Hard-hearted; rational; justice rules	33 — 43 — 58 — Caring for others selectively	68 — Soft-hearted; merciful; sympathetic — 100

CONSCIENTIOUSNESS	Flexible	Balanced	Focused
C1 Sense of competence	0 — Unprepared; inefficient; unsure	33 — Quite well prepared & confident	68 — Self-confident; planned; resourceful — 100
C2 Orderliness	0 — Disorganised; unmethodical	33 — 43 — Sometimes disorganised & untidy	68 — Neat; tidy; organised; meticulous — 100
C3 Sense of responsibility	0 — Unreliable; bending the rules	33 — 43 — Follows the rules most of the time	68 — Stick strictly to the rules; reliable — 100
C4 Need to achieve	0 — Easy-going; unambitious	33 — Relaxed about success	Driven; ambitious; enterprising — 100
C5 Self-discipline	0 — Distractable; procrastinating	42 — Quite focused, but can waste time	68 — Finisher; workaholic; self-pacing — 100
C6 Deliberateness	0 — Hasty; snap decisions	33 — 43 — Makes considered decisions	68 — Cautious; deliberate; thorough — 100

Figure 12.3 A Board Psychological Pattern: The NEO Survey. This figure illustrates the different personality types encompassed by a specific board. Each line represents an individual director. The NEO survey has five dimensions: emotionality, extraversion, openness, agreeableness, and conscientiousness. A spectrum has been developed for each dimension, for example, the extraversion dimension ranges from introvert to ambivert to extravert. Personalities are classified within these spectrums.
Source: IMD 2014.

on the past and tries to capture long-term issues while managing short-term matters. Dedication to the firm is also an important aspect of this pillar. Dedication goes beyond the allotted meeting time. It implicates, for example, the reasons someone decides to become a director.

Incentives differ for becoming a board member. Some seek this position to access networks and industry-specific information and to achieve an elevated status. Such incentives may negatively impact the person's dedication. Others become board members because they are highly motivated to make the firm successful.

Areas which the board should address include answering the following questions.

- Has the board clearly defined its role in the organization?
- Does the board have appropriate leadership?
- Are the CEO and his team adequate to organizational and strategic needs?
- Is compensation for board members suitable?
- Is the board following effective strategies?
- Is the board primarily concerned about monitoring or about supporting the executive team?
- Is the board using the best metrics to assess financial health?
- Does the board have a good understanding of the firm's risks and opportunities?
- Has the board anticipated urgent and emerging issues?
- Are executive sessions productive?

Consider, for example, the role of the board. An analysis of its role should be done regularly by an active board as the role gets transformed with context and individuals. The board should determine in what areas or matters it wants to be involved and to what degree it should be involved in these areas. The overriding criteria for choosing a role is that the contribution of the board must be *distinctive* (i.e., nobody else in the corporation does it) and *additive* (i.e., the involvement of the board makes the decision better and/or prevents the company from being exposed to unacceptable risks). Figure 12.4 shows an effective way of determining the role of the board. The vertical axis presents two areas on which the board can focus, support or monitoring, and the horizontal axis depicts where such focus can be placed in relation to the board—internal or external. For example, in a monitoring/external scenario, the role of the board would be to supervise the risk strategy that the management team is implementing.

The degree of involvement of the board varies across time according to the economic and social context. A well-defined list of board tasks and of the level of interaction chosen is also key to effective board work. Investor due diligence can thus include an analysis of whether the board appears well focused on the right tasks. Figure 12.5 provides a typical list of board tasks and the nature of the board's involvement for each task. For example, while performing a task related to policy formulation, the nature of the board's involvement is to approve the outcome of the process.

A good checklist for an investor to reflect on the first pillar would be:

1. How close to the heart of every board member does this company appear to be?
2. Where does each board member add value to this board?
3. How much confidence exists that individual board members are steering the company in the right direction?

Figure 12.4 Working Roles of the Board.   This figure shows a tool employed to determine the monitoring versus supporting roles of the board in particular situations. The matrix's vertical axis refers to chosen board priority and the horizontal axis underlines whether focus is external or internal. The different stars represent primary and secondary choices made by different board members, stressing the need to find a consensus for board priorities. Source: Cossin 2014.

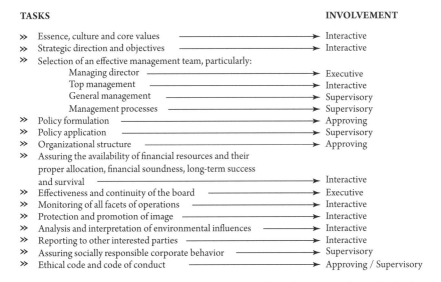

Figure 12.5 An Example of Board Tasks.   This figure lists a typical set of tasks that a board of directors performs and presents the nature of the board's involvement in each of those tasks. Source: Cossin 2014.

4. How much diversity exists on the board in terms of abilities, personalities, and competencies?

5. How clear does the board seem to be about the role of the board and each committee?

6. Does this board address future issues or does it focus on the past?

7. How does each director's knowledge compare to that of the ideal board member for this company?

THE SECOND PILLAR: INFORMATION ARCHITECTURE

If boards are to provide meaningful protection for investors, they must be in a position to challenge management and draw sufficient attention to dubious practices. To do this, board members must be prepared to invest the time necessary to understand the "big picture" of their organization. Even vigorously independent members are likely to prove ineffective unless they have both access to and understanding of all the relevant information (Roy 2011). All members should be able to express views that differ from those of the CEO without repercussions. Perhaps the most important characteristic of an effective board member is a willingness to challenge management, which represents the essence of independence.

The board should receive information about the essential activities undertaken by the company and the issues facing it. For example, jointly designed board briefings that include financials with forecasts, a CEO report, risks and opportunity maps, an analysis of key employee succession, and a summary of financial analysts' views contribute to the quality of the information architecture. Additionally, regular communication between management and the board is essential. Committee reports are also fundamental in creating the effective architecture of information. Adequate reports encompass analysis of specific issues rather than just recommendations. A key checkmark is whether the board is actively involved in designing the information and whether that information design changes with the firm as well as its environment and strategy. Yet, there is more to information than the formal information process. Informal channels are also important such as meetings with employees and informal meetings of the board. In short, a sophisticated but not overly complex information architecture is an important element to successful boards.

Another challenge for the board is to develop communication channels to the value-critical stakeholders. The right composition of the board enhances this communication. The board can also determine the need for having representative stakeholders among their members and/or in various subcommittees.

Beyond regular contact with large shareholders, many boards receive regular briefings by top management. At some banks, board members meet not only with the CRO but also individually with his or her team members. Some chairmen and board members have CEO-approved routines for visiting the shop floor or retail outlets, town hall meetings with factory employees, or management development seminars to sample the climate.

Boards also need information about the web reputation (new social media exposure) of the corporate brand, in addition to whistle-blowing channels for those on the frontline. In sum, to reduce exposure to future governance crises, boards require a program for each director to be in touch with specific value-critical stakeholders.

Information architecture is usually minimal for boards. Investments in information technology (IT) tend to be light compared to IT investments for executive teams. At the least, the information that the board receives should include the following: (1) a briefing including financials with forecasts, a CEO report, risk/opportunity maps, analysis of the performance of key employees, and a summary of financial analysts' views; (2) an informal management letter between meetings; (3) employee/customer surveys; (4) director outreach including plants, technology, and audits; and (5) committee reports including analysis not just recommendations.

A good checklist on information architecture for sophisticated investors follows:

1. Does the board know and track the business and its key value drivers on a timely basis?
2. Is the board well informed of competitive trends, regulatory changes, technological changes, and stakeholder evolution?
3. Does the board have enough information independent from management available for its judgment?
4. What informal processes of information exist for the board?
5. What is the board's involvement in designing the information architecture?
6. How involved are all board members?

THE THIRD PILLAR: STRUCTURES AND PROCESSES

A challenge facing the board is to establish and deploy efficient and complete board structures and processes (Ingley and van der Walt 2005; Minichilli, Zattoni, Nielsen, and Huse 2012). In terms of structures, the composition and size of the board contribute to its effectiveness. The board should regularly benchmark its current composition and structures against the ideal situation and act on any divergence. In terms of processes, many exist beyond running the board that involve the orientation of new directors to the board, strategy, evaluation processes, CEO and key managers' succession, risk assessment, board education, and regulation.

Key elements of the orientation of new directors include the following activities:

- Define composition of "ideal" board/desired candidate's profile.
- Conduct personality assessment of candidates.
- Assess new directors' business knowledge and client understanding.
- Develop and revise the integration plan for new directors.
- Disseminate company information and a board manual related to accepted behavior and directors' liability.
- Conduct strategic updates (e.g., board support/supervision role in company short/medium/long-term strategy).
- Introduce a mentoring process including e-mentoring methods.
- Set mechanisms for interaction between new directors and CEO/board chair.
- Set clear performance objectives for new directors.
- Establish a customized skill-development program for directors including e-learning tools.
- Launch a stakeholder engagement plan.
- Establish performance evaluation and feedback mechanisms.
- Initiate a process for managing expectations.
- Check on-boarding process for continuous improvement.
- Monitor/adjust skill-development programs.
- Revise/adjust the on-boarding process.

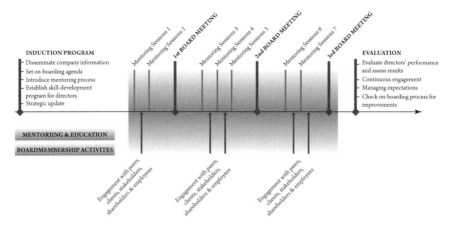

Figure 12.6 An Example of Process: On-Boarding.   This figure shows the major steps undertaken to incorporate new directors into the board. The process is designed to ultimately facilitate the integration of new board members to the organizational culture. Source: Cossin 2014.

The steps encompassed by the on-boarding process include mentoring and education programs as well as engagement with peers, clients, and shareholders. Figure 12.6 presents the major steps in the process.

The board strategy process also plays an important role in increasing effectiveness. The board strategic involvement occurs along three dimensions: co-creation, supervision, and support. Good processes will enrich the three dimensions. Typically, regular meetings complement retreats and external presentations complete internal ones. Focused, decision-oriented meetings complement long-term understanding of the industry and business from a strategic perspective. This process elaborates on various aspects including strengthening firm strategy by defining and aligning it with objectives and ensuring commitment. It also enhances the strategic reflection of the board and reinforces the interactions between management and board. The process creates a stronger basis for communicating the company's strategy both internally and externally. A well-designed strategy process ultimately enables boards to efficiently assess the company's strategic risks as well as its strategic opportunities.

Another decisive process is that of board evaluation. A poor evaluation process contributes to governance failure. Therefore, thriving boards engage in self-assessment or external assessment in terms of their roles, dynamics, and member performance. A good practice is to use available technology such as tablets for board evaluation during meetings, which provides results in "real-time" and thus offers an opportunity for careful and dynamic scrutiny beyond the one-year evaluations.

CEO succession is another critical process (Lafley and Tichy 2011). Successful succession planning aims at the transparency of selection, quality of the on-boarding process, and the smoothness of the transition. Hewlett-Packard (HP) serves as a case in point. In a six-year period, HP fired three CEOs (Behan 2011), a trend leading to corporate turmoil that negatively affected the company's brand reputation. In one of the cases, the HP board did not meet the new CEO before nomination, failing to identify a candidate that would fulfill HP's strategic vision.

In essence, the board's terms of reference should define the scope of its oversight responsibilities and how these duties are to be discharged in compliance with regulatory requirements. These terms of reference should be tailored to the company's specific needs and clearly outline the board's duties and responsibilities, including structure, process, and membership requirements. Ideally, it should describe the background and experience requirements for board members and set guidelines for the board's relationship with its subcommittees and management, supported by an appropriate structure and foundation, reasonable and well-defined responsibilities, and an understanding of current and emerging issues. Only through carefully designed processes can the board maximize its contribution to an organization.

While these building blocks apply to all entities, the agendas for effectively using them vary widely. Each board and its subcommittees must assess its own circumstances—financial situation, industry and stage of development, environment, and issues—to build its own, preferably a yearly, agenda. This process should be repeated on a regular basis.

Rotation of board members can provide a practical way to refresh and introduce new perspectives to the processes. Rotation also creates the opportunity for a greater number of board members to gain an in-depth and first-hand understanding of the functioning of the board, which can contribute to the board's cohesion. However, given the complex nature of the role, this needs to be balanced with the desire to have members that possess the necessary accumulated knowledge to discharge their responsibilities effectively.

When a company has no formal rotation policy, the board should evaluate each member's performance to help ensure that it meets the board's expectations. The chair of the audit committee should periodically assess the performance of board members. This assessment should be part of the overall board's evaluation of individual members (Spanberger 2011).

The board should implement a formal and rigorous assessment process that links to the board's evaluation process. This process may include interviews with the member being assessed, self-assessment by the member, and the assessment of members against standard criteria. The performance evaluation of individual members should consider several aspects. Expertise, inquiring attitude and independence, ability to take tough, constructive stands at meetings when necessary, understanding of the organization's business, willingness to devote the time needed to prepare for and participate in board meetings and deliberations are all important. Approach to conflict and whether the person helps the Board to manage conflict constructively and productively should also be considered. A specific board chair evaluation process also deserves attention.

A good investor checklist of structures and processes could start with the following:

1. What is the list of processes that truly matter for this board (e.g., strategy, evaluation, CEO succession, risk, board education, audit, regulatory compliance, and board succession)?
2. What information exists and what value does each of these processes contribute?
3. What assessment is conducted to ensure whether each is complete and sufficiently detailed?
4. Does this board have an appropriate committee structure and composition?
5. Are the reporting lines effective?

THE FOURTH PILLAR: GROUP DYNAMICS AND GOVERNANCE CULTURE

Effective boards foster a culture of productive interaction and rich, focused, and conclusive discussions. Strong boards are not consensual but strive on constructive dissent. Verhezen (2010) discusses the importance of dissent at the board level. Typically, a strong chair fosters a governance culture that leads to strong idea generation and discussions.

To achieve this requires a strong view of what the desired culture is, an understanding of the power of "walking away," a strong board for accidental dissent, and an interdisciplinary view of corporate governance. The underlying challenge consists of how to interact with dominant actors and strong personalities among the board members.

Typically, some unhealthy dynamics can develop over time in boards (Isaac 2013). The following is a list of such pathologies that threaten the firm's health: (1) sleepy board or routines board; (2) uninformed, uneducated, or unable board; (3) dominant chair or CEO board; (4) lifetime board; (5) disruptive board member; (6) set-up to fail board that ensures that the CEO fails; and (7) love board for whom the CEO can do no wrong.

Sometimes individual director characteristics create concern. For example, a director could engage in micro-management, be disruptive or overly aggressive, and dominate others. Other directors may be management's representative. Still others infrequently attend meetings or may be easily overwhelmed. Confronted with issues of this type, a board and its chair should follow procedures and deal with problems by giving concrete feedback.

Directors have both preferred (acceptable) and unacceptable behaviors (van Ees, Gabrielsson, and Huse 2009). Acceptable behaviors include independence and integrity, equal participation and mutual respect, openness and constructive dissent, knowledge acceleration, and external support and continuous education. By contrast, unacceptable behaviors include being imprudent and acting in an unlawful or unethical manner.

A strong chair fosters an effective board culture by fostering such primary board values as responsibility, accountability, moral authority, and the one voice principle. The chair should also stimulate discussion, encourage persistence and dissent, and build real consensus. Although the chair's role varies across time and contextual conditions, it should include the following dimensions: (1) lead and manage board discussion to keep focus and drive conclusions within time constraints; (2) provide rules of engagement; (3) be responsible for board processes; (4) set the agenda with management; and (5) represent moral authority.

An active board chair will do even more.

A good checklist for evaluating board dynamics could include the following questions:

1. How energetic does this board seem to be?
2. Do the board members seem to be listening to outside stakeholders?
3. Do they listen to each other?
4. Does the board seem to challenge the status quo?

5. Are board members disrespectful?
6. Is the board seemingly stuck?
7. Are the board members initiating creative solutions?
8. What is the overall reputation of the board chair?
9. Does the chair generate a strong governance culture?
10. Does this board seem to abide by the classic values of governance culture?

SUCCESS FACTORS OF AN EFFECTIVE BOARD

Table 12.1 presents an overview of the key success factors of an effective board, related to the four pillars.

Key Issues to Consider for Investors

Governance has become a key investment risk. Work can be done to assess and monitor this risk more effectively. Board failures occur mostly in a limited number of areas. Boards have been ineffective in the case of technical risk failures (such as in banking or in oil and gas). They have failed on redirecting strategy, on nominating a successful CEO or on addressing integrity issues. These areas of failures represent different symptoms of board ineffectiveness. Investors are thus better off supervising board effectiveness along the lines described above.

A sample of specific questions for an investor considering governance risks can include the following:

- What are the key factors of strengths and weaknesses of the board?
- Is the board well equipped to deliver effective risk oversight?
- Is a clear and defined link present between risk and strategy?
- Does the board have the right mix and number of board members to create added value?
- Is the board sufficiently literate on key business risks?
- Is the board structured for continued awareness?
- Are all roles clearly defined?
- Does the board do continuous improvement work on the four dimensions of people focus, information, processes, and group dynamics?
- How do board issues and conflicts of interest appear to be managed?

Mini Case: Governance at ICBC

Each institution has its own governance DNA. The Industrial and Commercial Bank of China Limited (ICBC), one of the largest commercial banks in China, drastically improved performance through a governance transformation (Cossin and Lu 2012b). As recently as June 1999, international institutions and analysts broadly considered ICBC as "technically bankrupt." Since its dual IPOs in 2007, ICBC has received a

Table 12.1 **Key Success Factors of an Effective Board**

Factors	People	Information	Structures and Processes	Group Dynamics/ Culture
Description	Focus Strategic coherence Competency Diversity	Getting needed information Sending the right signals to stakeholders	Efficient and complete board processes	Productivity of interaction Rich, focused, and conclusive discussions
Challenges	No "single correct template" Correct focus varies between organizations and over time	Importance of finding balance between too much and not enough information	Lack of board processes Invasion of corporate processes	Strong personalities Dominant actors
Typical Application	Executive meetings without the CEO	Management letter from CEO to board	The one-year agenda Evaluation processes	Open discussions on board member productivity
Don't	Avoid micro-management Encourage diversity of ideas and board composition but have focused discussions	Information overload	Short-term wins only because of random application	Force people to choose between voicing dissent and career health
Do	Clearly articulate priorities among board activities	Have a common information strategy and board/ management Prioritize	Self- and outside benchmark Understand what works and repeat successful processes	Understand the power of walking away Build board strong enough for accidental dissent

Note: This table illustrates the four pillars of effectiveness at play. It shows some of the challenges that each pillar can experience and provides examples of the application of the pillars. It also offers some "do's and don'ts" regarding the pillars.

multitude of best governance awards adding to its global reputation. But what does governance mean in a Chinese state-owned enterprise?

The ICBC's governance system has four tiers: the shareholders' general meeting, board of directors, board of supervisors, and senior management. Figure 12.7 depicts this structure and the specific reporting lines within it. The shareholding diversification reform was a historical stride forward compared to the state's sole ownership of the past. The state fully financed ICBC before 2005. The bank was then restructured as a joint-stock limited company and subsequently brought in Goldman Sachs, Allianz, and American Express as strategic investors. In 2006, ICBC further diversified its owner- ship through simultaneous IPOs in Hong Kong and Shanghai. This action resulted in systematically diversifying state ownership and also improving corporate governance. The shareholder meeting has the ultimate power to select directors and supervisors, decide their compensation, and decide on the operational policy, financing, investment, or dividend plans.

The board of directors is composed of three distinct groups: four executive direct- ors, six full-time non-executive directors, and six part-time independent directors. This structure is designed to provide effective checks and balances within the board. The executive directors focus more on the operational level details that help other directors have a deeper understanding of the real challenges and issues. The part-time independ- ent directors are designated to make objective judgments and express unbiased views

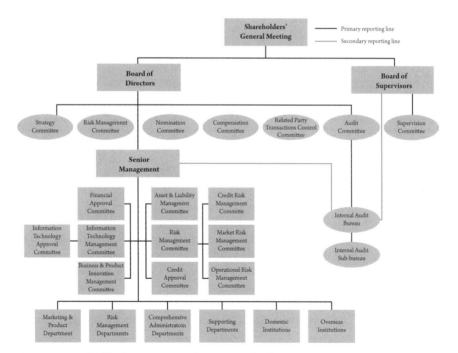

Figure 12.7 ICBC's GOVERNANCE SYSTEM.   This figure shows the governance system in place at the Industrial and Commercial Bank of China Limited (ICBC). Primary and secondary reporting lines are shown to illustrate the specificities of the system. Source: Cossin and Lu 2012a.

independently. Among the part-time independent directors are overseas banking professionals, academics, and regulators. The full-time non-executive directors sit on the board to represent the two state shareholders. They have extensive experience working in various government agencies directly involved in steering the country's economic reform. The non-executive directors and independent directors combined are expected to outnumber executive directors and hold key posts, including audit and compensation committees. Through the board committees, the three groups of directors openly voice opinions on the nomination, compensation, strategy, operational policy, financing, investment, or dividend plans. Under the direction of the board of directors, the senior management team executes strategy and is responsible for the daily operation and management activities.

To exercise checks on the management team and board directors so as to balance the power of directors, ICBC established a board of supervisors alongside that of directors. In the four-tier system, the board of supervisors monitors the performance of the directors and senior management members. A board of supervisors is composed of representatives of the shareholders (full-time) and the staff, workers, and external professionals (part-time). The governance system has two other components. Through a consultation and participation process, the party committee functions as a key stakeholder in the bank and expresses opinions on governance issues. Apart from the monitoring of the board of supervisors, the party disciplinary commissions operate at different levels of the bank, increase the number of controllers, and provide thorough monitoring. Such party monitoring can prevent misbehavior by managers and employees at all levels and can improve corporate governance, but defines a different mode of governance. Appointment of the CEO, for example, does not belong to the board.

ICBC's unique, sophisticated, and rich governance system shows that governance can differ widely across the world. Some facts remain: behavioral drivers of governance effectiveness include independence, integrity, equal participation, mutual respect, openness, and constructive dissent as well as personal engagement.

Summary and Conclusions

Companies are still struggling to develop best-in-class governance practices. In order to obtain the effective degree of risk oversight as set by the regulators and expected by shareholders, they need to enforce four key measures to obtain a higher added value. In particular, firms need to (1) ensure a higher degree of involvement and dedication as well as the right level of expertise at the board and subcommittees level; (2) address the information challenges to board knowledge for both external and internal information as well as formal and informal information routes; (3) ensure strong structures and processes; and (4) ensure productive board dynamics. Effective investor oversight regarding board performance in the four dimensions is critical to investment success.

Discussion Questions

1. Discuss the role of the board in an organization.
2. Discuss the factors making a board effective or ineffective.

3. Identify and explain conditions in which boards experience failure.
4. Identify and explain positive signals of effective governance.

References

Association of British Insurers. 2012. "Report on Board Effectiveness: Updating Progress, Promoting Best Practice." Available at http://www.ivis.co.uk/pdf/abi%20report%20on%20Board%20effectiveness%202012%20-%20final.pdf.

Bauer, Rob, Bart Frijns, Rogér Otten, and Alireza Tourani-Rad. 2008. "The Impact of Corporate Governance on Corporate Performance: Evidence from Japan." *Pacific-Basin Finance Journal* 16:3, 236–251.

Bates II, E. William, and Robert J. Leclere. 2009. "Boards of Directors and Risk Committees." *Corporate Governance Advisor* 17:6, 15–17.

Behan, Beverly. 2011, "Ray Lane's Intrigue at Hewlett-Packard." *Businessweek*. September 27. Available at http://www.businessweek.com/management/ray-lanes-intrigue-at-hewlettpackard-09272011.html.

Bhagat, Sanjai, and Brian Bolton. 2008. "Corporate Governance and Firm Performance." *Journal of Corporate Finance* 14:3, 257–273.

Bordean, Ovidiu-Niculae, Emil Lucian Crișan, and Cristiana Pop Zenovia. 2012. "A Multi-theory Approach of the Strategic Role of Boards." *Studies in Business and Economics* 7:2, 43–51.

Bradley, Nick. 2004. "Corporate Governance Scoring and the Link between Corporate Governance and Performance Indicators: In Search of the Holy Grail." *Corporate Governance* 12:1, 8–10.

Brown, Lawrence D., and Marcus L. Caylor. 2004. "Corporate Governance and Firm Performance." Available at http://ssrn.com/abstract=586423 or http://dx.doi.org/10.2139/ssrn.586423.

Bukhvalov, Alexander, and Barbara Bukhvalova. 2011. "The Principal Role of the Board of Directors: The Duty to Say 'No.'"*Corporate Governance* 11:5, 629–640.

Cheung, Yan-Leung, Aris Stouraitis, and Weiqiang Tan. 2010. "Does the Quality of Corporate Governance Affect Firm Valuation and Risk? Evidence from a Corporate Governance Scorecard in Hong Kong." *International Review of Finance* 10:4, 403–432.

Cossin, Didier, and Dinos Constantinou. 2011. "The Macondo Blowout: Decision Making in Difficult Times." Case Study *IMD-3-2188*. Lausanne: IMD.

Cossin, Didier, and Abraham Lu. 2012a. "The ICBC Path to Chinese Governance: Lessons for the Western and Emerging Markets." *European Financial Review*. Available at http://www.europeanfinancialreview.com/?p=6093.

Cossin, Didier, and Abraham Lu. 2012b. "Industrial and Commercial Bank of China: The Governance Model." Case Study *IMD-1-0335*. Lausanne: IMD.

de Larosière Group. 2009. "The High-Level Group on Financial Supervision in the EU." Available at http://ec.europa.eu/internal_market/finances/docs/de_larosiere_report_en.pdf.

Farzad, Roben. 2012. "How JP Morgan Lost $2 Billion without Really Trying." May 17. *Businessweek*. Available at http://www.businessweek.com/articles/2012-05-17/how-jpmorgan-lost-2-billion-without-really-trying.

Filatotchev, Igor, Yung-Chih Lien, and Jenifer Piesse. 2005. "Corporate Governance and Performance in Publicly Listed, Family-Controlled Firms: Evidence from Taiwan." *Asia Pacific Journal of Management* 22:3, 257–283.

Gompers, Paul, Joy Ishii, and Andrew Metrick. 2003. "Corporate Governance and Equity Prices." *Quarterly Journal of Economics* 118:1, 107–156.

Guerrera, Francesco, and Peter Thal-Larsen 2008. "Gone by the Board: Why the Directors of Big Banks Failed to Spot Credit Risks." *Financial Times*, June 25. Available at http://www.ft.com/cms/s/0/6e66fe18-42e8-11dd-81d0-0000779fd2ac.html#axzz2pk2lh0Bz.

Harford, Jarrad, Sattar A. Mansi, and William F. Maxwell. 2008. "Corporate Governance and Firm Cash Holdings in the US." *Journal of Financial Economics* 87:3, 535–555.

Ingley, Coral, and Nicholas van der Walt. 2005. "Do Board Processes Influence Director and Board Performance? Statutory and Performance Implications." *Corporate Governance: An International Review* 13:5, 632–653.

International Corporate Governance Network. 2009. "ICGN Global Corporate Governance Principles." Available at https://www.icgn.org/images/ICGN/files/icgn_main/ Publications/best_practice/global_principles/ICGN_Global_Corporate_Governance_ Principles_2009_July_2013_re-print.pdf.

Isaac, George. 2013. "The 'Toxic' Director: It Takes Only One to Derail the Board." *Directors and Boards* 37:5, 28–30.

Kiel, Geoffrey, and Gavin J. Nicholson. 2005. "Evaluating Boards and Directors." *Corporate Governance: An International Review* 13:5, 613–631.

Kirkpatrick, Grant. 2009. "The Corporate Governance Lessons from the Financial Crisis." *Financial Market Trends*. OECD. Available at http://www.oecd.org/finance/financial-markets/42229620.pdf.

Klapper, Leora F., and Inessa Love. 2004. "Corporate Governance, Investor Protection, and Performance in Emerging Markets." *Journal of Corporate Finance* 10:5, 703–728.

Kueppers, Robert. 2013. "Board Diversity: Let's Make It Personal." *NACD Directorship* 39:3, 74.

Ladd, Scott. 2010. "Risk Management by Boards Improving, Says Study." *Financial Executive* 26:8, 13.

Lafley, Alan George, and Noel Tichy. 2011. "The Art and Science of Finding the Right CEO: Lessons from P&G's Obsession with Succession." *Harvard Business Review* 89:10, 66–74.

Mahadeo, Jyoti, Teerooven Soobaroyen, and Vanisha Hanuman. 2012. "Board Composition and Financial Performance: Uncovering the Effects of Diversity in an Emerging Economy." *Journal of Business Ethics* 105:3, 375–388.

Marlin, Dan, and Scott W. Geiger. 2012. "The Composition of Corporate Boards of Directors: Does Industry Matter?" *Journal of Business and Economics Research* 10:3, 157–161.

Minichilli, Alessandro, Alessandro Zattoni, Sabina Nielsen, and Morten Huse. 2012. "Board Task Performance: An Exploration of Micro- and Macro-level Determinants of Board Effectiveness." *Journal of Organizational Behavior* 33:2, 193–215.

OECD. 2009. "Corporate Governance and the Financial Crisis: Key Findings and Main Messages." Available at http://www.oecd.org/corporate/ca/corporategovernanceprinciples/ 43056196.pdf.

Pirson, Michael, and Shann Turnbull. 2011. "Corporate Governance, Risk Management, and the Financial Crisis: An Information Processing View." *Corporate Governance: An International Review* 19:5, 459–470.

Roy, Marie-Josée. 2011. "Board Information: Meeting the Evolving Needs of Corporate Directors." *Management Research Review* 34:7, 773–789.

Spanberger, Peter. 2011. "A Respectful Approach to Director Assessment." *Directors and Boards* 35:3, 45–46.

van Ees, Hans, Jonas Gabrielsson, and Morten Huse. 2009. "Toward a Behavioral Theory of Boards and Corporate Governance." *Corporate Governance: An International Review* 17:3, 307–319.

Verhezen, Peter. 2010. "Giving Voice in a Culture of Silence: From a Culture of Compliance to a Culture of Integrity." *Journal of Business Ethics* 96:2, 187–206.

Wang, Tawei, and Carol Hsu. 2013. "Board Composition and Operational Risk Events of Financial Institutions." *Journal of Banking and Finance* 37:6, 2042–2051.

13

Inflation Risk

CLAUS HUBER

Managing Director, Rodex Risk Advisers LLC

FELIX GASSER

Head of Managed Futures, FRM Man Group Switzerland

NICOLAS BÜRKLER

Managing Partner, SIM Research Institute Inc.

Introduction

Global central banks flooding financial markets with cheap money during the credit crisis of 2008 have revitalized the debate around inflation and potential protection mechanisms. The purpose of this chapter is to examine how inflation could emerge in the 2010s compared to the 1970s and which instruments investors can use to protect their portfolios against inflation.

The chapter is organized as follows. The first section describes how inflation emerged in the 1970s, which was the last period of high inflation. This section also describes potential transmission mechanisms of inflation in the 2010s after the credit crisis of 2008 and how they could be affected by low interest rate levels, supply of credit to banks, emerging markets, and the high debt levels of the Western industrialized countries. The next section describes standard instruments for inflation protection such as equities, inflation-indexed bonds, gold, commodity futures, timber, and real estate. The third section discusses in more detail active investment strategies. Such strategies are similar to the approach based on trend-following used by commodity trading advisors (CTAs). This section deals with the anticipated large-scale inflation materializing as a long-term trend and how to navigate in this trend. This section also discusses how to measure trends, which environment is profitable for CTAs, and how CTAs behave during market stress and during the 1970s. The final section summarizes and concludes.

Inflation and Its Origins

The fear of inflation is often related to the massive expansion of monetary supply after a credit crisis. A glance through history can be helpful to better understand the effects of international central banks on money supply and debt levels.

THE LAST PERIOD OF HIGH INFLATION: THE 1970S

The 1970s was the decade with the highest inflation in the United States outside of war times. Several studies including Hooker (2002) identify the oil price shock in the early 1970s as a key driver in inflation, but the importance of oil has diminished since the early 1980s. Other causes are the high increases in nominal wages in the United States during the 1960s and the corresponding lower U.S. productivity.

In the early 1970s, the Nixon administration decided to reduce the U.S. debt by monetizing it via inflating the dollars in circulation. When the dollar fell versus other currencies such as the Swiss Franc or the Deutsche Mark, the Swiss and German central banks bought dollars and sold their own currencies to stabilize the dollar. Because of the gold standard, the central banks changed their dollars into gold, leading to a sharp reduction of the U.S. gold reserves. This action, which motivated the Nixon administration to abandon the gold convertibility of the dollar in 1971, led to a further decline of the dollar. The large-scale sales of their own currencies expanded the money stock in those countries resulting in high inflation rates in countries such as Germany, the United Kingdom, and Switzerland from the 1970s to the mid-1980s (Jordan and Rossi 2010). Notable differences existed in inflation rates. For example, the West German consumer price index (CPI) rose 7 percent in 1974–1975 while its U.K. counterpart climbed 25 percent during the same period (Laidler 2007).

U.S. monetary policy in the 1970s did not fight inflation because the Federal Reserve (Fed) opined that doing so was impossible at an acceptable cost (DeLong 1997). One of the costs could have been to restrict money supply while the supply shock of strongly rising oil prices still was being felt as a restraining input factor throughout the economy. The trade-off between lower unemployment and higher inflation was tilted toward the general acceptance of higher inflation as a reasonable price for lower unemployment. The modified Phillips curve proposed an inflation rate between 4 and 5 percent to achieve an unemployment rate of 3 percent or lower (Samuelson and Solow 1960). The Fed only obtained a formal mandate to fight inflation in the late 1970s (DeLong 1997).

Bataa, Osborn, Sensler, and van Dijk (2009) find that international inflation correlations have increased since the 1970s. This finding is not only true for the countries of the Eurozone but also for the United States and Canada. Oil price shocks had a large influence on inflation in the 1970s. Gómez-Loscos, Gadea, and Montañés (2012) find that this relationship weakened for the G7 countries until the 1990s but in the 2000s has gained strength again. The credit crisis of 2008 and its repercussions were the reasons for unprecedented central bank action globally, making monetary policy the most likely cause of inflation in the 2010s. Given that in 2013 the four most powerful central banks of the world (i.e., the Federal Reserve Board, European Central Bank, Bank of England, and Bank of Japan) have embarked on unprecedented monetary easing programs and the interconnectivity of the industrial countries, a reasonable assumption is that inflation might be back on the agenda in the near future. Historically, inflation at least partly had its roots in the most powerful economic force globally, namely, the United States.

CREDIT CRISIS, LIQUIDITY, MONETARY SUPPLY, AND INFLATION

Central banks flooded markets with liquidity in order to address the crisis of confidence among banks after the bankruptcy of Lehman brothers in September 2008. As columns

2 and 3 of Table 13.1 show, the Federal Reserve Board expanded the monetary basis dramatically.

Given the impressive rise of the monetary base, a challenging question is: How likely is a similar scenario as previously described? A typical starting point to explain the relationship between money supply and inflation is the quantity theory of money in Equation 13.1 (Friedman 1956):

$$MV = PY, \qquad (13.1)$$

where M represents the total amount of money in circulation, which is typically measured with a money aggregate like the money base; V is money velocity; P the price level; and Y the nominal gross domestic product (GDP). A simple interpretation of Equation 13.1 would be a rising P when M increases and Y and V stay the same. In a growing economy, the money base M should grow with about the same speed as the quantity of goods. The U.S. money supply has been vastly expanded by programs for purchasing securities such as quantitative easing (QE) and the Troubled Asset Relief Program (TARP). The first QE program started in November 2008, the second in November 2010, and the third in September 2012.

What happens with the expanded U.S. dollar money supply? Understanding this relationship requires taking a closer look at two components of the money supply: (1) currency in circulation (i.e., coins and notes); and (2) deposits held by banks at the Fed. As column 5 in Table 13.1 shows, the changes of currency in circulation since 2008 were between 4 and 10 percent a year. Currency in circulation grew but it did so at a much smaller pace than the monetary base (column 3 in Table 13.1).

Table 13.1 **Value of Currency in Circulation, Bank Credit, and U.S. Monetary Base: In Billions of Dollars as of December 31 of Each Year**

Year	U.S. Monetary Base ($ billions)	% Change	Currency in Circulation ($ billions)	% Change	Bank Credit of Commercial Banks ($ billions)	% Change
2006	812	NA	784	NA	8,122	NA
2007	825	2	792	1	8,926	10
2008	1,655	101	853	8	9,297	4
2009	2,019	22	888	4	8,973	−3
2010	2,011	0	942	6	9,163	2
2011	2,612	30	1,035	10	9,406	3
2012	2,673	2	1,127	9	9,980	6

Note: This table shows the strong growth of the U.S. monetary base since 2008. Currency in circulation is one component of the monetary base but it has not increased as strongly as the monetary base. Bank credit of commercial banks (i.e., the amount of money being lent by commercial banks) has also not kept pace with the growth of the monetary base.

Source: Federal Reserve 2013a.

Deposits of commercial banks in the central bank can be divided into required reserves and total reserves. Figure 13.1 shows the development of deposits for the United States. As represented by the gray area, excess reserves (total reserves minus required reserves) have risen strongly since 2008.

As Figure 13.1 shows, U.S. banks have not increased credit by a similar amount as implied by the rising money supply. Hence, banks do not lend money the Fed provides to them, but instead use the cheap central bank money to build excess reserves. Does this mean that the expansionary policy of the Fed is effective?

To answer this question requires understanding the motives of the Fed, which has been following two goals since the credit crisis (Keister and McAndrews 2009). First, the Fed wants to revive the economy. To this end, it defines a target interest rate, such as the Fed funds rate. Second, the Fed intends to stimulate the frozen interbank market by providing cheap financing but without initiating highly inflationary mechanisms such as in the 1970s and 1980s.

One method used since late 2008 is the payment of interest on bank reserves. In the past, banks did not receive interest payments on their reserves. This arrangement incentivized them to lend to generate interest income. The increasing credit supply should lead to falling market interest rates which, if bank reserves should expand strongly, could drop below the Fed's target interest rate and thereby undermine its

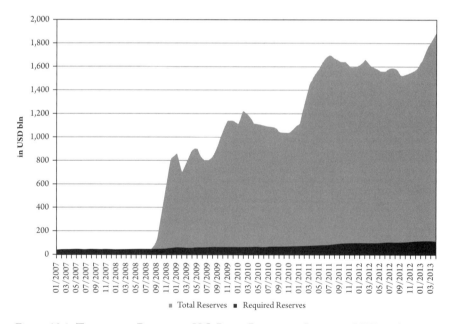

Figure 13.1 TOTAL AND REQUIRED U.S. BANK RESERVES: JANUARY 2007 TO APRIL 2013. This figure illustrates deposits of commercial banks in the central bank that can be divided into required reserves and total reserves. As represented by the gray area, excess reserves (total reserves minus required reserves) have risen strongly since 2008, meaning that banks have built reserves far higher than required by the Fed. Source: Federal Reserve 2013b.

monetary policy. A solution to this dilemma should prevent banks from lending below the target interest rate (Woodford 2000; Goodfriend 2002). Given that the Fed has paid interest on banks' reserves since October 2008, this incentive dampens banks' motivation to lend for interest rates below the Fed's target rate. Thus, the Fed can pursue macroeconomic policy independent of the provision of liquidity for the interbank market.

If banks do not lend money, does expanding liquidity make sense? Assume that bank A loaned money to bank B via the interbank market. If, due to the credit crisis, bank A cannot rely anymore on bank B paying back the loan, bank A will cancel the loan. Bank B must replace the loan with a different means of financing in the interbank market. Because other banks also do not trust each other, bank B's efforts to find alternative financing will be in vain. Bank B now has to cancel loans it has given to its clients to repay bank A. This reduces liquidity in the whole system and impedes investments. The Fed steps in and provides a loan to bank B, which uses this loan to repay bank A.

WHAT DOES INFLATION LOOK LIKE IN THE TWENTY-FIRST CENTURY?

As Figure 13.2 indicates, inflation has been much less volatile since the end of the 1990s (lower panel) and generally at lower levels compared to the 1970s (upper panel). Even the most recent recession due to the credit crisis of 2008 affected inflation to a much lesser degree than in the 1970s.

What are the reasons for the different behavior of inflation in the 1970s and in recent years? In the 1960s and early 1970s, errors in estimating GDP led to an overestimation of the output gap (e.g., in the United Kingdom) (Nelson and Nikolov 2002) and in Germany in the 1970s and 1980s (Gerberding, Seitz, and Worms 2005). Fearing to strap the economy by raising rates, central banks over-emphasized the risk of higher unemployment if they raised interest rates and thus kept them low too long. Since then, the methodological toolkit to estimate output gaps has been refined but much uncertainty is still involved in their real-time estimation (Dupasquier, Guay, and St. Aman 1999).

In the 1970s, the Federal Reserve Board was not an independent central bank. Given its political motivation, the Fed gave fighting unemployment a higher priority than fighting inflation. In the 2010s, inflation expectations are better anchored than they used to be in the 1970s (Simon, Matheson, and Sandri, 2013) based on well-communicated inflation targets and credible central banks.

As described by the Phillips curve, the relationship between unemployment and inflation has changed over time as unemployment has morphed from being more cyclical to being more structural. Cyclical unemployment is tied to fluctuations in economic activity (e.g., fewer workers are hired because of less demand for goods). In this case, reduced economic activity leads to lower wages. Structural unemployment occurs when the economy undergoes changes (e.g., from production-focused to more services-focused) and a mismatch exists between the skills of the workforce and the skills sought after by producers. Here, lower economic activity does not automatically mean reduced wages as the unemployed workforce does not have the required skills and therefore cannot compete with the employed workforce for jobs. Assuming that causes of inflation and how to address them are now better understood now than in

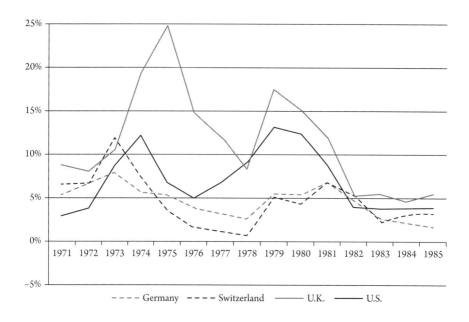

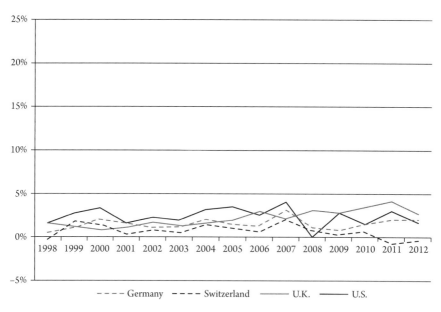

Figure 13.2 REALIZED INFLATION FOR GERMANY, SWITZERLAND, THE UNITED KINGDOM, AND THE UNITED STATES: 1971 TO 1985 AND 1998 TO 2012. This figure contrasts the inflation rates during the periods 1971 to 1985 (upper panel) and 1998 to 2012 (lower panel). The more recent inflation rates are lower and less volatile than in the first period. Source: OECD 2013.

the 1970s, how could the unprecedented monetary easing of Western central banks ultimately lead to rising prices?

INFLATION RISK FROM EMERGING MARKETS

Even if the direct route of inflation via the U.S. money supply and the commercial banks should not cause inflation to increase in a similar fashion as it did in the 1970s, a reasonable assumption is that the extremely low interest rate policy of the Western central banks will be inflationary for certain points in time. Market participants need to rely on them to tighten strings adequately (i.e., not too much to choke off fledgling economic activity and not too little to keep inflation under control). The exact timing for monetary fine tuning is very difficult and has not worked well in the past (Ip 2008).

The indirect route of cheap money is another option. In very low interest rate environments, investors look for other markets in search for yield. An alternative can be emerging markets, whose interest rates are typically higher than in Western industrialized countries and which lure investors with high growth potentials. Money from abroad fuels demand. Central banks of emerging markets face the problem of fighting domestic inflationary pressure by raising interest rates. This action widens the interest differential to the low interest countries and attracts even more capital.

Compared to the inflation rates of the Western industrialized countries, those of Brazil, Russia, India, and China (BRIC) are elevated: the average inflation rate of Brazil between 2007 and 2012 was 5.2 percent, Russia 9.2 percent, India 9.3 percent, and China 3.6 percent (OECD 2013). But a trend of increasing inflation rates does not exist. If anything, inflation rates declined in 2012 compared to previous years.

Emerging equity markets outperformed the MSCI World Equity index from early 2009 to early 2011 but underperformed after early 2011 until the third quarter of 2013. As cheap money from the developed world has not sustainably fueled equity markets in emerging markets, no inflationary pressure from those equity markets is apparent.

Another reason for rising prices could be increases in commodity prices. Browne and Cronin (2007) claim the existence of an empirical relationship between price developments in the commodity markets and inflation. Prices for some commodities have climbed noticeably. For example, prices for agricultural goods rose 17 percent from September 2008 to August 2013, those of food 13 percent and metals 10 percent (International Monetary Fund 2013a). In 2010, the International Monetary Fund (IMF) cited extraordinary macroeconomic policy support as one reason for the rebound in commodity prices since 2008 (International Monetary Fund 2010). Three years later, this reason was no longer mentioned as an influential factor for commodity price development (International Monetary Fund 2013b).

INFLATION AND THE EXPLOSION OF DEBT IN THE WESTERN INDUSTRIAL COUNTRIES

Governments of the industrial countries could be incentivized to tolerate higher than usual inflation even if the transmission mechanism between monetary expansion and inflation does not need to be in force in the 2010s. The Eurozone, the United States, and the United Kingdom have accumulated high levels of debt to save their banking systems and to stimulate their economies. Table 13.2 exhibits that the debt level of all countries reporting to the Bank for International Settlements (BIS) has increased by $13 trillion or 50 percent between September 2008 and March 2013. Most pronounced are the debt increases for Ireland (191 percent), the United Kingdom (171 percent), Spain (92 percent), and the United States (78 percent). Greece's debt has declined due to its debt restructuring. The United States issued 37 percent of the debt of the reporting BIS countries. Thus, events taking place in the United States will also affect other countries.

In European history, debt crises used to be much more often resolved by debasing a country's currency or devaluations than by debt restructurings (Sturzenegger and Zettelmeyer 2006). Before the Bretton Woods system was abolished in the 1970s, most currencies were covered by gold. Since then, no currency is covered by gold, but by faith in the prudent steering of the issuing central bank. This coined the expression "fiat" money, which is derived from the Latin word for "faith." When a currency is debased, the central bank prints as much money as it deems necessary.

During the credit crisis of 2008, the industrial countries supported their banking systems and economies. Expenses to support the jobless added to liabilities from healthcare and pension systems in aging societies. Under the assumption of an economic recovery, Figure 13.3 shows the debt levels of those countries are projected to stay at elevated levels.

Table 13.2 **Debt Levels and Changes of Select Countries since September 2008**

Country	Central Government Debt in $ Billions			Change vs. 09/08	
	September 2008 ($)	December 2009 ($)	March 2013 ($)	December 2009 (%)	March 2013 (%)
Greece	341	408	131	19	−62
Ireland	54	121	158	123	191
Italy	1,954	2,114	2,179	8	11
Japan	6,843	8,258	9,825	21	44
France	1,523	1,822	2,044	20	34
Germany	1,689	1,870	2,086	11	23
Spain	517	746	992	44	92
United Kingdom	1,011	1,387	2,190	37	117
United States	8,092	10,251	14,401	27	78
All BIS reporting countries	26,365	32,161	39,418	22	50

Note: This table shows the amounts of government debt in billions. Government debt has risen since the credit crisis 2008. The only exception in this table is Greece, which experienced a debt restructuring to avoid default.

Source: Bank of International Settlements 2013.

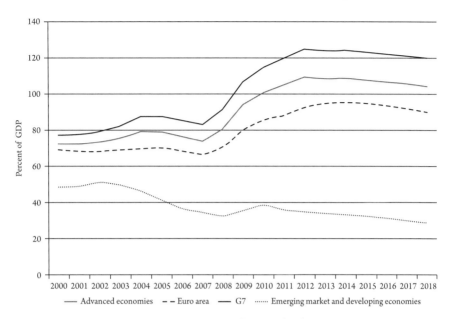

Figure 13.3 Public Debt as a Percent of GDP.   This figure shows the projections for the ratios of public debt provided by the IMF for different groups of countries. Debt ratios are projected to stay at elevated levels for the developed countries but are expected to decrease for emerging market and developing economies. Source: International Monetary Fund 2013b. Data after 2012 are projections.

How can the high debt levels be reduced? One way would be to inflate the debt away. Inflation historically occurred in countries with high levels of public debt when they were unable or unwilling to pay interest such as in Belgium, Spain, Italy, and Germany.

Politicians have another means to diminish government debt: austerity. This policy comprises highly unpopular actions such as reducing salaries and state benefits and increasing taxes. Often cited successful examples are the United Kingdom in the 1980s and Canada in the 1990s. Latvia serves as a role model for the credit crisis of 2008: GDP shrank by 23 percent between 2008 and 2009 but its household deficit fell from 10 percent to almost 0 percent. In 2010, Latvia's unemployment rate was above 20 percent. The IMF forecasts that Latvia will reach low double digits of unemployment by 2014. Typical negative effects from austerity measures could be observed in Latvia. For example, due to lack of employment perspectives, many Latvians emigrated, 12 percent of Latvia's overall population worked abroad in 2010, and marriages and birth rates declined strongly (Hudson and Sommers 2011). Austerity cannot be implemented easily. After the announcement of austerity measures in Greece in May 2010, violent protests with casualties occurred. A shrinking economy will contract even further in the presence of austerity measures.

The perspective of higher inflation over the next few years seems likely given globally expansive monetary and fiscal policy, rising government debts, and the unpopularity of austerity. The following section describes possible ways to protect against inflation.

Instruments for Inflation Protection

This section discusses briefly different asset classes and their suitability for inflation protection. Given the overview character of this chapter, the discussion does not distinguish between realized, expected, and unexpected inflation, but focuses on realized inflation.

EQUITIES

The first part of this subsection looks at the historical performance of equities during times of higher inflation and the second part focuses on the value drivers for stocks and their relation to inflation. The relationship between stocks and inflation is controversial. Several studies concentrate on the short-term relationship (monthly or quarterly data) of inflation and stock market return. For example, Fama and Schwert (1977) and Hagmann and Lenz (2005) suggest a negative relationship between stock market returns and inflation since the 1950s. Gorton and Rouwenhorst (2006) find the absolute values of correlations between stocks and inflation rise in longer time horizons. However, this correlation is negative and therefore stocks are unsuitable as an inflation hedge.

Israel in the 1980s can serve as an example for a close short-term relationship between strong inflation of more than 100 percent a year and the level of stock prices (Offenbacher 2002). Between 1984 and 1986 the increases of the Israeli CPI were closely matched by the performance of the Israel All Share Index. One reason for this was indexation of prices in the Israeli economy enabling corporations to quickly pass on higher prices for production inputs to customers.

Using a database of more than 200 years, Boudoukh and Richardson (1993) conclude that a positive relationship exists between inflation and stock market returns with the statistical significance increasing with a longer time horizon. Given that few investors have long-term horizons of 10 years and more, the following subsection focuses on an annual horizon.

The examples and studies discussed previously focused on empirical data. Concentrating on the value drivers of equities begs the question: Which relationship between inflation and stock market returns can be expected today? One possible explanation focuses on the value drivers of stocks shown in Equation 13.2: the price (P) of a stock can be written as the product of the earnings (E) and the valuation of the earnings (P/E ratio).

$$P = E\,(P/E). \tag{13.2}$$

The higher the P/E ratio, the more expensive is a unit of profit and the higher is the overall valuation of the stock market. If prices of commodity inputs rise and corporations cannot increase prices for the goods and they produce by the same order of magnitude, their P/E ratios will decline and their stock prices will fall.

The empirical evidence is less clear. Figure 13.4 exhibits the annual real P/E ratios for U.S. stocks, sorted by annual changes in the U.S. CPI. The sample covers 135 years from 1878 to 2012. On the left (right) of the chart are the P/E ratios corresponding to strong declines (increases) in the CPI. For strong declines of the CPI, a clear pattern of *P/E* ratios does not emerge: some are above 15 while others are at or below 10. On the right hand side of the chart, reflecting strong gains of the CPI, *P/E* ratios are generally lower than in the rest of the chart. Given current *P/E* ratios of about 16 for the S&P 500 index and Eurostoxx indices and assuming a strong increase of consumer prices of 5 percent or more (as in the right part of Figure 13.4), a decline of the *P/E* ratio can be expected.

The other important factor for evaluating the price of stocks in Equation 13.2 is earnings. Earnings depend mostly on economic growth, input costs, interest rates, leverage of the overall system, and labor costs. The two most interesting factors are leverage and interest rates.

Leverage describes the usage of debt by households, governments, non-financial, and financial corporations. Systemic leverage continually increased until the financial crisis of 2007–2008 and subsequently decreased (McKinsey 2012). As corporations use debt to maximize their return on equity (ROE) and further deleveraging can be expected, corporate earnings should not benefit. Several years of loose monetary policy have sent interest rates to all-time lows. This situation has helped corporations to reduce their interest payments on debt and increase profits. When central banks return to more "normal" interest rate levels, corporate earnings should decline. In summary, the efficacy of inflation protection from equities for the next few years given the empirical evidence cited above and the status of the drivers of equity valuations can be judged as weak.

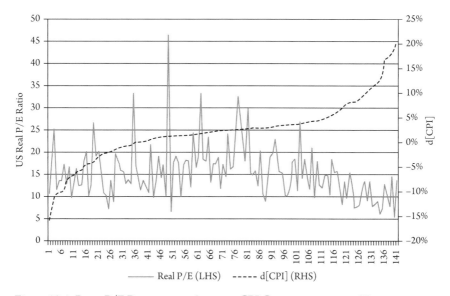

Figure 13.4 Real P/E Ratios and Annual CPI Changes for the United States: 1872 to 2012, Sorted by Annual CPI Changes. This figure displays the annual real P/E ratios for U.S. stocks, sorted by annual changes in the U.S. CPI. On the left (right) of the chart are the P/E ratios corresponding to strong declines (increases) in the CPI. Source: Raw data from the home page of Shiller 2013.

BONDS

The Fisher equation describes how bonds behave under inflation. In its simplest form shown in Equation 13.3, the Fisher equation establishes a relationship between nominal interest rates $[i_t]$, real interest rates $[r_t]$, and expected inflation $[E_{t-1}(\pi_t)]$:

$$i_t = r_t + E_{t-1}(\pi_t). \tag{13.3}$$

The buyer of a bond secures the nominal interest rate for the time to maturity of the bond. If the inflation expectations $[E_{t-1}(\pi_t)]$ rise, the nominal interest i_t increases leading to losses of the bond's value. Hence, nominal bonds are not suited for inflation protection.

The cash flows of inflation-indexed bonds are directly linked to an official statistical measure, such as the CPI. Inflation-indexed bonds have special characteristics. One of those is *basis risk*: the further the bond buyer's basket of goods is away from the basket used to calculate the CPI, the higher is the basis risk (Barnes, Bodie, Triest, and Wang 2010). A potential scenario could include a basket of primarily durable goods if the buyer of the inflation-indexed bond had protection against rising food prices in mind.

The buyers of inflation-indexed bonds are subject to sudden changes in the calculation method. For example, before June 2010, the British inflation-linked bonds were tied to the Retail Price Index, which includes housing costs. In June 2010, the British government changed this to the slower rising CPI, which excludes housing costs, and thus saves several millions of pounds of interest costs that escape bond holders. Official statistics measure inflation with a delay of several months for which the buyers of inflation-indexed bonds are compensated again with a delay. Because bond investors would have to invest 100 percent in inflation-indexed bonds in order to protect their portfolios, this does not leave capital to invest in other assets.

Consumers perceive inflation in a different way than measured by statistical measures such as CPI. One example is the introduction of the Euro notes and coins in the member states of the European Monetary Union in 2002. While official statistics show stable or even falling prices, the public perceived inflation as much higher.

PRECIOUS METALS

In fiat monetary systems, precious metals are the only "currencies" that are not someone else's liabilities and thus cannot be devalued just by printing more paper money. But how well will gold and other precious metals protect wealth from inflation? Two different arguments are available to answer this question. First, in a long-run comparison, the purchasing power of gold has been largely unchanged, even though variability has existed (Herbst 1983). Second, the opportunity costs are higher in a high inflation environment with high interest rates because an investment in gold will not return any interests or dividends. Thus, gold delivers poor inflation protection.

In practice, the timing of the investment determines much of gold's effectiveness. For example, an investor who bought gold in the early 1980s has not benefitted from gold's inflation hedging properties: inflation stood at 14 percent in 1980 and then declined over subsequent years. Because of the multiple opportunities in other assets with high returns, gold was a poor investment. Conversely, if an investor invested in gold in 1970, he would have bought effective protection from inflation for the decades that followed.

In addition to gold, other precious metals such as silver, platinum, and palladium may be considered for inflation protection. These precious metals have hybrid characteristics due to their industrial usage. For example, palladium and platinum are mostly used in automobile catalysts, connecting them to the global economy and car sales. Their price dynamics rely primarily on global economic growth and not on inflation. Conversely, silver serves a dual purpose (i.e., it can be used for both business purposes and as storage of value). Therefore, silver can also serve as an inflation hedge although the price volatility will be higher than gold's due to its industrial usage. In summary, gold and silver provide long-run protection against inflation, while other precious metals are insufficient. However, high volatility in gold and silver price makes market timing an essential element of strategy success.

FUTURES, EXCHANGE TRADED FUNDS, AND PHYSICAL COMMODITIES

Childers (2011) documents that industrial and precious metals futures have inflation betas higher than five and can provide leveraged protection against inflation. Therefore, investing a certain part of a portfolio in commodities may make sense.

Returns of commodity futures comprise two components: the price development of the commodity and the roll yield. Erb and Harvey (2006) find that the average excess returns of individual commodity futures contracts are indistinguishable from zero.

Roll yield is the yield due to a difference between the spot price and future prices or between two futures prices with different expiration dates. It occurs because futures contracts have a limited time until expiration. At expiration, investors need to roll their exposure into the next contract. If the next contract trades at a higher price than the current one, the commodity is in *contango*. That is, futures prices will be higher than spot prices. If the investor has to pay more for one contract than for their existing one, roll losses occur. Roll gains can occur when the next contract is cheaper than the existing one. This is called *backwardation* in which futures prices will be less than spot prices. A similar relationship exists with exchange-traded funds (ETFs) that invest in commodity futures (Guedj, Li, and McCann 2011). Because commodities move in trends, this favors active trading. Miffre and Rallis (2007) investigate different trading strategies and conclude that long commodity strategies tend to buy backwardated contracts while short commodity trading strategies tend to sell contangoed contracts.

Precious metals can be purchased physically relatively easily and stored in a safe place. An alternative to futures is the purchase of a physically covered precious metal ETFs whose issuer stores the metal bars and charges a fee for this service. For long-term investments, the direct physical purchase can be viable option.

COMMODITY AND MINING STOCKS

Corporations from the commodity sectors are highly dependent on economic growth and corresponding demand. Holding equity of such entities could be worthwhile because they process commodities, thereby adding value to the raw inputs and hence should be less influenced by price volatility of the underlying commodity. Thus, commodity stocks and commodity futures cannot be expected to exhibit similar price movements. Gorton and Rouwenhorst (2006) conclude that commodity stocks behave more like other equities than commodity prices.

TIMBER

Another possible alternative protection from inflation could be timber and timber production companies. Timber grows naturally and delivers a steady "carry income." In times of low prices, a timber company can just wait and let the forest grow. This option helps to endure uncertain times. According to Healey, Corriero, and Rozenov (2005), different returns for timber investment exist in different inflationary environments. Historically, the real return was always positive and well above the inflation rate. In high inflationary times (e.g., a timeframe from 1973 to 1981 with inflation averaged 9.2 percent), the returns on timber were 17.1 percent. In a medium inflation environment (inflation averaged 3.5 percent from 1982 to 1996), the returns on timber were 8.4 percent. In a low inflation environment (inflation averaged 1.7 percent from 1956 to 1965), the returns on timber were 4.4 percent. Similar conclusions can be drawn from correlation analysis (Forest Research Group 2007). An important feature of timber investment is its low liquidity. Mortimer (2009) points out that the buying and selling process can be lengthy and investment timing is non-trivial.

REAL ESTATE

The real estate literature often distinguishes between unsecuritized real estate investments (e.g., direct investments in buildings) and real estate investment trusts (REITs). Ibbotson and Siegel (1984) and Hartzell, Hekman, and Miles (1987) observe a close return relationship between unsecuritized real estate and inflation.

Direct investments in property generally are useful for inflation protection. This relationship is true if landlords can pass on higher costs to the tenants. However, supply and demand must be in equilibrium; no over-supply must exist due to over-heated construction activity and demand must be strong. During the most recent high inflation period in the 1970s and 1980s, vacancy rates for industrial buildings were lower than for office buildings. The owners of the industrial properties could pass on higher costs to their tenants via increased rents.

Another determinant of the efficacy of real estate as an inflation hedge is the duration of the rental contracts. With rising prices, landlords want to pass on higher costs with little delay. This situation becomes more difficult with contract maturities of five years and more. Conversely, long contract terms shield against falling prices or deflation.

Huang and Hudson-Wilson (2007) divide the return of an investment in U.S. property in price appreciation and rental income. They establish that price appreciation generates the greatest part of inflation protection, while rental income only provides a small part. The most effective inflation protection opportunities come from office buildings followed by apartments, warehouses, and retail property.

In contrast to unsecuritized real estate, REITs are not considered a good inflation hedge (Gyourko and Linneman 1988; Chan, Hendershott, and Sanders 1990). REIT returns tend to correlate more strongly with small cap stocks than with indicators of inflation. Benjamin, Sirmans, and Zietz (2001) provide a good overview about the characteristics of property as an inflation hedge.

After discussing buy-and-hold investments for inflation protection and some of their features in this section such as illiquidity, basis risk, timing risk, and roll yield, the next section deals with a non-traditional representative of inflation protection investments with active investment strategies.

Inflation Protection with Active Investment Strategies

The previous section provided a brief discussion of *futures contracts*, which are standardized investment contracts traded on regulated exchanges. Standardization and regulation enables liquid buy and sell transactions, which is a prerequisite for systematic and large-scale trading and hedging. Trend-following CTAs fall into the category of systematic investors. Because they use futures contracts almost exclusively, CTAs are also called *managed futures hedge funds*. The following section explains how investors can protect themselves against inflation through active trend following in liquid futures markets.

HOW TO PROFIT FROM INFLATION WITH TREND-FOLLOWING STRATEGIES

During periods of sustained inflation, passively held assets are exposed to the risk of devaluation. How can active trading strategies provide protection from inflation associated with large changes in prices of equities, bonds, and commodities? The answer is contingent on whether the price developments arising during inflationary scenarios are consistent and large enough to be profitably traded (i.e., strategies profit best from price trends triggered by inflation through active market exposure repositioning). Because CTAs manage investment funds specializing in generating returns from price trends, this section specifically focuses on their qualities from this perspective. CTAs do not exclusively trade price trends. However, because trend following is the dominant return and risk driver, CTAs are also called *trend followers*.

COMMODITY TRADING ADVISORS

Since the 1980s, the CTA investment strategy has increasingly attracted attention. The strategy originated from charting and technical analysis, which is basically time series and statistical price analysis. With the rise of personal computing in the 1990s, the assets under management for this strategy experienced rapid growth. CTAs have incorporated more sophisticated strategies and are now more established in the institutional investment industry with the help of computing and quantification. An additional key development for CTAs has been the implementation of electronic exchanges that allowed rule-based CTA strategies to become fully automated. However, the strategy goal remains unchanged: entering price trends at an early stage and exiting before major trend reversals, combined with a reduction in positioning during random market action.

In 2013, more than 200 different futures contracts trade across global exchanges, which allow CTAs to diversify across all asset classes and global economies in equity indices, bonds, currencies, and commodities. The diversification aims at enhancing opportunities to engage in new price trends. The key for success of these strategies is the frequency and duration of trends and the ability of CTAs to quantify trend strength with optimal position sizing. If trends are an integral part of the price finding process in free markets and if trends can be isolated statistically, then historical returns of CTAs are credible and indicative of performance.

PRICE TRENDS AND INFLATION HEDGING

Markets trade in equilibrium around a fair price level as long as all information is reflected.

Price trends emerge when new fundamental information has to work itself into market valuation. Important news events change the outlook positively or negatively and the price discovery process reflects this change with an autocorrelated (serial correlated) directional tendency. No individual investor knows the new fair price level because the interaction of all buyers and sellers determines that level. Directional price tendencies can be filtered with a lag from a pure random walk price action with the help of technical instruments such as moving averages (MA). This use of this filter is possible during the trend phase because the market price always moves away from its own average. If a market price moves away from its moving average, it indicates that a price trend is in process. The signaling of price trends with technical indicators is generally a weak indication of sustainable trends, resulting in only 35 to 45 percent profitable trades. This methodology is based on retaining exposure to the winners and eliminating exposure to the losers. The fewer profitable trending trades are larger than the more frequent smaller losses and contribute in the long run to a net profitable result (Kaufman 2005). CTAs capture price trends profitably due to systematic repetitions of this method across many markets. This methodology results in the characteristically volatile performance profile with the ability to profitably capture large price dislocations as triggered during substantial inflation.

MEASURING TRENDS

Methods based on quantifying serial correlation can measure the level of trendiness in price data in hindsight. For illustration purposes, this section considers the well-documented Welles Wilder trend indicator Average Directional Index (ADX) (Wilder 1978). The slightly altered ADX indicator is not used to forecast trends but to visualize ex post the causality between historical trends and CTA returns. A trendiness reading of 0 percent would indicate a year with no trends, and a 100 percent reading would indicate trends in all markets at all times. These extremes, which have never been recorded, are unlikely to occur. Analysts have used the 40 most liquid futures markets across all sectors to measure trends in recent history. Trend frequency measured with this method ranges from 35 to 55 percent, which is indicated in Figure 13.5 by the black bold line with the scale on the right. CTA returns are visualized by the gray bars of the Barclay CTA index scaled on the left-hand side.

Trendiness varies depending on the measurement method but averages below 50 percent. Randomness and lesser known price patterns, such as mean reversion, dominate the other 50 percent of price moves. CTAs can achieve profitable returns

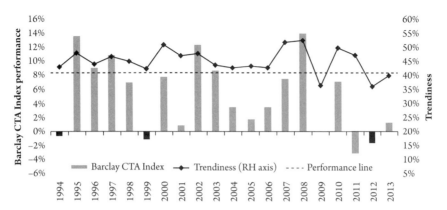

Figure 13.5 CAUSALITY BETWEEN MARKET PRICE TRENDINESS AND CTA PERFORMANCE. This graph compares market trendiness to the Barclay CTA Index to visualize the dependency of CTA returns from market trends. Source: Man Investment Database 2013.

with a minimum of 35 to 40 percent of markets trending by closing losing trades and letting profitable trend positions continue. The resulting position switching from non-trending to trending markets results in performance volatility but reduces maximum drawdown fat tail risk. Return distributions of CTAs are skewed to the right because they take many small losses bunching up near the mean on the left side of the return distribution. The fewer profitable trending positions that continue spread out across the right side of the return distribution, including outliers in the right tail. Hence, CTAs' left tails of the distribution are smaller than implied by their volatility. During market crises as triggered by a bear market or substantial inflation, the long or short position alignment with price trends results in a hedge for passive asset exposures.

CTA RETURNS DURING MARKET STRESS

As Figure 13.6 illustrates, the highest CTA returns have been generated during economic crises and especially during equity market corrections. Environments driven by fundamentally threatening and bearish circumstances such as the Russian crisis (scenario 1 in Figure 13.6), the Dot.com bubble burst (scenario 2), or the credit crisis of 2008 (scenario 3) have resulted in large price moves and profitable trends for CTAs. This performance profile is due to the fact that CTAs can go long and short futures on equities, bonds, commodities, and currencies. CTAs can capture moves to the downside by selling futures. This helps in crises when the global flight to quality leads to extended moves in markets such as government bonds, the U.S. dollar, gold, or specific commodities such as crude oil.

INFLATION AND TRENDS

Inflation is one of the most disruptive economic scenarios affecting all economic sectors and prices. If major economic zones such as North America or Europe are exposed, the

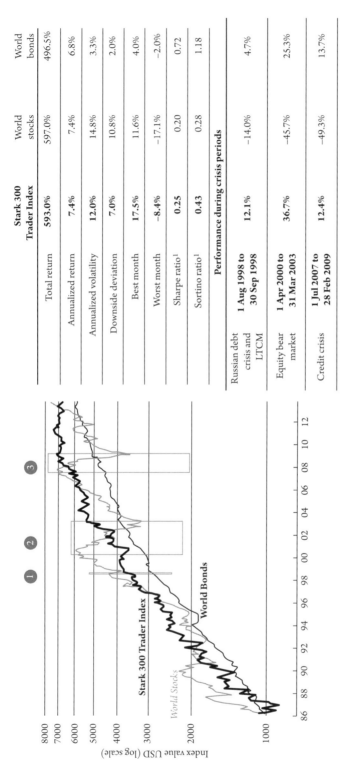

	Stark 300 Trader Index	World stocks	World bonds
Total return	593.0%	597.0%	496.5%
Annualized return	7.4%	7.4%	6.8%
Annualized volatility	12.0%	14.8%	3.3%
Downside deviation	7.0%	10.8%	2.0%
Best month	17.5%	11.6%	4.0%
Worst month	–8.4%	–17.1%	–2.0%
Sharpe ratio[1]	0.25	0.20	0.72
Sortino ratio[1]	0.43	0.28	1.18
Performance during crisis periods			
Russian debt crisis and LTCM	1 Aug 1998 to 30 Sep 1998	12.1%	–14.0%	4.7%
Equity bear market	1 Apr 2000 to 31 Mar 2003	36.7%	–45.7%	25.3%
Credit crisis	1 Jul 2007 to 28 Feb 2009	12.4%	–49.3%	13.7%

Figure 13.6 CTA RETURNS DURING CRISES SCENARIOS. The graph on the left shows three major equity market corrections compared with the Stark Trader 300 CTA index. The table on the right quantifies the negative performance correlation between world stocks and the CTA index during these crisis periods. Source: Bloomberg 2013; MSCI 2013; Stark & Co, Inc. 2013; and Man Investments Database 2013.

phenomenon is difficult to contain locally and it will typically permeate globally. This scenario existed in the 1970s as discussed previously. For an investor to be protected against inflation through trend-following strategies, the issue is whether inflation affects asset prices enough to trigger price trends, which then CTAs can capture. Due to rising prices for goods and services, inflation reduces the purchasing power of currencies, resulting in a depreciation of the affected exchange rate (Öner 2012).

The resulting value adjustments can result in the trend behavior of affected local currencies. Other markets will respond in accordance with their sensitivity to inflation. As a potential monetary substitute for cash, gold may appreciate and offer protection, while interest rates adjust higher in line with inflation expectations. Because interest rates determine the cost of capital, they have a downstream impact on many other markets. Higher interest rates typically drive commodity prices up due to storage and financing cost and can trigger a bear market in equities as fixed income investments become more attractive on a risk-adjusted basis.

The magnitude of price changes is correlated with high levels of inflation and can be traded with today's 200 global futures contracts across sectors and geographic locations. As inflation increases and becomes more threatening, its impact on price changes and trends grows correspondingly. Such an environment is supportive of CTA returns as providers of inflation protection.

PERFORMANCE OF CTAs DURING THE LAST BIG INFLATION

An analysis of the last major inflation episode in the 1970s shows that price levels of equities were slow to respond to rising inflation. Conversely, strong trends in gold, oil, grains, and currencies were much faster to emerge as observed in the Dow Jones Industrial Average (DJIA) and the gold chart depicted in Figure 13.7.

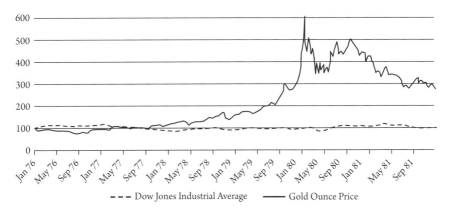

Figure 13.7 Dow Jones versus Gold: 1976–1981. This graph shows the potential magnitude of price dislocations by comparing the historic gold price against the Dow Jones Industrial Average (DJIA) during inflation in the 1970s. Both the DJIA and gold are indexed to 100 in January 1976 as a VAMI (value added monthly index) chart.
Source: Bloomberg 2013.

In the 1970s and early 1980s, trend following strategies were not yet computerized but supported by systematic "charting" techniques. Technical analysis used such techniques as point and figure charts, trend lines, or support and resistance break-outs to determine market direction. Technical analysis opened the door to systematic trading methodologies, which constitute the CTA industry today.

Figure 13.8 shows returns of four CTA pioneers during the inflation years of the 1970s and 1980s. The CTA returns are divided into the high inflation years up to 1983 with an average consumer price increase of 9.3 percent and the following years

| | Pre 1983 | | Post 1983 | |
| | Total Return | Annualized Return | Total Return | Annualized Return |
Fund	%	%	%	%
Millburn Ridgefield	473.9	34.4	47.9	8.1
Campbell Trust	95.1	25.0	76.5	12.0
Harvest Futures Fund	218.4	34.4	−8.5	−1.8
Trendlogic-D LP	357.8	50.0	29.4	5.3

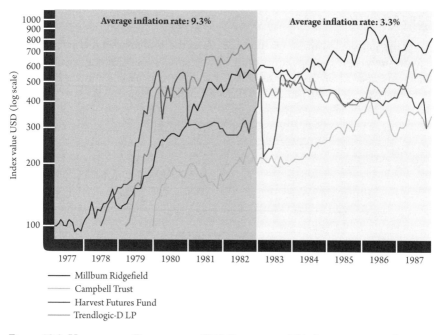

Figure 13.8 HISTORICAL RETURNS OF CTA PIONEERS.   This figure compares the performance of four CTA pioneers during different levels of inflation. Returns are divided into the high inflation years, with an average CPI of 9.3 percent, followed by the lower 3.3 percent inflation years. During high inflation, the strong market trends resulted in a record 25 to 50 percent return a year. The lower inflation environment resulted in more moderate CTA performance. Source: Man Investments Database 2013.

with a lower 3.3 percent increase. The table below Figure 13.8 shows the CTAs' returns. During the high inflation years before 1983, record returns of 25 to 50 percent per year resulted on the back of strong price trends.

Two of these CTAs, Millburn Ridgefield and Campbell Trust, are still in business today. The success of these two companies over the last 35 years can be interpreted as a testament to the fundamental existence of trends and the ability to follow trends profitably through times of turbulence.

Academic studies examine the suitability of trend-following CTAs as a way of inflation protection. Edwards and Park (1996) analyze the correlations of CTAs' returns with the U.S. CPI on both a monthly and annual basis and find positive dependencies. Irwin and Brorsen (1985) study the high inflation years at the end of the 1970s and the beginning of the 1980s and report similar results.

Summary and Conclusions

Investors fear inflationary effects building from central banks pumping unprecedented amounts of money into the financial system. This chapter describes how the U.S. central bank's interest payments on reserves reduced inflationary pressures in the 2010s compared with the 1970s and how the expansion of liquidity can help to revive a frozen interbank market. The toolkit of instruments for providing liquidity and supporting a troubled financial system is better understood today than it was a few decades earlier. However, concerns remain that inflation could arise from new sources such as the fast-growing emerging markets, the need of Western industrialized countries to inflate away their high debts, or based on the sheer size of liquidity pumped into the world economy.

The discussion of the usual suspects for inflation protection such as equities, inflation-protected bonds, gold and precious metals, futures and physical investments in commodities, timber, and real estate, touches on the pros and cons for each of those instruments. Equities, for example, provide inflation protection but only for longer time horizons. Inflation-indexed bonds face basis risk and are subject to changes of the index calculation method. For investments in gold, timing is essential. Futures have special characteristics including the roll yield and trend behavior. Timber provides renewable carry income and historically has proven to be a good inflation protection instrument, but tends to be illiquid. The efficacy of unsecuritized real estate depends on a type of property (e.g., apartments, warehouses, and retail property) and the duration of the rental contracts. Because REITs behave more like equities and less like changes in the CPI, they are less useful for inflation protection.

A common feature of these instruments is their buy-and-hold character. In contrast, active investment strategies as pursued by CTAs try to benefit from trends in financial markets by long and short positions in futures markets. If inflation emerges as a longer term trend, CTAs could be a natural candidate to provide inflation protection. After describing their historical development, CTAs' characteristic return properties are explained, and how they behaved in periods of market stress as well as during the last periods of high inflation in the 1970s. This chapter's message is that CTAs are a useful addition to protect portfolios against inflation.

Discussion Questions

1. Explain why an inflationary scenario can be expected after three decades of moderate price changes.
2. Discuss how central banks strategies toward inflationary concerns developed since the 1970s.
3. Discuss how standard investment instruments perform in an inflationary scenario and the difficulty in using these instruments as an inflation hedge.
4. Discuss why and how investors can use trend-following strategies as a hedge against inflation.

References

Bank for International Settlements. 2013. *BIS Quarterly Review Statistical Annex*. September 15. Basel, Switzerland: Bank of International Settlements. Available at http://www.bis.org/publ/qtrpdf/r_qt1309.htm.

Barnes, Michelle L., Zvi Bodie, Robert K. Triest, and J. Christina Wang, 2010. "A TIPS Scorecard: Are They Accomplishing Their Objectives?" *Financial Analysts Journal* 66:5, 68–84.

Bataa, Erdenebat, Denise R. Osborn, Marianne Sensier, and Dick van Dijk. 2009. "Structural Breaks in the International Transmission of Inflation." Working Paper, Centre for Growth and Business Cycle Research Discussion Paper Series 119.

Benjamin, John D., G. Stacy Sirmans, and Emily N. Zietz. 2001. "Returns and Risk on Real Estate and Other Investments: More Evidence." *Journal of Real Estate Portfolio Management* 7:3, 183–214.

Bloomberg. 2013. Bloomberg Service Center. Available at http://www.bloomberg.com/quote.

Boudoukh, Jacob, and Matthew Richardson. 1993. "Stock Returns and Inflation: A Long Horizon Perspective." *American Economic Review* 83:5, 1346–1355.

Browne, Frank, and David Cronin. 2007. "Commodity Prices, Money, and Inflation." European Central Bank Working Paper Series, No. 738, March.

Chan, K. C., Patric H. Hendershott, and Anthony P. Sanders. 1990. "Risk and Return on Real Estate: Evidence from Equity REITs." *Journal of the American Real Estate and Urban Economics Association* 18:4, 431–452.

Childers, Vincent L. 2011. "Inflation: An Ounce of Protection." *CFA Institute Conference Proceedings Quarterly* 28:2, 1–10.

DeLong, Bradford J. 1997. "America's Peacetime Inflation: The 1970s." In Christina D. Romer and David H. Romer, eds., *Reducing Inflation: Motivation and Strategy*, 247–280. Chicago: University of Chicago Press. Available at http://www.nber.org/chapters/c8886.

Dupasquier, Chantal, Alain Guay, and Pierre St. Aman. 1999. "A Comparison of Alternative Methodologies for Estimating Potential Output and the Output Gap." Working Paper, Bank of Canada.

Edwards, Franklin R., and James M. Park. 1996. "Do Managed Futures Make Good Investments?" *Journal of Futures Markets* 16:5, 475–517.

Erb, Claude B., and Campbell R. Harvey. 2006. "The Strategic and Tactical Value of Commodity Futures." *Financial Analysts Journal* 62:2, 69–97.

Fama, Eugene, and G. William Schwert. 1977. "Asset Returns and Inflation." *Journal of Financial Economics* 5:2, 115–146.

Federal Reserve. 2013a. "Currency and Coin Services." Available at www.federalreserve.gov/paymentsystems/coin_data.htm#value.

Federal Reserve. 2013b. "Aggregate Reserves of Depository Institutions and the Monetary Base." H.3 Statistical Release. Available at www.federalreserve.gov/econresdata/statisticsdata.htm.

Forest Research Group. 2007. "Inflation and Timberland Returns—Part 2." *Forest Research Notes* 4:4, 1–4.

Friedman, Milton. 1956. "The Quantity Theory of Money: A Restatement." In Milton Friedman Milton, ed., *Studies in the Quantity Theory of Money*, 3–21, Chicago: University of Chicago Press.

Gerberding, Christina, Franz Seitz, and Andreas Worms. 2005. "How the Bundesbank Really Conducted Monetary Policy." *North American Journal of Economics and Finance* 16:3, 277–292.

Gómez-Loscos, Ana, María Dolores Gadea, and Antonio Montañés. 2012. "Economic Growth, Inflation and Oil Shocks: Are the 1970s Coming Back?" *Applied Economics* 44:35, 4575–4589.

Goodfriend, Marvin. 2002. "Interest on Reserves and Monetary Policy." *Federal Reserve Bank of New York Economic Policy Review* 8:1, 13–29.

Gorton, Gary K., and Geert Rouwenhorst. 2006. "Facts and Fantasies about Commodity Futures." *Financial Analysts Journal* 62:2, 47–68.

Guedj, Ilan, Guohua Li, and Craig McCann. 2011. "Futures-Based Commodity ETFs." *Journal of Index Investing* 2:1, 14–24.

Gyourko, Joseph, and Peter Linneman. 1988. "Owner-Occupied Homes, Income-Producing Properties, and REITs as Inflation Hedges: Empirical Findings." *Journal of Real Estate Finance and Economics* 1:4, 347–372.

Hagmann, Matthias, and Carlos Lenz. 2005. "Real Asset Returns and Components of Inflation: A Structural VAR Analysis." Working Paper, Faculty of Business and Economics, University of Basel.

Hartzell, David, John S. Hekman, and Mike E. Miles. 1987. "Real Estate Returns and Inflation." *Journal of the American Real Estate and Urban Economics Association* 15:1, 617–637.

Healey, Thomas, Timothy Corriero, and Rossen Rozenov. 2005. "Timber as an Institutional Investment." *Journal of Alternative Investments* 8:3, 60–74.

Herbst, Anthony. 1983. "Gold versus U.S. Common Stocks: Some Evidence on Inflation Hedge Performance and Cyclical Behavior." *Financial Analysts Journal* 39:1, 66–74.

Hooker, Mark A. 2002. "Are Oil Shocks Inflationary? Asymmetric and Nonlinear Specifications versus Changes in Regime." *Journal of Money, Credit and Banking* 34:2, 540–561.

Huang, Haibo, and Susan Hudson-Wilson. 2007. "Private Commercial Real Estate Equity Returns and Inflation." *Journal of Portfolio Management* 33:5, 63–73.

Hudson, Michael, and Jeffrey Sommers. 2011. "The Spectre Haunting Europe: Debt Defaults, Austerity, and Death of the 'Social Europe' Model." Available at www.globalresearch.ca/index.php?context=va&aid=22846.

Ibbotson, Roger B., and Laurence B. Siegel. 1984. "Real Estate Returns: A Comparison with Other Investments." *Journal of the American Real Estate and Urban Economics Association* 12:3, 219–242.

International Monetary Fund. 2010. "Rebalancing Growth." *World Economic Outlook*, April.

International Monetary Fund. 2013a. "Primary Commodity Price System." Available at http://www.imf.org/external/np/res/commod/index.aspx.

International Monetary Fund. 2013b. "The Dog that Didn't Bark: Has Inflation Been Muzzled or Was It Just Sleeping?" *IMF World Economic Outlook*, April, 79–95. Available at http://www.imf.org/external/pubs/ft/weo/2013/01/index.htm.

Ip, Greg. 2008. "Fears of Stagflation Return as Price Increases Gain Pace." *Wall Street Journal Online*, February 21. Available at http://online.wsj.com/news/articles/SB120355396795281551.

Irwin, Scott H., and B. Wade Brorsen. 1985. "Public Futures Funds." *Journal of Futures Markets* 5:2, 149–171.

Jordan, Thomas J., and Enzo Rossi. 2010. "Inflation und die Geldpolitik der Schweizerischen Nationalbank." *Die Volkswirtschaft* 83:1, 21–25.

Kaufman, Perry. 2005. *Trading Systems and Methods*. Hoboken, NJ: John Wiley & Sons.

Keister, Todd, and James McAndrews. 2009. "Why Are Banks Holding So Many Excess Reserves?" Federal Reserve Bank of New York, Staff Report No. 380.

Laidler, David. 2007. "Successes and Failures of Monetary Policy since the 1950s, Conference Monetary Policy over Fifty Years." Available at http://www.bundesbank.de/Redaktion/EN/Downloads/Bundesbank/Research_Centre/Conferences/2007/2007_09_21_frankfurt_02_laidler_paper.pdf?__blob=publicationFile.

Man Investment Database. 2013. Man Group. Available at https://www.man.com/GB/home.

McKinsey. 2012. "Debt and Deleveraging: Uneven Progress on the Path to Growth." McKinsey Global Institute. Available at http://www.mckinsey.com/insights/global_capital_markets/uneven_progress_on_the_path_to_growth.

Miffre, Joelle, and Georgios Rallis. 2007. "Momentum Strategies in Commodity Futures Markets." *Journal of Banking and Finance* 31:6, 1863–1886.

Mortimer, Jeff. 2009. "Investing in Timberland: Another Means of Diversification." J.P. Morgan Investment Analytics and Consulting. Available at https://www.jpmorgan.com/tss/General/Timberland/1159351270237.

MSCI Inc. 2013. Available at http://www.msci.com/products/indices/.

Nelson, Edward, and Kalin Nikolov. 2002. "Monetary Policy and Stagflation in the UK." Working Paper, Bank of England.

OECD. 2013. "Consumer Prices (MEI)." *OECD StatExtracts*. Available at http://stats.oecd.org/Index.aspx?DataSetCode=MEI_PRICES.

Offenbacher, Edward A. 2002. "Dollarization and Indexation in Israel's Inflation and Disinflation: 'There's More than One Way to Skin a Cat'." Monetary Department, Bank of Israel.

Öner, Ceyda. 2012: "Inflation: Prices on the Rise." *International Monetary Fund*, March 28. Available at http://www.imf.org/external/Pubs/FT/fandd/basics/inflat.htm.

Samuelson, Paul A., and Robert M. Solow. 1960. "Analytical Aspects of Anti-Inflation Policy." *American Economic Review* 50:2, 185–197.

Shiller, Robert J. 2013. "Home Page of Robert J. Shiller." Online Data. Available at http://www.econ.yale.edu/~shiller/data/.

Simon, John, Troy Matheson, and Damiano Sandri. 2013. "World Economic Outlook." *International Monetary Fund*, April, 79–95.

Stark & Co. 2013. "Stark & Co, Inc. Managed Futures Research." Available at http://www.starkresearch.com/.

Sturzenegger, Federico, and Jeromin Zettelmeyer. 2006. *Debt Defaults and Lessons from a Decade of Crises*. Cambridge, MA: MIT Press.

Wilder, J. Welles, Jr. 1978. *New Concepts in Technical Trading Systems*. Greensboro, NC: Trend Research.

Woodford, Michael. 2000. "Monetary Policy in a World without Money." International Finance 3:2, 229–260.

14

Risk Aggregation and Capital Management

SUMIT MATHUR

Global Product Manager, SAS Institute Inc.

Introduction

A chief risk officer (CRO) invariably needs a meaningful picture of total risk in order to understand and proactively manage the risk profile of an organization bounded by an established risk appetite. *Risk aggregation* is a term used to describe aggregation of one or more types of risk across all the portfolios in order to obtain a picture of total risk rolled up at multiple levels in an aggregation hierarchy. The aggregation hierarchy may comprise legal entities, business units, and business lines. Risk aggregation becomes an important part of the risk planning, monitoring, and control in a risk management valechain. Economic capital (ECAP) of a financial institution aggregates many different risk types and presents them as one number that banks can then compare to Tier 1 capital (shareholder equity) to describe capital surplus or shortage.

In the risk aggregation process, some positions may naturally offset or hedge others within the same portfolio so that the net risk of the portfolio is always less than the sum of the risk of each individual position. For example, typical aggregation of repricing risk by asset liability management (ALM) systems allows netting off interest-rate sensitive assets with interest-rate sensitive liabilities to calculate the net repricing exposure in each time bucket. So for the risk managers, risk aggregation should lead to understanding net residual risk for macro hedging to enable attaining the target risk-return profile.

Risk aggregation and in particular capital aggregation is a widely discussed topic in many regulatory and non-regulatory references. Capital aggregation allows a financial institution to estimate total regulatory capital (RCAP) and ECAP for meeting the capital adequacy and internal capital adequacy assessment process (ICAAP) requirements. From a regulatory perspective, banks must have greater than or equal to 8 percent of risk-weighted assets (RWAs) as RCAP made up of at least a 4.5 percent of Tier 1 capital (shareholder equity) and the remaining as Tier 2 (qualified long-term debt).

Economic capital is the minimum amount of capital required to cushion unexpected losses (UL) measured at a pre-specified confidence level. The confidence level selected should to sufficient to sustain a high credit rating (AA or A) for the bank over a one-year horizon. ECAP is based on a bank's own judgment of economic risks by taking into account all the risk factors that may influence economic value of its portfolios. The notion of ECAP is closely linked to risk appetite and plays a pivotal role in ICAAP compliance. ECAP also supports decision-making at a business transaction level. Some examples of using the ECAP metric include: (1) determining the right price of various transactions in order earn risk-adjusted margins (2) evaluating hedging opportunities and optimization of risk; and (3) establishing risk-based limits taking into account ECAP risk contributions down to the business line or product level. The primary focus of this chapter is to describe risk aggregation involving credit risk and market risk with an objective of estimating a capital number for a bank.

Market practices for risk aggregation can be divided into two main approaches: a bottom-up approach and a top-down approach. The *bottom-up approach* is an integrated risk-measurement approach involving multifactor models that take into account the correlations and interactions between different risk types to provide an estimate of total risk of a position. In contrast, a *top-down approach* is a compartmentalized aggregation approach that first measures individual risk types such as market, credit, and operational risk and then produces a correlated aggregation of each of these silos. Under this approach, pre-aggregated market, credit, and operational risk estimates are inputs into a correlated aggregation process. For the bottom-up approach, however, overall risk is measured and aggregated concurrently. Different methodical choices are available under these approaches and banks make choices based on such factors as:

- *Trade-offs between accuracy and complexity*. A simple aggregation approach may be less accurate, but it may offer a good understanding of the logic and hence more explainable to senior management.
- *Errors involved in parameterization*. This is a factor associated with a complex approach where the amount of capital depends on parameters such as choosing the degrees of freedom in a Student-t copula.
- *Stability of the aggregated risk measure*. Financial institutions look for methods that lead to a more stable aggregated capital estimate compared to the ones that may result in the capital estimate varying widely from one reporting period to the other.
- *Nature of the business activities and characteristics of their portfolios*. For some banks with simple portfolios such as those including loans and mortgages, no need exists to include complex aggregation methods such as those requiring nonlinear correlated aggregations.

Risk Aggregation—The Notion of Capital

Capital can be computed in various ways. The required amount of capital on a balance sheet is guided by required RCAP and ECAP (based on ICAAP) estimates. Banks must meet the RCAP criteria equal to a minimum capital to risk adequacy ratio (CRAR) of 8 percent at any point of time. RCAP computation is prescriptive and is based on detailed guidelines for estimating risk for different asset classes. It involves a simple summation of RWAs at different levels to arrive at a total RWA and RCAP figure. Under each risk type, RWA is computed separately and then summed up as if they were perfectly correlated to get total RCAP. Compared to RCAP, the ECAP approach is more oriented to model the actual interactions or dependencies between different risk types in various portfolios. Since risks are imperfectly correlated and RCAP does not allow any diversification between risk types, some contend that RCAP should provide a more conservative estimate of capital. This argument, however, may not always be true if, for example, the interactions between risk types (e.g., market and credit risk) are nonlinear (BCBS 2009).

Breuer, Jandačka, Rheinberger, and Summer (2010) show that interactions between risks may lead to compounding effects where inter-risk correlations may actually be greater than 100 percent. They give an example of credit risk in a portfolio of foreign currency loans that depends on market risk factors. The authors point out that an element of wrong-way risk also exists where an adverse movement in market risk factors (e.g., foreign exchange movements) will lead credit risk to increase. Under these circumstances, RCAP will not provide a conservative estimate compared to ECAP.

Another factor that leads to the differences between the RCAP and ECAP frameworks is the risks considered in each of these approaches. ECAP also includes quantification of interest rate risk in banking book (IRRBB) under market risk capital using an economic value sensitivity approach that includes basis risk, repricing risk, yield curve risk, and optionality risk applicable for the banking book products. IRRBB is required to be estimated as a part of the Basel II (Pillar 2) Accord guidelines. Pillar 2 includes different types of risks but their treatment is based on judgment of the bank and the local regulator instead of having some defined common minimum quantitative standard as available under Pillar 1 for credit risk and market risk.

ECAP can be estimated for individual risk types at various confidence intervals. Aggregating ECAP requires banks to take into account the dependencies between risk types that are involved in the aggregation process. ECAP is always calibrated at a higher confidence interval that is consistent with either AA or A rating for a bank. A higher credit rating of a bank is a sign of confidence among its lenders and enables a bank to access wholesale funding at competitive rates thereby leading to higher profit margins. According to Jackson, Perraudin, and Saporta (2002), an AA rating for a bank would imply a 99.96 percent solvency standard. Compared to ECAP, RCAP is based on a lower confidence level of 99.90 percent.

The next two sections explain the risk aggregation within credit risk and market risk components before moving to inter-risk aggregation approaches.

Credit Risk Capital Based on a Structural Model

Credit risk generally has three dimensions involving risks: (1) counterparty default for portfolios that are held-to-maturity (HTM) and loans; (2) credit spread risk for trading portfolios or available-for-sale (AFS) portfolios; and (3) rating downgrade (transition) risk leading to mark-to-market losses for the HTM, trading, and AFS portfolios. Credit risk is typically measured over a one-year horizon at a sufficiently high confidence level usually around 99.97 percent in order to capture default events that are rare. The regulatory computation of credit risk capital uses an asymptomatic single risk factor (ASRF) model that Vasicek (1991) pioneers to fulfill the assumption of portfolio invariance in credit portfolios. Portfolio invariance works with an assumption that the idiosyncratic risk component of all the individual exposures cancels out each other completely when the size of the credit portfolio is very large and the individual exposure is very small. Therefore, at the outset RCAP for credit risk assumes that name concentration risk in credit portfolio is zero. RCAP's advanced calculation for credit risk is based on Merton's (1974) asset value model and single value systemic risk factor. Equation 14.1 shows the basic model. In general, credit risk correlated aggregation draws heavily from the specification of the asset value model, which is also known as the *structural model*.

$$A_i = w_i Z + \sqrt{1 - w_i^2}\, X_i, \tag{14.1}$$

where A_i is the asset value of firm i; w_i is the factor loading or sensitivity of systemic risk factor; Z is the single systemic risk factor (global parameter) that is a standard normal variable; Z can also be interpreted as square-root of the asset correlation of firm i; and X_i is the value of the idiosyncratic risk factor that is a standard normal variable.

Factors Z and X_i are totally independent of each other and both are normally distributed with a zero mean and standard deviation of 1. If the default threshold is set to a value γ_i, the firm will default if the asset value falls below this threshold (i.e., $A_i \leq \gamma_i$).

The probability of default (PD_i) conditional on realization of a stress value for Z_i can be written as shown in Equations 14.2 through 14.5:

$$PD_i\,(Z) = Prob\left(A_i \leq \Phi^{-1}\,(PD_i)|Z\right) \tag{14.2}$$

$$= Prob\left(w_i Z + \sqrt{1 - w_i^2}\, X_i \leq \Phi^{-1}\,(PD_i)\,|Z\right) \tag{14.3}$$

$$= Prob\left(X_i \leq \frac{\Phi^{-1}\,(PD_i) - w_i Z}{\sqrt{1 - w_i^2}}\right) \tag{14.4}$$

$$= \Phi\left(\frac{\Phi^{-1}\,(PD_i) - w_i Z}{\sqrt{1 - w_i^2}}\right). \tag{14.5}$$

The Basel II Accord's Internal Ratings Based (IRB) Approach (BCBS 2006) derives the stressed value of the single systemic risk factor as $Z = \Phi^{-1}(\alpha)$, where α is required to be set equal to $(1 - 99.9 \text{ percent}) = 0.001$. This value is a single market state that remains constant for regulatory credit risk calculations for any portfolio.

The factor sensitivity or factor loading w_i is pre-calibrated in the RCAP model as the square root of the asset value correlation or $\sqrt{R_i}$, where the asset value correlation is shown in Equation 14.6:

$$R_i = 0.12 \left[\frac{\left(1 - exp^{(-50PD_i)}\right)}{\left(1 - exp^{(-50)}\right)}\right] + 0.24 \left[\frac{1 - (1 - exp\,(-50PD))}{1 - exp\,(-50)}\right]. \tag{14.6}$$

This function is the asset correlation model for wholesale lending class of exposures. Asset value correlation in this model is a simple decreasing function of the PD.

If an exposure has an average PD of 5 percent, from Equation 14.5, the conditional PD of this exposure will be 28.45 percent. Assuming that its loss given default (LGD) is 30 percent, the RCAP for this exposure for credit risk or the conditional expected loss can be calculated in Equation 14.7:

$$RCAP\ (\%) = [(LGD)\ (Conditional\ PD\ -\ LGD\ (PD)]\ Maturity\ adjustment, \quad (14.7)$$

where the maturity adjustment $(b) = [(0.11852 - 0.05478)\ln (PD)]^2$.

This calculation results in a RCAP (%) of 0.07966. For a credit exposure (exposure at default (EAD)) of $1 million, the RCAP against this exposure will be $79,669. The maturity adjustment factor takes into account the capital required due to a transition in credit quality over an exposure's residual maturity. This example assumes that the residual maturity of this exposure is 2.5 years.

The marginal risk contribution of an individual exposure to the regulatory capital is only due to its own systemic risk component modeled with a single systematic risk factor. The RCAP does not consider pair-wise default correlation between obligors. With these assumptions the total RCAP is simply the sum of the RCAP of each of the individual exposures in credit portfolio. In practice, however, one systemic risk factor is insufficient to detail the risk of correlated defaults in a credit portfolio. Therefore, the ECAP for credit risk uses more sophisticated asset value modeling account for the dependence structure.

Considering the structural approach, a multifactor model for asset value correlations shown in Equation 14.8 is used to model asset value correlations. The asset value or equity returns of an individual counterparty is estimated through regression with benchmark market indices used to estimate the sensitivity (beta) of the asset value to each index, a factor loading (weight assigned to the systematic component) and an idiosyncratic (unexplained) component. Correlation among obligors or asset value correlation is then obtained from the correlation between the different indices used as benchmark variables.

$$A_i = w_i \sum_k \beta_{ik}\eta_k + \sqrt{1 - w_i^2}\ X_i. \quad (14.8)$$

In Equation 14.8, the single factor systemic risk component 'Z' that was used in Equation 14.1 is replaced by k correlated market indices. An example of the market indices could be the chemical industry index, banking index, and so on with β_{ik} being the sensitivity of asset value A_i with the market index η_k. Koyluoglu and Hickman (1998), Crouhy, Galai, and Mark (2000), and Gordy (2000) provide detailed discussions on credit risk structural models. The market indices used need a clear economic interpretation and can be backward linked to the primary macroeconomic risk factors such as gross domestic product (GDP), capacity utilization, inflation, and interest rates. Through this linkage, stress on macroeconomic factors, such as modeling an economic downturn, can be easily converted into constraints on the corresponding market indices that are assumed to be Gaussian distributed. A correlation matrix derived from pair-wise asset correlations of asset returns can be simulated directly using methods such as Cholesky decomposition and asset values compared with default threshold to arrive at a portfolio loss number at a desired percentile for calculating credit value-at-risk (VaR).

An assumption of multivariate normality of the risk factor distribution involving linear correlations is often unsuitable to model rare events using extreme value theory (EVT). Under a Gaussian model the number of simulated large loss events will be very sparse and the probabilities associated with large losses tend to taper off quickly (quadratic decay) leading to unreliable estimates of extreme losses in the tail. Banks may use methods such as importance sampling in simulating rare events with huge losses to improve the number of events available in the tail. Glasserman (2005) analyzes an importance sample on a normal copula by shifting the mean of underlying factors. Using different distributional assumptions of asset values, such as the Student-t or normal mixture distribution, may lead to heavier tailed distributions for capturing tail dependence and calculation of extreme value statistics.

Market Risk Capital

This section discusses some specific aspects of market risk VaR estimation. The RCAP norms for market risk capital for exposures in the trading book have undergone a vast change since the financial crisis of 2007–2008. According to the current regulatory norms, market risk regulatory capital is a sum of (1) 60-day average VaR, (2) stressed VaR, and (3) incremental risk charge (IRC) to cover the risk of default and credit migration on the non-securitized credit products measured at 99.9 percent confidence level. Banks usually quantify IRRBB as a part of market risk ECAP. The IRRBB is calculated for non-trading portfolios that include financial investments in the available-for-trading (AFT) and held-to-maturity (HTM) portfolios, and retail and commercial banking assets and liabilities. ECAP for market risk is usually measured at a 99 percent confidence level over a one-day horizon assuming that positions remain unchanged over this period.

The internal models approach (IMA) for market risk requires that banks compute VaR on a daily basis at a 99th percentile using a minimum one-year observation period. The daily VaR value is then scaled using the square root of time of one-day to a minimum 10-day holding period that represents an instantaneous price shock to measure end of period loss. Scaling of VaR from a one-day to a 10-day holding period works only with an assumption that asset returns are independent and identically distributed (i.i.d.). Therefore, if the returns are assumed to be normally distributed, but exhibit volatility clustering, scaling of the volatility using the square root formula will be incorrect. Positive autocorrelation would lead this scaling of VaR to underestimate the real volatility, whereas a negative autocorrelation (mean reversion) would lead to the scaling to overstate volatility. Additionally, the VaR calculation is an end-of-period measurement that ignores the profit and loss (P&L) distribution of each day up to the end of the period. Bakshi and Panayotov (2010) propose Intraday VaR (I-VaR) as an alternate measure that integrates an end-of-period risk VaR measure with the P&L over the trading horizon considering models that include jumps in the pricing process.

Common risk categories that are included in market risk ECAP computations include interest rates, equity, credit spread, foreign exchange, and commodity. The Basel II Accord does not specify any particular VaR method and therefore banks may use a method of their choice (i.e., the method that best suits their portfolios and business activities). Commonly available VaR approaches are variance-covariance or analytical VaR, Monte Carlo simulation, and historical simulation. Under the variance-covariance approach, the underlying risk factors are assumed to be multivariate normal and therefore can be fully modeled using linear correlations. This approach is also called linear VaR or delta-normal VaR and takes into account only the delta component shift in a risk factor value to estimate VaR. Therefore, this approach is unsuited for positions with nonlinear risk-return payoffs or that have higher order sensitivities. The variance-covariance basic structure assumes that the returns are i.i.d. thus resulting in an unconditional or a constant covariance matrix over time. Under this assumption, the variance covariance can be forecast using fixed weights over the sample period. However, when returns are normally distributed but exhibit autocorrelation, the covariance matrix forecast is obtained by modeling volatility as heteroskedastic and modeling volatilities is done using exponentially weighted mean averages (EWMA) and generalized autoregressive conditionally heteroskedasticity (GARCH) to forecast the variance-covariance matrix.

The historical simulation approach is a popular approach for estimating VaR because it is a nonparametric approach where VaR can be derived just from repricing a portfolio forward for each interval up to the measurement horizon based on historical changes in risk factor values over that interval. It obviates the need to make any distributional assumptions to model risk factors or forecasting a covariance matrix. Under the historical simulation approach, the functional forms and dependencies between the risk factors become a direct input from the historical risk factor data set.

The accuracy of this approach depends on both the number of observations in the data set and the behavior of the risk factor during the observation period. The number of observations has to be fairly large to enable meaningful estimation of VaR. Calculating 99 percent VaR with a four-year observation period (i.e., $250(4) = 1,000$ days) would lead to just 10 observation beyond the VaR threshold resulting in a lack of a fat tail. To overcome the data limitation, analysts use a bootstrapping methodology to create a data set of returns by randomly drawing an entire cross-section of returns with replacement from a historical sample as many times as required. For example, to create 200 returns after the VaR threshold measures at 99 percentile would require bootstrapping 20,000 sample vectors. In the absence of bootstrapping, historical simulation would require 80 years of returns. Another aspect concerns the behavior of the risk factors during the market regime when creating the historical data set. Therefore, the simple moving average volatility observed from this data set would be different from current market volatility. Many different approaches are available for updating volatility parameter such as the EWMA that gives greater weight to the recent variances and returns instead of equally weighing all returns or using GARCH.

Monte Carlo simulation is a full repricing approach that involves simulating thousands of paths of risk factors evolution using stochastic models to model uncertainty. For instance, to revalue a portfolio comprising fixed income instruments and calculate its VaR using the Monte Carlo method, the short rate or instantaneous spot rate is simulated using a one-factor short rate model. The positive side of this approach is that risk factors are modeled based on their actual distribution properties without making unrealistic assumptions (e.g., saying that all risk factors are jointly normally distributed as in variance-covariance approach). This approach also provides flexibility to model dependence between risk factors to arrive at correlated values of risk factors that will be used in repricing of various positions.

Risk Measures and Extreme Value Statistics

The risk metric chosen to sum up the total risk needs to be interpretable and reliable (i.e., reflect the real world) and lead to correct decisions around risk measurement, monitoring, and control. Risk managers need to be aware of the advantages and disadvantages of using a particular risk metric in summing up risks. VaR is by far the most popular measure used by financial institutions to measure the maximum loss amount at a specified probability over a given time horizon.

VaR has several limitations. Being a quantile measure, VaR only estimates the value of loss up to a specified threshold and therefore any loss beyond that threshold, even though large enough to materially impact solvency, gets completely ignored by VaR. VaR does not measure probability and losses associated with rare events that exist in the tail of a loss distribution. Reliance on VaR as the only risk measure means that extreme risks in the tail are not addressed and potential risk is always underestimated. Therefore, using VaR encourages risk managers to build positions that may result in extreme losses but still be within the specification of VaR limit. To address this limitation, stress testing must be done to measure the risk of loss at a threshold by shocking the underlying risk factors values. Revisions to the Basel II market risk framework in 2009 included stressed VaR as a part of total market risk capital.

Some criticize VaR for being an incoherent risk measure because it fails to be sub-additive where the loss distribution has fat tailed asset returns or belongs to a non-elliptical distribution family leading to an overestimation of risk. Absence of convexity (i.e., the property that ensures sub-additivity and positive homogeneity) makes VaR unreliable for portfolio optimization because it can result in multiple minima and maxima. Despite its limitations, VaR continues to be a popular measure due to the fact that it is a more elicitable measure of risk. According to Ziegel (2013), VaR presents better verification (backtesting) compared to other risk measures.

Expected shortfall (ES), also called tail VaR or conditional tail expectation (CTE), is another popular risk measure that satisfies all properties of risk measure coherence and may be used to supplement VaR. *Expected shortfall* is a tail measure that calculates an average tail loss over and above the VaR quantile α. It helps to provide an understanding of the size of loss that is otherwise hidden in VaR measure. Being a convex risk measure, managers can effectively use ES in portfolio optimization unless the underlying portfolio payoffs are linear in which case even VaR is a good optimization measure. One of the main limitations of ES is that it is practically impossible to backtest due to a lack of large losses in the observation window. Therefore, much of ES usage remains in the purview of non-regulatory calculations and therefore is not needed for regulatory capital measurement.

A critically important part of risk management is to understand the behavior of a distribution's tail when modeling asset returns. Both VaR and ES measures suffer from tail risk. Although the tail risk of ES is less than that of VaR, it does not explain the maximum loss or shape and size of the tail. Therefore, both VaR and ES suffer from underestimating risks in which asset returns being modeled have fat tails. Analysts can use extreme value theory (EVT) to model the extreme values in the tails. The peak-over-threshold (POT) model is a popular method to model the exceedances over some threshold to fit a generalized Pareto distribution (GPD) to the tail area. The POT model also describes the tail with a scale parameter (dispersion of the extreme events), a shape parameter (density of the extreme events or tail index), and location (average position of extreme events in the tail) that can be estimated using maximum likelihood estimation or regression methods. As Yamai and Yoshiba (2002) discuss, VaR-EVT and ES-EVT are derived analytically from the tail estimator of univariate or multivariate extreme value distribution as the case may be.

Risk Aggregation Framework

A risk management framework consists of different interconnected pieces including:

- *Risk appetite/tolerance.* This refers to the amount and type of risk that a bank is willing to take.
- *Risk limits/budgets.* These are limits set on maximum amount of risk that is permissible at a business line or a portfolio level.
- *Risk measurement.* This is the quantification of risk.
- *Risk aggregation or risk integration.* This refers to the process by which total risk across diverse risk portfolios is computed.
- *Risk optimization, monitoring, and control.* This involves attaining target risk levels, monitoring with respect to the limits, and taking actions to reduce risk.

Risk aggregation is an important aspect of a risk management framework that involves integrating different risks or risk types into a single metric at various levels in an organization hierarchy and rolling up to the topmost level. Understanding that different risk types are measured at different confidence levels and time horizons is important. For instance, for the RCAP computation, the confidence interval used for market risk VaR is 99 percent, and for credit risk and operational risk it is 99.9 percent. The time horizon over which market risk VaR needs to be scaled for capital purpose is for a 10-day holding period, whereas for credit risk and operational risk, VaR is measured over a one-year horizon. ECAP is calibrated at a fairly high confidence level that corresponds to the target rating (e.g., AA rating corresponding to a 0.03 percent chance of failure or 99.97 percent confidence level) over one year.

As previously mentioned, two approaches for risk aggregation are available: the top-down approach and the bottom-up approach. This section discusses these approaches in detail. The RCAP approach is a compartmentalized approach that adds individual risk types assuming a 100 percent correlation exits between risk types. Banks normally model aggregation of ECAP to derive diversification benefits between risk types. The diversification benefit is unavailable under the regulatory approach. The diversification effect in the total capital is important because it reduces the amount of capital required for a bank overall taking into account less than perfect correlation between the different risk types. Brockmann and Kalkbrener (2010) contend that these diversification benefits range between 10 and 30 percent for banks.

The compartmentalized approach assumes that exposures in a bank can be divided into sub-portfolios that are purely market risk or credit risk specific. Market risk capital for exposures in the trading book serves as a good case in point. Exposures in the trading book are marked-to-market on a daily basis and pertain to held-for-trading or available-for-sale category. The positions are held for no more than 90 days in the trading book, and banks compute the IRC at the 99.9 percent confidence level over a 90-day horizon to estimate risk of default or migration risk for these exposures. Although the IRC measures credit risk, it actually forms a part of market risk capital. Even if risk aggregation involves aggregating different risk types, market risk capital already makes an allowance for credit risk for trading assets. Conversely, if a loan exists in the banking book portfolio, is it exposed only to credit risk? The answer is no because an element of market risk on this loan exists due to changes in interest rates and foreign exchange rates if the loan exposure is in a different currency that affects near term earnings and the present value of future cash flows from that loan. Capital needed to cover the market risk of this loan is called IRRBB capital that measures an economic value sensitivity approach to measure repricing and yield curve risks.

Table 14.1 shows various financial asset categories in a bank, their accounting rules, portfolios (banking or trading book), and the risks that are measured based on the asset categorization and accounting basis. Generally speaking, demarcating an asset category as exposed to just one risk type is complex. Regulatory norms increasingly address this issue as they make IRC a part of market risk capital.

Another aspect of a risk aggregation framework is the direction and level at which risks need to be aggregated and reported. Most institutions want to nurture discipline involving planning and using capital at a business line level to enable allocating capital on a risk-adjusted return basis.

Another aspect of top-down aggregation is that risk is aggregated among risk types or business units. Usually banks aggregate ECAP and RCAP both at a business line level and risk types. Aggregating risk at a business unit level takes into account multiple risk factors based on risk factor sensitivity of positions of each business unit. Then capital is aggregated for all business units together through a correlated aggregation process to estimate diversified total risk at the bank level. Usually business unit level risk is used in allocating ECAP to business lines for risk-based performance management purposes, whereas total risk aggregated along risk types is used to estimate total ECAP requirements. Total ECAP rolled up from business units (and not risk types) will be misleading because different business units may have positions on the same risk factors (e.g., exposure to interest rates or foreign exchange rates) but in opposite directions (long versus short). When aggregating up from the business units, opposite positions would actually add and not net off as needed. Therefore, risk aggregation at a business line level is good mostly for calculating risk contributions and diversified ECAP leading to decision-making such as:

- Allocating and re-allocating capital to different business lines based on risk-adjusted returns that are measured in reference to capital attribution.
- Targeting shareholder value added at the individual business line level.
- Compensating business line managers based on risk-adjusted performance.
- Pricing products correctly within a business line based on their riskiness (measure of capital attribution).
- Monitoring and controlling risk based on limits or risk capital allocation.

Table 14.1 **Risk Aggregation and Accounting Treatment across Major Portfolios in a Bank**

Portfolio	Accounting Basis	Portfolio	Market Risk	Credit Risk
Loans and receivables	Amortized cost using effective interest method less impairment losses	Banking book	IRRBB capital (economic sensitivity)	Credit risk VaR
Trading assets	Fair value with gains and losses through P&L	Trading book	General risk VaR (base and stressed) capital	Specific risk charge (IRC capital)
Derivatives (OTC and traded) and securities financing transactions (SFTs)	Fair value basis on the balance sheet with gains/losses recognized in income statement	Banking book or trading book	General risk VaR (base and stressed) capital	Counterparty credit risk/credit valuation adjustment (capital charge)
		Investments		
Available-for-sale (AFS)	Fair value with gains and losses recognized in other comprehensive income included in shareholders' equity. Impairment losses and foreign exchange differences are recognized in P&L	Banking book or trading book	IRRBB capital (economic sensitivity) if in banking book or general risk VaR (base and stressed) capital if in trading book	Credit risk VaR is in banking book or specific risk charge (IRC capital) if in trading book
Held-to-maturity (HTM)	Amortized cost using effective interest method less impairment losses	Banking book	IRRBB capital (economic sensitivity)	Credit risk VaR

Risk Aggregation: The Top-Down Approach

Top-down approaches assume that risks are separable along the lines of credit risk and market risk. According to Cuenot, Masschelein, Pritsker, Schuermann, and Siddique (2006), banks compute market and credit risk independently (e.g., stress scenarios for market and credit risk may be inconsistent) and aggregate the two risks in a correlated aggregation process. The main motivation is to seek diversification benefits though imperfectly correlated risks resulting in reduced capital requirement compared to the RCAP approach. For risks to be measured in a top-down fashion, they are aggregated at various levels in a bank with different levels of diversification observed at each level.

Kuritzkes, Schuermann, and Weiner (2003) describe such a risk aggregation process through a building block approach comprising three levels at which risks are aggregated. Level 1 comprises stand-alone risks (pre-aggregation of individual credit risk and market risk). Level 2 comprises inter-risk aggregation for a group (correlated aggregation of credit risk and market risk). Level 3 comprises inter-group (aggregating capital for banking and insurance together). The authors conclude that the diversification benefit is the highest at Level 1 (intra-risk), decreases at Level 2 (inter-risk), and is smallest at Level 3. Other risk aggregation combinations may exist at a firm level.

Figure 14.1 shows an example of a bank rolling up its risk-based capital. The aggregation starts by aggregating the capital in a correlated aggregated process at the lowermost Level 1 (i.e., business line level), and then moving up along the organization hierarchy to Level 2 (i.e., business unit level), and finally to Level 3 (i.e., overall bank level). As capital gets rolled up in an aggregation hierarchy, diversification benefits are realized at each level. Banks plan total required capital based on the Level 3 (i.e., the total capital figure, which already imbibes a reduction in capital due to the diversification effects across many levels).

Dimakos and Aas (2004) assume pair-wise dependence between credit, market, and operational risk. The total risk is the sum of the unconditional credit risk and conditional marginal distributions (i.e., operational risk is conditional on credit risk and market risk is conditional on credit risk). According to their simulation results, total risk measured using confidence intervals between 95 and 99 percent is about 10 to 12 percent less than the sum of the individual risks. In their case, the value of the diversification ratio (calculated by dividing diversified capital by stand-alone capital) ranges from 0.88 to 0.90. Using the far tail confidence interval of 99.97 percent, Dimakos and Aas find that total risk is often overestimated by more than 20 percent using the additive method.

For top-down aggregation of pre-aggregated risks, the variance-covariance approach using a linear correlation matrix approach is commonly used where the inter-risk correlations are estimated using expert judgment or using a data series for which not all variables are observed simultaneously. More than 75 percent of the IFRI Foundation and CRO Forum (2007) surveyed banks favor this approach to integration. A major reason for its popularity is its simplicity given the fact that using a correlation matrix is entirely sufficient to describe the interdependence between risk types. This approach also provides for nesting of the correlation matrix to aggregate the individual risk types. For example, this method is used within the standard formula approach to the Solvency II Solvency Capital Requirement (SCR) as detailed in the Solvency II QIS 4 Technical

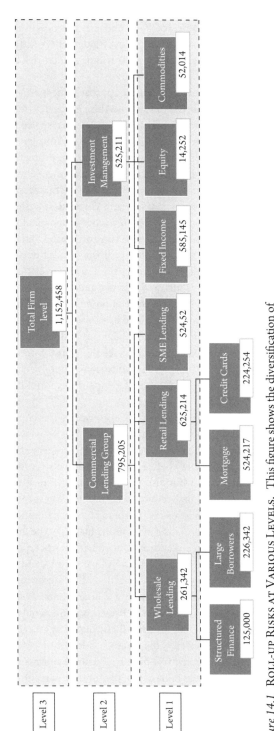

Figure 14.1 ROLL-UP RISKS AT VARIOUS LEVELS. This figure shows the diversification of capital that occurs in a risk aggregation process in a roll-up hierarchy consisting of three levels: Level 1, Level 2, and Level 3.

Standard Specification. The correlation parameters can be estimated in many ways. They may be modeled from time series of P&L between business units or trading desks derived from macroeconomic scenarios or expert judgment based on sensitivity of ECAP to linear pairs (e.g., credit risk and market risk or market risk and ALM) or using some external data.

Despite the popularity of the variance-covariance approach due to its simplicity, this approach suffers from several limitations. For example, this approach assumes that risks have a multivariate normal distribution, whereas in practice this is false because asset returns show asymmetry and have fat tails. So for risk distributions belonging to the elliptical family such as a Gaussian distribution, this may be a good method to aggregate risks. Others observe that ECAP estimated using the variance-covariance approach does not provide a stable measure, That is, this approach may fluctuate from one period to another because correlation is a point measure and correlation based on stressed risk factor data set will turn out to be higher. From a long-term capital planning perspective, banks do not want capital measurement to vary too much from one period to another. Correlation parameters are sensitive to the choice of asset portfolios regarding credit risk and market risk. Outliers also affect the linear correlation calculation compared to rank correlation measures such as Spearman and Kendall tau that are unaffected by outliers. Also, the linear or Pearson correlation measures of linear statistical dependency between two variables can be explained by normal distribution. The linear correlation measure fails to explain nonlinear dependencies that lead to a fatter tail of the loss distribution. Whereas the range of linear correlation varies from -1 to 1, nonlinear dependence between risk types may even lead to compounding effects (Breuer, Jandačka, Rheinberger, and Summer 2008). Such dependencies cannot be modeled in the variance-covariance aggregation.

A more sophisticated approach for top-down risk aggregation uses copulas. Copulas allow combining the marginal distributions of different risk types or asset returns into a multivariate distribution while also specifying the required dependency structure (nonlinearity and higher order dependencies) between the marginal distributions. Copulas are used not only in risk integration but also in individual risk measurement. Risk aggregation modeling using copulas first requires determining the marginal distribution of every risk component (risk type or risk factor). This means initially modeling the marginal distribution function consisting of an individual risk type and then modeling the dependence structure independent from the individual risk types. Rosenberg and Schuermann (2006) use the marginal distributions' parameters and their correlation measures using market data and values as reported in other studies and regulatory reports. They combine the marginal distributions by a Gaussian and a Student-t copula to point out the effects of positive tail dependence. Rosenberg and Schuermann report that the choice of the copula (Gaussian or Student-t) also affects aggregate risk besides other factors such as the business mix (i.e., the weights assigned to a bank's financial portfolios). The difference in aggregated risk produced using a normal copula rather than a Student's-t copula with 5 degrees of freedom is around 11 percent.

The Gaussian and Student-t copulas pertain to the family of elliptical copulas. A Gaussian copula is based on multivariate normal distribution and uses linear correlation matrix. McNeil, Frey, and Embrechts (2005) use a Spearman or Kendall's tau correlation to convert to a Pearson (linear correlation) matrix. The Gaussian copula has zero tail dependence and hence is unsuitable for modeling dependency with heavy tails.

Salmon (2009) blames the Gaussian copula for increasing the severity of the financial crisis of 2007–2008. A limitation of the Gaussian copula is that it is modeled by a single variable (i.e., linear correlation). This limitation is addressed in a Student-t copula because it also uses degrees of freedom. As the number of degrees of freedom increases, the Student-t copula approaches the Gaussian copula and tail dependency is reduced to zero. Student-t also has symmetric upper and lower tail dependency unlike a Gaussian copula. However, equal left and right tail dependency is not a perfect option for ECAP.

Another family of copulas used in risk aggregation is the Archimedean copulas consisting of Clayton and Gumbel as its most famous members. Archimedean copulas are actively used in the portfolio risk modeling literature because they allow for asymmetric tail dependence. These copulas are not derived from multivariate distribution but instead allow for generating various copulas based on the range of a generator function. Where the Clayton copula displays lower tail dependence and zero upper tail dependence, the analogous is true for the Gumbel copula.

Copulas provide flexibility around modeling dependencies between risk types and can also be easily simulated via a Monte Carlo simulation. However, selecting the right copula and its parameterization is a non-trivial exercise requiring a high level of technical expertise.

Risk Aggregation—The Bottom-Up Approach

The bottom-up approach to firm-wide risk aggregation has a practical appeal because it quantifies total risk of one or more positions in a single number at the outset instead of using pre-aggregated risks and then combing them by assuming a dependency structure between them. Integrating risk in the bottom-up approach is achieved by way of a joint modeling of risks factoring in the dependencies between credit and market risk factors. As the end result, it produces a joint loss distribution for a given portfolio. The effect that is being modeled through the bottom-up approach is that risks are inseparable. Therefore, an evolution of the credit and market risk factors together is necessary for accurate risk measurement. An inherent assumption in the bottom-up approach is that the portfolios cannot be bifurcated on the lines of risk factors. Therefore, an integrated risk modeling approach is needed to estimate total risk. Modeling this approach will not result in individual risk types being measured but it does provide the total risk of portfolios. For example, even if risk-free interest rates and credit spreads used in traditional structural credit risk models are often currently observable and uncorrelated, a bottom-up approach models credit transition, interest rates, and credit spreads jointly as stochastic and correlated variables.

Grundke (2005) examines the integration of credit and market risk for a portfolio of zero coupon bonds by introducing interest rate risk in credit risk structural model first in discounting of bonds and then as a risk factor that drives the asset returns. The author examines credit risk over a one-year horizon (as needed by credit risk measurement) assuming correlations between the risk-free rate, credit spreads, and firm asset returns. Grundke concludes that the lower the unconditional default probability and the longer the bonds' time to maturity, the higher is the difference between the unexpected loss measured with and without considering interest rate risk during the revaluation process at the risk horizon.

Barnhill and Maxwell (2002) use numerical simulation of the correlated risk factors (i.e., interest rate, foreign exchange spread, and credit) affecting a fixed income portfolio to measure VaR. They find that taking into account correlation between these risk factors leads to improved risk measurement.

Breuer et al. (2010) analyze hypothetical portfolios of foreign exchange denominated loans of rating BBB+ and B+ over a one-year horizon using an integrated model. They observe that compounding of risk takes place with the ratio of integrated risk to the sum of individual measures ranging from 1.94 to 8.22 at various confidence intervals when measuring ES. Kiesel, Perraudin, and Taylor (2003) use Monte Carlo simulations for a portfolio of zero coupon bonds and induce rating-specific credit spread volatility to a structural credit risk model. They observe that higher quality rating spreads exhibit considerable mean-reverting component volatility. According to their study, spread risk is important for issues with higher rating and assuming zero spread risk (deterministic spreads) seriously undermines the credit risk of higher rated portfolios.

Kijima and Muromachi (2000) propose a new simulation model for integrated credit and market risk for interest rate sensitive assets. They integrate interest rate risk into a reduced form credit model wherein default rate of obligors is modeled as correlated Vasichek processes as originally proposed by Hull and White (1990). In a reduced form credit model, the default time is modeled as a random variable whose distribution is arrived at exogenously usually by a Poisson process. Hull and White extend the one state variable interest rate model of Vasichek (1977) to be consistent with current term structure and current volatility of rates.

Alexander and Pezier (2003) propose a multifactor approach for aggregating credit and market risk in which profit and loss of different business units are linked through a linear regression model to changes in risk factors that include risk-free rates, credit spreads, equity indices, or implied volatilities. They model the risk factors using normal mixture distributions linked by a normal copula. A normal mixture distribution uses a probability weighted sum of normal density functions. It is used in place of normal distribution to better model the tail probabilities. A normal mixture distribution produces positive excess kurtosis and therefore has fatter tails compared to normal distribution. Comparing the ECAP estimated using the multifactor model with the actual ECAP data of three banks, Alexander and Pezier find that the simple summation of individual ECAP estimates are higher than that produced from their multifactor model. The main explanation of this result stems from the fact that empirical correlations between many risk factors are negative.

Despite the practical appeal of the bottom-up approach and the feasibility of modeling risks jointly, banks often separate the risks in order to understand and manage the individual risks more effectively. For example, a bank branch that offers loans to both corporate and retail clients typically cannot mitigate the market risks associated with changes in market rates. The loan origination centers such as a bank branch simply do not have access to the capital markets and are unaware of the residual risks and different types of derivatives instruments available to mitigate risks. Therefore, separating risks of the traditional banking book positions and consolidating management at a central unit level make sense because these managers have the best understanding of the bank's total risk and the expertise in managing such risks.

The process that banks have to insulate internal business units from changes in the market rates is to protect the margins of the business units. This process is called *funds transfer pricing* (FTP). It insulates the net interest margin (NIM) of individual business units that originate loans and deposits by taking the market risk component out and transferring it to the Treasury department. The Treasury department in turn consolidates and nets off this risk among all the participating business units and provides a macro-hedge to the residual risk.

Aggregate Risk Linked with Forward Looking Capital Planning

The economic outcome of the financial crisis of 2007–2008 was devastating. Banking regulators all over the world, especially in the United States and European Union (EU) where the impact of the crisis was great, issued more prescriptive regulations for addressing systemic risks. The main objective of these regulations is to define the systemic risk scenarios by way of adverse macroeconomic scenarios and templates for forward-looking capital planning of the so-called systemically important financial institutions (SIFIs). Based on the Dodd-Frank Act Stress Test (DFAST), the U.S. Federal Reserve performs an annual stress testing of large U.S. banks (i.e., banks with consolidated asset greater than $50 billion). These banks must formulate and report a sound capital plan under the adverse macroeconomic scenarios provided by the regulator.

Banks must measure the current risk (i.e., RWA based on current balance sheet and off balance sheet items) and also must estimate the future evolution of the assets and liabilities and estimate risk. Based on the projected RWA, banks show the regulators whether they will have a capital surplus or a capital deficit and then present a credible plan to mitigate any capital deficit. Thus, risk aggregation is now linked to other important variables that need to be modeled as an outcome of the same process. The objective is to make large banks adequately capitalized even if in the event of acute systemic problems over a three-year planning horizon. Regulators require detailed reports asking banks to breakdown various asset and liability portfolios to show their current and planned risk distribution. Mathur (2013) provides a complete interconnected framework of capital management in banks taking into account systemic risk scenarios.

The U.S. Comprehensive Capital Analysis and Review (CCAR) process requires a multi-period (nine quarters forward) analysis model of various businesses and their constituent portfolios. For each period, CCAR requires measurement of the impact on key financial variables such as profit and loss, incomes and expenses, RWA, and capital adequacy. For undertaking this annual activity, banks need an effective risk aggregation infrastructure that involves elements of business planning integrated with risk measurement and includes financial (accounting) and regulatory reporting.

Summary and Conclusions

Risk aggregation is an important process because it summarizes total risk of all portfolios into a single number often corresponding to the total capital a bank needs to provide a cushion for unexpected losses. Regulators expect banks to consider adverse macroeconomic scenarios and to summarize their impact on capital and profitability for future periods. Banks need to supplement VaR with other measures such as ES and EVT in order for risk managers to understand the scale and shape of the fat tails of asset returns. In the traditional methodologies available for risk aggregation, each individual risk type is measured and aggregated (e.g., aggregation of credit risk or aggregation of market risk, followed by combining credit and market risk to arrive at total risk). The choice of method allows or does not allow compounding of risks. For example, linear correlations are range bound between -1 and +1 and do not allow the possibility for summing risk to be greater than the individual parts. Bottom-up measurement approaches that take into account concurrent dependencies between credit and market risk factors can model cases that factor in wrong-way risk or the risk that worsening of market risk leads to worsening of credit risk.

Discussion Questions

1. Define risk aggregation and discuss its importance.
2. Explain the structural approach used to measure credit risk.
3. Explain the approaches used to measure market risk.
4. List various measures used in reporting total risk and discuss their relative strengths and weaknesses.
5. List various approaches for risk aggregation and discuss pros and cons of each.

References

Alexander, Carol, and Jacques Pezier. 2003. "Assessment and Aggregation of Banking Risks." Working Paper, 9th Annual Roundtable, International Financial Risk Institute.

Bakshi, Gurdip, and George Panayotov. 2010. "First-Passage Probability, Jump Models, and Intra-Horizon Risk." *Journal of Financial Economics* 95:1, 20–40.

Barnhill, Theodore M., and William F. Maxwell. 2002. "Modeling Correlated Interest Rate, Exchange Rate, and Credit Risk in Fixed Income Portfolios." *Journal of Banking and Finance* 26:2–3, 347–374.

BCBS. 2006. "International Convergence of Capital Measurement and Capital Standards." Available at http://www.bis.org/publ/bcbs128.htm.

BCBS. 2009. "Findings on the Interaction of Market and Credit Risk." Available at http://www.bis.org/publ/bcbs_wp16.htm.

BCBS. 2010. "Developments in Modeling Risk Aggregation." Joint Forum. Available at http://www.bis.org/publ/joint25.htm.

Breuer, Thomas, Martin Jandačka, Klaus Rheinberger, and Martin Summer. 2008. "Compounding Effects between Market and Credit Risk: The Case of Variable Rate Loans." Available at http://gloria-mundi.com/UploadFile/2010-6/62020101127090.pdf.

Breuer, T., Martin Jandačka, Klaus Rheinberger, and Martin Summer. 2010. "Does Adding Up of Economic Capital for Market and Credit Risk Amount to a Conservative Risk Estimate?" *Journal of Banking and Finance* 34:4, 703–712.

Brockmann, Michael, and Michael Kalbrener. 2010. "On the Aggregation of Risk." *Journal of Risk* 12:3, 45–68.

Crouhy, Michel, Dan Galai, and Robert Mark. 2000. "A Comparative Analysis of Current Credit Risk Models." *Journal of Banking and Finance* 24:1–2, 59-117.

Cuenot, Sylvain, Nancy Masschelein, Matthew Pritsker, Til Schuermann, and Akhtarur Siddique. 2006. "Interaction of Market and Credit Risk: Framework and Literature Review." Basel Committee Research Task Force Working Group.

Dimakos, Xeni K., and Kjersti Aas. 2004. "Integrated Risk Modeling." *European Journal of Operational Research* 230:24, 385–398.

Glasserman, Paul. 2005. "Importance Sampling for Portfolio Credit Risk." *Management Science* 51:11, 1643–1656.

Gordy, Michael. 2000. "A Comparative Anatomy of Credit Risk Models." *Journal of Banking and Finance* 24:1–2, 1896-1910.

Grundke, Peter. 2005. "Risk Measurement with Integrated Market and Credit Portfolio Models." *Journal of Risk* 7:3, 63–94.

Hull, John C., and Allan White. 1990. "Valuing Derivative Securities Using the Explicit Finite Difference Method." *Journal of Financial and Quantitative Analysis* 25:1, 87–100.

IFRI Foundation and CRO Forum. 2007. "Insights from the Joint IFRI/CRO Forum Survey on Economic Capital Practice and Applications."

Jackson, Patricia, William Perraudin, and Victoria Saporta. 2002. "Regulatory and 'Economic' Solvency Standards for Internationally Active Banks." Bank of England Working Papers 161, Bank of England.

Kiesel, Rudiger, William Perraudin, and Alex P. Taylor. 2003. "The Structure of Credit Risk: Spread Volatility and Rating Transition." *Journal of Risk* 6:1, 1–27.

Kijima, Masaaki, and Yukio Muromachi. 2000. "Evaluation of Credit Risk of Portfolio with Stochastic Interest Rate and Default Process." *Journal of Risk* 3:1, 5–36.

Koyluoglu, Ugur H., and Andrew Hickman. 1998 "Reconcilable Differences in Risk." *Risk* 11:10, 56–62.

Kuritzkes, Andrew, Till Schuermann, and Scott M. Weiner. 2003. "Risk Measurement, Risk Management and Capital Adequacy in Financial Conglomerates." Working Paper, Wharton Financial Institutions Center.

Mathur, Sumit. 2013. "Capital Management for Banking: Dawn of a New Era." Cary, NC: SAS Institute Inc. Available at http://www.sas.com/reg/wp/ca/58120.

McNeil, Alexander J., Rudiger Frey, and Paul Embrechts. 2005. *Quantitative Risk Management*. Princeton, NJ: Princeton University Press.

Merton, Robert C. 1974. "On the Pricing of Corporate Debt: The Risk Structure of Interest Rates." *Journal of Finance* 29:2, 449–470.

Rosenberg, Joshua V., and Til Schuermann. 2006. "A General Approach to Integrated Risk Management with Skewed, Fat-tailed Risks." *Journal of Financial Economics* 79:3, 569–614.

Salmon, Felix. 2009. "Recipe for Disaster: The Formula that Killed Wall Street." Available at http://www.wired.com/print/techbiz/it/magazine/17-03/wp_quant.

Vasicek, Oldrich A. 1977. "An Equilibrium Characterization of the Term Structure." *Journal of Financial Economics* 5:2, 177–188.

Vasicek, Oldrich A. 1991. "Limiting Loan Loss Probability Distribution." KMV Working Paper. Available at http://www.moodysanalytics.com/~/media/Insight/Quantitative-Research/Portfolio-Modeling/91-08-09-Limiting-Loan-Loss-Probability-Distribution.ashx.

Yamai, Yasuhiro, and Toshinao Yoshiba. 2002. "Comparative Analyses of Expected Shortfall and Value-at-Risk under Market Stress." Working Paper, Bank of Japan. Available at http://www.bis.org/cgfs/conf/mar02p.pdf.

Ziegel, Johanna F. 2013. "Coherence and Elicitability." Available at http://arxiv.org/abs/1303.1690.

Part Three

QUANTITATIVE ASSESSMENT OF RISK

15

Value-at-Risk and Other Risk Measures

MARKUS LEIPPOLD

Hans Vontobel Professor of Financial Engineering, Department of Banking and Finance,
University of Zurich and the Swiss Finance Institute

Introduction

Risk and return play a central role in financial theory. Return is easily measurable and is a percentage number indicating by how much the value of an investment or asset has changed from the previous period. But how should risk be measured? Over longer holding periods, return generation is associated with the risk taken. How can risk be measured to facilitate comparisons between investments?

Markowitz (1952) and Roy (1952) are early contributors to understanding how people view risk. Markowitz's work on portfolio theory received wide attention shortly after its publication. When Markowitz formalized the trade-off between risk and return, he set risk equal to the variance of the portfolio returns. Using variance as a risk measure has some deficiencies due to its symmetry property and inability to consider the risk of low probability events. If returns are not normally distributed and investors exhibit non-quadratic utility functions, alternative ways are needed to express the riskiness of an investment.

Although Roy (1952) received less attention than Markowitz, further development of his remarkable contribution occurred later. Roy's safety first principle was instrumental in the development of downside risk measures, which continued with the introduction of lower partial moments (LPMs) by Bawa (1975) and Fishburn (1977). LPMs provide an important generalization of the concept of semivariance introduced earlier by Markowitz (1959) and build a bridge to the risk measures used in today's financial industry.

For the discussion of modern risk measures, this chapter focuses specifically on value-at-risk (VaR) because of its high practical relevance and expected shortfall (ES), which is sometimes called conditional VaR (CVAR), and more generally on spectral risk measures. VaR is now an industry standard in financial risk management partly because it is based on a simple concept and its computational implementation is straightforward compared to many other risk measures. Because VaR has some deficiencies, financial economists developed other measures such as ES and spectral risk measures. These measures are built on theoretically solid ground and may potentially become more important in the future.

The remainder of the chapter is organized into eight sections. The next section introduces Roy's (1952) safety first principle and Markowitz's (1959) concept of semivariance. The second section discusses the LPMs that serve as a generalization of the semivariance as risk measures. Before continuing the presentation of VaR and ES, the chapter examines the properties that a "good" risk measure should share. Addressing this question in the third section enables critical assessment of the appropriateness of the risk measures used in practice such as VaR. The fourth section presents the concepts of VaR and ES as well as their advantages and shortcomings. The fifth section provides a further extension of ES to the so-called spectral risk measures. The sixth section examines the impact of VaR and ES constraints on the mean-variance investor. This section shows that imposing risk constraints can generate adverse effects. The seventh section discusses the use of risk measures from a regulator's perspective. The final section offers a summary and conclusions.

Shortfall Probability and Semivariance

According to Roy (1952), investors first want to make sure that they preserve a certain amount of principal rather than thinking in terms of some utility function. Therefore, investors aim at minimizing a very specific aspect of risk, namely the risk of falling short of some predefined threshold level. In mathematical terms, Roy suggests solving the optimization problem in Equation 15.1:

$$\min_{w_i, i=1,\dots,n} P(R_p \leq R_0), \qquad (15.1)$$

where R_0 denotes the threshold level and the portfolio return by $R_p = \sum_{i=1}^{n} R_i w_i$ given the return of $i = 1, \dots, n$ assets. The minimization of the shortfall probability $P(R_p \leq R_0)$ has a surprising link to the mean-variance optimization principle. To see the link requires reviewing Chebychev's inequality (Tchebichef 1867). Given a random variable x for which the variance is finite and given a constant $c > 0$, Equation 15.2 holds

$$P(|x - \mu| > c) \leq \frac{\sigma_x^2}{c^2}. \qquad (15.2)$$

Chebychev's inequality states that the probability of deviating more than a fixed constant c from the random variable's mean is constrained by the random variable's variance normalized by the square of the fixed constant c. This inequality does not require making any assumptions about the distribution of the random variable, except that its variance must be finite. Chebychev's inequality can be rewritten as Roy's shortfall probability in Equation 15.3:

$$P(R_p \leq R_0) = P(\mu_p - R_p \geq \mu_P - R_0) \leq \frac{\sigma^2}{(\mu_p - R_0)^2}. \qquad (15.3)$$

Hence, in a situation where no knowledge about the distribution of portfolio returns is available, except that their distribution is such that the variance is finite, minimizing the shortfall probability is equivalent to minimizing the variance normalized by the squared mean excess return as shown in Equation 15.4:

$$\min_w \frac{\sigma^2}{(\mu_p - R_0)^2}. \tag{15.4}$$

But this minimization is equivalent in Equation 15.5 for maximizing the Sharpe ratio (Sharpe 1963) of a portfolio, when the threshold level is set to equal the risk-free rate R_f:

$$\min_w \frac{\sigma^2}{(\mu_p - R_f)^2} \Leftrightarrow \max_w \frac{\mu_p - R_f}{\sigma^2}. \tag{15.5}$$

In the Markowitz setting, maximizing the Sharpe ratio would result in the well-known tangential portfolio, which in the capital asset pricing model (CAPM) equals the market portfolio. Thus, to minimize the probability of falling short some predefined threshold level when the exact distribution of portfolio returns is unknown, the Sharpe ratio should be adjusted (i.e., hold the market portfolio). This example provides some important insight into the fact that downside risk measures and portfolio optimization are closely linked concepts.

Roy (1952) is not alone in recognizing the importance downside risk. Subsequently, Markowitz (1959) recognizes the importance of Roy's ideas and indicates that investors should be interested in minimizing downside risk for two reasons. First, only the downside risk is relevant to investors, not the symmetric risk such as variance. Second, under the assumption of normally distributed returns, any downside risk measure would yield the same result as a variance risk measure. Markowitz realizes that if the normality assumption is inappropriate, then downside risk measures become relevant.

Markowitz (1959) proposes using semivariance to correct for the fact that variance is a symmetric measure that penalizes over- and under-performance equally. In contrast, *semivariance*, which is a measure that is concerned only with the adverse deviations below the mean value, is defined in Equation 15.6:

$$\sigma_{semi}^2 = E\left[\min\left(\sum_{i=1}^{n} w_i R_i - \sum_{i=1}^{n} w_i \mu_i, c\right)^2\right]. \tag{15.6}$$

Usually, the constant c is set equal to zero. Choosing different values for c in the above definition, permits incorporating some kind of downside risk aversion into the optimization. After proposing semivariance, Markowitz continued to rely on the variance measure as a representation of risk mainly because it is computationally simpler and required less computer power at that time.

Lower Partial Moments

Bawa (1975) and Fishburn (1977) introduce the LPM risk measures. The term "moments" originally comes from the world of physics. Mean and variance are moments of the first and second order but higher order moments also exist. Given a random variable X with cumulative distribution function $F_X(x)$ and reference level m, the moment of degree n is defined in Equation 15.7 as:

$$M_{n,m}(F_X(x)) = E((m - X)^n) = \int_{-\infty}^{\infty} (m - x)^n dF_X(x). \tag{15.7}$$

When the reference level m equals the mean of X, $M_{n,m}$ is called the n-th central moment of X. For example, skewness is the normalized central moment of third order and is a measure of symmetry. Positive (negative) skewness occurs when the right (left) tail of the distribution is long. Kurtosis is the fourth normalized central moment, which is usually expressed as excess kurtosis. The kurtosis value of a normal distribution is 3, whereas excess kurtosis is 0 or kurtosis -3. Some probability distributions with extreme kurtosis may exhibit fat tails, indicating that the probability of extreme events is much higher than implied by a normal distribution. In mathematical terms, a distribution is called *fat tailed*, as shown in Equation 15.8, if the decay of the tail has a power law that is

$$P(X > x) \sim x^{-\alpha} \text{ as } x \to \infty \text{ for } a > 0. \tag{15.8}$$

LPMs examine the moment of degree n below a certain threshold. Hence, they are just a generalization of what semivariance is to variance. The LPM_{q,R_0} is defined in Equation 15.9 by a power index q and a target rate of return R_0 as follows:

$$LPM_{q,R_0} = E\left[\min (R_p - R_0, 0)^q\right]^{1/q}. \tag{15.9}$$

Setting $q = 2$ results in the semivariance (semivolatility, respectively). This definition of LPMs does not take into account the probability of falling below the threshold level. Hence, downside risk measures based on LPMs are unconditional risk measures.

From an economic viewpoint, LPMs have an additional advantage. Although variance and semivariance are risk measures consistent with an investor having quadratic utility function only, LPMs are consistent with a much wider class of Neumann-Morgenstern utility functions. LPMs represent the whole range of human behavior, from risk seeking $(0 < q < 1)$ to risk neutral $(q = 1)$ and risk aversion $(q > 1)$. LPMs are also consistent with the concept of stochastic dominance (Bawa 1975). *Stochastic dominance* is a very powerful risk analysis tool based on the portfolio's cumulative probability curve, which allows one to determine whether one investment is superior to another. This approach avoids the complications of specifying preferences or beliefs and, as such, is an alternative rather than a substitute for the Markowitz approach. Although it theoretically works for all probability distributions and is general with respect to the underlying utility assumptions, this approach remains computationally impracticable without imposing some major simplifications (Kuosmanen 2004).

In practice, other frequently used downside risk measures are VaR and ES shortfall, also called conditional VaR or CVaR. These measures do not have such obvious links to utility theory as the mean-variance or LPM principles. However, before examining VaR and ES as risk measures, addressing a more general question might provide valuable guidance in determining what constitutes a "good" risk measure.

Coherent Risk Measures

Quantifying the risk of uncertainty in the future value of a portfolio is one of the key tasks of risk management. In mathematical terms, this quantification is achieved by modeling the uncertain payoff as a random variable to which a certain functional is then applied. Such functionals are then termed risk measures. Several endeavors are available in the financial literature to define such risk measures in an axiomatic setting (i.e., to find a set of premises that are so evident as to be accepted as true without controversy). Given a strong subjective component related to risk and its perception by individuals, such an axiomatic and objectivistic theory becomes even more important.

In actuarial science, Goovaerts, De Vylder, and Haezendonck (1984) present a seminal axiomatic approach to risk measures. Artzner, Delbaen, Eber, and Heath (1999) extend the use of their axiomatic approach to finance theory and define in a mathematically concise way some commonly shared principles for a risk measure used for financial applications. They call these risk measures *coherent*. Following Artzner et al., a coherent risk measure $\rho(X)$ applied to some portfolio value X satisfies the following four axioms.

- *Subadditivity*. Subadditivity means that the risk of two portfolios should be less than or equal to adding the risk of two separate portfolios. This property formalizes the principle of diversification and allows decentralization of the task of managing the risk arising from a collection of different positions. For instance, if separate risk limits are given to different trading desks, then the risk of the aggregate position is bounded by the sum of the individual risk limits. In mathematical terms and given two portfolios X and Y, the subadditivity property can be written as Equation 15.10:

$$\rho(X)+\rho(Y) \geq \rho(X+Y). \qquad (15.10)$$

- *Homogeneity*. A homogeneous risk measure implies that leveraging or deleveraging a portfolio gives rise to a proportional increase or decrease of risk. In mathematical terms, homogeneity is shown in Equation 15.11:

$$\lambda\rho(X) = \rho(\lambda X), \qquad (15.11)$$

where the constant λ denotes the amount of leverage (if $\lambda > 1$) and deleverage (if $\lambda < 1$), respectively.
- *Monotonicity*. The monotonicity property states that a portfolio Y, which is preferable to portfolio X under all possible scenarios, should have a risk measure assigned that is at least as high as the one of X.
- *Translation invariance*. Translation invariance implies that adding a risk-free cash position of an amount m to the portfolio reduces the risk by m shown in Equation 15.12:

$$\rho(X+m) = \rho(X) - m. \qquad (15.12)$$

Usually, the risk measure is normalized such that the measure $\rho(0) = 0$ (i.e., the risk of holding no asset is zero). These axioms provide an elegant mathematical framework for the study of coherent risk measure. The introduction of coherent risk measure subsequently spurred much interest from both academia and the finance industry. Financial economists have proposed many revisions to the axioms of coherent risk measures, replacing in particular positive homogeneity and subadditivity with the more general convexity property (Föllmer and Schied 2002, 2011; Frittelli and Gianin 2002), co-monotonic subadditivity (Kou, Peng, and Heyde 2013), or co-monotonic convexity (Song and Yan 2009).

Föllmer and Schied (2002) present an important and notable revision. They replace homogeneity and subadditivity by the weaker condition of convexity. In particular, a convex risk measure obeys Equation 15.13:

$$\rho(\lambda X + (1 - \lambda)Y) \leq \lambda\rho(X) + (1 - \lambda)\rho(Y) \qquad (15.13)$$

for $0 \leq \lambda \leq 1$. The following examples provide a way of gaining some intuition about this property. Consider the collection of possible future outcomes that can be generated with two strategies available to an investor: one investment strategy leads to X, while a second strategy leads to Y. By diversifying, spending only the fraction of the resources on the first possibility and using the remaining part for the second alternative results in $\lambda X + (1 - \lambda)Y$. Thus, the axiom of convexity gives a precise meaning to the idea that diversification should not increase risk.

More importantly, the convexity property helps to adjust for the possibility of liquidity risk. The homogeneity property states that an increase in leverage of any position leads to a proportional increase in risk. In the presence of liquidity risk, increasing the size of a position must increase its risk in a nonlinear way. Hence, the risk measure should not be positive homogeneous. The risk exposure might grow faster than linear in volume, which motivates the relaxed notion of convex measures of risk (Föllmer and Schied 2002; Frittelli and Gianin 2002; Heath and Ku 2004).

Some contend that besides the coherence axioms, the risk measure should be law-invariant in the sense that the risk $\rho(X)$ depends on the distribution function of X only. The concept of law invariance, first studied in this context by Kusuoka (2001), is linked to the existence of a single specific probability measure. Therefore, law invariance means that risk can be estimated from empirical data. Furthermore, law-invariance also directly relates to stochastic dominance. As Föllmer and Knispel (2013) show, a risk measure $\rho(X)$ is law-invariant, if and only if it respects first and second order stochastic dominance and satisfies co-monotonic convexity (i.e., if it satisfies the convexity condition for co-monotonic random variables). Co-monotonic random variables are characterized by a perfect dependence structure (i.e., they move up and down together in all cases). Hence, such variables provide no mutual hedge. Some authors also require a risk measure to be co-monotonic additive in the sense that for two co-monotonic variables X and Y, as shown in Equation 15.14:

$$\rho(X + Y) = \rho(X) + \rho(Y), \ X, Y \text{ co-monotonic.} \qquad (15.14)$$

Subadditivity alone does not yet imply co-monotonic additivity. Hence, for the diversification principle to be well embodied in the risk measure requires both subadditivity and co-monotonic additivity. With one of these properties absent, risk arbitrage would be possible. Lacking subadditivity, a portfolio can be split into suitable sub-portfolios to decrease the total risk. Lacking co-monotonic additivity, the portfolio could be merged with another co-monotonic portfolio to decrease the portfolio risk. Both practices run against the intuition of measuring risk. Hence, from an objectivistic perspective, both properties (i.e., subadditivity and co-monotonic additivity) make perfect sense. Nevertheless, from a practical side the impact and the relevance of consistency are still highly debated, especially in the context of regulation and capital allocation (Danielsson, Jorgensen, Samorodnitsky, Sarma, and de Vries 2013).

Value-at-Risk and Expected Shortfall

Regulation and internal risk management force the use of an internal model approach for measuring risk. Regulators favor VaR as a risk measure. Hence, with the backing of the regulators, VaR has become an industry standard in financial risk management. This is due partly to the fact that it is a simple concept and its computational implementation is straightforward compared to many other risk measures.

VaR is denoted by $VaR_\alpha(X, \tau)$, which is defined as the maximum potential loss that a portfolio X can suffer in the $100(1 - \alpha)$ percent best cases after time period τ. Alternatively, $VaR_\alpha(X, \tau)$ is the minimum potential loss that a portfolio X can suffer in the 100α percent worst cases after period τ. The scalar $\alpha \in]0, 1[$ is termed the confidence level. Hence, the philosophy behind the concept of VaR is to fix a threshold probability α (e.g., 1 percent) and define a position as acceptable if the probability to go bankrupt is smaller than α. However, the main problem with VaR is that it does not distinguish between these 100α percent worst cases. In other words, VaR does not distinguish between a bankruptcy of, for example, $1 million or $100 million. Nevertheless, VaR is a widely used instrument to control risk.

Studying the properties of VaR requires a more precise definition. Formally, given a well-defined random variable X and a confidence level α, the formal definition of the VaR is given by Equation 15.15:

$$VaR_\alpha(X, \tau) = \inf\{x : P(X < -x) \leq \alpha\}, \tag{15.15}$$

with $\alpha \in]0, 1[$. Hence, $VaR_\alpha(X, \tau)$ is just the quantile of the portfolio distribution. To illustrate the concept of VaR, Figure 15.1 shows a plot of the historical return distribution of an arbitrary portfolio. The vertical dashed line represents the VaR level. Because VaR is a quantile-based risk measure, it is a so-called point measure and does not consider any realization of portfolio returns beyond the VaR level.

Although appealing at first sight, VaR has some severe deficiencies. In general, VaR is not coherent because it fails to fulfill the subadditivity axiom for most distributions. VaR is only coherent for the family of elliptical distributions such as the normal distribution. However, even in the case of elliptical distributions, VaR is not necessary subadditive in multivariate cases. For VaR to be subadditive, this requires that the full joint distribution is a multivariate elliptical. An example can be constructed in which risk factors follow a Gaussian marginal distribution. But if the risk factors are dependent (e.g., by linking them via a copula), the VaR for the joint distribution may fail to be subadditive.

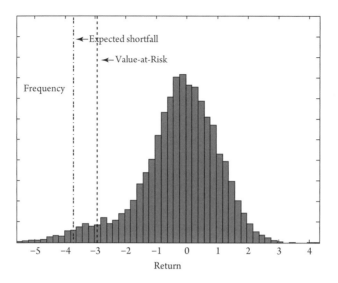

Figure 15.1 VALUE-AT-RISK AND EXPECTED SHORTFALL.   The figure plots the historical distribution of simulated portfolio returns together with the VaR and the ES level.

Therefore, studying only the marginal distribution to ward off a VaR violation is never sufficient (Acerbi 2007).

In contrast, the expected shortfall $ES_\alpha(X, \tau)$ is the expected value of the loss that portfolio X can suffer in the 100α percent worst cases in n days. Hence, unlike in the case of VaR, the losses beyond the VaR level should considered by taking the average loss beyond the confidence level α into account. In Figure 15.1, the ES is given by the vertical dash-dotted line. It takes all returns into account that are below the VaR level and expresses the portfolio risk as the average of these returns. ES is a coherent risk measure (Acerbi and Tasche 2002). Under appropriate technical conditions, ES is given by Equation 15.16a:

$$ES_\alpha(X, \tau) = \frac{1}{\alpha} \int_0^\alpha VaR_m(X, \tau)dm, \tag{15.16a}$$

which is equivalent to Equation 15.16b

$$ES_\alpha(X, \tau) \geq VaR_\alpha(X, \tau). \tag{15.16b}$$

Thus, ES is always a more conservative risk measure than VaR for a given confidence level α.

Both ES and VaR can be determined from statistical observations. Given N observations, an estimate of ES can be obtained as Equation 15.17:

$$\widehat{ES}_\alpha(X, \tau) = \frac{\sum_{i=1}^{\lfloor N\alpha \rfloor} X_i^{(\uparrow)}}{\lfloor N\alpha \rfloor}, \tag{15.17}$$

where the brackets $\lfloor \cdot \rfloor$ mean the integer floor and $X_i^{(\uparrow)}$ denotes the ordered (in ascending order) portfolio realizations after period τ. Given that the VaR is simply the historical quantile, it can be calculated as Equation 15.18:

$$\widehat{VaR}_\alpha(X, \tau) = X_{\lfloor N\alpha \rfloor}^{(\uparrow)}. \qquad (15.18)$$

Estimation involves a practical problem. Although the ES is a sound risk measure and preferable to VaR from a theoretical viewpoint, the standard errors of ES estimates are by a multiple larger than standard errors of VaR estimates. Although neglecting the severity of losses in the tail of the distribution results in a theoretically flawed risk measure, backtesting becomes easier because empirical quantiles are robust to extreme outliers, unlike typical estimators of ES. Furthermore, the estimation of risk measures, especially for VaR, suffers from the curse of dimensionality. Although estimating the risk in a one-dimensional setting is straightforward, the sparseness of the data in the tails of the distribution requires the application of sophisticated numerical methods to overcome the problem of dimensionality (Egloff and Leippold 2010).

To get some idea about the impact of estimation error, consider the following example in which the loss distribution illustrated in Equation 15.19 is assumed to follow a generalized Pareto distribution $G_{\kappa,\theta,\sigma}(x)$ (Embrechts, Klüppelberg, and Mikosch 1997):

$$G_{\kappa,\theta,\sigma}(x) = 1 - \left(1 + \kappa \frac{x - \theta}{\sigma}\right)^{-\frac{1}{\kappa}}. \qquad (15.19)$$

The generalized Pareto distribution is characterized by the tail index parameter κ, the scale parameter σ, and the threshold (location) parameter θ. When $\kappa = 0$ and $\theta = 0$, the generalized Pareto distribution is equivalent to the exponential distribution. When $\kappa = 0$ and $\theta = \sigma/\kappa$, the Pareto distribution is obtained. The mean of the generalized Pareto distribution is not finite when $\kappa \geq 1$. This case is irrelevant for financial application. The variance is not finite when $\kappa \geq 1/2$. Mandelbrot (1961, 1963), Fama (1963), and Mandelbrot and Taylor (1967) contend that the distribution of stock prices does not have a defined second moment (e.g., is stable Paretian) or, equivalently, has tails that are too fat to be consistent with a normal (Gaussian) distribution. Financial economists still debate whether financial assets have a finite variance.

Table 15.1 reports the results from a simulation exercise. VaR and ES are calculated from a sample of 10,000 random numbers following a generalized Pareto distribution with varying tail index parameter κ. For simplicity, set $\sigma = 1$ and $\theta = 0$. To calculate the error estimates, the VaR and ES calculation are performed 100,000 times. To get an idea about the accuracy of the estimation, the standard deviation of the estimate normalized by its average is reported. The VaR and ES estimates are used to create 95 percent confidence intervals. Inspection of Table 15.1 shows that the ratio of standard deviation and average is increasing for the 5 percent VaR from 0.02 to 0.09 by increasing the tail index from 0 to 0.9. At the same time, the ratio for the ES increases from 0.02 to 9.22 (i.e., by a factor of almost 600). This factor dramatically increases to almost 1300 when considering the 1 percent ES.

Table 15.1 Estimates of VaR and Expected Shortfall under Generalized Pareto Distributions

α = 0.05	Average		Standard Deviation		Ratio		Confidence Interval (95%)			
κ	VaR	ES	VaR	ES	VaR	ES	VaR		ES	
0	3.00	3.99	0.04	0.06	0.01	0.02	2.92	3.89	3.07	4.10
0.10	3.49	4.99	0.06	0.10	0.02	0.02	3.40	4.83	3.59	5.16
0.25	4.46	7.28	0.09	0.22	0.02	0.03	4.31	6.93	4.61	7.64
0.50	6.95	15.88	0.19	1.54	0.03	0.10	6.63	14.24	7.27	17.97
0.75	11.28	48.35	0.41	72.50	0.04	1.50	10.62	34.63	11.98	70.53
0.90	15.37	135.64	0.65	1,250.20	0.04	9.22	14.33	64.63	16.47	228.59

α = 0.01	Average		Standard Deviation		Ratio		Confidence Interval (95%)			
κ	VaR	ES	VaR	ES	VaR	ES	VaR		ES	
0	4.61	5.60	0.10	0.14	0.02	0.03	4.44	5.37	4.77	5.84
0.10	5.85	7.60	0.16	0.26	0.03	0.03	5.60	7.18	6.11	8.05
0.25	8.65	12.85	0.32	0.73	0.04	0.06	8.15	11.74	9.18	14.11
0.50	18.03	37.96	1.00	7.10	0.06	0.19	16.46	30.91	19.75	47.77
0.75	40.94	165.10	3.16	523.10	0.08	3.17	36.06	97.17	46.41	270.22
0.90	69.32	647.01	6.34	24,536.89	0.09	37.92	59.58	209.53	80.41	1,028.71

Note: This table reports the results from the Monte Carlo estimation of VaR and ES for different confidence levels α and tail indices κ.

Hence, when the loss distribution is fat-tailed, ES estimates are more affected by whether large and infrequent losses are realized in the simulation, given that the ES considers the entire right tail of the loss distribution. Yet, large and infrequent losses have less effect on VaR because they do not take losses beyond the VaR level into account. Therefore, the ES estimate becomes more volatile when the probability of infrequent and large losses is high, resulting in an estimation error significantly larger than the error of the VaR estimate.

Spectral Risk Measures

So far, the chapter has presented VaR and ES as two candidate measures for expressing risk. Both measures rely on the distribution of the portfolio, say $F(x) = P(X \leq x)$. The ES can be expressed in terms of the distribution function as shown in Equation 15.20:

$$ES_\alpha(X, \tau) = -\frac{1}{\alpha} \int_0^\alpha F^{-1}(m)dm. \tag{15.20}$$

ES attaches the same weight to all realizations below the α-quantile and neglects all realizations above the α-quantile. Hence, ES performs a risk-neutral weighting of all relevant losses.

From a risk manager's perspective, behaving like a risk-neutral manager regarding the losses beyond the confidence level as implied by ES could be useful. Therefore, an important issue is whether the above weighting scheme can be generalized. Acerbi (2002) formalizes the weighting of quantiles in canonical form by introducing the class of spectral risk measures. Given a non-increasing density function ϕ on the interval $[0, 1]$, a spectral risk measure is defined in Equation 15.21:

$$\rho_\phi(X) = -\int_0^1 F^{-1}(m)\phi(m)dm. \tag{15.21}$$

Hence, spectral risk measures provide a subjective weighting of the quantiles of the profit and loss distribution F. The weighting scheme is defined by the so-called risk spectrum ϕ, which has to satisfy some technical conditions. In particular, the property that the risk spectrum must be non-increasing means adding at least a constant or an increasing weight to increasing losses. In the constant case, it means that investors are risk-neutral with respect to losses, while increasing weights reflects risk aversion.

Balbás, Garrido, and Mayoral (2009) define further requirements on the risk spectrum ϕ in order to guarantee that all quantiles of the profit and loss distribution are well defined:

- The function ϕ needs to be positive on the whole unit interval (i.e., $\phi(m) > 0, \forall m \in [0, 1]$.)
- The function ϕ must be monotonic and strictly decreasing on the whole unit interval (i.e., $\phi(\alpha) > \phi(\beta)$ must exist for $0 \leq \alpha < \beta \leq 1$).
- The function ϕ fulfills $\lim_{m \to 0} \phi(m) = \infty$ and $\lim_{m \to 1}\phi(m) = 0$.

Interestingly, Wang, Young, and Panjer (1997) introduce these spectral risk measures earlier, but under a different name, in the theory of insurance risk. In insurance, the spectral risk measures are called *distorted expectation*.

Using the above definition of spectral risk measures enables casting the ES as a limiting case. In particular, the risk spectrum takes the following form in Equation 15.22:

$$\phi_{ES}(m) = \begin{cases} \frac{1}{\alpha}, & \text{for } m \in [0, \alpha) \\ 0, & \text{for } m \in (\alpha, 1] \end{cases}. \tag{15.22}$$

Although the function ϕ is non-increasing for the ES, it does not fulfill the requirements stated by Balbás et al. (2009). Given that it gives zero weight to some parts of the unit interval, some quantiles of the portfolio distribution are not considered. Further, ES does not utilize useful information in a large part of a loss distribution. Because ES only takes into account the mean loss below the quantile and not any higher moments of the losses, it fails to properly adjust for extreme low-probability losses. Consequently, ES fails to create the incentive to mitigate these losses. Furthermore, the class of coherent risk measures could be too large from the perspective of practical risk management applications.

In principle, expressing the VaR measure in terms of functions ϕ and Φ is possible, although VaR is not a coherent risk measure. In particular, the function ϕ takes the form shown in Equation 15.23:

$$\phi_{VaR}(m) = \delta(m - \alpha), m \in [0, 1], \tag{15.23}$$

where $\delta(m - \alpha)$ is the Dirac function taking infinite value at the point α and zero elsewhere. Hence, the specification of $\phi_{VaR}(m)$ violates the condition that this function must be non-increasing on the unit interval. Figure 15.2 plots the two corresponding risk spectra for VaR and ES. Panel A plots the VaR, which puts infinite weight at the confidence level α set to 10 percent. In contrast, the ES puts equal weight to all realizations below the confidence level of $\alpha = 0.10$.

Spectral risk measures that have previously been analyzed in the academic literature are exponential and power spectral risk measures (Cotter and Dowd 2006; Dowd and Blake 2006; Dowd, Cotter, and Sorwar 2008). The exponential spectral risk measure is obtained in Equation 15.24:

$$\phi_{exp}(m) = \frac{a\,e^{-am}}{1 - e^{-a}}, a \geq 0, m \in [0, 1]. \tag{15.24}$$

The power spectral risk measure is obtained using Equation 15.25:

$$\phi_{pow}(m) = b\,m^{b-1}, b \in (0, 1], m \in [0, 1]. \tag{15.25}$$

Although the exponential and power spectral risk measures fulfill the first two properties stated by Balbás et al. (2009), they fail to fulfill the third property.

Another example of a spectral risk measure, which appears in the literature on insurance risk and fulfills all the technical properties of Balbás et al. (2009), is the transformation suggested by Wang (2000) in Equation 15.26:

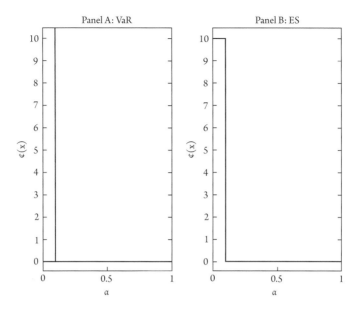

Figure 15.2 Risk Spectra for Value-at-Risk and Expected Shortfall. Panel A plots the risk spectrum for the VaR corresponding to the Delta function and Panel B plots the risk spectrum for the ES.

$$\phi_{Wang}(m) = \frac{n\left(N^{-1}(m) - N^{-1}(\zeta)\right)}{n\left(N^{-1}(m)\right)}, \zeta \in \left(0, \frac{1}{2}\right), m \in [0, 1], \qquad (15.26)$$

where $n(\cdot)$ and $N(\cdot)$ are the probability density and cumulative density function of the standard normal distribution. As with the previously analyzed specifications of the function ϕ, the specification of Wang also fulfills the technical conditions resulting in a well-defined and coherent (spectral) risk measure.

Figure 15.3 plots the risk spectra for the exponential risk measure (Panel A) and for the Wang transform (Panel B). In contrast to Figure 15.2, where the risk spectra of VaR and ES are analyzed, the spectral risk measures in Figure 15.3 give nonzero weights to all the portfolio realizations. Although gains obtain a weight, their weight is smaller than the weights attached to the losses, which reflects the risk aversion of the risk manager. However, in contrast to VaR and ES, the risk manager using a spectral risk measure is not fully ignorant about the upside of the portfolio.

Although many specifications of spectral risk measures are possible, no guidance is available as to why one specific measure should be preferred to another one. Even on a more general level beyond class of spectral risk measures, the selection of the appropriate risk measure continues to cause heated discussions and debates among regulators, bankers, and investment managers. However, the concept of risk is both complex and highly subjective. Every market participant has his own perception of risk. Although the major focus in academic research focuses on putting the "right" or "ideal" risk measure on an objective basis, all risk measures have drawbacks and limitations in practical applications. Therefore, Balzer (2001) concludes that no single universally

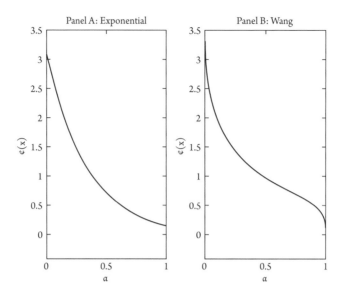

Figure 15.3 RISK SPECTRA FOR SPECTRAL RISK MEASURES.   Panel A plots the exponential spectral risk measure and Panel B plots the spectral risk measure based on the Wang transform.

acceptable risk measure exists. The flexibility in specifying spectral risk measures allows the choice of different measures in different situations but measures should rest on a solid theoretical foundation.

As in the case of VaR and ES, estimating spectral risk measures is straightforward. An estimate of a spectral risk measure $\rho_\phi(X)$ with risk spectrum ϕ given N portfolio realizations can be written as shown in Equation 15.27:

$$\hat{\rho}_\phi(X) = \Sigma_{i=1}^N X_i^{(\uparrow)} \hat{\phi}_i \tag{15.27}$$

with weights shown in Equation 15.28:

$$\hat{\phi}_i = \int_{(i-1)/N}^{i/N} \phi(m)dm. \tag{15.28}$$

Hence, from this representation the nature of spectral risk measures becomes obvious once again. A spectral measure is just a weighted average of all the outcomes of a portfolio sorted from worst to best. As discussed for VaR and ES, the problem of estimation error for spectral risk measures may be aggravated by the risk spectrum, as the risk spectrum puts more weight on the large losses than in the case of ES that imposes an equal weighting. Hence, whether large and infrequent losses are realized in the simulation have a greater effect on spectral measure estimates, resulting in even larger estimation errors. Ironically, with increases in investor risk aversion (i.e., the more weight is put on extreme events), larger estimation errors occur creating more concern about the accuracy of the risk estimate.

Risk Measures and Portfolio Allocation

This section provides an analysis of the impact of VaR and ES constraints on the investment set of a Markowitz investor (i.e., an investor who maximizes the expected return of the portfolio subject to some variance constraints). To simplify the analysis, assume selection from n assets that are normally distributed according to $r \sim N(\mu, \Sigma)$, where μ is an n-dimensional vector of expected portfolio returns and Σ is the corresponding $(n \times n)$-dimensional covariance matrix. The expression $W = \{w : \Sigma_i^n w_i = 1\}$ denotes the set of admissible portfolios expressed as a vector of fractions invested in the different assets. Under these assumptions, the portfolio return r_w is also normally distributed as shown in Equation 15.29:

$$r_w \sim N(w'\mu, w'\Sigma w). \tag{15.29}$$

Concentrating on the VaR constraint, the VaR can be expressed in terms of a critical return level $v(r_w, \alpha)$ in Equation 15.30:

$$v(r_w, \alpha) = z_\alpha \sqrt{w'\Sigma w} - w'\mu = z_\alpha \sigma_w - \mu_w, \tag{15.30}$$

where $z_\alpha = \Phi^{-1}(\alpha)$ is the inverse of cumulative density function of the standard normal distribution. Based on Merton (1972), the unconstrained mean-variance optimization solves Equation 15.31:

$$\min_{w \in W} \sigma_w^2, \text{ subject to } \mu_w = r^* \tag{15.31}$$

and its solution is given by the parabola in Equation 15.32:

$$B_M = \left\{ (\mu_w, \sigma_w) : \frac{\sigma_w^2}{\frac{1}{c}} - \frac{\left(\mu_w - \frac{b}{c}\right)^2}{\frac{d}{c^2}} = 1 \right\} \tag{15.32}$$

with constants $a = \mu'\Sigma^{-1}\mu$, $b = 1'\Sigma^{-1}\mu$, $c = 1'\Sigma^{-1}1$, $d = ac - b^2$. The mean-VaR trader solves a similar optimization problem, namely $\min_{w \in W} z_\alpha \sigma_w - \mu_w$, subject to $\mu_w = r^*$. The (μ, VaR)-efficient frontier is given in Equation 15.33:

$$B_V(\alpha) = \left\{ (v(r_w, \alpha), \sigma_w) : \frac{(v(r_w, \alpha) + \mu_w)^2}{\frac{z_\alpha^2}{c}} - \frac{\left(\mu_w - \frac{b}{c}\right)^2}{\frac{d}{c^2}} = 1 \right\}, \tag{15.33}$$

where $\alpha > \Phi\left(\sqrt{d/c}\right)$ must be guaranteed for a solution to exist. Hence, the set of admissible portfolios depends heavily on the confidence level α and the level of the VaR constraint. Depending on the VaR constraint and the level of α, portfolios with large standard deviation could be precluded as well as portfolios with small standard deviations. In such a situation, highly risk-averse investors will select a portfolio with a larger standard deviation, while slightly risk-averse investors will choose a portfolio with a smaller standard deviation. Figure 15.4 plots the mean-variance efficient frontier of a

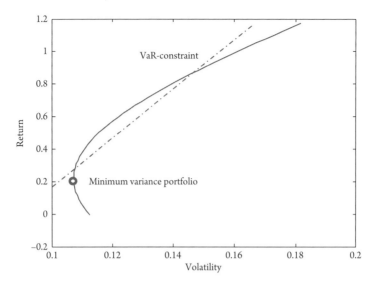

Figure 15.4 IMPACT OF STANDARD DEVIATION-BASED RISK MEASURES ON PORTFOLIO ALLOCATION.   The graph shows the impact of imposing a standard deviation-based risk measure such as VaR or ES on a mean-variance optimizer. The dash-dotted line represents the risk constraint.

Markowitz investor. Also, the VaR constraint $v(r_w, \alpha)$ is plotted for a given confidence level α. For reference, the minimum variance portfolio is marked on the efficient frontier. The portfolios above the dash-dotted line do not fulfill the VaR constraint. The presence of the risk constraint carves out portfolios of intermediate risk on the efficient frontier. Portfolios with very low risk and very high risk are still acceptable. Depending on the risk aversion, an investor might choose a portfolio that is riskier than he would have chosen without any risk constraint.

The fact that the risk constraint induces highly risk-averse investors to hold portfolios with larger standard deviations is counterintuitive. However, this result does not follow from the lack of coherency of the VaR risk measure. The same implications would be observed when replacing VaR by ES. To illustrate this concept, consider an ES-constrained mean-variance optimizer. Under the assumption of normally distributed returns, the critical expected shortfall return $\epsilon(r_w, \alpha)$ is obtained in Equation 15.34:

$$\epsilon(r_w, \alpha) = -E[r_w | r_w \leq -v(\alpha)] = \frac{\rho(z_\alpha)}{\alpha} \sigma_w - \mu_w, \qquad (15.34)$$

where $\rho(z_\alpha)$ is the standard normal probability density function taken at z_α. Obviously, as for the VaR constraint, the ES is linear in the portfolio's standard deviation σ_w and mean return μ_w. Therefore, imposing an ES constraint under the assumption of normally distributed returns has essentially the same effect that imposing a more conservative VaR constraint. Hence, ES constraints lead to the same conclusion as above (i.e., whether imposing ES and VaR risk constraints for portfolio optimization generates the intended effects is unclear a priori).

An important question concerns what happens when the return distribution is non-normal exhibiting skewness and excess kurtosis. As a first step, the impact of assuming asset returns follow a Student's t-distribution with λ-degrees of freedom could be analyzed so that the results show that both the VaR and the ES remain linear functions of the portfolio variance $w'\Sigma w$ and the expected return $w'\mu$. In particular, the following critical returns are obtained for the VaR and ES in Equation 15.35:

$$v(r, \alpha, \lambda) = t_{\alpha,\lambda} \sqrt{\frac{\lambda - 2}{\lambda}} \sqrt{w'\Sigma w} - w'\mu \qquad (15.35)$$

and Equation 15.36:

$$\epsilon(r, \alpha, \lambda) = \frac{\sqrt{\lambda - 2}}{\alpha} \int_0^\alpha \sqrt{\frac{1}{B_{1,2m-1}^{-1}\left(\frac{\lambda}{2}, \frac{1}{2}\right)} - 1} \; dm \sqrt{w'\Sigma w} - w'\mu, \qquad (15.36)$$

where $t_{\alpha,\lambda}$ is the α-quantile of the Student's t-distribution with λ-degrees of freedom and $B^{-1}(\cdot, \cdot)$ is the inverse of the regularized beta function. Therefore, leaving the assumption of normality in favor of the Student's t-distribution does not alter the qualitative effects previously discussed. The assumption only leads to more conservative risk constraints for a fixed confidence level. This result holds for both the Student's t-distribution and the whole class of elliptical distributions. Elliptical distributions include the normal distribution as a special case, as well as the Student's t-distribution and the Cauchy distribution. Elliptical distributions are called "elliptical" because the contours of equal density are ellipsoids (Fang and Anderson 1990). For this class of distribution, both the VaR constraint and the ES constraint can be shown in Equation 15.37 to be represented as a standard deviation-based risk measure:

$$\rho(r, c) = c \sqrt{w'\Sigma w} - w'\mu \qquad (15.37)$$

for some constant c (Embrechts, McNeil, and Straumann 1998). Furthermore, for elliptical distributions, the utility maximization under standard deviation-based risk measure constraints can be shown to be consistent with the standard utility maximization paradigm. Once leaving this class of distribution functions, consistency is no longer guaranteed (Alexander and Baptista 2002, 2004; Yamai and Yoshiba 2002b).

Risk Measures and Regulation

Ideally, regulation aims at maintaining and improving the safety of the financial industry by defining minimal capital standards. The 1996 Market Risk Amendment of the original Basel Accord brought an important conceptual innovation. The notion of risk on which the calculation of regulatory capital relied moved much closer to the notion of risk that was in use in the financial industry and in the academic literature.

The main goal was to align regulatory capital with "economic capital." The regulator acknowledged that financial institutions are in the best position to assess their market-based risk exposures. By allowing banks to use their internal models, the new regulatory approach seemed to suggest that relying on this knowledge might be the best way to cope with methodological problems of risk assessment in a rapidly changing economic environment.

VaR-based risk management already emerged as common market practice in the early 1990s. In the 1996 Market Risk Amendment, regulators chose VaR as the regulatory reporting tool and extended this practice to the highly nonlinear credit risk. Consequently, with the explicit encouragement of regulators, the VaR concept enjoyed further support and was finally adopted as the risk measurement standard.

The academic literature recognizes that VaR has some serious deficiencies. In particular, investors using VaR may be misled to construct positions that can generate unwarranted losses beyond the VaR level. Basak and Shapiro (2001) show this possibility for dynamic portfolio optimization and Yamai and Yoshiba (2002a) for portfolios involving far out-of-the-money options and for concentrated credit portfolios. Under extreme price fluctuations and dependence structures, VaR may underestimate risk due to its lack of coherency. Hence, VaR fails under extreme market scenarios (i.e., exactly in the situations when risk management should be effective).

ES or spectral risk measures helps to avoid the deficiencies of VaR. However, because these risk measures require more data to obtain a reliable estimate, their advantages may vanish for practical applications. When the loss distribution becomes more fat-tailed, the ES estimates become more varied due to infrequent and large losses, and their estimation error grows larger than the estimation error of VaR (Yamai and Yoshiba 2002c).

Analyzing both the coherency of risk measures and the incentive structures they may create are both important. Hellwig (1995, 1996) warns of the adverse effects created by using an internal model. According to Hellwig, banks may find that biasing their model development toward the goal of minimizing capital is desirable. Furthermore, whenever constraints on regulatory capital are defined, the possibility of adverse feedback effects should be considered. Basak and Shapiro (2001) and Leippold, Trojani, and Vanini (2006) provide a discussion of the equilibrium implications of VaR regulation. These authors find that VaR risk managers often optimally choose a larger exposure to risky assets than non-VaR risk managers and consequently incur larger losses when losses occur. Before the latest financial crisis, the academic literature discusses that VaR regulation may create severe adverse effects. The practice of determining capital based on VaR models helped the banking sector greatly reduce the amount of capital to be held against any given asset during the pre-crisis boom years. The regulatory adjustments of the post-financial crisis of 2007–2008 period mainly aim at correcting this mistake.

From the regulators' perspective, the ability to summarize risk in a single number is highly questionable, despite the beliefs of the propagators of VaR. Compressing all aspects and dimensions of risk into a single number ultimately has to lead to some loss of information. For VaR, this loss is substantial. It gives a misleading impression of precision and obfuscates the true underlying risks of one's position. A wiser approach would be to see more details of the position itself rather than some number out of a black box that is supposed to reflect its risks. VaR is a number that depends too much on unstated assumptions. Consequently, fully relying on this measure would be a mistake. However, the problem of unwarranted feedback effects caused by regulation with a coherent measure such as ES is still an open issue. Markets will adjust for the models they have to use. The resulting feedback effects and the impact on the safety of the financial system are hardly predictable.

Summary and Conclusions

This chapter has discussed different risk measures including VaR and ES as well as their weaknesses and theoretical shortcomings. VaR's main disadvantage is that it remains silent about the part of the loss distributions that should naturally be of interest for risk management, namely about the extreme events in the tail of the distribution. Moreover, VaR as a risk measure may discourage risk diversification due to the violation of the subadditivity axiom of coherent risk measures. The risk regulations set out by the Basel Committee build on these questionable VaR measures, which may give flawed estimates of market risk. From a regulatory viewpoint, VaR opens up moral hazard issues in manipulating VaR reports to fulfill any regulatory requirements.

The chapter favors using coherent risk measures such as ES or spectral risk measures. These measures provide an ideal approach for quantifying the impact of large losses and infrequent catastrophic events by adding relevant information from the tail of the loss distribution, which is the fundamental figure for effective risk management.

Despite their advantages, these risk measures have limitations. A particularly severe disadvantage arises from estimating risk measures that incorporate all the information from the tail of the loss distribution. When the underlying loss distribution is fat-tailed, the estimation errors of risk measures that do take into account the losses beyond the VaR level become much greater than those from estimating VaR itself.

Reducing the estimation error requires either increasing the sample size or using clever methods to reduce the errors such as importance sampling. However, this topic is beyond the scope of this chapter and is still part of active and highly mathematical research. Hence, the current findings suggest that reliance on a single risk measure should be avoided because each measure offers its own advantages. Complementing VaR with other measures and understanding their potential shortcomings allows for a clearer picture of a portfolio's risk profile and permits comprehensive risk monitoring.

Discussion Questions

1. Explain the circumstances under which VaR would be a "good" risk measure.
2. Discuss VaR's advantages and disadvantages.
3. Explain what a "good" risk measure should be and relate it to the coherency axioms.
4. Discuss the weighting schemes of VaR, ES, and a spectral risk measure and relate these weighting schemes to the "utility" function of the risk manager.
5. Identify the potential disadvantages of spectral risk measures.
6. Discuss the potential dangers of regulating financial markets using VaR and other risk measures.

References

Acerbi, Carlo. 2002. "Spectral Measures of Risk: A Coherent Representation of Subjective Risk Aversion." *Journal of Banking and Finance* 26:7, 1505–1518.

Acerbi, Carlo. 2007. "Coherent Measures of Risk in Everyday Market Practice." *Quantitative Finance* 7:4, 359–364.

Acerbi, Carlo, and Dirk Tasche. 2002. "On the Coherence of Expected Shortfall." *Journal of Banking and Finance* 26:7, 1487–1503.

Alexander, Gordon, and Alexandre Baptista. 2002. "Economic Implications of Using a Mean-VaR Model for Portfolio Selection: A Comparison with Mean-Variance Analysis." *Journal of Economic Dynamics & Control* 26:7, 1159–1193.

Alexander, Gordon, and Alexandre Baptista. 2004. "A Comparison of VaR and CVaR Constraints on Portfolio Selection with the Mean-Variance Model." *Management Science* 50:9, 1261–1273.

Artzner, Pilippe, Freddy Delbaen, Jean-Marc Eber, and David Heath. 1999. "Coherent Measures of Risk." *Mathematical Finance* 9:3, 203–228.

Balbás, Alejandro, José Garrido, and Silvia Mayoral. 2009. "Properties of Distortion Risk Measures." *Methodology and Computing in Applied Probability* 11:3, 385–399.

Balzer, Leslie. 2001. "Investment Risk: A Unified Approach to Upside and Downside Returns." In Frank Sortino and Stephen Satchell, eds., *Managing Downside Risk in Financial Markets: Theory, Practice and Implementation*, 103–105. Oxford: Butterworth-Heinemann.

Basak, Suleyman, and Alexander Shapiro. 2001. "Value-at-Risk Based Risk Management: Optimal Policies and Asset Prices." *Review of Financial Studies* 14:2, 371–405.

Bawa, Vijay S. 1975. "Optimal Rules for Ordering Uncertain Prospects." *Journal of Financial Economics* 2:1, 95–121.

Cotter, John, and Kevin Dowd. 2006. "Extreme Spectral Risk Measures: An Application to Futures Clearinghouse Margin Requirements." *Journal of Banking and Finance* 30:12, 3469–3485.

Danielsson, Jón, Bjørn N. Jorgensen, Gennady Samorodnitsky, Mandira Sarma, and Casper de Vries. 2013. "Fat Tails, VaR and Subadditivity." *Journal of Econometrics* 172:2, 283–291.

Dowd, Kevin, and David Blake. 2006. "After VaR: The Theory, Estimation, and Insurance Applications of Quantile-Based Risk Measures." *Journal of Risk and Insurance* 73:2, 193–229.

Dowd, Kevin, John Cotter, and Ghulam Sorwar. 2008. "Spectral Risk Measures: Properties and Limitations." *Journal of Financial Services Research* 34:1, 61–75.

Egloff, Daniel, and Markus Leippold. 2010. "Quantile Importance Sampling with Stochastic Approximation." *Annals of Statistics* 38:2, 1244–1278.

Embrechts, Paul, Claudia Klüppelberg, and Thomas Mikosch. 1997. *Modelling Extremal Events for Insurance and Finance*. New York: Springer.

Embrechts, Paul, Alexander McNeil, and Daniel Straumann. 1998. "Correlation and Dependency in Risk Management: Properties and Pitfalls." Working Paper, ETH Zürich.

Fama, Eugene. 1963. "Mandelbrot and the Stable Paretian Hypothesis." *Journal of Business* 36:4, 420–429.

Fang, Kai-Tai, and Theodore W. Anderson. 1990. *Statistical Inference in Elliptically Contoured and Related Distributions*. New York: Allerton Press.

Fishburn, Peter C. 1977. "Mean Risk Analysis with Below Target Returns." *American Economic Review* 67:2, 116–126.

Föllmer, Hans, and Thomas Knispel. 2013. "Convex Risk Measures: Basic Facts, Law-Invariance and Beyond, Asymptotics for Large Portfolios." In Leonard C. MacLean and William T. Ziemba, eds., *Handbook of the Fundamentals of Financial Decision Making, Part II*, 507–554. Singapore: World Scientific.

Föllmer, Hans, and Alexander Schied. 2002. "Convex Measures of Risk and Trading Constraints." *Finance and Stochastics* 6:4, 429–447.

Föllmer, Hans, and Alexander Schied. 2011. *Stochastic Finance: An Introduction in Discrete Time*, 3rd Edition. Berlin: Walter de Gruyter.

Frittelli, Marco, and Emanuela Rosazza Gianin. 2002. "Putting Order in Risk Measures." *Journal of Banking and Finance* 26:7, 1473–1486.

Goovaerts, Marc J., Florent De Vylder, and Jean Haezendonck. 1984. *Insurance Premiums.* Amsterdam: North-Holland.

Heath, David, and Hyejin Ku. 2004. "Pareto Equilibria with Coherent Measures of Risk." *Mathematical Finance* 14:2, 163–172.

Hellwig, Martin. 1995. "Systemic Aspects of Risk Management in Banking and Finance." *Swiss Journal of Economics and Statistics* 131:2, 723–737.

Hellwig, Martin. 1996. "Capital Adequacy Rules as Instruments for the Regulation of Banks." *Swiss Journal of Economics and Statistics* 132:2, 609–612.

Kou, Steven, Xianhua Peng, and Chris Heyde. 2013. "External Risk Measures and Basel Accords." *Mathematics of Operations Research* 38:3, 292–417.

Kuosmanen, Timo. 2004. "Efficient Diversification According to Stochastic Dominance Criteria." *Management Science* 50:10, 1390–1406.

Kusuoka, Shigeo. 2001. "On Law Invariant Coherent Risk Measures." *Advances in Mathematical Economics* 3, 83–95.

Leippold, Markus, Fabio Trojani, and Paolo Vanini. 2006. "Equilibrium Impact of VaR Regulation." *Journal of Economic Dynamics and Control* 30:8, 1277–1313.

Mandelbrot, Benoit. 1961. "Stable Paretian Random Fluctuations and Multiplicative Variation of Income." *Econometrica* 29:4, 517–543.

Mandelbrot, Benoit. 1963. "The Variation of Certain Speculative Prices." *Journal of Business* 36:4, 394–419.

Mandelbrot, Benoit, and Howard M. Taylor. 1967. "On the Distribution of Stock Price Differentials." *Operations Research* 15:6, 1057–1062.

Markowitz, Harry. 1952. "Portfolio Selection." *Journal of Finance* 7:1, 77–91.

Markowitz, Harry. 1959. *Portfolio Selection-Efficient Diversification of Investments.* New Haven, CT: Yale University Press.

Merton, Robert. 1972. "An Analytical Derivation of the Efficient Portfolio Frontier." *Journal of Financial and Quantitative Analysis* 7:4, 1851–1872.

Roy, Arthur D. 1952. "Safety First and the Holding of Assets." *Econometrica* 20:3, 431–450.

Sharpe, William F. 1963. "A Simplified Model for Portfolio Analysis." *Management Science* 9:2, 277–294.

Song, Yongsheng, and Jia-An Yan. 2009. "Risk Measures with Comonotonic Subadditivity or Convexity and Respecting Stochastic Orders." *Insurance: Mathematics and Economics* 45:3, 459–465.

Tchebichef, Pafnouti. 1867. "Des Valeurs Moyennes." *Journal de Mathématiques Pures et Appliquées* 2:12, 177–184.

Wang, Shaun. 2000. "A Class of Distortion Operators for Pricing Financial and Insurance Risks." *Journal of Risk and Insurance* 67:1, 15–36.

Wang, Shaun, Virginia R. Young, and Harry H. Panjer. 1997. "Axiomatic Characterization of Insurance Prices." *Insurance: Mathematics and Economics* 21:2, 173–183.

Yamai, Yasuhiro, and Toshinao Yoshiba. 2002a. "On the Validity of Value-at-Risk: Comparative Analysis with Expected Shortfall." *Monetary and Economic Studies* 20:1, 57–86.

Yamai, Yasuhiro, and Toshinao Yoshiba. 2002b. "Comparative Analysis with Expected Shortfall. (2): Expected Utility Maximization and Tail Risk." *Monetary and Economic Studies* 20:2, 95–115.

Yamai, Yasuhiro, and Toshinao Yoshiba. 2002c. "Comparative Analysis with Expected Shortfall. (3): Their Validity under Market Stress." *Monetary and Economic Studies* 20:3, 181–237.

16

Stress Testing

MARTIN ČIHÁK

Advisor, International Monetary Fund

Introduction

The financial instability of recent years has put the spotlight on tools for identifying vulnerabilities in financial institutions. Stress testing is a key method for quantifying vulnerabilities. It encompasses techniques for assessing resilience to extreme events. Outside of finance, stress testing is used in areas as diverse as cardiology, engineering, and software programming. In finance, stress testing has traditionally referred to asset portfolios, but recently it has been applied to whole financial institutions and financial systems.

This chapter discusses strengths and weaknesses of stress testing, focusing on common types of stress tests. It explains how to establish various shocks and how to interpret stress testing results. Other sources on stress testing include Blaschke, Jones, Majnoni, and Peria (2001), Čihák (2004a, 2004b, 2005, and 2007a), Jones, Hilbers, and Slack (2004), and International Monetary Fund and the World Bank (2005).

The chapter begins by providing a discussion of the stress testing process followed by an examination of the input data. Next, the chapter discusses stress tests for credit risk, interest rate risk, foreign exchange risk, interbank (solvency) contagion risk, liquidity tests and liquidity contagion, and stress testing scenarios. Finally, the chapter offers a summary and conclusions.

The Stress Testing Process

The stress testing process involves the following stages: (1) identifying vulnerabilities; (2) constructing a scenario; (3) mapping the scenario outputs into a form that is usable for an analysis of financial institutions' balance sheets and income statements; (4) performing the numerical analysis; (5) considering any second round effects; and (6) summarizing and interpreting the results (Jones et al. 2004; International Monetary Fund and the World Bank 2005). As Figure 16.1 shows, these stages are not necessarily sequential because some modification or review of each component of the process may be needed as work progresses.

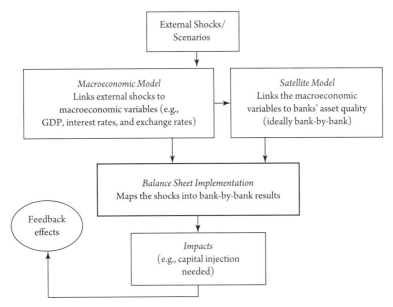

Figure 16.1 Stress Testing Process. This figure shows the key stages in the stress testing process from the assumed external shocks or scenarios to the estimated impacts. The figure also illustrates that the stages are not necessarily sequential because modification or review of each component of the process may be needed as work progresses and as feedback effects are taken into account.

VARIABLES OF INTEREST IN STRESS TESTING

Capitalization is a popular measure of expressing stress test results. An advantage of capitalization measures such as capital or equity-to-assets or capital-to-risk-weighted assets is that capital adequacy is a scaled measure, allowing comparison among institutions of different size. Also, bank regulators commonly use capitalization as a basic indicator of soundness. The disadvantage of this measure is that no straightforward link exists between capitalization and other variables such as the probability of the institution's default.

Another common measure for expressing the impact of stress tests is the capital injection needed to bring a bank to compliance with regulatory requirements, particularly the minimum capital adequacy requirement. The capital injection need can be expressed for example as a percentage of gross domestic product (GDP) to emphasize the macroeconomic relevance of the impact. It provides an upper bound on the potential fiscal costs of bank failure triggered by the stressful scenario. Mathematically, the capital needed can be calculated from the following accounting relationship in Equation 16.1:

$$\frac{C+I}{RWA+qI} = \rho, \qquad (16.1)$$

where C is the bank's existing total regulatory capital; I is the capital injection; RWA is its existing risk-weighted assets; q is the percentage of the capital injection that is immediately used to increase risk-weighted assets; and ρ is the regulatory minimum capital adequacy ratio (CAR). From Equation 16.1, the necessary capital injection can be expressed in Equation 16.2 as:

$$
\begin{aligned}
I &= \frac{\rho\,RWA - C}{1 - q\rho} \quad \text{if } C < \rho\,RWA; \\
&= 0 \quad \text{otherwise}.
\end{aligned}
\tag{16.2}
$$

If $q = 0$ (i.e., the capital injection is not used for an increase in RWA at least immediately), the capital injection can be calculated as $I = \rho RWA - C$. The values of the parameters ρ and q are assumed. If ρ is higher (say, if it exceeds the Basel Accord minimum of 8 percent), the necessary capital injection is higher. If risk-weighted assets increase as a result of the increase in capital (i.e., if $q > 0$), the necessary capital injection is higher but the impact of changes in q is generally rather small.

Stress test results can also be expressed in terms of profits. In a baseline scenario, banks would typically create profits. Stress testing evaluates impacts against such a baseline, as banks would normally use profits as the first line of defense. Therefore, estimating the "profit buffer" that banks would have in the baseline is useful. The profit buffer estimate can be based on the typical pattern of profits over several economic cycles.

Another way of expressing stress test results is in terms of the z-score, which is a measure of bank soundness (Boyd and Runkle 1993; Hesse and Čihák 2007). The attraction of the z-score comes from the fact that it is related to the probability of a bank's insolvency (i.e., the probability that the value of its assets becomes lower than the value of the debt). The z-score can be summarized as $z \equiv (k + \mu)/\sigma$, where k is equity capital as a percent of assets, μ is the average after-tax return as percent on assets, and σ is the standard deviation of the after-tax return on assets, as a proxy for return volatility. The z-score measures the number of standard deviations a return realization has to fall in order to deplete equity, under the assumption of normality of banks' returns. A higher z-score implies a lower insolvency risk.

Another possibility is to express stress test results in terms of loan losses, as done in stress tests presented by staff from Norges Bank (Evjen, Lund, Morka, Nordal, and Svendsen 2005) and the Bank of England (Bunn, Cunningham, and Drehmann 2005). Although this approach is relatively easy to implement, the drawback of using loan loss is that it does not take into account banks' buffers (profits and capital) against those losses. Loan losses may underestimate the overall impact if losses are concentrated in weak institutions.

For liquidity stress tests, the impacts have to be measured differently than for solvency tests. One option is to show the number of days for which a bank would be able to withstand an assumed liquidity shock without an external liquidity injection from say a central bank. Another option is to show results in terms of changes in commonly used liquidity ratios.

Another way to express stress tests is in terms of changes in ratings and probabilities of default (PDs). Ratings and PDs provide a way of combining solvency and liquidity risks into a single measure. Čihák (2007a) shows that this process can be performed by using an early warning system similar to those used in supervisory agencies for assessing soundness of banks (Sahajwala and Van den Bergh 2000). Although a supervisory early warning system usually consists of a set of ratios, Kraft and Galac (2007) point out that it may also include other variables that have power to identify weak banks such as overly high deposit rates. A typical off-site supervisory ranking system has a set of thresholds for each indicator, determining a numerical ranking to each of the indicators say with 1 indicating the best ranking and 4 the worst ranking. The rankings for the individual variables are weighted to derive an overall ranking for a bank. Converting the rankings into probabilities of default is possible using a "step function" illustrated in Figure 16.2. In practice, the parameters of such step functions are based on either expert estimates or calibrations using data from past situations of bank stress.

Figure 16.3 provides an illustration of such calibration for two variables—capital adequacy and nonperforming loans (NPLs) to total loans—and one threshold per variable. The dots represent bank-level observations, and the two bigger boxes indicate two banks that have actually failed. The supervisory ranking system attempts to single out the failed banks (i.e., the bigger boxes), minimizing the signal-to-noise ratio for the estimate. If the purpose is to capture all failed banks in Figure 16.3 (i.e., eliminate Type I errors), the early warning system characterized by the CAR threshold and the NPL threshold shown in the figure allows decreasing the percentage of banks misclassified as failures (i.e., Type II errors) from 88 percent (15/17 assuming no prior information) to 33 percent (1/3 for the "northwest" subset identified by the two thresholds). This difference represents a major improvement in forecast precision. Once such a calibrated ranking system is in place, a stress test can focus on calculating the impacts on the system's components (e.g., in the case of Figure 16.3, on capital adequacy and NPLs to total loans) and the ranking system could be

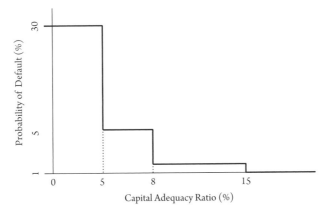

Figure 16.2 EXAMPLE OF A "STEP FUNCTION". This figure provides an example of a "step function" that maps bank rankings into probabilities of default. The parameters of such functions are usually based on expert estimates. They can also be informed by data from past cases of bank stress as illustrated in Figure 16.3.

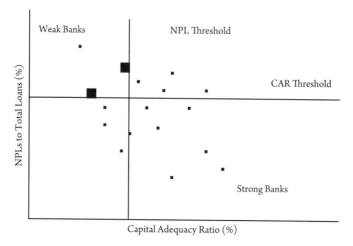

Figure 16.3 AN EXAMPLE OF CALIBRATING A SUPERVISORY EARLY WARNING
SYSTEM. This figure illustrates a calibration of an early warning system with two
variables—the capital adequacy ratio (CAR) and nonperforming loans (NPLs) to total
loans—and one threshold per variable. The dots represent bank-level observations and the
two bigger boxes indicate two failed banks. The supervisory ranking system attempts to
single out the failed banks (i.e., the bigger boxes), minimizing the signal-to-noise ratio for
the estimate. If the thresholds are set so that they capture all failed banks (i.e., eliminate
Type I errors), the early warning system decreases the percentage of banks misclassified as
failures (i.e., Type II errors) from 88 percent (15/17 assuming no prior information) to
33 percent (1/3 for the "northwest" subset identified by the two thresholds). This change
results in a major improvement in precision.

used to convert the post-shock values of these variables into post-shock rankings and
post-shock PDs.

Finally, calculating stress test impacts in terms of other variables that capture soundness of financial institutions and can be credibly linked to the development of risk
factors is possible. For example, instead of the accounting-based data discussed above,
the impacts can be presented in terms of market-based indicators of financial sector
soundness, such as relative prices of securities issued by financial securities, distance to
default for banks' stocks, or credit default swap premiums (Čihák 2007b). For example, distance to default, which uses stock price data to estimate the volatility in the
economic capital of the bank, is a version of the z-score for banks with stocks listed in liquid equity markets (Danmarks Nationalbank 2004). An advantage of the market-based
indicators is that they are available more frequently than accounting data. However,
their calculation requires the existence of deep markets from which such indicators can
be derived.

Input Data

Data availability is critical for stress test quality. Čihák (2007a) shows the types of data
usually needed for a basic stress test. These data include the following: (1) capital,

assets, and risk-weighted assets; (2) asset quality and structure of lending by sector and by size of borrower; (3) provisioning and collateral; (4) structure of assets, liabilities, and off-balance sheet items by time to repricing; (5) structure of the bond portfolio; (6) net open positions in foreign exchange and lending in foreign currency; (7) average profits and standard deviation of profits over time; (8) liquidity structure of assets and liabilities; and (9) bank-to-bank uncollateralized exposures.

Stress tests analyze the economic position (i.e., net worth) of banks. In principle, net worth should be aligned with the reported capital data, but in practice important differences exist between the economic net worth and the reported regulatory data on capital (e.g., when some bank assets are overvalued or when regulators accept as capital liabilities that in fact are not capital such as some long-term loans). The person carrying out stress tests should first adjust the input data for such biases. One example of such adjustments is when banks under provision NPLs. Another example is when banks do not "mark-to-market" bonds that they are holding in their portfolios.

The input data should reflect not only assets and liabilities but also off-balance sheet positions. For example, the net open positions in foreign currency should reflect the delta equivalents of foreign exchange options.

For interest rate risk calculations, having data on time to repricing is important. For example, from an interest rate risk perspective, a 20-year mortgage loan with an interest rate that can change every six months, should be treated the same as a six-month fixed rate loan, not as a 20-year loan. However, obtaining data on time to repricing may be difficult in some cases. In many countries, banks report instead a breakdown of assets by maturity or by residual maturity. While data on maturity or residual maturity are important for analyzing liquidity, using them as a proxy for time to repricing may lead to misleading results, which typically involves overstating the interest rate risk.

Additional data are needed for stress testing for other risks. For example, to carry out stress tests for equity price risk and commodity price risk, data on net open positions in equities and in commodities would be needed. The mechanics of the test would be similar to the direct foreign exchange solvency test. Also, breakdowns of assets and liabilities by residual maturity/time to repricing and currency would be needed to perform stress tests separately for foreign currency.

Credit Risk

Credit risk is the key type of risk in most banks. Three basic groups of approaches are available to modeling credit risk in stress tests. The first group includes mechanical approaches, typically used if data are insufficient or if shocks are different from past ones. The second group includes approaches based on loan performance data, such as probabilities of default, losses given default, NPLs, and provisions; and regressions, such as single equation, structural, and vector auto regression. The third group encompasses approaches based on nonfinancial corporate data, such as leverage or interest coverage, and household data.

A basic approach to modeling credit risk consists of assuming a generalized decline in asset quality. For example, assume that NPLs increase by a certain percentage, say 25 percent of the existing stock of NPLs. This means that a bank would have to undertake additional provisioning by 25 percent for each of the three groups that constitute NPL (substandard, doubtful, and loss loans). The increased provisioning requirements will reduce the value of the risk-weighted assets (RWA) as well as the capital. Regarding the impact on the RWA, a common assumption is that the full increase in NPL is subtracted from RWA. However, the impact on RWA may be smaller if the affected assets have a weight of less than one in the RWA. Calculating this impact more precisely requires having information of the distribution of NPL across risk-categories.

The crucial assumption in this calculation is that the increase in NPLs is proportional to the existing NPLs in these banks. In other words, if a bank had more NPLs in the past, it is assumed to have more new NPLs as a result of the shock. While this approach results in the most straightforward calculation, alternative approaches are available. For example, the new NPLs can be proportional to the overall stock of loans or to the stock of new performing loans.

Whether to use existing NPLs or existing performing loans as a basis for assessing future credit risk is an open question. This issue can and should be decided empirically by testing for factors explaining changes in NPLs if sufficient empirical data are available. In the absence of reliable or sufficiently detailed empirical data, stress testers have been resorting to simplifying assumptions. An example of this process would be assuming that the existing NPLs is correct if the existing bad loans are a good proxy for the quality of a bank's risk management and therefore of the risk faced by the bank going forward.

Studies attempt to link credit risk to macroeconomic variables using econometric models. For example, Pesola (2005) presents an econometric study of macroeconomic determinants of credit risk and other sources of banking fragility and distress in numerous European countries from the early 1980s to 2002. The International Monetary Fund (2003) presents an even broader cross-country analysis. For Austria, Boss, Krenn, Schwaiger, and Wegschaider (2004) provide estimates of the relationship between macroeconomic variables and credit risk. For Finland, Virolainen (2004) develops a macroeconomic credit risk model, estimating the probability of default in various industries as a function of a range of macroeconomic variables. For Norway, the Norges Bank has single equation models for household debt and house prices, and a model of corporate bankruptcies based on annual accounts for all Norwegian enterprises (Eklund, Larsen, and Berhardsen 2003). Several studies are available on this topic for Hong Kong, including single equation aggregate estimates (Peng, Lai, Leung, and Shu 2003) as well as panel estimates using bank-by-bank data (Gerlach, Peng, and Shu, 2004). For the Czech Republic, Babouček and Jančar (2005) estimate a vector autoregression model with NPLs and a set of macroeconomic variables. Similar models are also common in International Monetary Fund's Financial Sector Assessment Program missions (Čihák 2007a).

When interpreting the macroeconomic models of credit risk, consideration should be given to the fact that linear statistical models dominate the literature. The linear approximation may be reasonable when shocks are small, but non-linearities are likely to be important for large shocks: doubling the size of the shock may more than double its impact. Indeed, micro-level credit risk models often find a non-linear relationship between the scale of shocks and the likelihood of default. For macroeconomic shocks, Drehmann (2005) also reports a non-linear link to credit risk. Moreover, the models are subject to a version the Lucas critique (Lucas 1976). The critique points out that predicting the effects of a decision maker's decision entirely on the basis of relationships observed in historical data would be naive. Major stress, such as the one assumed in stress testing, may fundamentally alter the decision makers' behavior. As a result, data on past behavior may be of limited or no value. For example, when considering a scenario that involves de-pegging of a currency board, models estimated on past data are likely to say little about the impact of the exchange rate changes on credit risk. Other approaches, such as calibration that uses parameters based on experience from other countries, may be more appropriate in such situations.

To get a better picture of the impact of sector-specific shocks, a useful approach would be to select different shocks to economic sectors and calculate how a bank would be affected depending on its exposures to the respective sectors. One example is a "terrorist attack" scenario, increasing credit risk in the tourism and trade sectors. The calibration of the sector-specific shocks can be based on a historical scenario (e.g., a past terrorist attack in the country or a neighboring country) or on empirical models mapping macroeconomic and other explanatory variables into default rates in different sectors.

Interest Rate Risk

A financial institution incurs direct interest rate risk when the interest rate sensitivities of its assets and liabilities are mismatched. Calculating the direct impact of interest rate changes usually consists of two parts: reflecting flows and stocks. The first part works with the repricing gap information. It calculates the changes in interest income and interest expenses resulting from the "gap" between the flow of interest on the holdings of assets and liabilities in each bucket. The "gap" in each time band or time-to-repricing bucket shows how a given change in interest rates affects net interest income. It sorts assets and liabilities into time-to-repricing buckets (e.g., due in less than 3 months, due in 3 to 6 months, and due in 6 to 12 months). The second part of the calculation shows the impact of interest rate changes on the value of bonds held by the commercial banks. The calculations assume that the bonds are "marked-to-market" (i.e., changes in their market value have a direct impact on the capitalization of the banks). The impact of an interest rate change on the market value is approximated using the duration of the bonds held by the banks. Duration can be calculated from data on the parameters of the bonds and the structure of the bond portfolio (International Monetary Fund 2004).

The direct impact of higher nominal interest rates on capital and capital adequacy is typically negative, resulting from the fact that financial institutions operate with a duration gap between their assets and liabilities. *Duration of assets* (liabilities), D_A (D_L), is defined as the weighted average, term-to-maturity of an asset's (liability's) cash flow, the weights being the present value of each future cash flow as a percent of the asset's (liability's) full price. A formula is provided in paragraph 3.52 of International Monetary Fund (2004). Duration approximates the elasticity of the market values of assets and liabilities to the respective rates of return as shown in Equation 16.3:

$$\frac{\Delta A(r_A)}{A(r_A)} \cong \frac{-D_A \Delta r_A}{(1 + r_A)}, \quad \frac{\Delta L(r_L)}{L(r_L)} \cong \frac{-D_L \Delta r_L}{(1 + r_L)}, \tag{16.3}$$

where $A(r_A)$ and $L(r_L)$ are market values of assets and liabilities of the financial system, and r_A and r_L are annual interest rates of assets and liabilities (Bierwag 1987). The results are first-order approximations. For large changes in interest rates, second derivative terms need to be included to account for convexity of portfolios. Alternatively, the elasticity of bond prices to interest rate changes can be empirically estimated using past data. Differentiating the capital adequacy ratio with respect to the interest rate on assets and substituting from Equation 16.3 results in Equation 16.4:

$$\frac{\Delta[C(r_A, r_L)/A_{RW}(r_A)]}{\Delta r_A} \cong -\frac{(L/A_{RW})}{1 + r_A}\left(D_A - D_L\frac{1 + r_A}{1 + r_L}\frac{\Delta r_L}{\Delta r_A}\right)\frac{1 - \frac{\Delta A_{RW}}{A_{RW}}\frac{C}{\Delta C}}{1 - \frac{\Delta A}{A}\frac{C}{\Delta C}}.$$
$$(16.4)$$

Assuming that the risk-weighted assets move proportionally to total assets (i.e., $\Delta A_{RW}/A_{RW} = \Delta A/A$), Equation 16.4 can be simplified into Equation 16.5 as follows:

$$\frac{\Delta[C(r_A, r_L)/A_{RW}(r_A)]}{\Delta r_A} \cong -\frac{(L/A_{RW})}{1 + r_A}GAP_D, \qquad (16.5)$$

where GAP_D is the duration gap, defined as Equation 16.6:

$$GAP_D = D_A - D_L\frac{1 + r_A}{1 + r_L}\frac{\Delta r_L}{\Delta r_A}. \qquad (16.6)$$

Most financial institutions transform short-term, low-interest rate liabilities into long-term, higher interest rate assets. This means that $D_A > D_L, r_A > r_L$, and $GAP_D > 0$. Thus, an interest rate increase has a negative impact on the institutions' net worth and capitalization, leading to increased vulnerability.

In addition to direct interest risk, the financial institution is also exposed to indirect interest rate risk, resulting from the impact of interest rate changes on borrowers' creditworthiness and ability to repay. The indirect interest rate risk is a part of credit risk. Accounting for the interest rate-related credit risk is discussed in more detail in the section devoted to designing scenarios. An increase in nominal interest rates to the extent that it increases real interest rates and the difficulty of borrowers repaying their debts and obtaining new credit is likely to have a negative effect on the credit risk of the financial institutions' borrowers. Other things being equal, higher risk eventually translates into higher losses and a decline in the financial institutions' net worth. The effect of higher real interest rates on NPLs or loan losses depends on factors such as the borrowers' earnings in relation to interest and principal expenses, loan loss provisions, and the degree of collateralization of the loans.

Foreign Exchange Risk

Foreign exchange risk is the risk that exchange rate changes affect the local currency value of financial institutions' assets, liabilities, and off-balance sheet items. The risk consists of three components: (1) direct solvency risk resulting from banks' net open positions in foreign currency and those in local currency that are indexed to exchange rates; (2) the indirect solvency risk resulting from the impact of foreign exchange positions taken by borrowers on their creditworthiness and ability to repay, and thereby on financial institutions; and (3) foreign exchange liquidity risk resulting from liquidity mismatches in foreign currency. This section focuses on the direct and indirect solvency risk, leaving the foreign exchange liquidity risk for the section on liquidity stress testing.

International Monetary Fund (2004) defines the assessment of the direct foreign exchange risk using the net open position in foreign exchange. Let F denote the net open position in foreign exchange, C the capital, A_{RW} the risk-weighted assets (all in domestic currency units), and e the exchange rate in units of foreign currency per unit of domestic currency. A depreciation (decline) in the exchange rate leads to a proportional decline in the domestic currency value of the net open position (i.e., $\Delta e/e = \Delta F/F$ (for $F \neq 0$). Assume that this translates directly into a decline in capital (i.e., $\Delta C/\Delta F = 1$). Equation 16.7 shows the impact of the exchange rate shock on the ratio of capital to risk-weighted assets:

$$\frac{\Delta[C(e)/A_{RW}(e)]}{\Delta e} \cong \frac{\frac{F}{e}A_{RW} - C\frac{\Delta A_{RW}}{\Delta C}\frac{F}{e}}{A_{RW}^2} \cong \frac{1}{e}\frac{F}{C}\frac{C}{A_{RW}}\left(1 - \frac{\Delta A_{RW}}{\Delta C}\frac{C}{A_{RW}}\right),$$

(16.7)

where $\Delta C/\Delta e = \Delta F/\Delta e = F/e$. The symbol "$\cong$" means that the equation is only approximate for larger than infinitesimal changes. Equation 16.7 can be rewritten as Equation 16.8:

$$\Delta[C(e)/A_{RW}(e)] \cong \frac{\Delta e}{e}\frac{F}{C}\frac{C}{A_{RW}}\left(1 - \frac{\Delta A_{RW}}{\Delta C}\frac{C}{A_{RW}}\right),$$

(16.8)

where the term $\Delta A_{RW}/\Delta C$ can have values from 0 to 1, reflecting the degree of co-movement of capital and the risk-weighted assets (empirically, $\Delta A_{RW}/\Delta C$ could be estimated by a regression). In the case of $\Delta A_{RW}/\Delta C = 0$ (i.e., if the risk-weighted assets do not change), the change in the capital adequacy ratio equals the exchange rate shock times the exposure, measured as a product of the net open position to capital (F/C) and capital adequacy (C/A_{RW}). This measure is sometimes used as a short-hand calculation of the direct exchange rate stress test.

Equation 16.8 is a linear approximation that works well in unsophisticated financial systems. However, if financial institutions have large positions in foreign exchange options, the relationship between exchange rate changes and capital can become highly non-linear. In such cases, stress tests based on detailed decomposition of financial institutions' open positions are preferable.

For most banks, the direct foreign exchange solvency risk is small. Banks' net open positions in foreign exchange tend to be closely scrutinized by banks' risk managers and supervisors. Banks typically have explicit limits on these positions (e.g., 10 or 20 percent of capital) and they usually have to include the net open positions in the capital adequacy calculation. In general, the open positions tend to be small, making the direct impact relatively small.

Besides direct depreciation effects, an exchange rate change would also influence the corporate sector's creditworthiness and ability to repay. An exchange rate shock not only changes the domestic corporate sector's competitiveness relative to foreign firms but also influences the corporate balance sheets via firms' net open positions in foreign currencies. While banks' direct foreign exchange risk is typically tightly monitored and regulated by measures such as limits on banks' net open positions, their indirect foreign exchange risk often receives much less scrutiny. This is in part because monitoring it properly requires comprehensive knowledge of the foreign exchange exposures of bank's corporate and household counterparts. Such information is not always available to banks' risk managers and supervisors. When the indirect foreign exchange risk is analyzed in more depth, it often turns out to be more important than the direct one (Čihák 2007a). The indirect foreign exchange risk can get particularly sizeable during prolonged periods of exchange rate stability (e.g., in countries with closely managed exchange rate pegs). These can lull banks' counterparts into a false sense of security and into accepting sizeable foreign exchange exposures and saddling the banks with indirect foreign exchange risk.

To illustrate the calculation of the indirect risk in overall banking sector risk, denote the corporate sector's debt, equity, and open foreign exchange position as $Dc(e)$, $Ec(e)$, and $Fc(e)$, respectively. Assume that, similar to the case of banks' net open position, a percentage change in the exchange rate will translate into the same percentage change in the domestic currency value of the net open position, which will in turn lead to an equivalent change in the corporate sector's equity, i.e., $\Delta E_c / \Delta e = \Delta F_c / \Delta e = F/e$. The impact of the exchange rate on the corporate leverage (Dc/Ec) is then given by Equation 16.9:

$$\frac{\Delta[D_c(e)/E_c(e)]}{\Delta e} \cong \frac{\frac{\Delta D_c}{\Delta E_c}\frac{F_c}{e}E_c - D_c\frac{F_c}{e}}{E_c^2} \cong -\frac{1}{e}\frac{F_c}{E_c}\left(\frac{D_c}{E_c} - \frac{\Delta D_c}{\Delta E_c}\right). \tag{16.9}$$

Thus, if the corporate sector is short in foreign exchange, depreciation (decline) in the exchange rate would lead to an increase in its leverage. Corporate leverage is typically positively correlated with the share of banks' NPLs in total loans (denoted as NPL/TL) (i.e., $\Delta(NPL/TL)/\Delta(D_c/E_c) = a > 0$). The impact of a change in the exchange rate on the NPL/TL ratio can then be expressed as Equation 16.10:

$$\Delta(NPL/TL) \cong a\,\Delta[D_c(e)/E_c(e)] \cong -\frac{\Delta e}{e}\frac{F_c}{E_c}a\left(\frac{D_c}{E_c} - \frac{\Delta D_c}{\Delta E_c}\right). \tag{16.10}$$

If $\Delta D_c/\Delta E_c = 0$, the change in the NPL/TL ratio would equal the exchange rate change times the net open position, times the parameter a, which can be estimated empirically, as shown in International Monetary Fund (2003) and Boss et al. (2004). To find the impact on capital adequacy, assume that the credit shock moves some of the previously performing loans into the nonperforming category. Differentiating C/A_{RW} with respect to NPL/TL, and substituting for NPL/TL from Equation 16.10, results in Equation 16.11:

$$\Delta(C/A_{RW}) \cong \frac{\Delta e}{e}\frac{TL}{A_{RW}}\left(1 - \frac{C}{A_{RW}}\frac{\Delta A_{RW}}{\Delta C}\right)\pi\frac{F_c}{E_c}a\left(\frac{D_c}{E_c} - \frac{\Delta D_c}{\Delta E_c}\right), \qquad (16.11)$$

where provisions are assumed to be a fixed percentage (π) of NPLs and are deducted directly from capital.

The indirect effects make the analysis of foreign exchange rate risk more complex and dependent on additional assumptions or regression analysis. Adding to the complexity is the fact that the indirect exchange rate risk includes effects on both stocks and flows. To calculate the impact of exchange rate changes on the net present value (NPV) of the corporate sector, as in Equation 16.11, requires taking into account changes in the NPV of future earnings. For example, in export-oriented companies, depreciation tends to increase future earnings. The effect on NPV is similar to that of a long position in foreign currency. However, often a simpler approach is to calculate the impact on flows, by estimating the elasticity of earnings to interest and principal expenses with respect to the exchange rate, and then estimating the relationship between this variable and the ratio of NPLs to total loans. An alternative approach, data permitting, is to compile an indicator measuring the corporate sector's flow exposure, such as a ratio of foreign exchange earnings to total earnings, or a ratio of foreign exchange earnings to foreign exchange interest and principal expenses. Combining such data with a data set of past corporate failures allows for performing a more direct analysis of links between exchange rate changes and corporate defaults.

In the absence of more granular data, a useful way of approximating the effect of an exchange rate shock on credit risk is to assume that the change in the NPLs is proportional to the volume of foreign exchange loans in a bank. This assumption is based on the observation that depreciation increases the domestic currency value of these loans, which increases the difficulty for some borrowers, particularly for those with limited access to foreign currency, to repay.

Interbank (Solvency) Contagion Risk

Two basic types of the interbank (solvency) contagion stress tests are available: (1) the "pure" contagion stress test (Blåvarg and Niemander 2002) and (2) the "macro" contagion stress test (Elsinger, Lehar, and Summer 2003; Čihák, Heřmánek, and Hlaváček 2007). The "pure" contagion stress test shows what would happen with the capital of a bank if another bank (or group of banks) failed and defaulted on its interbank borrowing. This framework is actually a series of separate stress tests, showing for each bank what would be the direct impact of its failure on the capital of each of the other banks. The test is run in several iterations, as the initial failures (first iteration) can induce failures in other banks (second iterations), which can lead to yet other failures in subsequent iterations.

The "pure" contagion stress test is useful primarily because it provides a measure of systemic importance of individual banks: the bigger the decline in the system's capital or capital adequacy ratio, the more systemically important the bank whose default is assumed. The drawback of the "pure" test is that it does not reflect the different

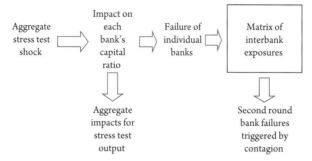

Figure 16.4 "Macro" Interbank Contagion. This figure summarizes the "macro" contagion stress test. In the test, adverse macroeconomic developments weaken the banking system and trigger one or more bank failures. For the failed banks, an interbank contagion exercise is conducted using the matrix of net interbank exposures. Then, a search is conducted for banks that fail in this first iteration. If no new failures occur, the exercise stops. If new failures occur, another iteration is run, calculating the impact of the additional failures on other banks. When the contagion-induced failures do not lead to other failures, the process stops.

likelihood of failures in different banks, an issue that is addressed by the "macro" interbank contagion test.

A "macro" contagion stress test models the case when macroeconomic developments trigger bank failures. The starting point for the "macro" interbank contagion is therefore the post-shock value of capital and risk-weighted assets. For the failed banks, an interbank contagion exercise is conducted using the matrix of net interbank exposures. Then, a search is conducted for banks that fail in this first iteration. If no new failures occur, the contagion test stops at this point. But if new failures exist, a second iteration is run looking at the impact of the additional failures on other banks. The process stops when the contagion-induced failures do not lead to other failures. Figure 16.4 shows this process.

The key difference between the "pure" and the "macro" contagion stress tests is that the "pure" contagion test assumes that a failure occurs in a single bank for some internal reason such as fraudulent behavior within the bank, and it does not distinguish the relative likelihood of the failure of various banks. Thus, the "macro" contagion test analyzes situations when all banks are weakened at the same time by a common external (typically macroeconomic) shock, which affects each bank differently depending on its exposures to the various risk factors, and makes some banks fail.

Liquidity Tests and Liquidity Contagion

Modeling liquidity risks is complex requiring very detailed, high frequency data. Moreover, modeling the impact of large liquidity shocks requires considering the broader liquidity management framework, in particular, the lender of last resort function of many central banks. At the same time, testing for liquidity risks is important.

From the late 1980s to the financial crisis of 2007–2008, much of the attention in risk management and prudential supervision was on capital, with relatively less attention paid to cash flows and analysis of liquidity (Goodhart 2006). The impact of the financial crisis reinforces the importance of understanding liquidity under stress.

The presentation of the stress test impact is different from the solvency tests discussed previously. The impact of liquidity shocks is typically shown in terms of the number of days the bank would be able to survive a liquidity drain without resorting to liquidity from outside (i.e., from other banks or the central bank). In general, supervisors usually see five days as an important threshold for a bank's ability to withstand a liquidity run. The reason is that after five days or less, banks will close for a weekend or a holiday, giving some "breathing time" for the bank management and supervisors to regroup, assess the situation, and decide on measures and public announcements to make. Of course, the growth of direct banking has partly diluted this general framework.

One example of liquidity test is a liquidity drain that affects banks depending on their volumes of demand and time deposits. The test is based on assumptions on the percentage of demand deposits and time deposits withdrawn daily and on the percentage of liquid assets and other assets that banks can convert to cash daily.

Another example is "liquidity contagion" in which the liquidity drain starts in the smallest or weakest banks and is tested to determine how this can affect the larger or stronger banks. The test allows for three possible measures of "bank safety": (1) total assets, (2) total assets with a premium for state ownership, and (3) pre-shock rating. In the first case, depositors perceive bank safety as linked to the size of the bank, approximated by total assets. In the second case, they also perceive state-owned banks safer than privately owned banks because of an explicit or implicit government guarantee in the former case. In the third case, depositors' perceptions of bank safety are correlated with the banks' recent financial performance. Liquidity contagion can also be thought of in terms of a similar "exposure" matrix as used in the solvency contagion, only instead of "net uncollateralized interbank lending," the value of the variable in the matrix for liquidity contagion would be the difference between bank A's and bank B's measure of "distance" as a proxy for exposure.

As part of liquidity stress tests, another possibility is to include the liquidity impact of government default with a bank run. The key assumption in this calculation involves the percentage of the government bonds that are in default.

Scenarios

The main reason for using scenarios rather than single factor shocks is that changes in several risk factors are typically interrelated. For example, a large increase in nominal interest rates can lead to an increase in real interest rates, which can contribute to an increase in NPLs. Banks are then hit not only by the direct impact of the nominal increase in interest rates but also by the indirect impact through credit risk.

Two main ways are available for asking questions about exposures in the financial system. The first way is to ask, for a given level of plausibility, which scenario has the worst impact on the system ("the worst-case approach"). The second way is to ask, for a given impact on the system, what is the most plausible combination of shocks that would need to occur to have that impact (known as "reverse stress test" or the "threshold approach").

When summing the impacts of shocks, taking into account concentration of risks is important. Simply aggregating losses caused by individual shocks could overlook situations when risks are concentrated in an institution or a group of institutions. Calculating the impacts bank-by-bank permits examining which banks are hit by the combination of shocks harder than others.

Combining solvency and liquidity risks is not a trivial matter but it can be done. Čihák (2007a) illustrates this combination using a supervisory early warning system to combine the changes in solvency and liquidity to identify the change in the supervisory rating, and the implied change in probability of default.

Figure 16.5 shows the process of scenario selection under the worst-case approach and the threshold approach (reverse stress test), for a simplified case when only two risk factors exist (e.g., changes in interest rates and exchange rates). Each ellipse depicts the set of combinations of the two risk factors with the same probability of occurrence. The shape of the ellipse reflects the correlation between the two factors, and its size reflects the level of plausibility (the larger the ellipse, the smaller is the plausibility). The diagonal lines depict combinations of the risk factors leading to the same overall impact, measured here by a change in the system's CAR. The impact increases with the size of the shocks to the risk factors, so the CAR decreases in the northeast direction.

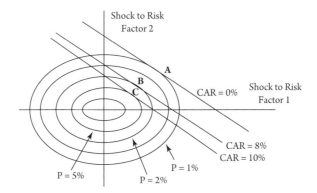

Figure 16.5 Worst-Case Approach vs. Threshold Approach. This figure shows scenario selection under the worst-case approach and the threshold approach (reverse stress test) for the case of two risk factors. Each ellipse depicts the set of combinations of the two risk factors with the same probability of occurrence. The shape of the ellipse reflects the correlation between the two factors, and its size reflects the level of plausibility (the larger the ellipse, the smaller is the plausibility). The diagonal lines depict combinations of the risk factors leading to the same overall impact, measured here by a change in the system's capital adequacy ratio (CAR). The impact increases with the size of the shocks to the risk factors, so the CAR decreases in the northeast direction. The diagonal lines do not have to be straight; they are only depicted here as such for simplicity. The worst-case approach and the reverse stress test are two essentially equivalent ways of analyzing the same problem.

The diagonal lines do not have to be straight; they are only depicted here as such for simplicity. Figure 16.5 illustrates that the worst-case approach and the reverse stress test are two essentially equivalent ways of analyzing the same problem.

The worst-case approach starts with selecting a level of plausibility (e.g., 1 percent), and searching for the combination of shocks with this level of plausibility that has the worst impact on the portfolio. This means searching for the point on the largest ellipse that lies as far northeast as possible. In Figure 16.5, point A reflects this scenario.

The reverse stress test starts with selecting the threshold (i.e., the diagonal line); it then searches for the most plausible (i.e., smallest) shocks reaching this threshold. This is straightforward if only one risk factor exists. If two risk factors are present, the correlation between the risk factors should be considered. For the specific correlation pattern in Figure 16.5, selecting a threshold of zero capital adequacy would lead again to the combination of shocks corresponding to point A.

Establishing the plausibility level of a scenario can be difficult in practice given that the scenario should be a low probability "tail" event. For risk factors with good time series of historical data (in particular, for market risks), the natural starting point is to base the scenarios on the past volatility and covariance patterns. Calibrating the shocks is particularly straightforward for single-factor stress tests: an exchange rate shock can be based on, say, three standard deviations of past exchange rate changes, corresponding roughly to a 1 percent confidence level. With multiple risk factors, the joint movement of the variables should be considered (e.g., by using stochastic simulations based on macroeconomic models). Such calculations are subject to various caveats. In particular, models can breakdown for large shocks. Nonetheless, the models, if used cautiously, can help to find a first-cut approximation of stress test scenarios.

In discussions on designing stress tests, too much emphasis is placed on establishing the "right" scenario. In theory, having internally consistent scenarios, as highlighted by Figure 16.5, is important. In practice, assessing such consistency is tricky because the scenarios should also be exceptional but plausible.

How can this challenge be addressed? One approach is to choose a concrete extreme historical scenario (e.g., the East Asian crisis of 1997 or the U.S. subprime mortgage crisis of 2007) and calculate what would be the impact of repeating such a scenario or an adaptation of such scenario in the present situation of the banking system. The main advantage is that historical scenarios are easy to communicate and to implement. Also, they are plausible because such a situation actually happened. Their main disadvantage is that past crises may provide only a limited guidance on what happens for future crises. Also, the probability level of a concrete extreme historical scenario may be hard to determine.

Another approach is to use an existing macroeconomic model (e.g., a model used by the central bank for macroeconomic forecasts and policy analysis) as a basis for stochastic simulations showing the distribution of the key risk factors in the case of shocks to the model's exogenous variables. The challenge of this approach often arises from the fact that such macroeconomic models typically do not include a measure of credit risk (e.g., NPLs to total loans, or another measure of asset quality). Therefore, this approach usually involves estimating a "satellite" model that links a measure of credit risk to the variables from the macroeconomic model. Unlike the macroeconomic model, the satellite model can be estimated (and generally should be, if adequate data are available) on individual bank and even individual borrower data. The estimates from the satellite model can then be used for the balance sheet implementation.

Finally, in attempts to identify the "right" scenario, sometimes turning the question around helps. This means that instead of identifying an adverse scenario and calculating its effect on capitalization or another soundness variable, the stress tester identifies an adverse effect and then tries to calculate what would have to happen to produce the assumed affect. As Figure 16.5 illustrates, these two approaches are conceptually identical. But for identifying the scenarios, as well as for communicating and discussing results, turning the question around can be helpful.

In summary, each method has advantages and disadvantages. Picking a scenario that is stressful and tells an interesting and consistent story is important. However, in most cases, identifying the "right" scenario is an equivalent of finding the Holy Grail. Much more important than fine-tuning scenarios is (1) being transparent about the underlying assumptions of the scenarios; (2) being transparent about the sensitivity of the results to those assumptions; and (3) showing how results with the same assumptions change over time. Showing results over time allows judgments to be made about the developments in both the overall pool of risks and the structure of risks faced by a financial system.

The stress test calculations presented here focus on the impacts of shocks arising from the macroeconomic environment and affecting the financial sector. From a macroeconomic perspective, an important issue is whether the shocks in the financial sector can have feedback effects that influence the macroeconomic environment.

One direct effect that can be easily incorporated into the financial programming framework employed by the IMF is an impact on capital on "Other Items Net" in the monetary survey and thereby on other macroeconomic variables. However, this is just one of many potential impacts. In some cases, the effects depend on the behavior of the institutions in situations of stress. For example, if banks attempt to sell off certain types of assets (e.g., real estate) in situations of stress, they may bring down the asset prices, with repercussion effects for other sectors (e.g., household consumption). Also, bank failures triggered by stress may result in a credit crunch. One way to approximate the potential macroeconomic impacts is to examine the capital injection needed to bring all banks to the minimum required capital adequacy ratio. This indicator does not capture all the potential macroeconomic effects, but it is a useful broad indicator of potential fiscal costs associated with averting failures in the banking system.

Summary and Conclusions

This chapter highlights the basic stress testing techniques and some challenges to be considered by anyone attempting stress testing. An important challenge relates to the data intensity of stress testing. Stress tests are conducted based on low-probability events. This assumption implies a lack of data for stress tests. Carrying out stress tests often requires simplifying assumptions. Thus, an analyst should be transparent about the nature of the assumptions.

Another challenge is that non-linearities are likely to kick in for the large shocks that are being contemplated in stress tests. Also, standard models tend to breakdown in crises. Past crises may not be a good guide for the future. As an example, a change in borrower characteristics may leave credit more vulnerable to interest rate risk.

To make things worse, the impact of shocks is distributed over time. Time is needed for asset quality to deteriorate and for that deterioration to have an impact. When a system finds itself in a crisis, that crisis will evolve over a period of time, sometimes many years. Therefore, modeling stressful scenarios has to consider the time dimension. For example, the Bank of England's stress tests look at impacts over a period of two to three years. Clarifying the benchmark scenario against which the stressful scenario is compared is important. Participants and authorities can take various mitigating measures, especially if they are looking at longer time periods. Also, feedback effects start playing a role over time.

Addressing these challenges requires keeping stress testing assumptions transparent. Clarifying the sensitivity of the results to the assumptions is also important. This clarification should be the one key message from this chapter: assumptions matter and they particularly matter in stress testing.

A related important step in addressing the stress testing challenges is to present stress test results over time. Presenting results over time helps to say whether the overall pool of risks has changed or whether the structure of risks has changed. Most financial stability reports still do not provide results over time, which makes interpreting the presented results more difficult (Čihák 2006).

Stress testing can be developed in a modular fashion, with additional modules capturing additional risks or elaborating on the existing ones. Many extensions are possible as more data become available. For example, an important extension relates to the modeling of the credit risk-macro nexus. Credit risk is the main source of risk in most financial systems. At the same time, it is the part where this exercise is perhaps the most simplified. Ideally, more detailed data on loan exposures and loan performance by economic sector would be needed in addition to data on the financial soundness of the corporate and household sectors. Analysts should ideally use time series of historical data to establish linkages between macroeconomic variables and loan performance or, in the absence of reliable time series, estimates from other countries could be used.

Discussion Questions

1. Assume that the interest rate sensitivities of a financial institution's assets and liabilities are perfectly matched. Discuss whether the institution has a zero interest rate risk.
2. Discuss whether the following statement is correct: For direct foreign exchange risk calculations, off-balance sheet positions need to be excluded from the net open position.
3. Identify which type of foreign exchange solvency risk is larger for most banks—direct or indirect—and explain why.
4. Discuss the differences between a "pure" and "macro" interbank contagion test.
5. Discuss whether the following statement is correct: The "worst-case approach" to stress testing allows for creating more stressful scenarios than the "threshold approach."

References

Babouček, Ivan, and Martin Jančar. 2005. "Effects of Macroeconomic Shocks to the Quality of the Aggregate Loan Portfolio." CNB Working Paper 1/2005, Czech National Bank. Available at http://www.cnb.cz/www.cnb.cz/en/research/cnb_wp/download/cnbwp_2005_01.pdf.

Bierwag, Gerald. 1987. *Duration Analysis.* Cambridge, MA: Harper & Row.

Blaschke, Winfrid, Matthew Jones, Giovanni Majnoni, and Maria Soledad Martinez Peria. 2001. "Stress Testing of Financial Systems: An Overview of Issues, Methodologies, and FSAP Experiences." IMF Working Paper 01/88. Washington, DC: International Monetary Fund.

Blåvarg, Martin, and Patrick Niemander. 2002. "Inter-bank Exposures and Systemic Risk." *Sveriges Bank Economic Review* 2002:2, 19–45.

Boss, Michael, Gerald Krenn, Markus Schwaiger, and Wolfgang Wegschaider. 2004. "Stress Testing the Austrian Banking System." *Österreichisches Bankarchiv* 11:04, 841–852.

Boyd, John, and David Runkle. 1993. "Size and Performance of Banking Firms." *Journal of Monetary Economics* 31:1, 47–67.

Bunn, Philip, Alastair Cunningham, and Mathias Drehmann. 2005. "Stress Testing as a Tool for Assessing Systemic Risks." *Bank of England Financial Stability Review*, June, 116–126. Available at http://www.bankofengland.co.uk/publications/Documents/fsr/2005/fsrfull0506.pdf.

Čihák, Martin. 2004a. "Stress Testing: A Review of Key Concepts." Czech National Bank Research Policy Note 2/2004. Available at http://www.cnb.cz/en/pdf/IRPN_2_2004.pdf.

Čihák, Martin. 2004b. "Designing Stress Tests for the Czech Banking System." Czech National Bank Research Policy Note 3/2004. Available at http://www.cnb.cz/en/pdf/IRPN_3_2004.pdf.

Čihák, Martin. 2005. "Stress Testing of Banking Systems." *Finance a úvěr/Czech Journal of Economics and Finance* 55:9–10, 418–440.

Čihák, Martin. 2006. "How Do Central Banks Write on Financial Stability?" IMF Working Paper 06/163. Washington, DC: International Monetary Fund. Available at www.imf.org/external/pubs/ft/wp/2006/wp06163.pdf.

Čihák, Martin. 2007a. "Introduction to Applied Stress Testing." IMF Working Paper 10/282. Washington, DC: International Monetary Fund. Available at http://www.imf.org/external/pubs/ft/wp/2007/wp0759.pdf.

Čihák, Martin. 2007b. "Systemic Loss: A Measure of Financial Stability." *Finance a úvěr/Czech Journal of Economics and Finance* 57:1–2, 5–26.

Čihák, Martin, Jaroslav Heřmánek, and Michal Hlaváček. 2007. "New Approaches to Stress Testing the Czech Banking Sector." *Finance a úvěr/Czech Journal of Economics and Finance* 57:1–2, 41–59.

Danmarks Nationalbank. 2004. "Market-Based Risk Measures for Banks." *Financial Stability 2004.* Copenhagen: Denmark National Bank.

Drehmann, Matthias. 2005. *A Market Based Macro Stress Test for the Corporate Credit Exposures of UK Banks.* Available at http://www.bis.org/bcbs/events/rtf05Drehmann.pdf.

Eklund, Trond, Kai Larsen, and Eivind Berhardsen. 2003. "Model for Analyzing Credit Risk in the Enterprise Sector." Available at http://www.norges-bank.no/english/publications/economic_bulletin/2001-03/eklund-larsen.pdf.

Elsinger, Helmut, Alfred Lehar, and Martin Summer. 2003. "Risk Assessment for Banking Systems." 14th Annual Utah Winter Finance Conference Paper, EFA 2003 Annual Conference Paper 437.

Evjen, Snorre, Arild Lund, Kjersti Haare Morka, Kjell Nordal, and Ingvild Svendsen. 2005. "Monetary and Financial Stability in Norway: What Can We Learn from Macroeconomic Stress Tests?" *BIS Papers* 22. Basel: Bank for International Settlements. Available at http://www.bis.org/publ/bppdf/bispap22u.pdf.

Gerlach, Stefan, Wensheng Peng, and Chang Shu. 2004. "Macroeconomic Conditions and Banking Performance in Hong Kong: A Panel Data Study." Hong Kong Monetary Authority

Research Memorandum. Available at http://www.info.gov.hk/hkma/eng/research/RM_macro_and_banking.pdf.

Goodhart, Charles. 2006. "A Framework for Assessing Financial Stability?" *Journal of Banking and Finance* 30:12, 3415–3422.

Hesse, Heiko, and Martin Čihák. 2007. "Cooperative Banks and Financial Stability." IMF Working Paper 07/02. Washington, DC: International Monetary Fund.

International Monetary Fund. 2003. "Financial Soundness Indicators—Background Paper." May 14. Washington, DC: International Monetary Fund.

International Monetary Fund. 2004. *Financial Soundness Indicators Compilation Guide.* Washington, DC: International Monetary Fund.

International Monetary Fund and the World Bank. 2005. *Financial Sector Assessment: A Handbook.* Washington, DC: International Monetary Fund and World Bank.

Jones, Matthew, Paul Hilbers, and Graham Slack. 2004. "Stress Testing Financial Systems: What to Do When the Governor Calls." IMF Working Paper No. 04/127. Washington, DC: International Monetary Fund.

Kraft, Evan, and Tomislav Galac. 2007. "Deposit Interest Rates, Asset Risk and Bank Failure in Croatia." *Journal of Financial Stability* 2:4, 337–355.

Lucas, Robert. 1976. "Econometric Policy Evaluation: A Critique." Carnegie-Rochester Conference Series on Public Policy 1, 19–46.

Peng, Wensheng, Kitty Lai, Frank Leung, and Chang Shu. 2003. "The Impact of Interest Rate Shocks on the Performance of the Banking Sector," Hong Kong Monetary Authority Research Memorandum. May. Available at http://www.info.gov.hk/hkma/eng/research/RM07-2003.pdf.

Pesola, Jarmo. 2005. "Banking Fragility and Distress: An Econometric Study of Macroeconomic Determinants." Bank of Finland Research Discussion Paper 13. Helsinki: Bank of Finland. Available at http://www.bof.fi/eng/6_julkaisut/6.1_SPn_julkaisut/6.1.5_Keskustelualoitteita/0513netti.pdf.

Sahajwala, Ranjana, and Paul Van den Bergh. 2000. "Supervisory Risk Assessment and Early Warning Systems." Basel Committee on Banking Supervision Working Paper 4. Available at http://www.bis.org/publ/bcbs_wp4.pdf.

Virolainen, Kimmo. 2004. "Macro Stress Testing with a Macroeconomic Credit Risk Model for Finland." Bank of Finland Discussion Paper 18/2004.

17

Risk Management and Regulation

DAVID E. ALLEN

Adjunct Professor, Centre for Applied Financial Studies, University of South Australia, and
Visiting Professor, School of Mathematics and Statistics, University of Sydney

ROBERT J. POWELL

Associate Professor, School of Business, Edith Cowan University

ABHAY K. SINGH

Lecturer, School of Business, Edith Cowan University

Introduction

Earlier chapters in this book introduced different risk measurement concepts and considered various ways of analyzing, assessing, controlling, and hedging risk. This chapter considers the regulation of risk, which is appraised in the context of global financial markets and institutions with particular reference to the financial crisis of 2007–2008 also called the global financial crisis (GFC).

The management and regulation of risk should be considered in the context of the processes at work within the financial system as reflected in the financial institutions operating within it and the various associated markets comprising the international financial system. The chapter begins by considering both the roles of institutions and markets before considering the various types of risk in the context of the operations of the financial system. It also examines its integral components and the manner in which the various manifestations of risk need to be monitored, managed, and regulated.

Financial markets are linked around the globe via a vast network of international telecommunications. The growth of the World Wide Web is the most recent and fundamental advance. The financial instruments traded in these markets include more standard financial claims such as fixed income and equity securities, foreign exchange transactions, plus the vast array of derivative securities such as futures, options, and swaps.

If the instruments are highly standardized, they can trade in regulated, open markets including online outlets. However, financial intermediaries focus on more specialized transactions. Financial intermediaries provide customized products and services that are less susceptible to standardization. A *financial intermediary* is an entity that connects savings-surplus and savings-deficit agents. A classic example of a financial intermediary is a bank that transforms its deposits into loans. Through the process of financial intermediation, certain assets or liabilities are transformed into different assets or liabilities.

As such, financial intermediaries channel funds from people who have extra money (savers) to those who do not have enough money (borrowers) to carry out a desired activity. Lenders and borrowers have conflicting needs. For example, most lenders prefer lending short term, while most borrowers prefer borrowing long term. As a result, most intermediation is done indirectly in which intermediaries understand and reconcile the different needs of lenders and borrowers. Financial intermediaries play a special role in the economy. Financial intermediaries take advantage of economies of scale to reduce transaction costs, while financial institutions assist in the process of risk sharing and diversification. Financial institutions also overcome the problems of adverse selection and moral hazard.

Adverse selection refers to the perverse outcome that a tightening of conditions to avoid risk may paradoxically attract higher risks. A common example is that of insurance companies that might increase the price of insurance policies and as a result attract a higher risk clientele. These individuals are prepared to pay the higher premiums as they perceive their risks as being relatively high justifying the increased premium expenditure. The problem is related to a lack of full information on the part of the insurer about the true risks faced by its customers.

Moral hazard is similarly related to asymmetric information on the part of two parties to a transaction. Potential borrowers may have an incentive to claim that they are low risk when in fact they are high risk. If a financial institution has a continuing and long-standing relationship with customers, its ability to monitor their accounts and cash balances may give a more accurate picture of their true risks and reduce the problem of moral hazard.

A financial system provides a system of clearing payments for facilitating trade. Primary markets exist for issuing securities of various types (e.g., stock exchanges for equity issuance), while secondary market functions provide liquidity for the purchase and sale of existing securities. The primary market functions permit risk capital issuance and the pooling of financial resources. They also provide a means of reallocating consumption and savings across individuals and entities as well as across national borders and through time. Securities can be repackaged into portfolios; investments can be professionally managed; and risks can be pooled. Risk management and reallocation are key functions of financial markets and institutions.

Allen (2001) queries whether financial institutions "matter" and points to the treatment of financial institutions as a "veil" in the standard theory of finance, which treats them as being unimportant. The counterargument is that issues such as agency costs, which are taken seriously in corporate finance but not in asset pricing theory, cause financial institutions to matter. This chapter considers a view that proved to be very prescient in terms of the recent events triggered by the GFC as well as the causes of the crisis and the responses by regulators.

The Links between Economic Circumstances and Regulation

The context and nature of current financial market regulations and attitudes about risk management are more intelligible if they are placed in a historical and economic context. This section considers responses by U.S. authorities to the events of the early decades of the twentieth century.

THE REGULATORY RESPONSE TO THE GREAT DEPRESSION

Calomiris (2010) suggests that the three most important regulatory responses by U.S. authorities to the Great Depression in the context of banking were Regulation Q limits on bank interest payments, the exclusion of underwriting activities from depository banks, and the creation of federal deposit insurance. He notes that regulators consciously designed these responses either to perpetuate unit banking or to facilitate continuing adherence to the real bills doctrine, which is the goal of Regulation Q and the separation of investment banking from commercial banking. Calomiris regards these aspects of the U.S. banking system and regulation as causing the most harm to banks and the economy during the 1930s. Unit banking made banks less diversified and more fragile. The real bills doctrine led to a tightening of credit policy and an increase in interest rates in a counter-cyclical manner exacerbating economic contractions.

The impact of these measures was long lasting. Calomiris (2010) comments that unwinding the Regulation Q limits on deposit interest required more than half a century. The regulators realized the impact after the limits had produced large-scale disintermediation from banking that occurred in the 1960s and 1970s. This was a rational response by depositors seeking higher rates of return in reaction to the accelerating inflation of that era and the limited nominal interest rates permitted under Regulation Q.

Keynesian economics (Keynes 1919, 1936) greatly influenced the response to the Great Depression. Keynes viewed that private sector decisions may lead to inefficient macroeconomic outcomes. Such decisions necessitate policy responses by the authorities, such as appropriate central bank monetary policy and fiscal policy measures by the government, in order to ensure demand equates to output over the business cycle. Keynes (1937, p. 221) suggests the following:

> This that I offer is, therefore, a theory of why output and employment are so liable to fluctuation. It does not offer a ready-made remedy as to how to avoid these fluctuations and to maintain output at a steady optimum level. But it is, properly speaking, a Theory of Employment because it explains why, in any given circumstances, employment is what it is.

Thus, the general approach at the time was of a greater readiness to intervene in market processes and to fix interest rates and exchange rates. The government regulated the banks as a group of identifiable homogeneous institutions with a key role to play in providing credit and implementing monetary policy.

The prospect of changed economic conditions in the immediate post–World War II period led the authorities to create important changes in the institutional framework that had subsequent implications for financial innovation and risk management. The reaction to the Great Depression of the 1930s saw the instatement of the Bretton Woods system of global monetary management, which was formalized in July 1944 and set up the rules for commercial and financial relations among the world's major industrial powers. The agreement led to the creation of the International Monetary Fund (IMF) and the International Bank for Reconstruction and Development (IBRD). The core of the agreement involved a system in which each country tied its currency to the U.S. dollar and managed its exchange rate with a role given to the IMF for bridging temporary imbalances of payments. The focus was on regulation and intervention rather than permitting markets the freedom to respond to market conditions.

Financial Innovation and the Circumvention of Regulation

Van-Horne (1984, p. 621) describes financial innovation as being "one of the bedrocks of our financial system." He suggests that financial innovations may be products or processes, are rarely completely new, and frequently involve modifying an existing idea. A viable financial innovation usually must make the markets more efficient in an operational sense and/or more complete in the sense of spanning more contingencies. A margin or spread often exists between the rate at which institutions raise funds to finance intermediary activities and the rate they charge for providing the required means of funding or service. A financial innovation may reduce the cost or size of this spread or provide the service in a more convenient form. One example would be the switch to providing financial services via the Internet as represented by online banking, brokering, and security trading services. Financial innovations often arise in response to regulatory barriers, profit opportunities, or some form of market incompleteness.

Benston and Smith (1975, p. 215), who analyze financial intermediation in terms of the way in which intermediation can serve to provide reductions in costs, state:

> We view the role of the financial intermediary as creating specialized financial commodities. These commodities are created whenever an intermediary finds that it can sell them for prices which are expected to cover all costs of their production, both direct costs and opportunity costs.

The authors provide an example of how the New York Stock Exchange (NYSE) provides a market for trading securities in which listed securities are traded in one location with listing requirements that serve to reduce information and search costs.

A recent phenomenon, partly engendered by the growth of the World Wide Web, is the reduction in search costs produced by the web and the development of efficient search engines such as Google. This change is gradually leading to an increasing fragmentation of markets as physical locations are becoming less important. These technical and communications developments are also leading to the demise of traditional stock broking services and market-making services, as these can now be provided over the web, and the use of electronic trading mechanisms continues to grow. Thus, technical change and advances in communications systems stimulate financial innovation given that finance and financial markets are often concerned with creating and transmitting information.

ECONOMIC DEVELOPMENTS, REGULATORY RESPONSES, AND FINANCIAL INNOVATION

The economic system continually evolves. The first section mentioned the regulatory response to the Great Depression and some post–World War II initiatives. Other changes based on prevailing economic circumstances gradually overtook these changes. The development of swaps provides a good example of how economic circumstances and regulatory restrictions can lead to financial innovation.

Under the Bretton Woods system, the United Kingdom had to undertake a fixed rate of exchange relative to other currencies. The Bank of England accomplished this strategy by using the Exchange Equalization Account (EEA), in which it held foreign exchange that could be used to purchase sterling. However, in the 1950s and 1960s, the dollar replaced the sterling as a reserve currency and current account surpluses were unavailable to provide the required foreign exchange. Sterling was subject to a series of exchange crises. Britain adopted a dual exchange market in which all capital transactions undertaken by residents and nonresidents took place at the financial exchange rate, and all current transactions took place at the official exchange rate. The imbalance of supply and demand meant that U.K. residents faced a premium in buying foreign currency. This imbalance led to several financial innovations that ultimately launched a more active swaps market.

Currency swaps emerged in the 1970s to circumvent the restrictions faced in the United Kingdom. If U.K. companies had a desire to borrow in U.S. dollars, they had to pay a premium to do so. To avoid this, U.K. companies set up back-to-back loan agreements with U.S. companies wanting to borrow in sterling. U.S. companies would borrow U.S. dollars on behalf of U.K. companies, and they would do likewise in sterling for their U.S. counterparts. Thus, this exchange restriction led to the development of parallel or back-to-back loans. These transactions set the stage for the construction of swaps.

IBM and the World Bank initiated the first interest rate swap in 1981. IBM had large amounts of Swiss franc and German deutsche mark debt and payment obligations in Swiss francs and deutsche marks. Interest rates were much higher at the time in the United States than in Germany or Switzerland. IBM and the World Bank worked out an arrangement in which the World Bank borrowed dollars in the U.S. market and swapped the dollar payment obligation to IBM in exchange for taking over IBM's Swiss franc and deutsche mark obligations (Arnold 1984). From this inaugural agreement, the swap market has expanded to the extent that now trillions of dollars of swaps are arranged in a massive global market. The Bank for International Settlements (BIS) suggests this amount stood at $24.740 billion at the end of 2012.

By the 1980s, strong pressure existed from economic and political forces in some of the developed nations to increase the exposure of national financial systems to the effects of market forces. The international markets were becoming globalized and inter-linked. The 1970s had seen increasing competition from foreign banks that started to open branches in London. The traditional distinction between banking and building society activities in the United Kingdom began to breakdown. Tremendous growth in the Eurobond market occurred in the 1970s. International trading in the securities of multinational firms began to develop. The possibility of continuous global 24-hour trading arranged across the major financial centers started to emerge. The removal of foreign exchange trading controls in 1979 was one of the first major financial reforms by the Thatcher administration. Twenty-four hour trading in the foreign exchange markets became virtually possible and included London as a major center. The Euronote market expanded rapidly in the early 1980s and banks moved into the securitization market, which further eroded the distinctions between bank and non-bank financial intermediaries.

Then in 1986, the "Big Bang" took place in the United Kingdom. These reforms, encouraged by the Thatcher administration, included the abolition of fixed commission charges and of the distinction between stockjobbers and stockbrokers on the London Stock Exchange. The switch was also made from open-outcry to electronic, screen-based trading. At that time, regulators expressed concern that a stock exchange club excluding foreigners and operating a different dealing system from that of the United States was in danger of becoming outdated and was likely to suffer a consequent loss of business.

In the United States, various deregulatory changes were underway and eventually instituted under the Reagan administration. Legislators made a series of moves to deregulate the activities of savings and loans associations (S&Ls) or "thrifts," and the passage of the 1982 Garn-St. Germain Depository Institutions Act deregulated them almost entirely. This Act permitted commercial lending and competition with money market mutual funds, but led to subsequent problems. For example, between 1981 and 1986, the percentage of thrift assets in home mortgage loans shrank from 78 percent to 56 percent as thrifts pursued more risky leading opportunities such as commercial real estate. The passage of the Tax Reform Act of 1986 meant that many of the previous tax shelters were no longer available to real estate investors, causing a drop in demand and a crisis in the industry with many thrift insolvencies. In 1989, Congress created the Office of Thrift Supervision to regulate S&Ls. Related legislation formed the Resolution Trust Corporation (RTC) to dissolve and merge troubled institutions resulting in a virtual reduction by half of the number of institutions. Auerback and Slemrod (1997) discuss the economic impact of the Tax Reform Act.

More radical changes in the context of banking took place in the 1990s including the Riegle-Neal bill in 1994 to eliminate previous interstate banking restrictions. The restrictions on the combination of investment and retail banking inherent in the Glass-Steagall Act were gradually loosened. In 1996, bank holding companies received permission to earn up to 25 percent of their revenues in investment banking. In 1999, the passage of the Gramm-Leach-Bliley Act, which had the support of the Federal Reserve Chairman Alan Greenspan and the Treasury Secretary Robert Rubin, removed the Glass-Steagall Act entirely. In 2000, the Commodity Futures Modernization Act was enacted, which ensured most over-the-counter (OTC) derivative contracts, including credit default swaps, did not fall under regulation by the Commodity Futures Trading Commission (CFTC).

These changes set the scene for some developments that lead to the GFC, which will be considered subsequently. They are also a feature of the dynamic nature of the evolution of global financial markets that Kane (2012) interprets as a dialectical process.

REGULATORY DIALECTIC

Kane (2012) describes the continual dynamic interplay between economic and technical developments and regulatory imposition and innovation to circumvent the regulatory restrictions as a "regulatory dialectic." Kane (p. 3) suggests the following:

> The Hegelian Dialectical Model seeks to explain institutional change as a process of Conflict Generation, Conflict Resolution, and Conflict Renewal. The process has three stages: Thesis-Antithesis-Synthesis. The predictive power of this evolutionary model comes from positing that each synthesis serves as a thesis to be challenged afresh by new ideas and experience.

Kane indicates that applying this approach to regulation means that as quickly as the regulatory authorities pass new regulation, innovative financial entities will develop new ways of avoiding their grasp. This chapter returns to this argument when the discussion turns to the events leading up the GFC.

The ability to innovate and change the nature of both the financial intermediaries and the financial instruments used for a given purpose led to a call for the regulation of financial functions, not the classes of intermediaries per se, as was the case before the 1980s. An example in Australia is provided by the building societies that were lightly regulated. Building societies are the equivalent of "thrifts" in the United States, accepting funds on deposit, paying interest on them, and repackaging them into much larger loans for property purchase, By contrast, the banks were relatively heavily regulated until the deregulation in Australian financial markets during the early 1980s. This difference prevailed despite the fact that both offered many similar services. The functional view of regulation is the framework for capturing this view and would treat banks and building societies performing the same functions in a similar fashion in terms of their regulation.

A FUNCTIONAL VIEW OF FINANCIAL REGULATION

Merton and Bodie (1995) discuss a conceptual framework for analyzing fundamental institutional changes in financial systems. This framework's objectives are designed to improve understanding of how and why financial institutions change. The framework should assist in facilitating the making of accurate predictions about how financial institutions are likely to evolve and to assist and guide the development of business strategy and public policy in this arena.

The central pillar of their approach is a focus on functions rather than institutions as the lens through which to perceive change. Merton and Bodie (1995) contend that economic functions, such as size and risk transformation by intermediaries or the hedging and pooling of risks, change less over time and across borders than the institutional and market framework for pursuing these functions.

According to Merton and Bodie (1995), institutional structure follows function and competition, and innovation among institutions results in greater efficiency in the performance of these functions. They apply their approach to analyzing key public policy issues facing the international financial system such as accounting for risk, derivatives regulation, deposit insurance reform, pension reform and privatization, and the international harmonization of regulatory policies.

The evolution of the financial system is described by using the term *innovation spiral* in which organized markets and intermediaries compete with each other in a static sense and complement each other in a dynamic sense. The continuing process of innovation drives the financial system toward achieving greater efficiency.

To illustrate the core concept embodied in the functional view, Merton and Bodie (1995) enumerate the many ways in which an investor could take a levered position in the S&P 500 stock constituents. They suggest the following transactions:

1. Buying each stock individually on margin in the cash stock market.
2. Investing in an S&P 500 index fund and financing the purchase from a bank.
3. Going long on a future contract on the S&P 500 index.
4. Going long on an OTC forward contract on the S&P 500 index.
5. Entering into a swap contract to receive the total return on the S&P 500 index and pay the London Interbank Offered Rate (LIBOR) or some other standard interest rate.
6. Going long on exchange-traded calls and short puts on the S&P 500 index.
7. Going long on OTC calls and shorting puts.
8. Purchasing an equity-linked note that pays based on the S&P 500 index and financing it with a purchase agreement.
9. Purchasing from a bank a certificate of deposit with its payments linked to the return on the S&P 500 index.
10. Buying on margin or purchasing the capital appreciation component of a unit investment trust (e.g., Super Shares or SPDRs) that holds the S&P 500 index.
11. Borrowing to buy a variable-rate annuity contract that has its return linked to the S&P 500 index.

The authors also suggest that from an economic theory point of view all these are equivalent. In a neoclassical economics world, the role of institutional arrangements is regarded as a market friction. Thus, if transactions costs are assumed away, institutions cease to matter.

If the institutional view of the market is adopted, then all transactions that achieve the same economic purpose will be regulated in different ways. In case 1, the operation involves the stock market, case 3 involves forward contracts traded in the futures market, while case 4 involves the OTC market. Case 5 involves swaps, which are different instruments but they also trade on the OTC. Case 6 involves traded puts and calls and so on. The point is that although all of these markets and the instruments within them are subject to different institutional arrangements, costs, and regulation, the economic purpose of the transactions is identical.

The regulatory authorities have moved toward adopting this conceptual framework to some degree. Successive Basel Agreements by the BIS provide a good example.

Regulation and the Basel Agreements

The Bank for International Settlements (BIS) was originally set up in 1930 to deal with German reparation payments required under the Treaty of Versailles following the conclusion of World War I. The BIS has a mission to act as a banker for central banks, to assist central banks in their pursuit of monetary and financial stability, and to promote international cooperation in those areas. The Basel Committee of the BIS acts as a global standard-setter for the prudential regulation of banks and provides a forum for cooperation on banking supervisory matters.

The Basel I Accord was released in July 1988 with the intention of strengthening the soundness and stability of the international banking system and providing a fair framework for capital adequacy that would have consistency in its application in different countries. Its primary focus was on credit risk and the risk-weighting of assets (Basel Committee on Banking Supervision 1988).

In the Basel I Accord, bank assets are ranked and grouped into five categories according to their level of credit risk. Cash, bullion, government securities, and government guaranteed securities are given a zero risk weighting. Claims on domestic public sector entities are allocated discretionary weightings between 0 percent and 50 percent. Claims on other banks are given a 20 percent weighting, while loans secured against property require a 50 percent weighting, and corporate debt and other claims require a 100 percent weighting.

The capital base consists of two tiers. Tier 1 comprises paid-up share capital/common stock plus disclosed reserves. Tier 2 consists of undisclosed reserves, asset revaluation reserves, general provisions/general loan-loss reserves, hybrid (debt/equity) capital instruments, and subordinated debt. Banks have to hold a minimum of 8 percent of their risk-weighted assets as Tier 1 capital. Tier 3 capital included an even greater variety of debts made up of subordinated issues, undisclosed reserves, and general loss provisions.

Tier 1 capital ratio = Tier 1 Capital/All risk-weighted assets.
Total capital ratio = Tier 1 + Tier 2 + Tier 3 Capital/All risk-weighted assets.
Leverage ratio = Total capital/Average weighted assets.

Clearly, if the Basel I Accord was to be successful, the banks had to maintain adequate capital ratios. The requirement to maintain these ratios could act as a constraint on their ability to write further loans. One way of trying to avoid the constraints of some of these restrictions is to engage in regulatory capital arbitrage by means of securitization. Suppose a bank has $1 million in mortgage loans for which it has to hold 4 percent capital or $40,000. It can securitize the loans by forming a collateralized debt obligation (CDO). The bank sells them to a specially created special purpose vehicle (SPV) that issues bonds to investors, backed by the SPV pool. These bonds are backed by the regular mortgage payments on the mortgages. If the credit rating agencies offer a higher rating to the investments higher in the tranche structure, the bank can lower the risk weights on those tranches. A "tranche" is a French word referring to a slice or portion. In a financial context, tranche refers to a financial instrument that can be divided up into smaller subsets. The lowest tranches in the CDO may have more concentrated risk but by means of the process of reducing the average perceived risk, their capital requirements may be lowered.

The existence of agencies that were either government owned (e.g., Government National Mortgage Corporation or Ginnie Mae) or government related (e.g., Federal National Mortgage Association or Fannie Mae and the Federal Loan Mortgage Corporation or Freddie Mac) greatly assisted the process of securitization. Congress created these agencies with a view to assisting in the goal of promoting home ownership but the big advantage from the viewpoint of the process of securitization is that the market perceived them as being low-risk.

Ginnie Mae began issuing mortgage-backed securities (MBS) in 1970 and the other two entities soon followed. An advantage of using these conduits was that the market perceived them as being of low risk, with a perception that the U.S. government stood behind them. Thus, the banks could sell their mortgages to Ginnie Mae, which would package and sell them with an improved credit rating. The banks could then buy them back and require less regulatory capital to support them. The Basil I Accord permitted the U.S. banks to give such securities a 20 percent risk weighting as they were in the public sector debt category that attracted a 20 percent risk weight. Figure 17.1 summarizes this process.

Critics expressed other concerns about the potential impact of the Basel I Accord on bank activities including the view that it was insufficiently sensitive to risk. The risk-weighting framework reflected broad categories of loans and not entity risk, as reflected in, for example, credit ratings. The Basel II Accord, first published in 2004, expanded the definition of risks for which capital had to be put aside to include types of financial and operational risks that the banks and the economy face. The Basel II Accord was aimed at promoting stronger risk management practices that included more risk-sensitive capital requirements. One major innovation was adopting greater use of risk

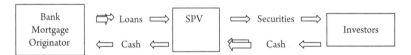

Figure 17.1 THE PROCESS OF SECURITIZATION.   This figure demonstrates the process of securitization. The bank mortgage originator typically attracts deposits from short-term depositors seeking to earn interest on their deposits with the ability to withdraw them on short notice when they want to use them. These deposits would be repackaged into longer term mortgage loans that remain on the bank's books. The process of securitization involves transferring the mortgage loans into the SPV that repackages them and sells them to investors who hold them to receive the mortgage repayments and interest. The cash paid for these repackaged securities flows back to the SPV. The bank can now make further loans and reduce its capital requirements because the loans are no longer on its books. Alternatively, if the repackaged loans have a better average credit rating, the bank could repurchase them to have these loans as assets earning a return on its books. The improved credit rating would mean the bank needs less capital to support the loans. So again, the bank can issue more loans and increase its earnings.

assessments provided by the banks' internal systems as inputs to capital calculations (Bank of International Settlements 2006).

The revised framework involved three pillars. The first pillar of the Basel II Accord, similar to the Basel I Accord, centered on credit risk, but was expanded to incorporate the standardized approach, an internal ratings based (IRB) approach, and a credit risk securitization framework. The measure also included inputs from operational risk and market risk. The other two pillars incorporated the supervisory review process and the role of market discipline.

The intention was to capture via consolidation all the activities of a bank including banking and other relevant financial activities (both regulated and unregulated) conducted within a group containing an internationally active bank. Activities under the first pillar (i.e., the maintenance of an adequate capital base) involved assessing credit risk based on either the standard approach, as introduced in the Basel I Accord or the two IRB approaches of varying degrees of sophistication.

Banks could measure operational risk in various ways. The basic indicator approach used a metric based on 15 percent of average annual gross income (ignoring loss years) over the previous three years, to calculate an amount of capital to be set aside to meet operational risk. Banks could also use the most sophisticated advanced measurement approach (AMA) based on their own model as an operational risk metric approved by local regulators. The AMA framework had to include the application of four data measurements: (1) internal loss data (ILD), (2) external data (ED), (3) scenario-based analysis (SBA), and (4) business environment and internal control factors (BEICFs). Between these two extremes, banks could also use a standardized approach in which they would segment their gross income into categories and apply a risk weight or beta coefficient for that type of income to calculate a weighted capital requirement.

Value-at-risk (VaR) is the preferred method of measuring market risk apart from using duration-based metrics for the analysis of bond price sensitivity to interest rate changes. Sir Dennis Weatherstone first adopted the use of VaR in 1989 when he was the chief executive officer (CEO) of JP Morgan and requested a daily summary of the company's risk position. In 1998, client demand for the application of this method was sufficient for the corporate risk management component of the firm to be spun off into the RiskMetrics Group. This spinoff served to popularize the use of VaR as a metric and it was adopted in the Basel II Accord. The next section provides a discussion of the attributes of VaR as a metric. The Basel III Accord, which was a response to the GFC, is discussed in a section following the consideration of the GFC.

VALUE-AT-RISK

Value-at-risk (VaR) describes the loss that can occur over a given period, at a given confidence level, due to exposure to market risk. More technically, VaR is the loss in market value of an asset over a given time period that is exceeded with a probability θ. For a time series of returns r_t, VaR_t is defined as shown in Equation 17.1:

$$\Pr{t} < VaR{t}|t - 1 = \theta, \qquad (17.1)$$

where θ is usually set at 1 percent or 5 percent reflecting the probability of breaching a lower tail quantile. A 1 percent VaR is the 1 percent breach of the return level at the 1 percent quantile in the left-hand tail of the distribution conditioned in this time series sense on the information set known in the previous period I_{t-1}. One problem with this measurement is the need to know the nature of the distribution to fit the quantile. In the early applications of VaR, banks used normal distributions. However, financial return distributions are frequently skewed and have fat tails (i.e., positive excess kurtosis), and therefore using normal distributions may lead to underestimating the probability of extreme events. Gloria Mundi (2013) provides a description of the various methodologies for the modeling of VaR. Duffie and Pan (1997) provide a comprehensive survey of the VaR concept and Beder (1995), JP Morgan and Reuters (1996), Stambaugh (1996), Jorion (1997), and Pritsker (1997) offer further discussion.

Despite its broad adoption, VaR has shortcomings. As a decision tool, VaR has certain limiting mathematical properties such as the lack of subadditivity, convexity, and monotonicity (Artzner, Delbaen, Eber, and Heath 1997, 1999). Another limitation is that VaR provides a probability for the breach of a particular quantile, but it says nothing about the size of the breach or likely losses beyond VaR. Businesses are most likely to fail during times of extreme risk. An alternative to VaR is *conditional value-a-risk* (CVaR), which measures losses beyond VaR. CVaR is becoming a popular alternative as it measures losses beyond VaR. A further advantage is that CVaR does not demonstrate the undesirable mathematical properties of VaR. Pflug (2000) shows that CVaR is a coherent risk measure having such desirable properties as convexity and monotonicity. In a decision theory framework, these two characteristics ensure a unique optimum exists. CVaR has been applied to portfolio optimization problems (Andersson, Mausser, Rosen, and Uryasev 2001; Rockafellar and Uryasev 2000, 2002; Alexander and Baptista 2003; Alexander, Coleman, and Li 2003; Rockafellar, Uryasev, and Zabarankin 2006).

Allen and Powell (2007a, 2007b) report a linkage between industries that are risky from a credit perspective (lending to companies in those industries) and those that are risky from a market perspective (share price volatility). The authors incorporate industry VaR and CVaR techniques into structural probability of default (PD) models as well as transition matrix credit VaR models.

Practical limitations to the application of VaR as a risk metric exist. To model a distribution of returns on a portfolio requires that the composition of the portfolio in question remains unchanged over the specified period. If long time horizons are involved, many investment positions and their portfolio weights may change. The VaR of the original portfolio may be of little relevance. If a historical simulation approach is adopted that uses variances and covariances in calculating VaR, then the assumption is that historical correlations are unchanged and do not vary in times of market stress. This assumption may be incorrect.

THE SECOND AND THIRD PILLARS OF THE BASEL II ACCORD

The second and third pillars of the Basel II Accord concern the supervisory review process and the third pillar involves market discipline. Under the second pillar, the institution must maintain sound monitoring and risk assessment procedures and address the various types of risk such as credit risk, operational risk, market risk, interest rate risk, liquidity, and other risks. The bank needs to develop effective systems for monitoring and reporting its risks. The third pillar involving market discipline is more likely to be effective if investors, regulators, and other interested parties are fully informed about the banks risk management, monitoring, and reporting procedures. The fairly slow process of adopting and implementing the Basel II Accord was overtaken by economic events and the commencement of the GFC in 2007.

The Global Financial Crisis

Gorton (2009a, 2009b, 2010) examines the GFC and surveys the literature. The complexity of the GFC and the related literature it spawned prompted Gorton and Metrick (2012, p. 128) to provide a reader's guide to "key facts and mechanisms in the build-up of risk, the panics in short-term debt markets, the policy reactions, and the real effects of the financial crisis." Low (2012) provides an alternative review of conflicting views about the origins of the crisis. The GFC had its origins in the U.S. subprime mortgage and credit crisis. It moved from the subprime mortgage markets to the credit markets and then produced shocks to short-term interbank markets as liquidity evaporated, particularly in structured credit and then on to stock markets globally.

Gorton's (2010) view is that the GFC had many similarities to previous crises, except that in 2007, the majority of investors and institutions had never heard of the markets that were involved and had little knowledge of their workings or purposes. Instruments and terms such as subprime mortgages, asset-backed commercial paper conduits, structured investment vehicles, credit derivatives, securitization, or repo markets were not in the common vocabulary. Gorton stresses that the securitized banking system is a real banking system that permits institutional investors and firms to make enormous, short-term deposits but it is still vulnerable to a panic. He suggests that the crisis that began in August 2007 may be understood not as a retail panic involving individuals, but as a wholesale panic involving institutions consisting of large financial firms "running" on other financial firms, making the system insolvent. Gorton and Metrick (2012) suggest the means for regulating the "shadow banking system" that was at the core of this process.

What were the major events in the development of the GFC? The first signs of trouble were in the U.S. housing market. Figure 17.2 shows the unseasonably adjusted 10-year composite index for the Standard & Poor's Case-Shiller Home Price Index, which is a constant-quality house price index for the United States. As Figure 17.2 indicates, the index peaked in 2006 and then started to fall. This pattern led to a weakening in the MBS market. Shiller (2004) warned of the dangers of an over-heated U.S. housing market well before the onset of the crisis in 2007.

Subprime mortgages were designed to encourage home ownership by higher risk mortgage borrowers. Such mortgages were a financial innovation with a design feature that linked their success to an assumption of continuing U.S. house price appreciation. They were financed by securitization and were constructed to reflect the major features of the subprime mortgages. Sets of these mortgages, or subprime tranches, were

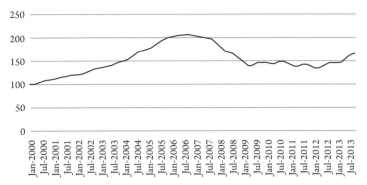

Figure 17.2 S&P/Case-Shiller 20-City Composite Home Price Index. The S&P/Case-Shiller Indices are designed to measure changes in the total value of all existing single-family housing stock. The method used involves sampling all available and relevant transaction data to create matched sale pairs for pre-existing homes. The indices are calculated monthly and a three-month moving average calculation method is adopted. Home sales pairs are accumulated in rolling three-month periods on which the repeat sales methodology is applied. They do not include new constructions or non-single-family dwellings. Source: S&P/Case-Shiller Home Price Index Series 2013.

often sold into CDOs. In turn, off-balance sheet vehicles such as a partnership, a trust, or a company were formed for this specific purpose, and then money market mutual funds might purchase these products. The characteristics of SPVs used for off-balance sheet purposes are typically that they are thinly capitalized, have no independent management or employees, are structured so they cannot go bankrupt, and are frequently managed by trustees. The use of credit default swaps (CDSs) to try to offset the risk further complicated the process of securitization. This combination of off-balance sheet investment vehicles, securitization, derivatives, and repurchase agreements came to be called the *shadow banking system*. The problem was that this system was not transparent and when mortgage defaults began to accumulate in the U.S. housing market, outside investors had difficulty understanding what was happening in this shadow banking system or deciding the nature of the actual risks. This situation is an example of an information asymmetry problem. In reaction to the shadow banking system, financial institutions began to refuse to deal with each other and then the panic spread from one sector to another and across the globe.

The problems started in the subprime market in 2007 and then surfaced at Freddie Mac, one of the key agencies in the securitization process for mortgages, in April 2007, followed by Bear Stearns in June 2007. This set off a ripple effect across the globe with French bank BNP Paribas suspending three funds in August 2007. This suspension caught the attention of central banks that began to coordinate their efforts to increase liquidity in the financial system.

Further consequences followed and on September 14, 2007, the U.K. bank Northern Rock sought and received a liquidity support facility from the Bank of England. The bank had problems in the credit markets leading it to be the first U.K. bank to experience a run in over a century. Northern Rock was eventually taken into state ownership.

By March 2008, JPMorgan Chase had acquired Bear Stearns at $2 per share in a fire sale to avoid bankruptcy. Federal authorities took over Fannie Mae and Freddie Mac on September 7, 2008. Bank of America bought Merrill on September 14, 2008, and Lehman Brothers filed for bankruptcy protection. Within a few days, the Federal Reserve lent support to American International Group (AIG). The U.S. authorities then proposed a $700 million emergency bail-out fund for purchasing toxic assets. By October 2008, the financial crisis spread to Europe. England, China, Canada, Sweden, Switzerland, and the European Central Bank cut rates in a coordinated effort to aid the world economy. Nine of the major U.S. banks participated in a Federal government support program: (1) Bank of America, (2) JPMorgan Chase, (3) Wells Fargo, (4) Citigroup, (5) Merrill Lynch, (6) Goldman Sachs, (7) Morgan Stanley, (8) Bank of New York Mellon, and (9) State Street.

A global economic shock resulted as the crisis spread and resulted in European bank failures. Large reductions in the market values of equities and commodities occurred around the globe. A crisis in global liquidity resulted as banks refused to lend to one another and to customers. The universal response by financial institutions was to de-lever in order to payback obligations, which caused credit spreads to widen. This effect, in turn, had a major impact on the real economy resulting in a synchronized global negative shock and causing international trade to decrease.

Low (2012) reviews some of the literature generated in response to the GFC and suggests that the reasons behind it are complex and difficult to disentangle. He addresses 21 books on the topic, 11 by academics and the rest by journalists and a former Treasury Secretary. He points out that even the starting date of the crisis is open to dispute. Should it be at the peak of the U.S. housing market in mid-2006, or the liquidity crunch in the shadow banking system in late 2007, or when Lehman's file for bankruptcy in September 2008?

This chapter mentions a few of the academic approaches that apparently reveal more heterogeneity than other accounts. Shiller (2008) views the crisis primarily as a response to an unraveling of a bubble in housing prices. He suggests a general contagion of mistaken beliefs about the future course in prices. Gorton (2010) ascribes it to an asymmetric information problem in the repo market which translated into a liquidity crunch. Low (2012) suggests that Gorton's argument that originating mortgage loans to distribute them via securitization and re-packaging, leaving others holding the risk, does not square with the fact that some institutions that fared the worst retained toxic securities on their own balance sheets and suffered the consequences for it.

Akerlof and Shiller (2009) show the results of a study in which they sought to rehabilitate Keynes's concept of "animal spirits" into the analysis in the context of the "originate to distribute" view point. In contrast to Gorton (2010), who views the problem as lying in complex structure of the MBS, Akerlof and Shiller see a more willful disposition on the part of the vendors to conceal and be deceptive. Stiglitz (2010) also adopts a form of the "originate to distribute" view but focuses on the misalignment of incentives in the large financial institutions that is attached to the "too big to fail" concept. These institutions could take excessive risk because they were too big to fail. Such institutions were secure in the knowledge that they were large and essential to the functioning of the financial systems of the American and global economy so that their excessive risk-taking would not be penalized.

Regulatory Responses to the Global Financial Crisis

The U.S. Congress enacted the Dodd-Frank Wall Street Reform and Consumer Protection Act in 2010. This Act featured a broad set of financial reforms including the creation of a new Financial Stability Oversight Council (FSOC), a reallocation of banking oversight responsibility, authority for regulators to impose enhanced size and liquidity based standards for those institutions considered systemically important, and heightened capital requirements. The FSOC had the authority to require that systemically important non-bank financial companies and interconnected holding companies have resolution plans for circumstances of financial distress or "living wills." A prescription intended to restrict banks and bank holding companies engaging in certain types of proprietary trading was added, plus a requirement that banks engaging in securitization retain at least 5 percent of the credit risk on their own balance sheets. New provisions were added enabling the authorities to resolve any financial problems that might lead to failures in bank holding companies. The Federal Reserve and the Federal Deposit Insurance Corporation (FDIC) published implementing regulations for living wills in November 2011. The U.S. Treasury continues to monitor the situation via the FSOC and is gradually winding down the Troubled Asset Relief Program (TARP) program. Also present was a requirement that most swap contracts, including credit derivative swaps, would have to be settled through clearing houses. The intention was to provide market information and greater transparency (Allen, Kramadibrata, Powell, and Singh 2013).

The IMF provides a continuing and valuable source on the global responses to the GFC in its annual series of "Global Financial Stability" reports. For example, the reports note the expected contraction of world GDP by 1.3 percent in 2009 (International Monetary Fund 2009a). The reports also note that establishing the conditions for a return to sustained growth required coordinated financial and macroeconomic policies. Additionally, the IMF reports also address the potential issue of national-level policies exacerbating cross-border strains.

In terms of policies for the global financial sector, the reports note that priorities remained in ensuring that financial institutions have (1) access to liquidity; (2) policies for identifying and dealing with distressed assets; and (3) and the ability to recapitalize the weak but viable institutions and resolving failed institutions. While the pre-crisis focus had been on financial health of individual institutions, this emphasis was insufficient and regulators needed to take into account the risk of both individual and systemic failures.

Different responses to the GFC emerged from governments and central regulatory regimes around the world. Table 17.1 summarizes typical government and central bank responses as offered by the IMF (International Monetary Fund 2009b). These responses include a move to lower interest rates and to provide liquidity support, government supported recapitalizations, liability guarantees, and asset purchase schemes.

Although global financial and market conditions have improved, problems in the Euro area remain where banks at the periphery continue to be challenged by elevated funding costs, deteriorating asset quality, and weak profits, while companies across the area remain challenged by a debt overhang (International Monetary Fund 2013). The IMF report also warns that accommodating monetary policies and regimes of

Table 17.1 **Central Bank Responses to the GFC**

Central Bank—Monetary Policy and Liquidity Support

Interest rate change	Reduction of interest rates
Liquidity support	Reserve requirements, longer funding terms, more auctions and/or higher credit lines
	Domestic system lender of last resort: broader set of eligible institutions, wider collateral rules, and/or eligible collateral
	Other liquidity support (e.g., support of money market funds)
	Foreign exchange lender of last resort: forex swap lines (with other central banks) and forex repos

Government—Financial Sector Stabilization Measures

Recapitalization	Capital injection (common stock/preferred equity)
	Capital injection (subordinated debt)
Liability guarantees[1]	Enhancement of depositor protection
	Debt guarantee (all liabilities)
	Debt guarantee (new liabilities)
	Government lending to an individual institution
Asset purchases[2]	Asset purchases (individual assets, bank by bank)
	Asset purchases (individual "bad bank")
	Provisions of liquidity in context of bad asset purchases/removal
	On-balance-sheet "ring-fencing" with toxic assets kept in the bank
	Off-balance-sheet "ring-fencing" with toxic assets moved to a "bad bank"
	Asset guarantees

[1]Includes the Federal Reserve's liquidity support to AIG for toxic asset removal to a special-purpose vehicle, coupled with government's loss sharing.

[2]Includes business loan guarantees as part of financial sector stabilization measures (e.g., the United Kingdom, Germany); for some countries, asset purchases were not conducted by the government, but (also) by the central bank (or a central bank-sponsored) agent, such as in the case of the United States and Switzerland.

Source: IMF staff estimates.

low interest rates could lead to further investment portfolio distortions. Problems also remain regarding the "too-big-to-fail" issue, OTC derivatives reform, accounting convergence, and shadow banking regulation. This situation resulted in the development of the Basel III Accord.

The Basel III Accord

The third Basel Accord or Basel III is a further global, voluntary regulatory standard on bank capital adequacy, stress testing, and market liquidity risk. Originally agreed by the

Basel Committee on Banking Supervision in 2010–2011, with an introductory schedule from 2013 until 2015 has since been extended until March 31, 2018. The Basel III Accord was a direct response to the GFC and focuses on increasing bank liquidity and reducing bank leverage. The goal is to improve the financial system's ability to absorb financial shocks and to limit the transfer of these shocks to the real economy (Bank for International Settlements 2010b).

The original requirement in the Basel III Accord stated that banks should increase their holdings of common equity to 4.5 percent from 2 percent in Basel II and their Tier 1 capital from 4 percent to 6 percent of risk-weighted assets. To increase safeguards, the Basel III Accord introduced further capital buffers; a 2.5 percent mandatory "capital conservation buffer," plus the authorities were to be given additional discretion to introduce an additional 2.5 percent requirement in periods of high credit growth known as the "discretionary counter-cyclical buffer."

The Basel III Accord introduced a new leverage ratio set at a minimum of 3 percent calculated by dividing Tier 1 capital by the bank's average total consolidated assets. The U.S. Federal Reserve Bank announced in July 2013 that the minimum Basel III leverage ratio would be 6 percent for eight systemically important financial institutions banks (also known as too big to fail) and 5 percent for their bank holding companies.

The Basel III Accord involves two further measures to safeguard liquidity. According to the Bank of International Settlements (2010a, p.1):

> The first objective is to promote short-term resilience of a bank's liquidity risk profile by ensuring that it has sufficient high-quality liquid assets to survive a significant stress scenario lasting for one month. The Committee developed the Liquidity Coverage Ratio (LCR) to achieve this objective. The second objective is to promote resilience over a longer time horizon by creating additional incentives for banks to fund their activities with more stable sources of funding on an ongoing basis. The Net Stable Funding Ratio (NSFR) has a time horizon of one year and has been developed to provide a sustainable maturity structure of assets and liabilities.

Many criticisms to these proposals have followed the development of the Basil III Accord. Fears exist that requiring tighter capital controls in time of distress may exacerbate economic cycles—the pro-cyclical argument. The changes could affect bank profitability and lending capabilities. Financial institutions are likely to seek new ways around them, via the regulatory arbitrage process mentioned previously, and they may try to arbitrage across national borders if different national regulatory authorities implement the suggested changes to differing degrees. The liquidity ratios may change the attractiveness to institutions of long-term vis-à-vis short-term funding.

Summary and Conclusions

This chapter reviews some aspects of risk management and regulation with particular emphasis on the series of Basel accords and the response to the recent GFC.

The chapter stresses the financial system and processes involved in financial intermediation continually evolve and develop in a dynamic fashion. Changes in regulation trigger new rounds of innovation and regulatory arbitrage. Thus, the regulators are in a constant struggle to try to keep up with changed economic circumstances and market practices.

Kane's (2012) concept of a regulatory dialectic is evident in the aftermath of the GFC in Europe. The European experience can be contrasted with that of the United States where the economy is regaining speed. The Bureau of Economic Analysis released data suggesting that the U.S. economy was growing at 3.6 percent in the third quarter of 2013. By contrast, in the 28 member European Union (EU), GDP fell by one half percent in 2012 and was flat in 2013. A major difference between the EU and the United States is the common currency across the former that restricts exchange rate policy and has been a major contributor to the European sovereign debt crisis. This debt crisis refers to the difficulties faced by some countries in the eurozone to repay or refinance their government debt without the assistance of third parties.

These difficulties have led to changes of governments in various countries, high unemployment rates, and a series of actions including financial support measures such as the European Financial Stability Facility and European Stability Mechanism. The European Central Bank has also tried to lower interest rates and maintain money flows between European banks.

This debt crisis is partly a banking crisis, as one major problem is cross-border holdings by banks of other countries sovereign debt. Deflation rather than inflation is also a current risk and austerity programs have led to general high unemployment. On average, 12 percent of the labor force is unemployed and youth unemployment in countries such as Greece exceeds 50 percent. A real possibility exists that the Euro area will fragment and break up.

In conclusion, the impact and after-effects of the GFC have been very different in Europe than in the United States. This difference is partly the result of a complex set of economic and regulatory circumstances in terms of EU members being at different stages of economic development, the complications attached to a single currency union, and lax fiscal policy on the part of some governments. These circumstances provide an example of the complex interplay, among regulation, market innovation, and economic consequences. The United States, whose expansionary home ownership policies combined with financial innovation subsequently led to some developments triggering the GFC, has now moved on economically. In contrast, Europe remains mired in economic difficulties partly because it faces a very different set of regulatory circumstances. Learning about the regulatory responses and financial innovations that are likely to follow from this complex set of economic and political circumstances should be of great interest to market participants and others.

Acknowledgments

The authors are very grateful to the editors for their careful guidance and suggested revisions.

Discussion Questions

1. Discuss the nature of financial intermediation.
2. Explain the securitization process.
3. Identify several factors that drive financial innovation.
4. Define regulatory arbitrage.
5. Discuss the primary objectives of the Basel Accords.

References

Akerlof, George A., and Robert J. Shiller. 2009. *Animal Spirits: How Human Psychology Drives the Economy, and Why It Matters for Global Capitalism.* Princeton, NJ: Princeton University Press.

Alexander, Gordon J., and Alexandre M. Baptista. 2003. "CVaR as a Measure of Risk: Implications for Portfolio Selection." Working Paper, School of Management, University of Minnesota, Saint-Paul.

Alexander, Siddharth, Thomas F. Coleman, and Yuying Li. 2003. "Derivative Portfolio Hedging Based on CVaR." In Giorgio Szego, ed., *New Risk Measures in Investment and Regulation,* 321–336. New York: John Wiley & Sons.

Allen, David E., and Robert J. Powell. 2007a. "Structural Credit Modelling and Its Relationship to Market Value at Risk: An Australian Sectoral Perspective." Working Paper, Edith Cowan University.

Allen, David E., and Robert J. Powell. 2007b. "Transitional Credit Modelling and Its Relationship to Market at Value at Risk: An Australian Sectoral Perspective." Working Paper, Edith Cowan University.

Allen, David E., Akhmad Kramadibrata, Robert J. Powell, and Abhay K. Singh. 2013. "Understanding the Regulation Impact: US Funds of Hedge Funds after the Crisis." In Greg. N. Gregoriou, ed., *Reconsidering Funds of Hedge Funds: The Financial Crisis and Best Practices in UCITS, Tail Risk, Performance, and Due Diligence,* 503–514. Oxford: Academic Press.

Allen, Franklin. 2001. "Do Financial Institutions Matter?" *Journal of Finance* 56:4, 1165–1175.

Andersson, Fredrik, Helmut Mausser, Dan Rosen, and Stanislav Uryasev. 2001. "Credit Risk Optimization with Conditional Value-at Risk Criterion." *Mathematical Programming* 89:2, 273–291.

Arnold, Tanya S. 1984. "How to Do Interest Rate Swaps." *Harvard Business Review* September–October, 96–101.

Artzner, Phillipe, Freddy Delbaen, Jean-Marc Eber, and David Heath. 1997. "Thinking Coherently." *Risk* 10:November, 68–71.

Artzner, Phillipe, Freddy Delbaen, Jean-Marc Eber, and David Heath. 1999. "Coherent Measures of Risk." *Mathematical Finance* 9:3, 203–228.

Auerbach, Alan J., and Joel Slemrod. 1997. "The Economic Effects of the Tax Reform Act of 1986," *Journal of Economic Literature* 35:2, 589–632.

Bank for International Settlements. 2006. "Basel II: International Convergence of Capital Measurement and Capital Standards. A Revised Framework Comprehensive Version." Communications, CH-4002. Basel, Switzerland: Bank of International Settlements.

Bank for International Settlements. 2010a. "Basel III: International Framework for Liquidity Risk Measurement, Standards and Monitoring." Communications, CH-4002. Basel, Switzerland: Bank of International Settlements.

Bank for International Settlements. 2010b. "Basel III: A Global Regulatory Framework for More Resilient Banks and Banking Systems." Communications, CH-4002. Basel, Switzerland: Bank of International Settlements.

Basel Committee on Banking Supervision. 1988. "International Convergence of Capital Measurement and Capital Standards." Basel, Switzerland: Basel Committee on Banking Supervision.

Beder, Tanya. 1995. "VaR: Seductive but Dangerous." *Financial Analysts Journal* 51:5: 12–25.

Benston, George J., and Clifford Smith. 1975. "A Transactions Cost Approach to the Theory of Financial Intermediation," *Journal of Finance* 31:2, 215–231.

Calomiris, Charles W. 2010. "The Political Lessons of Depression-Era Banking Reform." *Oxford Review of Economic Policy* 26:3, 540–560.

Duffie, Darrell, and Jun Pan. 1997. "An Overview of Value at Risk." *Journal of Derivatives* 4:3, 7–49.

Gloria Mundi. 2013. "All About Value-at-Risk." Available at http://www.gloriamundi.com.

Gorton, Gary. 2009a. "The Subprime Panic." *European Financial Management* 15:1, 10–46.

Gorton, Gary. 2009b. "Information, Liquidity, and the (Ongoing) Panic of 2007." *American Economic Review, Papers and Proceedings* 99:2, 567–572.

Gorton, Gary. 2010. Slapped by the Invisible Hand: The Panic of 2007. Oxford: Oxford University Press.

Gorton, Gary, and Andrew Metrick. 2012. "Getting up to Speed on the Financial Crisis: A One-Weekend-Reader's Guide." *Journal of Economic Literature* 50:1, 128–150.

International Monetary Fund. 2009a. *Global Financial Stability Report: Responding to the Financial Crisis and Measuring Systemic Risk*. Washington, DC: International Monetary Fund.

International Monetary Fund. 2009b. *Global Financial Stability Report: Navigating the Financial Challenges Ahead*. Washington, DC: International Monetary Fund.

International Monetary Fund. 2013. *Global Financial Stability Report: Old Risks: New Challenges*. Washington, DC: International Monetary Fund.

Jorion, Phillipe. 1997. Value at Risk: *The New Benchmark for Managing Financial Risk*. New York: McGraw-Hill.

JP Morgan and Reuters. 1996. *RiskMetrics Technical Document*. Available at http://www.riskmetrics.com/rmcovv.html.

Kane, Edward J. 2012. "The Inevitability of Shadowy Banking." Paper presented at the Federal Reserve Bank of Atlanta, April 10, Financial Markets Conference Financial Reform: The Devil's In the Details, Atlanta, Georgia.

Keynes, John Maynard. [1919] 2004. The Economic Consequences of the Peace. New Brunswick,NJ: Transaction Publishers.

Keynes, John Maynard. [1936] 2007. The General Theory of Employment, Interest and Money. Basingstoke, Hampshire: Palgrave Macmillan.

Keynes, John Maynard. 1937. "The General Theory of Employment." *Quarterly Journal of Economics* 51:2, 209–232.

Low, Andrew W. 2012. "Reading about the Financial Crisis: A Twenty-One-Book Review." *Journal of Economic Literature* 50:1, 151–178.

Merton, Robert C., and Zvi Bodie. 1995. "A Conceptual Framework for Analyzing the Financial Environment." In Dwight B. Crane, Kenneth A. Froot, Scott P. Mason, André Perold, Robert C.Merton, ZviBodie, Eric R. Sirri, and Peter Tufano, eds., The Global Financial System: A Functional Perspective, 3–31. Boston: Harvard Business School Press.

Pflug, Georg. 2000. "Some Remarks on Value-at-Risk and Conditional-Value-at-Risk." In Stanislav Uryasev, ed., *Probabilistic Constrained Optimisation: Methodology and Applications*, 272–281. Dordrecht, The Netherlands/Boston: Kluwer Academic Publishers.

Pritsker, Mathew. 1997. "Evaluating Value-at-Risk Methodologies: Accuracy versus Computational Time." *Journal of Financial Services Research* 12:2/3, 201–242.

Rockafellar, R. Tyrrell, and Stanislav Uryasev. 2000. "Optimization of Conditional Value-at-Risk." *Journal of Risk* 2:3, 21–41.

Rockafellar, R. Tyrrell, and Stanislav Uryasev. 2002. "Conditional Value-at-Risk for General Loss Distributions." *Journal of Banking and Finance* 26:7, 1443–1471.

Rockafellar, R. Tyrrell, Stanislav Uryasev, and Michael Zabarankin. 2006. "Master Funds in Portfolio Analysis with General Deviation Measures." *Journal of Banking and Finance* 30:2, 743–776.

Shiller, Robert J. 2004. "Household Reaction to Changes in Housing Wealth." Cowles Foundation Discussion Paper No. 1459.

Shiller, Robert J. 2008. *The Subprime Solution: How Today's Global Financial Crisis Happened and What to Do about It*. Princeton, NJ: Princeton University Press.

Stambaugh, Robert. F. 1996. "Risk and Value-at-Risk." *European Management Journal* 14:6, 612–621.

S&P/Case-Shiller Home Price Indices. 2013. Available at http//www.spindices.com/index-family/real-estate/sp-case-shiller.

Stiglitz, Joseph E. 2010. "Risk and Global Economic Architecture: Why Full Financial Integration May Be Undesirable." Working Paper 15718, National Bureau of Economic Research.

Van-Horne, James C. 1984. "Of Financial Innovations and Excesses." *Journal of Finance* 40:3, 620–631.

18

Risk Budgeting

GREGG FISHER

Chief Investment Officer, Gerstein Fisher

TIM NGUYEN

Director of Alternative Investments, University of Connecticut

Adjunct Professor, Brown University

CRISTIAN I. TIU

Associate Professor of Finance, School of Management, University at Buffalo–SUNY

Introduction

Risk budgeting or *risk management* is the process by which risk is identified, measured, decomposed, and managed. Despite general agreement on its definition, risk budgeting has many implementations. These implementations range from making risk management a process completely complementary to that of portfolio creation to making it entirely subservient to the latter. This chapter describes several practices and tools used to measure risk and identify its sources.

Although risk is a broad concept, this chapter focuses specifically on financial risk. In the context of this chapter, *financial risk* is the risk that a portfolio created to maximize a certain investment objective (a process referred to as *asset allocation*) is suboptimal. This concept of risk is as customizable as the criteria used to create portfolios. For example, if a portfolio is created to minimize the standard deviation, then the relevant risk to that portfolio is the concern that the standard deviation may become too high. Once this risk (i.e., standard deviation) has become too high, identifying which portfolio components are responsible for the risk elevation becomes vital. For a risk measure to lend itself to decomposition across different portfolio components requires satisfying certain mathematical conditions. Marrying asset allocation with risk management requires that the criterion used in asset allocation lend itself to becoming a good risk measure.

Should investors use risk management? After a disastrous recession caused in part by lax credit risk controls and after witnessing staggering trading losses that risk management systems failed to catch, the answer seems to be an unequivocal "yes." The practice of risk management also seems to pay off. For example, a study by Ernst

& Young (2012, p. 1) finds that "companies with more mature risk management practices outperform their peers financially." Whether investment managers resort to internal risk management controls, institutional investors prefer it and legislation may require such controls. For example, the Dodd-Frank Wall Street Reform and Consumer Protection Act of 2010 (Dodd-Frank) calls for the Federal Reserve to create uniform standards for the management of risks by systemically important financial organizations. Institutional investors typically include risk management questions in their due diligence questionnaires. Risk management has emerged as an integral part of the investment process.

Who should use risk management? Focusing on what type of investors should use the process is less important than modeling the risk management process for a generic investor who encompasses several known investor types. This process is especially true when allowing for decentralization, a case in which an investor can not only take active risk but also decide the definition of active investing. Despite restricting the discussion of specific cases to known asset allocation criteria, the proposed risk management approach to risk measures can be extended to other areas.

In addition to the main source of financial risk, investors can explore many other portfolio characteristics excluded from the asset allocation decision. For example, the risk that a key fund manager leaves her firm may not formally be part of the asset allocation decision, but managers may estimate this risk separately. Managers may not determine whether to include geographic exposure as a part of the asset allocation process, but they may choose to include it as part of the risk management process to ensure that exposure to one particular area does not become too large. This chapter does not focus on how these measures can be integrated in the risk management process. Yet, being informed about the value of these risk measures could provide a clear portfolio picture to the risk manager seeking to measure risk.

The chapter also offers a few warnings to risk managers. Some address basic measurements such as portfolio returns or identify the sources of risk. These warnings are not meant to deter from measuring risk but serve as a caution to carefully interpret measures that are part of the portfolio management process. The measures are also useful to risk managers who rely on off-the-shelf risk management software that calculates but often does not interpret, risk statistics.

This chapter has the following structure. First, a section on asset allocation details some current asset allocation practices and discusses compatibility with known risk measures. Next, the chapter describes desirable properties of risk measures, followed by comments on popular risk measures, an illustration showing how risk can be decomposed, and two examples. A discussion of issues with risk management rounds out the chapter, preceding the summary and conclusions.

Asset Allocation

As used in this chapter, *risk* is the degree to which a portfolio is suboptimal. Understanding this type of risk also requires clarifying what is meant by an optimal portfolio. In investments, this optimality criterion drives the asset allocation. Hence, the following discussion of potential asset allocation criteria can be used in conjunction with risk measures that are relatively well understood. The main point is that the criterion to be optimized in asset allocation can be tailored to the investor's type. The chapter provides examples of such a procedure.

Asset allocation refers to the portfolio choice among several asset classes in contrast to choosing assets within the same class. Its first phase consists of understanding the opportunity set or more precisely selecting the possible asset classes to which capital is allocated. Disagreements exist about what constitutes an asset class. For example, are hedge funds an asset class? A voluminous literature body is dedicated even to allocation problems with the simplest opportunity set such as one consisting of equity and fixed income (Wachter 2010). A second step consists of postulating the statistical properties of the assets in the opportunity set. These two steps can be consistent across many types of investors. The third step in asset allocation involves understanding the criteria that the portfolio must satisfy (i.e., selecting the utility function). This utility function should be highly customized to investor type. Consider the following examples:

- An individual investor seeks to minimize the standard deviation of his or her portfolio. In this case, the investor may want to form a portfolio that has the minimum standard deviation of all portfolios meeting the returns objective. Markowitz (1959) addresses this type of case.
- A university is concerned about its endowment portfolio meeting a minimum required return in order to preserve the fund's purchasing power after the fund makes a payout to the university. In this case, the optimization problem is that of a downside risk from a pre-specified minimum return target (Harlow 1991).
- A bank is worried that its capital requirements are not met and wants to minimize its average returns conditional on these returns being lower than the capital requirement. In this case, the bank may want to minimize the conditional value-at-risk (CVaR). Rockafellar and Uryasev (2000) offer optimization as a methodology for accomplishing this goal.

These three examples of utility functions share one mathematical property that makes them especially suited for risk measurement. This property known as *homogeneity* is defined and discussed in the next section. Below are examples of criteria for optimization that an investor might consider, but they are not homogeneous:

- The probability that the returns do not fall under a certain amount (e.g., 10 percent), more than a specific number of times (e.g., four times) in a certain time period (e.g., four years). This criterion is useful for an investor who prefers to avoid large negative returns, which may attract bad publicity.
- The probability that the returns exceed a certain threshold (e.g., 15 percent) in a given year. This criterion is useful to an investor attempting outperformance that, in contrast to the criterion mentioned previously, may generate positive headlines.

Although more examples abound, asset allocation is not the subject of this chapter. Therefore, this discussion concludes by commenting on how to construct a utility function from a set of unrelated criteria.

To create a proprietary utility function, assume several optimization criteria such as the ones enumerated in this section, $U_0, U_1, \ldots, U_K$. Because the possible optimization criteria may include complicated, non-linear functions that are difficult to optimize, reducing the number of portfolio candidates may make sense. One way to achieve this goal is to suppose that U_0 is a criterion that may yield a number of portfolio candidates (e.g., U_0 is a downside risk and minimizing U_0 produces an efficient downside risk frontier). In this case, a subset of the optimal frontier may be used as candidate portfolios for the rest of the given criteria. Assume that the portfolio candidates are $P_1, \ldots, P_N$. Then by combining the criteria $U_1, \ldots, U_K$ by first normalizing each criterion across portfolios, Equation 18.1 emerges:

$$\widehat{U_k}(P_n) = \frac{U_k(P_n)}{\sum_{n=1}^{N} U_k(P_n)}. \qquad (18.1)$$

Next, attribute to each criterion a weight, according to its importance. Denoted by w_k the weight assigned to criterion U_k form the proprietary utility function of the investor as Equation 18.2:

$$\widehat{U(P_n)} = \sum_{k=1}^{K} w_k \widehat{U_k}(P_n). \qquad (18.2)$$

Next, find the optimal portfolio as $P^* = argmax_n \, \widehat{U(P_n)}$. Note that the last optimization problem is simply to select the optimal portfolio from N available portfolios.

Asset allocation and risk management are based on statistics that are mutually compatible. Modern portfolio theory, however, promotes asset allocation methods that spread the risk contributions equally among portfolio components rather than specifying a criterion for optimization. This approach is known as *risk parity* (Asness, Frazzini, and Pederson 2012).

RISK STATISTICS PROPERTIES

Next, the chapter turns to a discussion on measuring risk. As mentioned previously, the risk measure should ideally be compatible with the one used in the asset allocation process. This section outlines several mathematical properties that may be satisfied by risk measures. In the following discussion, a generic risk measure is denoted by ρ, outlining desirable mathematical properties that a risk measure must satisfy.

Monotonicity
For two portfolios with returns $R_1 \geq R_2$, the following relationship should hold: $\rho(R_1) \geq \rho(R_2)$. In other words, a portfolio with lower performance is riskier than an outperforming portfolio.

Homogeneity
If λ is a positive constant, then $\rho(\lambda R) = \lambda \rho(R)$. In other words, if the portfolio returns double, the risk will also double. This property turns out to be very useful in the mathematical decomposition of risk. To see why, Equation 18.3 assumes that a portfolio is the weighted sum of several components (i.e., for a set of weights $w_1 + \cdots + w_N = 1$),

$$R = w_1 R_1 + \cdots + w_N R_N. \tag{18.3}$$

If the measure of risk is homogeneous, and if one simplifies the notation for the risk measure of such a combined portfolio to $\rho(w_1, \ldots, w_N)$, then it follows that $\varepsilon\rho\,(w_1, \ldots, w_N) = \rho(\epsilon w_1, \ldots, \epsilon w_n)$. Taking the derivative with respect to ϵ and making $\varepsilon = 1$, Equation 18.4 shows the risk decomposition formula.

$$\rho(w_1, \ldots, w_N) = w_1 \frac{\partial\rho}{\partial w_1} + \cdots + w_N \frac{\partial\rho}{\partial w_N}. \tag{18.4}$$

The n-th component in Equation 18.4 represents the contribution of component n to the risk of the entire portfolio. The relative risk contribution of a component is not determined solely by the weight of the component in the portfolio, but it also depends on the marginal risk, $\partial\rho/\partial w_n$. The marginal risk represents the rate at which the total portfolio risk changes as the weight of the n-th component changes. In particular, it takes into account the correlation effects resulting from pooling all the components to form the portfolio. In a similar vein, the relative risk contribution of the n-th component is equal to $\frac{\partial\rho}{\partial w_n}/\rho(w_1, \ldots, w_N)$. In certain cases in which the risk measure is not homogeneous, different techniques may be employed to realize a risk decomposition expression similar to Equation 18.4.

Equation 18.4 may be used to separate the risks associated with market moves over which an investor may have very little control from risks generated by active investment decisions that may be reversed. These active investment decisions may consist of selecting certain securities in lieu of an index, or attempting to time the markets by over- or under-weighting an asset or an asset class. In order to see how, assume that the investor is supposed to track a benchmark index with returns B, but he invests (actively) in a portfolio that generates the returns R. Equation 18.5 decomposes the investor's portfolio:

$$R = B + (R - B), \tag{18.5}$$

which is a portfolio consisting of three assets weighted with the weights $w_1 = 1$ assigned to B, $w_2 = 1$ assigned to R, and $w_3 = -1$ assigned to B. The sum of the last two components, $(R - B)$, represents the manager's active investment. The weights add up to one. When Equation 18.4 is applied, a decomposition formula with three terms emerges. The first term of the formula reflects the contribution of the benchmark B to the overall portfolio risk. This risk cannot be controlled at least not by a price-taking investor. The sum of the next two terms represents the contribution of the active part of the portfolio, namely $(R - B)$, to the overall portfolio risk. The investor can control this risk because the decision to invest actively can be reversed in favor of a more passive investment strategy.

Convexity (Coherence)
If $\varepsilon \in [0, 1]$, then $\rho\left[\varepsilon R_1 + (1 - \varepsilon)R_2\right] \leq \epsilon\rho(R_1) + (1-\varepsilon)\rho(R_2)$. This property hints at diversification: the risk of a combination of portfolios is smaller than the weighted sum of their risks. One good example is the standard deviation. Because of the diversification

effect, the standard deviation of a portfolio is smaller than the (positive-weighted) sum of individual standard deviations. *Coherence* is a property attesting that the risk measure is consistent with the idea of diversification. Not all risk measures exhibit this property.

Examples of Risk Measures

The following is a discussion of specific risk measures. Besides defining the measures, the section offers recommendations about when to use each measure.

STANDARD DEVIATION

Standard deviation is the most widely used risk measure. It is consistent with the idea of diversification (i.e., coherence). Standard deviation is also compatible with criteria used in asset allocation. For example, if the investor is mean-variance efficient, then she performs the asset allocation by minimizing the standard deviation. The relevant risk is that the standard deviation is higher than the minimum risk level for a given return. Standard deviation is also homogenous and amenable to decomposition as in Equation 18.4 (Pearson 2002).

Should standard deviation be used as a risk criterion? Consider the counterarguments. The main counterargument is that a portfolio may have a high standard deviation if it deviates up from the mean. However, a high unexpected return could be desirable. High unexpected returns should not represent events with a probability that needs to be minimized. In reality, portfolios should only be "punished" when their returns deviate below the mean. A counterargument is that this conclusion is irrelevant: portfolios of institutions that measure and minimize risk are large and diverse. Further, if the assets are not completely correlated, then the overall returns, as a weighted sum of many random variables, are close to normal because of the law of large numbers. Therefore, portfolio returns are symmetric and the downside deviations from the mean of the portfolio are just half of all the deviations. Because standard deviation measures deviations in both directions from the mean, high performance is not being punished by using standard deviation rather than downside risk. This argument is fallacious because in down markets, correlations increase, and the assumptions of the law of large numbers are violated. Consequently, using standard deviation is not equivalent to using downside risk as a measure of optimization.

VALUE-AT-RISK

Value-at-risk (VaR) of a portfolio is calculated based on a percentile of its returns. Its most popular implementation uses the 95th percentile of returns (ranked from the lowest to the highest). VaR gained popularity as a risk measure used by banks, but whether its popularity will survive the Basel III Accord, which requires banks to impose more than just VaR limits on their capital, is unclear (Georg 2011). VaR is homogenous, for which Equation 18.4 can be applied.

Consider three shortcomings of using VaR. First, the temptation exists to use an exact formula, which is useful to evaluate 95 percent VaR of a normally distributed returns series: $VaR = \mu - 1.65\,\sigma$ where μ is the expected return and σ is the standard deviation of the return series. This formula is correct only if the returns are normally distributed.

Second, VaR is not a coherent risk measure. Why is VaR inconsistent with the idea of diversification? VaR is a measure intended to capture, in a sense, the worst outcomes. "Putting eggs in multiple baskets" almost ensures that one of the baskets will experience the "worst outcome." For example, assume two zero coupon bonds, both with independent default probabilities equal to 4 percent (one year forward) and with recovery rates of 30 percent. The 95 percent VaR is zero for both bonds taken separately. However, since the probability of at least one of the bonds defaulting is $1 - (0.96)^2 = 7.84$ percent, the 95 percent VaR of the equally weighted portfolio of both bonds is strictly positive.

Third, using VaR can sometimes yield confusing results. Assume that a portfolio consists of stocks 1 and 2, equally weighted, and with the returns presented in Table 18.1. Each realization of returns is presented in a separate row in the table and has equal probabilities. The 80 percent VaR of the portfolio is then 1.50 percent. The question is, however, which asset contributes the most to VaR—stock 1 or stock 2? The first row of the table shows that the highest contribution to VaR comes from stock 2, whereas in the second row, it is generated by stock 1. The reduction of the allocation to the stock with the highest contribution results in an impasse. In practical implementations, this problem is resolved by using a "neighborhood approach" (i.e., using, as a 95 percent VaR, an average between the 93 percent, 94 percent, 95 percent, 96 percent, and 97 percent VaR or another neighborhood of 95, other than 93 to 97).

CONDITIONAL VALUE-AT-RISK

Conditional value-at-risk (CVaR) is a risk measure meant to overcome some of VaR's shortcomings. It is defined as $CVaR = E(R \mid R < M)$ (the average of returns smaller than VaR). Because CVaR is homogeneous and coherent, the decomposition Equation 18.4 applies.

Table 18.1 **Hypothetical Value-at-Risk**

Returns			VaR Contributions	
Stock 1 (%)	Stock 2 (%)	Portfolio (%)	Stock 1 (%)	Stock 2 (%)
1.0	2.0	1.5	0.5	1.0
2.0	1.0	1.5	1.0	0.5
5.0	5.0	5.0	2.5	2.5
5.0	5.0	5.0	2.5	2.5
5.0	5.0	5.0	2.5	2.5

Note: The table presents the decomposition of VaR in a portfolio consisting of two stocks. Columns 1 and 2 present the historical returns and Columns 3 and 4 show VaR contributions.

DOWNSIDE RISK

The downside risk (DR) of a portfolio with returns R, from a pre-specified level of return M, is defined as $DR^2 = E\left[\max\left(M - R\right)^2\right]$. Downside risk is a more realistic risk than the standard deviation measure because it "punishes" only returns that fall short of an objective return, but it is mathematically less tractable, for optimization purposes, than the standard deviation. Although downside risk is consistent with the idea of diversification for a fixed M, it is not homogeneous. Thus, downside risk does not lend itself to the simple decomposition of Equation 18.4. However, an analogous formula can be developed as in the following. Let $I = 1_{\{R \leq M\}}$ and starting with the definition of downside risk and expanding, Equation 18.6 assesses each component's contribution to the overall downside risk as follows:

$$
\begin{aligned}
DR^2 = E\left[(M - R)^2 I\right] &= E[I\,(M - R)\,\textstyle\sum_{n=1}^{N} w_n\,(M - R_n)] \\
&= \textstyle\sum_{n=1}^{N} w_n E\left[I\,(M - R)\,(M - R_n)\right] = \textstyle\sum_{n=1}^{N} w_n \widehat{DRDR_n} \rho_n,
\end{aligned}
\tag{18.6}
$$

where $\widehat{DR_n} := \sqrt{E\left[I(M - R_n)^2\right]}$ is the risk that the n-th portfolio component falls short of M on the set on which the entire portfolio falls short of M, and $\rho_n := \frac{E[I(M-R)(M-R_n)]}{DRDR_n}$ is the "down-correlation" between the entire portfolio R with the n-th component R_n. Simplifying by DR in Equation 18.6 results in the downside risk decomposition shown in Equation 18.7:

$$
DR = \sum_{n=1}^{N} w_n \widehat{DR_n} \rho_n.
\tag{18.7}
$$

Equation 18.7 is intuitive and contains three main elements. The first element is w_n, the dollar weight of the n-th component of the portfolio. The higher the dollar weight of a component, the higher is its downside risk contribution. The second element, $\widehat{DR_n}$, is the risk that one component falls short of the return objective M exactly when the entire portfolio falls short of M. The n-th component's downside risk contribution is higher if, on the set on which the entire portfolio falls short of the return objective M, the returns of the n-th component also fall short of M. Finally, the contribution is determined by the downside correlation ρ_n between the returns of the n-th component and the returns of the entire portfolio. Calculations of downside risk often use the mean returns, $E[R]$, in place of the target return M. If downside risk is calculated that way, then downside risk is homogeneous and the decomposition in Equation 18.4 can be applied directly.

MAXIMUM DRAWDOWNS

The *maximum drawdown* represents the worst possible return over a certain time period. It is calculated in the following manner. Assume monthly returns of a portfolio, $R_1, \ldots, R_T$. Returns can be formed over a time period such as a quarter for every month in the sample: $R_3^Q = R_1 + R_2 + R_3, \ldots, R_T^Q = R_{T-2} + R_{T-1} + R_T$. The first quarterly drawdown is the negative of the smallest of the $R_3^Q, \ldots, R_T^Q$. The second maximum drawdown is the negative of the next smallest returns. The maximum drawdown is homogeneous and consistent with the idea of diversification.

Examples of Managing Risk

This section illustrates the use of risk management in two examples. Both examples demonstrate how a risk manager may isolate active risk within a portfolio. The first example focuses on the case of a decentralized institution and the second example applies to an institutional investor.

RISK MANAGEMENT FOR DECENTRALIZED INVESTORS

The first example follows Reed, Tiu, and Yoeli (2011) and outlines risk management for a decentralized investor. Assume that the investor is performing an asset allocation based on downside risk minimization. The authors illustrate the downside risk composition of a fictitious decentralized fund, XYZ, which is structured as follows. The fund invests in U.S. equity and inflation hedge securities, employing a manager for each asset class. The chief investment officer (CIO) of the fund decides that the optimal long-term allocation is 50 percent to each asset class. Because of temporary market conditions, the CIO decides to engage in marketing timing for both markets. He employs a tactical shift in the asset allocation to include only 40 percent to U.S. equity and 60 percent to inflation hedge securities. If the entire fund consists of $100 million, then the managing director for U.S. equity receives $40 million to invest and allocates $20 million to a large cap fund and $20 million to a small cap fund. The managing director for inflation hedge securities receives $60 million and splits the allocation between Treasury inflation-protected securities (TIPS), which receive $40 million, and commodities, which receive $20 million.

Another active investment decision made within the fund is how to evaluate the performance of investments. The CIO may be responsible for establishing indices against which the performance of asset classes in which the fund invests are evaluated. In the case in question, the CIO benchmarks the performance of the U.S. equity portfolio using the Russell 3000 index (R3000), and the performance of the inflation hedge portfolio using the Merrill Lynch Inflation Linked (MLIL) securities index. The managing director of each asset class may also establish benchmarks based on the indices against which the performance of internal investment is evaluated. For the XYZ fund, the assumption is that the U.S. equity managing director uses the S&P 500 index (SP500) to evaluate the performance of large cap managers and the Russell 2000 (R2000) index to evaluate the performance of small cap managers. Similarly, the managing director for inflation hedge uses the MLIL index to evaluate TIPS managers, and the Goldman Sachs Commodities Index (GSCI) to evaluate the performance of the commodities managers in which she invests. Table 18.2 details the hypothetical portfolio.

To reflect the long-term investment strategy, as well as the timing and security selection decisions, the hypothetical portfolio returns may be decomposed as shown in Equation 18.8:

Table 18.2 **A Hypothetical Portfolio**

Asset Class	Index	Benchmark Portfolio (%)	Actual Portfolio (%)
U.S. Equity	Russell 3000	50	40
Large-cap manager	S&P 500		20
Small-cap manager	Russell 2000		20
Inflation Hedge	ML Inflation Linked	50	60
TIPS Manager	ML Inflation Linked		40
Commodities Manager	GSCI		20

Source: Reed, Tiu, and Yoeli 2011.

$$
\begin{aligned}
R =\ & (0.5\,R3000 + 0.5\,MLIL + (-0.1\,R3000 + 0.1\,MLIL) \\
& + 0.2\,(SP500 - R3000) + 0.2\,(R2000 - R3000) \\
& + 0.4\,(MLIL - MLIL) + 0.2\,(GSCI - MLIL) \\
& + 0.2\,(M1 - SP500) + 0.2\,(M2 - R2000) \\
& + 0.4\,(M3 - MLIL) + 0.2\,(M4 - GSCI).
\end{aligned}
\tag{18.8}
$$

In Equation 18.8, M1 to M4 represent the outside managers' returns. The first row represents the returns generated by the long-term investment strategy undertaken by the fund, plus the returns generated by the decision to time the two asset classes in which the fund invests. The second row represents the risks brought by the difference in benchmarks in U.S. equity. The managing director for the U.S. equity asset class evaluates the performance of her external managers using benchmarks different from the benchmark against which her performance is evaluated. Unless the R3000 index is replicated by an equally weighted mix of the S&P 500 index and the R2000 index, a difference exists between the benchmarks for the entire asset class and the sub-benchmarks used to evaluate the performance of outside managers. The third row illustrates the same benchmark differences for the inflation hedge. Finally, the last two rows illustrate the active risk taken by managers.

Both the decisions to reallocate tactically (i.e., away from the long-term asset allocation), as well as the decision to establish benchmarks, contribute to the overall portfolio risk and returns. For example, tactical allocations may generate negative returns and benchmarks may incentivize managers to make investment decisions that may further the downside.

Table 18.3 presents the returns, as well as the risk decomposition of the hypothetical fund of Reed, Tiu, and Yoeli (2011), with Panel A detailing returns and Panel B risk. As Panel A shows, the largest contribution to the portfolio's overall mean return of 11.78 percent is generated by the tactical decision to overweight the allocation to the inflation hedge asset class. The worst contributor to performance is the tactical decision to underweight U.S. equity. Overall, the tactical allocation makes a positive contribution to returns (equal to –0.84 percent + 5.12 percent). This contribution differs from what would be obtained by decomposing the portfolio solely across the asset classes in which the fund is invested, namely, U.S. equity and inflation hedge securities.

Table 18.3 **XYZ Returns and Risk Decomposition**

Benchmark Assets	Intermediate Benchmarks	Contributions				
		Asset Allocations (%)	Tactical (%)	Intermediate Benchmarking (%)	Active (%)	Total (%)
Panel A. Return decomposition						
U.S. Equity		4.18	−0.84			3.88
	Large cap			−0.02	0.17	
	Small cap			0.13	0.25	
Inflation hedge		2.56	5.12			7.90
	TIPS			0.00	0.09	
	Commodities			−0.02	0.15	
Total					11.78	11.78
Panel B. Downside risk decomposition						
U.S. Equity		2.60	−0.50			2.90
	Large cap			−0.10	0.10	
	Small cap			0.60	0.20	
Inflation hedge		0.90	0.20			2.90
	TIPS			0.00	0.10	
	Commodities			1.60	0.10	
Total					5.08	5.80

Note: The table presents the decomposition of returns and downside risk for the decentralized fund XYZ.

In the policy portfolio of the fund, the main return contributor is the U.S. equity asset class that generates 4.19 percent of the returns, while only 2.56 percent comes from inflation hedge securities. However, if the portfolio was decomposed solely across asset classes and investment decisions are not considered, then the main return contributor would be the inflation hedge securities, which generates 7.90 percent of the returns, as compared to only 3.88 percent generated by the U.S. equity. Because the risk statistic considered by Reed et al. (2011) is downside risk, assets generating higher returns may reduce overall portfolio risk, which is somewhat contrary to the intuition that higher expected returns are associated with higher risk.

Panel B of Table 18.3 presents the risk decomposition of the hypothetical portfolio. The largest contribution to portfolio returns is the tactical decision to overweight the inflation hedge securities relative to the long-term asset allocation prescription. The largest contribution to risk comes from the asset allocation decision to invest 50 percent of the portfolio in U.S. equity (a long-term asset allocation decision). The active decision to invest in commodities as an inflation hedging asset has the (negative) effect of reducing returns by 0.02 percent, while simultaneously increasing the risk by 1.60 percent. This result would be an investment decision that should be challenged and perhaps reversed based on its contribution to portfolio overall returns and risk. All the external managers add returns to the portfolio while increasing the risk, an observation consistent to the rewards-for-risk idea.

A useful exercise is to contrast the results of the simultaneous risk decomposition presented in Panel B of Table 18.3 with what would have been obtained if the portfolio decomposition occurred across the two asset classes only (U.S. equity and inflation hedge securities). If the risk decomposition is performed on these asset classes exclusively, each has an equal contribution to total downside risk (2.9 percent of the total of 5.8 percent). Taking this result in isolation combined with the fact that inflation hedge securities are an asset class with lower expected returns, the CIO may be incentivized to shift the asset allocation away from the inflation hedge securities.

The simultaneous decomposition yields a different conclusion. The inflation hedge securities provide a much smaller contribution of 0.9 percent to risk in the asset allocation policy, relative to that of 2.6 percent coming from U.S. equity. The primary reason for the high downside risk generated by the manager of the inflation hedge securities is a mismatch between the benchmark of the entire asset class—the MLIL index—and the benchmark employed for the sub-asset class of commodities, which is the GSCI. Because a third of the portfolio is invested in commodities, which are considerably riskier than TIPS, the manager of the inflation hedge securities generates a much higher risk than if she simply invested passively in her benchmark index. Using the classical risk decomposition across asset classes, one would not have arrived at this conclusion.

Risk Reduction for U.S. Equity Investors

The risk decomposition has the advantage that it measures individual risk contributions holistically in the context of a specific portfolio. In particular, the risk decomposition takes into account the correlations between different asset classes. When correlations between assets are lowered, risk contributions decline and may even result in lower overall portfolio risk.

This example from Fisher and Tiu (2013) illustrates how to lower the downside risk of a portfolio by actively "tilting" an asset class toward a factor with which other asset classes have low correlations. The authors start with the observation that the momentum factor as discussed in Jegadeesh and Titman (1993) and Carhart (1997) is relatively uncorrelated with other U.S. equity factors, such as value or growth. This finding can be exploited by creating portfolios that track growth or value indices but that are composed of high-momentum stocks. Fisher and Tiu's choice is to form a growth strategy using high momentum stocks and then to compare how this strategy performs relative to a "normal" growth strategy, such as investing in the R3000 Growth index. They provide the details of forming this strategy (dubbed "growth-to-momentum" or GTM) with an outline of its performance in Figure 18.1. Figure 18.1 shows that the GTM strategy outperforms, in absolute terms, its natural growth benchmark, the R3000 Growth index.

This chapter focuses on the risk analysis of the active investment decision to substitute this strategy in place of the R3000 Growth index in different equity portfolios. Following Fisher and Tiu (2013), three possible investment portfolios are highlighted.

- Portfolio 1 consists of an equally weighted mix of growth and value indices.
- Portfolio 2 consists of 50 percent of a growth index, 10 percent of the R2000 Value index, and 40 percent of the Russell 1000 (R1000) Value index.
- Portfolio 3 consists of an equally weighted mix of a growth index and R2000 Value and R1000 Value indices.

Such portfolio can be formed in two different ways, depending on the growth strategy used in its construction. More precisely, the more traditional R3000 Growth index or the GTM strategy can be used. The objective of this analysis is to evaluate the impact of this active decision on the downside risk of the portfolio formed. More precisely, does

Figure 18.1 THE VALUE OF $1 INVESTED IN THE GTM STRATEGY. The figure presents the value of $1 invested in usual growth and value indices as well as in the GTM strategy. Source: Fisher and Tiu 2013.

the active decision to invest in the GTM portfolio rather than in the R3000 Growth index help the investor reach a minimum required return?

In order to estimate downside risk, Fisher and Tiu (2013) investigate return objectives that either an individual investor or an institution, such as a foundation of a university endowment, may seek to achieve. They consider returns between 6 and 9 percent. For every such return target, they calculate the downside risk of the portfolio formed using the GTM strategy as a growth component relative to a minimum return. They then use Equation 18.7 to decompose the risk of the portfolio and especially to isolate the active decision to replace the R3000 Growth index with the GTM strategy.

For Portfolio 3, for example, Equation 18.9 shows the portfolio returns R^P:

$$\begin{aligned} R^P &= (1/3)\, R^{R1000V} + (1/3)\, R^{R2000V} + (1/3)\, R^{GTM} \\ &= (1/3)\, R^{R1000V} + (1/3)\, R^{R2000V} + (1/3) R^{R3000G} \\ &\quad + (1/3)\big[R^{R3000G} - R^{GTM}\big]. \end{aligned} \tag{18.9}$$

The last component, $(1/3)\big[R^{R3000G} - R^{GTM}\big]$, represents the contribution of replacing the R3000 Growth index with the GTM strategy when setting up the portfolio. Table 18.4 presents the overall downside risk statistics for each portfolio and the contributions of the active decision to tilt growth to momentum. As Table 18.4 shows, the active decision to employ the GTM strategy resulted in lowering the downside risk of the investment portfolio for all three portfolios and the target returns considered. That is, the tilt to momentum facilitated attaining the minimum required return in each of the cases considered. For example, in the case of Portfolio 1 and that of a target return of 6 percent, the overall downside risk is equal to 3.19 percent, of which the active decision to tilt to momentum contributes –0.07 percent. These results are consistent across all the cases analyzed.

As observed in Equation 18.9, three possible sources exist that may make the contribution of the active component to tilt momentum small. Specifically, the contribution of the component to the overall downside risk may be small because of the following factors:

- The weight of the components in the portfolio, w_n, is small, or
- The downside risk of the component relative to the entire portfolio return being lower than the target return, $\widehat{DR}_n$, is lower, or
- The downside correlation between the component and the portfolio, on the set on which the portfolio does not meet the required return, ρ_n, is low.

In this case, the downside risk contribution of the active decision to tilt the growth component to momentum is negative. The only way this can happen is if either the component weight or the downside correlations are negative and not both simultaneously. Here, the weights are always positive. Thus, the downside correlations, ρ_n, are negative in all cases considered.

Table 18.5 presents the breakdown of the risk contribution of the active tilt to momentum, more specifically, the downside risk statistics relative to the entire portfolio not reaching the target returns and the downside correlations. The active tilt

Table 18.4 **Downside Risk Decomposition of Typical Investment Portfolios**

	MAR = 6%		MAR = 7%		MAR = 8%		MAR = 9%	
	DR(%)	Corr	DR(%)	Corr	DR(%)	Corr	DR(%)	Corr
				Portfolio 1				
50% R3000V	3.06	0.96	3.10	0.96	3.13	0.96	3.17	0.96
50% R3000G	3.74	0.96	3.78	0.96	3.82	0.96	3.86	0.96
GTM vs. R3000G	0.38	−0.35	0.38	−0.35	0.39	−0.35	0.40	−0.34
				Portfolio 1				
10% R2000V	3.02	0.94	3.05	0.94	3.09	0.94	3.13	0.94
40% R1000V	3.67	0.94	3.71	0.94	3.74	0.94	3.78	0.94
50% R3000G	3.72	0.94	3.76	0.95	3.80	0.95	3.84	0.95
GTM vs. R3000G	0.37	−0.31	0.37	−0.31	0.36	−0.32	0.38	−0.32
				Portfolio 1				
33% R2000V	3.01	0.97	3.04	0.97	3.08	0.97	3.12	0.97
33% R1000V	3.67	0.95	3.71	0.95	3.74	0.95	3.78	0.95
33% R3000G	3.72	0.93	3.76	0.93	3.80	0.93	3.84	0.93
GTM vs. R3000G	0.36	−0.30	0.36	−0.30	0.37	−0.30	0.38	−0.29

Individual conditional downside risk and correlations

Note: The table presents the decomposition of the downside risk (DR) relative to a pre-specified target for different investment portfolios in which the GTM strategy replaces a typical growth strategy. The table covers four levels of annual minimum acceptable returns (MAR).

Source: Fisher and Tiu 2013.

differs substantially from the other portfolio components. In particular, the downside correlations of the active tilt with the rest of the portfolio are negative for all cases of minimum required returns considered. This finding means that the active tilt decreases the downside risk of the portfolio, enabling the investor to reach the target returns easier.

Table 18.5 also reveals several other facts about the portfolios that have been formed. For example, the downside risk of each of the "classical" components used (i.e., the R1000 Value index, R2000 Value index, R3000 Value index, and R3000 Growth index) are about equal conditional on the entire portfolio falling short of its average, attesting to the similarity in risk between these indices. For example, for Portfolio 1 and a target return of 6 percent, the stand-alone downside risk of the R3000 Value index

Table 18.5 **Individual Downside Risk Statistics and Downside Correlations**

	MAR = 6%		MAR = 7%		MAR = 8%		MAR = 9%	
	$\widehat{DR}_n$ (%)	ρ_n	$\widehat{DR}_n$ (%)	ρ_n	$\widehat{DR}_n$ (%)	ρ_n	$\widehat{DR}_n$ (%)	ρ_n
			Portfolio 1					
50% R3000V	3.06	0.96	3.10	0.96	3.13	0.96	3.17	0.96
50% R3000G	3.74	0.96	3.78	0.96	3.82	0.96	3.86	0.96
GTM vs. R3000G	0.38	−0.35	0.38	−0.35	0.39	−0.35	0.40	−0.34
			Portfolio 1					
10% R2000V	3.02	0.94	3.05	0.94	3.09	0.94	3.13	0.94
40% R1000V	3.67	0.94	3.71	0.94	3.74	0.94	3.78	0.94
50% R3000G	3.72	0.94	3.76	0.95	3.80	0.95	3.84	0.95
GTM vs. R3000G	0.37	−0.31	0.37	−0.31	0.36	−0.32	0.38	−0.32
			Portfolio 1					
33% R2000V	3.01	0.97	3.04	0.97	3.08	0.97	3.12	0.97
33% R1000V	3.67	0.95	3.71	0.95	3.74	0.95	3.78	0.95
33% R3000G	3.72	0.93	3.76	0.93	3.80	0.93	3.84	0.93
GTM vs. R3000G	0.36%	−0.30	0.36	−0.30	0.37%	−0.30	0.38%	−0.29

Note: The table reports individual, conditional, downside risk statistics $(\widehat{DR}_n)$, and downside correlations from the downside (ρ_n). The table covers four levels of annual minimum acceptable returns (MAR).

Source: Fisher and Tiu 2013.

component is equal to 3.06 percent, while that of the R3000 Growth index component of the same portfolio is equal to 3.74 percent. In other words, when restricted to the set on which the entire Portfolio 1 does not meet its returns objective of 6 percent, the risks that the R3000 Value index and that the R3000 Growth index returns fall short of 6 percent are about the same. This result alludes to the impossibility of achieving full downside diversification using only the traditional indices. Downside diversification is achieved through the tilt to momentum, which ensures that the growth stocks picked in each of Portfolios 1 to 3 have a negative downside correlation with the portfolios.

The high downside correlation of each of the traditional components with the entire portfolio further shows the impossibility of achieving substantial downside diversification using only the traditional indices. For example, as Table 18.5 shows, for Portfolio 3 and a return objective of 9 percent, the downside correlations of each of the R2000 Value, R1000 Value, and R3000 Growth indices with the returns of Portfolio 3 are equal to 0.97, 0.95, and 0.93, respectively. By contrast, the downside correlation of the active component with Portfolio 3 and for a return target of 9 percent is equal to −0.29. Apparently, tilting growth to momentum and using the GTM strategy in lieu of a traditional growth index has the potential to induce downside diversification effects that enable an investor to reach a preset target return easier.

Challenges in Risk Management

Both budgeting and managing risk present challenges. This section outlines some potential problems faced by a manager attempting to introduce the concepts of risk decomposition.

MEASUREMENT

The first challenge is measurement. What data should be used to measure and decompose risk? Although this chapter uses monthly returns and annualized the risk statistics, other choices are available. One challenge is to select the appropriate frequency. For risk statistics developed using second moments such as standard deviation or downside risk, Merton (1980) contends that higher frequency data are desirable. However, the correspondence between returns measured at different frequencies depends on whether these returns are calculated arithmetically or geometrically. Compounding returns while changing the compounding method may alter the risk profile of the returns and yield incorrect risk estimates. To illustrate, assume two returns, r_1 and r_2, that they are normal, independent and identically distributed (i.i.d.), with mean zero and variance s^2. Assume that r_1 and r_2 are continuously compounded. The correct two-period return is then $(r_1 + r_2)$, whose variance is equal to $2s^2$. However, if the returns are compounded geometrically, the two-period return is equal to $[(1 + r_1)(1 + r_2) - 1] = r_1 r_2 + r_1 + r_2$. The variance of this random variable is equal to $s^2(2 + s^2) > 2s^2$. If returns are compounded geometrically, one could incorrectly conclude that the level of risk increased. If such a conclusion is followed by a managerial decision to reduce risk, then the compounding error will result in lowering the expected returns of the portfolio.

PORTFOLIO DYNAMICS

The decomposition outlined in Equation 18.4 or Equation 18.7 assumes that portfolio weights are fixed. However, these weights vary in time as does the composition of a portfolio. Despite the fact that such a time variation in individual security weights is obvious (e.g., only in rare cases could an investor rebalance every individual security in the portfolio), risk is often measured when keeping weights constant. A typical approach is to calculate portfolio weights taking one snapshot of positions, and then to assume that those are the true weights. If asset returns, co-vary with the weights, then assuming fixed weights could result in misstating the portfolio risk.

DATA SAMPLING AND RETURNS DISTRIBUTIONS

Risk calculations differ when making different assumptions about the distribution of returns. For example, VaR can be calculated as VaR $= \mu - 1.65\sigma$. This calculation assumes that returns are normal and this assumption may not always be satisfied. Another potential source of errors is assuming that simple estimates from the entire sample extend to the entire sample. Assume that a risk manager calculates maximum drawdowns using 10-month periods for the S&P 500 index (i.e., the maximum loss incurred by an investor in the index for a period of 10 consecutive months). In 2005, the maximum drawdown was –42.87 percent (continuously compounded). This result corresponded to the period from December 1973 to September 1974. Yet, assuming that this is the true maximum drawdown for the S&P 500 index would be a mistake. In February 2009, for example, the index incurred a 10-month drawdown of –64.45 percent, which is 50 percent more severe than the drawdown incurred in 1974.

MISMATCH BETWEEN RISK AND UTILITY FUNCTION

A mismatch between risk and the utility function can occur if the criteria used to form the portfolio differ from the statistics used to track risk. For example, the most popular portfolio construction criterion is minimizing variance, while perhaps the most popular measure of risk is VaR. For a normal distribution, minimizing variance (subject to a fixed expected return) is equivalent to maximizing VaR. However, when normality assumptions are relaxed, the two concepts are no longer equivalent.

Summary and Conclusions

Risk budgeting is the process by which investors decide on the optimal amount of risk to take in their portfolios and then manage it. Compared to asset allocation, risk budgeting is a new process. The success of risk budgeting depends on the degree to which it is consistent with asset allocation. This chapter has outlined a few popular risk measures and explained how the risk of a portfolio can be decomposed across its components. An important feature of this decomposition is that market risk (e.g., experiencing unexpected volatility) should be separate from decision risk (e.g., the active decision to differ from an index). Although little can be done to decrease market risk, the decisions to invest in assets that are "too risky" can be reversed and the portfolio's overall risk level can be brought down to its optimal point.

The chapter also presented challenges encountered in the most basic part of the risk management process. For example, inconsistency in returns compounding may misstate portfolio risk. Assuming that sample estimates can be extended to the entire distribution may also result in risk estimations that are incorrect. Although adhering to these practices is advisable, risk managers should understand that their data may be limited.

Discussion Questions

1. Discuss the importance of measuring risk in a way that is consistent with the criterion used for asset allocation.
2. Discuss why VaR is not a coherent risk measure and why having coherence risk measures is important.

3. Discuss why dollar weights differ from risk weights in a portfolio.
4. Some contend that the method used to compound returns is important but others argue that compounding, high (low) returns always leads to high (low) returns. Thus, the method is irrelevant as long as it is used consistently. Critique the validity of this argument.
5. Explain the difference between VaR and CVaR.
6. Maximum drawdowns become more severe as more data become available. Discuss whether this statement implies that risk increases over time.

References

Asness, Cliff S., Andrea Frazzini, and Lasse H. Pedersen. 2012. "Leverage Aversion and Risk Parity." *Financial Analysts Journal* 68:1, 47–59.

Carhart, Mark M. 1997. "On Persistence in Mutual Funds Performance." *Journal of Finance* 52:1, 57–82.

Ernst & Young. 2012. "Turning Risk into Results." *Ernst & Young Research Papers*. Available at http://www.ey.com/Publication/vwLUAssets/Turning_risk_into_results.

Fisher, Gregg, and Cristian I. Tiu. 2013. "Grazing Correlations." Working Paper, Gerstein Fisher.

Georg, Co-Pierre. 2011. "Basel III and Systemic Risk Regulation—What Way Forward?" Working Paper, University of Jena.

Harlow, W. V. 1991. "Asset Allocation in a Downside Risk-Framework." *Financial Analysts Journal* 47:5, 28–40.

Jegadeesh, Narasimhan, and Sheridan Titman. 1993. "Returns from Buying Winners and Selling Losers: Implications for Stock Market Efficiency." *Journal of Finance* 48:1, 65–91.

Markowitz, Harry M. 1959. *Portfolio Selection: Efficient Diversification of Investments*. New York: John Wiley & Sons.

Merton, Robert C. 1980. "On Estimating the Expected Return on the Market: An Exploratory Investigation." *Journal of Financial Economics* 8:4, 323–361.

Pearson, Neil D. 2002. *Risk Budgeting—Portfolio Problem Solving with Value-at-Risk*. New York: John Wiley & Sons.

Reed, Andrea, Cristian I. Tiu, and Uzi Yoeli. 2011. "Decentralized Downside Risk Management." *Journal of Investment Management* 9:1, 72–98.

Rockafellar, R. Tyrrell, and Stan Uryasev. 2000. "Optimization of Conditional Value-at-Risk." *Journal of Risk* 2:3, 21–41.

Wachter, Jessica. 2010. "Asset Allocation." NBER Working Paper, Paper Number 16255.

19

Risk-Adjusted Performance Measurement

PILAR GRAU CARLES

Senior Lecturer in Economics, Rey Juan Carlos University

Introduction

The literature on risk-adjusted performance measures (RAPMs) began with the seminal study of Sharpe (1966) presenting what is now known as the Sharpe ratio. Since then, researchers and practitioners have created various measures in an attempt to correct some of the Sharpe ratio's shortcomings. Each alternative measure has one feature in common: the ability to compare the excess return obtained in an investment to the risk incurred. The measures differ largely in how risk is measured.

RAPMs have grown in importance in the last few years for two main reasons. First, with the development of investment funds, investors need a tool with which to evaluate the performance of different investment fund managers. Second, the introduction of the Basel II and III Accords regulatory framework requires banks to maintain provisions for possible losses due to the risks incurred. The regulatory framework requires banks to consider both performance and risk.

This chapter focuses on the analysis of measures to evaluate performance. These measures are then used to rank investments and portfolio managers who make investment decisions based on risk-return trade-offs. No consensus exists concerning the best RAPM for assessing an investment. Some authors such as Eling and Schuhmacher (2007) find that the choice of a performance measurement is irrelevant because they all lead to the same ranking. Yet, others such as Zakamouline (2010) and Caporin and Lisi (2011) find that different measurements give rise to different investment rankings.

Risk-Adjusted Performance Measures

The main difference between RAPM values is how they measure risk. The Sharpe ratio is based on the mean-variance paradigm and uses standard deviation as a measurement of total risk but this presents several problems. The literature widely acknowledges that asset returns do not follow a normal distribution (i.e., return distributions often present extreme data and asymmetry). Furthermore, the Sharpe ratio does not consider loss and gain variability separately. In his paper on portfolio selection, Markowitz (1959) claims that downside deviation is a better risk measurement than standard deviation.

This chapter focuses on five main methods for classifying RAPMs based on either volatility according to standard deviation, Value-at-Risk (VaR), linear regression, lower partial moment, or the drawdown concept. Another possible classification consists of distinguishing between measures that assume a normal distribution of performance, using mean and variance, such as the Sharpe ratio, excess return on Normal VaR and on normal conditional Sharpe ratio; measures that consider the upper orders of a distribution, such as the adjusted Sharpe ratio and modified VaR Sharpe ratio; and measures that do not take a specific distribution into account, such as those based on lower partial moments and drawdown. Although this chapter discusses only the most commonly used RAPMs in the literature, Cogneau and Hubner (2009) note that more than 100 RAPMs exist.

Table 19.1 shows the monthly returns of a financial asset for three years, together with the benchmark returns and a statistical summary of the series. These data are used to show the value of each of the RAPM described.

THE SHARPE RATIO

The *Sharpe ratio* (SR), also known as reward-to-volatility ratio, is the oldest and most commonly used measurement of performance based on standard deviation as a measurement of risk. Equation 19.1 shows the SR, which divides an asset's excess return relative to a benchmark, generally the volatility risk-free interest rate measured by the asset's standard deviation.

$$SR_i = \frac{E(R_i) - R_f}{\sigma_i}, \tag{19.1}$$

where $E(R_i)$ represents the average return for a security i; R_f is the risk-free interest rate; and σ_i is the standard deviation of the returns. The Sharpe ratio is typically used to evaluate portfolios in which case p representing a portfolio replaces i in Equation 19.1.

Investors use the SR to choose from investment alternatives. Specifically, a risk-averse investor will choose the investment that provides the highest SR. Assume that the mean annualized return for portfolios A and B are 11.2 and 9.8 percent with a standard deviation of 6.4 and 4.5 percent, respectively. In this case, portfolio A provides a higher expected return than portfolio B, but with a higher risk, as measured by the standard deviation. Also assume a market (benchmark) mean annualized return of 10.6 percent with a standard deviation of 5.8 percent. If the annualized return on the risk-free asset is 3 percent, the SRs for the three options are:

$$SR_A = \frac{11.2 - 3.0}{6.4} = 1.28 \quad SR_B = \frac{9.8 - 3.0}{4.5} = 1.51 \quad SR_M = \frac{10.6 - 3.0}{5.8} = 1.3$$

Based on this ratio, an investor would choose portfolio B because it provides the highest excess return per unit of risk as measured by the portfolio's standard deviation.

Because of its simplicity, the SR is one of the most popular RAPMs. It indicates how much additional return is received from the additional volatility of maintaining an asset with risk relative to a risk-free asset. Thus, investors prefer higher SRs. For example, in

Table 19.1 Sample Data Using Three Years of Monthly Return Data and Summary Statistics

Time Period	Asset (%)	Benchmark (%)	Monthly Risk-free Rate = 0.005%	Asset	Benchmark
	2009				
01-01	12.10	11.30			
02-01	4.20	3.50			
03-01	−12.30	−11.90			
04-01	−2.80	−2.20			
05-01	3.40	3.10		Asset	Benchmark
06-01	−3.70	−3.80	Monthly return	0.010	0.008
07-01	4.30	4.10	Annualized return	0.113	0.089
08-01	10.00	8.20	Monthly standard deviation	0.050	0.047
09-01	−3.15	−3.20	Annualized standard deviation	0.172	0.162
10-01	1.50	1.80	Skewness	0.126	−0.029
11-01	0.60	0.30	Kurtosis	3.791	3.642
12-01	−1.90	−2.00	Excess kurtosis	0.791	0.642
	2010				
01-01	2.00	1.30			
02-01	2.80	2.60			
03-01	−0.90	−1.00			
04-01	4.60	4.70			
05-01	1.30	1.50			
06-01	−3.80	−3.90			
07-01	2.60	2.70			
08-01	2.70	2.80			
09-01	0.40	0.50			
10-01	1.90	2.00			
11-01	3.00	2.80			
12-01	−5.90	−6.00			
	2011				
01-01	−0.80	−0.90			
02-01	1.70	1.60			
03-01	4.10	4.00			

(continued)

Table 19.1 (**continued**)

Time Period	Asset (%)	Benchmark (%)	Monthly Risk-free Rate = 0.005%
04-01	1.80	1.70	
05-01	−3.70	−3.80	
06-01	12.50	11.10	
07-01	−3.40	−3.50	
08-01	−4.20	−4.30	
09-01	3.50	3.60	
10-01	−1.60	−1.80	
11-01	7.50	6.70	
12-01	−3.80	−4.20	

Note: The table shows the monthly performance of a financial asset for three years, together with the benchmark and a statistical summary of the series showing average monthly return and annualized return, standard deviation, annualized standard deviation, skewness, and kurtosis.

the case of portfolio B, the Sharpe ratio shows that the investment obtained an excess return relative to the risk-free asset that was 1.51 times the added risk. Furthermore, a negative SR shows that the investment underperformed the risk-free asset.

The SR has an interpretation in the capital asset pricing model (CAPM) because it is the slope of the capital allocation line (CAL) within the mean-variance Markowitz efficient frontier as shown in Figure 19.1. In other words, the Sharpe ratio is the slope of a

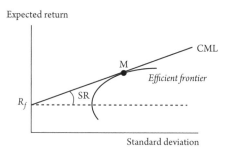

Figure 19.1 THE CAPITAL MARKET LINE AND THE SHARPE RATIO. This figure shows a graphical representation of the capital market line (CML) and the efficient frontier. The CML, which is a type of capital allocation line (CAL), is the graph of all possible combinations of the risk-free asset (R_f) and the risky asset, the line begins at the intercept of the minimum return and no risk (i.e., the entire portfolio is invested in the risk-free rate). The efficient frontier can be plotted as portfolios that have the greatest expected return for each level of risk involved. M is the market portfolio, which is where the highest feasible CAL is tangent to the efficient frontier. The Sharpe ratio (SR) is the slope of the CML.

line connecting the risk-free rate of return with the asset (generally a portfolio) of interest on the mean-standard deviation plane. Thus, the objective of finding the greatest possible slope is achieved by selecting the portfolio with the highest Sharpe ratio.

The SR has some shortcomings that investors need to consider. For example, it assumes the return series follows a normal distribution. This measure can lead to incorrect decisions when used with returns that deviate from a normal distribution, which is usually the case for some assets such as hedge funds. The SR is also difficult to interpret with continuous negative values, meaning negative returns or returns that do not exceed those of the risk-free asset.

According to the CAPM, excess returns cannot be negative, as in that case investors would select the risk-free option. Some maintain that in the case of negative returns, having more variability is desirable because the sign would be more likely to change. Thus, a less negative SR would imply less loss per risk unit. Others disagree and contend that greater variability is always less desirable. Israelsen (2005) and Scholz (2007) propose refinements of the SR to solve the problem of its possible negativity.

Moreover, according to Spurgin (2001) and Goetzmann, Ingersoll, Spiegel, and Welch (2007), the SR is prone to manipulation through so-called information-free trading strategies. Manipulation of the SR consists of selling the upside return potential, creating a distribution with high left-tail risk. With these strategies, a fund manager increases fund performance without actually adding value.

MODIGLIANI RISK-ADJUSTED PERFORMANCE OR M^2

One modification of the SR leading to the same ranking as the original is the Modigliani risk-adjusted performance or M^2 or the *Modigliani–Modigliani* measure of RAPM (Modigliani and Modigliani 1997). This measure is much easier to interpret than SR because M^2 has the advantage of being in units of percent return as shown in Equation 19.2:

$$M_i^2 = R_i + SR_i(\sigma_i - \sigma_b), \tag{19.2}$$

where σ_b is the benchmark standard deviation. Figure 19.2 shows a graphic representation of the M^2. If a vertical line is drawn from benchmark risk σ_b, its cut-off point with the SR line obtains the same performance as the SR but in benchmark risk units; it is known as the M^2, and enables a comparison of portfolios with different risk levels.

Using data for portfolios A and B, the M^2 is calculated as follows:

$$M_A^2 = 11.2 + 1.29(5.8 - 6.4) = 10.43 \text{ and } M_B^2 = 9.8 + 1.51(5.8 - 4.5) = 11.76.$$

So investors would again choose portfolio B.

THE ADJUSTED SHARPE RATIO

Many assets present a statistical distribution of return with asymmetry and kurtosis when compared to a normal distribution. Skewness quantifies the degree to which the distribution exhibits symmetry in which a perfectly symmetrical distribution having

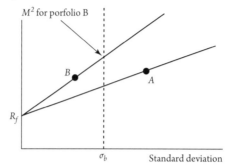

Figure 19.2 GRAPHIC REPRESENTATION OF M. This figure shows a graphical representation of the Modigliani performance measure. The cut of the vertical line from the benchmark risk with the Sharpe line is the M^2, which enables comparing portfolios with different risk levels.

a skewness of zero. An asymmetrical distribution with the mass of the distribution concentrated on the right has negative skewness and if the mass of the distribution is concentrated on the left, skewness is positive. Furthermore, kurtosis, which refers to the peakedness of a distribution, quantifies whether the shape of the data distribution matches the Gaussian distribution. A common practice is to use the excess kurtosis relative to a normal distribution. Excess kurtosis for a normal distribution is zero. Distributions with negative excess kurtosis (less peaked or flatter than normal) are called *platykurtic* and distributions with positive excess kurtosis (more peaked than normal) are called *leptokurtic*.

Pézier and White (2008) propose introducing these statistical measures in the SR calculation using the *adjusted Sharpe ratio (ASR)*, illustrated in Equation 19.3, which includes a penalty factor for negative skewness and excess kurtosis:

$$ASR_i = SR_i \left[1 + \left(\frac{S}{6} \right) SR_i - \left(\frac{K - 3}{24} \right) SR_i^2 \right], \qquad (19.3)$$

where S and K are the skewness and kurtosis of the return distribution, respectively.

The ASR takes into account the fact that investors prefer positive asymmetry and negative excess kurtosis, so it penalizes those portfolios exhibiting characteristics to the contrary. In other words, if S is negative and $K - 3$ is positive, the ASR will be smaller than the traditional SR. Both measurements give the same result if returns are normally distributed.

THE DOUBLE SHARPE RATIO

The SR ratio also presents a methodological problem. Because the requirements for calculating expected returns and standard deviation are measured incorrectly, the sampling distribution of the ratio may be difficult to determine due to the presence of the random denominator that defines the ratio. To solve this problem, Morey and Vinod

(2001) stress that sampling error substantially contributes to estimation error when considering expected returns and volatilities in financial portfolios. They propose using the so-called *double Sharpe* (DSh) ratio as shown in Equation 19.4:

$$DSh_i = \frac{Sharpe_i}{s_i^{sh}}, \tag{19.4}$$

where s_i^{sh} is the standard deviation of the SR estimate or the estimation risk. Bootstrap methodology is used to estimate s_i^{sh}. The initial idea behind bootstrapping is that a relative frequency distribution of an estimator calculated from the resamples can be a good approximation to its sampling distribution. This modification seeks to control for estimation error by capturing the standard deviation of the SR via a bootstrap approach.

To illustrate and compare all the ratios Table 19.1 provides three-year monthly returns of an asset and its benchmark. Equations 19.1, 19.2, 19.3, and 19.4 yield the following results: SR using raw data = 0.103, annualized Sharpe ratio = 0.354, ASR (annualized) = 0.359, M^2 = 0.120, and DSh = 0.601.

The difference between SR and the ASR is very small because of the small positive skewness and excess kurtosis. M^2 is the only measure that can be interpreted because it measures in percentage the return of the asset, adjusted for the risk relative to the benchmark.

Performance Measures Based on Value-at-Risk

In the early 1990s, several financial institutions proposed a new risk measure to quantify a firm's exposure to market risk by a single number commonly known today as Value-at-Risk (VaR). VaR is defined as the expected maximum loss over a chosen time horizon within a given confidence interval, $P(loss > VaR) \leq 1 - \alpha$, where $1 - \alpha$ is the confidence level, typically 0.95 and 0.99. Thus, if VaR for an asset is $100 million at a one-week, 95 percent confidence level, a 5 percent chance exists that the value of the asset will drop more than $100 million in any given week.

Formally, VaR is a quantile of the probability distribution F_x, that is, the x corresponding to a given value of $0 < \alpha = F_X(x) < 1$, as shown in Equation 19.5, which means that

$$VaR_\alpha(X) = F_X^{-1}(\alpha), \tag{19.5}$$

where F_X^{-1} denotes the inverse function of F_X.

Figure 19.3 shows a graphical representation of the VaR value. In the graph, VaR shows how much the portfolio can lose in the worst 5 percent case.

Because of its intuitive appeal and simplicity, VaR has become a standard risk measure worldwide. Bank regulators use VaR to determine minimum capital adequacy requirements. For example, the Basel Committee on Banking Supervision suggested in 1995 that banks use their own internal VaR models in order to determine their minimum capital reserves.

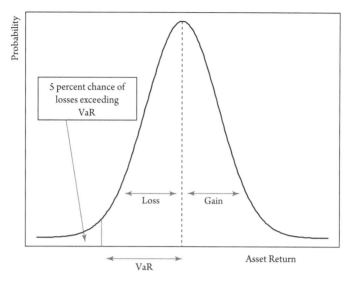

Figure 19.3 A GRAPHIC REPRESENTATION OF VaR$_{0.5}$. This figure illustrates the concept of VaR with a 95 percent confidence level.

The use of VaR instead of traditional performance ratios presents several advantages. First, VaR is a more intuitive measure of risk because it measures maximum loss at a given confidence interval over a given time period. Second, traditional measures do not distinguish between upside or downside risk, but investors are usually more interested in possible losses. Finally, several confidence levels can be used.

The excess return of an asset compared to VaR gives the Sharpe-VaR performance measure as illustrated in Equation 19.6.

$$Sharpe\ VaR_{i,\alpha} = \frac{E(R_i) - R_f}{VaR_{i,\alpha}} \tag{19.6}$$

A problem associated with this method involves different ways of calculating VaR. The simplest measure, assuming a normal distribution, uses standard deviation as a basis for the VaR calculation and looks at the tail of the distribution, as illustrated in Figure 19.3. In general, if the negative return distribution of a portfolio is $F_R \sim N(\mu, \sigma^2)$, VaR at a given confidence level is shown in Equation 19.7 as Normal VaR:

$$Normal\ VaR_\alpha = \mu + z_\alpha \sigma, \tag{19.7}$$

where μ is the mean, σ the standard deviation and z_α the quantile of standard distribution.

Historical VaR uses historical returns to calculate VaR using order statistics. The order statistics of a random sample are the sample values placed in ascending order. Let $R^{(1)} \geq R^{(2)} \geq \cdots \geq R^{(T)}$ be the order statistics of the T returns, where losses are positive, then *Historical VaR$_\alpha$*$(R) = R^{(T\alpha)}$. Historical VaR is simple to implement, makes no assumption about the likely distribution of the returns, and takes into account fat tails and asymmetries. However, Historical VaR has a major drawback because it is based on historical data assuming that the future will look like the past. For instance, if the sample period or window does not have many large price changes, Historical VaR will be low, but the actual VaR will be large if returns are more volatile during the sample period. This scenario will result in highly variable estimates that do not take the real economic climate into account.

Modified VaR, unlike Normal VaR, considers not only first and second moments (mean and standard deviation), but also third and fourth moments (skewness and kurtosis). The Cornish-Fisher expansion analytically adjusts the normal quantile for the standard normal distribution to include estimates for skewness and excess kurtosis as shown in Equation 19.8:

$$z^{Cornish\ Fisher} \approx z + \frac{1}{6}(z^2 - 1)S + \frac{1}{24}(z^3 - 3z)(K - 3) - \frac{1}{36}(2z^2 - 5z)S^2, \quad (19.8)$$

where z is the normal quantile for the standard normal distribution; S is skewness; and K is kurtosis, whereas $K - 3$ is excess kurtosis. Modified VaR is then based on Equation 19.9:

$$Modified\ VaR_\alpha = \mu + z^{Cornish\ Fisher}\sigma. \quad (19.9)$$

The Cornish-Fisher expansion penalizes assets than exhibit negative skewness and excess kurtosis by making the estimated quantile more negative. As a result, VaR increases. The expression, however, also rewards assets with positive skewness and negative excess kurtosis by making the estimated quantile less negative, thereby reducing VaR.

The Sharpe VaR is similar to the Sharpe ratio but measures excess return to risk-free assets relative to risk as measured by VaR in Equation 19.6. It can be modified similarly to compute the Normal Sharpe VaR, Historic Sharpe VaR, or, Modified Sharpe VaR.

The greatest problem when measuring risk by VaR is that the measure does not always meet the *subadditivity axiom*, a property according to which a portfolio's total risk should be the sum of the individual risks of each of its components or less. This property means that is possible to combine two portfolios X and Y, in such a way that $VaR\ (X + Y) > VaR(X) + VaR(Y)$. This relationship is counterintuitive because investing in independent portfolios generally reduces risks.

As a result, Artzner, Delbaen, Eber, and Heath (1999) conclude that VaR is not a coherent risk measure. To overcome the subadditivity problem and provide more information about the shape of the tail of the distribution, an alternative measure has also been proposed known as Expected Shortfall (ES) or Conditional VaR (CVaR). CVaR describes the expected loss if VaR is exceeded, so CVaR of a return series is the negative value of the expected value of the return when the return is less than its α-quantile. Formally, Equation 19.10 shows CVaR of X as:

$$CVaR(X) = \mathbb{E}(X|X > VaR_\alpha)(X). \quad (19.10)$$

Table 19.2 **Results of Value-at-Risk-based Sharpe Measures**

Measure	Asset	Measure	Asset
Gaussian VaR$_{0.05}$	0.0731	Gaussian VaR$_{0.01}$	0.0496
Modified VaR$_{0.05}$	0.0758	Modified VaR$_{0.01}$	0.0476
Historical VaR$_{0.05}$	0.1114	Historical VaR$_{0.01}$	0.0512
Gaussian CVaR$_{0.05}$	0.0566	Gaussian CVaR$_{0.01}$	0.0427
Modified CVaR$_{0.05}$	0.0563	Modified CVaR$_{0.01}$	0.0373
Historical CVaR S$_{0.05}$	0.0566	Historical CVaR$_{0.01}$	0.0419

Note: This table shows the results of Sharpe VaR and Sharpe CVaR measures using the sample data in the Table 19.1 with 95 and 99 percent confidence levels. VaR measures are calculated assuming normality of data in the case of Gaussian VaR, correcting for skewness and kurtosis in the modified VaR, and using order statistics in the case of the historical method.

CVaR can also be calculated using the methods described above, assuming normality (Normal CVaR), using historic data (Historical CVaR) or with the Cornish-Fisher correction (Modified CVaR). In this case, the performance ratio would be *the Sharpe Conditional VaR* (Sharpe CVaR)

$$Sharpe\ CVaR_{i,\alpha} = \frac{E(R_i) - R_f}{CVaR_{i,\alpha}} \qquad (19.11)$$

where $CVaR_{i,\alpha}$ can be calculated using one of the above methods.

Table 19.2 shows the results of the Sharpe VaR and Sharpe CVaR measures for the different ways of calculating VaR with 95 and 99 percent confidence levels. The Gaussian and modified VaR values are very similar because, as Table 19.2 shows, the data present little asymmetry and excess kurtosis.

Performance Measures Based on Linear Regression

Performance measures based on linear regression originate from the CAPM. The CAPM assumes the existence of a market portfolio and CML. Its purpose is to deduce how to price risky assets in market equilibrium. In this case, Equation 19.12 shows the expected return on any single asset is proportional to the expected excess return on the market portfolio:

$$R_i - R_f = \beta_i(R_m - R_f), \qquad (19.12)$$

where R_i is the expected risky asset return and R_m is the expected market return. The coefficient β_i represents the asset return's sensitivity to changes in the market return. In the absence of market equilibrium, Equation 19.3 shows that:

$$R_i - R_f = \alpha_i + \beta_i(R_m - R_f) \qquad (19.13)$$

with $\alpha_i \neq 0$. In this case, any asset with a positive alpha has an expected return that is in excess of its equilibrium return and should be bought, and any asset with a negative alpha has an expected return that is below its equilibrium return and should be sold (see Figure 19.4). With the current price of the asset, a CAPM model can be estimated for its equilibrium price and the decision can be make about whether the asset is overpriced or underpriced.

TREYNOR RATIO

Another measure that can be used to evaluate assets is the *Treynor ratio* (TR), proposed by Treynor (1965). This numerator defines excess return of a portfolio relative to the risk-free rate of return, but rather than divide by the total risk (using the standard deviation as the Sharpe ratio does), the Treynor ratio divides the excess return by the systematic risk of the asset as given by the asset's beta and illustrated in Equation 19.14:

$$TR_i = \frac{E(R_i) - R_f}{\beta},\qquad(19.14)$$

where β is the intercept coefficients defined in Equation 19.13. In other words, β is the sensitivity of the asset's excess return to changes in the market portfolio's excess return.

Figure 19.4 shows the security market line (SML), which is a graphical representation of the CAPM. The SML represents the investment's opportunity cost when investing in a combination of the market portfolio and the risk-free asset. The *x*-axis represents the risk (β), and the *y*-axis represents the expected return. The market risk premium is the slope of the SML. Any given point on the SML shows expected return

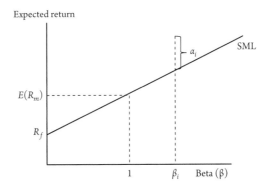

Figure 19.4 THE SECURITY MARKET LINE. This figure shows the security market line (SML), which is a graphical representation of the CAPM, and α and β values. The SML represents the investment's opportunity cost when investing in a combination of the market portfolio and the risk-free asset (R_f). Any given point on the SML shows the expected return for a security with the corresponding beta, which represents systematic risk. The Y intercept of the SML is the risk-free return. In the figure, a positive alpha means the asset has outperformed the market.

for a security with the corresponding β. Securities that plot above the SML are considered good (undervalued) investments, while those below the SML are not because they are overvalued.

The TR can be a useful measure for comparing a diversified portfolio with relatively little unsystematic risk. A fund manager with a higher TR than another manager with a similar beta is exhibiting better relative performance. The TR is a popular measure, but it has an important disadvantage. It ignores specific risk, only considering systematic risk, and also is based on the veracity of the CAPM model.

JENSEN'S ALPHA

Jensen (1967) proposes another performance measure known as *Jensen's alpha*. As Equation 19.15 shows, *Jensen's alpha* is the excess return on a portfolio over that which could be predicted for the portfolio based on the CAPM.

$$Jensen\ alpha_i = \alpha_i = R_i - [R_f + \beta_i(R_m - R_f)]. \tag{19.15}$$

If the Jensen alpha is positive, then the portfolio manager is doing better than predicted by the CAPM, given its beta value. The manager is "beating the market" in the sense of achieving a higher return than the portfolio's risk profile merits using the CAPM. A negative Jensen's alpha means that the manager is "underperforming the market" by achieving a lower return than predicted by the CAPM. Higher alpha values imply better active manager performance.

APPRAISAL RATIO

As Equation 19.16 shows, the *appraisal ratio* uses Jensen's alpha in the numerator, which is excess return adjusted for systematic risk, divided by the specific risk or standard deviation of the asset's return distribution:

$$Appraisal\ ratio_i = \frac{\alpha_i}{\sigma_\epsilon}, \tag{19.16}$$

where σ_ϵ is the portfolio's unsystematic risk or residual standard deviation. The appraisal ratio measures managers' performance by comparing funds' alpha (active return) to the specific (active) risk. The higher the ratio, the better is the manager's performance. Thus, the appraisal ratio is a measure of how much excess return the fund manager brings to a fund per unit of active risk.

Smith and Tito (1969) propose a logical alternative to the appraisal ratio known as the modified Jensen alpha. Instead of dividing by systematic risk, Equation 19.17 shows that the modified Jensen alpha divides excess return by β :

$$Modified\ Jensen\ alpha_i = \frac{\alpha_i}{\beta_i}. \tag{19.17}$$

In arbitrage pricing theory, introduced by Ross (1976), the CAPM is extended to multiple risk factors, giving rise to multifactor return models. However, obtaining a consistent portfolio ranking using Jensen's alpha is difficult because the ranking is highly dependent on the number of factors used (Alexander and Dimitriu 2005).

For example, using the sample data provided in Table 19.1, the results of the CAPM estimation related parameters and the linear regression measures using Equations 19.12, 19.13, 19.14, 19.16, and 19.17 are as follows. Beta = 1.0576 represents the asset return sensitivity to changes in the market return. Jensen' alpha = 0.0196, which is positive but very small, so the manager is doing almost similar than the predicted by the CAPM. The Treynor ratio = 0.0459 measures of the excess return per each unit of market risk. The modified Jensen alpha = 0.0185 measures the systematic risk-adjusted return per unit of systematic risk. The appraisal ratio = 1.5441, which measures the abnormal returns per unit of risk that could be diversified away by holding a market index portfolio.

Performance Measures Based on Partial Moments

Another approach that avoids some problems arising from abnormal return performance is based on *lower partial moments* (LPMs). LPMs measure risk by only considering deviations beneath a previously defined threshold. Following Kaplan and Knowles (2004), an LPM of order m can be estimated using Equation 19.18:

$$ LPM_m = \frac{1}{n} \sum_{i=1}^{n} min[R_i - \tau; 0]^m, \tag{19.18} $$

where n is the number of returns; R_i is a single return realization; and τ is the minimum return threshold.

This statistic gives rise to the notion of minimum return threshold or lowest acceptable return, so measures based on LPMs are more sensitive to extreme risks than measures based on volatility or standard deviation. The choice of minimum threshold is important. If the minimum threshold is too small, it will not appropriately consider the risks of the investment. If the minimum threshold is too large, it will not be good for detecting what is considered as a good investment. In fact, the major criticism for using LPM as a risk measure comes from the fact that the set of sample returns deviating from the threshold may be very small. Sortino (2001) recommends calculating downside deviation by means of a continuous fitted distribution rather than the discrete distribution of observations especially in cases of a small number of observations. He proposes using a lognormal distribution, or a fitted distribution based on a relevant style index, to construct the returns below the threshold to increase the confidence in the results. However, Shadwick and Keating (2002) point out some shortcomings of this method and recommend caution when calculating performance. Practitioners may want to choose several standardized threshold values for reporting results in different scenarios.

Furthermore, the choice of the order of the LPMs determines the weighting of the largest negative deviations from the target. If the order is 1, the statistic is also known as downside potential and can be considered the mean or expected loss. If the order is 2, the LPMs correspond to semi-variance or downside deviation. Thus, the order of the LPMs is chosen according to the investor's preference, with higher orders corresponding to a greater aversion to risk.

An advantage of measuring risk with LPMs is that they do not require any parametric assumptions about the distribution moments and no constraints exist regarding the form of underlying distribution. However, the most important criticism of using this measure is related to the choice of the threshold because it determines the size of the set of sample returns and the order of the LPMs also determines the weighting of negative deviations. The application of LPMs of order 1, 2, and 3 for performance measure calculation enables calculating such measures as the Omega ratio, Sortino ratio, and Kappa 3.

OMEGA RATIO

The *Omega ratio* (Ω) is an LPM-based performance measure originally developed by Shadwick and Keating (2002). A requirement for determining the Omega ratio is knowing $F(x)$, which is the cumulative distribution of one-period return, calculated by Equation 19.19:

$$\Omega(L) = \frac{\int_{L}^{b} [1 - F(x)]dx}{\int_{a}^{L} F(x)dx}, \tag{19.19}$$

where L is the minimum return threshold and a and b are the upper and lower bounds of the distribution. Following Kazemi, Schneeweis, and Gupta (2004), the *Omega-Sharpe ratio* can be converted to a ranking statistic in a similar form to the SR as shown in Equation 19.20.

$$Omega - Sharpe\ ratio_i = \frac{\overline{R}_i - \tau}{LPM_{1(\tau)}}. \tag{19.20}$$

Because the Omega-Sharpe ratio = $\Omega - 1$, it ranks portfolios in the same order as the Omega ratio. The main advantage of the transformed version is that it is more like the SR and therefore more intuitive.

SORTINO RATIO

Sortino and Van Der Meer (1991) offer another LPM-based measure called the *Sortino ratio*, which is the excess return on a threshold τ and the downside deviation δ. The downside deviation, or semi-standard deviation, measures the variability of underperformance below a minimum target rate. The minimum target rate could be the risk-free rate, the benchmark, zero or any other fixed threshold required by the client. All positive returns are included as zero in calculating semi-standard deviation or downside risk as shown in Equation 19.21:

$$Sortino\ ratio_i(\tau) = \frac{\overline{R}_i - \tau}{\delta}, \tag{19.21}$$

where δ is the downside deviation or lower partial moment of order 2.

The Sortino ratio includes the minimum return threshold and is more sensitive to extreme risks than the SR or other risk measures based on volatility measured by standard deviation. If the downside deviation is interpreted as the square root of the LPMs of order 2, the Sortino ratio can be rewritten as Equation 19.22

$$Sortino\ ratio_i(\tau) = \frac{\overline{R}_i - \tau}{\sqrt{LPM_{2(\tau)}}}. \tag{19.22}$$

When compared to the Omega ratio, the Sortino ratio uses an LPM of order 2 and assumes investors are more risk averse.

KAPPA RATIO

Kaplan and Knowles (2004) propose a generalization of this type of measure in the form of the *Kappa ratio* (K_n). Equation 19.23 shows the general form of this measure:

$$K_n(\tau) = \frac{\overline{R}_i - \tau}{\sqrt[n]{LPM_{n(\tau)}}}. \tag{19.23}$$

If $n = 1$, this results in the Omega ratio (K_1) and if $n = 2$, this results in the Sortino ratio (K_2). The most commonly used n value in the literature for the Kappa ratio is $n = 3$. However, the Kappa ratio is difficult to interpret, so it is only used to order the performance of different assets.

UPSIDE-POTENTIAL RATIO

Sortino, Van Der Meer, and Plantinga (1999) propose the *upside potential ratio* (*UPR*), assuming that investors are risk-seeking above certain thresholds and risk-averse beneath those thresholds. The numerator only uses the returns that exceed the threshold, while the denominator is the downside deviation and uses the returns that fall short of the threshold. Equation 19.24 shows the formula:

$$UPR_i(\tau) = \frac{UPM_1(\tau)}{\sqrt{LPM_{2(\tau)}}}. \tag{19.24}$$

Based on this statistic, Farinelli, Ferreira, Rossello, Thoeny, and Tibiletti (2008) propose a generalization of the previous statistics in the *Farinelli-Tibiletti* (p, q, τ), which consists of a ratio between the upper partial moment (UPM) of order p and the LPM of order q as shown in Equation 19.25

$$Farinelli - Tibiletti_i(p, q, \tau) = \frac{\sqrt[p]{UPM_p(\tau)}}{\sqrt[q]{LPM_q(\tau)}}, \tag{19.25}$$

where parameters p and q are selected according to the investor's preferences (Zakamouline 2010).

Table 19.3 **Results of Measures Based on Partial Moments**

Measure	$\tau = 0.006$	$\tau = 0.005$	$\tau = 0.004$
Omega-Sharpe ratio	0.2469	0.3141	0.3849
Sortino ratio	0.1305	0.1647	0.2000
Kappa 3	0.0946	0.1187	0.1435
Upside potential ratio	0.7659	0.7624	0.7693

Note: This table shows the results of the partial moments measures calculated using the sample data in Table 19.1 with three different thresholds: at the risk-free rate of 0.005 and at 0.006 and 0.004.

Table 19.3 shows the results of the statistics based on the LPM with three thresholds of 0.006, 0.005 (risk-free), and 0.004. Using the example data provided in Table 19.1 and using three different thresholds, the upside potential ratio, calculated using Equation 19.24, provides almost the same results using the three selected threshold values. For the other cases including the Omega-Sharpe ratio, Sortino ratio, and Kappa 3, the higher the threshold, the smaller is the ratio.

Performance Measures Based on Drawdown

This last category of RAPMs uses drawdown in the denominator to measure risk. An asset's *drawdown* is the loss incurred over a certain time period.

CALMAR AND STERLING RATIO

The *Calmar ratio* is a RAPM in which maximum drawdown is the greatest loss that an investor can occur by buying an asset at its highest value and selling it at its lowest value (Young 1991). As Equation 19.26 shows, the Calmar ratio measures the annualized rate of return over an investment's absolute drawdown value:

$$Calmar\ ratio = \frac{R_p}{D_{Max}}, \tag{19.26}$$

where D_{Max} is the absolute value of greatest drawdown of the period and R_p is the portfolio return. Analysts typically use at least a three-year return series for these calculations. Multiple variations of the Sterling ratio exist with the original definition of the *Sterling ratio* adding an excess risk measure to maximum drawdown, traditionally 10 percent. The choice of 10 percent is arbitrary and intends to compensate for the fact that the average of the maximum drawdowns is always smaller than the maximum drawdown.

$$Sterling\ ratio = \frac{R_p}{D_{Max} + 10\%}. \tag{19.27}$$

BURKE RATIO

The *Burke ratio* measures risk by the square root of the sum of the square of the *d* drawdowns of an asset as Equation 19.27 shows (Burke 1994):

Table 19.4 **Results of Measures Based on Drawdowns**

Measure	Asset
Calmar ratio	0.7475
Sterling ratio	0.4499
Burke ratio	0.5376
Modified Burke ratio	3.2256

Note: This table shows the results of the partial moments measures calculated using the sample data in Table 19.1. Using drawdowns as risk measure four different measures are calculated: the Calmar ratio, Sterling ratio, Burke ratio, and Modified Burke ratio, which is the Burke ratio multiplied by the square root of the number of data.

$$Burke\ ratio = \frac{R_p - R_f}{\sqrt{\sum_{j=1}^{d} D_j^2}}, \tag{19.28}$$

where d is the number of drawdowns; D_j the jth drawdown; and R_p the portfolio return.

The Burke ratio is less sensitive to outliers than the Calmar ratio. Because the Burke ratio uses the square of the drawdowns, the larger drawdowns are more heavily weighted than the smaller drawdowns, implying that a few large losses represent a greater risk than many small ones. The *modified Burke ratio* uses the ulcer index in the denominator, as Equation 19.29 shows:

$$Modified\ Burke\ ratio = \frac{R_p - R_f}{\sqrt{\sum_{j=1}^{d} \frac{D_j^2}{n}}}, \tag{19.29}$$

where n is the total number of observations.

Using the example data shown in Table 19.1, applying Equation 19.26, and using the maximum drawdown to reflect the investor's risk, the Calmar ratio is 0.7475 based using the average drawdown over the period of analysis. Equation 19.27 results in a Sterling ratio equal to 0.4499. Dividing the excess return by the square root of the sum of the square of the drawdowns (Equation 19.28) the Burke ratio for the sample data is 0.5376 and, finally introducing the modification of Equation 19.29 in the denominator, the calculus of the modified Burke ratio leads to a ratio of 3.2256. Table 19.4 summarizes these results.

Risk-Adjusted Performance Measure Applications

In portfolio selection theory, a typical problem is to determine how to choose assets from a larger group to build an optimal portfolio. The traditional method comes from Markowitz portfolio theory using a mean-variance approach (Markowitz 1959). In this theory, a portfolio is characterized by reward and risk, measured by expectation and variance or standard deviation, respectively. If a risk-free asset is available, mean-variance optimization merely involves maximizing the portfolio's SR. As a result, the SR continues to be the most popular RAPM, despite its shortcomings.

This measure, however, can only be used when the standard deviation is an appropriate measure of risk and the distribution function of the returns is symmetrical and similar to a normal distribution. On most occasions, the distribution functions of the returns of many types of assets are non-normal. Researchers and practitioners have proposed measures other than the mean-variance paradigm to solve this problem. Investors use most measures to evaluate the performance of alternative investments and to compare, analyze, rank, and choose assets. Two questions arise. Which performance measure should be used? Does the performance measure selected affect investment decisions?

An initial requirement to finding the right answer to these questions is to know whether all measures rank investments in the same way. According to Eling and Schuhmacher (2007) and Eling (2008), the choice of measure is irrelevant because they all provide the same rankings. The authors calculate the rank correlation between some alternative measures to the SR. Because the rankings obtained present a very high positive correlation, they suggest that the choice of the performance measure is irrelevant.

Others, however, disagree that the performance measure is irrelevant (Adcock, Areal, Rocha, Ceu, Oliveira, and Silva 2010; Zakamouline 2010; Caporin and Lisi 2011; Grau, Doncel, and Sainz 2013). Using the same data as Eling (2008), Zakamouline (2010) concludes that Eling's results are based on a reduced subset of measures and are solely supported by the value of the coefficients of the Spearman rank correlation. Although the correlations are high, many funds move from one position to another in the rankings. In fact, about 30 percent of the funds in the sample undergo ranking changes of more than 1.5 deciles and the largest change is an average of about four deciles. This means that although rank correlation is high, the rankings obtained relative to the SR differ. Moreover, based on the data used in the studies, most return distributions are approximately normal: 60 percent in the Eling and Schuhmacher (2007) and 80 percent in Eling (2008). Additionally, the remaining samples show deviations from normality that are not very high with low asymmetry and moderate kurtosis, so measures based on normality or that use parametric computing will produce similar rankings.

Zakamouline (2010) also notes that Eling and Schuhmacher (2007) and Eling (2008) use monthly data, so the results are only applicable to investments with a one-month investment horizon. According to Zakamouline, the rank correlation is lower with longer time horizons. Finally, a simulation analysis shows that distribution moments (asymmetry and kurtosis) play an important role in alternative performance measures. He concludes that funds with higher SRs undergo greater changes in their rankings, while higher SRs also correspond to higher asymmetry and kurtosis values.

Using U.K. investment trust data, Adcock et al. (2010) compare alternatives to the SR and conclude that the measures used provide similar results while investment strategies are similar. Yet, when using simulated return samples, they conclude that the choice of the performance measure does affect the performance assessment of investment portfolios.

Caporin and Lisi (2011) compare more measures and analyze equity data. They find little correlation with the SR for some measures and conclude that the degree of association can depend on the asset in question and the sample period. Caporin and

Lisi also find that rank correlations vary over time. Finally, they propose a way to reduce the number of measures forming groups of measures and considering only those carrying different information. Of the 80 measures studied, they conclude than 57 show redundant information that is similar to that of the 23 measures that they finally choose.

Using data from investment funds in the United Kingdom, Grau et al. (2013) conclude that different measures give different rankings despite the high correlations, which are unstable over time. The disagreement between the measures is greater the larger the difference between the higher moments in the distribution of profits.

Schuhmacher and Eling (2012) attempt to explain their results that all measures give rise to similar rankings by showing that measures based on partial moments, VaR, and other alternatives are strictly increasing functions of the SR. This finding is true under the distributions that maintain the location and scale properties (i.e., when all analyzed funds follow the same distribution and in case of three or four parameter distributions, shape parameter remain fixed).

In practice, investors often use the described measures for ex post comparisons of different investment funds or strategies. Yet, investors rarely use these measures for ex ante optimization. In fact, little experience exists in using measures not based on the mean-variance paradigm. Regarding the traditional approach for other target function specifications, only a few attempt to use VaR, with a small number of assets and unrealistic assumptions (Biglova, Ortobelli, Rachev, and Stoyanov 2004; Farinelli et al. 2008). The main reason for the poor development of other specifications of the objective function is the difficulty involved in optimizing portfolios with such target functions. This difficulty is because some resulting problems are non-convex and cannot be solved with standard methods. Thus, little evidence exists of the added utility of these measures when used for portfolio optimization.

Using heuristic optimization, Gilli and Schumann (2011) find that measures based on partial moments, drawdown, and quantiles can present better results than the benchmark (minimum variance). Their results improve when using long-term returns. They use heuristic optimization techniques, specifically threshold accepting, which do not require data to be approached by parametric functions and can solve non-convex optimization problems that cannot be solved by classic optimization methods. Gilli and Schumann also find that all the tested measures are sensitive to relatively small changes in the data.

Different measures consider different information about asset performance and how it relates to risk-free assets and benchmark portfolios. Thus, the preferences of each specific investor must be identified in order to know which measures are best adapted to their individual characteristics. Using a set of measures is also advisable because some measures are unstable over time.

Summary and Conclusions

RAPMs take on different forms depending on the benchmark used and how risk is measured. They can be classified as being based on volatility, VaR, linear regression, LPMs, and drawdowns. All of these measures have both advantages and disadvantages and their resulting rankings sometimes differ. Sample size influences rank correlations.

Such correlations are not time irrelevant. Although some measures may be redundant, they can also vary with different methods and parameters.

The SR ratio often does not provide enough and accurate information for making appropriate investment decisions. As stated previously, distribution moments can play an important role in risk-adjusted performance values, especially when finding the ratio that best fits an investor's preferences aimed at making the best possible investment.

Although some common performance measures produce highly correlated rankings, some alternative measures, especially those taking into account higher moments and tail behavior, provide different rankings. This outcome is a logical result because different measures carry different information about asset returns and their relationship with the risk-free asset and the benchmark. Thus, using different performance measures to analyze or select assets should consider the priorities of the investor. Using more than one measure, different data set lengths, and different frequencies is often desirable.

Discussion Questions

1. Stochastic dominance implies that if the same return can be obtained with two different investments, X and Y, yet the likelihood of a return exceeding a threshold α is greater for X, investors will prefer X over Y. Strict dominance occurs if $P_X(R > \alpha) > P_Y(R > \alpha)$ and weak dominance if $P_X(R > \alpha) \geq P_Y(R > \alpha)$ for any α. Provide an example showing that the Sharpe ratio does not respect weak dominance.
2. Discuss countering views as to whether a higher or lower negative Sharpe ratio is better.
3. Relative to the Kappa index, considerable debate exists about which order and threshold values are best for ranking funds. Indicate what the following options imply: (a) a higher Kappa order and (b) a high threshold value relative to a value equal to the risk-free value.
4. Discuss the advantages and disadvantages of using VaR as a risk measurement.
5. Discuss the consequences of using drawdown to evaluate a manager's ability.

References

Adcock, Christopher J., Nelson Areal, Manuel J. Rocha, Maria Ceu, Benilde Oliveira, and Florinda Silva. 2010. "Does the Use of Downside Risk-Adjusted Measures Impact the Performance of UK Investments Trusts?" The 23rd Australasian Finance and Banking Conference 2010 Paper. Available at http://ssrn.com/abstract=1662627.
Alexander, Carol, and Anca Dimitriu. 2005. "Detecting Switching Strategies in Equity Hedge Funds Returns." Journal of Alternative Investments 8:1, 7–13.
Artzner, Philippe, Freddy Delbaen, Jean M. Eber, and David Heath. 1999. "Coherent Measures of Risk." Mathematical Finance 9:3, 203–228.
Biglova, Almira, Sergio Ortobelli, Svetlozar T. Rachev, and Stoyan Stoyanov. 2004. "Different Approaches to Risk Estimation in Portfolio Theory." Journal of Portfolio Management 31:1, 103–112.

Burke, Gibbons. 1994. "A Sharper Sharpe Ratio." *Futures* 23:3, 56.

Caporin, Massimiliano, and Francesco Lisi. 2011. "Comparing and Selecting Performance Measures Using Rank Correlations." Economics Discussion Papers, No 2011-14, Kiel Institute for the World Economy.

Cogneau, Phillipe, and Georges Hubner. 2009. "The (More Than) 100 Ways to Measure Portfolio Performance Part 2: Special Measures and Comparison." *Journal of Performance Measurement* 14:1, 56–69.

Eling, Martin. 2008. "Does the Measure Matter in the Mutual Fund Industry?" *Financial Analysts Journal* 64:3, 54–66.

Eling, Martin, and Frank Schuhmacher. 2007. "Does the Choice of Performance Measure Influence the Evaluation of Hedge Funds?" *Journal of Banking and Finance* 31:9, 2632–2647.

Farinelli, Simone, Manuel Ferreira, Damiano Rossello, Markus Thoeny, and Luisa Tibiletti. 2008. "Beyond Sharpe Ratio: Optimal Asset Allocation Using Different Performance Ratios." *Journal of Banking and Finance* 32:10, 2057–2063.

Gilli, Manfred, and Enrico Schumann. 2011. "Risk–Reward Optimisation for Long-Run Investors: An Empirical Analysis." *European Actuarial Journal* 1:2, 303–327.

Goetzmann, William, Jonathan Ingersoll, Matthew Spiegel, and Ivo Welch. 2007. "Portfolio Performance Manipulation and Manipulation-Proof Performance Measures." *Review of Studies* 20:5, 1503–1546.

Grau, Pilar, Luis M. Doncel, and Jorge Sainz. 2013. "Risk-Adjusted Measures in Mutual Fund Performance. Are They Indifferent?" Working Paper, Rey Juan Carlos University.

Israelsen, Craig L. 2005. "A Renement to the Sharpe Ratio and Information Ratio." *Journal of Asset Management* 5:6, 423–427.

Jensen, Michael C. 1967. "The Performance of Mutual Funds in the Period 1945–1964." *Journal of Finance* 23:2, 389–416.

Kaplan, Paul D., and James A. Knowles. 2004. "Kappa: A Generalized Downside Risk-adjusted Performance Measure." *Journal of Performance Measurement* 8:3 42–54.

Kazemi, Hossein, Thomas Schneeweis, and Raj Gupta. 2004. "Omega as a Performance Measure." *Journal of Performance Measurement* 8:3, 16–25.

Markowitz, Harry M. 1959. *Portfolio Selection: Efficient Diversification of Investments*. Cowles Foundation, Monograph No. 16. New York: John Willey & Sons, Inc.

Modigliani, Franco, and Leah Modigliani. 1997. "Risk-adjusted Performance." *Journal of Portfolio Management* 23:2, 45–54.

Morey, Mathew R., and Hrishikesh D. Vinod. 2001. "A Double Sharpe Ratio." *Advances in Investment Analysis and Portfolio Management* 8, 57–65.

Pézier, Jacques, and Anthony White. 2008. "The Relative Merits of Alternative Investments in Passive Portfolios." *Journal of Alternative Investments* 10:4, 37–49.

Ross, Stephen A. 1976. "The Arbitrage Theory of Capital Asset Pricing." *Journal of Economic Theory* 13:3, 341–360.

Scholz, Hendrik. 2007. "Refinements to the Sharpe Ratio: Comparing Alternatives for Bear Markets." *Journal of Asset Management* 7:5, 347–357.

Schuhmacher, Frank, and Michael Eling. 2012. "A Decision-Theoretic Foundation for Reward-to-Risk Performance Measures." *Journal of Banking and Finance* 36:7, 2077–2082.

Shadwick, William F., and Con Keating, 2002. "A Universal Performance Measure." *Journal of Performance Measurement* 6:3, 59–84.

Sharpe, William F. 1966. "Mutual Fund Performance." *Journal of Business* 39:1, 119–138.

Smith, Keith V., and Denis A. Tito, 1969. "Risk-Return Measures of Ex Post Portfolio Performance." *Journal of Financial and Quantitative Analysis* 4:4, 449–471.

Sortino, Frank A. 2001. "From Alpha to Omega." In Frank A. Sortino and Stephen Satchell, eds., *Managing Downside Risk in Financial Markets*, 51–58. Oxford: Reed Educational and Professional Publishing.

Sortino, Frank A., and Robert Van Der Meer. 1991. "Downside Risk." *Journal of Portfolio Management* 17:4, 27–31.

Sortino, Frank A., Robert Van Der Meer, and Auke Plantinga. 1999. "The Dutch Triangle." *Journal of Portfolio Management* 26:1, 50–57.

Spurgin, Richard B. 2001. "How to Game Your Sharpe Ratio." *Journal of Alternative Investments* 4:3, 38–46.

Treynor, Jack L. 1965. "How to Rate Management of Investment Funds." *Harvard Business Review* 43:1, 63–75.

Young, Terry W. 1991. "Calmar Ratio: A Smoother Tool." *Futures* 20:1, 40.

Zakamouline, Valeriy. 2010. "The Choice of Performance Measure Does Influence the Evaluation of Hedge Funds." *Available at SSRN 1403246.* .

20

Risk Attribution Analysis

PHILIPPE BERTRAND

Professor of Finance, Aix-Marseille University, IAE Aix-en-Provence, CERGAM (EA 4225) and KEDGE Business School and Aix-Marseille School of Economics

Introduction

Competition among financial institutions has led to the development of performance analysis that examines the qualities of portfolio managers who use active investment strategies. Performance analysis allows for the investment process to receive an overall evaluation. The fundamental question addressed is: Does a given manager provide an actual value-added service with respect to a simple index replication (i.e., a passive investment strategy) or to a given benchmark?

As a by-product, Fama (1970) contends that performance analysis is a test of the market efficiency, which is based on different definitions of information. An active manager tries to take opportunities from particular information (public or private) that may not be reflected by current market prices. Analyzing a manager's performance requires the following:

- Introducing specific performance measures that take account of different types of risk. Therefore, several risk measures can be considered in order to evaluate the risk associated to the performance. Chapter 19 addresses this topic.
- Attributing this performance.
  - What are the exact contributions of each investment decision to the overall portfolio performance?
  - Does the manager exhibit skill or luck?
  - Compared with the benchmark, does the performance come from security selection or market timing?
- Examining the performance consistency
  - Is past performance a good indicator of future performance?

Using a benchmark portfolio is common practice in the financial management industry. A benchmark portfolio allows relative performance evaluation. Performance attribution separates a portfolio's excess returns with respect to a benchmark to active investment decisions such as asset allocation and security selection. Fama (1972) offers perhaps the first work to address this question in the context of the capital asset pricing model (CAPM). Fama's approach suggests that a portfolio's excess return over the risk-free rate can be decomposed into risk-bearing and security selection.

Being primarily interested in risk attribution, this chapter relies on a static framework, namely on a single-period analysis. In analyzing relative portfolio performance over long periods such as a quarter or a year, several portfolio rebalancings are likely to occur during this period. In such a situation, a multi-period performance attribution methodology must link periodic returns over time in an efficient way. Menchero (2004) provides a comparison of methods and especially for the optimized linking algorithm. The current framework is essentially equivalent to a holding-based approach in which the portfolio is analyzed each period on a buy-and-hold basis. Aspects linked to the return calculation (i.e., time-weighted returns versus money-weighted returns) and an attribution approach (i.e., a holding-based approach versus a transaction-based approach) are left aside to focus on risk attribution. Bacon (2008) offers more information on these topics.

A common practice in the financial management industry is to combine portfolio risk attribution with performance attribution. Performance attribution considered alone is insufficient and can be misleading. The rationale for risk attribution is that investors such as institutional or retail customers, as well as fund managers, need to identify the major sources of risk in their portfolios. Stand-alone risk measures such as volatility are insufficient because of correlations between assets.

Following Mina (2003), Bertrand (2005), and Menchero and Hu (2006), risk attribution began to be widely used in the performance attribution process. Bertrand's paper was perhaps the first to address the topic of risk-adjusted performance attribution, subsequently developed by Menchero (2007) and Bertrand (2009). As Biglova and Rachev (2007) point out, Bertrand (2005) is unique in proving that the underlying portfolio optimization program is consistent with risk attribution.

The organization of the chapter follows. The next section provides a brief review of the first models dealing with performance decomposition. The following section contains the basic method of internal performance attribution, called the Brinson, Hood, and Beebower model, and presents an example highlighting the limitation of this method with respect to risk. The next two sections present the risk attribution method based on a decomposition of tracking-error volatility and the method of risk-adjusted performance attribution in the context of tracking-error portfolio optimization (Bertrand 2005, 2008, 2009). The final section provides a summary and conclusions.

Performance Decomposition

Performance attribution tries to decompose the excess performance into identified terms by taking more account of the management process than of traditional performance measures of Treynor (1965), Sharpe (1966, 1994), and Jensen (1968). This section covers the first historical attempts to address the performance attribution problem.

THE FAMA DECOMPOSITION

Following the work of Treynor (1965), Sharpe (1966, 1994), and Jensen (1968), Fama (1972) proposes a finer breakdown of performance that separates overall fund performance, which is its return in excess of the risk-free rate, into two parts: selectivity (i.e., security selection skill) and portfolio risk. Fama's analysis is rooted in the CAPM framework. A portfolio P is compared to a naively managed portfolio C, which consists of investing a weight x on the riskless asset, and $(1 - x)$ on the market portfolio, such that the portfolio beta of C is equal to the beta of P: $\beta_C = \beta_P$. Portfolio C is the efficient portfolio, which has the same systematic risk as portfolio P and does not require forecast ability. Equation 20.1 shows this relationship:

$$\overline{R_C} = (1 - \beta_P)\, R_f + \beta_P \overline{R_M}. \tag{20.1}$$

Portfolio P may be less diversified. This risk may allow for an excess performance compared to the performance of portfolio C. Fama proposes the decomposition shown in Equation 20.2:

$$\underbrace{\overline{R_P} - R_f}_{\text{Total performance}} = \underbrace{\left[\overline{R_P} - \overline{R_C}\right]}_{\text{Selectivity}} - \underbrace{\left[\overline{R_C} - R_f\right]}_{\text{Risk}}. \tag{20.2}$$

The selectivity term measures the performance part due to the systematic risk undertaken by the fund manager. It is equal to the Jensen alpha. Although portfolios P and C have the same systematic risk, their total risks are different. If portfolio P is the main source of the investor's wealth, then total risk is the pertinent risk measure. In that case, portfolio P must be compared with a naive portfolio with the same total risk rather than the same systematic risk.

EXTERNAL ATTRIBUTION

By external attribution, these methods use only information exogenous to the portfolio management process, namely the time series of the portfolio and benchmark returns. They allow determining the fund manager's ability to forecast or time the global evolution of the market and to select assets well. Among the best known methods are the Treynor and Mazuy (1966) and Henriksson and Merton (1981) models.

In order to determine the quality of the forecast concerning the global evolution of the market, Treynor and Mazuy (1966) examine the evolution of the portfolio's beta with respect to market evolution. Typically, a successful market timing strategy is associated with a beta that is greater than 1 when the market is bullish and less than 1 when the market is bearish. If the fund manager has no market timing goal, then the portfolio's beta is constant. For that purpose, Treynor and Mazuy introduce a quadratic extension of the single factor model in order to allow for a convex relationship between portfolio return and market return. Then, without specific risk, points with components (R_{Mt}, R_{Pt}) would be on the straight line with equation: $R_{Pt} = \beta_P R_{Mt}$, where R_{Mt} is the market return at time t; R_{Pt} is the portfolio returns at time t; and β_P is the portfolio beta with respect to the market. With specific risk, but still with a constant β_P, one would observe a set of points such as in Figure 20.1.

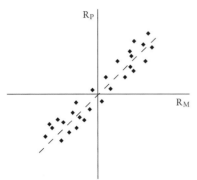

Figure 20.1 LINEAR REGRESSION OF R_P ON R_M WITHOUT MARKET TIMING ($\boldsymbol{\beta}_P$ = CSTE). If the fund manager has no market timing goal ($\boldsymbol{\beta}_P$ = cste) and in the presence of specific risk, one would observe a set of points such as in the following figure. Without specific risk but still with no market timing goal, points with components (R_{Mt}, R_{Pt}) would be on the straight line.

As soon as the fund manager tries to forecast the market evolution and modifies the beta accordingly, one would observe points in Figure 20.1 above the regression line for various market return values R_{Mt}. The set of points would be adjusted with respect to a convex curve, if the market timing strategy is successful, as shown in Figure 20.2.

Treynor and Mazuy (1966) propose a statistical method based on this property. More precisely, in order to allow for a convex relationship between R_{Mt} and R_{Pt}, they introduce the quadratic equation shown in Equation 20.3:

$$R_{Pt} - R_{ft} = \alpha_P + \beta_P(R_{Mt} - R_{ft}) + \delta_P(R_{Mt} - R_{ft})^2 + \varepsilon_{Pt}. \qquad (20.3)$$

If the coefficient δ_P is significantly different from zero, then the conclusion is that the fund manager has used a market-timing strategy (with success if $\delta_P > 0$ and failure if $\delta_P < 0$). Moreover, the alpha coefficient is still viewed as the fund manager's ability to select assets with returns above the equilibrium values given by the CAPM.

Henrickson and Merton (1981) assume that the fund manager can forecast whether $R_{Mt} > R_{ft}$ or $R_{Mt} < R_{ft}$. This assumption leads to the following regression model in Equation 20.4:

$$R_{Pt} - R_{ft} = \alpha_P + \beta_P(R_{Mt} - R_{ft}) + \delta_P D(R_{Mt} - R_{ft})^2 + \varepsilon_{Pt} \qquad (20.4)$$

with $D = 1$ if $R_{Mt} > R_{ft}$, and $D = 0$ if $R_{Mt} < R_{ft}$.

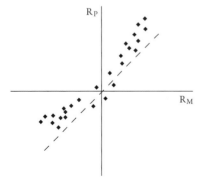

Figure 20.2 LINEAR REGRESSION OF R_P ON R_M WITH SUCCESSFUL MARKET TIMING (VARIABLE β_P). This figure indicates that as soon as the fund manager tries to forecast the market evolution and modifies beta accordingly, one would observe points above the regression line (compared to Figure 20.1) for various market return values R_{Mt}. The set of points would be adjusted with respect to a convex curve, if the market timing strategy is successful.

Then, the beta can take two values: $\beta_P + \delta_P$ (respectively β_P) is the portfolio beta when the market return is higher (respectively smaller) than the riskless return. A market-timing strategy is successful if δ_P is positive and statistically signicant. The fund manager's ability to select assets is determined by the Jensen alpha.

Internal Attribution

This section presents the internal performance attribution model. This method of performance attribution uses the time series of the portfolio and benchmark weightings. Brinson, Hood, and Beebower (1986) and Brinson, Singer, and Beebower (1991) introduce the most basic model of internal performance attribution.

ASSET CLASSES VERSUS RISK FACTORS

The Brinson et al. (1986) model is developed in terms of the classical asset classes' approach as shown in next section. Grinold and Kahn (2000) and Clarke, De Silva, and Murdock (2005) introduce a factor approach to asset allocation in the literature, which is also addressed in Chapter 5 of this book. A natural question to ask is: Why switch portfolio building from asset classes to risk factors? Asset classes are categories such as equities, bonds, and real assets. Ideally, asset classes should be as less correlated as possible. But many underlying common factors drive the returns of asset classes, leading to a high correlation between asset classes returns. The idea is to develop return and risk models directly in terms of factors, much as in the spirit of the arbitrage pricing theory (APT) (Ross 1976). The expected outcome is to be able to build portfolios that are better diversified and more efficient than those obtained by usual methods. A problem still remains of choosing the set of factors that better explains the returns of individual assets under management. This is a challenging task that may be guided by a statistical method such as principal component analysis as well as by economic and/or financial theory. Performance and risk attribution can also be performed in a risk factor framework. However, this chapter presents the standard and original approach of Brinson et al. (1986) to simplify the presentation.

THE BRINSON, HOOD, AND BEEBOWER MODEL

Brinson et al. (1986) propose the following method. Consider a managed portfolio P and a benchmark portfolio B containing n asset classes $i = 1, \ldots, n$. The benchmark is a consequence of an investment policy. The following notation is adopted.

- U denotes the universe of assets, $l = 1, \ldots, m = |U|$.
- $\{U_1, \ldots, U_n\}$ is a partition of the set U and is the set of n asset classes, $i = 1, \ldots, n \leq m$.
- R_l is the return of asset l (in vector notation: $\mathbf{R}$ where bold notations are used for vector and matrix). R_l is a random variable if ex ante returns are considered or a sample of observations if ex post data are analyzed.
- $\overline{R}_l$ is the expected (or sample mean) return of asset l (in vector notation: $\overline{\mathbf{R}}$).

- σ_{kl} is the covariance between the returns of assets k and l (in matrix notation: $\mathbf{V}$).
- z_{pl} (respectively z_{bl}) is the weight of asset l in the managed (respectively the benchmark) portfolio (in vector notation: $\mathbf{z_p}$ and $\mathbf{z_b}$).
- $w_{pi} = \sum_{l \in U_i} z_{pl}$ (respectively $w_{bi} = \sum_{l \in U_i} z_{bl}$) is the weight of asset class i in the managed (respectively the benchmark) portfolio.
- $w_{pl}^{(i)} = \dfrac{z_{pl}}{\sum_{l \in U_i} z_{pl}}$ and $w_{bl}^{(i)} = \dfrac{z_{bl}}{\sum_{l \in U_i} z_{bl}}$ are the weights of asset l in the asset class i of the portfolio and of the benchmark ($\mathbf{w_p}^{(i)}$ and $\mathbf{w_b}^{(i)}$ are the m-dimension vectors with elements $w_{pl}^{(i)}$ and $w_{bl}^{(i)}$ for $l \in U_i$ and zero otherwise).
- $R_{pi} = \sum_{l \in U_i} w_{pl}^{(i)} R_l$ (respectively $R_{bi} = \sum_{l \in U_i} w_{bl}^{(i)} R_l$) is the return of asset class i in the portfolio (respectively the benchmark).

Total value added by the portfolio managers is defined in Equation 20.5:

$$S = R_p - R_b = \sum_{i=1}^{n} \left(w_{pi}.R_{pi} - w_{bi}.R_{bi} \right) = \sum_{l=1}^{m} \left(z_{pl} - z_{bl} \right) R_l. \tag{20.5}$$

Equation 20.6 shows the expected or sample mean value:

$$\bar{S} = \bar{R}_p - \bar{R}_b = \sum_{i=1}^{n} \left(w_{pi}.\bar{R}_{pi} - w_{bi}.\bar{R}_{bi} \right) = \sum_{l=1}^{m} \left(z_{pl} - z_{bl} \right) \bar{R}_l. \tag{20.6}$$

The aim of portfolio attribution is to breakdown total value added into its main sources: asset allocation and security selection. As will be shown, an interaction term is required to obtain Equation 20.6.

Asset Allocation

When searching for the origin of excess performance, a problem occurs due to the allocation effect for one particular asset class. Indeed, the high weighting (respectively the low weighting) of an asset class leads to the low or high weighting of at least one another class.

One would expect to consider the following measure of asset allocation effect for asset class i: $\left(w_{pi} - w_{bi} \right) \bar{R}_{bi}$. The data contained in Table 20.1 show that this measure is not well adapted.

The last column in Table 20.1 leads to the conclusion that the high weighting of asset class 1 is judicious and that the relatively bad global performance of the portfolio is due to the low weighting of asset classes 2 and 3. Nevertheless, the fund manager has highly weighted an asset class that has a return smaller than the mean return of the benchmark (8 percent compared to 10.5 percent).

This example indicates the importance of accounting for the difference between the class return and the mean (or expected) benchmark return. Therefore, Equation 20.7 measures the contribution of asset class i to the total expected value added:

$$\overline{AA}_i = \left(w_{pi} - w_{bi} \right) \left(\bar{R}_{bi} - \bar{R}_b \right). \tag{20.7}$$

Table 20.1 **Asset Allocation**

Asset Class	w_{pi} (%)	w_{bi} (%)	$\overline{R}_{bi}$ (%)	$(w_{pi}-w_{bi})\overline{R}_{bi}$ (%)
1	25	15	8	0.8
2	40	45	10	−0.5
3	35	40	12	−0.6
Total	100	100	$\overline{R}_b=10.50$	−0.3

Note: The table shows that the term $\left(w_{pi} - w_{bi}\right)\overline{R}_{bi}$ is inappropriate to account for the allocation effect. The portfolio manager's decision to over-weight asset class 1 is not judicious because the return on asset class 1 is below the benchmark return. Therefore, the contribution of asset class 1 to asset allocation should be negative.

In turn, Equation 20.8 measures the total asset allocation effect:

$$\overline{AA} = \sum_{i=1}^{n} \left(w_{pi} - w_{bi}\right)\left(\overline{R}_{bi} - \overline{R}_b\right) = \sum_{i=1}^{n} \left(w_{pi} - w_{bi}\right)\overline{R}_{bi}. \tag{20.8}$$

Table 20.2 indicates the different cases and Table 20.3 applies this method to the previous example. Note that the poor performance of the portfolio with respect to the benchmark is mainly due to the high weighting of asset class 1, which is intuitive. Additionally, the poor global performance is the same as previously noted (−0.3 percent).

This is due to the relationship noted in Equation 20.9:

$$\sum_{i=1}^{n} (w_{pi} - w_{bi})R_b = 0 \text{ since } \sum_{i=1}^{n} w_{pi} = \sum_{i=1}^{n} w_{bi} = 1. \tag{20.9}$$

The *allocation effect* is also known as the *timing effect* as it can be understood as modifying "portfolio's asset class i beta" (i.e., the sensitivity of portfolio return to benchmark's asset class i return).

Table 20.2 **Contribution to Asset Classes**

	Over-performance Class i: $(\overline{R}_{bi} - \overline{R}_b) > 0$	Under-performance Class i: $(\overline{R}_{bi} - \overline{R}_b) < 0$
Over-weighting Class i: $(w_{pi} - w_{bi}) > 0$	Good Decision $(w_{pi}-w_{bi})(\overline{R}_{bi}-\overline{R}_b) > 0$	Bad Decision $(w_{pi}-w_{bi})(\overline{R}_{bi}-\overline{R}_b) < 0$
Under-weighting Class i: $(w_{pi} - w_{bi}) < 0$	Bad Decision $(w_{pi}-w_{bi})(\overline{R}_{bi}-\overline{R}_b) < 0$	Good Decision $(w_{pi}-w_{bi})(\overline{R}_{bi}-\overline{R}_b) > 0$

Note: This table displays the four cases that may arise regarding the contribution of an asset class to portfolio outperformance.

Table 20.3 **Asset Allocation Revisited**

Asset Class	w_{pi} (%)	w_{bi} (%)	$\bar{R}_{bi}$ (%)	$(w_{pi}-w_{bi})(\bar{R}_{bi}-\bar{R}_b)$ (%)
1	25	15	8	−0.25
2	40	45	10	0.03
3	35	40	12	−0.08
Total	100	100	$\bar{R}_b=10.50$	−0.30

Note: This table shows that when using the correct method, the results become consistent with financial intuition.

Selection Effect

Equation 20.10 gives the contribution to the total outperformance of the choice of security within each asset class:

$$\overline{SE}_i = w_{bi}\left(\bar{R}_{pi} - \bar{R}_{bi}\right). \tag{20.10}$$

Equation 20.11 shows the total selection effect:

$$\overline{SE} = \sum_{i=1}^{n} w_{bi}\left(\bar{R}_{pi} - \bar{R}_{bi}\right). \tag{20.11}$$

The choice of the benchmark weight for asset class i is justified in order not to interfere with the allocation effect. The difference $(R_{pi} - R_{bi})$ is different from zero as soon as the fund manager's weighting of the assets included in asset class i is different from the benchmark's one. Therefore, this framework allows for the measurement of the selection effect.

Interaction

The sum of the two preceding effects is not equal to the total outperformance of asset class i, S_i. To ensure equality requires adding a term referred to as *interaction*, which is defined by Equation 20.12:

$$\bar{I}_i = \left(w_{pi} - w_{bi}\right)\left(\bar{R}_{pi} - \bar{R}_{bi}\right). \tag{20.12}$$

This equation can be interpreted as the part of the excess expected return jointly explained by the two preceding effects. It can also be defined as an extension of the effect of security selection which would be the security selection effect on the over- or under-weighted part of asset class i. This relationship provides Equation 20.13:

$$\bar{S} = \sum_{i=1}^{n} \left(w_{pi}.\bar{R}_{pi} - w_{bi}.\bar{R}_{bi}\right) = \sum_{i=1}^{n} \left(\overline{AA}_i + \overline{SE}_i + \bar{I}_i\right). \tag{20.13}$$

Sometimes the selection and the interaction effect are grouped together in a single term of selection as shown in Equation 20.14:

$$\overline{SE}'_i = w_{pi}\left(\overline{R}_{pi} - \overline{R}_{bi}\right). \tag{20.14}$$

AN EXAMPLE OF PERFORMANCE ATTRIBUTION

Consider a fund with a benchmark consisting of 35 percent in domestic stocks, 50 percent in domestic bonds, and 15 percent in international stocks. Suppose that the management period corresponds to one year and the weighting of asset classes has been determined through a strategic asset allocation that is not modified during the given period. The numerical values are given in Table 20.4 with the measures of the three effects in Table 20.5 .

The benchmark and the portfolio generate returns equal to 9.35 percent and 10.10 percent, respectively. This excess performance is decomposed into 0.45 percent for the allocation effect, 0.23 percent for the asset selection, and 0.075 percent for the interaction effect.

This chapter does not address the relative importance of asset allocation policy (i.e., the benchmark in the current setup) with respect to active portfolio management (i.e., timing, selection, and interaction effects). This debate started with the publication of

Table 20.4 **Portfolio Characteristics**

Asset Classes	w_{pi}	w_{bi}	$\overline{R}_{pi}$	$\overline{R}_{bi}$
Stock (Domestic)	40	35	13.00	12.00
Bond (Domestic)	40	50	6.75	7.00
Stock (International)	20	15	11.00	11.00
Total	100	100		$\overline{R}_b=9.35$

Note: This table provides the statistics for an example of a managed portfolio against a given benchmark.

Table 20.5 **Performance Attribution**

Asset Classes	Allocation Effect	Selection Effect	Interaction Effect
Stock (Domestic)	0.13	0.35	0.050
Bond (Domestic)	0.24	−0.13	0.030
Stock (International)	0.08	0.00	0.000
Total	0.45	0.23	0.075

Note: This table shows the complete performance attribution of the managed portfolio of Table 20.4.

Brinson et al. (1986). Xiong, Ibbotson, Idzorek, and Chen (2010) review the main arguments and Kritzman and Page (2003) also offer insights into this debate.

INSUFFICIENCY OF PERFORMANCE ATTRIBUTION METHOD

As Bertrand (2005) notes, the previous method of performance attribution exhibits an intrinsic weakness in that it does not consider risk. In order to highlight the bias involved in excluding risk, consider a simple example. Assume that a fund manager follows the principles of portfolio choice theory as developed by Markowitz (1952). However, instead of finding the portfolio that minimizes the total return variance for a given expected total return, the portfolio manager has to find the portfolio with minimum tracking-error variance (TEV) for a given expected total return relative to the benchmark. Following Roll (1992), the set of all such portfolios will be called the TEV efficient frontier. Bertrand (2010) provides comparisons of various portfolio optimization programs under the TEV constraint. Thus, the manager's decision process is based on expected return as well as on the expected tracking-error risk of the assets under management.

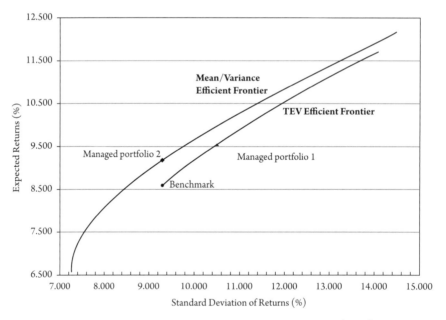

Figure 20.3 MEAN/VARIANCE AND TRACKING-ERROR VARIANCE (TEV) EFFICIENT FRONTIERS. This figure displays a portfolio manager's benchmark, which lies below the efficient frontier and is consequently not mean-variance efficient. In this framework, the portfolio manager can select an optimal portfolio on the TEV efficient frontier depending on the manager's tracking-error variance constraint and/or risk aversion (e.g., Managed portfolio 1). Managed portfolio 2 on the efficient frontier is also an example of a suboptimal portfolio in this context.

For expositional purpose, three asset classes each with two assets will serve as a hypothetical benchmark. Suppose also that this benchmark is not mean variance efficient, which is in general the case as shown by Grinold (1992). Because the distribution of the returns is supposed to be multivariate normal, the manager has perfect knowledge of the expectations and the variances of the returns of the six assets, as well as the correlation between the different assets' returns.

In this idealized world, the manager determines the TEV efficient frontier. She will select an optimal portfolio on the TEV efficient frontier depending on her TEV constraint and/or her risk aversion. Thus, the decision variable is the vector of the weights of the individual assets.

Figure 20.3 illustrates a situation in which the manager seeks to outperform her benchmark while controlling her tracking-error risk (or relative risk). In this example, the benchmark and managed portfolio 1 have an expected return of 8.60 percent and 9.60 percent, respectively; a standard deviation of 9.30 percent and 10.57 percent, respectively; and the standard deviation of the tracking error, T, is equal to 2.24 percent.

As Table 20.6 shows, even in this perfect world, the performance attribution will penalize some of the fund manager's optimal choices. The total excess return of the portfolio relative to the benchmark is 1.00 percent, of which 0.5081 percent is due to the allocation decision, 0.5308 percent is due to the security selection, and −0.0389 is due to the interaction term.

Although the manager selected the portfolio in an optimal manner with optimal information, the performance attribution is negative for some attributes. For example, the decision to underweight the asset class 3 leads to a negative contribution of −0.002 percent to the total portfolio outperformance relative to the benchmark.

Although these results seem paradoxical, the attribution of performance is incomplete because the analysis neglected risk. A well-known fact is that each optimal decision that contributes negatively to the outperformance can be interpreted in terms of relative risk reduction.

Table 20.6 **Performance Attribution Portfolio 1**

Asset Class	Portfolio Weight (%)	Benchmark Weight (%)	Weight Difference (%)	Allocation Effect (%)	Selection Effect (%)	Interaction Effect (%)	
	w_{pi}	w_{bi}	$w_{pi} - w_{bi}$	$(w_{pi}-w_{bi})$ $(R_{bi}-R_b)$	$w_{bi}(R_{pi}-R_{bi})$	$(w_{pi}-w_{bi})$ $(R_{pi}-R_{bi})$	
1	65.80	40.00	25.80	0.2320	−0.0270	−0.0170	
2	14.73	40.00	−25.27	0.2780	0.0120	−0.0070	
3	19.47	20.00	−0.53	−0.0020	0.5460	−0.0140	Total
	100.00	100.00	0.00	0.5081	0.5308	−0.0389	1.0

Note: This table provides the complete performance attribution of Managed portfolio 1 of Figure 20.3. Although this portfolio is mean-TEV optimal, the performance attribution is negative in some attributes.

Risk Attribution

This section presents the risk decomposition framework and then applies it to tracking-error risk measures. The section concludes by applying the risk attribution methodology developed here to the previous example.

THE GENERAL FRAMEWORK

As Litterman (1996) points out, some portfolio risk measures, such as the variance or the volatility of portfolio returns, are homogeneous of degree α in the portfolio weights. This means that when all portfolio weights are multiplied by a common factor $h > 0$, the portfolio risk is increased by h^α. Thus, Euler's homogeneous function theorem can be applied to such portfolio risk measures. Consider for example the variance of portfolio returns defined in Equation 20.15:

$$\sigma_P^2(z_{P1}, \ldots, z_{Pm}) \equiv \sigma_P^2(\mathbf{z_p}) = \mathbf{z_p'} \mathbf{V} \mathbf{z_p} = \sum_{k=1}^{m} \sum_{l=1}^{m} z_{pk}.z_{pl}.\sigma_{kl}. \quad (20.15)$$

It is a homogeneous function of degree 2 as shown in Equation 20.16

$$\sigma_P^2(h.\mathbf{z_p}) = h^2 \sigma_P^2(\mathbf{z_p}). \quad (20.16)$$

Euler's theorem gives Equation 20.17:

$$2.\sigma_P^2(\mathbf{z_p}) = z_{p1} \frac{\partial \sigma_P^2(\mathbf{z_p})}{\partial z_{p1}} + \ldots + z_{pm} \frac{\partial \sigma_P^2(\mathbf{z_p})}{\partial z_{pm}}$$
$$\sigma_P^2(\mathbf{z_p}) = \frac{1}{2}\left(z_{p1}(2\sigma_{1p}) + \ldots + z_{pm}(2\sigma_{mP})\right) \quad (20.17)$$
$$\sigma_P^2(\mathbf{z_p}) = z_{P1}\sigma_{1P} + \ldots + z_{Pm}\sigma_{mP},$$

where

$$\sigma_{kp} = Cov(R_k, R_p) = Cov\left(R_k, \sum_{l=1}^{m} z_{pl}.R_l\right) = \sum_{l=1}^{m} z_{pl}.\sigma_{kl}, \, k = 1, \ldots, m$$

Equation 20.17 can be written as illustrated in Equation 20.18:

$$\sigma_P^2(\mathbf{z_p}) = cov\left(z_{P1}R_1, R_P\right) + \ldots + cov\left(z_{Pm}R_m, R_P\right)$$
$$= cov\left(\sum_{k=1}^{m} z_{Pk}R_k, R_P\right), \quad (20.18)$$

which is the usual decomposition of the variance as a sum of covariance terms. Thus, for risk measures such as variance or volatility, risk decomposition does not rely on the computation of any partial derivatives.

Restating the result of Equation 20.17 in terms of portfolio volatility by dividing both sides of Equation 20.17 by the portfolio volatility is straightforward as illustrated in Equation 20.19:

$$\sigma_P(\mathbf{z_p}) = z_{P1}\frac{\sigma_{1P}}{\sigma_P(\mathbf{z_p})} + \ldots + z_{Pm}\frac{\sigma_{mP}}{\sigma_P(\mathbf{z_p})}. \tag{20.19}$$

Equations 20.17 and 20.19 are fundamental in risk attribution. They help identify the main source of risk in a portfolio. The risk contribution of asset k, $z_{Pk}\frac{\partial\sigma_P^2(z_P)}{\partial z_{Pk}}$, is the amount of risk that comes from investing z_{Pk} in asset k. The sum of risk contributions over all securities equals total risk as measured by the variance or the volatility of portfolio return.

The term $\frac{\partial\sigma_P^2(z_P)}{\partial z_{Pk}}$ is the marginal risk or risk sensitivity for asset k. It represents, other things being equal, the marginal impact on total risk of a small change in the weight of asset k, z_{Pk}. If the term's sign is positive, then increasing the weight of the asset at the margin will increase the total risk. If the term's sign is negative, then increasing the weight of the asset at the margin will reduce the total risk. Thus, assets with negative marginal risk can be considered as hedging instruments. Litterman (1996) points out that one important limitation exists to this approach. The decomposition process is a marginal analysis, which implies that the analysis is only valid for small changes in asset weights. Thus, this approach does not cover cases involving a major change, such as removing one asset entirely from the portfolio.

TRACKING ERROR RISK ATTRIBUTION

A measure is needed for the effect on portfolio risk both of the decision to over (or under) weight each asset class in the benchmark and of asset selection inside each asset class. Moreover, this measure needs to be consistent with the portfolio management context, namely a benchmarked portfolio. Thus, a natural candidate should be relative risk as measured by the TEV or by its square root, denoted by T. The results of the previous section can be directly applied to the tracking error of the portfolio return relative to the benchmark return.

As Mina (2003) and Bertrand (2005) show, the total standard deviation of the tracking error, T, of the portfolio relative to the benchmark can be expressed as Equation 20.20:

$$
\begin{aligned}
T = \frac{T^2}{T} &= \frac{(\mathbf{z_p} - \mathbf{z_b})'\mathbf{V}(\mathbf{z_p} - \mathbf{z_b})}{\sqrt{(\mathbf{z_p} - \mathbf{z_b})'\mathbf{V}(\mathbf{z_p} - \mathbf{z_b})}} = \frac{Cov(s,s)}{T} \\
&= \frac{1}{T}Cov\left(\sum_{l=1}^{m}(z_{pl} - z_{bl})R_l, \sum_{l=1}^{m}(z_{pl} - z_{bl})R_l\right) \\
&= \frac{1}{T}\left[Cov\left(\sum_{i=1}^{n}(w_{pi} - w_{bi})(R_{bi} - R_b), S\right)\right. \\
&\quad + Cov\left(\sum_{i=1}^{n}w_{bi}(R_{pi} - R_{bi}), S\right) \\
&\quad \left. + Cov\left(\sum_{i=1}^{n}(w_{pi} - w_{bi})(R_{pi} - R_{bi}), S\right)\right] \\
&= \frac{1}{T}[Cov(AA, S) + Cov(SE, S) + Cov(I, S)].
\end{aligned}
\tag{20.20}
$$

Alternately, Equation 20.21 illustrates the use of the second definition of the selection effect:

$$T = \frac{1}{T}\left[Cov\,(AA, S) + Cov\,(SE', S)\right]. \tag{20.21}$$

Equation 20.22 gives a meaningful interpretation of the previous decomposition of the tracking error. The relative risk contribution of a given asset class, i, can be written as:

$$Cov(AA_i, S) = \left(w_{pi} - w_{bi}\right) Cov\left(R_{bi} - R_b, R_p - R_b\right). \tag{20.22}$$

Thus, an asset allocation decision, AA_i, reduces the total relative risk whenever it is: (1) over-weighted (i.e., $w_{pi} - w_{bi} > 0$) and the excess return of asset class i in the benchmark over the benchmark return, $R_{bi} - R_b$, covaries negatively with total portfolio excess return, $R_p - R_b$; or (2) under-weighted (i.e., $w_{pi} - w_{bi} < 0$) and the excess return of asset class i in the benchmark and benchmark return, $R_{bi} - R_b$, covaries positively with total portfolio excess return, $R_p - R_b$.

Moreover, the relative risk contribution of a given stock selection decision within an asset class, i, can be expressed as Equation 20.23:

$$Cov(SE_i, S) = w_{bi} Cov\left(R_{pi} - R_{bi}, R_p - R_b\right). \tag{20.23}$$

Thus, a stock selection decision, SE_i, reduces the total relative risk whenever the excess return of asset class i in the portfolio relative to that in the benchmark, $R_{pi} - R_{bi}$, covaries negatively with total portfolio excess return with respect to the benchmark, $R_p - R_b$.

As Menchero and Hu (2006) point out, Equation 20.19 can be written as either Equations 20.24 or 20.25.

$$T = \sum_{i=1}^{n}\left[\sigma(AA_i)\,\rho(AA_i, S) + \sigma(SE_i)\,\rho(SE_i, S) + \sigma(I_i)\,\rho(I_i, S)\right] \tag{20.24}$$

$$= \sum_{i=1}^{n}\left[\left(w_{pi} - w_{bi}\right)\sigma\left(R_{bi} - R_b\right)\rho(AA_i, S) + w_{bi}\sigma\left(R_{pi} - R_{bi}\right)\rho(SE_i, S)\right. \tag{20.25}$$
$$\left.+ \left(w_{pi} - w_{bi}\right)\sigma\left(R_{pi} - R_{bi}\right)\rho(I_i, S)\right]$$

with Equation 20.26:

$$\sigma(AA_i) = \sigma\left(\left(w_{pi} - w_{bi}\right)\left(R_{bi} - R_b\right)\right), \quad \sigma(SE_i) = \sigma\left(w_{bi}\left(R_{pi} - R_{bi}\right)\right) \quad \text{and}$$
$$\sigma(I_i) = \sigma\left(\left(w_{pi} - w_{bi}\right)\left(R_{pi} - R_{bi}\right)\right) \quad \text{and}$$
$$\frac{Cov(X_i, S)}{T} = \frac{Cov(X_i, S)}{\sigma(S)} = \sigma(X_i)\,\rho(X_i, S)\,, \quad X_i = \{AA_i, SE_i, I_i\}. \tag{20.26}$$

Equation 20.25 leads to a meaningful interpretation. Consider, for example, the first term, which measures the contribution of the allocation decision to tracking error. It is the product of three quantities:

- The allocation decision variable, $(w_{pi} - w_{bi})$, is controlled directly by the asset manager. If it is equal to zero, the allocation decision variable does not contribute to the tracking error.
- The stand-alone risk of the relative return of asset class i is $\sigma(R_{bi} - R_b)$. If $R_{bi} = R_b$, then the allocation decision again contributes zero to the tracking error. This situation is very unlikely to occur because the benchmark would contain only the assets inside asset class i.
- The third term, $\rho(AA_i, S)$, reflects the degree of the linear dependence between the return of the allocation effect and the relative return. If this correlation is zero (or at least very close to zero), the allocation decision has no impact (or at most a weak impact) on the portfolio's tracking error. This relationship is true even though the volatility of the allocation effect is not zero. This situation can be a good opportunity for the portfolio manager to increase return without increasing relative risk of her portfolio.

Similar interpretations can be performed for the selection and the interaction effect.

AN EXAMPLE OF RISK ATTRIBUTION

Referring to the previous example in which the performance attribution of managed portfolio 1 in Figure 20.5 seemed to be paradoxical. Recall that this portfolio is TEV optimal. Table 20.7 indicates the tracking-error volatility of each component of the performance attribution process proposed in the previous example.

Once risk attribution is introduced, the portfolio manager's decisions become consistent again. According to proposition 2 of Bertrand (2005), for a managed portfolio belonging to the TEV efficient frontier, if a choice (asset allocation or stock selection) generates a negative performance, it also generates a relative risk reduction, and is thus justified. Thus, the paradoxical result of the preceding section is resolved.

Instead of a TEV efficient portfolio, assuming a mean/variance efficient frontier portfolio such as the managed portfolio 2 in Figure 20.3, Bertrand (2005) shows that

Table 20.7 **Risk Attribution**

Asset Class	$Cov(AA_i, S)$	$Cov(SE_i, S)$	$Cov(I_i, S)$	Total
1	0.5205	−0.0596	−0.0385	0.422
2	0.6231	0.0258	−0.0163	0.633
3	−0.0047	1.2234	−0.0323	1.186
Total	1.1388	1.1896	−0.0871	2.241

Note: This table shows that each decision leading to a bad performance is now clearly identified as a decision contributing to reducing relative risk and is thus justified.

some inconsistencies between performance attribution and risk attribution remain. Thus, some choices (asset allocation or stock selection) can lead to an underperformance and also to a positive contribution to relative risk.

Risk-Adjusted Performance Attribution

This section presents the method of risk-adjusted performance as introduced in Bertrand (2005) and Menchero (2007). The information ratio attribution is applied to TEV-efficient portfolios. Bertrand shows that the component information ratio is the same across all TEV frontier portfolios. This presentation relies on Bertrand (2009).

THE GENERAL FRAMEWORK

The *information ratio*, which is the ratio of excess return over tracking-error volatility as defined in Jorion (2003) and Bertrand (2010), serves a measure of risk-adjusted performance. Bertrand (2005) discusses risk-adjusted performance attribution: the risk attribution decomposition method appears in Equation 20.27. He examines the consistency between performance and risk attribution for TEV efficient portfolios and establishes a property on the component information ratio of these portfolios. Similarly, Xiang (2006) and Menchero (2007) propose a method of decomposition of the information ratio of the whole portfolio without considering whether portfolios are efficient (e.g., mean-variance or TEV). In Equation 20.27, the information ratio of the portfolio is given by (selection and interaction effects are grouped):

$$IR_P = \frac{\overline{R}_p - \overline{R}_b}{\sigma\left(\overline{R}_p - \overline{R}_b\right)} = \frac{\overline{S}}{T} = \sum_{i=1}^{n}\left(\frac{\overline{AA_i + SE_i}}{T}\right) = \sum_{i=1}^{n}\sum_{m=1}^{2}\left(\frac{\overline{X}_{im}}{T}\right).$$ (20.27)

$$X_{i1} = AA_i, \ X_{i2} = SE_i$$

By multiplying and dividing by the contribution of X_{im} to the tracking error, $Cov(X_{im}, S)/T$, Equation 20.28 emerges:

$$IR_P = \sum_{i=1}^{n}\sum_{m=1}^{2}\left(\frac{Cov(X_{im}, S)}{T^2}\frac{\overline{X}_{im}}{Cov(X_{im}, S)\ T}\right).$$ (20.28)

Substituting Equation 20.26 into Equation 20.28 leads to the expression in Equation 20.29:

$$IR_P = \sum_{i=1}^{n}\sum_{m=1}^{2}\left(\frac{\sigma(X_{im})\ \rho(X_{im}, S)}{T}IR(X_{im})\right)$$ (20.29)

with $IR(X_{im}) = 1/\rho(X_{im}, S)\ \overline{X}_{im}\ \sigma(X_{im})$.

The first term of the right member of Equations 20.28 and 20.29 is interpreted as the risk weight of decision im and will be denoted RW_{im}. These weights sum to unity as expected. The second term is defined as the information ratio of the component X_{im}. It is the product of the stand-alone information ratio of the decision im, $\overline{X}_{im}/\sigma(X_{im})$, and a factor, $1/\rho(X_{im}, S)$, which reflects the inclusion of the decision within a portfolio. This factor takes into account the diversification effect.

Thus, the analysis of the information ratio attribution involves three levels:

- The *stand-alone* information ratio of the decision im, $\dfrac{\overline{X}_{im}}{\sigma(X_{im})}$ which is of the sign of $\overline{X}_{im}$.
- The *component* information ratio, $IR(X_{im})$, whose sign depends on that of $\overline{X}_{im}$ and $\rho(X_{im}, S)$. Thus, when $\rho(X_{im}, S)$ is negative, its sign is opposite to that of $\dfrac{\overline{X}_{im}}{\sigma(X_{im})}$.
- The *contribution* of the component X_{im} to the information ratio of the portfolio, IR_P, $\dfrac{\overline{X}_{im}}{T}$. Its sign depends only on that of $\overline{X}_{im}$.

Table 20.8 summarizes the different cases for the sign of the three terms of the information ratio decomposition. First, note that the sign of the risk weight depends only on the sign of the coefficient of correlation, $\rho(X_{im}, S)$. Two cases must be distinguished according to the sign of $\rho(X_{im}, S)$:

- $\rho(X_{im}, S) > 0$: Whether $\overline{X}_{im} > 0$ or $\overline{X}_{im} < 0$, the results for the three levels of the analysis of the information ratio are consistent with one another. Namely, their signs are the same. For example, the case at the bottom/left means that a decision that generates an underperformance and that contributes positively to relative risk, exhibits a negative component information ratio and also contributes negatively to the portfolio information ratio.
- $\rho(X_{im}, S) < 0$: Whatever the sign of the performance attribution term, conflicts exist between some of the three terms of the decomposition.

Based on the case at the top/right, a decision that generates an outperformance and that decreases relative risk exhibits a negative component information ratio, although the contribution to the information ratio is positive. Thus, a good decision is poorly rated by $IR(X_{im})$ and well rated by $\dfrac{\overline{X}_{im}}{T}$ since its risk weight, RW_{im}, is negative.

Table 20.8 **Sign of the Three Terms of the Information Ratio Decomposition**

	$\rho(X_{im}, S) > 0 \ (RW_{im} > 0)$	$\rho(X_{im}, S) < 0 \ (RW_{im} < 0)$
$\overline{X}_{im} > 0$	$\dfrac{\overline{X}_{im}}{\sigma(X_{im})} > 0,\ IR(X_{im}) > 0,\ \dfrac{\overline{X}_{im}}{T} > 0$	$\dfrac{\overline{X}_{im}}{\sigma(X_{im})} > 0,\ IR(X_{im}) < 0,\ \dfrac{\overline{X}_{im}}{T} > 0$
$\overline{X}_{im} < 0$	$\dfrac{\overline{X}_{im}}{\sigma(X_{im})} < 0,\ IR(X_{im}) < 0,\ \dfrac{\overline{X}_{im}}{T} < 0$	$\dfrac{\overline{X}_{im}}{\sigma(X_{im})} < 0,\ IR(X_{im}) > 0,\ \dfrac{\overline{X}_{im}}{T} < 0$

Note: This table displays the sign of the three levels in the analysis of the information ratio attribution as a function of the coefficient of correlation $\rho(X_{im}, S)$ and the expected excess return, $\overline{X}_{im}$.

The case at the bottom/right leads to another conflict. The decision leads to an underperformance as well as a relative risk reduction. It is also a legitimate decision that is well rated by $IR(X_{im})$ and poorly rated by $\frac{X_{im}}{T}$ because of its negative risk weight.

INFORMATION RATIO ATTRIBUTION: TEV FRONTIER PORTFOLIOS

Proposition 2 of Bertrand (2005) establishes that for any TEV efficient portfolio, the information ratio of each component of the risk attribution decomposition is the same and is equal to the information ratio of the whole portfolio, IR_P. The expression "information ratio" is used here as a ratio of an outperformance over relative risk. This latter is defined as the contribution of the decision (allocation or selection) to the total relative risk of the managed portfolio as measured by the volatility of the tracking error, T as shown in Equation 20.30:

$$IR\,(AA_i) = \frac{\left(w_{pi} - w_{bi}\right)\left(\overline{R}_{bi} - \overline{R}_b\right)}{\dfrac{Cov(AA_i, S)}{T}} = IR_P$$

$$IR\,(SE_i) = \frac{w_{pi}\left(\overline{R}_{pi} - \overline{R}_{bi}\right)}{\dfrac{Cov(SE_i, S)}{T}} = IR_P.$$

(20.30)

An assumption is that the benchmark is not mean variance efficient, which is in general the case, as shown by Grinold (1992) and supposed by Roll (1992). Thus, if the managed portfolio is selected on the TEV efficient frontier, the appropriate risk attribution is the standard deviation of the tracking error for each component of the decomposition. Indeed, if a choice (asset allocation or security selection) generates negative performance, it also generates a relative risk reduction, and is thus justified.

Moreover, the uniformity of the information ratio for all the components of the decomposition is the consequence of some equilibrium that has been reached between expected excess return and relative risk of each decision (allocation and selection). In other words, the portfolio solutions to the TEV optimization program are Pareto optimal and this property is preserved by the decomposition of the excess return of the portfolio into allocation contribution and selection contribution.

Summary and Conclusions

This chapter discusses the basic performance model of Brinson, et al. (1986) as well as its limitations arising from not accounting for risk. Performance attribution is a useful tool that can help portfolio managers analyze the source of their performance relative to a benchmark portfolio. Since Sharpe (1964) introduced the CAPM, financial theory argues that the equilibrium of financial markets imply a trade-off between asset's covariance risk (i.e., beta) and an asset's expected return. This trade-off must also apply to attribution analysis. Thus, risk attribution must be introduced to complement performance attribution and makes justifying portfolio manager's choices possible. This was previously penalized by the performance attribution method alone. The next step is to combine the two attribution measures into a single one: a measure of risk-adjusted performance attribution.

Acknowledgments

The author gratefully acknowledges Palgrave Macmillan for giving permission to use materials previously published by the author in the *Journal of Asset Management* 5:6 (2005) and 10:2 (2009).

Disclaimer

This material contains the current opinions of the author but not necessarily those of Aix-Marseille University or KEDGE Business School and such opinions are subject to change without notice.

Discussion and Questions

1. Discuss why considering performance attribution alone can be misleading in evaluating portfolio performance. Identify what the process lacks to be consistent with financial theory.
2. Discuss why risk attribution is defined by tracking-error volatility decomposition and not by volatility decomposition.
3. Discuss the different decompositions of the standard deviation of the tracking error.
4. Discuss why risk attribution applied to Markowitz efficient portfolios does not lead to perfect consistency with performance attribution.
5. Discuss an issue arising when undertaking risk-adjusted performance attribution.

References

Bacon, Carl R. 2008. *Practical Portfolio Performance Measurement and Attribution*. Hoboken, NJ: John Wiley & Sons.

Bertrand, Philippe. 2005. "A Note on Portfolio Performance Attribution: Taking Risk into Account." *Journal of Asset Management* 5:6, 428–437.

Bertrand, Philippe. 2008. "Risk Attribution and Portfolio Optimizations under Tracking-Error Constraints." *Journal of Performance Measurement* 13:1, 53–66.

Bertrand, Philippe. 2009. "Risk-Adjusted Performance Attribution and Portfolio Optimizations under Tracking-Error Constraints." *Journal of Asset Management* 10:2, 75–88.

Bertrand, Philippe. 2010. "Another Look at Portfolio Optimization under Tracking-Error Constraint." *Financial Analysts Journal* 66:3, 78–90.

Biglova, Almira, and Svetlozar Rachev. 2007. "Portfolio Performance Attribution." *Investment Management and Financial Innovations* 4:3, 7–22.

Brinson, Gary P., L. Randolph Hood, and Gilbert L. Beebower. 1986. "Determinants of Portfolio Performance." *Financial Analysts Journal* 42:4, 39–44.

Brinson, Gary P., Brian D. Singer, and Gilbert L. Beebower. 1991. "Determinants of Portfolio Performance II: An Update." *Financial Analysts Journal* 5:6, 40–48.

Clarke, Roger G., Harindra de Silva, and Robert Murdock. 2005. "A Factor Approach to Asset Allocation." *Journal of Portfolio Management* 32:1, 10–21.

Fama, Eugene F. 1970. "Efficient Capital Markets: A Review of Theory and Empirical Work." *Journal of Finance* 25:2, 383–417.

Fama, Eugene F. 1972. "Components of Investment Performance." *Journal of Finance* 27:3, 551–567.

Grinold, Richard C. 1992. "Are Benchmark Portfolios Efficient?" *Journal of Portfolio Management* 19:1, 34–40.

Grinold, Richard C., and Ronald N. Kahn. 2000. *Active Portfolio Management*, 2nd Edition. New York: McGraw-Hill.

Henriksson, Roy D., and Robert C. Merton. 1981. "On Market Timing and Investment Performance. II. Statistical Procedures for Evaluating Forecasting Skills." *Journal of Business* 54:4, 513–533.

Jensen, Michael. 1968. "The Performance of Mutual Funds in the Period 1945-1964." *Journal of Finance* 23:2, 389–416.

Jorion, Philippe. 2003. "Portfolio Optimization with Constraints on Tracking-Error." *Financial Analysts Journal* 59:5, 70–82.

Kritzman, Mark, and Sébastien Page. 2003. "The Hierarchy of Investment Choice." *Journal of Portfolio Management* 29:4, 11–23.

Litterman, Robert. 1996. "Hot Spots^{TM} and Hedges." Working Paper, Goldman Sachs Risk Management Series.

Markowitz, Harry M. 1952. "Portfolio Selection." *Journal of Finance* 7:1, 77–91.

Menchero, Jose. 2004. "Multiperiod Arithmetic Attribution." *Financial Analysts Journal* 60:4, 76–91.

Menchero, Jose. 2007. "Risk-Adjusted Performance Attribution." *Journal of Performance Measurement* 11:2, 22–28.

Menchero, Jose, and Jummin Hu. 2006. "Portfolio Risk Attribution." *Journal of Performance Measurement* 10:3, 22–33.

Mina, Jorge. 2003. "Risk Attribution for Asset Managers." *RiskMetrics Journal* 3:2, 33–55.

Roll, Richard. 1992. "A Mean/Variance Analysis of Tracking Error." *Journal of Portfolio Management* 18:4, 13–22.

Ross, Stephen. 1976. "The Arbitrage Theory of Capital Asset Pricing." *Journal of Economic Theory* 13:3, 341–360.

Sharpe, William F. 1964. "Capital Asset Prices: A Theory of Market Equilibrium under Conditions of Risk." *Journal of Finance* 19:3, 425–442.

Sharpe, William F. 1966. "Mutual Fund Performance." *Journal of Business* 39:1, 119–138.

Sharpe, William F. 1994. "The Sharpe Ratio." *Journal of Portfolio Management* 21:1, 49–58.

Treynor, Jack. 1965. "How to Rate Management of Investment Funds." *Harvard Business Review* 43:1, 63–75.

Treynor, Jack, and Kay Mazuy. 1966. "Can Mutual Funds Outguess the Market?" *Harvard Business Review* 44:2, 131–136.

Xiang, George. 2006. "Risk Decomposition and Its Use in Portfolio Analysis." *Journal of Performance Measurement* 9:2, 26–32.

Xiong, James X., Roger G. Ibbotson, Thomas M. Idzorek, and Peng Chen. 2010. "The Equal Importance of Asset Allocation and Active Management." *Financial Analysts Journal* 66:2, 1–9.

Part Four

RISK MANAGEMENT AND ASSET CLASSES

21

Risk and Mortgage-Backed Securities in a Time of Transition

HAROLD C. BARNETT

Adjunct Professor, Marshall Bennett Institute of Real Estate, Roosevelt University

Introduction

Managing risk is particularly problematic after a market crash. The market for private label mortgage-backed securities (MBS) grew at an unsustainable pace into late 2006. The subprime segment of the MBS market then unraveled and caused an implosion of the real estate finance and housing markets. The United States and global economies are still digging their way out of the great deleveraging that followed. This chapter provides an assessment of the risk associated with residential MBS before and after that market crashed.

The chapter begins with a summary of growth and contraction in homeownership and the MBS market through the first half of 2013. The second section examines the misleading evaluations of MBS default risk by securitizer Goldman Sachs and credit rating agencies (CRAs) that produced toxic loans and contributed to massive market failure. The third section focuses on the shortcomings of market discipline, litigation and enforcement, and regulation and their roles going forward in creating a sustainable MBS market that can support homeownership. The final section provides a summary and conclusions.

The MBS Market in 2013

A *mortgage-backed security* is a pool of mortgages packaged into a security. The government sponsored enterprises (GSEs), namely, Fannie Mae and Freddie Mac, issue MBS in which all investors not only hold a proportionate claim over interest and principal payments but also face the same risk of loss. In contrast, private label MBS are divided in tranches. The tranches are structured so that investors in the top or senior tranche are the last to suffer loss in case of delinquency and default, while investors in the lower or subordinate tranches are the first to absorb loss.

The GSEs and the Federal Housing Administration (FHA) were the core under-writers of the residential housing market until the early 2000s. Fannie Mae and Freddie

Mac, established as government agencies but eventually privatized, bought pools of mortgages, packaged them, and sold them as securities. They provided a guarantee against loss from delinquency and default. Investors assumed that MBS issued by GSEs posed minimal risk of loss because taxpayers would ultimately provide a backstop. Fannie Mae and Freddie Mac went under government conservatorship in 2008 and required a $188 billion bailout. Investor expectations that taxpayers would cover the losses were correct. MBS issued by the GSEs are usually referred to as agency issues and are underwritten using agency guidelines. The FHA provides insurance against loss on its approved mortgages but does not own mortgages or package them for sale.

The private label residential MBS market began to expand in the early 2000s to profit from a refinancing and a housing boom. In 2001, there were $1,086 billion in agency MBS issues and $149 billion in private label MBS. By 2005, agency issues had fallen to $983 billion while private label issues had risen to $726 billion. As the market peaked and crashed, private label issues declined from $509 billion in 2007 to $32 billion in 2008 and $4.2 billion in 2012. Private label issues have rebounded since 2012 increasing to $32 billion in mid-2013. After the crash, the GSEs took up much of the slack rising to $1,730 billion in 2012 (Securities Industry and Financial Market Association 2013). FHA has minimal down payment requirements and its share of the market declined as the private label market expanded. After the crash, the FHA is again a source of financing for borrowers who can only provide a minimal down payment.

The prime mortgages issued by the agencies had the most demanding standards in terms of borrower credit scores, employment, down payment, financial assets, and collateral. The prime mortgage market was also the most demanding with respect to verification of borrower and property characteristics. Alt-A loans went to borrowers who might have good credit but could not satisfy all agency guidelines. By contrast, subprime was the weakest segment of the MBS market. The subprime market emerged for borrowers with weak credit and who posed a greater risk of delinquency and default. With less demanding guidelines to qualify and less emphasis on verification, the subprime market lent itself to predatory lending (i.e., the lender misleads the borrower), predatory borrowing (i.e., the borrower misleads the lender), and combinations of the two (Barnett 2013). Alt-A and subprime mortgages securitized by the private sector had no ultimate guarantor and hence passed on default risk to investors. The originators took their fees upfront.

Figure 21.1 shows the transformation of homeownership including the substantial impact of the expansion and collapse of the private label MBS market. The homeownership rate increased from 64 percent in the early 1990s to a peak of 69 percent in 2006. As of the first quarter of 2013, the rate has fallen back to 65 percent. This percentage change represents some 5 million housing units that went from owner-occupied to foreclosed, bank-owned, investor-owned, or abandoned. This is equal to about two and a half times the number of housing units in Rhode Island, slightly less than the total number in Illinois, or over a third the number in California.

Home price inflation was a major driver of the mortgage and housing booms. Single-family home prices increased by nearly 90 percent between 2000 and the end of 2006 according to the S&P Case-Shiller index. Prices in the "sand" states (California, Florida, Arizona, and Nevada) exceeded the national average while other states experienced far less home price appreciation. The expectation of rising prices motivated

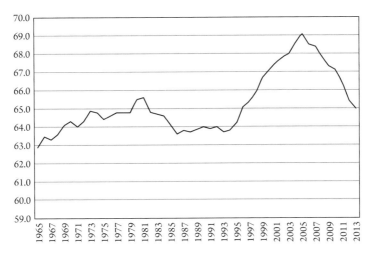

Figure 21.1 HOMEOWNERSHIP RATES: 1965–2013. The figure illustrates the increase in homeownership (in percent) from the mid-1990s to 2006 and the decline thereafter.
Source: U.S. Census Bureau 2013.

investors to buy and flip properties and allowed homeowners to take cash out of their increasingly valuable properties. Rising prices were a safety valve. Rising housing prices increased homeowner equity and provided an opportunity to sell or refinance when problems arose.

Competition for properties to buy, loans to securitize and sell (known as the "originate to distribute" model), and an increase in the supply of funds to the mortgage market drove up prices. Since income growth fell far short of the growth in debt loads, delinquency rates and defaults began to accelerate in 2006 and shake confidence in the sustainability of the riskier segments of the mortgage market. A huge structure of speculative debt grew on top of the MBS market. Short-term loans financed much of the debt. As creditors acknowledged the loss in value of the underlying collateral, they stopped renewing these loans causing the entire structure of debt to collapse. Home prices fell about a third nationally and far more in the "sand" states.

Falling home prices drove many borrowers *underwater* (i.e., the value of their homes were now worth less than the balance on their mortgages). The fall in value eliminated the ability to refinance as a safety valve and induced some investors and homeowners to just walk away from their debt. The economy went into recession at the end of 2007 adding an increasing number of prime borrowers to the pool of homeowners already in default. Many Alt-A and subprime borrowers joined the default pool earlier having acquired mortgage debt that was unsustainable before the recession. The rate of homeowners 90 days or more delinquent increased from about 1 percent in early 2005 to more than 5 percent in 2010. The rate of foreclosure increased from less than 0.5 percent in 2005 to around 4 percent by 2011. Real estate owned by banks rose from nearly zero in 2005 to about 1 percent of U.S. properties in 2011 (Aragon, Peach, and Tracy 2013). As of late 2013, the GSEs and FHA finance roughly 90 percent of home loans. A small private label market exists that mainly packages loans to high net worth individuals.

Disclosure and Rating of Risk before the Fall

This section considers basic determinants of MBS risk and examines whether securitizers disclosed and CRAs affirmed that the risk of MBS default was increasing to unsustainable levels.

Mortgage loan risk depends largely on the ability to repay based on monthly income and debt. Income and employment should be stable and predictable. Certainty of debt obligations is greater if rates are fixed rather than variable, if payments are fully amortized rather than interest only, if no negative amortization exists, and if rate adjustments will not cause payment shocks. Financial reserves provide a cushion against lost income. Credit scores provide a history of willingness and/or ability to honor debt obligations.

The debt-to-income ratio (DTI) is a short-hand measure of a borrower's ability to repay. Stated income loans without verification of income and no-documentation (no-doc) loans raise the risk of default. The appraised value of the property relative to borrower's equity is an important determinant of risk. The lower the ratio of loan-to-value (LTV), the more equity the borrower has in the property and the less likely is the borrower to default. A property purchased for investment or as a second home is considered riskier than one purchased as a primary residence (i.e., owner-occupied).

Lender guidelines define the standards a borrower and property must satisfy for loan approval. Underwriting views risk as *layered* meaning that additional risk elements can have a multiplicative impact on the probability of default. When selling the loan, the lender represents and warrants borrower and property characteristics and generally agrees to repurchase the loan if a material breach occurs. The lender's financial viability is a major determinant of its ability to honor this obligation.

The documentation accompanying Goldman Sachs issues of predominantly subprime MBS pools provides a timeline of risk. Goldman, an important player in the subprime MBS market, predicted and bet on a market implosion before many of its competitors. Subprime was the riskiest segment of the MBS market and a major contributor to financial and housing market collapse.

Figure 21.2 presents credit ratings and projected losses for 32 MBS pools comprising primarily subprime residential mortgages securitized by Goldman Sachs during 2005–2007. The columns in the figure represent Moody's Investor Services ex post projection of loss for these Goldman Sachs Alternative Mortgage Products (GSAMP) Trust MBS pools. Losses for 2005 issues are generally in the 5 to 25 percent range, while projected losses for the 2006–2007 issues are in the 20 to 40 percent range. As of March 2009, Moody's projected $7.4 billion in losses, representing a 27 percent reduction in value, for this $27 billion worth of GSAMP issues. As of June 2010, Moody's projected loss was $9.4 billion, a 35 percent reduction in value (Barnett 2011).

In Figure 21.2, the solid line represents the percentage of principal balance in each MBS issue rated less than AAA by Standard and Poor's and less than Aaa (triple-A) by Moody's Investor Services. The senior tranches in each issue received the same ratings from both CRAs. On average, 81 percent of principal balances are rated triple-A. Between 16 and 23 percent of issues are rated less than triple-A. More striking is the fact that projected losses began to increase for MBS designated as 2005 issues and remain

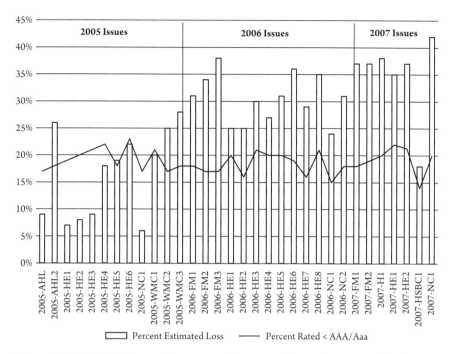

Figure 21.2 GSAMP Trusts Projected Loss and Credit Ratings. This figure illustrates the percentage of GSAMP MBS issues rated less than triple-A and the projected loss on each issue as of March 2009. Source: Moody's Investor Service 2010 and the U.S. Securities and Exchange Commission, EDGAR Database.

in a substantially higher range for those designated as 2006–2007 issues. In contrast, no similar stepwise change occurs in credit ratings (Barnett 2011).

Standard and Poor's and Moody's are designated as Nationally Recognized Statistical Rating Organizations (NRSRO). The Securities and Exchange Commission (SEC) requires investment grade CRA ratings of an MBS for purchase by pension funds, insurance companies, banks, and other institutional investors. Securitizers pay the CRAs for their ratings, creating an apparent conflict of interest.

The assessment of default risk by Goldman Sachs as presented in this chapter is derived from two sources: a confidential presentation to its board of directors (Goldman Sachs 2007) and the narratives of risk factors in a sample of the GSAMP MBS prospectuses. Goldman Sachs presentation to its board includes a timeline of major events in the subprime sector and the Goldman response. In the first half of 2006, Goldman told the directors that the subprime market was growing and Goldman was increasing its long position. Goldman was becoming concerned about an increase in early payment defaults, a breach of representations and warranties that require the lender to repurchase the loan.

In the second half of 2006 and into the first quarter of 2007, Goldman reported a substantial deterioration in underwriting standards and increased fraud. Widespread mortgage originator defaults followed. Bank regulators were issuing underwriting guidance for non-traditional mortgage products. As Morgenson and Rosner (2011) note, regulators warned lenders to consider the ability of a borrower to make payments over the life of the loan, not just at an introductory or 'teaser' rate. Finally, bids for subprime loans were falling below the cost of origination. Goldman's credit department was stepping up its due diligence of originators and of loan collateral valuations. The department was scaling back its purchase of riskier loans and was marking down its residual assets to reflect market deterioration. Goldman was also reversing its long position via purchases of collateralized debt obligations (CDOs).

Goldman Sachs informed its board that, as of March 2007, large originators were experiencing an equity market sell-off. The securitization market for subprime had slowed substantially. Early payment default claims continued to increase. Goldman was halting purchases of subprime loan pools and tightening its credit terms.

Risk disclosures by Goldman Sachs to MBS investors were consistent with the subprime market assessments presented to its board. The prospectus for the GSAMP Trust 2006-HE3, issued in spring 2006, provided investors boiler plate warnings about subprime loans. These loans were riskier than those underwritten with Fannie Mae and Freddie Mac guidelines. Borrowers may have impaired or unsubstantiated credit histories. Interest only loans could stress borrowers when rates reset and the loan becomes fully amortized. Violation of federal, state, and local laws could result in losses on mortgage loans, and some authorities considered predatory lending an issue with subprime originators. Loan prepayment could impose a loss on investors. As Barnett (2011) notes, GSAMP prospectuses reviewed here are available through the SEC EDGAR database.

Goldman Sachs further disclosed that borrowers were increasingly financing their homes with new mortgage products, such as stated income and no-money-down loans, and little historical data existed on these new mortgage products. Delinquencies and defaults could exceed anticipated levels as borrowers faced potentially higher monthly payments.

These standard subprime disclosures were not suggestive of a major uptick in the risk of default. However, the observations about "new mortgage products" and "little historical data" can be taken as warnings that credit ratings could be underestimating the likelihood of default associated with these riskier loans. Interest rates were rising that could also cause delinquencies and defaults "to exceed anticipated levels." These two considerations suggest an increased risk of default for this vintage MBS. Figure 21.2 reveals the divergence between credit ratings and projected loss on this and other GSAMP issues.

The prospectus for GSAMP Trust 2006-NC2, issued about six months later in the second half of 2006, advises investors of additional risks. This MBS contained loans originated by New Century Financial, the second largest subprime originator and a major supplier of mortgages to Goldman Sachs. The prospectus notes that adjustable rate mortgages (ARMs) are underwritten on the basis of a judgment that the borrower initially will have the ability to make monthly payments. Although not called as such in the prospectus, a borrower is qualified on a low "teaser" rate, not on a fully indexed rate, and income may be insufficient to make payments when rates increase. Moreover, loans included in the issue may not conform to the originator's underwriting standards. Investors were again informed that stated income loans do not involve verification by the originator. The recitation of these additional factors acknowledges the greater risk of default associated with late 2006 MBS issues.

The Prospectus for GSAMP Trust 2006-FM3 offers further warnings about default risks that are relevant for MBS issued in the second half of 2006. This trust was one of several to securitize mortgages originated by Fremont Investment and Loan, one of the top 10 subprime originators. Fremont had made changes to its loan origination guidelines because loans under the previous guidelines were experiencing increased levels of delinquency and foreclosure. Goldman Sachs warned investors that they could not be assured that mortgages in the current trust would perform better under the new guidelines.

Goldman Sachs reported additional problems with Fremont in a supplement to the prospectus for a 2007 issue, GSAMP Trust 2007-FM2. Goldman Sachs informed investors that deterioration in Fremont's financial position and regulatory status could adversely affect the lenders ability to repurchase loans with a material breach of representations and warranties. Further, Fremont's parent corporation had announced a regulator cease-and-desist order that required Fremont to not operate with inadequate underwriting, not market ARMs in an unsafe and unsound manner, and not make mortgage loans without adequately considering the borrower's ability to repay.

As if anticipating the collapse of the subprime bubble, the prospectus for GSAMP Trust 2007-NC1, another pool of New Century Financial loans and the last MBS issue included in Figure 21.2, notes recently increased levels of delinquency and default in the subprime mortgage market. Combined with deterioration in general real estate market conditions, these problems were resulting in a substantial increase in demand for repurchase of early payment default loans. This demand caused deterioration in the financial performance of many subprime lenders and in some cases they ceased operation. Goldman Sachs informed investors that they face a heightened risk because the originators may be unable to repurchase loans that do not satisfy their representations and warranties.

These final disclosures clearly suggest a substantial increase in default risk by the second half of 2006 and into early 2007. While the CRAs had the same information available to them, their risk assessments remained virtually unchanged until the end of Goldman Sachs subprime securitization in early 2007. A clear disconnect exists between the Goldman Sachs risk narratives and the CRA ratings. Because the Goldman assessments are verbal, how they would translate into a range of values in Figure 21.2 is a matter of speculation. Recall that risk is layered and each additional element can have a multiplicative impact on the probability of default.

To provide scale and a neutral starting point, assume that Goldman Sachs subprime mortgage market disclosures in early 2006 implied default risk consistent with that of the CRAs. Goldman does warn of developing problems—early payment default, new loan products, and a decline in loan performance predictability—that could increase risk. By the second half of 2006, Goldman Sachs adds more risk factors—deterioration in underwriting standards, increased fraud, inability of borrowers to pay after rate adjustments, and exceptions to guidelines—that suggest a further step up in credit risk. Another step up in risk occurs in early 2007 as Goldman Sachs starts to unwind its long positions, delinquency and defaults increase, and originators can no longer honor their representations and warranties.

A line representing the Goldman Sachs narrative of credit risk would increase stepwise from mid-2006 to mid-2007. In contrast, the CRA credit risk line remains essentially flat implying Standard and Poor's and Moody's did not incorporate available market and securitizer data in their risk assessments. As a result, the CRAs misled investors and contributed to the MBS bubble and its collapse. At the same time, Goldman Sachs warned investors of enhanced risk while publishing the CRA credit ratings that contradicted its warnings. Goldman Sachs hid behind the imprimatur of triple-A ratings. Investors who never read past the CRA ratings in a prospectus or had their risk aversion assuaged by discussion of credit enhancements suffered for their trust.

MBS are highly complex structured financial instruments. Despite the wealth of information contained in a prospectus, MBS are far from transparent. Consequently, investors need to have trust in the integrity of CRAs and securitizers. That trust was often misplaced. An originate-to-distribute model drove originators while CRAs followed an issuer-pays model. These models involve considerable conflict of interest. CRAs and securitizers have been sued for misrepresentation and fraud.

The CRAs have successfully argued that ratings are opinions protected as free speech under the First Amendment as a defense against lawsuits that allege they contributed to the collapse of the subprime mortgage market (Stempel and Walder 2011). The Department of Justice (DOJ) filed a civil suit alleging that Standard & Poor's engaged in a scheme to defraud investors in MBS and CDO deals. The DOJ alleges that the CRA conduct was egregious and goes to the very heart of the recent financial crisis. The First Amendment is not a defense against fraud (U.S. Department of Justice 2013).

The Federal Housing Finance Agency (FHFA), the conservator of Fannie Mae and Freddie Mac, brought lawsuits against Goldman Sachs and 16 other large securitizers claiming misrepresentation and fraud and demanding compensation for losses suffered on over $200 billion of MBS sold to the GSE. In contrast to the focus on borrower characteristics and loan terms, the FHFA suit provides evidence of misrepresentation regarding the subject properties that served as collateral in 40 Goldman Sachs MBS issues. The suit alleges that Goldman Sachs misstated several key risk-related statistics (Federal Housing Finance Agency 2011). FHFA data provides strong evidence that on average 12.7 percent of the properties in the 40 MBS pools were investment properties or second homes despite the fact that Goldman Sachs designated them as owner-occupied. The average was about the same for pools designated as 2005, 2006, and 2007 issues.

The prospectuses of Goldman Sachs claimed that no loans had an LTV greater than 100 percent. Data presented by FHFA, using automated valuation method appraisals of the properties at the time of the transactions, demonstrate that the percentage of loans with LTV greater than 100 percent increased from about 10 percent for 2005 issues to 14.8 percent for 2006 issues and to 19.7 percent for 2007 issues. This evidence further supports the case for a stepwise increase in the risk posed by the Goldman Sachs MBS issues.

Overestimating appraised values allows a borrower to purchase or refinance based on the property value rather than on the ability to repay. A borrower with an ARM who had his loan reset to a higher interest rate could have monthly payment temporarily reduced through refinancing. The cumulative impact of misrepresenting LTV was to boost house price inflation.

Investors must rely on securitizers to conduct due diligence on originators to guarantee that the characteristics of the pooled loans are what the prospectuses say they are. The prospectuses of Goldman Sachs state that the scope of due diligence on originators depends on the credit quality of the mortgage loans. The reputation for low quality loans originated by many Goldman Sachs suppliers would have justified extensive due diligence. Goldman Sachs, like other securitizers, hired third-party firms to perform due diligence.

The FHFA suit reports that Clayton, a leading due diligence firm, had informed Goldman Sachs that Clayton had rejected 23 percent of the mortgage loans Goldman Sachs submitted to it between 2006 Q1 and 2007 Q2 as falling outside of applicable underwriting guidelines. Goldman Sachs subsequently included 29 percent of these loans in MBS pools without proper consideration and analysis of compensating factors. Further, the suit alleges that Goldman Sachs would demand a discount from originators for some of these loans but did not pass the discount on to investors.

Putting Humpty Dumpty Back Together

Three primary interdependent mechanisms exist to constrain the issuance and sale of assets that pose excessive risk to investors: market discipline, litigation and enforcement, and regulation. This section examines how each failed and the role each might play in reviving a private label MBS market.

MARKET DISCIPLINE

Markets can discipline issuers of risky assets by selling them, calling short-term loans collateralized by the asset, or betting against them through short sales and credit default swaps. But, with notable exceptions (Lewis 2010), these options rarely occurred before the MBS downgrades of early 2007. Like former Federal Reserve chairman Alan Greenspan, many investors and speculators put great faith in the self-correcting power of free markets and failed to anticipate the self-destructive power of wanton mortgage lending (Andrews 2008).

In April 2007, Moody's released a report projecting cumulative losses of between 6 and 8 percent for loans backing 2006 vintage subprime MBS. In July 2007, as new MBS volume cratered, Standard and Poor's and Moody's downgraded hundreds of MBS and placed CDOs backed by MBS on watch lists for possible downgrades. Major and minor subprime originators, including all those that supplied Goldman Sachs, lost their financial backing and were either acquired by banks or declared bankruptcy.

Fannie Mae and Freddie Mac together owned or guaranteed some $5 trillion of debt and required a $188 billion bailout from the federal government. The FHFA became their conservator. They owed billions in guaranty payments to agency MBS investors and suffered a loss in the value of agency MBS held in their portfolios. Private label MBS acquired in part to satisfy their commitment to support low- and moderate-income housing lost substantial value.

Fannie Mae and Freddie Mac currently account for about two-thirds of residential originations and MBS issues. Their issues are still purchased, held by investors, and considered safe because investors assume that the federal government backs their issues. Interestingly, Fannie Mae states in its single-family MBS prospectus that it alone, not the U.S. government, is responsible for making payments under its guarantee (Fannie Mae 2013a). Fitch Ratings, however, does affirm a triple-A rating for the GSE due to its direct financial support from the government and despite a negative outlook on U.S. sovereign debt (Fitch Ratings 2012a). As of July 2012, Standard and Poor's and Moody's have not rated any of Fannie Mae MBS issues (Fannie Mae 2012) although Standard and Poor's did downgrade U.S. government sovereign debt.

On July 21, 2010, President Obama signed the Dodd–Frank Wall Street Reform and Consumer Protection Act (Dodd-Frank Act). On the same day Standard and Poor's, Moody's, and Fitch asked that their ratings not be used in new bond sales (Shrivastava 2010). The Dodd-Frank Act requires that when CRAs assign credit grades to asset-backed securities (ABS), they be subject to the same expert liability that applies to law firms and accountants. This Act exposes the CRAs to lawsuits by investors (Verschoor 2013). Since such disclosures are required when a security is registered with the SEC, the refusal of the CRAs to allow their ratings to be disclosed froze up the market for ABS. The SEC then issued a "no action" letter indicating that it would not bring enforcement actions against issuers that did not disclose ratings in prospectuses. This action removed the expert-liability threat for the CRAs. The SEC subsequently extended this non-enforcement stance indefinitely (Morgenson 2013).

The CRAs are attempting to regain legitimacy by upgrading their loan loss models to incorporate factors that caused the crash. Notably, estimates of change in home values are now a prime driver for predicting loss. In a recent loan loss model by Fitch Ratings, a borrower's true equity in the property is expressed in terms of a sustainable LTV ratio. The model predicts sustainable prices using factors that are fundamental to the housing market including unemployment rates, income, rental prices, population, housing starts, and mortgage rates. It essentially deflates bubbles and predicts home prices consistent with trends in economic fundamentals. The Fitch model also uses borrower and loan attributes that are predictive of loss: credit scores, loan documentation, loan purpose, loan term, DTI ratios, property type, and occupancy (Fitch Ratings 2012b).

The Dodd-Frank Act has imposed requirements on securitizers and CRAs with respect to MBS disclosure. Credit rating reports must now disclose information on originators and their past experience with loan repurchases, third-party due diligence on mortgage loans, and representations and warranties. The impact of Dodd-Frank is apparent in CRA ratings reports for private label MBS issues.

The private label market accounted for $1.2 trillion in issues in 2006 and 2007 and a small but growing $32 billion up to mid-2013 (Securities Industry and Financial Market Association 2013). JP Morgan Chase (JPMorgan) issued three private label MBS securities in 2013 worth a total of $1.4 billion. The JPMorgan issues contain non-conforming jumbo loans for high net worth individuals. The GSEs will insure conforming mortgage loans up to $417,000 in most counties and up to $625,500 in high cost counties (Fannie Mae 2013b).

The report by credit rating agency DBRS for the third of these JPMorgan issues identifies and documents strengths that include the following: high quality credit attributes exist such as low LTV, strong credit reports, and full documentation; all loans are current; borrowers are high-income borrowers with substantial reserves;

third-party due diligence firms conducted property valuation, credit and compliance and fraud reviews on 100 percent of the loans in the pool; and strong representations and warranties exist for most counterparties. The borrowers are at the upper end of the income distribution with average loan balance of $887,015, average income greater than $543,000 and average liquid assets in excess of $2.4 million. DBRS notes some weakness in representations and warranties. It also notes financial stress for minor originators that limits their ability to fulfill repurchase obligations. DBRS consequently raised expected default risk and requires the securitizer to provide an additional financial cushion against loss. As required by Dodd-Frank, DBRS links the rating report to a detailed disclosure of representations and warranties for this and prior JPMorgan private label issues (DBRS 2013).

Private label issues have an appeal to some investors seeking higher yield, but they are a risky corner of the MBS market. Most investors prefer the main arena with federal guarantees. After the fact, the market is imposing discipline on the private label market.

LITIGATION AND ENFORCEMENT

Investors and insurers who suffered losses due to alleged misrepresentation and fraud associated with MBS issues have brought lawsuits seeking compensation individually or as a class. Lenders often required mortgage insurance when the LTV ratio was greater than 80 percent. Federal agencies have brought civil and criminal complaints alleging misrepresentation and fraud.

Litigation and enforcement in the aftermath of the mortgage meltdown has resulted in compensation for investors and insurers. The D&O Diary website tracks subprime and credit crisis-related securities class action lawsuits. As of April 30, 2013, courts awarded plaintiffs $9.36 billion including $2.4 billion to shareholders from Bank of America's merger with Merrill Lynch (D&O Diary 2013). In its lawsuits against 17 securitizers who sold some $200 billion of toxic MBS to Fannie Mae and Freddie Mac, the FHFA has so far reached settlements with General Electric Co., Citigroup Inc., UBS AG, and JP Morgan Chase & Co. The FHFA did not release the terms of the settlements with General Electric and Citigroup. UBS agreed to pay $885 million to settle, an amount reported to be equal to the loss on the loans involved. The JP Morgan settlement is for $5.1 billion to cover losses related to at least $33 billion in MBS sold to the GSEs (Barrett, Fitzpatrick, and Timiraos 2013). Settlements overall appear to fall short of damages.

As reported previously, Moody's projection of a loss on the $27 billion in MBS sold by Goldman Sachs to Fannie Mae and Freddie Mac was estimated at $7.4 billion in 2009 and increased to $9.4 billion in 2010. If the $200 billion MBS sold by all 17 securitizers to Fannie Mae and Freddie Mac had a similar 30 percent loss, the damages would amount to $60 billion. The SEC reportedly brought 175 lawsuits against individuals and corporations. Most suits do not involve high-profile defendants with substantial executive responsibilities. A *Wall Street Journal* article lists 138 of these suits (Eaglesham 2013)

A jury found Ralph R. Cioffi and Mathew M. Tannin, Bear Stearns hedge fund managers, not guilty of criminal securities fraud in 2009. Cohen (2009) relates their role in the collapse of Bear Stearns. Allegedly, these managers lied to investors about the precarious state of the highly leveraged funds they oversaw (Kouwe 2009). Cioffi and Tannin subsequently settled related civil charges in 2012, agreeing to pay $1.05 million in disgorgement and civil penalties and were barred from SEC-regulated industries for three and five years, respectively. Cioffi also settled charges that he had not told investors about redemptions of his own money from one of the troubled funds he managed (U.S. Securities and Exchange Commission 2012).

At the top of the corporate ladder, Angelo R. Mozilo, founder and former chief executive of Countrywide Financial, the nation's largest mortgage lender and a major originator of toxic loans, settled insider trading allegations with the SEC in 2011. The regulator contends that Mozilo sold $140 million in Countrywide stock in 2006 and 2007 as he recognized the company was failing. From 2000 to 2008, he received total compensation of $521.5 million. His settlement with the SEC was for $67.5 million of which the Bank of America, which acquired Countrywide, and insurers paid $45 million. Federal prosecutors subsequently dropped a criminal investigation against Mozilo (Morgenson 2011).

More recently, a jury found Fabrice Tourre, a Goldman Sachs vice president, guilty of violating federal securities law by intentionally misleading investors. The case involved the Abacus 2007-ACI synthetic CDO, which was allegedly designed to fail. The jury found that Tourre misled investor ACI Financial Guaranty Corp. into believing that hedge fund Paulson and Co. was taking a long position on the CDO. In fact, Paulson had hand-picked the riskiest referenced subprime tranches and was shorting the CDO (Baer, Bray, and Eaglesham 2013). Paulson made $1 billion on the deal as the MBS market crashed. Tourre was high profile because Goldman Sachs had previously settled with the SEC over the Abacus deal for $550 million without accepting or denying responsibility.

REGULATION

Mortgage market discipline has been countercyclical, eroding during expansion and becoming most restrictive as the housing market imploded. The possibility of litigation and enforcement clearly did not deter misrepresentation and fraud. If market discipline fails to discipline and litigation and enforcement are insufficient to deter, the burden of promoting sustainability falls on regulation. Conservatives argue that Congress and regulatory agencies drove Fannie Mae and Freddie Mac to provide loans to lower and middle-income individuals who were unqualified borrowers. The GSEs held toxic loans in their portfolios but they did not issue them. These issues were private label MBS containing subprime and Alt-A loans issued in a poorly regulated private market place.

More than a year after the collapse of the housing market, the Federal Reserve approved a final rule for "higher-priced mortgage loans," applicable to all lenders, prohibiting any lender from making a loan without regard to the borrower's ability to repay the loan from income and assets other than the home's value. Lenders must verify the income and assets relied upon in determining ability to repay. A *high priced loan* is one with an interest rate that is 1.5 percentage points or more above the average for prime mortgages if a first lien and 3.5 percentage points or more above that benchmark if a second lien. The high-priced metric would encompass most subprime market loans and would exclude those in the prime market (Board of Governors of the Federal Reserve System 2008).

The Dodd-Frank Act expanded upon lender responsibilities and liability in originating mortgage loans. It created the Consumer Financial Protection Bureau (CFPB) within the Federal Reserve to write some of the new regulations and to insure compliance. The Dodd-Frank Act requires banks that securitize loans to keep 5 percent of the credit risk on their balance sheets unless issued with government backing. Controversy over implementation of this rule is discussed later in this section. On January 10, 2013, the CFPB issued ability to repay rules (ATR Rule) that create a range of lender liability scenarios (Consumer Financial Protection Bureau 2013; Noto, Chanin, and Gabai 2013). The rules took effect on January 10, 2014.

Origination of a loan covered by a minimum ATR standard requires a reasonable and good faith effort to verify the borrower's ability to repay based on income, assets, employment, debt obligations, DTI ratio, and credit history. Stated income and no-documentation loans are not permitted. There is no limit on points and fees, no limitations on certain loan features (e.g., negative amortization, interest only, and balloon payments), and no requirement for a 30-year term. However, considerable penalties are available for failure to meet the ATR standard including ordinary Truth in Lending remedies, recovery of fees and charges, and an extended window to bring suit alleging violation of these rules. Failure to meet the standard can be used as a defense in foreclosure proceedings. Lenders and securitizers argued that the subjectivity surrounding "good faith" and "reasonable" under the ATR standard would expose them to excessive liability and would likely dry up the mortgage market.

In response to these concerns, the ATR Rule provides the option of a Qualified Mortgage (QM), with a safe harbor and a rebuttable presumption for the lender and securitizer, in exchange for origination of a more restrictive mortgage product. A *safe harbor* limits liability if the lender acts in good faith. A *rebuttable presumption* means that the lender is presumed to have acted in good faith unless proven otherwise. A *Qualified Mortgage* is a regularly amortized 30-year loan, underwritten to standards enumerated in the ATR Rule, with limited points and fees (generally 3 percent of the loan amount), and a maximum DTI ratio of 43 percent. If an ARM, the borrower must be qualified on the highest rate that may apply over the first five years of the loan. With some exceptions, a QM cannot have negative amortization, be interest-only, or have balloon payments.

A loan can also be QM if it can be sold to or guaranteed or insured by Fannie Mae, Freddie Mac, FHA, or other federal mortgage programs. In this instance, it does not have to meet the 43 percent DTI standard and is subject to the agency underwriting standards as opposed to the newer standards provided in the ATR Rule. This special rule will expire no later than 2021.

The ATR Rule is very specific about what points and fees fall within the 3 percent cap. Lenders often used the compensation for loan originations, included under the cap, as an incentive to steer borrowers to higher priced subprime loans even if they qualified for prime loans. Failure to correctly apply points and fees can disqualify creditors from QM safe harbor and rebuttable presumption protection.

High priced mortgage loans that meet all other QM conditions only receive a rebuttable presumption. Jumbo loans are ineligible for purchase by the GSE. Those loans that have a DTI greater than 43 percent cannot be QM and will fall under the basic ability to repay rules with neither a safe harbor nor rebuttable presumption. The JPMorgan private label MBS discussed previously had an average DTI less than 30 percent.

The Dodd-Frank Act also mandates that banks issuing MBS retain 5 percent of the risk (i.e., have "skin in the game") unless the MBS is issued with government backing. This would align securitizer and investor interests and deter banks from securitizing unsustainable loans and passing them off as triple-A rated. Banks would not have to retain risk if loans are Qualified Residential Mortgages (QRM), a category to be defined by federal regulators and to be at least as restrictive as QM. An April 2011 proposal would require loans to have a 20 percent down payment to be QRM. Most recently, an August 27, 2013, proposal would equate QRM requirements with existing QM requirements. The proposal would allow lenders to satisfy risk retention requirements if they satisfied this more limited QRM requirement (Petrasic and Kowalski 2013). Debate continues over whether skin in the game is required to achieve market discipline, whether ability to repay or down payment is a more important factor in determining risk, and whether regulation should be less restrictive to support housing market recovery (Timiraos and Zibel 2013).

CoreLogic performed an analysis of 2.2 million loans to determine the impact of QM and QRM on loan originations once the Dodd-Frank Act's special exclusions expire in 2021 (Khater 2013). Sequentially applying the QM requirements, CoreLogic found that only 52 percent of the loans qualify under QM. The 43 percent DTI requirement had the greatest impact, removing 24 percent of the loans. Low documentation (low doc) and no documentation (no doc) exclusions removed 16 percent of the loans. They were in the system for loan modifications and refinance. Credit scores less than 640, which would make the loan equivalent to subprime, removed 5 percent. A 10 percent down payment requirement under a hypothetical QRM rule would eliminate another 12 percent of loans. In total, only 40 percent of the loans examined would satisfy both QM and QRM.

CoreLogic also examined the impact of QM and QRM for removing the layered risk of serious delinquency from the loan pool. The DTI requirement removed 36 percent of the risk, a credit score greater than 640 removed 28 percent, and a 10 percent down payment removed 18 percent. Low doc or no doc removed 9 percent of the risk. Overall, the two rules removed 60 percent of the loans and more than 90 percent of the risk.

According to CoreLogic, a 10 percent down payment will have a greater impact on the purchase market where only 25 percent of loans would qualify for both QM and QRM. For jumbo loans, which account for 10 percent of originations, 62 percent would meet QM standards. QRM has no impact on jumbo loans because they already have low down payments.

Summary and Conclusions

An absence of market discipline combined with lax government regulation and enforcement allowed increasingly unsustainable private label securitizations to boost homeownership and precipitate a market crash. Deleveraging and the financial crisis of 2007–2008 followed. Economic conditions drove subprime and then prime borrowers to foreclosure and resulted in underwater valuations. Hedge funds and other cash rich investors have bought up many foreclosed and abandoned properties as rentals.

Analysis of Goldman Sachs securitizations demonstrates that an ability to repay standard gave way to an expectation of continuously rising home prices and new affordability mortgage products designed to feed loans into MBS. Both securitizers and CRAs misrepresented the risk of default for these MBS.

As of October 2013, 90 percent of loans are originated under Fannie Mae, Freddie Mac, and FHA. The GSEs have substantially tightened lending standards and provide a taxpayer guarantee against loss. The private label market is limited to high net worth borrowers. Many of these loans are held in portfolios rather than securitized.

The Dodd-Frank Act of 2010 produced restrictive ability to repay standards and may yet result in a skin-in-the-game rule for securitizers or a mandatory down payment for borrowers. Congress is debating the future of the mortgage market. The Senate would have private capital provide the first guarantee against loss with taxpayers covering "catastrophic" loss. The House advocates a purely private mortgage market. The current Congress is unlikely to agree on what Fannie Mae and Freddie Mac will look like after conservatorship. Whatever platform evolves, regulators must conservatively balance homeownership goals against risk to taxpayers and not being overly supportive of Wall Street (Kane 2012).

For a more inclusive private label market to emerge, investors and mortgage insurers must come to believe that originators and securitizers are not engaging in any substantial misrepresentation and fraud when packaging yield and risk into MBS. In this regard, the ability to repay and QM rules can protect borrowers and by extension investors. Enforcement of a strict adherence to the ability to repay standard will help promote growth in a private label market. Originators and securitizers on their part must believe that sufficient profit and manageable liability exists to grow the private label MBS market. Risk retention would align securitizer interests with those of investors. Equating QRM to QM may short circuit this goal. An open question is whether private capital will accept the necessary risk and responsibility.

The GSEs and FHA allow purchase mortgages with low down payment. However, credit issues, student loan debt, and a scarcity of financial assets exclude many foreclosed and first time homeowners from the housing market. They will rent the properties once owned by prime and subprime borrowers. Homeownership rates are still above their 1965–1995 average. The challenge remains to promote both sustainable homeownership and affordable rentals (Calmes 2013).

Discussion Questions

1. Discuss borrower and property characteristics that lenders should consider in qualifying someone for a mortgage.
2. Describe differences between the CFPB's ability to repay standards and the "affordability products" originated in the subprime market.
3. Discuss how the over valuation of properties contributed to the housing bubble associated with the financial crisis of 2007–2008 and how CRAs are now attempting to determine sustainable home prices.
4. Describe the difference between a loan issued under the ATR standard and one that is classified as a Qualified Mortgage.

References

Andrews, Edmund L. 2008. "Greenspan Concedes Error on Regulation." *New York Times.* Available at nytimes.com/2008/10/24/business/economy/24panel.html.

Aragon, Diego, Richard Peach, and Joseph Tracy. 2013. "Distressed Residential Real Estate: Dimensions, Impacts, and Remedies." Federal Reserve Bank of New York. Available at http://libertystreeteconomics.newyorkfed.org/2013/07/distressed-residential-real-estate-dimensions-impacts-and-remedies.html.

Baer, Justin, Chad Bray, and Jean Eaglesham. 2013. "'Fab' Trader Liable in Fraud." *Wall Street Journal.* Available at http://online.wsj.com/article/SB10001424127887323681904578641843284450004.html.

Barnett, Harold C. 2011. "Assessing Risk on Subprime Mortgage Backed Securities: Did Credit Rating Agencies Misrepresent Risk to Investors." Available at SSRN.com/abstract=1899631.

Barnett, Harold C. 2013. "And Some with a Fountain Pen: Mortgage Fraud, Securitization, and the Subprime Bubble." In Susan Will, Stephan Handelman, and David C. Brotherton, eds., *How They Got Away With It: White Collar Criminals and the Financial Meltdown,* 104–129. New York: Columbia University Press.

Barrett, Devlin, Dan Fitzpatrick, and Nick Timiraos. 2013. "J. P. Morgan Settles with FHFA." *Wall Street Journal.* Available at http://online.wsj.com/news/articles/SB10001424052702303615304579157931846055864.

Board of Governors of the Federal Reserve System. 2008. "Board Issues Final Rule Amending Home Mortgage Provisions of Regulation Z (Truth in Lending)." Available at federalreserve.gov/newsevents/press/bcreg/20080714a.htm.

Calmes, Jackie. 2013. "Obama Outlines Plans for Fannie Mae and Freddie Mac." *New York Times.* Available at nytimes.com/2013/08/07/us/politics/obama-fannie-mae-freddie-mac.html.

Cohen, William D. 2009. *House of Cards.* New York: Doubleday

Consumer Financial Protection Bureau. 2013. "General Comparison of Ability-to-Repay Requirements with Qualified Mortgage." Available at files.consumerfinance.gov/f/201308_cfpb_atr-and-qm-comparison-chart_V2_final.pdf.

DBRS. 2013. "J.P. Morgan Mortgage Trust 2013-3 Mortgage Pass-Through Certificates, Series 2013-3." Available at dbrs.com/issuer/19452.

D&O Diary. 2013. "Subprime and Credit Crisis-Related Lawsuits Settlements, Dismissals and Denials." Available at dandodiary.com/2008/06/articles/subprime-litigation/the-list-subprime-lawsuit-dismissals-and-denials/index.html.

Eaglesham, Jean. 2013. "Wall Street's Top Cop Tries to Rebuild Its Reputation." *Wall Street Journal.* Available at http://online.wsj.com/article/SB10001424127887323864604579064961041032146.html.

Fannie Mae. 2012. "Basics of Fannie Mae Single-Family MBS." Available at fanniemae.com/resources/file/mbs/pdf/basics-sf-mbs.pdf.

Fannie Mae. 2013a. "Single-Family MBS Prospectus." Available at fanniemae.com/syndicated/documents/mbs/mbspros/SF_March_1_2013.pdf.

Fannie Mae. 2013b. "Loan Limits." Available at http://www.fanniemae.com/singlefamily/loan-limits.

Federal Housing Finance Agency. 2011. "FHFA Complaint against Goldman Sachs." Available at http://www.fhfa.gov/webfiles/22589/fhfa%20v%20goldman%20sachs.pdf. Access is through FHFA web page http://www.fhfa.gov/Default.aspx?Page=110.

Fitch Ratings. 2012a. "Fitch Affirms Fannie Mae and Freddie Mac at 'AAA'—Outlook Negative." Available at fitchratings.com/creditdesk/press_releases/detail.cfm?print=1&pr_id=775632.

Fitch Ratings. 2012b. "U.S. RMBS Loan Loss Model Criteria." Available at fitchratings.com/creditdesk/reports/report_frame.cfm?rpt_id=715454.

Goldman Sachs. 2007. "Presentation to GS Board of Directors, Subprime Mortgage Business." Hearing on Wall Street and the Financial Crisis: The Role of Investment Banks, United States Senate, Permanent Subcommittee on Investigations, Committee on Homeland

Security and Government Affairs, Exhibit 22. Available at hsgac.senate.gov//imo/media/doc/Financial_Crisis/042710Exhibits.pdf?attempt=2.

Kane, Edward J. 2012. "Missing Elements in the U.S. Financial Reform: A Kübler-Ross Interpretation of the Inadequacy of the Dodd-Frank Act." *Journal of Banking and & Finance* 36:3, 654–661.

Khater, Sam. 2013. "The Mortgage Market Impact of Qualified Mortgage Regulation." CoreLogic. Available at corelogic.com/downloadable-docs/MarketPulse_2013-February.pdf.

Kouwe, Zachery. 2009. "Bear Stearns Managers Acquitted of Fraud Charges." *New York Times*. Available at dealbook.nytimes.com/2009/11/10/2-ex-fund-managers-found-not-guilty-of-fraud//.

Lewis, Michael. 2010. *The Big Short*. New York: W. W. Norton & Company Ltd.

Moody's Investor Service. 2010. "Moody's Current Loss Projections for 2005–2008 Jumbo, Alt-A, Option ARM and Subprime RMBS." Available at https://www.moodys.com/researchdocumentcontentpage.aspx?docid=PBS_SF211961.

Morgenson, Gretchen. 2011. "Case on Mortgage Official Is Said to Be Dropped." *New York Times*. Available at nytimes.com/2011/02/20/business/20mozilo.html?_r=0.

Morgenson, Gretchen. 2013. "Hey, S.E.C., That Escape Hatch Is Still Open." *New York Times*. Available at nytimes.com/2011/03/06/business/06gret.html.

Morgenson, Gretchen, and Joshua Rosner. 2011. *Reckless Endangerment*. New York: Times Books/Henry Holt & Company.

Noto, Thomas J., Leonard N. Chanin, and Joseph Gabai. 2013. "CFPB Ability to Repay Rules Issued." Morrison & Foerster LLP. Available at http://www.mofo.com/files/Uploads/Images/130128-CFPB-Ability-to-Repay-Rules-Issued.pdf.

Petrasic, Kevin L., and Amanda J. Kowalski. 2013. "Regulators Re-Propose Dodd-Frank QRM Rule—More Flexibility for 'Skin in the Game'." Paul Hastings LLP. Available at https://www.paulhastings.com/docs/default-source/PDFs/re-proposed-qrm-rule.pdf.

Securities Industry and Financial Market Association. 2013. "U.S. Mortgage-Related Securities Issuance and Outstanding." Available at http://www.sifma.org/research/statistics.aspx.

Shrivastava, Anusha. 2010. "Bond Sales? Don't Quote Us, Request Credit Firms." *Wall Street Journal*. Available at http://online.wsj.com/article/SB10001424052748704723604575379650414337676.html.

Stempel, Jonathan, and Noeleen Walder. 2011. "Rating Agencies Win Dismissal of Lawsuits." Reuters. Available at http://www.reuters.com/article/2011/05/11/us-ratingagencies-ruling-idUSTRE74A4OK20110511.

Timiraos, Nick, and Alan Zibel. 2013. "Easing of Mortgage Market Curb Weighed." *Wall Street Journal*. Available at online.wsj.com/article/SB10001424127887324144304578624331793965730.html.

U.S. Census Bureau. 2013. *Current Population Survey/Housing Vacancy Survey, Series H-111 Reports, Table 14.* Available at http://www.census.gov/housing/hvs/data/histtabs.html.

U.S. Department of Justice. 2013. "Department of Justice Sues Standard & Poor's for Fraud in Rating Mortgage-Backed Securities in the Years Leading Up to the Financial Crisis."Available at http://www.justice.gov/opa/pr/2013/February/13-ag-156.html.

U.S. Securities and Exchange Commission. 2012. "Court Approves SEC Settlements with Two Former Bear Stearns Hedge Fund Portfolio Managers; SEC Bars Managers from Regulated Industries." Available at sec.gov/litigation/litreleases/2012/lr22398.htm.

Verschoor, Curtis C. 2013. "Credit Rating Agency Performance Needs Improvement." AccountingWeb. Available at accountingweb.com/article/credit-rating-agency-performance-needs-improvement/22074.

22

Credit Value Adjustment

JAMES T. MOSER

Executive in Residence, Kogod School of Business, American University

Introduction

Since the financial crisis of 2007–2008, market participants and regulators have paid heightened attention to the bilateral contractual relationships created within the $700 trillion-dollar over-the-counter (OTC) derivatives markets. Previously, management of these relationships largely focused on keeping loss probabilities low with respect to individual credits while emphasizing the use of diversification at the portfolio level. The financial crisis revealed weaknesses in past practices. Among the lessons drawn from that credit crisis is the spectacular failure of credit ratings as a means for determining capital adequacy and the realization of a sizable systematic component in the sense of the capital asset pricing model (CAPM) to default risk. The once relied-upon system of ratings, essentially rank-orderings of default probabilities, provided by agencies paid for by corporate and government contract issuers proved insufficiently reliable as substantial and widespread downgrades became common over the course of the crisis.

As a result, these exposures now garner increased attention. This line of thought originates with Merton's (1974) work on pricing corporate debt obligations. Considering the right to default as an option offers a scheme for determining the usefulness of entering into a contractual relationship and then for providing a framework to manage the exposures inherent in every credit relationship. Merton's research led to the development of considerable insight into the economics of corporate debt. The very large exposures created by derivative contracts, especially the OTC segment of those markets, prompted a line of research that adapts Merton's approach to value credit exposures created by such contracts. The method is termed *credit value adjustment* (CVA), which is a valuation exercise that values the credit exposure an entity has to its contract counterparties.

This chapter first motivates the rationale for developing CVA via a description of the exposure created by a simple interest-rate swap contract, which is the most common of the OTC contracts. After recognizing these exposures, the chapter then explains how market attention turned toward contract innovations that substantially mitigated bilateral credit exposure. Ultimately, the financial crisis of 2007–2008 demonstrates the insufficiency of those efforts. That insufficiency then elevated attention to pricing approaches.

With this background, the chapter develops a one-period, unilateral CVA model. Subsequently, the chapter extends that model to the multi-period case. This model enables exploring certain aspects of credit risk exposures particularly the relevance of correlations for the efficacy of netting arrangements and the factors affecting credit risk valuations. Next, the CVA model is extended to the bilateral case. The chapter then reviews implementing CVA under the Basel III Accord guidelines. A summary section completes the chapter.

The Need for CVA

This section establishes the purpose for CVA calculation. It proceeds by considering the credit-risk exposure created via a simple interest-rate swap agreement. On establishing these exposures, the section covers the steps addressing these exposures and ends by covering the adequacy of those steps.

CREDIT EXPOSURE CREATED BY A VANILLA INTEREST-RATE SWAP

Figure 22.1 is the standard depiction of an interest-rate swap. In the contract, counterparty A is obligated to make a payment to counterparty B based on a fixed rate determined at the contract's inception. In return, counterparty B is obligated to make a payment based on a variable rate such as LIBOR (London Interbank Offered Rate) or OIS (Overnight Indexed Swap). Applying these rates to the contract's notional amount determines the respective dollar amounts payable. Payment amounts are the net of these obligations so that counterparty A is obligated to pay $Max\,(0, \bar{r} - r_{t_1})\,N$, where N is the notional amount of the contract, $\bar{r}$ is the contracted fixed rate, and r_{t_1} is the contract's floating rate at time t_1. Counterparty B is obligated to pay $Max\,(0, r_{t_1} - \bar{r})\,N$. For this one-period depiction, the extant credit exposure for each party is the prospect of default by its counterparty in which case the amount at risk is the amount payable at the contract settlement date t_1.

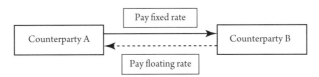

Figure 22.1 Vanilla Interest-Rate Swap. This figure shows that counterparty A is obligated to make a payment to counterparty B based on a fixed rate determined at the contract's inception. In return, counterparty B is obligated to make a payment based on a variable rate such as LIBOR (London Interbank Offered Rate) or OIS (Overnight Indexed Swap). The amounts due will be the products of the respective rates and a notional amount that is determined at contract inception.

At some earlier date, say at t_0, the expected loss amount for counterparty A will be $p^B\left(t_0, t_1 | \varphi_B, r_{t_1} > \bar{r}\right) Max\left(0, r_{t_1} - \bar{r}\right) N$ where $p^B(t_0, t_1)$ is the probability determined at t_0 that counterparty B will default on its payment due at t_1 given A's information about counterparty B (denoted φ_B) and that the floating rate exceeds the fixed rate. Similarly, the expected amount loss amount for counterparty B is $p^A\left(t_0, t_1 | \varphi_A, \bar{r} > r_{t_1}\right) Max\left(0, \bar{r} - r_{t_1}\right) N$, where $p^A(t_0, t_1)$ is the probability determined at t_0 that counterparty A will default on its payment due at t_1 given B's information about counterparty A (denoted φ_A) and that the fixed rate exceeds the floating rate. This setup demonstrates that determining the expected loss amounts depends on obligated payment amounts and probabilities of default determined by each counterparty conditioned on their information about each other and their expectations about the difference between fixed and floating rates at time t_1.

Typically, swaps include multiple payments so that their value is comparable to the price difference of a fixed-rate bond and a floating-rate bond, where interest and principal payments on each bond are time matched over the tenor (i.e., life) of the contract. At contract inception, this difference is zero reflecting that neither counterparty willingly enters the contract at a disadvantage to its counterparty. This relationship implies that for each payment date, the considerations previously discussed must be made to determine expected loss. Additionally, given that default of its counterparty does occur, each counterparty must determine the amount it can expect to recover through bankruptcy proceedings. These amounts determine loss given default (LGD).

Despite the apparent difficulties of determining credit-risk exposure, derivative markets experienced considerable growth in OTC contracts such as the one depicted in Figure 22.1 as well as many others of considerably greater complexity. The Bank of International Settlements (BIS) (2013) reports notional amounts worldwide reached 693 trillion dollars in its semiannual survey dated June 2013. Although the due amounts on those contracts will be a small fraction of their notional amounts, and therefore expected losses smaller yet, those later amounts when aggregated across market participants are substantial. The potential that losses may be concentrated in certain institutions has led to systemic risk concerns. As those amounts grew, market participants increasingly sought measures to mitigate their loss exposures.

EVOLUTION OF STEPS TO MITIGATE CREDIT EXPOSURE

The first measures to mitigate credit exposures were steps to standardize contract terms. In 1985, the International Swap Dealers' Association (ISDA), later renamed International Swaps and Derivatives Association, adopted the predecessor of what would later become *ISDA Master Agreement*, which is a boilerplate contract that standardized substantial portions of interest-rate and foreign-exchange swap contracts. Such standardization initially focused on establishing a common vocabulary for swap contracts with the idea of preventing defaults arising from differences in understanding.

As markets for swap contracting expanded, participants recognized the need for measures to mitigate further their counterparty credit exposures. Netting and close-out arrangements were among the very early important measures. These addressed issues arising in cases where default involved multiple contracts between counterparties, in terms of the above interest-rate example, when counterparty A and B have multiple contracts with each other. Rather than treating each pay or collection as separate obligations, the net amount of those obligations across their extant contracts determines the closeout amount due or payable. This step dealt with *cherry picking where* the conservators of a defaulting counterparty attempt to collect on contracts where the defaulting counterparty is due some amount while it defaults on contracts where it is obligated to pay. From those efforts came netting agreements covering groups of contracts between counterparties involved in bilateral contract positions.

Subsequently, participants developed procedures that standardized the use of collateral. This very important step facilitated negotiations between counterparties of unequal credit standing to attempt to equalize their respective credit exposures. Early on, collateral requirements focused on upcoming payment amounts. Based on current obligations, which in the case of interest swaps is the difference between fixed and floating interest-rate levels, counterparties could anticipate the amount of the next payment. For example, if the floating rate exceeds the fixed rate by 1 percent per annum on a $100 million notional amount, the next reset payment on a contract settled quarterly would be $250,000. Addressing the exposure buildups that can result from rate changes, contracts specified collateral terms specifying threshold amounts, so that collateral would be required once a due amount exceeded the threshold level. If default occurs, the loss would be limited to the remaining uncollateralized amount.

DEALING WITH THE REMAINING CREDIT RISK

Despite the steps undertaken by the ISDA to deal with credit exposures, problems remained. The most striking problem was the bankruptcy of Lehman Brothers in 2008. According to a report given to its creditors (Lehman Brothers Holdings Inc. 2009), Lehman was a counterparty in more than 900,000 derivatives contracts involving over 6,000 ISDA Master Agreements. Although presumed "too big to fail" (TBTF), Lehman failed in September 2008. The realization that the contracts of an organization formerly understood to be TBTF might be less than bulletproof prompted reconsideration of credit risk. On the morning of Lehman's Chapter 11 filing announcement, the rating agencies lowered their ratings on Lehman. For example, Standard and Poor's counterparty rating dropped from single A to SD (Selective Default). This change prompted recognition that credit ratings were less reliable than previously thought. Lehman's default and the liquidity crisis that followed brought to the forefront a developing understanding that despite private efforts such as those by the ISDA, substantial levels of credit risk remained.

Among these revelations were issues involving collateralization practices. Those practices envisioned a world in which default events would be limited to one-off events. In such a world, the market can safely regard counterparty defaults as uncorrelated events. The aftermath of Lehman scotched that worldview. In general, threshold amounts described previously could adequately deal with a world of uncorrelated credit exposures but proved lacking when integrating default prospects across multiple counterparties.

Similarly, accepted collateral procedures in OTC markets allow substantial periods before collateral receipt actually covers existing exposures. Termed the "margin period of risk," operational considerations include the time for resolving disputes over collateral amount due as well as the time for the necessary delivery and settlements to occur. Recognizing this issue, the Basel III Accord stipulates that capital requirements be based on a presumption that 20 business days pass before collateral is in place to cover a derivatives exposure. Previously, under the Basel II Accord, the period was 10 business days. The creators of the Basel III Accord deemed the increase necessary after considering the extreme loss of liquidity during 2008. Pykhtin and Zhu (2006) provide a discussion of the coverage of CVA under the Basel II Accord.

As Gregory (2012) describes, risk mitigants do not eliminate risk. Instead, risk mitigation replaces one risk with another (i.e., risk mitigation is risk substitution). In this instance, collateral collected from a counterparty substitutes liquidity risk for the credit exposure that an entity has to that counterparty. This relationship occurs because no assurance exists that the sale of the collateral by the surviving entity will not be on "fire sale" terms. As an extreme but entirely plausible example, consider the case where a positive correlation exists between the value of collateral intended to mitigate an exposure and the value of the failing entity. In that case, the collateral value declines as the failing entity's value decreases. Such *wrong-way risk* undermines what the entity may have presumed to be its mitigated risk.

These considerations along with weaknesses revealed in the last half of 2008 prompted the adoption of a more holistic perspective on credit risk. From this situation, more careful thinking emerged about replacement costs, increased consideration of reliance on funding availability, and reconsideration of the effectiveness of previous risk-mitigation procedures. The next section introduces CVA as a means to value risk exposure.

Building a CVA

This section first constructs a high-level perspective on CVAs and then proceeds to develop a one-period CVA model. This process sets the stage for a CVA specification covering the multiple-period case. The section ends with coverage of some recent work by Brigo and Morini (2010) that reconsiders the determination of closeout amounts.

A HIGH-LEVEL PERSPECTIVE ON CVA

Much contemporary thought about credit risk traces to insights formalized by Merton (1974). His insight is to construe the value of a risky contract as the value of a riskless contract accompanied by an option on the underlying risk source. Merton introduces this line of thinking in the context of corporate debt. The risky corporate bond promises to pay at its maturity date a par amount. However, the prospects of the firm that issued the bond determine its ability to make that payment. Those prospects determine the riskiness of the bond. Supposing those prospects riskless, bondholders can be confident that the firm will honor its promises to redeem the bonds at par value. Reality dictates that the firm's prospects are typically not riskless. In good states, the firm's prospects are favorable because revenues generated by assets are sufficient for the firm to redeem its bonds at their par values. Should the firm's results turn out to be poor and revenues insufficient to enable redemption, then the firm's owners default and the bondholders take over the firm. That is, the owners give up their ownership and turn over the assets to the bondholders in exchange for the bondholders relinquishing their claims to the firm's promised interest payments and redemption at par value of the bonds purchased from the firm. This exchange of the firm's assets for the dropping of bondholder claims constitutes an option. It is a put option because the owners of the firm retain the right to sell the firm's assets to the bondholders at the par value of the outstanding bonds. The sale extinguishes the bondholder claim to the par payment specified by the bonds.

Framing this model using the terminology of options, the equivalent position for a bondholder entering into a risky debt position is a long position in a risk-free bond and selling the owners of the firm an option that allows them to relinquish the firm's assets in lieu of paying the par value of the firm. In the Merton construction, this framework is a one-period model so the value of the option is the value of the right to default on the debt obligation. Employing methods similar to those developed by Black and Scholes (1973) and Merton (1973), the value of this default option is determined by the value of the promised payment (i.e., the bond's par value), the value of the firm's assets, volatility of those assets, time until default can occur, and the risk-free rate of interest.

This perspective provides a useful framework for the valuation of credit risk. Merton's (1973) one-period model of a corporate bond is readily extended to a single-payment, interest-rate swap contract. In one period, counterparty A expects to receive from its contract with counterparty B the current difference between the floating rate and the fixed rate. Noting its exposure, counterparty A has called for and obtained from counterparty B collateral fully covering that amount. Should the floating rate not change, counterparty A can be confident that it will receive the amount it is due. Because the floating rate varies, counterparty A has a risk exposure. The value of that exposure, as with Merton's corporate bond case, is determined by the product of the floating-to-fixed-rate spread and the contract notional value, the volatility of that spread, a *pro rata* share of the assets of counterparty B, time until the payment is due (or defaulted on), and the risk-free rate of interest. According to Merton's perspective, the value of the risky position held by counterparty A is equivalent to the value of a risk-free position with counterparty B and the market value of an option giving counterparty B the right to default by handing over the collateral already posted along with a *pro rata* share of its assets.

The ability to value exposure is useful. First, valuation concentrates attention on the cost incurred when entering a contract. Suppose, for example, that the goal of the contract is to hedge an unwanted interest-rate exposure. On recognizing that entry into the contract creates a risk exposure, absent valuation of that exposure, discerning the extent of advantage obtained by establishing the hedge position will be difficult. For example, the case may arise that the value locked in by the hedge is less than the credit risk exposure created by the hedging contract. In that instance, the intended hedger may want to shop for another counterparty or possibly forgo consideration of the hedge position entirely.

Second, if alternative counterparties are unavailable, valuation enables identifying negotiable contract terms that stand to achieve a lower valued risk exposure. Negotiating these terms can bring the value of the risk exposure down to a level that obtains the desired interest-rate hedge at acceptable cost. For example, steps that can reduce the value of the credit risk are reducing the collateral threshold amount or the period of margin risk or even requiring over collateralization. Absent a valuation scheme, consideration of the trade-offs inherent in such contracts is likely ad hoc and unreliable.

Craine (1992) provides an early example of the Merton approach to credit risk management. His work deals with the credit risk exposure of a futures clearinghouse. A futures clearinghouse interposes itself between the buy (long positions) and sell (short positions) sides of the contracts that trade on the exchange. In so doing, the clearinghouse takes on credit exposure to both the buy side and the sell side. To manage that exposure, all contracts are marked-to-market on at least a daily basis so that at the beginning of each trading period, the amounts owed to the clearinghouse are zero. Nevertheless, the clearinghouse has credit exposure in that price changes during the day may exceed the ability of some participants to fulfill their payment obligations when contracts are next marked-to-market.

Craine (1992) treats the value of those exposures as one-period default options that enable futures contract holders to walk away from their contracts. Because the clearinghouse is short these options, clearinghouse officials have incentives to minimize their value. Officials achieve control over their exposures (i.e., the value of these options) by stipulating margin requirements. Such requirements are best termed performance bonds because they bond the performance of market participants. On receipt of margin deposits by market participants, the clearinghouse collateralizes its exposures. The collateral it collects, in turn, lessens the value of the extant options. Craine contends that the clearinghouse sets margin levels to drive the current market value of these options to zero. The clearinghouse substantially reduces its risk exposures. Its remaining credit risk exposures arise from increases in the volatility of the contract prices traded on the exchange.

CALCULATING THE CVA

As the previous section states, the CVA on any contract is the market value of the risk exposure. A general expression for this can be written as Equation 22.1:

$$CVA \equiv PV - \widetilde{PV}, \tag{22.1}$$

where PV is the present value of a default-free contract and $\widetilde{PV}$ is the present value of an identically structured contract having default risk. Because a counterparty will only default in states where it owes some amount, a need exists for a representation that defines those amounts for each period over the life of the contract and expresses their sum in present value terms.

To develop this approach, consider an entity at the beginning of the first period t. At the end of the period, the entity learns two things: the value of its extant contracts with its counterparty and whether that counterparty will default. Developing expectations for each of these scenarios enables the entity to determine an expectation for the loss it may realize at the end of the current period.

For each contract, if at the end of period t the value of that contract is zero or less and the counterparty defaults, then no credit exposure exists because the counterparty is not under an obligation to pay on that contract. Conversely, if the value of the contract at the end of period t is positive and the counterparty defaults, then the entity realizes a loss on the contract. The amount of loss is the contract's value. Thus, for an individual contract the exposure in period t can be written as Equation 22.2:

$$E_t^i = max[V_i(t, T), 0], \qquad (22.2)$$

where $V_i(t, T)$ is the value at time t of contract i whose expiry date is T. Inclusion of the termination date of the contract T stipulates that the loss amount will be the market value of an identically specified contract having a remaining tenor of $T - t$.

Instances of multiple contracts with a single counterparty implies that exposure to that counterparty will be determined over all contracts with that counterparty. The maximum exposure to the counterparty is then the sum of all the exposures to that counterparty. In other words, the exposure at time t is defined as the sum over all contracts: $E_t \equiv \sum_i E_t^i = \sum_i max[V_i(t, T), 0]$. However, netting arrangements such as those defined by the ISDA Master Agreement can, and often do, substantially reduce exposure by allowing the entity to set off the amounts it owes to a defaulting counterparty against the amounts the counterparty owes to the entity. Contracts coming under a *netting agreement*, which is an agreement specifying the settlement procedures for a group of contracts between two counterparties should either counterparty default comprise a *netting set*. The netting agreement will specify how the amount owed on the netting set is determined when a counterparty defaults. This amount, termed the *closeout amount*, is the final settlement on the extant contracts comprising the netting set.

In this case, the $max()$ function on the sums is less than or equal the sum of the constituent sum functions. This result, known as subadditivity, implies that the closeout amount will often be less than the maximum exposure; that is $E_t^{NS} = max(\sum_i V_i(t, T), 0)$, where E_t^{NS} is the exposure of the netting set at time t. This subadditivity property often produces substantial netting benefits, the extent of which depends on the correlation between contracts comprising the netting set. To illustrate this netting benefit, Gregory (2012) derives a simple formula for the ratio of net to gross exposure assuming exposures are normally distributed. His formulation, written in contract units rather than units of contract notional value, provides a mechanism that illustrates the benefits obtained from netting arrangements. Gregory refers to the formulation as the *netting factor* that he writes as Equation 22.3:

$$Netting\ Factor = \frac{\sqrt{n + n(n-1)\bar{\rho}}}{n}, \qquad (22.3)$$

where n is the number of contracts in the netting set and $\bar{\rho}$ is the average of the correlations across exposures within the netting set. By inspection, when the average of the correlations is unity, the netting factor is unity indicating the netted exposure equals the gross exposure so that no netting benefit exists. Any lower average correlation drives the net-to-gross exposure ratio lower indicating an increasing netting benefit as correlations decline. Similarly, holding the average of the correlations constant but less than unity, as the number of contracts in the netting set rises, the netting benefit increases.

This result occurs because increasing the number of exposures increases the odds of setting off existing exposures.

Having specified the exposure entailed by the netting set, the next step is considering the extent of recoverable loss as the entity becomes a general claimant on the assets of the failing counterparty. Most often, this amount is specified as a constant, hence the amount is assumed independent of the other arguments determining the CVA value. Some authors instead specify a LGD, which Equation 22.4 shows:

$$LGD = (1 - R)E_t^{NS}, \tag{22.4}$$

where R, the recovery rate, is the average amount per dollar of loss deemed recoverable through bankruptcy proceedings. Given that default will occur, discounting the LGD at the risk-free rate is appropriate. This is can be represented as Equation 22.5:

$$\wedge = 1_{\{t_0 < \tau < t_1\}} e^{-r(t_1 - t_0)} (1 - R)E_t^{NS}, \tag{22.5}$$

where $1_{\{t_0 < \tau < t_1\}}$ is an indicator function taking the value one if the argument is true, otherwise its value is zero. In this case, the argument is that default occurs at time τ which falls within the period beginning at t_0 and ending at t_1 (the current period) and r is the continuously compounded risk-free rate of interest.

A risk-neutral investor values the credit exposure as Equation 22.6

$$CVA = E^{RN}(\wedge) = (1 - R)E^{RN}(E_t^{NS})PD(t_0, t_1), \tag{22.6}$$

where $E^{RN}(\ )$ is the expectations operator for a risk-neutral investor and $PD(t_0, t_1)$ is the probability of default during the period that begins at t_0 and ending at t_1. Default probabilities deriving from the term structure of credit default swaps, the above equation gives the unilateral, one-period CVA. Because this is a market valuation, the CVA is the price the counterparty should expect to pay to obtain protection from default on its netting set.

CALCULATING THE MULTIPLE-PERIOD CVA

Because many OTC derivative contracts require payments beyond the current period, they create exposures for multiple periods into the future. Such contracts necessitate methods that generate forward-looking scenarios of market conditions that enable computation of contract values $(V_i(t, T))$ for dates between t and T. Parameterization is through one of two methods of a specification for the following geometric Brownian motion process denoted in Equation 22.7:

$$dX(t) = \mu(t)X(t)dt + \sigma(t)X(t)dW_t, \tag{22.7}$$

where $\mu(t)$ is the mean drift term and $\sigma(t)$ the standard deviation of the diffusion process. The first parameterization method employs a historical time series of market rates and prices, whereas the second obtains the necessary parameters from current prices. The well-known solution to the geometric process is Equation 22.8:

$$X(t_i) = X(t_{i-1})e^{\left[\bar{\mu}_{i-1,i} - \frac{1}{2}\bar{\sigma}_{i-1,i}^2\right]}(t_k - t_{k-1}) + \bar{\sigma}_{i-1,i}^2 \sqrt{t_k - t_{k-1}}\,\tilde{\varepsilon}, \qquad (22.8)$$

where $\tilde{\varepsilon}$ is a standard normal random variable and

$$\bar{\mu}_{i,j} = \frac{1}{t_j - t_i}\int_{t_i}^{t_j}\mu(s)ds \qquad \bar{\sigma}_{i,j}^2 = \frac{1}{t_j - t_i}\int_{t_i}^{t_j}\sigma^2(s)ds.$$

On generating driver variables for each scenario, computed values for the contracts comprising the netting set at discrete dates over the tenor of the contracts and expected exposures of the netting set determined.

The multi-period CVA integrates across time to obtain Equation 22.9:

$$CVA = E^{RN}(\wedge) = (1 - R)\int_0^T E^{RN}[E_t^{NS}|t = \tau]dPD(0, t_1). \qquad (22.9)$$

RECONSIDERING THE CLOSEOUT AMOUNT

The above CVA treats the closeout amount as being risk-free. Thinking along these lines derives, at least in part, from thinking of CVA as being unilateral. This is to say an entity has exposure to a counterparty that will either default or not while considering the entity itself to be at all times default free. Under those circumstances a closeout arrangement, either in the form of a cash payment that the surviving counterparty can use to obtain a replacement for the defaulted contract or a replacement for the contract by a new counterparty, could be regarded as free of default risk. As Brigo and Morini (2010) point out, this is an unlikely circumstance.

To illustrate this point, consider what happens if a counterparty defaults. If the surviving entity has an extant negative exposure at the time of bankruptcy, the conservators representing the creditors of the defaulting party will collect that payment. Considering only the correlation of defaults due to the respective idiosyncratic risks of the two counterparties, treating the conservator's claim as risk-free does seem a reasonable approximation of its value. This conclusion is because considering credit risk strictly idiosyncratic, the odds that the surviving counterparty will also default is small in most cases. However, among the lessons of the financial crisis of 2007–2008, the standout lesson is that default correlations also derive from systematic risks to use the term associated with asset pricing models, or systemic risk to use the term favored by regulators of the institutional organizations.

Turning to the positive exposure that the surviving entity may have to its counterparty, the former considerations also apply but one must also consider the ISDA specifications for closeout arrangements. On this point, the International Swaps and Derivatives Association (2009, p. 13) states:

> In determining a Close-out Amount, the Determining Party may consider any relevant information, including, without limitation, one or more of the following types of information:

(i) quotations (either firm or indicative) for replacement transactions supplied by one or more third parties that may take into account the creditworthiness of the Determining Party at the time the quotation is provided and the terms of any relevant documentation, including credit support documentation, between the Determining Party and the third party providing the quotation.

The 2009 Protocol contradicts the notion of a risk-free amount. On default of a counterparty, the surviving organization will present for recovery its claims in the full amount of the cost to obtain replacement contracts. Dealer quotes for replacement contracts will include adjustments that consider the credit risk of the surviving counterpart. In other words, counterparties who consummate deals with the surviving counterparty to replace its defaulted contracts will include a CVA in their offers for the replacement contracts. Those costs will be included in determining the close out amount. Therefore, regarding close out amounts as risk-free is inappropriate.

Furthermore, the ISDA Protocol undermines the logic of a unilateral CVA. If a counterparty fails and its replacement contracts include a CVA, then the surviving counterparty must have presented a credit risk exposure to the failed counterparty. In other words, credit risk exposure is in all, or nearly all, cases bilateral and the fact of default by the counterparty to the original netting set does not imply the surviving counterparty could not have defaulted. Each counterparty was at risk that the other might default, one did, but because both could have defaulted the CVA valuation must consider the credit risks bilaterally.

Valuing a Bilateral CVA

To this point, the chapter has developed a valuation scheme for a CVA that seeks to obtain a market value for the credit risk created in a bilateral contract. The previous section's coverage of Brigo and Morini (2010) on closeout arrangements points out that credit exposure is *bilateral* because each party to a contract has exposure to the other. This section extends the CVA concept to the bilateral case.

GOING BEYOND A UNILATERAL CVA

A bilateral CVA requires two additional considerations over those required to construct a unilateral CVA. First, on recognizing that each counterparty to a bilateral contract has an exposure, one expects that rational counterparties will incorporate their valuation of the exposures taken on as part of their consideration of the deal. The assumption of rationality stems from an understanding that the value of the exposure created by taking on the counterparty risk should exceed the value gained from the contract when considered independent of its credit exposure. Further, each counterparty should value its *net exposure* (i.e., the value of the risk posed by the counterparty—the CVA—net of the risk it poses to its counterparty). The latter of these is termed a *debit value adjustment* (DVA).

Second, recall that in a multi-period contract the unilateral CVA is the integral of expected default amounts discounted to obtain their current-period value. In a bilateral arrangement, the entity conducting the valuation must include the possibility that it has defaulted at some prior date. Consider that an entity has determined its unilateral CVA for a two-period contract is $5,000 for each period. When computing its bilateral CVA, the entity must include the possibility that it might default in one period eliminating its exposure in the second period. Hence, provided the entity has a nonzero probability of default, a bilateral CVA will be less than a unilateral CVA. Recognizing that a debit value adjustment is a mirror image of the CVA, the same reasoning will apply to the DVA (i.e., default of the entity's counterparty eliminates exposure that the entity's counterparty has to the entity).

Incorporating both of these considerations, a general expression for the bilateral CVA (BCVA) can be written as Equation 22.10:

$$BCVA = CVA^B + DVA^B, \tag{22.10}$$

where CVA^B the previously introduced CVA is adapted to include the possibility of default by either counterparty and DVA^B is the debit value adjustment also adapted for the bilateral case.

Equation 22.10 has two parts. CVA^B is the credit value adjustment portion now adjusted for the possibility that the entity may default before its counterparty. Equation 22.11 expands this portion:

$$CVA^B = (1 - R_C) \int_0^T E^{RN}[E_t^{NS}|t = \tau_C, t < \tau_E]dPD(0, t_1), \tag{22.11}$$

where R_C is the expected recovery rate should the entity's counterparty default. This term, sometimes written as LGD in which case it is LGD_C, indicates the amount of unrecoverable loss should the counterparty default. The term $E^{RN}[E_t^{NS}|t = \tau_C, t < \tau_E]$ is the risk-neutral, conditional expectation of the netting set value at time t. In the prior unilateral case, the conditional expectations operator represented the likelihood of counterparty defaulting at time τ, which is now being denoted as τ_C. In the bilateral case, the conditional expectation must include the possibility that the entity has not defaulted as of time t. The reasoning for this is simple. If the entity defaults before time t, then the contract is void at date t and the counterparty cannot default on a voided contract. Defining τ_E as the date of the entity's default, the condition states that the entity will, at some future date, default on its contracts. Of course, the situation may occur where $T < \tau_E$ (i.e., that the terminal date of the longest-dated contract included in the netting set comes before the date that entity defaults on whatever contracts it does have open).

Because the DVA represents the counterparty's exposure to the entity, the second term of the bilateral CVA is a mirror image of the CVA as shown in Equation 22.12:

$$CVA^B = (1 - R_E) \int_0^T E^{RN}[E_t^{NS}|t = \tau_E, t < \tau_C]dPD(0, t_1), \tag{22.12}$$

where R_E is the expected recovery rate for the counterparty given that the entity defaults. Again, some authors write this as the LGD. In that case, the term would be denoted as LGD_E or the LGD by the entity. The conditional expectation term now reverses the default incidence to say that the entity defaults at time t and the counterparty has not previously defaulted so as to void the contract.

Implementation of CVAs by Regulatory Authorities

This section covers the Basel III Accord requirement that banks incorporate CVA into their capital charge. The section begins with a background for the reasoning for this capital charge and a discussion of actuarial and risk-neutral approaches for inclusion of credit risk into the regulatory capital requirements. A second section covers the BIS implementation.

BACKGROUND TO INCORPORATION OF CVA INTO REGULATORY CAPITAL CHARGES

The Basel Committee on Banking Supervision (2011, p. 3) states:

> Banks will be subject to a capital charge for potential mark-to-market losses (i.e. credit value adjustment—CVA—risk) associated with a deterioration in the credit worthiness of a counterparty. While the Basel II standard covers the risk of a counterparty default, it does not address such CVA risk, which during the financial crisis was a greater source of losses than those arising from outright defaults.

In his comments shortly after release of the Basel III Accord framework, Hervé Hannoun, Deputy General Manager for the BIS, elaborated by explaining that two-thirds of the losses during the crisis were mark-to-market losses due to CVAs as opposed to the one-third of the losses realized from actual defaults.

Despite having recognized the importance of CVAs, the BIS implementation described by Rosen and Saunders (2012) falls short of its implementation by financial institutions and accounting firms. This outcome may derive from bankers having two perspectives on CVAs prompting banking regulators to accommodate. One approach is along the lines developed in the previous sections of this chapter. This being that CVA is not a measure of an entity's risk exposure but a price for having undertaken that risk exposure. The advantage of this approach comes through the objectivity obtained when adopting a market valuation for an institution's credit risk exposures.

However, this approach is at odds with traditional banking practice that measures the extent of risk undertaken and manages those exposures by carrying reserve balances. Under this approach, the bank creates an expense based on the loan losses it expects to realize in subsequent periods. The bank carries the balance of those expenses as a reserve account that it nets against the loan account (i.e., in this instance, the loss reserve account is a contra-asset account). On realizing a loss, the bank takes a charge against its reserve account. In periods of deteriorating loan quality, charges taken against earnings accumulate in the loss reserve account because actual losses in any single period are more often less than the amount of increase. As conditions improve, release of excess charges often boosts earnings. As a result, reported earnings and the bank's net worth are less volatile.

The approach is actuarial in that it uses historical probabilities to determine expensed amounts. This contrasts to the risk-neutral probabilities used to value loss exposures. This difference can be important. Using historical probabilities relies on repetition of the events captured in the collected data history. Conversely, risk-neutral probabilities are market based and can be viewed as consensus estimates that incorporate the above-mentioned actuarial information but also any other information relevant to default probabilities. Although CVA can be calculated using historical probabilities, the result may differ substantially from the price an institution would actually pay to hedge its credit risks. In particular, as market assessments of risk rise (fall), actuarial approaches will tend to undervalue (overvalue) CVA.

BIS SCHEME FOR IMPLEMENTING CVA IN CAPITAL CHARGES

The Basel III Accord stipulates that banks using internal models include in their capital estimates provisions for a 99 percent, 10-day value-at-risk (VaR) calculation of the CVAs computed on a unilateral basis (Basel Committee on Banking Supervision 2011). The requirement is three times the equal-weighted sum of both VaR and stressed VaR.

Rosen and Saunders (2012) give the required unilateral credit value calculation in Equation 22.13:

$$CVA = LGD \sum_{i=1}^{n} max[0, q_i] \left(\frac{EE_{i-1} + EE_i}{2} \right), \tag{22.13}$$

where the EE_i are discounted unconditional exposures at time t_i and the q_i are default probabilities imputed from differences in the term structure of credit spreads between period t_i and period t_{i-1} as shown in Equation 22.14

$$q_i = exp \left(-\frac{s_{i-1} t_{i-1}}{1 - R} \right) - exp \left(-\frac{s_i t_i}{1 - R} \right), \tag{22.14}$$

where s_i is the credit spread at time t_i. Division by $1 - R$ restates each credit spread by an amount the market expects to be unrecoverable. Because credit spreads incorporate default probabilities along with expectations of unrecoverable losses, the division adjusts for the expected recovery amount to obtain the probability of default provided the recovery expectation matches that of the market.

The issue, raised by both Rosen and Saunders (2012) and Hull and White (2012), is the lack of independence between the imputed probabilities and the exposures. Although the Basel III Accord guidance assumes these amounts are independently determined, considerable evidence fails to support this assumption. Lack of independence is called *wrong-way risk*, a term that refers to instances where a positive relationship exists between default probability and the associated exposure amounts. An example would be an entity whose exposure is to a counterparty paying the variable rate on an interest-rate swap. Should the counterparty have a substantial duration gap (i.e., the Macaulay duration of its assets is much higher than for its liabilities), increases in interest rates lead to a decline in net worth. Therefore, the probability of counterparty default is increasing as the extent of exposure to that counterparty increases. Rosen and Saunders suggest a method to estimate a conditional expectation. Hull and White take a different approach by considering a Taylor-series approximation of the CVA, which they refer to as a delta-gamma method.

Summary and Conclusions

Because CVA amounts were for many years not a material expense, they went unreported. Matters changed substantially as the financial crisis of 2007–2008 revealed a far greater extent of credit exposure. Additionally, the events of the crisis led to increased attention to finding improved methods of pricing credit risk exposures. These efforts confront a long-held presumption that valuing OTC products such as interest-rate swaps could ignore considering the completeness of those markets. For many years the OTC markets experienced few states of the world combining large exposures and high default probabilities but this is no longer the case.

The financial crisis generated much academic interest on developing valuation schemes that are both useful and efficiently calculated. Similarly, regulatory attention is focused anew on the problem of default, especially the correlated defaults that comprise systemic risk. Much work remains to be done. This chapter has described current research but this work is very much on going and as such is unsettled.

Discussion Questions

1. Using the Merton (1974) model, describe how credit risk embedded in corporate debt can be understood as an option.
2. Summarize three measures that the ISDA undertook to mitigate the credit risk inherent in OTC derivatives.
3. List and describe the three components of a unilateral CVA.
4. Using a vanilla interest-rate swap, describe the determinants of CVA for both counterparties.
5. Describe the circumstances leading to including CVA in the Basel III Accord and how the CVA requirement might be expected to alleviate future problems.

References

Bank of International Settlements. 2013. *Statistical Release OTC Derivatives Statistics at End-June 2013*. Monetary and Economic Department. Available at http://www.bis.org/publ/otc_hy1311.pdf.

Basel Committee on Banking Supervision. 2011. "Basel III: A Global Regulatory Framework for More Resilient Banks and Banking Systems." Available at http://www.bis.org/publ/bcbs189.pdf.

Black, Fischer, and Myron Scholes. 1973. "The Pricing of Options and Corporate Liabilities." *Journal of Political Economy* 81:3, 637–654.

Brigo, Damiano, and Massimo Morini. 2010. "Dangers of Bilateral Counterparty Risk: The Fundamental Impact of Closeout Conventions." Available at http://ssrn.com/abstract=1709370.

Craine, Roger. 1992. "Are Futures Margins Adequate." Working Paper, University of California at Berkeley.

Gregory, Jon. 2012. *Counterparty Credit Risk and Credit Value Adjustment: A Continuing Challenge for Global Financial Markets*, 2nd Edition. Chichester, UK: John Wiley and Sons Ltd.

Hull, John, and Alan White. 2012. "CVA and Wrong Way Risk." Working Paper, Joseph L. Rotman School of Management, University of Toronto.

International Swaps and Derivatives Association, Inc. 2009. "Close Out Amount Protocol." Available at http://www.isda.org/isdacloseoutamtprot/docs/isdacloseoutprot-text.pdf.

Lehman Brothers Holdings Inc. 2009. First Creditors Section 341 Meeting, slides 19–20, January 29. Available at http://www.lehmanbrothersestate.com/LBH/Project/default.aspx#L.

Merton, Robert C. 1973. "Theory of Rational Option Pricing." *Bell Journal of Economics and Management Science* 4:1, 141–183.

Merton, Robert C. 1974. "On the Pricing of Corporate Debt: The Risk Structure of Interest Rates." *Journal of Finance* 29:2, 449–470.

Pykhtin, Michael, and Steven Zhu. 2006. "Measuring Counterparty Credit Risk for Trading Products under Basel II." In Michael K. Ong, ed., *Basel Handbook*, 2nd Edition, 123–162. London: Risk Books.

Rosen, Dan, and David Saunders. 2012. "CVA the Wrong Way." *Journal of Risk Management in Financial Institutions* 5:3, 252–272.

23

Risk Management and Hedge Funds

RAZVAN PASCALAU

Associate Professor, SUNY Plattsburgh

Introduction

According to Barclay Hedge (2013), a hedge fund database, the total number of assets under management (AUM) grew from $26 billion in 1988 to $1,946 billion in the second quarter of 2013. This number is likely to grow at an even higher rate after the removal of the ad ban on hedge fund advertising as part of the Jumpstart Our Business Startups Act (JOBS Act).

Now, more than ever, a need exists for adequate risk management tools to separate the well-managed hedge funds from the poorly managed ones. The hedge funds data vendors already employ and provide a host of useful risk management tools. Drawdown (e.g., worst and average) measures, financial ratios (e.g., Sharpe, Calmar, efficiency, Sortino, and Sterling ratios), and other risk measures (e.g., correlation with various indexes and betas) are available to investors for assessing and comparing the risk profiles of hedge funds.

Recent research shows, however, that these measures may be insufficient to accurately and adequately manage hedge fund risk. For instance, Kang, In, Kim, and Kim (2010), who build on previous studies such as Fung and Hsieh (2001), Lo (2001), Mitchell and Pulvino (2001), and Agarwal and Naik (2004), demonstrate the asymmetric dependence between hedge funds and the equity market. Their study finds that hedge funds are exposed nonlinearly to market risks at least in the short run. Liang and Park (2007) also analyze the risk-return trade-off in hedge funds and find that the left-tail risk as captured by the expected shortfall (ES) and tail risk (TR) measures explain the cross-section variation in returns, unlike the measures mentioned above. Liang and Park also show that ES is superior to value-at-risk (VaR) as a downside risk measure.

The financial crisis of 2007–2008 demonstrates the importance of liquidity and operational risk measures in addition to the more traditional financial risk measures used in the standard risk management practice. For instance, Teo (2011) highlights the importance of favorable redemption terms to investors. This study shows that within this group of more liquid funds, the high net inflow funds outperform the low net inflow funds by 4.79 percent per year on a risk-adjusted basis. The findings of Teo, which build on the theoretical work of Brunnermeier and Pedersen (2009), assert that initial losses by speculators precipitate further investor redemptions that force hedge fund asset sales at fire sale prices, thereby inducing further investor withdrawals. Hence, as liquidity providers, those hedge funds with high liquidity risk exposure outperform the portfolio of funds with low liquidity risk by 5.80 percent a year.

A different stream of the literature considers the impact of operational issues on the risk-return trade-off. In particular, the focus has been on clearly identifying and measuring operational risk. Brown (2012) states that according to the Basel II Accord, *operational risk* is the risk of direct or indirect losses due to failed internal processes, people, or systems or even due to external events. He contends that while developing operational risk measures in an asset management context is challenging due to the secretive nature of hedge funds in particular, several avenues are worth pursuing.

For example, Brown, Fraser, and Liang (2008) study the value and the importance of operational risk using a brief period of mandatory disclosure as required by the Securities and Exchange Commission (SEC) in February 2006. More specifically, the SEC adopted several rule changes and amendments to the Investment Advisers Act of 1940 that required hedge fund managers to register as investment advisers by February 1, 2006. To be compliant with these new regulations, the SEC required hedge fund managers to file Form ADV. Some hedge fund and mutual fund managers, who are classified as "investment advisers," already filed this form. Although the rule changes were short lived given that the U.S. Court of Appeals for the District of Columbia Circuit repealed them on June 23, 2006, they provided a wealth of data on hedge funds' potential conflicts of interest and past legal and regulatory problems.

Brown et al. (2008) propose several operational risk measures. First, one operational risk variable indicates if the fund has external relationships conflicts of interest. Such conflicts include whether the fund recommends securities in which a related party has an ownership interest, if the company buys and sells between itself and the clients, or if the fund uses external research from the same broker that executes its trades. Brown et al. find that the coefficients on all of these variables are large, positive, and statistically significant, which indicates a positive correlation between potential conflicts of interest and legal or regulatory problems. Further, these proxies for operational risk are negatively related to historical performance. Finally, the authors combine these observed variables into one construct of operational risk by defining a linear combination of these variables that maximally correlates with the cross-section of Form ADV disclosures that match a hedge fund database. Brown et al. call this measure the *ω-score*. Regression fund returns on the operational risk ω-score shows that operational risk has a negative and significant impact on fund performance, all things being equal. Further, in a separate study Brown, Goetzmann, Liang, and Schwarz (2009) use the ω-score and find that operational risk is even more significant than financial risk in explaining fund failure. This study also uncovers a positive relationship between financial risk and operational risk.

The remainder of the chapter is organized as follows. The first section discusses the established tools and current practice of measuring and managing hedge fund risk investment. The next section demonstrates and evaluates empirically some risk measures using recent hedge fund data. Next, a discussion involves the recent risk management advances in the world of alternative investments, focusing on tail risk and operational risk measures. The final section offers a summary and conclusions.

Measuring and Managing Hedge Fund Risk

Before discussing risk management, the concept of risk must be defined. Indeed, investors may have different concepts of risk including a deviation from a benchmark, an average, or any situation where an investor may lose money. Although volatility is a simple and appealing risk measure due to its ease of computing and understanding, it may not suffice in the context of hedge funds. Fung and Hsieh (2002) demonstrate that hedge fund returns display strong skewness and kurtosis properties that render the simple measure of standard deviation insufficient. Therefore, in the context of hedge funds, investors should consider several risk measures that incorporate the asymmetric and "fat tails" nature of hedge fund returns. This chapter considers several measures but Lhabitant (2006) provides a more in-depth discussion.

DOWNSIDE RISK MEASURES

In contrast to return volatility as a measure of risk, downside risk measures assign a higher weight to the negative returns and also consider the possibility of a non-normal return distribution. Assume a time series of hedge fund returns, $R_t, t = \overline{1, T}$, where the investor has a pre-specified target rate of return, R^*. Equation 23.1 shows the computation of the measure of downside risk:

$$\text{Downside risk} = \frac{1}{T} \sqrt{\sum_{t=1}^{T} \delta_t^2} \qquad (23.1)$$

where

$$\delta_t = \begin{cases} R^* - R_t, & \text{if } R_t < R^* \\ 0, & \text{otherwise} \end{cases}.$$

The target rate is often set equal to the average historical return, in which case this measure is called *semi-deviation*. Risk-averse investors who may be especially worried about losing money and institutional investors who typically have minimum return requirements or benchmarks may find this measure useful.

DRAWDOWN STATISTICS

Drawdown is the (percentage) decline in net asset value (NAV) from the highest historical return level or the peak-to-valley rate of return. In a drawdown, the rate of return (ROR) is by definition negative. Several drawdown measures exist such as the worst, average, and current drawdown. Equation 23.2 denotes the worst drawdown based on the value-added monthly index (VAMI), where VAMI is computed as $VAMI = (1 + ROR_t) \times VAMI_{t-1}$, as the growth in value of a $1,000 investment.

$$\text{Worst drawdown} = \left(1 - \frac{\text{Valley VAMI}}{\text{Peak VAMI}}\right) \times 100. \qquad (23.2)$$

An *average downturn* is the average continuous negative return over an investment period. Equation 23.3 denote D_j as the jth drawdown over the entire period and d as the total number of draw-downs over the same entire period:

$$\text{Average drawdown} = \left| \sum\nolimits_{j=1}^{j=d} \frac{D_j}{d} \right|. \tag{23.3}$$

Some investors consider only the largest drawdowns and therefore restrict d to a predetermined maximum limit. The *current drawdown* is computed as the average return from the most recent peak. The *average recovery time* (ART) is the average time in a recovery from a drawdown measured from the low point of the drawdown to a new peak. In the empirical analysis that follows, if a hedge fund is in an ongoing drawdown, the assumption is that the current drawdown is over for purposes of computing the ART.

BENCHMARK-RELATED STATISTICS

Although hedge funds often market themselves as absolute performers, they frequently produce ratios to compare their performance with that of a market index or some other benchmark. For instance, among some intuitive benchmark-related statistics popular with investors are the *up percentage ratio* (i.e., number of periods in which the fund outperformed the benchmark when the benchmark was up), the *down percentage ratio* (i.e., number of periods in which the fund outperformed the benchmark when the benchmark was down), and the *ratio of negative months to total months*, which is also a good indicator of the downside risk of the fund.

Beta, another important relative measure, measures how risky a fund may be as compared to a market index such as the S&P 500, the Dow Jones Industrial Average (DJIA), or the Nasdaq or Russell 2000. Given that hedge funds claim to deliver absolute performance, which is supposed to be independent of market conditions, hedge funds should display betas less than one. However, since beta focuses only on the impact of the overall stock market and ignores all other idiosyncratic risks, beta may be an incomplete explanation of the risk-return trade-off. Therefore, a low beta but high volatility fund simply means low exposure to the market but high specific risk.

RISK-ADJUSTED PERFORMANCE MEASURES

Although most comparisons of hedge funds usually focus on absolute (or total) return, investors need to be aware of the different risk characteristics of hedge funds relative to other pooled investments such as mutual funds. Thus, a fair comparison requires that the measures considered include both the returns and the risks a hedge fund generates.

Several measures relate to measuring excess performance over a benchmark, which is the so-called *alpha*. These measures are of interest to both investors and money managers because the former ultimately care about the ability of the manager to generate alpha and not simply following a passive strategy.

The Sharpe Ratio

The *Sharpe ratio* measures the excess return per unit of volatility of a fund as shown in Equation 23.4:

$$\text{Sharpe ratio} = \frac{R_{\text{HF}} - R_{\text{F}}}{\sigma_{\text{HF}}}, \qquad (23.4)$$

where R_{HF} is the average return of a particular hedge fund; R_F is the risk-free asset; and σ_{HF} is the annualized standard deviation of monthly ROR or the annualized standard deviation of quarterly ROR. The Sharpe ratio may be expressed on an annual or monthly basis. The risk-free asset is usually the three-month Treasury bill return.

The Calmar Ratio

The *Calmar ratio* is a statistic that combines a fund's return with the drawdown risk to enable investors to see the potential opportunity gain versus opportunity loss of investing with a particular manager. It is calculated by dividing a fund's compound annualized ROR over a certain period such as three years and dividing it by the fund's maximum drawdown. The lower this ratio is, the worse the investment performed over the specified period.

The Efficiency Ratio

The *efficiency ratio* generally measures how well a company uses its assets and liabilities internally. In the context of hedge funds, the *efficiency ratio* is computed by dividing the compound annual ROR over the annualized standard deviation of monthly ROR. An improvement of this ratio translates into improved profitability. Analysts usually use this measure to compare funds within the same strategy area.

The Sortino Ratio

The Sortino ratio reconsiders the issue of performance measurement from the perspective of downside risk. The key idea is that the most important risk component is not volatility, but rather the risk of not achieving the return to an investment goal. Hence, unlike the Sharpe ratio, the Sortino ratio in Equation 23.5 measures the incremental return over a minimum acceptable return (MAR) divided by the downside deviation below the MAR:

$$\text{Sortino ratio} = \frac{R_{\text{HF}} - \text{MAR}}{\text{DD}}, \qquad (23.5)$$

where R_{HF} denotes the average percentage hedge fund return and *MAR* indicates the minimum acceptable return, respectively; and *DD* is the downside deviation of returns below *MAR*. The Sortino ratio can accommodate different degrees of target returns as well as different downside deviations for different minimum acceptable rates.

The Sterling Ratio

The Sterling ratio also compares historical reward and risk (Lhabitant 2006). As Equation 23.6 shows, the Sterling ratio is calculated by dividing the average annual rate of return for the past three calendar years to the average of the maximum annual drawdown in each of those three years plus 10 percent:

$$\text{Sterling ratio} = \frac{\text{Compound Annual ROR}}{\text{Max Draw D} + 10\%}. \tag{23.6}$$

The plus 10 percent definition is included (somewhat arbitrarily) to provide a similar value to the Calmar ratio.

NON-TRADITIONAL RISK MEASURES

Recent findings in the hedge fund literature emphasize the nonlinearity of hedge fund returns with respect to market returns and several risk factors (Fung and Hsieh 1997, 2001, 2004; Mitchell and Pulvino 2001; Agarwal and Naik 2004; Fung, Hsieh, Naik, and Ramadorai 2008). Fung and Hsieh (2001, 2004) emphasize option-like traits of hedge fund returns and recommend including lookback straddle returns as a systematic factor. A *lookback straddle option* is an exotic option where the holder can "look back" and set the strike price for the call at the lowest price during the option's life, whereas for the put the holder can set the strike at the highest price, respectively. Further, Mitchell and Pulvino (2001) show that returns from risk arbitrage resemble the payoff from selling uncovered index put options. Other risk factors identified in the literature include lookback straddles on interest rates and equity securities, out-of-the-money index put options, and liquidity.

The ability of fund managers to generate alpha rests with their ability to produce returns in addition of a passive strategy that simply follows the risk factors mentioned previously. For instance, Equation 23.7 outlines some popular risk factors:

$$r_{it} = \alpha + \beta_1 \text{PTFSBD} + \beta_2 \text{PTFSX} + \beta_3 \text{PTFSCOM} + \beta_4 \text{Bond Factor}$$
$$+ \beta_5 \text{Equity Factor} + \beta_6 \text{Credit Spread} + \beta_7 \text{Size Spread} \tag{23.7}$$
$$+ \beta_8 \text{US Dollar Index} + \varepsilon_t,$$

where $t = 1, \ldots T$ months is the length of the time series sample; α_{it} is the manager's contribution (Fung-Hsieh alpha) of fund i for month t; r_{it} is the fund return in excess of the risk-free rate (e.g., three-month Treasury bill rate); *PTFSBD* is the excess return of the PTFS bond lookback straddle; *PTFSFX* is the excess return of the PTFS currency lookback straddle; *PTFSCOM* is the excess return of the commodity lookback straddle; *Bond Factor* is the change in the monthly market yield of the 10-year Treasury constant maturity yield; *Equity Mkt Factor* is the S&P 500 index monthly total excess return; *Credit Spread* is the monthly change in the Moody's Baa yield minus 10-year Treasury constant maturity yield; and *Size Spread* is the Russell 2000 market index return less the S&P 500 index total return. In all cases, excess returns are computed by subtracting the three-month Treasury bill rate. The appraisal ratios are obtained by dividing the fund alphas over the residual standard deviation. Brown, Goetzman, Ibbotson, and Ross (1992) contend that the appraisal ratio provides a measure of performance reasonably robust to the lookback bias frequently encountered when ranking managers by performance. *Lookback bias* is a bias that occurs in hedge fund databases when a fund withholds data after observing poor performance (say before liquidation) or delays reporting returns when those are poor. Thus, because of lookback bias, the last few months of return data cannot be recovered in those cases where the fund liquidates because of poor performance. Agarwal and Naik (2000) contend that this measure is especially relevant for hedge funds because it accounts for differences in leverage.

Other nontraditional measures discussed in the literature include the approach of Gupta and Liang (2005) using the extreme value theory to estimate VaR and address capital adequacy and risk estimation issues in the hedge fund industry. In the context of hedge funds, VaR has also been estimated using a fat tailed generalized error distribution and the Cornish-Fisher expansion (Bali and Gokcan 2004).

However, the VaR measure cannot tell how big the eventual loss is going to be when the VaR level is breached. Therefore, Agarwal and Naik (2004) and Liang and Park (2007) among others propose two alternative measures. The first measure is the *expected shortfall*, which measures the potential loss once the VaR level is breached. This risk measure is also known as conditional VaR, tail conditional expectation, conditional loss, or loss. The second risk measure is *tail risk*, introduced by Bali, Demirtas, and Levy (2005). Tail risk measures the deviation from the mean only when the return is lower than VaR.

An Empirical Demonstration of Hedge Fund Risk Management

To demonstrate some risk management tools previously discussed, this section employs a data set from Barclay Hedge (2013) that spans January 2000 to August 2012. It contains monthly live and dead funds return data net of all fees reported to Barclay Hedge on a voluntary basis. The analysis is performed from the point of view of regular hedge fund investors using some standard tools. The analysis is based on the formation of several equally weighted portfolios where the common denominator is the strategy pursued. Tables 23.1 and 23.2 show the results, while Figures 23.1 through 23.6 contain graphs illustrating some more relevant risk measures.

For instance, the total risk of a portfolio as measured by the standard deviation of annual returns is highest for the Equity Short and Activist hedge funds, respectively. The Activist, Equity Short, and Emerging Markets focused hedge funds exhibit the highest average losing ROR. Furthermore, the drawdown measures provide useful information. Thus, the worst drawdown (see Figure 23.1 for details) ranks the Equity Short fund as the riskiest portfolio. For instance, for this hedge fund category, the drop from the highest NAV point is 44.44 percent. According to this measure, the Emerging Markets, Equity Long Only, and Activist groupings also register relatively high decreases in NAV at more than 30 percent. The average drawdown and current drawdown measures confirm the findings that classify the Equity Short, Activist, and Emerging Markets portfolios among the riskiest ones. The Sector Specific portfolios display a relatively high average drawdown risk.

Although the risk measures have primarily focused on the risk side of the risk-return trade-off, investigating whether the riskier funds provide adequate compensation for

Table 23.1 A Basic Risk Analysis of Equally Weighted Portfolios across Hedge Fund Classifications

Fund Category	N	Annual Return	Standard Deviation	Average Losing ROR	Average Winning ROR	Worst Draw-down	Average Draw-down	Current Draw-down	Average Recovery	Sharpe Ratio
Activist	13	3.322	20.810	-4.648	4.544	30.832	13.734	27.587	1.629	0.029
Arbitrage	80	6.269	8.706	-1.752	1.946	12.439	4.926	10.200	2.294	1.3116
Balanced	68	1.599	7.572	-1.777	1.679	16.299	6.087	14.317	2.819	0.031
Convertible arbitrage	224	7.151	7.454	-1.636	1.580	16.458	5.440	10.236	2.621	1.035
Distressed securities	201	9.089	11.840	-2.449	2.452	23.994	6.563	17.848	2.748	0.869
Emerging markets	1,249	5.680	18.706	-4.230	3.923	33.767	13.239	26.910	3.231	0.377
Equity long only	1,433	6.970	16.866	-3.686	3.700	31.291	10.923	23.739	3.381	0.380
Equity long/short	1,789	7.098	11.982	-2.496	2.670	20.123	7.419	15.890	2.969	0.454
Market neutral	387	3.536	7.8117	-1.760	1.763	13.032	5.119	10.475	2.773	0.282
Equity short	45	3.429	23.012	-4.615	5.318	44.444	18.964	39.722	4.604	0.019
Event driven	345	9.638	11.515	-2.382	2.549	21.180	6.401	12.338	3.013	0.733
Fixed income	1,140	9.704	8.197	-1.979	1.701	14.231	5.752	8.911	2.905	2.006
Macro	468	6.194	12.345	-2.626	2.806	18.101	7.157	13.837	2.717	0.427
Arbitrage	130	6.968	5.262	-1.174	1.214	7.955	2.285	4.347	2.491	0.981
Multi-strategy	357	8.014	8.618	-1.896	1.855	15.434	5.1797	10.550	2.847	1.051
Options	130	10.562	17.168	-4.212	3.554	20.520	8.7850	8.785	3.564	0.807
Sector	965	7.748	17.887	-3.814	3.963	28.780	11.2530	22.448	3.043	0.470
Volatility trading	31	28.484	13.301	-2.628	3.697	11.076	5.7948	8.701	2.073	1.181

Table 23.2 Additional Risk Measures of Equally Weighted Portfolios across Hedge Fund Classifications

Fund Category	N	Efficiency Ratio	Sortino Ratio	Sterling Ratio	% Losing Months	% Winning Months	Correlation S&P 500	Alpha S&P 500	Beta S&P 500
Activist	13	0.243	0.333	1.153	42.107	57.892	0.368	−0.272	1.064
Arbitrage	80	1.732	2.575	0.300	36.932	63.069	0.126	0.470	0.124
Balanced	68	0.220	0.240	0.322	44.266	55.733	0.537	−0.040	0.664
Convertible arbitrage	224	1.673	2.427	0.690	29.343	70.657	0.244	0.505	0.151
Distressed securities	201	1.141	2.743	0.758	29.832	70.168	0.397	0.646	0.334
Emerging markets	1,249	0.532	1.213	0.752	39.367	60.632	0.468	0.268	0.605
Equity long	1,433	0.538	1.066	0.561	39.946	60.0536	0.624	0.296	0.658
Equity long/short	1,789	0.701	1.127	0.440	39.875	60.125	0.295	0.405	0.271
Market neutral	387	0.610	0.878	0.297	40.596	59.403	0.053	0.247	0.033
Equity short	45	0.191	0.111	0.1679	47.777	52.223	−0.564	0.987	−0.869
Event driven	345	1.057	2.878	0.904	32.295	67.705	0.384	0.643	0.316
Fixed income	1,140	2.562	5.070	0.794	25.826	74.174	0.242	0.587	0.148
Macro	468	0.626	0.834	0.443	40.930	59.069	0.200	0.381	0.190
Arbitrage	130	1.520	3.642	0.602	26.492	73.507	0.3134	0.533	0.116
Multi-strategy	357	1.518	2.503	0.703	30.030	69.970	0.246	0.606	0.160
Options	130	1.036	3.053	0.628	31.413	68.586	0.092	0.894	0.173
Sector	965	0.650	1.364	0.610	40.164	59.836	0.398	0.505	0.519
Volatility trading	31	1.347	6.399	0.546	34.013	65.986	0.084	2.210	0.157

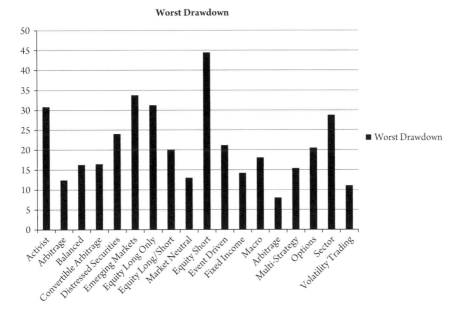

Figure 23.1 THE WORST DRAWDOWN ACROSS HEDGE FUND STYLES. This figure shows the average worst drawdown across the hedge fund portfolios.

the additional risk is the next step of the analysis. The evidence is mixed. As Figure 23.2 shows, the Sharpe ratio finds that the risk-adjusted return is lowest for the Equity Short and Activist portfolios. Therefore, while these two portfolios are among the riskiest ones, they do not appear to adequately compensate investors for the additional risks. The Fixed Income, Arbitrage, and Volatility Trading portfolios provide the highest risk-adjusted returns, respectively. However, one deficiency of the Sharpe ratio is that it treats the upside volatility and downside volatility the same, whereas the investors worry more about the downside risks. Hence, the Sterling (see Figure 23.3 for details) and Sortino (see Figure 23.4 for details) ratios should provide a better picture of the more relevant risk-return trade-offs.

According to the Sterling ratio, the Activist portfolio displays the highest maximum drawdown risk-adjusted return. Yet, the Equity Short portfolio has the lowest Sterling ratio among all portfolio classifications. In contrast, the Event Driven and Fixed Income classifications provide the second and third highest drawdown risk-adjusted returns. However, the Sortino ratio, which adjusts the return for the downside deviation below the minimum acceptable return, ranks the Activist and Equity Short portfolios as the lowest performing funds. At the opposite end, the Sortino ratio confirms the Volatility Trading and Fixed Income portfolios as the highest performing ones, adjusting for downside risk. Further, according to the efficiency ratio (see Figure 23.5 for details) the Fixed Income portfolio ranks best, followed by the Arbitrage and Statistical Arbitrage portfolios, respectively.

Table 23.1 and 23.2 present additional useful risk measures. For example, risk-averse investors also worry about the percentage losing months, correlation with the market, as

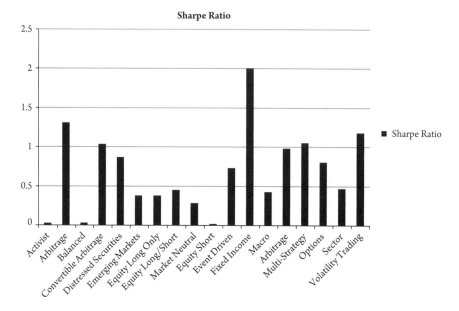

Figure 23.2 THE SHARPE RATIO ACROSS HEDGE FUND STYLES. This figure shows the average Sharpe ratio across the hedge fund portfolios.

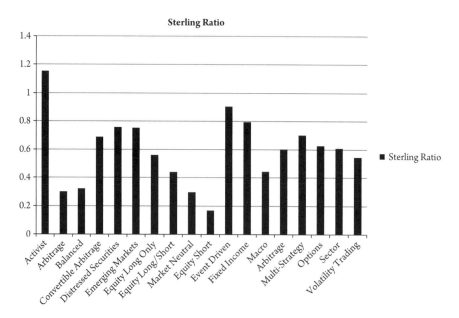

Figure 23.3 THE STERLING RATIO ACROSS HEDGE FUND STYLES. This figure shows the average Sterling ratio across the hedge fund portfolios.

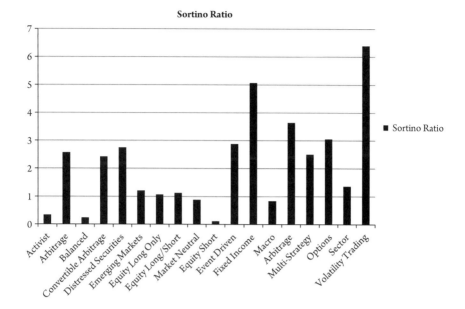

Figure 23.4 THE SORTINO RATIO ACROSS HEDGE FUND STYLES. This figure shows the average Sortino ratio across the hedge fund portfolios.

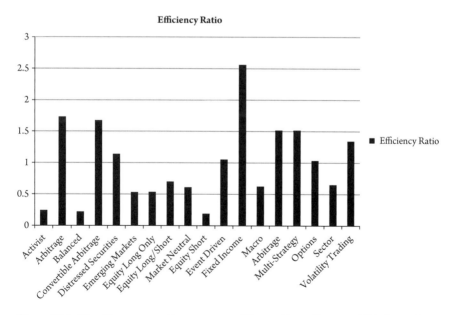

Figure 23.5 THE EFFICIENCY RATIO ACROSS HEDGE FUND STYLES. This figure shows the average efficiency ratio across the hedge fund portfolios.

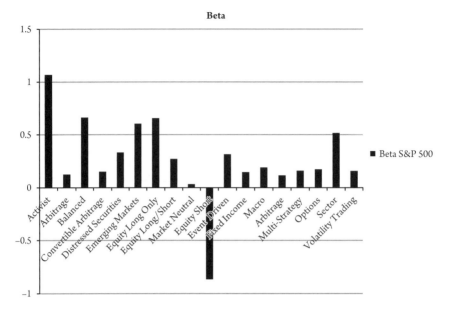

Figure 23.6 THE AVERAGE BETA ACROSS HEDGE FUND STYLES. This figure shows the average beta measured against the S&P 500 index across the hedge fund portfolios.

well as the degree of systematic risk each classification brings in the portfolio. An inspection of the percentage losing months measure confirms that the Activist and Equity Short portfolios rank as the riskiest ones at 42.11 percent and 47.78 percent of the time, respectively. However, the correlation coefficient and beta measures (see Figure 23.6 for details) relative to the S&P 500 index show that the Equity Short hedge funds provide negative co-movement with the market and act as an appropriate hedge. The alpha of the Equity Short portfolio is second highest below that of the Volatility Trading.

As expected, the Equity Long Only, Balanced, Emerging Markets, and Distressed Securities portfolios display relatively high degrees of correlation with the market, whereas the Market Neutral, Options, and Volatility Trading portfolios have little co-movement with the overall stock market. The beta measure generally confirms this finding and also finds that the Activist portfolio displays the highest exposure to market risk.

To summarize, the risk measures discussed in the previous section and demonstrated empirically in the current section show several ways in which average investors can compare and contrast the relative performance of various hedge fund portfolios and potentially use a combination of those tools to select those funds according to their risk appetite. The next section contends, however, that an even more important metric investors need to consider involves a hedge fund's operational risks.

Operational Risk Measures

In a series of papers, Brown, Goetzmann, Liang, and Schwartz (2008, 2009, 2012) propose that an important component of hedge fund risk management is managing operational risk. In a series of publications, the Basel committee identifies that most types of operational risks involve breakdowns in internal controls and corporate governance that relate to such areas as unethical behavior or outright fraud and major failure of information of information technology systems. Several spectacular hedge fund collapses have occurred that were in major part due to unsuspected operational risks.

For instance, Amaranth Advisors whose loss of $6 billion is the highest for a hedge fund, collapsed in 2006 over natural gas futures bets in part due to faulty risk models. After an intensive investigation, the Commodity Futures Trading Commission (CFTC) charged Amaranth with attempting to manipulate natural gas futures prices. Long-Term Capital Management (LTCM) was another famous hedge fund collapse triggered in part by the failure of its computer models to recommend switching positions in the presence of losses of hundreds of millions of dollars per day. The Bayou Hedge Fund group was notorious for defrauding its clients. Managers of this hedge fund misappropriated funds for personal use, lied to investors, and even set up a fake accounting firm to provide false and misleading audited financial results. The fund filed for bankruptcy in 2006 and its owners eventually received long prison sentences. In 2012, the High Court of the United Kingdom charged the founding director of the $600 million hedge fund Weavering Capital with offenses that included false accounting, fraudulent trading, fraud by abuse of position, and forgery. Finally, the manager of the Asenqua Beta Fund and Fireside LS Fund was found guilty in June 2013 of fraud and making false statements to investors that the funds were affiliated with well-known lawyers and auditors. The list of collapsed hedge funds could continue.

What the description of hedge fund failures shows is that hedge fund operational risks are real and have not decreased over time. This finding calls for potential metrics that can identify and predict operational risks accurately. However, while developing operational risk measures is difficult even in the more established field of banking, the lack of data and suitable metrics amplify the estimation problem in the case of hedge funds.

As Brown (2012) contends, the challenges to developing quantitative metrics of operational risk are threefold. First, operational issues are diverse in nature as they involve processes, people, and systems and one or more of these can fail in various ways often simultaneously. Second, due to the secretive nature of hedge funds, a lack of proper information and adequate data to measure such risks exists. Third, operational risks may overlap or be masked by market and credit risks as in the Bernie Madoff affair in 2008 in which the extensive fraud surfaced only in the aftermath of the liquidity and financial crisis of that year.

Besides all of these issues, no regulatory framework or agency requires hedge funds to report risks along the seven operational risk classifications as in the Basel II Accord (Basel Committee on Banking Supervision 2002, 2009). In fact, the Investment Company Act of 1940 guarantees the secretive nature of hedge funds. However, a recent set of papers by Brown et al. (2008, 2009, 2012) contributes to this area and provides a promising research agenda. These papers build on a short-lived yet valuable mandatory disclosure requirement by the SEC to reveal several pieces of information including fund characteristics such as potential conflicts of interest and past and legal and regulatory problems.

In particular, in December 2004 the SEC adopted a new rule and amendments to the Investment Advisers Act of 1940 that required hedge fund managers to register as investment advisers by February 1, 2006. This Act concerned hedge funds with at least 14 clients, AUM of more than $25 million, and lock-up periods of less than two years. In order to comply with this requirement, the SEC required managers to file Form ADV. Although the U.S. Court of Appeals for the District of Columbia Circuit later abrogated this new legal requirement in June 2006, it provided a rare opportunity to investigate a large and less biased sample of hedge fund disclosures. Among others, these disclosures required information that could potentially indicate fraud, degree of compliance with the laws and existing regulations, ownership data, and so forth. Brown et al. (2008) then link the Form ADV disclosures to fund characteristics to obtain a quantifiable measure of operational risk which they claim is different from market risk.

Brown et al. (2008) link the ADV forms to the TASS hedge fund database in order to establish the connection between hedge fund disclosures and fund characteristics. Among the main findings, they show that legal and regulatory problems are associated with conflicts of interest that are both external and internal to the firm, concentration of ownership, and reduced leverage. For the latter, prime brokers and other providers of liquidity and leverage would be expected to do their own due diligence before lending. But with those funds that display reduced leverage, such due diligence is less likely. The authors confirm that external conflicts of interest and concentration of ownership negatively influence the returns of those funds that report legal and regulatory problems.

To clearly identify and measure the impact of operational risks, Brown et al. (2009) use canonical correlation analysis to construct a univariate measure of operational risk. To be more precise, this measure relies on hedge fund variables that prior research associates with the probability of fund failure. The canonical correlation approach requires a linear combination of those variables that maximally correlate with the cross-section of operational risk variables identified in the ADV disclosures. The new risk tool is called the ω-score and it correlates positively with all of the Form ADV variables related to operational risk exposure. Further, Brown et al. (2008) show that funds displaying a higher ω-score experience poor returns in the future. This finding is strengthened in Brown et al. (2009), who find that operational risks as measured by the ω-score are more indicative of fund failure than financial risks.

The insight from this research is that savvy investors need to do their due diligence before committing to a certain hedge fund. Indeed, Brown, Fraser, and Liang (2008) maintain that due diligence is an important source of alpha and effective operational due diligence can eliminate or reduce problematic funds and avoid future losses resulting from operational risks. However, due diligence is generally an expensive process and many investors or hedge fund portfolio managers may not have enough cash to pay for it. Brown, Gregoriou, and Pascalau (2012) show that the ability to afford this operational due diligence is a major factor in explaining the survival of funds of hedge funds since 2000.

However, the ADV form does not reveal much information on the other important operational risk component that has to do with internal people processes or systems. One solution to this problem is to hire private consultants who can then perform the operational due diligence on behalf of investors.

In a subsequent paper, Brown et al. (2012) investigate a database of 444 proprietary due diligence reports performed on behalf on fund investors that provide a host of information on failures of processes, people, and systems. Serious operational issues involved misrepresentations of past returns, AUM, and other legal and regulatory problems affecting the fund. A striking finding is that 90 percent of the hedge funds analyzed inaccurately reported no past or present legal or regulatory issues facing that respective fund. Even more, in one case a fund was facing 22 lawsuits that the investors would have had no idea existed in the absence of the due diligence (DD) report.

A main contribution of Brown et al. (2012) is to propose a more direct canonical-based measure of operational risk, which unlike the indirect one of Brown et al. (2008, p. 1) is "based on evidence of imperfect or failed internal processes taken directly from the DD reports themselves, including data on informational contradictions and variables related to honesty." The study shows that this new operational risk measure can be successfully used out-of-sample to predict that exposure to operational risk increases the chance of poor subsequent performance and fund failure.

To be more specific, some variables used in constructing this measure include whether:

- the securities in the fund are priced entirely or partially by the manager or are priced completely externally;
- the fund's NAV has been previously restated, the number of signatures required to move money from a bank or the prime broker;
- money movements are restricted to certain locations;
- signature controls on all money movements require an internal or independent third party, personnel turnover, the percent of independent board members; and
- the fund is audited by a "big four" accounting firm; and whether the fund has had previously regulatory issues or lawsuits.

The results are surprising. Brown et al. (2012) find that in 16 percent of the cases the fund's and administrator's versions of the signatures did not match and in 3.6 percent of the cases funds disagreed with the administrator on the portfolio pricing process. Further, in 18 percent of the cases the fund's NAV could not be verified independently and 14 percent of the due diligence reports reflected performance discrepancies or verification problems. Finally, a manager verbally overestimated, on average, his fund's NAV by $300 million, and in 6 percent of the cases Brown et al. found strategic misstatements about past problems the fund had faced.

The operational risk measure that Brown et al. (2012) propose employs all the variables listed above and uses a linear combination of them that maximally correlates with factors shown to contribute to fund failure. The latter variables related to a fund's death include average monthly returns from previous year, the monthly standard deviation and first-order autocorrelation from the previous year, the size at the beginning of the period, fund age, fees, leverage, lockup provision, and the advance notice period. The ω-score is the linear correlation of the due diligence variables and the TASS variables. Finally, the study validates the ω-score as a measure of Basel-defined operational risk by performing an out-of-sample test, which reveals that exposure to this risk measure leads to an increased likelihood of subsequent poor performance.

Summary and Conclusions

This chapter summarizes the state-of-the-art practices in the risk management of hedge funds and also assesses the latest contributions in the area involving measures of operational risk. Thus, besides traditional measures such as the standard deviation of annual returns, Sharpe ratio, and simple correlation with various market indexes, the chapter considers both theoretically and empirically drawdown and downside deviation risk measures, the Sortino, Sterling, and efficiency ratios among others. The chapter also discusses the appraisal ratio, which is a newer risk-adjusted performance measure.

Finally, drawing upon the recent work of Brown et al. (2008, 2009, 2012), the chapter finds that researchers have made substantial progress quantifying the operational risks of hedge funds. The studies by Brown et al. propose a quantitative measure of operational risk called the ω-score, which is a linear combination of fund variables indicative of operational risk and fund characteristics that past literature has associated with fund failure. A higher ω-score is associated with poor subsequent fund performance. Therefore, the ω-score promises to serve as yet another tool in the arsenal of the typical hedge fund investor for fund selection purposes.

Discussion Questions

1. List and explain several examples of hedge fund downside and drawdown risk measures.
2. Discuss the advantages of risk-adjusted returns relative to absolute return measures. In particular, compare and contrast the Sharpe ratio with the Sortino, Sterling, and Calmar ratios.
3. Discuss the nonlinear payoff structure of hedge fund returns and provide an example of how hedge fund returns need to be adjusted for risk in this case.
4. Discuss the possible types and the importance of operational risks for managing hedge fund risks. Provide an example of how to quantify operational risks in the hedge fund context.

References

Agarwal, Vikas, and Narayan Y. Naik. 2000. "Multi-Period Performance Persistence Analysis of Hedge Funds." *Journal of Financial and Quantitative Analysis* 35:3, 327–342.

Agarwal, Vikas, and Narayan Y. Naik. 2004. "Risks and Portfolio Decisions Involving Hedge Funds." *Review of Financial Studies* 17:1, 63–98.

Bali, Turan G., K. Ozgur Demirtas, and Haim Levy. 2005. "Is There a Relation between Downside Risk and Expected Returns?" Working Paper, Baruch College.

Bali, Turan G., and Suleyman Gokcan. 2004. "Alternative Approaches to Estimating VAR for Hedge Fund Portfolios." In Barry Schachter, ed., *Intelligent Hedge Fund Investing*, 253–277. London: Risk Books.

Barclay Hedge. 2013. Available at http://www.barclayhedge.com/research/indices/ghs/mum/HF_Money_Under_Management.html.

Basel Committee on Banking Supervision. 2002. "Operational Risk Data Collection Exercise—2002." Basel, Switzerland: Bank for International Settlements.

Basel Committee on Banking Supervision. 2009. "Observed Range of Practice in Key Elements of Advanced Measurement Approaches (AMA)." Basel, Switzerland: Bank for International Settlements.

Brown, Stephen J. 2012. "Quantitative Measures of Operational Risk: An Application to Funds Management," Working Paper, Stern School of Business, New York University.

Brown, Stephen, Thomas Fraser, and Bing Liang. 2008. "Hedge Fund Due Diligence: A Source of Alpha in a Hedge Fund Portfolio Strategy." *Journal of Investment Management* 6:4, 23–33.

Brown, Stephen, Greg N. Gregoriou, and Razvan Pascalau. 2012. "Is It Possible to Overdiversify? The Case of Funds of Hedge Funds." *Review of Asset Pricing Studies* 2:1, 89–110.

Brown, Stephen J., William N. Goetzmann, Roger G. Ibbotson, and Stephen A. Ross. 1992. "Survivorship Bias in Performance Studies." *Review of Financial Studies* 5:4, 553–580.

Brown, Stephen, William Goetzmann, Bing Liang, and Christopher Schwarz. 2008. "Mandatory Disclosure and Operational Risk: Evidence from Hedge Fund Registration." *Journal of Finance* 63:6, 2785–2815.

Brown, Stephen, William N. Goetzmann, Bing Liang, and Christopher Schwarz. 2009. "Estimating Operational Risk for Hedge Funds: The ω-Score." *Financial Analysts Journal* 65:1, 43–53.

Brown, Stephen, William N. Goetzmann, Bing Liang, and Christopher Schwarz. 2012. "Trust and Delegation." *Journal of Financial Economics* 103:2, 221–234.

Brunnermeier, Markus K., and Lasse Heje Pedersen. 2009. "Market Liquidity and Funding Liquidity." *Review of Financial Studies* 22:6, 2201–2238.

Fung, William, and David A. Hsieh. 1997. "Empirical Characteristics of Dynamic Trading Strategies: The Case of Hedge Funds." *Review of Financial Studies* 10:2, 275–302.

Fung, William, and David A. Hsieh. 2001. "The Risk in Hedge Fund Strategies: Theory and Evidence from Trend Followers." *Review of Financial Studies* 14:2, 313–341.

Fung, William, and David A. Hsieh. 2002. "Benchmarks of Hedge Fund Performance: Information Content and Measurement Biases." *Financial Analysts Journal* 58:1, 22–34.

Fung, William, and David A. Hsieh. 2004. "Hedge Fund Benchmarks: A Risk Based Approach." *Financial Analyst Journal* 60:5, 65–80.

Fung, William, David A. Hsieh, Narayan Y. Naik, and Tarun Ramadorai, 2008. "Hedge Funds: Performance, Risk, and Capital Formation." *Journal of Finance* 63:4, 1777–1803.

Gupta, Anurag, and Bing Liang. 2005. "Do Hedge Funds Have Enough Capital? A Value-at-Risk Approach." *Journal of Financial Economics* 77:1, 219–253.

Kang, Byoung Uk, Francis In, Gunky Kim, and Tong Suk Kim. 2010. "A Longer Look at the Asymmetric Dependence between Hedge Funds and the Equity Market." *Journal of Financial and Quantitative Analysis* 45:3, 763–789.

Lhabitant, Francois-Serge. 2006. *Handbook of Hedge Funds.* Hoboken, NJ: John Wiley & Sons.

Liang, Bing, and Hyuna Park. 2007. "Risk Measures for Hedge Funds: A Cross-Sectional Approach." *European Financial Management* 13:2, 333–370.

Lo, Andrew W. 2001. "Risk Management for Hedge Funds: Introduction and Overview." *Financial Analysts Journal* 57:6, 16–33.

Mitchell, Mark, and Todd Pulvino. 2001. "Characteristics of Risk and Return in Risk Arbitrage." *Journal of Finance* 56:6, 2135–2175.

Teo, Melvin. 2011. "The Liquidity Risk of Liquid Hedge Funds." *Journal of Financial Economics* 100:1, 24–44.

Part Five

HEDGING RISK

24

Options

KIT PONG WONG

Professor and Director, School of Economics and Finance, University of Hong Kong

GREG FILBECK

Samuel P. Black III Professor of Finance and Risk Management, Black School of Business, Penn State Erie, the Behrend College

H. KENT BAKER

University Professor of Finance, Kogod School of Business, American University

Introduction

Options are part of a larger class of financial instruments known as derivatives. A *derivative* is a security that derives its value from the value or return of another asset or security. Derivative securities play an important role in promoting efficient prices and reducing transaction costs. Although some criticize derivatives for their risky nature, many market participants use them to manage and reduce existing risk exposure.

In finance, an *option* refers to a contract giving the buyer (the owner) the right, but not the legal obligation, to buy or sell an underlying asset or instrument at a predetermined price called the *exercise* or *strike price* on or before a predetermined future date called the *exercise date*. Thus, the option buyer only acts if doing so is profitable. Each option contract is between two counterparties (a buyer and a seller) with specified terms including the quantity and class of the underlying assets, strike or exercise price, expiration date, and settlement terms.

The option buyer has the right to decide whether the trade will eventually occur while the seller of the option has the obligation to perform if the buyer exercises the option. The option buyer pays the seller an option premium to obtain this right. The *option premium* is the price of the option. A *call option* is an option to buy an asset at a predetermined price at some time in the future; a *put option* is an option to sell an asset at a predetermined price at some time in the future.

For example, assume the buyer pays $4 (the option premium) to purchase a call option from the seller over the next three months for $40 (the exercise price). Note that the option premium is on a per share basis. The seller keeps the $4 premium regardless of what happens to the stock's price over the period. If the buyer exercises the option, the seller receives the $40 exercise price and must deliver to the buyer a share of the specified stock. If the price of the stock falls to $40 or below, the buyer has no obligation to exercise the option.

Two common forms of options are American and European options. With an *American option*, the owner can exercise the option on any trading day until the option's expiration date also called *expiry*. By contrast, the owner of a *European option* can exercise the option only on the option's expiration date. If two options are identical in every way, except one is an American option and the other is a European option, the value of the American option should be equal to or greater than that of the European option. The reason is that an American option provides more flexibility due to its exercise feature than a European option.

OPTION MARKETS AND TYPES

Contracts similar to options have been used since ancient Greek times. Today, options are traded either on an exchange or over the counter (OTC). *Exchange-traded options* or *listed options* are regulated, standardized, and liquid. In the United Stated, the Options Clearing Corporation (OCC) for Chicago Board Options Exchange (CBOE) backs transactions. Standardization helps to ensure accurate pricing. Expiration on most exchange-listed options is within two to four months but exchanges also list equity options called *long-term equity anticipatory security* (LEAPs) with expiration dates longer than a year. Examples of exchange-traded options include stock options, bond options and other interest rate options, index options, and options on futures. Listed stock options are normally for 100 shares, which are adjusted for stock splits after issuance of the contracts.

In contrast, the OTC market is largely unregulated and has bilateral, customized contracts between a single buyer and seller, which are facilitated by dealers or market-makers. Market participants face *counterparty risk*, which is the probability that the other party will not perform as promised. Trading occurs through two private parties who individually tailor the options to meet specific business need. Institutions are the primary buyers in the OTC options market. Commonly traded OTC options include options on bonds, currencies, swaps (swaptions), and interest rate options.

Several major types of options are available based on the underlying instruments: (1) financial options, (2) options on futures, and (3) commodity options. Financial options include a broad array of equity options as well as options based on Treasury bonds, interest rates, currencies, and stock indices. Options on futures give the holder the right to buy or sell a specified futures contract by a given date at a specified futures price (i.e., the strike price). Commodity options give the holder the right to buy or sell a fixed quantity of some physical asset at a fixed price (i.e., the strike price). Most of this chapter focuses on commodity options.

OPTION POSITIONS AND BASIC STRATEGIES

The buyer of an option is said to be *long* the option, and the seller (writer) of an option is said to be *short* the option. Because each option has a buyer and seller, four possible options positions are available. A *long call* is when the buyer of a call option has the right to buy an underlying asset. A *short call* is when the seller (writer) of a call option has the obligation to sell the underlying asset. With a *long put*, the buyer of a put option has the right to sell the underlying asset. With a *short put*, the seller (writer) of a put option has the obligation to buy the underlying asset.

To illustrate, consider the potential payoff from buying a call on a specific stock. Although the following example is from a speculator's perspective, options can also be used as hedges by combining several positions. A trader who expects a stock's price will increase might buy a call option at a fixed price instead of buying the stock itself. Why do this? For the same initial investment, the buyer can control a much larger number of shares through the option contract instead of buying the shares because of greater leverage. This is because the right to buy 100 shares of the stock (the call option), whose cost is the option premium, is much less than the cost of initially buying the 100 shares of stock at the current market price. If the stock price at expiration exceeds the exercise price, the call option is *in the money*. However, the deal is not profitable until the stock price exceeds the exercise price by more than the option premium. If the option has value, the buyer can either exercise the option or sell it in the secondary options market. If the stock price at expiration is lower than the exercise price (i.e., the call option is *out of the money*), the call buyer will let the call contract expire worthless and only lose the amount paid for the option premium. If the stock price equals the exercise price, a call option is said to be *at the money*.

To illustrate how options can be used for hedging purposes, let's examine two simple strategies: a protective put and a covered call. A *protective put strategy* involves owning the underlying asset (e.g., taking a long position in a stock) and buying a put option on that same asset. This strategy is designed to protect a stock from a decline in value. A long position gives the holder the right to sell the asset at a fixed price for a given time period. Thus, as the underlying asset value decreases, the option becomes more valuable and may be constructed to offset the corresponding unrealized losses in the underlying asset. This relationship provides the downside protection to insulate against net losses in the hedged position. If the value of the underlying asset increases, the put option loses value (options cannot take on negative values), but the underlying asset would experience unrealized gains and retain upside potential. Because options represent an opportunity, but not an obligation, the buyer would not exercise the put option, which would essentially expire worthless.

Another well-known options strategy is *writing covered calls*, which involve buying a stock or holding a previously purchased long stock position and selling a call. The term *covered* means that the stock covers the obligation to deliver the stock assumed by writing the call. Basically, the call writer is trading the stock's upside potential for the call premium. If the stock price increases above the exercise price, the buyer will exercise the call and the writer of the call option will receive a specified amount (i.e., the exercise or strike price). If the stock price decreases, the buyer will not exercise the call and any loss incurred by the call writer will be partially offset by the premium received from selling the call.

OPTIONS AND HEDGING

Options, futures, and swaps all offer risk management opportunities for underlying exposures. Options differ from futures and swaps in fundamental ways. Options offer an asymmetrical payoff profile, while futures and swaps have payoff profiles that are symmetrical in nature. In other words, options strategies can be constructed to allow for the retention of upside potential while providing downside protection.

In contrast, hedging using futures or swaps is a zero sum game. A short position in a futures contract represents an obligation to sell or settle at a fixed price over a stated time frame. For example, while decreases in the value in the long position of the underlying asset can be offset by increases in a short position in a futures contract, any gains occurring with an increase in the value of the long position in the underlying asset would be offset by corresponding losses in the decreased value of the short position. Thus, losses can accrue with positions in futures or swaps, whereas long option values cannot be negative.

The desirable asymmetric payoff profile of an option comes with a cost. The cost, known as a *premium*, reflects the market's assessment of worth of the opportunity presented. In contrast, futures or swaps contracts are typically established without an associated cost at initiation.

This chapter focuses on commodities as one application of option hedging. Camerer (1982) points out that commodities options offer three benefits unavailable with futures contracts. First, the option contract requires initially establishing a premium with no other requirement for the long position, whereas futures contracts, while initially costless, require additional deposits (margin) if equity positions do not meet minimum requirements. Second, option prices adjust instantly to new market information, whereas futures contracts have daily price movement limits that may result in new information taking several trading days to be fully reflects. Third, option contracts allow producers to hedge price and quantity risk, whereas futures contracts only allow for the hedging of price risk.

This chapter explores competitive firm behavior facing both price uncertainty and a revenue shock. Two common theories are introduced to describe the hedging process: the separation theorem or full-hedging theorem. Neither of these theories holds when the revenue shock prevails resulting in a need to consider the correlation between the random output price and the revenue shock.

The rest of this chapter is organized as follows. The next section provides a brief overview on the valuation of options. The following section reviews the literature and delineates the model of the competitive firm under joint revenue and output price risk. The firm can trade unbiased commodity futures contracts for hedging purposes. The following section examines a benchmark wherein the revenue shock is absent. The subsequent section derives the firm's optimal production and hedging decisions. The final section concludes.

Valuation of Options

Commodity option valuation models originated from the early work of Black and Scholes (1973). The basis of the Black-Scholes model is an arbitrage relationship between the risk-free rate of return and the return on a portfolio containing the option and the asset underlying the option. This differential-equation-based model assumes equilibrium of a risk-free rate return based on the arbitrage relationship assumption. The model also concludes that a Gaussian distribution is applicable. The option model involves solving the differential equation, which results in an option price that is a function of the strike price, underlying asset's current price, standard deviation of the asset, risk-free rate, and time until maturity. Black's (1976) commodity option pricing formula varies the inputs in the model determining value based on a futures contract on the same commodity that has the same expiration date without a requirement for an expected spot price for commodities in the future. Black's model assumes that underlying futures prices are proportional to commodity options prices and futures prices are independent and identically distributed based on assumptions of normality.

Myers and Hanson (1993) develop an alternative framework based on empirical evidence suggesting that these assumptions are violated, and models commodity option prices based on time-varying volatility and positive excess kurtosis through the use of a generalized autoregressive conditional heteroskedastic (GARCH) model. They contend that their model improves Black's model when using historical volatility estimates. Luft and Fielitz (1986) expresses similar concerns for implications associated with an assumption of normality but argues that the Black model works reasonably well with shorter time lags between the option's variance estimate and subsequent trading (i.e., if not applied to a thinly traded market). Subsequent research has tackled a variety of complex deviations of the original models including stochastic term structures of convenience yields and interest rates (Miltersen and Schwartz 1998; Nakajima and Maeda 2007), jump pricing in option pricing (Hilliard and Reis 1999), commodity volatility modeling (Anderluh and Borovkova 2008), and commodity storage costs (Hinz and Fehr 2010).

Commodity Options

Commodity options are the right to buy or sell a specified quantity of a commodity, or commodity futures contract, at a specified price. Camerer (1982) argues that commodity options offer price efficiency allowing both producers and investors to hedge quantity as well as price risk for crops. Factors such as demand and supply, weather conditions, and seasonality affect price risk. Through commodity options, only the premium is lost regardless of how much underlying commodity prices change, offering a desirable asymmetric payout profile for market participants who need to hedge their assets against price volatility.

Since the seminal work of Sandmo (1971), the theory of the competitive firm has been the subject of considerable research in decision-making under uncertainty (Batra and Ullah 1974; Chavas 1985; Wong 1996, 2014; Viaene and Zilcha 1998; Broll and Wong 2013). One important strand of this literature concerns the behavior of the competitive firm when a commodity futures market exists for hedging purposes (Danthine 1978; Holthausen 1979; Feder, Just, and Schmitz 1980; Broll and Zilcha 1992; and Broll, Wong, and Zilcha 1999). Danthine finds that optimal production depends only on the futures prices and is independent of hedging decisions. Holthausen, who also develops a model of the competitive firm under price uncertainty, finds that the firm will select an output level depending exclusively on the forward price. This decision is found to be independent of the firm's risk aversion and the probability distribution of the uncertain price.

From these early studies, two theories emerge regarding production decisions and price uncertainty. First, the separation theorem states that the firm's production decision depends neither on the risk attitude of the firm nor on the incidence of the output price uncertainty. Second, the full-hedging theorem states that the firm should completely eliminate its output price risk exposure by adopting a full-hedge should the commodity futures market be unbiased. The full-hedging theorem is analogous to a well-known result in the insurance literature that a risk-averse individual fully insures at an actuarially fair price (Mossin 1968). A corollary of the full-hedging theorem is that no other hedging instruments, options in particular, would have a hedging role that is over and above that of futures, thereby rendering futures to be the most preferred hedging instrument (Battermann, Braulke, Broll, and Schimmelpfenning 2000). Indeed, Lapan, Moschini, and Hanson (1991) analyze the production and hedging decisions and show that the competitive firm uses options only when it perceives the futures price and/or option premiums as biased. In this regard, options appear more like a speculative device than a hedging instrument. They also show that Danthine's (1978) separation result continues to hold when using options if no basis risk exists or if risk aversion can be described by a constant absolute risk aversion (CARA) utility function. Under CARA and a fixed output, increases in futures prices will result in increases in the supply of futures and options. Aradhyula and Choi (1993) extend Lapan et al.'s work by showing that unbiased pricing is not a necessary condition for the separation theorem to hold.

The following discussion examines the robustness of the separation and full-hedging theorems when the competitive firm is confronted with not only the output price uncertainty but also a multiplicative shock to its revenue as in Adam-Müller (1997). Such a revenue shock may come from various sources including uncertain exchange rates, production uncertainty, credit risk, and many others. Unlike Adam-Müller, this shock is allowed to be correlated with the output price uncertainty. For example, the prevalence of incomplete exchange rate pass-through gives rise to a negative correlation between the random spot exchange rate and the prevailing output price (Wong 2003b). As Goldberg and Knetter (1997) document, a 10 percent depreciation of the U.S. dollar would be associated with an increase in U.S. import prices of approximately 5 percent at the aggregate level. Gust, Leduc, and Vigfusson (2010) and Marazzi and Sheets (2007) find that the sensitivity of U.S. import prices to the exchange rate has gradually declined from 0.5 in the 1980s to 0.2 in the past decade. Using annual political and exchange rate risk ratings from the International Country Risk Guide of the Political Risk Services, Kim and Song (2010) document a positive correlation between these two measures. While the output price risk is hedgeable by trading commodity futures and option contracts, the revenue shock is neither hedgeable nor insurable.

When the revenue shock prevails, both the separation and full-hedging theorems fail to hold. The correlation between the revenue shock and the random output price is shown to play a pivotal role in determining the firm's optimal production and hedging decisions. Specifically, if this correlation is non-positive, the firm optimally produces less as compared to the benchmark output level when the revenue shock is absent. Doing so allows the firm to limit its risk exposure to the unhedgeable revenue shock. If, in addition, the firm's preferences satisfy the reasonable property of prudence (Kimball

1990, 1993), the prudent firm's optimal hedge position consists of an under-hedge in the futures position and a long put option position. However, if the correlation is sufficiently positive, a canonical example is constructed under which the firm optimally produces more, not less, than the benchmark level, and opts for an over-hedge in the futures position and a short put option position. The firm's optimal production and hedging decisions as such depend not only on the risk attitude of the firm, but also on the joint distribution of the random output price and the revenue shock. Operational hedging and financial hedging are used as complements to better cope with the multiple sources of uncertainty.

This chapter contributes to the burgeoning literature on the hedging role of options. Moshini and Lapan (1992) indicate that separation between production and hedging decisions can still hold after prices are known allowing for some input decisions. When the profit function is quadratic (convex) in price, and assuming unbiased futures and options pricing, the optimal futures hedge for a risk averse firm equals expected output is a short straddle option position. A short straddle involves a short position in both a call and put option. They further argue that the use of options for hedging purposes raises expected utility through income risk reduction. This induced convexity makes options a useful hedging instrument. Moschini and Lapan (1995), Brown and Toft (2002), Wong (2003b), Lien and Wong (2004), and Korn (2009) show that firms facing both hedgeable and nonhedgeable risks would optimally use options for hedging purposes. Even with price and production uncertainty, Sakong, Hayes, and Hallam (1993) show that maximization expected utility can be achieved for producers who can use futures and options markets. With production uncertainty, they contend that optimality is achieved for the producer through purchasing of put options and taking an underhedged position in the futures market. Simulation results further illustrate that hedging the minimum expected yield in the futures market and hedging downside risk using put options for the remaining expected production is a successful strategy. The results are further enhanced when local production influences national prices and if risk aversion is higher at low-income levels.

The hedging demand for options in the case of a convex pricing function arises from the fact that the two sources of uncertainty interact in a multiplicative manner that affects the curvature of profit functions. Frechette (2001) demonstrates the value of options in a hedge portfolio when transaction costs exist, even though markets themselves may be unbiased. Futures and options are shown to be highly substitutable and the optimal mix of them is rarely one-sided. Lien and Wong (2002) justify the hedging role of options with multiple delivery specifications in futures markets. The presence of delivery risk creates a truncation of the price distribution, thereby calling for the use of options as a hedging instrument. They further point out the flexibility of multiple delivery specifications in terms of commodity grades and location causes failure of futures prices convergence to spot prices of the par-deliver grade at the par-delivery location. Thus, hedgers face an additional price (delivery) risk. Lien and Wong find that a hedging role exists for options when futures markets allow for multiple delivery specifications.

Chang and Wong (2003) theoretically derive and empirically document the merits of using currency options for cross-hedging purposes, which are due to a triangular parity condition among related spot exchange rates. Wong and Xu (2006) as well as

Adam-Müller and Panaretou (2009) show that the presence of liquidity risk truncates a firm's payoff profile, thereby making options particularly suitable for the hedging need. Benninga and Oosterhof (2004) show that firms whose private state prices differ from the market state prices use options.

The Model

Consider the competitive firm under output price uncertainty according to Sandmo (1971). There is one period with two dates, 0 and 1. The firm possesses a von Neumann-Morgenstern utility function, $U(\Pi)$, defined over its profit Π, at date 1. The firm is risk averse so that $U'(\Pi) > 0$ and $U''(\Pi) < 0$ for all $\Pi > 0$. The risk-averse behavior of the firm can be motivated by managerial risk aversion (Stulz 1984), corporate taxes and costs of financial distress (Smith and Stulz 1985), and/or capital market imperfections (Stulz 1990; Froot, Scharfstein, and Stein 1993). Indeed, Tufano (1996) provides evidence that managerial risk aversion is a rationale for corporate risk management in the gold mining industry.

To begin, the firm produces a single commodity according to a deterministic cost function, $C(Q)$, where $Q \geq 0$ is the output level chosen by the firm at date 0, and $C(Q)$ is compounded to date 1. The firm's production technology exhibits decreasing returns to scale so that $C(Q)$ satisfies that $C(0) = C'(0) = 0$, and that $C'(Q) > 0$ and $C''(Q) > 0$ for all $Q > 0$. At date 1, the firm sells its entire output, Q, at the then prevailing per-unit output price, $\tilde{P}$, that is not known ex ante. Let $F(P) : [\underline{P}, \overline{P}] \to [0,1]$ be the marginal cumulative distribution function (CDF) of $\tilde{P}$, where $0 < \underline{P} < \overline{P}$. As in Adam-Müller (1997), the firm's revenue at date 1 is subject to a multiplicative shock, $\tilde{\theta}$, which is a positive random variable with unit mean. Let $G(\theta) : [\underline{\theta}, \overline{\theta}] \to [0,1]$ be the marginal CDF of $\tilde{\theta}$, where $0 < \underline{\theta} < 1 < \overline{\theta}$. To allow the possible correlation between $\tilde{\theta}$, and $\tilde{P}$, let $H(\theta, P) : [\underline{\theta}, \overline{\theta}] \times [\underline{P}, \overline{P}] \to [0,1]$ be their joint CDF. Throughout the chapter, random variables have a tilde ($\sim$) while their realizations do not.

While the revenue shock, $\tilde{\theta}$, is neither hedgeable nor insurable, the firm can hedge its output price risk exposure to $\tilde{P}$ by trading infinitely divisible commodity futures and put option contracts at date 0, each of which calls for delivery of one unit of the commodity at date 1. Because of the put-call parity, payoffs of any combinations of futures, calls, and puts can be replicated by any two of these three financial instruments, thereby rendering one of them to be redundant. Restricting the firm to use only commodity futures and put option contracts is without any loss of generality.

The futures price is predetermined at $P^f \in (\underline{P}, \overline{P})$. The commodity put option contracts have a single strike price, $K \in (\underline{P}, \overline{P})$, and an exogenously given option premium, $\Phi > 0$, per contract. In principle, the strike price, K, should also be a choice variable of the firm. If K is very close to $\underline{P}$, the put option contracts would be out of the money almost surely and thus have little use to the firm. On the other hand, if K is very close to $\overline{P}$, the put option contracts would be in the money almost surely and thus are not different from the futures contracts. Hence, if K is a choice variable, the firm should optimally choose K such that the put option contracts are neither too out of the money nor too in the money so as to further improve the hedge effectiveness (Ahn et al. 1999).

The firm's profit, $\tilde{\Pi}$, at date 1 is given by Equation 24.1:

$$\tilde{\Pi} = \tilde{\theta}\tilde{P}Q + \left(P^f - \tilde{P}\right)X + \left[\Phi - max\left(K - \tilde{P},\, 0\right)\right]Y - C(Q), \qquad (24.1)$$

where X and Y are the numbers of the commodity futures and put option contracts sold (purchased if negative) by the firm at date 0, respectively. The pair (X, Y) is referred to as the firm's hedge position. The futures position, X, is said to be an under-hedge, a full-hedge, or an over-hedge, depending on whether X is smaller than, equal to, or greater than the output level, Q, respectively. Conversely, the put option position, Y, is said to be a long or short position, depending on whether Y is negative or positive, respectively.

The firm's ex ante decision problem is to choose an output level $Q \geq 0$, and a hedge position (X, Y) at date 0 so as to maximize the expected utility of its profit at date 1 shown in Equation 24.2

$$max_{Q \geq 0, X, Y} E\left[U(\tilde{\Pi})\right], \qquad (24.2)$$

where $E(\cdot)$ is the expectation operator with respect to the joint CDF, $H(\theta, P)$, and $\tilde{\Pi}$ is given by Equation 24.1. The first-order conditions for Equation 24.2 are given by Equation 24.3, 24.4, and 24.5:

$$E\left\{U'(\tilde{\Pi}^*)\left[\tilde{\theta}\tilde{P} - C'(Q^*)\right]\right\} = 0, \qquad (24.3)$$

$$E\left[U'(\tilde{\Pi}^*)\left(P^f - \tilde{P}\right)\right] = 0, \qquad (24.4)$$

and

$$E\left\{U'(\tilde{\Pi}^*)\left[\Phi - max\left(K - \tilde{P}, 0\right)\right]\right\} = 0, \qquad (24.5)$$

where an asterisk $(*)$ signifies an optimal level. The second-order conditions for Equation 24.2 are satisfied given risk aversion and the strict convexity of the cost function.

To focus on the firm's pure hedging motive, the commodity futures and put option contracts are assumed hereinafter to be fairly priced in that $P^f = E(\tilde{P})$ and $\Phi = E\left[max\left(K - \tilde{P},\, 0\right)\right]$. Using the covariance operator, $Cov(\cdot, \cdot)$, with respect to the joint CDF, $H(\theta, P)$.

Equations 24.3, 24.4, and 24.5 can be written as Equation 24.6, 24.7, and 24.8, respectively:

$$E(\tilde{P}) + Cov(\tilde{\theta},\, \tilde{P}) - C'Q^* = -\frac{Cov\left[U'(\tilde{\Pi}^*),\, \tilde{\theta}\tilde{P}\right]}{E\left[U'(\tilde{\Pi}^*)\right]}, \qquad (24.6)$$

$$Cov\left[U'(\tilde{\Pi}^*),\ \tilde{P}\right] = 0,\tag{24.7}$$

and

$$Cov\left[U'(\tilde{\Pi}^*),\ max\left(K - \tilde{P},\ 0\right)\right] = 0,\tag{24.8}$$

where Equation 24.6 takes into account the fact that $E\left(\tilde{\theta}\right) = 1$.

Benchmark Case without Revenue Risk

In this section, a benchmark case in which the revenue shock is absent (i.e., $\tilde{\theta} \equiv 1$) is considered. Equations 24.6, 24.7, and 24.8 as such become Equations 24.9, 24.10, and 24.11, respectively:

$$E(\tilde{P}) - C'(Q^\circ) = -\frac{Cov\left[U'(\tilde{\Pi}^\circ),\tilde{P}\right]}{U'\left(\tilde{\Pi}^\circ\right)},\tag{24.9}$$

$$Cov\left[U'(\tilde{\Pi}^\circ),\tilde{P}\right] = 0,\tag{24.10}$$

and

$$Cov\left[U'(\tilde{\Pi}^\circ),\ max(K - \tilde{P},0)\right] = 0,\tag{24.11}$$

where a naught ($\circ$) signifies an optimal level, and $\tilde{\Pi}^\circ$ is given by Equation 24.1 with $\tilde{\theta} \equiv 1$. Solving Equations 24.9, 24.10, and 24.11 simultaneously yields the following proposition:

Proposition 1. Given that the commodity futures and put option contracts are fairly priced, and that the revenue shock is absent, the competitive firm's optimal output level, Q°, is the unique solution to Equation 24.12:

$$E(\tilde{P}) = C'(Q^\circ)\tag{24.12}$$

and its optimal hedge position, (X°, Y°), consists of a full-hedge (i.e., $X^\circ = Q^\circ$) and no options (i.e., $Y^\circ = 0$).

Proof. Substituting Equation 24.10 into Equation 24.9 yields Equation 24.12. Suppose that $X^\circ = Q^\circ$ and $Y^\circ = 0$. The firm's profit at date 1 becomes $E(\tilde{P})Q^\circ - C(Q^\circ)$, which is non-stochastic. In this case, Equations 24.10 and 24.11 are satisfied simultaneously, thereby implying that $X^\circ = Q^\circ$ and $Y^\circ = 0$, are indeed the firm's optimal hedge position.

The intuition for Proposition 1 is as follows. Substituting $\tilde{\theta} \equiv 1$, $P^f = E(\tilde{S})$, and $\Phi = E\left[max(K - \tilde{P},\ 0)\right]$ into Equation 24.1 yields Equation 24.13:

$$\tilde{\Pi} = E\left(\tilde{P}\right) Q - C(Q) + \left[\tilde{P} - E\left(\tilde{P}\right)\right] (Q - X)$$

$$+ \left\{ E\left[max\left(K - \tilde{P}, 0\right)\right] - max\left(K - \tilde{P}, 0\right)\right\} Y. \qquad (24.13)$$

Inspection of Equation 24.13 reveals that the firm could have completely eliminated its output price risk exposure had it chosen a full-hedge (i.e., $X = Q$) and used no options (i.e., $Y = 0$) within its own discretion. Alternatively, the degree of output price risk exposure to be assumed by the firm should be totally unrelated to its production decision. The firm as such chooses the optimal output level, Q°, that maximizes $E(\tilde{P})Q - C(Q)$, which gives rise to Equation 24.12. Because the commodity futures and put option contracts are fairly priced, the firm optimal opposition is to completely eliminate its output price risk exposure by adopting a full-hedge (i.e., $X^{\circ} = Q^{\circ}$) and using no options (i.e., $Y^{\circ} = 0$). These results are simply the celebrated separation and full-hedging theorems emanated from the literature on the behavior of the competitive firm under output price uncertainty. In this benchmark case, options play no role as a hedging instrument (Lapan et al. 1991; Battermann et al. 2000).

Optimal Production and Hedging Decisions

Because the revenue shock is neither hedgeable nor insurable, the firm's profit at date 1 must be stochastic. Equation 24.1 as such implies the relationship described in Equation 24.14

$$Cov\left[U'(\tilde{\Pi}^{*}), \tilde{\Pi}^{*}\right] = Cov\left[U'(\tilde{\Pi}^{*}), \tilde{\theta}\,\tilde{P}\,Q^{*} - \tilde{P}X^{*} - max\left(K - \tilde{P},\ 0\right)Y^{*}\right]$$

$$= Cov\left[U'(\tilde{\Pi}^{*}), \tilde{\theta}\,\tilde{P}\right]Q^{*} < 0, \qquad (24.14)$$

where the second equality follows from Equations 24.7 and 24.8, and the inequality follows from $U''(\Pi) < 0$. If $Cov(\tilde{\theta}, \tilde{P}) \leq 0$, Equations 24.6 and 24.14 imply that $E(\tilde{P}) > C'(Q^{*})$. It then follows from Equation 24.12 and the strict convexity of the cost function that $Q^{*} < Q^{\circ}$, thereby invoking the following proposition.

Proposition 2. Given that the commodity futures and put option contracts are fairly priced, the competitive firm's optimal output level, Q^{*}, is less than the benchmark output level, Q°, if the revenue shock, $\tilde{\theta}$, and the random output price, $\tilde{P}$, are either uncorrelated or negatively correlated.

The intuition for Proposition 2 is as follows. Substituting $P^{f} = E(\tilde{P})$ and $\Phi = E\left[max\left(K - \tilde{P},\ 0\right)\right]$ into Equation 24.1 yields Equation 24.15:

$$\tilde{\Pi}^{*} = E\left(\tilde{P}\right) Q^{*} - C\left(Q^{*}\right) + (\tilde{\theta} - 1)\tilde{P}\,Q^{*} + \left[\tilde{P} - E\left(\tilde{P}\right)\right]\left(Q^{*} - X^{*}\right)$$

$$+ \left\{ E\left[max\left(K - \tilde{P},\ 0\right)\right] - max\left(K - \tilde{P},\ 0\right)\right\} Y^{*}. \qquad (24.15)$$

The prevalence of the revenue shock induces the firm to reduce its output so as to limit the risk exposure that comes from the third term on the right-hand side of Equation 24.15. Taking expectations on both sides of Equation 24.15 yields Equation 24.16:

$$E(\tilde{\Pi}^{*}) = E(\tilde{P})Q^{*} - C(Q^{*}) + Cov(\tilde{\theta}, \tilde{P})Q^{*}. \tag{24.16}$$

If $\tilde{\theta}$ and $\tilde{P}$ are negatively correlated (uncorrelated), the last term on the right-hand side of Equation 24.16 is decreasing in (invariant to) output, which reinforces (has no effect on) the firm's risk reduction incentive, thereby rendering $Q^{*} < Q^{\circ}$.

For tractability, the revenue shock, $\tilde{\theta}$ and the random output price, $\tilde{P}$, are assumed to be related in the following manner (Chang and Wong 2003; Wong 2003a, 2013):

$$\tilde{\theta} = 1 + \beta\big[\tilde{P} - E(\tilde{P})\big] + \tilde{\varepsilon}, \tag{24.17}$$

where β is a constant, and $\tilde{\varepsilon}$ is a zero-mean random variable independent of $\tilde{P}$. According to Equation 24.17, $\tilde{\theta}$ and $\tilde{P}$ are negatively or positively correlated depending on whether β is negative or positive, respectively. They are uncorrelated if $\beta = 0$.

As Kimball (1990, 1993) convincingly argues, i.e., $U'''(\Pi) > 0$, is a reasonable behavioral assumption for decision making under multiple sources of uncertainty. Prudence measures the propensity to prepare and forearm oneself under uncertainty, vis-à-vis risk aversion that is how much one dislikes uncertainty and would turn away from it if one could. As Leland (1968), Drèze and Modigliani (1972), and Kimball (1990) show, prudence is both necessary and sufficient to induce precautionary saving. Furthermore, prudence is implied by decreasing absolute risk aversion (DARA), which is instrumental in yielding many intuitively appealing comparative statics under uncertainty (Gollier 2001). As Bonilla and Vergara (2013) point out, prudence is consistent with not only DARA, but also increasing absolute risk aversion (IARA). To see this, take the following utility function (Pratt 1964) as an example:

$U(\Pi) = -(\theta - \Pi)^{\gamma}$, where θ and γ are positive constants such that $\theta > \Pi$ and $\gamma > 2$. The Arrow-Pratt measure of absolute risk aversion is then given by $A(\Pi) = -U''(\Pi)/U'(\Pi) = (\gamma - 1)/(\theta - \Pi)$. Since $A'(\Pi) = (\gamma - 1)/(\theta - \Pi)^{2} > 0$ and $U'''(\Pi) = \gamma(\gamma - 1)(\gamma - 2)(\theta - \Pi)^{\gamma - 3} > 0$, it is evident that $U(\Pi) = -(\theta - \Pi)^{\gamma}$ exhibits both IARA and prudence.

The following proposition characterizes the optimal hedge position, (X^{*}, Y^{*}), when the firm's preferences satisfy prudence.

Proposition 3. Given that the competitive exporting firm is prudent and has access to the fairly priced commodity futures and put option contracts for hedging purposes, and that the revenue shock, $\tilde{\theta}$, and the random output price, $\tilde{P}$, are characterized by Equation 24.17 with $\beta \leq 0$, the firm's optimal hedge position, (X^{*}, Y^{*}) consists of an under-hedge (i.e., $X^{*} < Q^{*}$) and a long put option position (i.e., $Y^{*} < 0$). The intuition for Proposition 3 is as follows. Substituting Equation 24.17 into Equation 24.15 yields Equation 24.18:

$$\tilde{\Pi}^{*} = E(\tilde{P})Q^{*} - C(Q^{*}) + \beta\,\tilde{P}\big[\tilde{P} - E(\tilde{P})\big]Q^{*} + \tilde{\varepsilon}\,\tilde{P}Q^{*} + \big[\tilde{P} - E(\tilde{P})\big](Q^{*} - X^{*})$$

$$+ \big\{E\big[max(K - \tilde{S}, 0)\big] - max(K - \tilde{S}, 0)\big\}Y^{*}. \tag{24.18}$$

If $\beta < (>) 0$, the third term on the right-hand side of Equation 24.18 is negatively (positively) correlated with $\tilde{P}$ since $Cov \beta \, \tilde{P} \left[\tilde{P} - E \left(\tilde{P} \right), \, \tilde{P} \right] = \beta \, E \left\{ \tilde{P} \left[\tilde{P} - E \left(\tilde{P} \right) \right]^2 \right\} < (<) 0$, which induces the firm to opt for a long (short) futures position. Furthermore, this term is quadratic and concave (convex) in the realized output price, P, if $\beta < (>) 0$, which induces the firm to opt for a long (short) put option position to create a convex (concave) payoff that better copes with the associated risk exposure. This impact on the hedge position is referred to as the *correlation motive*.

The random variable, $\tilde{\varepsilon}$, in the fourth term on the right-hand side of Equation 24.18 can be interpreted as a zero-mean background risk. The firm, being prudent, has a precautionary motive to shift its profit at date 1 from states with small background risk to states with large background risk so as to mitigate the loss of utility (Eeckhoudt and Schlesinger 2006). As is evident from this term, the magnitude of the background risk increases with an increase in the realized value of $\tilde{P}$. The precautionary motive as such calls for a long futures position and a long put option position. If $\beta < (>) 0$, the correlation motive reinforces (counteracts) the precautionary motive. Combining these two motives with the full-hedging motive in the absence of the revenue shock (see Proposition 1), the prudent firm's optimal hedge position consists of an under-hedge (i.e., $X^* < Q^*$) and a long put option position (i.e., $Y^* < 0$), if $\beta \leq 0$, and the optimal hedge position becomes ambiguous if $\beta > 0$.

An Example

To gain more insight into the firm's optimal production and hedging decisions, a reasonable example that has a closed form solution is constructed. Suppose that the revenue shock, $\tilde{\theta}$, and the random output price, $\tilde{P}$, are characterized by Equation 24.17 such that $\tilde{\varepsilon}$ is a standard normal random variable. Suppose further that $\tilde{P}$ takes on three possible values, $P_1, P_2,$ and P_3, with $0 < P_1 < P_2 < P_3$. Let p_i be the probability that $\tilde{P} = P_i$ for $i = 1, 2,$ and 3, where $0 < p_i < 1$ and $\sum_{i=1}^{3} p_i = 1$. The expected output price is therefore given by $E(\tilde{P}) = \sum_{i=1}^{3} p_i P_i$. The put option contracts have a single strike price, $K \in (P_1, P_2]$, and the premium per contract, $\varPhi = \sum_{i=1}^{3} p_i \, max \, (K - P_i, 0) = p_1 (K - P_1)$. The firm's preferences exhibit constant absolute risk aversion (CARA) so that $U(\varPi) = -e^{-\alpha \varPi}$, where $\alpha > 0$ is the constant coefficient of absolute risk aversion.

The first-order conditions for this example are given by Equations 24.19, 24.20, and 24.21:

$$E \left\{ \sum_{i=1}^{3} p_i \, e^{-\alpha [\varPi^*(P_i) + \tilde{\varepsilon} P_i \, Q^*]} \left\{ \left[1 + \beta \left(P_i - \sum_{j=1}^{3} p_j P_j \right) + \tilde{\varepsilon} \right] P_i - C'(Q^*) \right\} \right\} = 0,$$
(24.19)

$$E \left\{ \sum_{i=1}^{3} p_i \, e^{-\alpha [\varPi^*(P_i) + \tilde{\varepsilon} P_i \, Q^*]} \left(\sum_{j=1}^{3} p_j P_j - P_i \right) \right\} = 0$$
(24.20)

and

$$E\left\{\sum_{i=1}^{3} p_i\, e^{-\alpha[\Pi^*(P_i)+\tilde{\varepsilon}P_i\, Q^*]} \left[p_1\,(K - P_1) - max\,(K - P_i, 0)\right]\right\} = 0 \qquad (24.21)$$

$$\Pi^*(P_i) = P_i\, Q^* + \left(P_i - \sum_{j=1}^{3} p_j P_j\right)(\beta\, P_i\, Q^* - X^*)$$
$$+ \left[p_1\,(K - P_1) - max\,(K - P_i, 0)\right] Y^* - C\,(Q^*).$$

It follows from Equations 24.20 and 24.21 that Equation 24.22 is true.

$$\Pi^*(P_1) - \frac{\alpha}{2}(P_1\, Q^*)^2 = \Pi^*(P_2) - \frac{\alpha}{2}(P_2\, Q^*)^2 = \Pi^*(P_3) - \frac{\alpha}{2}(P_3\, Q^*)^2 \quad (24.22)$$

which follows from the fact that $\tilde{\varepsilon}$ is a standard normal random variable. Substituting Equation 24.22 into Equation 24.19 yields Equation 24.23:

$$E(\tilde{P}) - C'(Q^*) + \beta\, Var(\tilde{P}) - \alpha\, E(\tilde{P}^2)Q^* = 0, \qquad (24.23)$$

where $Var(\tilde{P})$ is the variance of $\tilde{P}$. Define the following constant:

$$\beta^\circ = \alpha\,\frac{E(\tilde{P}^2)Q^\circ}{Var(\tilde{P})} > 0, \qquad (24.24)$$

where Q° is given by Equation 24.12). Substituting Equations 24.12 and 24.24 into Equation 24.23 yields Equation 24.25:

$$C'(Q^\circ) - C'(Q^*) + Var(\tilde{P})\left(\beta - \frac{\beta^\circ Q^*}{Q^\circ}\right) = 0. \qquad (24.25)$$

If $\beta > (<)\beta^\circ$ but $Q^* \leq (\geq) Q^\circ$, the strict convexity of $C(Q)$ implies that the left-hand side of Equation 24.25 is positive (negative), a contradiction. Hence, $Q^* > (<)$ Q° must be true if $\beta > (<)\beta^\circ$. These results are consistent with the findings of Proposition 2 that $Q^* < Q^\circ$ should $\tilde{\theta}$ and $\tilde{P}$ be uncorrelated or negatively correlated (i.e., $\beta \leq 0$). Indeed, for all $\beta \in (0, \beta^\circ)$, it remains true that $Q^* < Q^\circ$. However, if $\beta > \beta^\circ, Q^* > Q^\circ$ must be true, which is a novel result. This is particularly the case when the firm is not too risk-averse (i.e., when α is close to zero so that the threshold value, β°) is also close to zero. A positive correlation between $\tilde{\theta}$ and $\tilde{P}$ is then likely to be sufficient to induce the firm to produce beyond the optimal output level in the benchmark case of no revenue shock.

Solving Equation 24.22 yields Equation 24.26:

$$X^* = Q^* + \left\{\beta - \left[\frac{P_2 + P_3}{P_2 + P_3 - E(\tilde{P})}\right]\frac{\alpha Q^*}{2}\right\}[P_2 + P_3 - E(\tilde{P})]Q^* \qquad (24.26)$$

and

$$Y^* = \frac{(P_2 - P_1)(P_3 - P_1)}{K - P_1} \left(\beta - \frac{\alpha Q^*}{2} \right) Q^*, \qquad (24.27)$$

where Q^* is given by Equation 24.23. Since $P_2 + P_3 - E(\tilde{P}) = P_1 + (1 - p_2)(P_2 - P_1) + (1 - p_3)(P_3 - P_1) > 0$, Equations 24.26 and 24.27 imply that $X^* < Q^*$ and $Y^* < 0$ if $\beta \leq 0$, which are consistent with the findings of Proposition 3.

When $\beta = \beta^\circ$, it follows from $Q^* = Q^\circ$ and Equation 24.24 that Equation 24.28 is true.

$$\beta^\circ - \left[\frac{P_2 + P_3}{P_2 + P_3 - E(\tilde{P})} \right] \frac{\alpha Q^\circ}{2}$$

$$= \frac{\{2[P_2 + P_3 - E(\tilde{P})]E(\tilde{P}^2) - (P_2 + P_3) Var(\tilde{P})\}\alpha Q^\circ}{2[P_2 + P_3 - E(\tilde{P})] Var(\tilde{P})}. \qquad (24.28)$$

Since $[P_2 + P_3 - E(\tilde{P})]E(\tilde{P}^2) = (P_2 + P_3) Var(\tilde{P}) + [p_1 P_1 (P_2 + P_3 - P_1) + (p_2 + p_3) P_2 P_3]E(\tilde{P}) > (P_2 + P_3) Var(\tilde{P})$, Equations 24.26 and 24.28 imply that $X^* > Q^*$ when $\beta = \beta^\circ$. Differentiating Equation 24.23 with respect to β yields $\partial Q^*/\partial \beta = Var(\tilde{P})/[C''(Q^*)] + \alpha E(\tilde{P}^2)]$. It follows that Equation 24.29 is true.

$$\frac{\partial}{\partial \beta} \left\{ \beta - \left[\frac{P_2 + P_3}{P_2 + P_3 - E(\tilde{P})} \right] \frac{\alpha Q^*}{2} \right\}$$

$$= \frac{2 [P_2 + P_3 - E(\tilde{P})] \left[C'' (Q^*) + \alpha E(\tilde{P}^2) \right] - \alpha (P_2 + P_3) Var(\tilde{P})}{2 [P_2 + P_3 - E(\tilde{P})] \left[C'' (Q^*) + \alpha E(\tilde{P}^2) \right]}. \qquad (24.29)$$

Since $C''(Q) > 0$ and $[P_2 + P_3 - E(\tilde{P})] E \left(\tilde{P}^2 \right) > (P_2 + P_3) Var (\tilde{P})$, the right-hand side of Equation 24.29 is positive. It then follows from Equations 24.26 and 24.28 that there exists a threshold value, $\beta^* \in (0, \beta^\circ)$, such that $X^* < (>)Q^*$ if $\beta < (>)\beta^*$. Proposition 3 implies that the correlation motive counteracts the precautionary motive whenever $\beta > 0$. As β increases, the correlation motive gets stronger and soon dominates the precautionary motive once β exceeds the threshold, β^* thereby rendering the optimality of an over-hedge (i.e., $X^* > Q^*$).

Since $\beta^* - \alpha Q^*/2 = \alpha E (\tilde{P}) Q^*/2 [P_2 + P_3 - E (\tilde{P})] > 0$, Equation 24.27 implies that $Y^* > 0$ when $\beta = \beta^*$. Since $\partial Q^*/\partial \beta = Var (\tilde{P}) / \left[C'' (Q^*) + \alpha E (\tilde{P}^2) \right]$, it follows that Equation 24.30 is true.

$$\frac{\partial}{\partial \beta} \left(\beta - \frac{\alpha Q^*}{2} \right) = \frac{2C''(Q^*) + \alpha \left[E(\tilde{P}^2) + E(\tilde{P})^2 \right]}{2 \left[C''(Q^*) + \alpha E(\tilde{P}^2) \right]} > 0. \qquad (24.30)$$

Equations 24.27 and 24.30 then imply that there exists a threshold value, $\beta^{**} \in (0, \beta^*)$, such that $Y^* < (>)0$ if $\beta < (>)\beta^{**}$. For all $\beta \in (\beta^{**}, \beta^*)$, it must be true that $X^* < Q^*$ and $Y^* > 0$. Hence, this example suggests that the correlation motive is more profound in affecting the put option position than the precautionary motive, when contrasted to the futures position. Furthermore, even when a full-hedge (i.e., $X^* = Q^*$) is optimal, which is the case when $\beta = \beta^*$, the firm includes a short put option position (i.e., $Y^* > 0$) in its optimal hedge position, thereby making the full-hedging theorem never hold in this example.

Summary and Conclusions

After providing an overview of options and valuation, this chapter examines the behavior of the competitive firm under joint revenue and output price risk. The firm can trade fairly priced commodity futures and put option contracts for hedging purposes. This chapter shows that neither the separation theorem nor the full-hedging theorem holds when the revenue shock prevails. Specifically, if the correlation between the random output price and the revenue shock is non-positive, the firm optimally produces less as compared to the benchmark output level when the revenue shock is absent. If, in addition, the firm's preferences satisfy the reasonable property of prudence, the prudent firm's optimal hedge position consists of an under-hedge in the futures position and a long put option position. However, if the correlation is sufficiently positive, a canonical example is constructed under which the firm optimally produces more, not less, than the benchmark level, and opts for an over-hedge in the futures position and a short put option position. The firm's optimal production and hedging decisions as such depend not only on the risk attitude of the firm but also on the joint distribution of the random output price and the revenue shock. Operational hedging and financial hedging are used as complements to better cope with the multiple sources of uncertainty.

Discussion Questions

1. Distinguish between a call option and a put option.
2. Explain how exchange-traded options differ from OTC options.
3. Define the separation and full-hedging theorems.
4. Explain why the separation and full-hedging theorems hold in the context of the competitive firm under output price uncertainty.
5. Identify possible reasons that support the hedging role of options.
6. When the multiplicative revenue shock prevails, the competitive firm optimally uses options for hedging purposes. Identify the key factors that drive the firm to include options in its optimal hedge position.

Acknowledgments

Professor Wong thanks Axel Adam-Müller, Udo Broll, and Jason Yi for their helpful comments and suggestions.

References

Adam-Müller, Axel F. A. 1997. "Export and Hedging Decisions under Revenue and Exchange Rate Risk: A Note." *European Economic Review* 41:7, 1421–1426.

Adam-Müller, Axel F.A., and Argyro Panaretou. 2009. "Risk Management with Options and Futures under Liquidity Risk." *Journal of Futures Markets* 29:4, 297–318.

Ahn, Dong-Hyun, Jacob Boudoukh, Matthew Richardson, and Robert F. Whitelaw. 1999. "Optimal Risk Management Using Options." *Journal of Finance* 54:1, 359–375.

Anderluh, Jasper, and Svetlana Borovkova. 2008. "Commodity Volatility Modelling and Option Pricing with a Potential Function Approach." *European Journal of Finance* 14:2, 157–184.

Aradhyula, Satheesh V., and E. Kwan Choi. 1993. "Production, Hedging, and Speculative Decisions with Options and Futures Markets: Comment." *American Journal of Agricultural Economics* 75:3, 745–747.

Batra, Raveendra, and Aman Ullah. 1974. "Competitive Firm and the Theory of Input Demand under Price Uncertainty." *Journal of Political Economy* 82:3, 537–548.

Battermann, Harald L., Michael Braulke, Udo Broll, and Jörg Schimmelpfennig. 2000. "The Preferred Hedge Instrument." *Economics Letters* 66:1, 85–89.

Benninga, Simon Z., and Casper M. Oosterhof. 2004. "Hedging with Forwards and Puts in Complete and Incomplete Markets." *Journal of Banking and Finance* 28:1, 1–17.

Black, Fischer. 1976. "The Pricing of Commodity Contracts." *Journal of Finance* 3:1-2, 167–179.

Black, Fischer, and Myron Scholes. 1973. "The Pricing of Options and Corporate Liabilities." *Journal of Political Economy* 81:3, 637–654.

Bonilla, Claudio A., and Macos Vergara. 2013. "Credit Rationing or Entrepreneurial Risk Aversion? A Comment." *Economics Letters* 120:2, 329–331.

Broll, Udo, and Kit Pong Wong. 2013. "The Firm under Uncertainty: Real and Financial Decisions." *Decisions in Economics and Finance* 36:2, 125–136.

Broll, Udo, and Itzhak Zilcha. 1992. "Exchange Rate Uncertainty, Futures Markets and the Multinational Firm." *European Economic Review* 36:4, 815–826.

Broll, Udo, Kit Pong Wong, and Itzhak Zilcha. 1999. "Multiple Currencies and Hedging." *Economica* 66:264, 421–432.

Brown, Gregory, and Klaus Bjerre Toft. 2002. "How Firms Should Hedge." *Review of Financial Studies* 15:4, 1283–1324.

Camerer, Colin. 1982. "The Pricing and Social Value of Commodity Options." *Financial Analysts Journal* 38:1, 62–66.

Chang, Eric C., and Kit Pong Wong. 2003. "Cross-Hedging with Currency Options and Futures." *Journal of Financial and Quantitative Analysis* 38:3, 555–574.

Chavas, Jean-Paul. 1985. "On the Theory of the Competitive Firm under Uncertainty When Initial Wealth Is Random." *Southern Economic Journal* 51:1, 818–827.

Danthine, Jean-Pierre. 1978. "Information, Futures Prices, and Stabilizing Speculation." *Journal of Economic Theory* 17:1, 79–98.

Drèze, Jacques H., and Franco Modigliani. 1972. "Consumption Decisions under Uncertainty." *Journal of Economic Theory* 5:3, 308–335.

Eeckhoudt, Louis, and Harris Schlesinger. 2006. "Putting Risk in Its Proper Place." *American Economic Review* 96:1, 280–289.

Feder, Gershon, Richard E. Just, and Andrew Schmitz. 1980. "Futures Markets and the Theory of the Firm under Price Uncertainty." *Quarterly Journal of Economics* 94:2, 317–328.

Frechette, Darren L. 2001. "The Demand for Hedging with Futures and Options." *Journal of Futures Markets* 21:8, 693–712.

Froot, Kenneth A., David S. Scharfstein, and Jeremy C. Stein. 1993. "Risk Management: Coordinating Corporate Investment and Financing Policies." *Journal of Finance* 48:5, 1629–1658.

Goldberg, Pinelopi Koujianou, and Michael M. Knetter. 1997. "Goods Prices and Exchange Rates: What Have We Learned?" *Journal of Economic Literature* 35:3, 1243–1272.

Gollier, Christian. 2001. *The Economics of Risk and Time*. Cambridge, MA: MIT Press.

Gust, Christopher, Sylvain Leduc, and Robert J. Vigfusson. 2010. "Trade Integration, Competition, and the Decline in Exchange-Rate Pass-Through." *Journal of Monetary Economics* 57:3, 309–324.

Hilliard, Jimmy E., and Jorge A. Reis. 1999. "Jump Processes in Commodity Futures Prices and Option Pricing." *American Journal of Agricultural Economics* 81:2, 273–286.

Hinz, Juri, and Max Fehr. 2010. "Storage Costs in Commodity Option Pricing." *SIAM Journal of Financial Mathematics* 1:1, 729–751.

Holthausen, Duncan M. 1979. "Hedging and the Competitive Firm under Price Uncertainty." *American Economic Review* 69:5, 989–995.

Kim, Jang-Chul, and Kyojik Song. 2010. "Investment Barriers and Premiums on Closed-End Country Funds." *International Review of Economics and Finance* 19:4, 615–626.

Kimball, Miles S. 1990. "Precautionary Saving in the Small and in the Large." *Econometrica* 58:1, 53–73.

Kimball, Miles S. 1993. "Standard Risk Aversion." *Econometrica* 61:3, 589–611.

Korn, Olaf. 2009. "How Firms Should Hedge: An Extension." *Journal of Futures Markets* 30:9, 834–845.

Lapan, Harvey, Giancarlo Moschini, and Steven D. Hanson. 1991. "Production, Hedging, and Speculative Decisions with Options and Futures Markets." *American Journal of Agricultural Economics* 73:1, 66–74.

Leland, Hayne E. 1968. "Saving and Uncertainty: The Precautionary Demand for Saving." *Quarterly Journal of Economics* 82:3, 465–473.

Lien, Donald, and Kit Pong Wong. 2002. "Delivery Risk and the Hedging Role of Options." *Journal of Futures Markets* 22:4, 339–354.

Lien, Donald, and Kit Pong Wong. 2004. "Optimal Bidding and Hedging in International Markets." *Journal of International Money and Finance* 23:5, 785–798.

Luft, Carl F., and Bruce D. Fielitz. 1986. "An Empirical Test of the Commodity Option Pricing Model Using Ginnie Mae Call Options." *Journal of Financial Research* 9:2, 137–152.

Marazzi, Mario, and Nathan Sheets. 2007. "Declining Exchange Rate Pass-Through to US Import Prices: The Potential Role of Global Factors." *Journal of International Money and Finance* 26:6, 924–947.

Miltersen, Kristian R., and Eduardo S. Schwartz. 1998. "Pricing of Options on Commodity Futures with Stochastic Term Structures of Convenience Yields and Interest Rates." *Journal of Financial and Quantitative Analysis* 33:1, 33–59.

Moschini, Giancarlo, and Harvey Lapan. 1992. "Hedging Price Risk with Options and Futures for the Competitive Firm with Production Flexibility." *International Economic Review* 33:3, 607–618.

Moschini, Giancarlo, and Harvey Lapan. 1995. "The Hedging Role of Options and Futures under Joint Price, Basis, and Production Risk." *International Economic Review* 36:4, 1025–1049.

Mossin, Jan. 1968. "Aspects of Rational Insurance Purchasing." *Journal of Political Economy* 76:4, 553–568.

Myers, Robert J., and Steven D. Hanson. 1993. "Pricing Commodity Options When the Underlying Futures Price Exhibits Time-Varying Volatility." *American Journal of Agricultural Economics* 75:1, 121–130.

Nakajima, Katsushi, and Akira Maeda. 2007. "Pricing Commodity Spread Options with Stochastic Term Structure of Convenience Yields and Interest Rates." *Asia–Pacific Financial Markets* 14:1-2, 157–184.

Pratt, John W. 1964. "Risk Aversion in the Small and in the Large." *Econometrica*, 32:1/2, 122–136.

Sakong, Yong, Dermot J. Hayes, and Arne Hallam. 1993. "Hedging Production Risk with Options." *American Journal of Agricultural Economics* 75:2, 408–415.

Sandmo, Agnar. 1971. "On the Theory of the Competitive Firm under Price Uncertainty." *American Economic Review* 61:1, 65–73.

Smith, Clifford W., and René M. Stulz. 1985. "The Determinants of Firms' Hedging Policies." *Journal of Financial and Quantitative Analysis* 20:4, 391–405.

Stulz, René M. 1984. "Optimal Hedging Policies." *Journal of Financial and Quantitative Analysis* 19:2, 127–140.

Stulz, René M. 1990. "Managerial Discretion and Optimal Financial Policies." *Journal of Financial Economics* 26:1, 3–27.

Tufano, Peter. 1996. "Who Manages Risk? An Empirical Examination of Risk Management Practices in the Gold Mining Industry." *Journal of Finance* 51:4, 1097–1137.

Viaene, Jean-Marie, and Itzhak Zilcha. 1998. "The Behavior of Competitive Exporting Firms under Multiple Uncertainty." *International Economic Review* 39:3, 591–609.

Wong, Kit Pong. 1996. "Background Risk and the Theory of the Competitive Firm under Uncertainty." *Bulletin of Economic Research* 48:3, 241–251.

Wong, Kit Pong. 2003a. "Currency Hedging with Options and Futures." *European Economic Review* 47:5, 833–839.

Wong, Kit Pong. 2003b. "Export Flexibility and Currency Hedging." *International Economic Review* 44:4, 1295–1312.

Wong, Kit Pong. 2013. "International Trade and Hedging under Joint Price and Exchange Rate Uncertainty." *International Review of Economics and Finance* 27:C, 160–170.

Wong, Kit Pong. 2014. "Regret Theory and the Competitive Firm." *Economic Modelling* 35, forthcoming.

Wong, Kit Pong, and Jianguo Xu. 2006. "Liquidity Risk and the Hedging Role of Options." *Journal of Futures Markets* 26:8, 789–808.

25

Futures

LUDWIG B. CHINCARINI, CFA

Professor of Finance, University of San Francisco

Introduction

Financial markets allow investors to manage their risks. In particular, sophisticated financial markets can sometimes allow investors to discard risks they do not want and transfer risk to another period when they are better suited to absorb it and alter the very nature of the risks faced.

Using futures accomplishes much of this risk transfer. Often, two parties exist within a risk transfer process: one party, the *speculator*, takes on risk, while the other party, the *hedger*, reduces or transfers risk. Both roles are extremely important for a well-functioning financial market (Angel and McCabe 2009). The speculator who takes on risk provides a valuable service for those who want to hedge risk. Futures are types of derivatives contracts that allow this transfer to take place. A *futures contract* is an agreement, originally between a buyer and a seller, to exchange a particular good for a specific price at a date in the future. A contract common to all market participants specifies the terms. Although some contend that too many derivatives exist, the time periods in which society has been most inconvenienced involve a lack of available futures contracts, not an abundance of them. For example, real estate futures lack sufficient liquidity, which increases the difficulty of using them to hedge housing risk.

Hedging is the common term used to refer to transforming risks. The term originated during the 1500s to refer to evading or dodging something. In finance, *hedging* is the act of making a financial transaction in order to offset movements in a security in which the investor has a financial interest. Investors might engage in the total or partial elimination of the risk being faced.

Many investors choose to hedge risks. Some hedgers are mainstream corporations with businesses subject to risk and thus use futures to hedge their business risk. Others are financial investors who use futures to reduce or limit their exposure to risks associated with the market place. Still other hedgers are individuals looking to reduce some specific element of their risks.

This chapter discusses how to use futures to hedge risk. This presentation includes using commodity futures, equity futures, interest rate futures, and other futures contracts. The chapter is organized as follows. The first section discusses the universe of futures contracts including the trading and pricing of futures. Next, the chapter discusses concepts for using futures to manage risk followed by a discussion of selected hedging examples. The final section provides a summary and conclusions.

The Futures Universe

Both futures and forwards are available to hedge risk. A *forward contract* is a contractual obligation between two parties to exchange a particular good for a specific price at a date in the future. Futures are similar. Although futures and forwards have some similarities, futures contracts differ from forward contracts in several ways. For example, futures contracts are marked-to-market, traded on exchanges, and are subject to government regulation. Forward contracts are private contracts constructed between two parties on the over-the-counter (OTC) market and are usually not regulated. Futures contracts are highly standardized whereas forward contracts are customized contracts satisfying the needs of the parties involved. A single clearinghouse is the counterparty to all futures contracts, which frees traders from having to worry about default because the counterparty to each contract is the clearinghouse. By contrast, forwards are contracts with the originating counterparty and hence face potential counterparty (default) risk.

An investor can buy or sell a futures contract and any profit depends on the movement of the underlying asset or security. For example, suppose that a futures position increases in value when coffee prices increase, then the appropriate strategy would be to buy the coffee futures contract if the investor wanted to profit from a rise in coffee prices. Typically, if coffee prices went up, the futures position would increase in value and if coffee prices went down, the futures position would decrease in value. The daily process of adjusting contract values is called mark-to-market.

Although this futures trading appears to be like gambling, it is not. If the only exposure is to the futures contract, then the investor is taking on more risk. This risk, however, is beneficial to society because it absorbs risk that others are unwilling to take. Often, the investor's futures position is added to an already existing exposure to the coffee market. For example, a coffee producer already has a large exposure to coffee prices based on his business. The coffee producer might sell a futures contract to minimize the fluctuations in profits due to changes in coffee prices.

THE TYPES OF FUTURES CONTRACTS

Many categories of futures contracts are available. For example, futures contracts may trade based on the underlying markets of commodities, equity indices, foreign exchange, interest rates, metals, real estate, and even weather.

Commodity Futures
Commodity futures represent some of the most important futures contracts for hedging by helping farmers, manufacturers, and other businesses reduce unwanted risks. Various types of commodity futures exist including agricultural futures and energy futures. Agricultural commodities include corn, soybeans, wheat, hog, cattle, milk, rice, lumber, butter, cotton, cheese, sugar, and coffee. Although onion futures once traded, the Onion Futures Act banned this contract in 1958. The law was passed due to pressure from

onion farmers who were upset at two onion traders, San Siegel and Vincent Kosuga, who attempted to manipulate the onion market. Despite the oddity of having this particular futures trading prohibited, the ban currently remains in effect. Energy commodities include natural gas, crude oil, ethanol, coal, and propane. The trading of commodities is a detailed and complicated task. Riley (2004) provides a video offering an overview of the commodities trading industry.

Equity Index Futures

Investors use equity futures for various reasons such as creating leveraged portfolios, gaining cheap exposure to equities, and hedging purposes. Hedging can take several forms. For example, if an investor has a long exposure to equities, but worries that the stock market will decline, he can short or sell futures contracts to reduce his exposure. A *long position* in a security means that an investor has bought the security, while a *short position* in a security indicates that an investor has sold the security without owning it and benefits from a decline in value. Investors can also use futures to hedge the risk of other transactions such as writing options or rebalancing a portfolio. Equity futures are available on many major stock market indices internationally. In the United States, these futures include contracts on such indices as the S&P 500, Nasdaq, Dow Jones Industrial Average (DJIA), Russell 2000, and various sectors of the U.S. economy.

Foreign Exchange Futures

One of the most actively traded financial instruments is foreign exchange futures. Foreign exchange is central to international business. Companies tap into the foreign exchange markets to hedge business risk associated with cross-border transactions. Businesses are not the only ones that use currency futures to hedge. Global money managers also use futures to hedge their investments in other currencies so as to protect their investments.

Currency trading totals more than $4 trillion daily (Bank of International Settlements 2010). Futures contracts exist on many currencies globally including on the yen–U.S. dollar (traders refer to this currency as the yen-dollar), pound–U.S. dollar (the cable), euro–U.S. dollar, Australian dollar–U.S. dollar (aussie-dollar), Swiss franc–U.S. dollar (dollar-swissy), Canadian dollar–U.S. dollar (loonie), Brazilian real–U.S. dollar, Chinese yuan–U.S. dollar, New Zealand dollar–U.S. dollar (Kiwi), Mexican peso–U.S. dollar, and many other currencies versus the U.S. dollar in Asia, Latin America, Europe, and Africa.

Interest Rate Futures

Futures contracts are also available based on the movement of all types of underlying interest rates including interest rates between different currencies in the interbank market, government interest rates, and even the federal funds rate, which the Federal Reserve (Fed) manipulates to set short-term interest rates.

Metal Futures

Metal futures consist of three categories: base metals, industrial metals, and precious metals. Base metal futures include aluminum, copper, iron ore, lead, nickel, steel, tin, and zinc. Industrial metal futures include lumber, polyethylene, rubber, and glass while precious metals include gold, palladium, and silver.

Real Estate Futures

The real estate market was the principal cause of the financial crisis of 2007–2008 (Chincarini 2012). Due to its importance in the economy, futures contracts were created that are based on an index of home prices in major cities in the United States and elsewhere. As of 2013, futures are traded on the basis of real estate prices in Boston, Chicago, Denver, Las Vegas, Los Angeles, Miami, New York, San Diego, San Francisco, Washington, DC, and a composite of 10 of the largest metropolitan areas including all of the above cities.

Weather Futures

Futures contracts exist that trade on weather conditions in various cities of the world. Weather derivatives represent one of the most impressive accomplishments of well-developed markets because they allow businesses to smooth out fluctuations in the demand for their products as weather conditions change.

THE MECHANICS OF FUTURES TRADING

Futures contracts trade on well-organized exchanges such as the Chicago Mercantile Exchange group (CME group), London International Financial Futures Exchange (LIFFE), Sydney Futures Exchange (SFE), and European Exchange (Eurex). Every futures contact is standardized so both buyers and sellers know the specifications in advance. The contract specifications include the asset, contract size, delivery arrangements, delivery months, price quotes, and price and position limits. The asset represents the underlying security for which the futures contract is based. For example, when delivering cotton, the futures contract specifies exactly what type of cotton must be delivered. The contract size indicates the level of exposure to the underlying asset from taking a position on one contract of the futures contract. For example, when buying one S&P eMini futures contract, the current value of the S&P 500 index is multiplied by $50. The delivery arrangements specify acceptable delivery terms for the underlying asset when the futures contract expires. For example, for corn futures on the CME, various cities are available where a short seller can deliver the actual corn. The delivery months specify the months and exact day at which the futures contract expires and delivery or cash settlement must be completed. *Price and position limits* are limits on the trading and ownership for investors who use futures. The limits are established to protect the futures market from one entity having a position that is so large on the exchange that they could either exert manipulative influence on the price of that futures contract or if they were to go bankrupt could cause a major disruption in the price of that futures contract.

For example, CME cattle futures require that one contract or 40,000 pounds of cattle that are 55 percent choice, 45 percent select, yield grade three live steers as defined by the United States Department of Agriculture (http://www.usda.gov) be delivered to several locations in approved livestock yards in Wray, Colorado; Dodge City, Kansas; Pratt, Kansas; Syracuse, Kansas; Clovis, New Mexico; Columbus, Nebraska; Norfolk, Nebraska; North Platte, Nebraska; Ogallala, Nebraska; Texhoma,

Oklahoma; Worthing, South Dakota; Amarillo, Texas; and Tulia, Texas. Delivery may be made on any business day of the contract month, and the first seven business days in the succeeding calendar month, provided a certificate has been tendered as prescribed by certain rules except that live graded deliveries may not be made before the seventh business day following the first Friday of the contract month. The contract expirations and thus delivery months are February, April, June, August, October, and December (CME Group 2013).

The futures prices are quoted in cents per pound. Thus, valuing a single contract requires multiplying the futures price by 40,000 and dividing by 100 to express in dollars. Trading on futures is allowed on the open outcry (i.e., the trading floor) from 9:05 a.m. to 1:00 p.m. Central Standard Time Monday through Friday and on the CME Globex electronic trading platform continuously from 9:05 a.m. on Monday morning to 1:55 p.m. on Friday Central Standard Time. Globex trading is halted daily between 4:00 p.m. and 5:00 p.m. (CME Group 2013). Positions are limited to 6,300 contracts in any non-spot contract month (i.e., any maturity other than the nearest term future contract) and as high as 450 in the spot contract.

Futures contracts allow investors to trade with a small equity position, known as the *initial margin*. The margin requirement varies by contract, but is typically between 5 to 15 percent of the underlying position. The exchange requires initial margin to ensure that all participants in the futures market can honor their buy or sell positions. During the life of the contract, the exchange marks the position to the market price every day (i.e., changes in value are reflected directly in the margin account). If the position moves against one of the buyers or sellers, the exchange may initiate a margin call to request more cash to maintain the existing position. The *maintenance margin* is the smallest amount of margin an investor can have before receiving a margin call for additional funds. If the investor cannot supply the additional funds, called *variation margin*, the futures exchange will close the position on his behalf. The main purpose of margin in the futures exchange is to act as collateral and maintain an orderly system for trading.

Capital gains taxes are different for futures contracts than for other financial investments. In the United States, any profit is treated as 60 percent long-term capital gains and 40 percent short-term capital gains. Thus, when an investor reverses a futures contract, the taxes on any gains are taxed partially at the long-term capital gains rate and partially at the short-term capital gains rate. This tax advantage can make futures much more attractive for short-term traders than trading in underlying equities or other instruments. For natural hedgers that use futures, taxes are recognized differently depending on the net position of the underlying and the futures profits and losses due to hedging. A *natural hedger* is one that uses futures to hedge his real business risks, such as a coffee producer that sells coffee futures to hedge the risk of coffee price changes.

When trading futures, the volume and open interest of the contracts is important. *Volume* represents the number of transactions on a given day and indicates trading frequency and liquidity. *Open interest* is a count of all the transactions ever initiated for that contract. A larger open interest indicates more buyers and sellers of a futures contract. In some sense, open interest is analogous to the market capitalization of a stock. The *market capitalization* of a stock represents the total dollar value of all shares held by investors indicating the market value of the company.

Trading futures contracts for hedging purposes is not always simple and straightforward. If an investor is hedging for a specific short-term horizon and a futures contract with a maturity equal to that horizon is available, then the hedging process is less complicated. However, many hedgers need to hedge their positions for a longer horizon than the length of existing futures contracts, which forces them to roll their hedges forward. Rolling a hedge forward involves initially taking a shorter-term futures contract, reversing it before delivery, and taking another position in a contract that extends the hedge into the future. This rolling strategy introduces *rollover risk* into the hedging process, which is discussed later in the chapter. Occasions exist when the underlying asset does not have a matching futures contract. Thus, the investor must engage in *cross-hedging*, which involves using other futures contracts that are not perfectly correlated to the underlying asset. This process introduces another source of risk in hedging, known as *basis risk*. Finally, the question arises as to how much exposure to hedge. For example, an individual who wants to hedge an equity portfolio must decide whether to hedge the current value of the portfolio or the perceived future value of the portfolio.

THE PRICING OF FUTURES TRADING

Although the primary focus of this chapter is on using futures contracts to hedge risk, understanding the inherent pricing of futures can aid an investor who wants to hedge the contracts. Most of the theoretical pricing models for futures are developed based on eliminating arbitrage in the financial markets. Such modeling links the pricing of the spot rate in an asset to the futures rates with different maturities. However, different underlying financial instruments have different pricing schemes based on such idiosyncrasies as whether they are storable, exhibit seasonality, and have sufficient liquidity.

Using continuous compounding, the general relationship between the futures price, $F_{0,T}$, and the spot price, S_0, is given by Equation 25.1:

$$F_{0,T} = S_0 e^{(c-y)T}, \tag{25.1}$$

where c is the *cost of carry* for the underlying asset, which is the storage cost plus any interest required to finance the asset minus any income earned on the asset; y is the *convenience yield*, which represents a benefit to owning the asset; and e is a mathematical constant that is the base of the natural logarithm, representing continuous compounding of the returns.

For example, for equity futures on underlying equity indices, the cost of holding the asset is the "risk-free" rate of interest that could be obtained investing in short-term deposits and the benefit to holding the asset (the portfolio) is the dividend rates paid on the stocks. Thus, Equation 25.2 shows the relationship between the spot value of the equity index and the futures contract maturing at time T:

$$F_{0,T} = S_0 e^{(r-q)T}, \tag{25.2}$$

where r is the risk-free rate of interest and q is the dividend rate on the index. In this case, no convenience yield exists.

Some commodities such as gold can be loaned out (leased) and thus, income is generated to the holder of gold. Gold also incurs storage costs. In general, if the cost of storing gold is larger than the income from leasing, a positive storage cost exists and the relationship between a gold futures maturing at time T and the spot price of gold is exhibited in Equation 25.3:

$$F_{0,T} = S_0 e^{(r+u)T},$$ (25.3)

where r is the risk-free rate of interest and u is the net storage costs of gold.

In many markets, the futures relationship can be well specified in advance with reasonably known quantities. In some markets, however, the term structure of futures prices behaves rather oddly. The *term structure of futures prices* is the relationship between the maturities of future contracts and their corresponding price structure. In such cases, the only way to match the term structure of futures prices with the spot price is to add a term structure of convenience yields. Often, the term structure of convenience yields indicates some kind of demand and supply imbalance in the markets, but it is not always easy to determine. In some markets, the underlying commodity is not storable, which makes having a well-formed equation between the spot and futures markets impossible. Examples include the weather derivatives market because future weather cannot be stored, the electricity market because electricity is very difficult to store, and other markets that are somewhat difficult to store.

Concepts for Managing Risk

The idea of using futures contracts to hedge positions is quite simple. If an investor has financial exposure (a long position) to a good or financial instrument and wants to temporarily reduce this exposure, he can do so by selling a futures contract with a value changing in the opposite direction as the value of his underlying exposure. Because futures contracts have specific contract details that must be considered when hedging, a calculation is required to determine the number of contracts needed to offset underlying risk. Also, sometimes, the hedger cannot find a perfect hedge but must find a cross-hedge using a futures contract that is closely related to the underlying exposure. A cross-hedge, for example, would be hedging heating oil with crude oil futures. In order to determine the appropriate amount of hedging requires finding what is known as the *optimal hedge ratio.*

THE NUMBER OF FUTURES CONTRACTS TO HEDGE

Every futures contract has standardized specifications. Thus, if an investor or a company has a long exposure to 375,000 pounds of coffee, he will need to know how to translate that into the number of appropriate futures contracts to hedge the position. Equation 25.4 shows the general formula as:

$$N_f = \frac{N_A}{qS_0},$$ (25.4)

where N_f is the number of futures contracts needed to hedge the position; q is the futures contract multiplier; N_A is the notional value that the user would like to hedge; and S_0 is the underlying value of the index for equity portfolios and is equal to one for all other futures contracts. Thus, if the investor used coffee futures on the CME, then one contract represents 37,500 pounds of coffee. He should sell 10 coffee futures contracts: $N_f = 375,000/[(37,500)(1)]$.

For commodities where corresponding futures contracts exist, the hedging problem is relatively simple. However, often a future contract will not exist that is similar to the item that needs to be hedged. This situation makes determining the correct amount of futures contracts to buy to hedge more difficult.

THE OPTIMAL NUMBER OF FUTURES CONTRACTS

The purpose of hedging is to reduce or completely remove the changes in value from an underlying exposure over a specific time period. In mathematical terms, Equation 25.5 illustrates this relationship:

$$\Delta V_P = \Delta V_u - h\Delta V_f, \tag{25.5}$$

where ΔV_P is the change in the value of the entire position consisting of the underlying asset and the futures hedge; ΔV_u is the change in the value of the underlying asset; ΔV_f is the change in the value of the futures position; and h is the number of contracts hedged as chosen by the hedger. A hedger who wants to remove all risk of the underlying asset over the time horizon should choose a value of h that would make $\Delta V_P = 0$.

Several ways are available to compute the optimal hedge ratio including regressions on dollar returns as expressed in Equation 25.5, on percentage returns as expressed in Equation 25.6, and on log returns as expressed in Equation 25.6, but using log returns. In most cases, the differences are small and insignificant. In some cases, however, these differences matter and a hedger should be careful to compute hedges correctly. Terry (2005) provides a detailed discussion of this subject. Throughout this chapter, hedge ratios are computed from regression analysis on percentage returns. This actual hedge ratio should be multiplied by S_{t-1}/F_{t-1} to get true minimum variance hedges, but for most examples in this chapter, this ratio is very close to one.

The expression for hedging in percentage terms is done such that for every unit of the underlying asset hedged, one wants to choose an h, such that the returns of the underlying asset and the returns of the futures hedge offset each other as illustrated in Equation 25.6:

$$r_H = r_u - hr_f, \tag{25.6}$$

where r_H, r_u, and r_f are the total hedged returns, unhedged underlying returns, and futures returns, respectively. One way to choose the h is to use historical data to see how the changes in the futures prices are related to changes in the underlying asset and then to select the h that makes the entire position closest to zero. Mathematically, this is usually done by minimizing the variance of the deviation in returns as shown in Equation 25.7:

$$\min_{h} \text{Var}\left(r_u - hr_f\right). \tag{25.7}$$

One way to find the h that minimizes this variance is to estimate the parameters on historical data using a linear regression. Thus, a regression can be run on a sample of historical daily return data. Alternatively, another frequency such as monthly or quarterly may be chosen. Equation 25.8 shows the regression specification:

$$r_{u,t} = \alpha + \beta r_{f,t} + \varepsilon_t, \tag{25.8}$$

where the estimate of β, $\hat{\beta}$, is the estimate used for h, which is also known as the *optimal hedge ratio*. Equation 25.9 shows the more comprehensive formula for the number of futures contracts to purchase to hedge a position:

$$N_f = \frac{hN_A}{qS_0}, \tag{25.9}$$

where h is chosen from either a historical regression as described previously, or given a value of one for futures that trade on the exact equivalent underlying instrument, or chosen by a more complicated procedure. In this chapter, the focus is on $h = 1$ or the optimal h based upon regression analysis.

Selected Hedging Examples

This section uses the hedging concepts discussed previously with actual data to give real-world hedging examples. The nuances associated with some hedging examples are discussed.

EQUITIES

Portfolio managers often use futures contracts to hedge their portfolios. One example of such hedging needs might arise from worries in the market place. Suppose a portfolio manager is managing a $500 million dollar portfolio of U.S. equities. The portfolio is a mix of many different stocks but not perfectly related to any one of the major indices. If the portfolio were an exact replica of such indices as the S&P 500, Nasdaq, or DJIA, then the portfolio manager could use any of the futures contracts on these indices to hedge the portfolio with a hedging parameter, h, equal to one. Unfortunately, the portfolio is not exactly like these futures contracts.

Table 25.1 shows the estimated optimal hedge ratios for the portfolio using three types of futures contracts: the S&P 500 futures contract, Nasdaq futures contact, and DJIA futures contact. The optimal hedge ratios are estimated from different periods since 1990. Focusing on the beta estimates for the S&P 500 index, the beta estimates are very unstable over time. For example, the beta or optimal hedge ratio was 0.96 for the 1990–1994 period, but 0.60 for the 2005–2009 period. Additionally, the $\bar{R}^2$, a measure of the goodness of fit of the estimation, is very low ranging from 0.08 to 0.32. Overall, this indicates that these futures are not very suitable to hedge the returns of this portfolio.

Table 25.1 **Hedging Parameters for an Equity Portfolio over Various Horizons**

Time Period	Mean	Standard Deviation	S&P 500 Futures			
			Correlation	Beta	Constant	$\bar{R}^2$
1990–1994	22.51	19.96	0.57	0.96	0.01	0.32
1995–1999	23.80	26.51	0.45	0.83	0.00	0.19
2000–2004	11.17	21.47	0.31	0.41	0.01	0.08
2005–2009	4.00	17.92	0.54	0.60	0.00	0.28
1990–July 2013	15.53	20.98	0.43	0.60	0.01	0.18

	Nasdaq Futures			
	Correlation	Beta	Constant	$\bar{R}^2$
1990–1994	NA	NA	NA	NA
1995–1999	NA	NA	NA	NA
2000–2004	–0.06	–0.04	0.01	0.01
2005–2009	0.41	0.36	0.00	0.16
1990–July 2013	NA	NA	NA	NA

	Dow Jones Futures			
	Correlation	Beta	Constant	$\bar{R}^2$
1990–1994	NA	NA	NA	NA
1995–1999	NA	NA	NA	NA
2000–2004	0.37	0.48	0.01	0.12
2005–2009	0.57	0.67	0.00	0.31
1990–July 2013	NA	NA	NA	NA

Note: This figure contains hedging summary statistics for hedging a portfolio with the S&P 500, Nasdaq, and Dow Jones futures contracts over various periods of time. Mean is the average annualized return of the Berkshire Hathway portfolio. Standard deviation is the annualized standard deviation of monthly returns of the Berkshire Hathway portfolio. Correlation is the correlation of the futures contract with the Berkshire Hathaway stock return (the portfolio). Beta is the optimal hedge ratio estimated over the specific period between the futures contract and the portfolio. Constant is the constant in the OLS regression to estimate the optimal hedge ratio. $\bar{R}^2$ represents the fit of the OLS regression. NA is not available.

During this lifetime of this portfolio, two major drops in value are observed. The first drop of 42 percent occurred in the portfolio from April 30, 1999, to February 29, 2000. The second major drop in the value of this portfolio was during the financial crisis of 2007–2009. From December 31, 2007, to February 28, 2009, the portfolio dropped by 44 percent. If investors or portfolio managers had been worried about either the Internet bubble or the housing bubble, they might have used futures to hedge the portfolio from potential drops in the market.

Suppose the value of the portfolio on each of these start dates was $100 million, the portfolio manager wants to hedge the potential decline in the market and determines the best futures contract to use for this portfolio is the S&P 500 futures contact. On April 30, 1999, the portfolio manager would have sold short 251 contracts as illustrated in Equation 25.10:

$$N_f = \frac{hN_A}{qS_0} = \frac{0.8391\,(100M)}{250\,(1335.18)} = 251.38, \tag{25.10}$$

where the value of the S&P 500 index was 1335.18 on April 30, 1999, and the optimal hedge ratio was determined by a historical linear regression over the period January 1, 1990, to April 30, 1999. Thus, the portfolio manager would sell 251 contracts to hedge the entire portfolio. Although this sounds large, the S&P 500 futures contract is an extremely liquid contract and on April 30, 1999, had an open interest of 1,890,564 contracts and a volume on that day alone of 357,728 contracts. Thus, 251 contracts would represent a very small percentage of the overall volume in order to hedge this portfolio.

Another complication is that this hedge uses the near-term futures contract. Thus, the portfolio manager would have to roll over the near-term futures contract as it expired into the new near-term futures contract until the hedging horizon had passed. Although small costs are involved to rolling the contract forward, an overall evaluation of the performance of this hedging procedure is necessary because none of the futures contracts are very well suited to hedge this portfolio as previously established. Equation 25.11 defines the total profits or losses from the hedging program:

$$P/L = 100M\,(r_P) + N_f q\,(F_{t+k} - F_t), \tag{25.11}$$

where r_P is the total return of the portfolio over the investment horizon and $(F_{t+k} - F_t)$ is the difference in futures prices over the investment horizon from a continuous series of near-term futures rolls that includes the drag from rolling the futures.

Table 25.2 contains the hedging effectiveness over the two periods of distress for this portfolio. In the first period, the portfolio dropped by 42 percent, even though the S&P 500 index actually did not decline. Thus, the hedge actually worsened the performance of the manager. Although this result is disturbing for advocates of hedging, recall that in the regression output, the S&P 500 futures contracts were not a good hedge for this equity portfolio.

In the second period, the portfolio dropped by 44 percent and the S&P 500 futures contract dropped in value by about 50 percent. However, because the optimal hedge ratio was only 0.633, the resulting decline of the hedged position was only 32 percent. Overall, this relationship helped to reduce the losses of the main portfolio substantially. Thus, over the financial crisis period, the portfolio would have only dropped by 13 percent after accounting for the futures hedge. The futures hedge reduced the portfolio's losses by $32 million. Thus, despite the fact that the S&P 500 futures contract does not represent a good hedge instrument for this portfolio, it was able to provide a very useful cushion during a market crash. If the market increased, the futures contract would have limited the gains. This illustrates the role of hedging.

Table 25.2 **Hedging Effectiveness for a Portfolio during Market Downturns**

Period	Total Returns (%)			
	Portfolio	*Futures Position*	*Hedged Position*	*Dollars Saved*
April 30, 1999, to February 29, 2000	−42.40	2.22	−44.64	−2.2 million
December 31, 2007, to February 27, 2009	−44.49	−31.84	−12.65	32.0 million

Note: This table presents the total returns of the Berkshire Hathaway stock returns (the portfolio) over the given investment horizon. Futures position is the futures hedge position return over the investment horizon. Hedged position is the returns for the total position of the portfolio plus the hedged futures position. Dollars saved is the total number of dollars that were saved from an initial $100 million portfolio by hedging. The optimal hedge ratio used is 0.833 for the first period and 0.633 for the second period.

Using equity futures to hedge portfolios is useful in various circumstances. Chincarini (2004) notes one of the most unique circumstances. Mutual fund managers typically have small daily flows of new funds entering or exiting their portfolios. Thus, for most mutual funds, the daily cash management of the inflows and outflows is not a major issue. However, for some mutual funds that have large inflows and outflows near the end of the trading day, sufficient time or liquidity is not present to make the trades before the market closes. Thus, funds could be left with a large overnight cash position leaving them exposed to risk. One way to reduce this risk is to invest the large cash flows into equity futures, which trade after hours and have liquidity that the stock market may not possess. This arrangement can improve the returns for owners of the mutual fund.

FIXED INCOME

Fixed income futures are useful for various hedging purposes. For example, a portfolio manager might want to use the probability of the Fed raising or lowering of interest rates as a method to hedge a position on the slope of the yield curve. The first step for the portfolio manager is to compute the probability that the Fed will raise rates from market prices. The methodology of Bieri and Chincarini (2005) is used for this purpose. Futures-based expectations before a Federal Open Market Committee (FOMC) meeting can be interpreted as a meaningful measure of the target rate expected to prevail after the meeting only if the target rate is not changed between meetings and never twice in the same month. Although the Chicago Board of Trade (CBOT) introduced Fed funds futures in October 1988, it was not until 1994 that the FOMC began announcing changes in its policy stance and abandoned inter-meeting rate changes. Equation 25.14 shows the rate implied by the Fed funds futures contract is defined as a time-weighted average of a pre-meeting and expected post-meeting target rate:

$$i_t^f = i_t^{\text{pre}} \frac{d_1}{B} + \left[p i_t^{\text{post}} + (1 - p) i_t^{\text{pre}} \right] \frac{d_2}{B}, \tag{25.14}$$

where i_t^f is the futures rate implied by relevant contract; i_t^{pre} is the target rate prevailing before the FOMC meeting; i_t^{post} is the target rate expected to prevail after the FOMC meeting; p is the probability of a target rate change; d_1 is the number of days between previous month end and FOMC meeting; d_2 is the number of days between FOMC meeting and current month end; and B is the number of days in month. Solving Equation 25.14 for p, Equation 25.15 shows the probability of a change in the target rate.

$$p = \frac{i_t^f - i_t^{pre}\left(\frac{d_1}{B} + \frac{d_2}{B}\right)}{\left(i_t^{post} - i_t^{pre}\right)\frac{d_2}{B}}. \tag{25.15}$$

Besides assuming no inter-meeting changes, this specification also assumes that the Fed has only two policy options: shift the target rate by a pre-specified amount or leave it unchanged. For ease of computation, this amount is assumed to be 25 basis points because the Fed has not changed rates by any other amount since August 1989. For example on March 2, 2000, the Fed fund target rate was 5.75 percent. Fed fund futures were trading at 5.83 percent. The FOMC meeting was scheduled for March 21, 2013. Using the formula above, one could calculate that the probability of a Fed tightening (raising rates by 25 bps) was at 65.88 percent.

Given the estimated probability of a Fed tightening, the portfolio manager with a flattening or steeping yield curve trade, may have wanted to alter this by using futures contracts of different maturities. Galitz (1995), Bieri and Chincarini (2005), Chincarini (2012), and Fabozzi (2012) provide more information about this method of hedging and other more complicated methods.

COMMODITIES

Commodity futures are very important futures contracts because they allow businesses and farmers to hedge the uncertainties of their businesses. This section discusses some commodities and their relationship to hedging practices.

Soybeans

For typical bond or equity investors, soybeans illustrate the vast differences between agricultural markets and strictly financial markets. At any given time, soybean futures trade actively for many maturity dates up to three years. Thus, hedgers can hedge the price risk of soybeans up to three years without having to roll their contracts.

Although most financial futures have a term structure that is slightly upward sloping due to the cost of interest, many commodity markets including soybeans have oddly shaped term structures. Figure 25.1 shows the soybean term structure as of September 30, 2011. The relationship between the spot price of a commodity and the futures price is complex. Soybean futures tend to have higher futures prices in expiration months during planting season, while having lower futures prices in expiration months during harvesting season. In theory, this makes sense. More risk to soybeans exists during the planting season because of limited supply. However, during the harvesting season, the market is flooded with supply and prices tend to be lower. Of course,

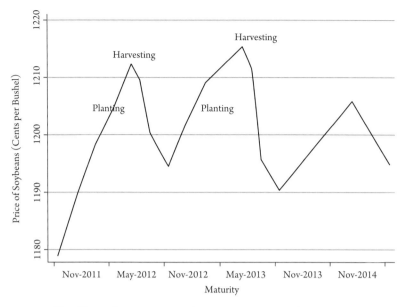

Figure 25.1 THE TERM STRUCTURE OF SOYBEAN PRICES ON SEPTEMBER 30, 2011.
This figure presents the price of soybeans in cents per bushel for soybean futures contracts
of different maturities as of September 30, 2011. Planting refers to the time period when
farmers typically plant soybeans and harvesting refers to the time period where farmers
typically harvest soybeans.

the shape of the term structure of soybean prices depends on the sensitive interaction
between the types of hedgers and speculators in this market.

Coffee

A coffee farmer may want to use coffee futures to hedge the future price of coffee during harvest time. If coffee prices drop due to a fall in demand, a lower price could lead to a loss in profits for the farmer. Another example of a natural coffee hedger might be a coffee retailer, such as Coffee Bean, Starbucks, or another coffee shop. Such retailers must continuously buy coffee from coffee farmers. If prices suddenly rise, profits could decline, and the coffee store may be forced to pass on higher input costs to its consumers.

The process for hedging coffee is similar to that of other commodities. After determining the volume to hedge, the hedger must choose the appropriate coffee futures contract and number of contracts and initiate the transaction. For example, if a retail store purchases coffee beans to make coffee and wants to hedge the possibility of an increase in future coffee prices, it can use coffee futures traded on the New York Mercantile Exchange (NYMEX). Suppose the estimated purchase was for 400,000 pounds of coffee. Each coffee future represents 37,500 pounds of coffee. Thus, the coffee retailer would ideally want to purchase 10.66 contracts. Because fractional contract positions are impossible, the retailer may choose to purchase 10 or 11 contracts. In the summer of 2010, this strategy would have benefited retailers tremendously. Dunkin Donuts, Green Mountain, Maxwell House, and Starbucks suffered from the rise in coffee prices passing some increases onto consumers in the form of higher prices.

Continuing this example, the cost of coffee was $1.37 per pound (using near-term futures) on June 10, 2010. During the summer, due to bad weather in South America, coffee prices rose to $1.931 per pound by September 8, 2010. On those two days, futures prices of the July 2011 contract were $1.4035 and $1.921 per pound, respectively. Thus, for a coffee retailer that did not hedge, coffee costs rose based on an example of 400,000 pounds by $224,000. A retailer that hedged coffee prices using July 2011 coffee futures would have observed an increase in their futures position of $194,062.50 or $213,468.75, depending on whether the retailer used 10 or 11 futures contracts, respectively. Thus, the hedged position would have resulted in net increase in coffee costs of just $30,337.50 or $10,931.25 depending on the number of contracts. This arrangement would have permitted the coffee retailer to gain a competitive edge with consumers. A strategic issue with hedging is whether one's competitors' hedge. If so, a given retailer may decide to hedge.

Another example of how futures can hedge uncertainties relates to Hurricane Katrina. This Atlantic tropical cyclone with winds as high as 174 miles per hour hit New Orleans over the period from August 23, 2005, to August 30, 2005, resulting in 1,833 deaths. One generally unknown implication of Hurricane Katrina is that it caused coffee futures prices to soar. This relationship may seem odd as New Orleans is not a center for coffee production. However, New Orleans houses a warehouse with around 27 percent of the U.S. inventory of coffee beans. At the time, this percentage translated to about 1.6 million bags of coffee. Markets were worried initially that the hurricane had damaged the coffee in the warehouses. The futures price of coffee rose by 5.8 percent and 4.2 percent for September and December futures, respectively, over the period from August 22, 2005, to September 1, 2005. When investors realized that the hurricane had not damaged the warehouse, futures prices dropped by 3.7 percent and 4.7 percent, respectively, between August 22 and September 8. Proctor & Gamble and Sara Lee also processed much of their coffee in New Orleans at the time as well. Fortunately, the disaster did not have a major effect on coffee production. Companies concerned about this possibility could have used coffee futures to hedge this risk.

Natural Gas

Natural gas futures trade on the NYMEX and Intercontinental Exchange (ICE) with maturities extended to five years. Figure 25.2 illustrates that the term structure of natural gas has an appearance similar to a sine or cosine curve. This behavior is partly due to the fact that the majority of homes (56 percent) as well as many restaurants, lodging facilities, offices, hospitals, and retail buildings in the United States use natural gas. Natural gas also generates about one-fifth of the domestically produced electricity in the United States. Much greater demand exists in winter months than in summer months. Natural gas is difficult to transport. Thus, as storage tanks are filled in summer and depleted in the winter, the price of natural gas increases.

The term structure in natural gas has led to considerable speculation in natural gas markets, including the bets that led to the collapse of Amaranth Advisors (Chincarini 2007a, 2008, 2013b). In order for liquidity to exist for natural hedgers of a commodity such as natural gas, speculators must enter the market and/or natural hedgers must have a different line of business that requires the opposite hedge. Amaranth Advisors speculated on the behavior of natural gas futures of different calendar months.

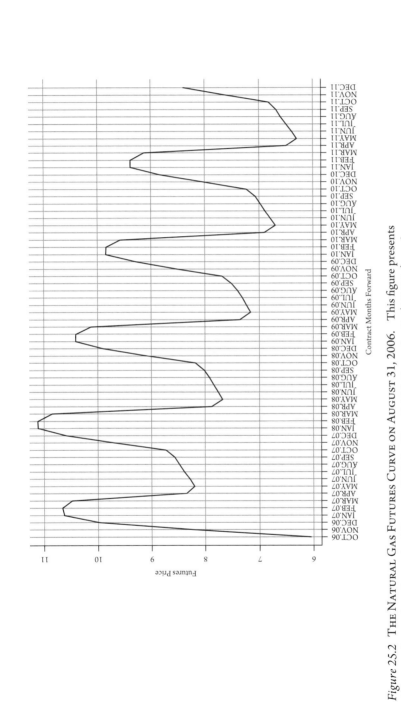

Figure 25.2 The Natural Gas Futures Curve on August 31, 2006. This figure presents the price of natural gas futures in dollars per 10,000 million British thermal units (MMBtu) as of August 31, 2006. For example, Dec 06 refers to the natural gas futures that expire in December 2006.

The firm essentially took long positions on winter month contracts and short positions on summer month contracts. Although this position was speculative, the hedge fund itself was hedging some of its risk by entering into long and short positions. That is, Amaranth Advisors was attempting to hedge general movements in natural gas prices. Unfortunately, the firm took positions in the natural gas market much too large relative to the size of its hedge fund and ultimately went bankrupt when market prices moved against Amaranth Advisors.

Natural hedgers can use natural gas futures contracts to hedge the fluctuations in the demand for heating in winter months and/or the demand for air conditioning in summer months. Due to the natural gas futures pattern, winter hedgers typically pay more for hedging than summer hedgers. However, in recent years, the premium for winter months is less pronounced, which makes winter hedging less expensive. Many reasons may explain this recent pattern including the more efficient use of liquefied natural gas.

Frozen Concentrated Orange Juice

Anyone familiar with the movie *Trading Places* is aware of the key role played by frozen concentrated orange juice (FCOJ) futures. In the movie, the characters of Winthorpe and Valentine get an advanced viewing of a crop report and make a fortune selling FCOJ at a higher price. Although these characters represent the speculators, rather than hedgers, many businesses involved in the production and distribution of orange juice can benefit by using FCOJ futures to hedge possible price uncertainties.

Changes in weather conditions in orange-producing regions can cause dramatic effects on orange prices as supply might be limited. Florida is the world's second largest orange producer after Brazil. Thus, in January 2012, when freezing temperatures in Florida damaged the orange crop, FCOJ prices skyrocketed. This situation can be particularly problematic for businesses that rely on buying or selling of oranges. In December of 2011, the average price of the March 2012 FCOJ futures contract was $1.67 per pound. By January 10, 2012 when the problems emerging from the freeze became evident, prices rose to $2.08 per pound. That is, FCOJ futures prices rose by 24 percent. This type of increase could be disastrous for a business in the orange industry and hedging might have been beneficial.

Crude Oil

Many businesses use oil as an input to their production process. Thus, changing oil prices can lead to a profit or loss unrelated to the core function of their businesses. As a result, many airline companies, trucking companies, and other businesses use oil futures to lock in their future oil price costs. The concept is similar to the hedging of other underlying securities. In 2011, oil expenses represented 38 percent or $6.1 billion of Southwest Airlines' operating costs. Southwest Airlines (2013, p. 4) stated:

> In 2012, the Company again experienced significant fuel and oil expense as fuel prices remained volatile and at historically high levels. In addition, for the eighth consecutive year Fuel and oil expense represented the Company's largest or second largest cost and was the Company's largest cost for the second consecutive year.

The Company enters into fuel derivative contracts to manage its risk associated with significant increases in fuel prices; however, because energy prices
can fluctuate significantly in a relatively short amount of time, the Company
must also continually monitor and adjust its fuel hedge portfolio and strategies
to address not only fuel price increases, but also fuel price volatility and hedge
collateral requirements.

One problem with hedging the price of jet fuel is that it is typically unavailable for
trading on exchanges. Thus, airlines use cross-hedging with products that are not perfectly correlated with the underlying movements of jet fuel as illustrated by Southwest
Airlines (2013, p. 25):

Because jet fuel is not widely traded on an organized futures exchange, there
are limited opportunities to hedge directly in jet fuel. However, the Company
has found that financial derivative instruments in other commodities, such
as West Texas Intermediate (WTI) crude oil, Brent crude oil, and refined
products, such as heating oil and unleaded gasoline, can be useful in decreasing its exposure to jet fuel price volatility.

The actual details of Southwest's hedging program are publicly unavailable. However, assuming that the firm uses a combination of OTC or customized derivatives as
well as oil futures, Southwest might select West Texas Intermediate (WTI) Crude oil
futures or Brent Crude oil futures. Suppose the airline wanted to lock-in the price of
142,000 gallons of fuel based on expected use over the next three months and choose to
hedge with WTI futures. Each contract represents 1,000 barrels and each barrel represents 42 gallons of oil. Thus, one contract represents 42,000 gallons of oil. However, the
airline company is interested in hedging jet fuel costs, rather than crude oil prices.

Collecting data on an index of jet fuel prices (e.g., from Bloomberg's New York
Harbor 54-grade Jet Fuel Spot Market index), a regression analysis of the movement
in crude oil futures prices in comparison to jet fuel returns can illustrate implementing a
hedging strategy. Depending on the contract maturity selected, the hedging parameters
can differ. For example, over the 1995–2013 period, the optimal hedge ratio for crude
oil for the 1-, 3-, 6-, 12-, and 24-month contract was 0.86, 0.97, 1.10, 1.22, and 1.22,
respectively. Using the one-year futures contract to hedge 142,000 gallons of jet oil,
Equation 25.16 shows the number of contracts needed:

$$N_f = \frac{hN_A}{qS_0} = \frac{1.22(142,000)}{42,000} = 4.124. \tag{25.16}$$

Thus, Southwest could take a long position on four WTI futures contracts (rounded to
the nearest whole number). If oil prices rise in the next year, the airline will pay more
for fuel, but this increase will be offset by the gains on the futures contracts.

Consider an investor who wants to hedge jet fuel risk using WTI oil futures contracts.
A simple method to study this relationship is to back test the hedging strategy. Starting
at the end of 1999, a regression from 1995 to 1999 is used to compute the optimal hedge
ratio based on the purchase of a two-year futures contract for the purpose of comparing

the gains/losses at the end of the two-year horizon on the cost of fuel compared to the gains/losses from the futures hedging. The process is repeated for the next two-year period in order to produce out-of-sample results.

Figure 25.3 shows the change in costs over each two-year hedging period from 2000 to 2012. For each period, the first bar in the graph represents the change in costs in jet fuel. Thus, if positive, this means that jet fuel became more expensive by a given percentage. The second number represents percentage change in profits from the crude oil futures hedge. Thus, a positive number reflects a positive gain on the future's position. The third number represents the net change in costs to the firm when combining both the futures position and the change in the costs of jet fuel.

Over the 2002–2004 period, the cost of jet fuel per gallon rose by 62 percent. This change would have been devastating for an airline. By using a two-year futures contract to hedge with a historical optimal hedge ratio, the futures position generated a return of 132 percent. Thus, the hedge did not serve as a perfect hedge, but it did generate an additional 70 percent in revenue. A similar story occurred over the 2004–2006 period. Over the 2008–2010 and 2010–2012 periods, the futures strategy worked more effectively as a hedge. Although jet fuel prices increased by 39 percent from 2010 to 2012, the futures hedge generated a 31 percent return leaving the net increase in costs of about 8 percent.

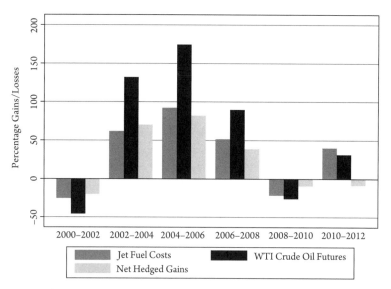

Figure 25.3 THE HEDGING PERFORMANCE OF JET FUEL USING WEST TEXAS INTERMEDIATE OIL FUTURES.   This figure presents the returns for jet fuel costs, WTI crude oil futures, and a hedged portfolio. Jet fuel costs represent the percentage change in price for jet fuel prices over the specified period. The WTI crude oil futures represent the percentage change in price for crude oil futures over the same period. The net hedged gains are the returns to a hedger that is hedging the price of jet fuel costs with crude oil futures. For example, in the period 2002–2004, jet fuel costs increased by 62 percent, WTI crude oil futures increased by 132 percent, and thus the net hedged gains increased by 70 percent.

Overall, hedging using oil futures can be very useful. An example of the intricacies of oil hedging and how hedging using futures can go wrong is the Metallgesellschaft debacle (Culp and Miller 1994). This study shows that a strategy of using futures to hedge forward contracts may fail dramatically when contracts need to be rolled over and margin calls occur on the futures contracts.

FOREIGN EXCHANGE

The foreign exchange market is one of the largest markets in the world facilitating global business. Many international companies sell their products in multiple countries and have offices in multiple countries. The revenues, profits, and costs of these businesses fluctuate for various reasons such as changes in the prices of inputs, demand for products, and value of the exchange rate between countries. Many businesses prefer to smooth the fluctuations due to exchange rate movements and do so by hedging with either currency futures or options.

Portfolio managers also invest in financial instruments in multiple countries in equities and bonds. Often, these global portfolio managers have specific skill in finding relatively valuable equity or bond markets, but have no opinion about the direction of the currency. Thus, their portfolios might be unnecessarily harmed by exchange rate fluctuations, and they may choose to hedge this exposure through currency futures. Other portfolio managers may have more active views on currencies and use currency futures to hedge parts of this risk and enhance other parts of this risk.

Consider a global portfolio manager who invests in equities in the United States, Europe, and Japan. In order to simplify the analysis, the S&P 500, Euro Stoxx 50, and Nikkei 225 indices will serve as proxies for the international equity portfolios. The analysis covers the 2000–2013 period. From 1995 to 2000, the optimal hedge ratios are estimated based on a regression of currency spot on the three-month futures returns (Chincarini 2007b). Both these estimates and a hedge ratio of one can be used to compare the return-risk characteristics of the portfolios with and without hedging. In order to compute the optimal hedge ratios, the parameters must be estimated that minimize the variance of the dollar-hedged portfolio returns minus the local currency returns. Equation 25.17 illustrates how to minimize the variance:

$$R_\$^H - R = \sum_{i=1}^N w_i s_i (1 + R_i) - \sum_{j=1}^N h_j R_{j,F}, \tag{25.17}$$

where $R_\$^H - R$ is the dollar portfolio returns minus the local currency returns; w_i is the weight of the portfolio in each of the three equity markets; s_i is the currency return; R_i is the equity return in country i's local currency; h_j is the hedging parameter for each currency; and $R_{j,F}$ is the return of the futures contract in each currency. Chincarini (2007b) offers more details associated with this calculation. In order to compute the optimal hedge parameters, h, Equation 25.18 estimates the following linear regression over the in-sample period:

$$\sum_{i=1}^N w_i s_i (1 + R_i) = \alpha + \beta_1 R_{1,F} + \beta_2 R_{2,F} + \beta_3 R_{3,F} + \varepsilon, \tag{25.18}$$

where β_i is the estimate for each currency's optimal hedge ratio, h.

The hedge ratios estimated from 1995 to 2000 are 0.44 for Europe and 0.20 for Japan. The link between European and Japanese near-term futures to the spot exchange rate is strong. Table 25.3 shows the result of maintaining this hedging parameter for the entire hedging period and comparing it to not hedging and a hedge ratio of one in each currency.

From Table 25.3, if the portfolio manager had no currency risk whatsoever (a theoretical concept), the portfolio return would have been –9.69 percent over the 13 years. This result is attributable primarily to the financial crisis of 2007–2008 that caused equity markets to collapse. The S&P 500 index partially recovered posting a return over the period of 14.73 percent. However, the Japanese market was down 27.81 percent and the Europe market by nearly 44 percent over this period.

The unhedged portfolio did better by 4 percent over the period. The main reason for this was that the Euro appreciated relative to the U.S. dollar (32.22 percent) and the Japanese Yen also appreciated but to a lesser degree (4.72 percent). Thus, the currency return helped offset the poor returns from these countries. These findings might also suggest that during this period the Fed engaged in more monetary easing than did the European Central Bank. The hedged portfolio with weights equal to the initial weights in the portfolio without rebalancing these weights led to a –12.31 percent return

Table 25.3 **Global Portfolio Currency Hedging Performance**

	Total Return	Standard Deviation	Maximum	Minimum
Local currency portfolio	–9.69	4.41	10.29	–18.92
Unhedged portfolio	–5.03	4.70	10.37	–18.43
Hedged ($h = 1$)	–12.31	4.70	23.51	–5.30
Hedged (optimal parameters)	–19.52	4.70	15.60	–13.20
S&P 500	14.73	4.44	13.18	–21.76
Euro Stoxx 50	–43.56	5.43	14.69	–21.48
Nikkei 225	–27.81	5.79	20.07	–23.83
Dollar–Euro Spot	32.22	3.10	10.10	–9.66
Dollar–Yen Spot	4.72	3.35	17.67	–9.24
Dollar–Euro 1st Future	31.29	3.05	9.61	–9.86
Dollar–Yen 1st Future	3.43	3.33	17.33	–9.70

Note: This table presents the returns and volatility from a global equity portfolios invested in the United States, Japan, and Europe at the start of 2000 until the end of July 2013. Initial portfolio weights were 50 percent in the S&P 500 index, 30 percent in the Nikkei 225, and 20 percent in the Euro Stoxx 50. Local currency is the theoretical return to investing in each local currency. Unhedged is the global portfolio return without currency hedging; Hedged ($h = 1$) is hedging with a hedge equal to the weight of the portfolio in each currency. Hedged (optimal parameters) is the hedging based on the linear regression optimal parameters estimated from 1995 to 2000. Returns are in percent. Standard deviation is the monthly standard deviation of returns. Maximum and minimum are maximum and minimum monthly returns over the period, respectively.

over the period. This was also true of the optimally hedged portfolio, which produced the worse return at –19.52 percent. These results were due to being short the foreign currencies during a time that they actually did better than the U.S. dollar.

The monthly return volatility of both hedged and unhedged portfolios was comparable. If a positive attribute can be assigned for hedging over this period, it is reflected in the minimum monthly return. The worst monthly return for the hedged portfolios was –5.30 percent (hedged with $h = 1$) and –13.20 percent (for optimally hedged). This result is better than the unhedged portfolio. Nevertheless, over this time horizon and for this particular portfolio invested in the United States, Japan, and Europe, a decision not to hedge the currency risk would have resulted in superior results.

In addition to hedging currency risk, portfolios can be constructed to provide an average real return or protect the investor against inflation risk (Bruno and Chincarini 2010a, 2010b, 2011). An exchange traded fund (ETF) with ticker symbol CPI has recently made this type of hedging available to investors.

REAL ESTATE

Real estate is a major investment for many individuals. A massive price appreciation or bubble in real estate prices occurred from 1999 to 2007 followed by the crash of real estate prices from 2007 to 2009. A resurgence in the real estate market prices occurred from 2009 to 2013.

Until recently, trading or hedging real estate risk was very difficult. In 2006, the CME introduced real estate futures contracts for many of the major metropolitan cities in the United States. Thus, investors theoretically could use these futures to hedge exposure to real estate. Such investors could include investment groups holding stakes in real estate portfolios, mortgage portfolio investors, construction companies or real estate developers, and individual homeowners planning on selling or buying in the future.

Unfortunately, these future contracts might not be very useful for hedging. Bertus, Hollans, and Swidler (2008) investigate how well Las Vegas home price futures contracts could hedge Las Vegas real estate housing exposure. Their evidence shows that these futures do not work well for construction companies that build in a very specific region. Real estate futures are also less useful for new housing construction because the futures are based on indices that consider repeat sales. Bertus et al. also find a very unstable hedging parameter over time. Because the authors use the underlying indices and not the futures contract, they ignore another important problem: real estate futures prices trade at premiums, which may erode the value from any hedging over a specific horizon.

The premium problem can be understood by examining trading on May 16, 2013. As Table 25.4 shows, the futures prices on this day implied that San Francisco home prices were expected to increase by 23 percent over the next two and a half years, by 18 percent in Los Angeles, 18 percent in Washington, DC, and 16 percent in Miami. Thus, if a hedger wanted to hedge real estate prices in San Francisco for two and a half years, they would pay a 22.65 percent premium, which might defeat the purpose of hedging the price risk (Chincarini 2013a). Gorton and Rouwenhorst (2006) provide additional information on the returns from commodity futures.

Table 25.4 **The Market's Prediction of Housing Prices**

Period	San Francisco	Los Angeles	Washington, DC	Miami
May 16, 2013	148.23	182.04	186.57	153.97
May 13	150.20	184.60	187.40	154.60
August 13	159.40	193.60	196.00	158.80
November 13	164.00	198.80	200.40	164.00
February 14	162.40	196.60	198.80	162.40
May 14	161.60	194.60	198.40	162.60
August 14	167.00	200.60	199.80	166.20
November 14	171.00	206.60	207.20	170.00
May 15	166.20	200.60	199.00	167.60
November 15	176.40	211.20	213.40	175.00
November 16	181.80	215.60	220.40	178.80
Implied return (%)	22.65	18.44	18.13	16.13

Note: This table presents futures contracts for home prices in four U.S. cities as of May 16, 2013. The futures contracts are based upon the underlying value of the Case-Shiller home prices indices. The implied return is the implied returns of futures contracts from May 16, 2013, to November 2016 ignoring interest rate changes.

Because real estate futures are thinly traded, determining whether any company or individual can use them to hedge a substantially large position is unclear. For example, on May 16, 2013, a total of nine positions existed in these contracts for the city of San Francisco. This dynamic limits the ability of using these futures. The illiquidity in these contracts may partly stem from the fact that some real estate futures are not very useful in hedging housing exposure. Future research should consider studying both the ability of futures prices to accurately predict housing prices and the effectiveness of hedging over various horizons after accounting for the premium cost.

WEATHER

Weather futures contracts for various cities trade based on the temperature, amount of rainfall, and amount of snowfall. The CME introduced weather derivatives in 1999. These futures are based on the underlying temperature in 18 U.S. cities, 9 European cities, and 2 Asian cities. The futures prices are based on heating degree days (HDD) and cooling degree days (CDD) in each city. These are measures of heat and cold and are computed using a specific formula (Chincarini 2011).

A natural gas or oil supplier to the city might have *volumetric risk*, which is based on external factors that may affect the demand for the supplier's product. For example, if a particular city is warmer than usual during the winter, the residents will demand less natural gas or oil to heat their homes. Thus, a company may want to hedge this risk by using weather futures.

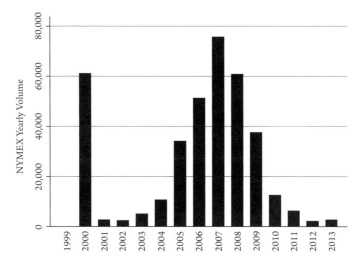

Figure 25.4 THE TOTAL VOLUME OF HDD WEATHER FUTURES ON THE NYMEX. This figure presents the yearly volume of HDD weather futures traded on the NYMEX for all cities in the United States. The yearly volume was computed by adding up the total volume on every day of the year for every city in which HDD futures trade.

On any given day, a hedger can buy or sell the HDD or CDD contracts. The HDD contract size is $20. Thus, on February 28, 2006, the March monthly HDD contract for Atlanta closed at 305. This quote indicated that one futures contract would represent the exposure of $6, 100 ($20 × 305). Of course, the number of futures contracts would be determined by the dollar amount that the business would like to hedge. In March 2006, Atlanta was colder than expected. Thus, the month's HDD at maturity was 349 and was the closing value of the futures contract. Thus, a hedger who bought this contract to hedge against a warmer winter would have lost $880 per futures contract. Of course, the increased heating demand in Atlanta would have offset this loss.

For a hedger of the weather, the market should be efficient otherwise, the futures hedger may overpay or underpay for protection. Chincarini (2011) shows that despite being a relatively new market and having lower volume than more established futures markets, the weather futures market is very efficient. In fact, the market for futures is so efficient that it predicts future weather better than the forecasts produced by the National Weather Service MOS Global Forecast System. This situation is reassuring for using these markets to hedge volumetric risk in various cities of the world.

As Figure 25.4 shows, from its inception in 1999, the weather futures market peaked in trading volume in 2007. Since then, the market volume has declined, which could relate to low natural gas prices and thus a lower need to hedge.

Summary and Conclusions

This chapter introduced the concept of managing business risk using futures contracts. Hedging is very useful for various businesses. Applications include a portfolio manager managing equities, bonds, commodities, real estate, or any other investment. It also includes main street corporations that want to hedge the uncertainties of prices or quantity demanded of their business products.

Hedging risks requires an understanding of what futures contracts are available for hedging as well as a methodology for finding the correct amount of futures contracts to hedge. The chapter discussed several methods to obtain the correct hedge ratio for different futures contracts. Besides finding the correct amount of futures contracts to hedge, measuring ex post the performance of the hedges is also important. In some of examples, the hedge was not extremely useful, while in other examples the hedge was very useful. This depended on several factors including whether the futures contract was closely related to the investment being hedged, whether the future correlation of the futures and the investment remained as it did in the past, and whether losses from rolling the futures contracts through time existed. Overall, the results were quite reassuring when the investor used the optimal hedge ratio to hedge the investment.

Some futures contracts have storable commodities, allowing for investment arbitrage, which makes these markets efficient. However, even in markets where the storage of the underlying asset is impossible and thus also makes arbitrage impossible, hedgers can use futures to hedge their business risk because these markets can often be as efficient as storable good markets.

Although the benefits of using futures to manage business risk are enormous, every hedging opportunity must be handled differently. A hedger should be aware of the basic concepts of hedging and analyze them carefully before engaging in a futures hedge. This means that a hedger should look beyond the simple models of this chapter to more advanced techniques in estimating the optimal hedge ratio. These include more sophisticated econometric models that have been extensively researched during the last 20 years.

Acknowledgments

The author thanks Jim Angel for detailed comments as well as Frank Ohara, Nicholas Tay, Jim Riley, and Steven Yau for other helpful comments. The author also thanks Brandon Carlson, Prescilla Gines, Duc Ta, Zach Hoffman, Sutinee Tangsirivanich, Odontuya Natsagdorj, and Siradee Techasrisuko for their research assistance.

Discussion Questions

1. Comment on the validity of the following statement. "A naive ratio of one is completely useless for hedging. Either find the optimal hedge ratio or don't hedge at all."
2. Discuss whether hedging is useless in markets where the commodity is not storable given the lack of a relationship tying the futures price to the spot price.
3. Discuss whether an airline company can hedge its oil demand given that jet oil futures do not trade with sufficient liquidity on the exchanges.
4. Describe how hedgers can use weather futures and commodity futures to hedge both price and quantity risk simultaneously.
5. Explain why some hedging techniques might be superior to others.

References

Angel, James, and Douglas M. McCabe. 2009. "The Ethics of Speculation." *Journal of Business Ethics* 90:3 Supplement, 277–286.

Bank of International Settlements. 2010. "Triennial Central Bank Survey—Foreign Exchange and Derivative Market Activity." *Monetary and Economics Department Publication*, September. Basil, Switzerland: Bank of International Settlements.

Bertus, Mark, Harris Hollans, and Steve Swidler. 2008. "Hedging House Price Risk with CME Futures Contracts: The Case of Las Vegas Residential Real Estate." *Journal of Real Estate Financial Economics* 37:3, 265–279.

Bieri, David, and Ludwig Chincarini. 2005. "Riding the Yield Curve: A Variety of Strategies." *Journal of Fixed Income* 15:2, 6–35.

Bruno, Salvatore, and Ludwig Chincarini. 2010a. "A Historical Examination of Optimal Real Return Portfolios for Non-US Investors." *Review of Financial Economics* 19:4, 161–178.

Bruno, Salvatore, and Ludwig Chincarini. 2010b. "Optimal Real Return Portfolios." *Investments and Wealth Monitor*, July/August, 35–39.

Bruno, Salvatore, and Ludwig Chincarini. 2011. "A Multi-Asset Approach to Inflation Hedging for a US Investor." *Journal of Portfolio Management* 37:3, 102–115.

Chincarini, Ludwig. 2004. "Managing Cash Flows in Sector Portfolios." *Derivatives Uses, Trading, and Regulation* 10:1, 27–45.

Chincarini, Ludwig. 2007a. "The Amaranth Debacle: Failure of Risk Measures or Failure of Risk Management." *Journal of Alternative Investments* 10:3, 91–104.

Chincarini, Ludwig. 2007b. "The Effectiveness of Global Currency Hedging after the Asian Crisis." *Journal of Asset Management* 8:1, 34–51.

Chincarini, Ludwig. 2008. "A Case Study on Risk Management: Lessons from the Collapse of Amaranth Advisors, L.L.C." *Journal of Applied Finance* 18:1, 152–174.

Chincarini, Ludwig. 2011. "No Chills or Burns from Temperature Surprises: An Empirical Analysis of the Weather Derivatives Market." *Journal of Futures Markets* 31:1, 1–33.

Chincarini, Ludwig. 2012. *The Crisis of Crowding. Quant Copycats, Ugly Models, and the New Crash Normal.* Hoboken, NJ: John Wiley & Sons, Inc.

Chincarini, Ludwig. 2013a. "Should You Put Your Money in Real Estate?" Available at http://ludwigbc.com/should-you-put-your-money-in-real-estate/.

Chincarini, Ludwig. 2013b. "A Case Study of Amaranth Advisors." In Betty J. Simkins and Russell Simkins, eds., *Energy, Finance, and Economics*, 543–578. Hoboken, NJ: John Wiley & Sons.

CME Group. 2013. *CME Rulebook.* Chicago: CME Group. Available at http://www.cmegroup.com/rulebook/CME/.

Culp, Christopher, and Merton Miller. 1994. "Hedging a Flow of Commodity Deliveries with Futures: Lessons from Metallgesellschaft." *Derivatives Quarterly,* Fall, 7–15.

Fabozzi, Frank. 2012. *Bond Markets, Analysis and Strategies.* Upper Saddle River, NJ: Prentice-Hall.

Galitz, Lawrence. 1995. *Financial Engineering: Tools and Techniques to Manage Financial Risk.* Burr Ridge, IL: McGraw-Hill.

Gorton, Gary, and K. Geert Rouwenhorst. 2006. "Facts and Fantasies about Commodity Futures." *Financial Analysts Journal* 62:2, 47–68.

Riley, Jim. 2004. "The Commodities Market: Yesterday, Today, and as a Career." November 30. Available at http://ludwigbc.com/rileycommodities/.

Southwest Airlines. 2013. "Annual Report." *Southwest Airlines Annual Report*, February 6.

Terry, Eric. 2005. "Minimum-Variance Futures Hedging under Alternative Return Specifications." *Journal of Futures Markets* 25:6, 537–552.

26

Swaps

DIMITRIS TSOUKNIDIS

Senior Lecturer in Finance, European Business School London, Regent's University London

ELIAS BOUKRAMI

Principal Lecturer in Banking and Finance, European Business School London,
Regent's University London

Introduction

This chapter examines the basic types of swaps contracts, their uses and properties, and their effectiveness in hedging different types of risks. Swaps form an important class of derivatives contracts that may be used for risk management purposes and applications. A *swap agreement* is typically an over-the-counter (OTC) agreement between two parties to exchange their future cash flows. The cash flows to be "swapped" are calculated on the basis of a notional value for a reference asset. Typically, the swap agreement explicitly states the dates and terms of the exchange of cash flows between the two parties. The main market players involved in trading swap contracts are dealers, traders, and other institutional or private investors interested in hedging risks.

Swaps instruments are mainly popular because they offer the potential user the opportunity to exchange cash flows on interest rates of debt obligations, currencies, or other products based on their risk exposures and hedging preferences. Swaps also provide an inexpensive and relatively easy way for two market participants to agree today to exchange cash flows in the future according to their views on the movement of underlying variables such as interest rates and currencies. By swapping streams of cash flows based on an outstanding amount called the *notional amount*, the two entities can hedge their interest rate risk, currency risk, or other types of risk exposures.

Figures published in the end-of-year 2012 report of International Swaps and Derivatives Association (ISDA) (2013) show that the notional amount outstanding of OTC derivatives before any adjustments for double counting (i.e., excluding foreign exchange (FX) transactions), increased by 6.7 percent between 2007 and 2012 increasing from \$529.7 trillion on December 31, 2007, to \$565.2 trillion by the end of 2012. According to the Bank of International Settlements (BIS) (2013), OTC interest rate derivatives, after adjusting for double counting, reached \$341.2 trillion, a slight increase from \$338.7 trillion recorded in December 2007. Thus, interest rate swaps contracts account for the largest part of derivatives positions on interest rates. The respective figures for interest rate swaps were $246.1 trillion in December 2012 down from $251.2 trillion in December 2007. Figures show that interest rate swaps represent more than 70 percent of OTC interest rate derivatives.

Swaps contracts are also important in the financial markets because of their size measured in notional values. For instance, the notional value of OTC interest rate derivatives outstanding in the U.S. market was $393.1 trillion in 2007, rising steadily to reach $504.1 trillion in 2011, and slightly deteriorating to $489.7 trillion in 2012 as stated in International Swaps and Derivatives Association (2013) report, based on data from the Bank of International Settlements (2013). From these figures, the percentage of cleared interest rate derivatives was 16.1 percent in 2007 rising steadily to 39.2 percent in 2011 and finally reaching 53.5 percent in 2012 according to International Swaps and Derivatives Association (2013) based on data from LCH Clearnet's SwapClear and CME Group clearing houses. *Cleared swap contracts* refer to the case where an intermediary stands between the payments of the two parties and guarantees the exchange of cash flows between them. These figures clearly indicate the increased interest of the investors for cleared derivatives or equivalently for derivatives involving a stock exchange between the two parties involved in the deal. This high interest for cleared derivatives can be attributed to the increasing effect of the subprime financial crisis on the investors risk aversion.

The financial crisis of 2007–2008 led financial market participants to invest heavily in credit default swap (CDS) instruments and eventually led several large U.S. financial institutions to experience extreme losses or failure including Lehman Brothers, Fannie Mae, Freddie Mac, Merrill Lynch, Washington Mutual and AIG. The very existence of the financial system was in doubt during this period. The swap market and especially CDS contracts raised several concerns and caused regulatory actions regarding the default risk exposures of the participants in the swap market. These concerns and severe skepticism further enhanced the discussion around the introduction of the Basel I, II, and III accords that imposed a series of risk-based capital adequacy reforms for financial institutions.

The remainder of this chapter is organized in the following manner. The next section presents the basic types of swaps contracts followed by a section containing typical examples of hedging risk with swaps for the interest rates and foreign exchange markets. The following section explains the role of the swap dealer and then focuses on the hedging properties of swaps for the balance sheet of a financial institution. The section after examines alternative measures of swaps' hedging effectiveness, and the last section concludes the chapter.

Swaps and Other Derivatives Contracts

A *swap contract* is most typically a bilateral OTC agreement where the two parties agree to exchange a specified series of payments over a predetermined period. That is, swap contracts can be viewed as a series of future or forward contracts with maturities matching the swap payments. In future or forward contracts, the two parties agree over specified cash flows for usually a single time period. In this way, even if swaps are very similar to futures or forwards contracts because the cash flows to be exchanged are explicitly specified in the contract, they are dissimilar to other derivative products such as options where the cash flows cannot be explicitly defined before the contract is exercised.

Comparing the differences between swaps and other derivatives products can reveal several important properties of swaps contracts associated with investors' risk exposures and their future prospects for the market. First, swaps usually involve symmetric cash flows (i.e., the parties involved in a swap have symmetric profit/loss opportunities), whereas other derivatives such as options contracts have asymmetric cash flows (i.e., for a given premium the option buyer is exposed to unlimited profits or limited losses). Second, swap contracts usually involve an intermediary who stands between the two parties of the swap agreement and mitigates the default risk entailed in the exchange of the cash flows. The intermediary also helps to reduce monitoring and information costs. Such costs can be large in OTC forward agreements. Thus, swaps contracts cleared through an intermediary offer an effective way to reduce such risks and costs. In practice, the majority of swap contracts are cleared through third-party dealers.

Another difference between swaps and other derivatives such as forward contracts is that swaps are marked-to-market at the payment dates whereas the forward contracts are marked-to-market only at their maturity date. *Marked-to-market* refers to the case where each position is settled daily against the spot market closing price of the day. Thus, a forward agreement entails higher default risk when compared to swaps contracts. This higher default risk is because forwards are not marked-to-market continuously like futures or options contracts, or even marked-to-market at the cash flow payment dates like swaps but only at maturity. Forwards contracts usually have no intermediary because they are OTC products and do not involve any up-front fee payment, whereas swaps involve a small fee for the intermediary. Finally, swaps usually have longer maturities than other derivative contracts making them ideal for long-term hedging purposes bearing a relatively small initial cost. However, when financial institutions use derivatives instruments such as swaps or even futures and options to reduce risk, they also limit potential excess returns from risk taking.

Benchmark uses of Swaps

The total size of their notional values can be used to classify the most important swaps: interest rate swaps are the most important ones, followed by currency swaps and credit default swaps. The first two types are very effective for hedging interest rate risk and currency risk, respectively. However, different types of swaps correspond to different underlying assets following the same principle (i.e., cash flows are computed on the specific underlying asset). The different expectations of the two parties regarding the future movement of the underlying asset usually motivate this exchange of cash flows.

INTEREST RATE SWAP EXAMPLE

Both financial and non-financial firms widely use interest rate swaps to maximize the value for both parties of a swap deal by exploiting a notion called *comparative advantage*. For example, in an interest rate swap, a higher rated company currently at

AA– may have a better (lower) spread offered by a financial institution for a credit facility in both the fixed and floating rate markets, rather than a lower rated company. Even if the firm has a better (lower) offer in both fixed and floating markets, its *comparative advantage* will exist in one of the two markets where its advantage is larger compared with the offers of the lower rated company (i.e. the counterparty of the swap deal). For this firm, the motive to exploit its comparative advantage by setting a swap agreement is determined by the future prospects of the firm for the interest rates evolution. Prospects for high interest rates in the future dictate that a fixed interest rate exposure is favorable, whereas prospects for lower interest rates in the future dictate that a floating interest rate exposure is favorable.

The respective parties usually arrange an interest rate swap agreement through a financial institution that acts as an intermediary and provides temporary "warehousing". *Interest rate swaps* involve "swapping" cash flows, such as interest rate payments, computed upon a notional value of debt between two parties. In the case of swap interest rates, these cash flows are usually denominated in the same currency and the swap contract explicitly states the dates when the cash flows are due to be exchanged.

For example, assume fund A has a current value of $50 million consisting of investments in fixed-income long-term instruments such as corporate bonds paying an average of 5 percent. The portfolio manager of fund A expects the interest rates to increase in the near future. Thus, he is seeking to replace his fixed-rate assets with floating-rate assets to benefit from the anticipated increase in interest rates. An inexpensive, easy, and flexible way to do so is by entering a swap agreement with counterparty B who has exactly the opposite expectations (i.e., expects interest rates to fall and wants to hedge this interest rate risk by transforming the floating rate portfolio into a fixed-rate one). Funds A and B agree to "swap" the cash flow of $2.5 million a year, which represents the proceeds from the interest rate earned in the fixed-rate portfolio of fund A, for a cash flow based on the short-term floating interest rate, which is earned on the value of fund B. The short-term interest rate upon which the floating-rate cash flows are tied is usually the London Interbank Offered Rate (LIBOR). *LIBOR* is the interest rate at which large financial institutions lend and borrow each other and is usually available for eight different time periods ranging from overnight to one-year maturity. Hence, in this swap agreement fund A will pay a 5 percent fixed cash flow on a value of $2.5 million (0.05 x $50 million) and receive a payment of LIBOR on the same notional principal (LIBOR x $50 million). So the net cash flow for fund A would be (LIBOR - 5 percent) x $50 million. In a swap agreement only the cash flows are exchanged, not the principal (notional) values. Based on this framework of "swapping" cash flows between two parties, restructuring the balance sheet of a firm or a financial institution can be achieved through similar swap contracts. Thus, swaps contracts can be very effective risk management tools.

CURRENCY SWAP EXAMPLE

The following example illustrates hedging currency risk through a swap contract. Suppose that a corporation has $100 million corporate debt outstanding with a 10 percent coupon. The firm has a client who will be paying its obligation in British pounds. Thus, having a debt outstanding denominated in British pounds instead of U.S. dollars would be much safer because the currency rate between U.S. dollar and British pound can fluctuate substantially. In other words, the firm is interested in hedging the currency risk between the dates of the payments for the issued bond (i.e., the date of coupon and principal payments), and the corresponding prevailing foreign exchange rates at these dates between U.S. dollar and British pound. Hence, the firm has a strong incentive to enter a swap agreement with another market player with exactly the opposite needs in currency denomination or with exactly different prospects regarding the evolution of the $/£ currency.

For example, if the prospects of the counterparty are that the British pound will depreciate in the future against the U.S. dollar, then this scenario creates substantial risk because the counterparty will have to pay more pounds for obtaining the same amount of dollars in the future. Thus, counterparty may seek ways to hedge this risk. In this setting, a mutually beneficial agreement between the two parties would be to "swap" the annual payments of the corporate bond issue denominated in U.S. dollars (USD) with an amount of British pounds (GBP). By doing so, firm A avoids the currency risk from GBP being appreciated against the USD and firm B avoids the risk of GBP being depreciated against the USD.

Another reason for such an agreement might be that one party might have obligations denominated in GBP, but finds access to more favorable (cheaper) financing opportunities in the U.S. credit market instead of the British one. This scenario would create a strong incentive to enter into a swap agreement in order to access the U.S. capital market and swap the payments of USD for GBP at pre-determined exchange rates and time periods.

THE COMPARATIVE ADVANTAGE ARGUMENT

The comparative advantage argument helps to provide a better understanding of the benefits of an interest rate swap. This argument exploits the case when firms are offered different rates of borrowing depending on their default risk and the terms of the loan agreement. For example, a firm with a better credit rating may be offered lower borrowing interest rates in a credit facility, both for fixed and floating interest rates. In principle, a firm would choose to borrow money at the lowest interest rate available (i.e., the fixed or floating interest rates when compared to another firm with a lower credit rating). However, a common issue arises when the better rated company has a different preference rather than the lowest offered interest rate when compared to the worse rated company. Then an opportunity exists for the two firms to construct a swap agreement and benefit mutually from the comparative advantage of the better rated company in a specific interest rate. Thus, the swap agreement enables the two companies to transform a fixed-rate loan to a floating rate one and vice versa.

An example of such an interest rate swap involves two firms: Simons Utilities (SU) and Browns Properties (BP). In a swap agreement, both companies should benefit in order to have an incentive to be part of the agreement. Further assume that the benefit from the swap agreement will be split equally between the two firms. Assume that these two companies want to borrow $500 million for a period of five years. Further assume that SU desires to borrow using a floating interest rate instrument linked to the three-month LIBOR, whereas BP prefers using a fixed interest rate instrument. The desires of the two companies may be a combination of their prospects about the interest rates

Table 26.1 **Interest Rates Offered to Simons Utilities and Browns Properties**

	Fixed Rate(%)	*Floating Rate*	*Relative Difference*	*Desired Exposure*
Simons Utilities	3.00	Libor	NA	Floating rate
Browns Properties	4.00	Libor + 40bps	NA	Fixed rate
Absolute difference	1.00	0.40%	0.60%	NA

Note: This table presents the fixed and floating interest rates offered to Simons Utilities and Browns Properties for a bank loan. The absolute difference and relative difference refer to the difference in each market and the difference of the two differences, respectively. The column titled "Desired Exposure" indicates the market to which each company wants to be exposed after the agreeing to a swap contract.

movements and/or their individual strategy and current capital structure of their balance sheets. Table 26.1 shows that the two firms have the following offerings regarding the interest rates charged for a credit facility of $500 million.

Because SU has a better credit rating (AA+) rather than BP (BBB+), SU is offered lower interest rates in both the fixed and the floating interest rate markets. As Table 26.1 shows, the advantage of SU in the fixed rate offering (1 percent) is larger than its advantage in the floating rate one (0.4 percent) when compared to the figures offered to BP. Therefore, SU has a comparative advantage over BP in the fixed rate market rather than the floating market. The net benefit to be split between the two companies can be found by subtracting the absolute differences in the fixed and floating offers. In this example, the benefit to be distributed between the two companies is 0.6 percent (found by subtracting 0.4 percent from 1 percent), so each company under the swap agreement will be paying the interest rate desired, which will be lower than the one offered by 0.3 percent (found by splitting the 0.6 benefit in equal parts). Splitting the potential benefit from a swap agreement is a matter of negotiation between the two parties involved.

If the two firms decide to negotiate a swap, then the simplest way to benefit from the comparative advantage of SU in the fixed rate market would be for the two firms to take the loans offered to them that do not match their preferences. This arrangement would involve SU taking the floating rate agreement and another firm (firm B) taking the fixed rate agreement. Then SU, which took the floating rate agreement even if it wants a fixed interest rate, pays the floating rate (LIBOR) to BP in order to remove the exposure in the floating interest rate, whereas BP does exactly the opposite (i.e., pays the fixed rate back to SU so the firm is left with a floating rate). Figure 26.1 illustrates the swap agreement graphically.

As Table 26.2 shows, under this swap contract, SU pays 3 percent to the outside lending financial institution and LIBOR to BP, whereas it receives 3.3 percent from BP. Accordingly, BP pays LIBOR + 0.4 percent to the outside lending financial institution and 3.3 percent to SU, and receives LIBOR from SU. The net value of this exchange of cash flows would be that the two firms end up with the desired interest rate, which is discounted by as much as half the benefit of the swap (0.3 percent).

In this way, SU ends up paying a fixed interest rate, which is in accordance with the firm's desire and will be also discounted by 0.3 percent and BP ends up paying floating

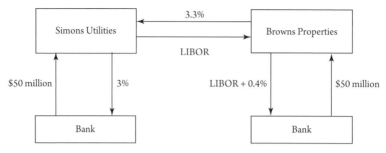

Figure 26.1 Cash Flows Exchanged Through an Interest Rate Swap
Agreement.   This figure depicts the design of the interest rate swap contract between
Simons Utilities and Browns Properties.

Table 26.2 **Interest Rate Cash Flows between Simons Utilities (SU) and Browns**
Properties (BP)

	SU Interest Flow	*BP Interest Flows*
SU borrows fixed rate funds	−3.00%	
BP borrows floating rate funds		− (LIBOR + 0.4%)
Swap: SU lends the fix rate to BP	3.30%	−3.30%
BP lends the floating rate sum to SU	− LIBOR	+ LIBOR
Net payoff	(LIBOR − 0.3%)	3.70%
Net payoff if borrowed without swap	LIBOR	8.00%
Gains from swap (equal split)	0.30%	0.30%

Note: This table presents the interest rate related cash flows which are exchanged between Simons
Utilities and Brown Properties according to the interest rate swap agreement between them.

rate exactly as desired, which will be discounted again by 0.3 percent. With a notional
amount of $50 million, each company could save $150,000 a year or $750,000 over the
loan period. In case an intermediary is involved, the potential benefit of the swap must
be reduced by an amount representing the profit of the intermediary involved with the
agreement to mitigate the credit risk entailed in the swap agreement for both parties.

A key issue in the previous example is when and under which circumstances a difference in the offered interest rates for two different firms can be exploited through
a swap agreement for the mutual benefit of both parties. Because of the size of the
swap market, the expectation is that such arbitrage opportunities should have vanished.
However, such differences continue to exist mainly because in the floating rate agreements, the lender has the option to review the offered interest rate in specific periods,
say six months. The lender has the opportunity to re-adjust the offered floating interest
rate according to the changing creditworthiness of the obligor or the changing dynamics
of interest rates in the economy. Because this option is unavailable in the fixed interest
rate offerings, this difference between the fixed and floating interest rates gives rise to
such arbitrage opportunities.

The Swap Dealer

The popularity of swaps contracts has grown dramatically in the financial markets worldwide. Part of this growth can be attributed to the fact that financial institutions use swaps in response to the volatile interest rates and foreign exchange rates. However, several factors apart from interest rates and currency rates may have affected commercial bank swap activity. For example, banks' earnings have decreased over time as a result of interest rates deregulation, greater competition or losses incurred in traditional banking business such as granting loans to emerging countries, energy firms, and the agricultural and real estate sectors. These practices have led banks to emphasize fee-based business to enhance their earnings. Such fee-based business may include acting as an intermediary for a bilateral swap agreement. Further, serving as an intermediary is also profitable due to the current flat rate deposit insurance system that tends to encourage excessive risk-taking by financial institutions.

In many swap agreements, a swap dealer might be willing to act as an intermediary for the exchange of the cash flows and collect in return a fee linked with the notional value of the swap contract. In fact, the popularity and growth of swaps markets can also be attributed to the willingness of financial institutions to act as market makers. A swap dealer acts as an intermediary by creating an OTC secondary market for swaps in return of a fee, which serves as collateral to the risks associated with the swaps contracts. For example, assume a swap dealer is willing to take a specific position on a swap agreement by paying a fixed rate and receiving a floating rate over LIBOR. In order to match this swap, the dealer will search for possible counterparties willing to hold the opposite position (i.e., paying a floating rate over LIBOR and receiving a fixed rate). By matching the two parties' positions, the swap dealer has achieved neutrality of his position versus the fluctuation of interest rates. This neutrality is due to the fact that the market maker pays a floating rate over LIBOR in the one swap contract and receives the same amount from another. The same principle also holds for the fixed rate part of a swap agreement. However, by standing between the two parties in a swap agreement, the swap market maker is exposed to substantial default risk because one or both of the parties may default on their payments due. Thus, the swap dealer charges a fee, which is usually expressed as a bid-ask spread, for all the transactions between the users of swaps and the market maker.

Financial institutions typically earn considerable profits by acting as settlement agents (i.e., collecting and paying the net difference in the interest rate payments), and serving as guarantors of the agreement. The fees depend on the complexity of the swap agreement and the amount of services that the bank provides. Some banks keep a record of standardized swap products but others are more flexible regarding the terms of the agreement. The flexibility depends heavily on the financial health of the counterparties involved and the size of the agreement. Margins on a plain vanilla swap vary from 10 to 15 basis points a year for simple contracts and could be much more for complex products designed to meet a client's specific requirements. When the bank acts as a guarantor of an interest rate swap agreement, the default risk is transferred from the swapping parties to the bank. In this way, even if the bank collects fee income, it exposes itself to default risk (i.e., one or both the parties may not honor the swap agreement).

The incentive of collecting a swap-related fee in order to act as an intermediary along with the competitive nature of the banking industry can lead the banks to underprice their risks. Such mispricing is frequent in the banking industry because banks have gone beyond their initial role of acting as market makers and participate in a competitive market of fee hunting. As market makers, banks take the opposite side of every swap transaction as the bank is the counterparty for each party of the deal. Thus, the parties of a swap contract have an agreement only with the bank and are unaware of who might be on the other side of the swap. Following this structure allows banks to sell one leg of the swap and locate a matching counterparty for the deal.

Hedging Risks with Swaps

As described in previous sections, swaps are important instruments for managing risks faced by financial institutions such as interest rate risk and foreign exchange risk. Market participants seek to maximize their profits and at the same time to avoid exposing themselves to excessive risks associated with their core operation (i.e., lending capital to firms and individuals for investment/consumption purposes). Also, financial institutions need to assess the ability of their obligors to repay their debt with a favorable risk-return profile for them. For example, the fluctuation of interest rates directly affects the valuation of the assets that the financial institution holds (Wright and Houpt 1996). Therefore, most financial institutions seek to manage their interest rate risks by relying on either on-balance sheet or off-balance sheet activities.

On-balance sheet activities are an integral part of asset and liability management. These activities involve adjusting all or part of banks' assets and/or liabilities in a way that an unfavorable interest rate movement will not harm the market valuation of the assets or the liabilities included in the balance sheet. Thus, with the help of swaps contracts, a financial institution can immunize its exposure to interest rate risk. Although asset/liability management is an on-balance sheet way to manage interest rate risk exposure, it could also be applied in managing the foreign exchange risk exposure of the institution.

Typically, financial institutions perform asset/liability management by estimating the interest rate GAP of their balance sheets and the duration of their assets. *Interest rate GAP* refers to the difference between the interest rate sensitive assets minus the interest rate sensitive liabilities for a specific maturity. Most typically, when banks want to measure the total effect of interest rate changes on profitability, they use the GAP measure. The *GAP measure* is defined as the difference between the amount of interest rate sensitive assets minus the interest rate sensitive liabilities (i.e., the assets and liabilities whose values may vary with interest rate changes over some given time horizon). Among the ways that the GAP measure can be expressed is the dollar GAP which is the simplest form. *Duration GAP* is a more complete measure of interest rate risk and complements the simple GAP analysis. Its main focus is on the impact of interest rates movements on the bank's value as reflected by the duration of the rate sensitive assets/liabilities.

The off-balance sheet activities are mainly *hedging techniques* and allow firms to achieve the same results as the on-balance sheet activities but without affecting the figures of their balance sheet. In other words, the difference is that the valuation of assets and liabilities of the bank on the balance sheet is not altered. Avoiding presenting the changes on assets and liabilities values on the balance sheet can be achieved since all the necessary adjustments to immunize the bank's portfolio against interest rate risk are performed as off balance sheet activities. These adjustments mainly concentrate within large banks as discussed in previous sections and involve using derivatives, which enable off-balance sheet activities. Thus, derivatives complement existing strategies based on conventional GAP and duration GAP techniques but are not adequate to replace them.

For example, assume that a financial institution has a positive duration GAP (i.e., the duration of interest rate sensitive assets is more than the duration of the interest rate sensitive liabilities). *Duration* is a measure of the sensitivity of the assets' prices to the interest rate changes. Thus, for high duration assets or liabilities, interest rates movements can result in significant changes in their values which eventually affect the balance sheet of the financial institution. In order to reduce this interest rate risk exposure, a financial institution could enter into a swap contract with another market player who has negative GAP duration and for this reason has exactly the opposite risk. In this way, one party could swap any floating rate liability's cash flows for fixed rate ones. This interest rate swap will enable both banks to reduce their GAP durations and thus the risks they face due to the interest rate risk. A financial institution could also use these swaps contracts for speculative purposes when it wants to deepen its duration GAP and exposure itself further to interest rate changes with an expectation of higher profits.

Measuring Swaps Hedging Effectiveness

Various studies examine the effectiveness of hedging risks using derivatives products and in particular swaps. This section reviews the most notable contributions in the area and explores the effects of managerial incentives and monitoring mechanisms on derivatives use for hedging purposes.

CONTEMPORARY BANKING THEORY

The contemporary theory of financial intermediation suggests that banks offer brokerage and qualitative asset transformation (QAT) services. Bhattacharya and Thakor (1993) and Dos Santos (2009) provide a survey of relevant theories on the contemporary banking theory. The traditional brokerage services provided by commercial banks usually include transactions accounts and origination or renewal of loan contracts. As QAT providers, banks transform or modify claims, mainly deposits, with respect to credit risk, liquidity, duration, and divisibility.

One of the fundamental causes of the savings and loan (S&L) crisis during the decades of 1980s and 1990s was the extensive use of duration and liquidity transformations resulting into excess interest rate risk. For this reason many bankers started using derivatives to hedge interest rate risk (Puri, Rocholl, and Steffen 2011). However, financial institutions were encouraged by the mispriced deposit insurance and tried to hedge their positions using on- or off-balance sheet activities. During the period of the S&L crisis, another emerging pattern was the extreme duration mismatches in many financial institutions balance sheets. The latter highlighted the need to effectively manage interest rate risk and to provide an incentive-compatible deposit-insurance contract. With the collapse of the S&L industry, many commercial banks witnessed losses in their residential loans (Blaško and Sinkey 2006). Given the necessary conditions (i.e., if a major upswing happens in the interest rates and in the absence of off-balance sheet measures of hedging in most of the financial institutions), the duration mismatches between short-maturity assets and long-maturity liabilities may expand and result in another S&L type crisis for real-estate lending depositories.

Because on-balance sheet methods of managing interest rate risk (e.g., duration matching) may conflict with customers' preferences for products and services, banks have employed two additional tools for managing interest rate risk: (1) securitization, through which a financial institution can repackage assets such as mortgages or corporate loans and sell them as new products; and (2) derivatives contracts, which employ off-balance sheet techniques to manage portfolio risks. Securitization is an effective way to remove risk from the balance sheet of the bank and transfer it to the buyers of the securitized assets. Loutskina (2011) analyzes the importance of securitization for financial institutions during the periods before and after the financial crisis of 2007–2008. The author finds evidence that by allowing banks to transform difficult to sell loans into easy to sell funds the securitization process increases the lending ability of the financial institutions. By this extra source of funding (i.e., the securitization), banks are more tolerate to cost of funds shocks.

SWAPS USE AND RISK EXPOSURES

The issue of derivatives use and especially swaps by financial institutions has been of great concern to both regulatory bodies and market players. The documented large growth in derivatives transactions confirms how fast moving and sophisticated modern banking has become. The types of financial services in which banks engage have become increasingly complex in theory and practice. However, a clear relationship between the use of derivatives and the bank's risk exposures has not been defined explicitly. This topic has generated much attention from both academics and practitioners. Researchers have developed several theoretical models and adopted different empirical methodologies to investigate the market implications of using derivatives.

Although many studies examine how the use of derivatives affects a firm's risk, results are mixed and sometimes controversial. For example, Allayannis and Ofek (2001) and Makar and Huffman (2001) contend that using currency derivatives for hedging foreign exchange risk substantially reduces the exchange rate risk banks face. Moreover, their findings signal the existence of cross-sectional differences on how foreign exchange derivatives use reduces foreign exchange risk exposure. By examining a sample of firms during the S&L crisis, Brewer, Jackson, and Moser (1996) suggest that concerns with interest rate derivatives products lead to higher risk. The authors claim that increased derivatives use seems to be linked with lower risk exposures. In a related study, Smithson and Simkins (2005) provide evidence that interest rate movements have a great effect on the stock returns of financial sector companies. However, such companies do not necessarily face higher exposure to interest rate risk. Industrial firms typically face higher risk exposures because they are considerably more sensitive to exchange rates. This finding implies that using derivatives products to mitigate interest rate risk is not solely focused on financial institutions but also includes industrial firms. Chaudhry and Reichert (1999) contend that using interest rate swaps decreases the systemic or non-systemic risk of commercial banks holding large assets.

In a related study, Choi and Elyasiani (1997) stress the relative influence of risk reduction involving exchange rates compared to the reduction in interest rate risk. Brewer et al. (1996) use a sample of S&Ls and show that using interest rate derivatives decreases the systematic and idiosyncratic risk. They also find that institutions that observed a greater use of derivatives witness a larger growth in their fixed-rate mortgages portfolio. In summary, this first group of academics (Brewer et al. 1996; Choi and Elyasiani 1997; Allayannis and Ofek 2001; Makar and Huffman 2001; Smithson and Simkins 2005) support the view that interest rate derivatives and swaps in particular help to reduce the risk exposure of financial institutions.

Another strand of the literature focuses on the relationship between interest rate risk exposure and banks' derivatives usage. For example, Gorton and Rosen (1995) provide evidence that using interest rate swaps leads to higher interest rate risk exposure. They also claim that other bank products and services exposures may offset to certain extent. Further, Gorton and Rosen (1995) confirm that the magnitude of the offsetting effect depends on the size of the bank, the status of the bank as a swap dealer, and the volume of its activity in this business. Last, the authors suggest that interest rate swaps used by commercial banks are positively correlated with interest rate risk exposure.

A third view supported by Hentschel and Kothari (2001) supports the idea that no relationship exists between a bank's risk and using derivatives. The main argument is that banks use derivatives to be involved as intermediaries and generate profit from the fees involved. Using a large panel of non-financial U.S. firms, they examine how stock return volatility, interest rate level, and exchange rates are related to the extent of derivative use. The authors find no statistically significant relationship between derivatives use andrisk exposures. Thus, they conclude that even large derivative positions will have a small effect on their risk exposures for most firms. Overall, evidence provided by academic research still enables an ongoing debate on the relationship between the use of swaps contracts and any reduction in firm's risk exposure.

ALTERNATIVE MEASURES OF SWAP RISK EFFECTS

Most of the empirical works on derivatives and their impact on a firm's risk exposures in the banking industry exhibit some methodological limitations. One of the main limitations is that most studies use the notional amount of derivatives in measuring the extent of the use of derivative products. However, higher notional amounts do not necessarily imply a higher risk exposures. For instance, a bank may have a high notional value of derivatives, but may be proactive enough to match its derivatives positions with other positions in the spot market or with the opposite positions in the derivatives market. The relationship between bank stock returns volatility and their interest rate swap activity has changed over time. It is particularly affected by the current phase of the financial markets business cycle (i.e., bull vs. bear markets).

Another limitation is that some studies lack a control sample. i.e., previous studies focus only on financial institutions which are present or past users of swaps, but exclude non-users . Moreover, interest rate swaps could have an effect on increasing the volatility of high volatile stocks and reducing the volatility of less volatile stocks. Previous studies also base their analyses on a cross-section panel of banks by using on balance sheet data to measure the risk. Such studies should focus on market-based measures of risk in order to capture any time dynamics and the market's sentiment.

Another way to quantify the substantial change in banks' risk profile due to swaps use involves focusing on stock returns volatility changes during periods before and after using swap contracts. The time window is usually between 90 and 200 days around the *event day*, which is the date of the initiation of swap use by the bank. This widely used technique enables researchers to avoid using the notional outstanding amount. However, this type of analysis introduces various limitations as discussed by Mazouz (2004). As previously stated, sample selection bias is another major concern when performing similar analysis because the sample used should contain both users and non-users of derivatives contracts.

Employing a control sample is not entirely new in the context of stock volatility. Yet, the way in which the control sample is constructed is a matter of debate. The control sample is designed to account for the possible volatility changes that may be caused by factors other than derivatives use and to avoid any biases resulting from the effect of market completeness, trading location or thin trading. Previous studies using the control sample technique, which takes into consideration market wide conditions movements and dynamics, ignore to some extent the latter effects. Control sample methodology allows researchers to mitigate some bias that may be caused by the measurement of the derivative use. This bias refers to the possibility that derivative use is an endogenous decision for an already swap user. Future studies in the area could consider examining the dual effect of the interest rate swaps, which refer to the increase in volatility of already volatile stocks and the decrease in volatility of the stable stocks due to performing hedging operations through swaps contracts.

Summary and Conclusions

This chapter examined several theories and risks directly related to the introduction and use of swaps contracts. Also, this chapter focused on the types and properties of swaps contracts and their hedging effectiveness. Several practical examples on how to manage risks through swaps contracts such as interest rate risk and currency risk were presented and analyzed in depth.

Broadly speaking, the trading of OTC derivatives and swaps by both financial and non-financial firms has experienced an unprecedented growth over the past two decades. An obvious benefit of using derivatives is that financial managers can reduce the volatility of their firm's cash flows in order to avoid business or financial risks. Other reasons for doing so could be that managers are risk-averse or that their personal compensation is directly related with firm performance. Another incentive to use swaps contracts is to maximize shareholders value through the mitigation of risks. However, irrespective of the actual objective, either reducing the volatility of their cash flows or maximizing shareholders' value, hedging risks through swaps contracts requires a deep knowledge and understanding of the mechanics and the complexity of the market.

The vast amount of research conducted in the last 20 years sheds some light on the uses of OTC derivatives and especially swaps in hedging risks. By using swaps, managers can increase shareholders value, reduce the cost of financial distress, lower the cost of external borrowing, or decrease payable taxes. As previously discussed, the results of empirical studies on the impact of using swaps on a firm's risk exposure are strongly debated along with the emergence of different schools of thought on the issue.

For example, some market participants support the view that OTC derivative products reduce a firm's risk and increase shareholders' value. This view is controversial in the light of recent cases of derivatives products misuse by middle-level managers in large financial institutions. Such cases include the French bank Société Générale, which lost $6 billion in 2007 because of the practices of one single junior trader in the derivatives market. An almost identical case involved a junior trader of Swiss bank UBS in 2011 involving trades carrying notional values far above his trading limit allowance. Such notable cases of derivatives misuse indicate that trader incentives can be much stronger in creating unhedged risk exposures in the market than any limitations of the market structure or any contract misspecifications in swaps contracts. Thus, equally important to the understanding of the mechanics of derivatives and especially swaps are the ethics involved when trading or using derivatives products along with the correct assessment of the risk exposures.

Discussion Questions

1. Mowal Plc. is offered a bank loan at a fixed rate of 6 percent or a floating rate of LIBOR + 0.5 percent. Sika Ltd. can borrow at a floating rate of LIBOR + 0.25 percent or a fixed rate of 5.25 percent.
   • Determine the individual benefits of both companies entering into an interest rate swap contract.
   • Assuming that a financial intermediary makes this arrangement and charges a fee of 0.25 percent, explain the benefit for the two companies.
2. Discuss the main benefits of entering into a swap contract involving a financial intermediary.
3. Explain how an interest rate swap works.
4. Al Maya Plc. can borrow capital at a fixed rate of 8.5 percent or a floating rate of LIBOR + 0.5 percent. Dil Plc. has been offered a fixed rate of 7.75 percent and a floating rate of LIBOR + 0.25 percent. A financial institution has agreed to act as an intermediary for a swap between the two parties at a fee of 0.10 percent for each party. Assuming the two companies share the benefits of the swap equally, demonstrate how a swap contract can reduce the cost of borrowing to each company.
5. Discuss the effects of using a swap on a firm's risk exposure.

References

Allayannis, George, and Eli Ofek. 2001. "Exchange Rate Exposure, Hedging, and the Use of Foreign Currency Derivatives." *Journal of International Money and Finance* 20:2, 273–296.

Bank of International Settlements. 2013. "Semiannual Over-the-Counter (OTC) Derivatives Markets Statistics." Available at http://www.bis.org/statistics/derstats.htm.

Bhattacharya, Sudipto, and Anjan. V. Thakor. 1993. "Contemporary Banking Theory." *Journal of Financial Intermediation* 3:1, 2–50.

Blaško, Matej, and Joseph F. Sinkey, Jr. 2006. "Bank Asset Structure, Real-Estate Lending, and Risk-Taking." *Quarterly Review of Economics and Finance* 46:1, 53–81.

Brewer, Elijah, III, William E. Jackson, III, and James T. Moser. 1996. "Alligators in the Swamp: The Impact of Derivatives on the Financial Performance of Depository Institutions." *Journal of Money, Credit and Banking* 28:3, Part II, 482-497.

Chaudhry, Mukesh K., and Alan K. Reichert. 1999. "The Impact of Off-Balance Sheet Derivatives and Interest Rate Swap on Bank Risk." *Research in Finance* 17:1: 275–300.

Choi, Jongmoo Jay, and Elyas Elyasiani. 1997. "Derivative Exposure and the Interest Rate and Exchange Rate Risks of U.S. Banks." *Journal of Financial Services Research* 12:2–3, 267–286.

Dos Santos, Paulo L. 2009. "On the Content of Banking in Contemporary Capitalism." *Historical Materialism* 17:2, 180–213.

Gorton, Gary, and Richard Rosen. 1995. "Corporate Control, Portfolio Choice, and the Decline of Banking." *Journal of Finance* 50:5, 1377–1420.

Hentschel, Ludger, and S. P. Kothari. 2001. "Are Corporations Reducing or Taking Risks with Derivatives?" *Journal of Financial and Quantitative Analysis* 36:1, 93–118.

International Swaps and Derivatives Association. 2013. "OTC Derivatives Market Analysis Year-End 2012." Available at http://assets.isda.org/media/467fbf64/438d9f0f.pdf/.

Loutskina, Elena. 2011. "The Role of Securitization in Bank Liquidity and Funding Management." *Journal of Financial Economics* 100:3, 663–684.

Makar, Stephen D., and Stephen P. Huffman. 2001. "Foreign Exchange Derivatives, Exchange Rate Changes, and the Value of the Firm: U.S. Multinationals' Use of Short-Term Financial Instruments to Manage Currency Risk." *Journal of Economics and Business* 53:4, 421–437.

Mazouz, Khelifa. 2004. "The Effect of CBOE Option Listing on the Volatility of NYSE Traded Stocks: A Time-Varying Variance Approach." *Journal of Empirical Finance* 11:5, 695–708.

Puri, Manju, Jörg Rocholl, and Sascha Steffen. 2011. "Global Retail Lending in the Aftermath of the US Financial Crisis: Distinguishing between Supply and Demand Effects." *Journal of Financial Economics* 100:3, 556–578.

Smithson, Charles, and Betty J. Simkins. 2005. "Does Risk Management Add Value? A Survey of the Evidence." *Journal of Applied Corporate Finance* 17:3, 8–17.

Wright, David M., and James V. Houpt. 1996. "An Analysis of Commercial Bank Exposure to Interest Rate Risk." *Federal Reserve Bulletin*, February, 115–128.

27

Credit Derivatives

UDO BROLL

Professor of Economics, Technische Universität Dresden, Faculty of Business and Economics

SIMONE RAAB

Senior Researcher, Universität Augsburg, Faculty of Business and Economics

PETER WELZEL

Professor of Economics, Universität Augsburg, Faculty of Business and Economics

Introduction

Credit derivatives are financial contracts written on the credit risk of an underlying loan or portfolio of loans. They allow the separation of credit risk from the loan, making this kind of risk tradable and putting a price tag on it. Trade of credit risk can be desirable for various reasons ranging from hedging, portfolio diversification, regulatory capital relief, and strategic motives to speculation. U.S. banks created derivative contracts based on credit risk during the mid-1990s to reduce the capital reserve requirement of their loan business (Helm, Geffen, and Capistron 2009). From that time until 2007, the total volume of credit derivatives outstanding grew explosively (Duffie 2008) and then the financial crisis of 2007–2008 caused a sharp reduction (International Monetary Fund 2013). In fact, some observers blamed the use of credit derivatives for the near collapse of the world financial system. Warren Buffett called them "financial weapons of mass destruction" when used for speculative purposes (Berkshire Hathaway Inc. 2003, p. 15). George Soros referred to derivatives as "toxic" and wanted them to be banned (Soros 2009).

This criticism notwithstanding, the volume of trade in credit derivatives is still substantial with large notional amounts outstanding of some types such as credit derivatives on sovereign debt, which have increased in recent years (International Monetary Fund 2013). Much theoretical and empirical research focuses on their role in the financial system. Undoubtedly, imperfections exist in credit derivatives markets, which need to be analyzed and, if necessary, met by regulatory measures. Such imperfection, however, should not conceal the potential value of these instruments as a sophisticated way of managing credit risk.

This chapter first takes a brief look at the basics and some institutional facts of credit derivatives and then presents a stylized model of bank risk management using credit derivatives. The model permits us to capture important aspects of credit risk transfer and of decision-making in a bank and to derive recommendations in a coherent framework. Next, the chapter modifies the model to discuss the impact of higher market transparency in the sense of publicly available information in the loan market on a bank's use of credit derivatives, their price, and loan volume. The extensive economic literature on credit derivatives examines a plethora of other questions concerning credit derivatives. The chapter then outlines the most important insights, before concluding with a brief summary.

Institutional Aspects

Credit derivatives are financial contracts traded over-the-counter (OTC) to provide insurance against credit risk. The protection buyer pays a premium to the protection seller and receives a payment in the case of a pre-defined credit event such as bankruptcy, payment default, rescheduling, or rating downgrade. However, they differ from insurance in many ways. For instance, the holder of a credit derivative does not need to hold the underlying exposure that creates the credit risk. Market participants, therefore, can use credit derivatives for both hedging and speculative purposes. Furthermore, sellers of protection against credit risk are not regulated and do not operate like insurance companies.

Credit derivatives exist in many variants. If they are unfunded, the protection seller has to put up money on an ex post basis if a credit event occurs. A credit default swap (CDS) is the most important variant of this type. A CDS most closely resembles an insurance policy. In case of a funded credit derivative, the protection seller makes an initial payment to be used to settle credit events. Credit-linked notes and collateralized debt obligations (CDOs) belong to this group. Reference entities can be single-name or multi-name. In the latter case, the credit event is defined on the performance of a specific basket of credits.

Credit derivatives transfer credit risk separately from the ownership of the underlying reference entity. They allow users to manage their exposure to credit risk arising from financial instruments such as commercial loans or sovereign debt. For example, a commercial bank holding a bond issued by some manufacturing company or a government may want to hedge against a potential default of the bond issuer. The commercial bank can buy a CDS to insure itself against loss and shift the credit risk to a third party, the CDS seller, while keeping the bond on its books. Buying a credit derivative as insurance against partial or total borrower default amounts to replacing credit risk by counterparty risk (i.e., the risk that the protection seller will be unable to fulfill its obligations in case of a credit event).

This chapter focuses on the CDS, which is the most important instrument to transfer credit risk. The Bank for International Settlement (BIS) reports a CDS notional amount outstanding of $25.0 trillion and a gross market value of $0.8 trillion compared to a total of $632.5 trillion and $24.7 trillion for all OTC derivatives and $489.7 trillion and $18.8 trillion for interest rate derivatives, the dominant type of derivative, for the second half of 2012 (Bank for International Settlements 2013). Notional amounts are the nominal values of all deals concluded, corrected for double counting. Gross market values are the sums of the absolute values at market prices of all open contracts where contracts with positive and negative replacement values with the same counterparty are not netted. Whereas notional amounts indicate market size, analysts use gross market values to evaluate the market risk in derivatives transactions.

Commercial banks as financial intermediaries taking deposits and giving loans are natural sellers of credit risk in CDS markets. By transferring credit risk to a third party, a bank can reduce the risk of being unable to fulfill its obligation against its depositors. It can also spare regulatory capital, which in turn can be used for further loan business. Under the so-called substitution approach included in the Basel II and Basel III Accords, a loan hedged by a CDS gets the risk weight of the counterparty (Pausch and Welzel 2013). This hedged position enables a bank to reduce its risk-weighted assets and as a consequence the amount of regulatory capital required. Data on the CDS market show the dominant role of banks as sellers of credit risk. However, financial institutions, especially banks, dominate the CDS market on both sides (D'Arcy, McNichols, and Zhao 2009; Bank for International Settlements 2013). Thus, banks also act as counterparties in the CDS market. Non-financial institutions account for less than 1 percent of the CDS volume.

From the perspective of a bank, buying protection via a CDS reduces risk. At the same time, this operation enables the bank to take on new credit risk. Instefjord (2005) is among the first to analyze the full impact on a bank's stability. He concludes that, depending on the elasticity in the loan market, credit derivatives can even increase bank risk. Financial institutions serve as the main buyers of credit risk and raise additional concerns about systemic stability. Ideally, banks would use CDS to transfer credit risk to a large number of small diversified investors. In reality, credit risk is transferred only within the financial sector. To make matters worse, a high concentration of counterparties exists that makes contagion more likely. According to the European Central Bank (2009), the 10 largest CDS dealers were counterparties to 72 percent of all CDS trades. Concentration seems to have increased more after the financial crisis of 2007–2008. A recent antitrust investigation of the European Commission also points to potential market failure in the CDS market.

According to the Bank for International Settlements (2013), 37 percent of the underlying exposure to the reference entities underlying the CDS comes from non-financial firms, 26 percent from financial firms, and 12 percent from sovereigns. The share of CDS on debt of sovereigns has been increasing in the last decade.

In the aftermath of the financial crisis of 2007–2008, some criticized the structural opacity of credit risk transfer. With CDS markets generating a vast number of bilateral deals within the financial industry, little was known about where credit risk actually resided. Some suggested using central counterparties (CCPs) such as ICE Clear Europe or ICE Trust US as entities interposing between the counterparties of a CDS and acting as buyer to every seller and as seller to every buyer as a measure to make CDS markets more transparent. Recently, central clearing through CCPs amounted to about 11 percent of original CDS trades (Bank for International Settlements 2013).

Against the background of the surge of economic and financial research on the use of credit derivatives as financial instruments to transfer credit risk from banks to third parties, the next two sections illustrate how the availability of such derivatives affects a bank's asset-liability management, and what can be said about the optimal level of hedging against this type of risk. The focus is primarily on the role of banks as buyers of protection (i.e., as sellers of credit risk). After introducing a basic framework to analyze the role of CDS for a bank, the framework will be extended to clarify the role of market transparency.

Managing Credit Risk with Credit Derivatives

Along with liquidity risk, credit risk is the oldest and most important form of risk faced by commercial banks. Large-scale borrower defaults can force a bank into bankruptcy. Hence, managing credit risk is a major challenge for bank management. Traditionally, banks met this challenge through selecting and monitoring borrowers (i.e., creating a well-diversified loan portfolio). However, modern financial instruments and global risk-sharing markets offer new ways to manage credit risk more efficiently.

This study features a risk-averse bank management facing risk from commercial, industrial, and sovereign loans. Hedging credit risk by offsetting an open position with an opposite one in the financial market is important for financial intermediaries concerned about both profitability and risk of their operations. As risk management is crucial for the bank, the issues of how it is optimally determined and how it adjusts to changes in the banking environment deserve closer scrutiny.

The economic literature provides various reasons for active risk management of a bank, ranging from risk aversion of managers who have bank-specific human capital and may hold a large share of their wealth in the bank's stock, to owners not being fully diversified, convex taxation, the cost of financial distress, and capital market imperfections (Froot, Scharfstein, and Stein 1993; Froot and Stein 1998). Thus, owners and managers of a bank can be made better off by reducing the variance of the bank's cash flow or bank's value.

Credit derivatives are financial contracts with payoffs connected to a credit-related event such as downgrade or outright borrower default. A bank can use credit derivatives to transfer all or some of the credit risk of a loan to a third party. By buying credit derivatives, the bank can take additional risks that may improve the risk-return properties of its total portfolio. In general, credit derivatives are financial instruments that allow selling or buying the risk of a loan separately from the loan itself. This process is most relevant for banks that are the dominant players in the markets for credit derivatives. A bank choosing to manage credit risk exposure with credit derivatives must consider basis risks, liquidity costs, and transaction costs.

A BASIC BANKING FIRM MODEL WITH CREDIT DERIVATIVES

This section introduces a banking firm model in the tradition of the industrial organization approach to banking (Freixas and Rochet 2008) augmented by credit risk (Wong 1997). At the beginning of the period, the bank chooses its assets and liabilities positions and its hedging policy to maximize expected utility of final wealth $EU(W)$. Random shocks in credit repayment reduce expected utility of final wealth

W, if utility U is a strictly concave function. With risk aversion, marginal utility is positive, $U' > 0$ and decreasing in final wealth, $U'' < 0$. Consider a bank with market power that takes deposits D and makes loans L. Let the loan rate r_L be negatively related to the commercial and industrial loan volume L (i.e., $L'(r_L) < 0$ which represents a downward-sloping demand for loans). Furthermore, normal supply conditions imply a positive relationship between the deposit rate r_D and the volume of deposits D. For simplicity assume that the supply of deposits is perfectly elastic at the given deposit rate. The bank's shareholders contribute a given equity capital K with a required rate of return r_K on their investment, where $r_K > r_D$, which reflects the risk premium shareholders demand for holding equity as opposed to deposits. By bank regulation of the Basel Accord type, the bank is subject to the capital adequacy requirement shown in Equation 27.1:

$$kL \le K. \tag{27.1}$$

The parameter k, $0 < k < 1$, is the minimum capital-to-loan ratio. It represents in a highly stylized fashion the Cooke ratio or solvency ratio known from banking regulation. To keep the model as simple as possible, this framework ignores interbank market transactions. Including interbank lending and borrowing would not lead to qualitative changes in the results. The bank has a given equity capital K. Equity, deposits, and loans are connected in the bank's balance sheet constraint shown in Equation 27.2:

$$L = K + D. \tag{27.2}$$

Loans are subject to credit risk $\tilde{\theta}$ (i.e., debtors will default on an ex ante uncertain share $\tilde{\theta} \in [0, 1]$ of the loan portfolio's interest and principal). The random end-of-period profit $\tilde{\pi}$ for the bank's shareholders is given by Equation 27.3:

$$\tilde{\pi} = (1 - \tilde{\theta})(1 + r_L)L(r_L) - (1 + r_D)D - (1 + r_K)K. \tag{27.3}$$

Since in equilibrium $r_L > r_D$, the bank will give loans up to the limit set by regulation (i.e., the capital requirement is binding). Substituting the bank's balance sheet constraint (Equation 27.2) and the binding capital requirement (Equation 27.1) into Equation 27.3 yields Equation 27.4:

$$\tilde{\pi} = [r_L - r_C - \tilde{\theta}(1 + r_L)]L(r_L) \tag{27.4}$$

for the end-of-period profit where $r_C = (1 - k)r_D + kr_L$ is the bank's weighted average cost of capital.

At the beginning of the period the bank chooses its loan rate r_L to maximize the expected value of its owners' utility as shown in Equation 27.5:

$$EU(\tilde{\pi}) = EU\left[(r_L - r_C - \tilde{\theta}(1 + r_L))L(r_L)\right]. \tag{27.5}$$

The first-order condition for maximization is given by Equation 27.6:

$$EU'(\tilde{\pi})\left[(1-\tilde{\theta})L(r_L{}^*) + (r_L{}^* - r_C - \tilde{\theta}(1+r_L{}^*))L'(r_L{}^*)\right] = 0, \qquad (27.6)$$

where E is the expectation operator and an asterisk indicates the loan rate in the optimum.

USING CREDIT DERIVATIVES WITH NO BASIS RISK

Suppose now that a financial instrument has a perfect negative correlation with the credit risk enabling the bank to transfer credit risk to or from a third party. Using such a risk-sharing market with no basis risk leads to a modified profit function in Equation 27.7:

$$\tilde{\pi} = \left[r_L - r_C - \tilde{\theta}(1+r_L)\right]L(r_L) + H(\tilde{\theta} - \theta_f). \qquad (27.7)$$

The bank exchanges a fixed payment $\theta_f H$ against a stochastic payment, $\tilde{\theta}H$. The credit derivative corresponds to a CDS. Notice that the volume H of hedging contracts is not constrained. The term θ_f is the given price of the credit derivative. This assumption leads to the expected utility maximization shown in Equation 27.8:

$$\max_{r_L, H} EU(\tilde{\pi}). \qquad (27.8)$$

Assume that the price of the credit derivative is unbiased (i.e., $\theta_f = E(\tilde{\theta})$). The first-order condition for the optimum loan rate and hedging volume leads to the following claim:

Proposition 1. Suppose a credit derivative with no basis risk and an unbiased price. The bank's optimal loan rate and hedge volume are given by Equations 27.9 and 27.10:

$$(1-\theta_f)L(r_L^*) + \left[r_L^* - r_C - \theta_f(1+r_L^*)\right]L'(r_L^*) = 0 \qquad (27.9)$$

$$H^* = (1+r_L^*)L(r_L^*). \qquad (27.10)$$

Equation 27.9 is a (Fisher) separation result. The bank's optimal loan rate only depends on cost and demand conditions and on the forward rate θ_f. Decisions are taken as if there were no uncertainty (i.e., the bank's beliefs about the distribution of credit risk and its risk aversion play no role for its optimal choice of an asset and liability position). The full hedge result in Equation 27.10 is a consequence of the unbiased price of the credit derivative. The bank buys full insurance against credit risk by selling all risk in the forward market.

A biased derivative price does not affect the separation result in Equation 27.9 which only depends on the absence of basis risk. However, for $\theta_f \neq E(\tilde{\theta})$ the bank's beliefs and the degree of risk aversion will affect the hedging quantity H. A so-called speculative hedge will arise with potential under- or over-hedging and even the possibility that the bank will become a provider of credit risk insurance. Even under an unbiased risk-sharing market, an under- or over-hedge can be optimal, when taking into account background risk in the sense of Franke, Schlesinger, and Stapleton (2011). Broll and Wong (2013) provide an analysis of additive and multiplicative background risk.

CREDIT DERIVATIVES WITH BASIS RISK

Using a credit derivative, a bank can lock in a return of its loan business with certainty in advance. However, assuming a case of a perfect negative correlation between credit risk and credit derivative is a highly stylized one. The case will prevail only when hedging is conducted bilaterally between a seller and a buyer who design a specific derivative contract based on the seller's credit risk. Whenever the stochastic properties of the reference entity underlying the credit derivative deviate from the credit risk to be hedged, the seller of credit risk-in this case the bank-will retain some of the risk. Such basis risk will occur, for example, for a mismatch between the maturities of the credit derivative and the bank's loan portfolio, or when using a standardized credit derivative that has stochastic properties different from the ones of the credit risk to be hedged. Credit derivatives with basis risk are no longer perfect bilateral forward contracts, but rather imperfect futures contracts. Thus, the next step is to analyze the consequences of such basis risk for the bank's optimal loan rate and hedging decisions.

Consider the case where the bank cannot find a hedging instrument that perfectly offsets its credit risk. Characterizing optimal decisions under basis risk becomes difficult. Some results may be obtained by focusing on a linear relationship between credit risk $\tilde{\theta}$ and the underlying $\tilde{g}$ of the credit derivative. The model presented in this section assumes regression dependence in the sense of Benninga, Eldor, and Zilcha (1983).

Assumption 1. $\tilde{\theta}$ is linearly regressable on $\tilde{g}$ in the following form shown in Equation 27.11:

$$\tilde{\theta} = \alpha + \beta\tilde{g} + \tilde{\varepsilon}, \tag{27.11}$$

where α is a constant, the regression coefficient β can be positive or negative, and $\tilde{\varepsilon}$ is a random variable stochastically independent of $\tilde{g}$ with mean zero and standard deviation σ_ε. Using σ to denote standard deviations of random variables and cov for the covariance operator, Equation 27.12 shows the correlation coefficient ρ between $\tilde{\theta}$ and $\tilde{g}$:

$$\rho = \frac{\text{cov}(\tilde{\theta}, \tilde{g})}{\sigma_\theta \sigma_g} = \frac{\beta\sigma_g}{\beta\sigma_g + \sigma_\varepsilon} \tag{27.12}$$

which is strictly decreasing in σ_ε, the closeness of the relationship between credit risk to be hedged and the risk of the reference entity underlying the credit derivative used. When σ_ε equals zero, $\tilde{\theta}$ and $\tilde{g}$ are perfectly correlated, which results in the case of no basis risk. A perfect hedge is created if $\sigma_\varepsilon = 0$ (see Proposition 1), and an imperfect or cross hedge, if σ_ε is positive (see Proposition 2 that follows). The term σ_ε can be interpreted as a measure of the incompleteness of the credit derivative market.

The bank now exchanges a fixed payment $g_f H$ against a stochastic payment $\tilde{g}H$ leading to the new profit definition in Equation 27.13:

$$\tilde{\pi} = \left[r_L - r_C - \tilde{\theta}(1 + r_L) \right] L(r_L) + H(\tilde{g} - g_f). \qquad (27.13)$$

To focus on non-speculative hedging, unbiasedness is assumed (i.e., $g_f = E(\tilde{g})$). Separation no longer holds when maximizing with respect to the loan rate and the hedging volume and substituting into Equation 27.11. Rewriting the first-order condition for H, Equation 27.14 emerges:

$$\mathrm{cov}\left[U' \left(\tilde{g}(H^* - \beta(1 + r_L^*)L) - (\alpha + \tilde{\varepsilon})(1 + r_L^*)L + (r_L^* - r_C)L - g_f H^* \right); \tilde{g} \right] = 0. \qquad (27.14)$$

Due to the stochastic independence of $\tilde{\varepsilon}$ and $\tilde{g}$, this condition can only hold if the hedge ratio is expressed as shown in Equation 27.15:

$$\frac{H^*}{(1 + r_L^*)L(r_L^*)} = \beta. \qquad (27.15)$$

Inspection of this result leads to the following claim:

Proposition 2. In the presence of basis risk, the bank hedges a fixed portion β (hedge ratio) of the credit risk.

The hedge ratio β of this so-called beta-hedge can be determined by estimating the regression Equation 27.11. Because residual uncertainty exists in this case, the end-of-period profit is still random, indicating that due to basis risk a portion of credit risk cannot be hedged away. Recall that the separation result discussed earlier no longer holds. The optimal loan rate depends on risk preferences and the joint probability distributions of credit risk and the risk of the reference entity underlying the credit derivative.

The extent of optimal hedging depends on the slope of the regression of credit risk on the hedge instrument. Determining which hedge instrument to use is an empirical question. Comparing two underlyings g_1 and g_2, the bank will choose the one with the lower σ_ε (i.e., the higher coefficient of determination in the estimation of Equation 27.11).

Financial contracts other than credit derivatives can also serve as candidates for hedging a loan portfolio. For instance, macro derivatives can be used. The beta-hedge rule, which was derived for an aggregate loan portfolio, can be generalized to a disaggregated bank loan portfolio.

HEDGING EFFECTIVENESS

The risk-reducing quality of a financial hedging instrument can be further evaluated using the concept of hedging effectiveness (HE) (Ederington 1979). *Hedging effectiveness* is defined as one minus the ratio of the variance of end-of-period profit with hedging, $\tilde{\pi}$, over the variance of end-of-period profit without hedging, $\tilde{\pi}_0$, as shown in Equation 27.16:

$$HE = 1 - \frac{\text{var}(\tilde{\pi})}{\text{var}(\tilde{\pi}_0)}. \tag{27.16}$$

If a perfectly correlated financial hedging instrument were available, hedging effectiveness would be equal to one because the full hedge implies $\text{var}(\tilde{\pi}) = 0$ (Proposition 1). The presence of basis risk, $\sigma_\varepsilon > 0$, leads to an (imperfect) beta-hedge (Proposition 2), and due to $\text{var}(\tilde{\pi}) > 0$ to a hedging effectiveness $HE < 1$. When the bank follows the beta-hedge rule from Proposition 2, the following result for the hedging effectiveness emerges.

Proposition 3. Under the beta-hedge rule, $H = \beta(1+r_L)L(r_L)$, hedging effectiveness is equal to the square of the correlation coefficient between credit risk and the underlying of the hedge instrument used, that is, $HE = \rho^2$.

The proof is as follows. Since $\text{cov}(\tilde{\theta}, \tilde{g}) = \beta\text{var}(\tilde{g})$ and $\sigma_\theta = \beta\sigma_g + \sigma_\varepsilon$, combining these expressions with Equation 27.12 and 27.16, Equation 27.17 emerges:

$$HE = \left(\frac{\beta\sigma_g}{\beta\sigma_g + \sigma_\varepsilon}\right)^2 = \rho^2. \tag{27.17}$$

Choosing the instrument with the highest hedging effectiveness and choosing the one with the lowest standard deviation of the residuals in the regression between credit risk and risk of the reference entity underlying the derivative used leads to the same decision.

HEDGING CREDIT RISK UNDER STATE-DEPENDENT PREFERENCES

This section examines the behavior of a banking firm with state-dependent preferences. Imagine bank owners or managers who value profits differently based on economic conditions. For instance, during a recession a given level of profit may create more utility than during a boom. Let $U(\tilde{\pi}, \tilde{s})$ be the preferences where $\tilde{s}$ is a state variable (i.e., the utility function is state-dependent). The following proposition shows that the beta-hedge rule may no longer be optimal in this case. Considering different values of $\tilde{s}$ as states of the business cycle, this implies that the banking firm takes the business cycle of the economy into consideration when deriving its optimal use of credit derivatives.

By assumption the utility function, $U(\tilde{\pi}, \tilde{s})$, satisfies $U_1(\tilde{\pi}, \tilde{s}) < 0$, $U_{11}(\tilde{\pi}, \tilde{s}) < 0$, and $U_{12}(\tilde{\pi}, \tilde{s}) < 0$, where subscripts 1 and 2 denote partial derivatives with respect to the first and the second argument, respectively. Under this specification, a lower value of $\tilde{s}$, indicating weaker economic conditions, leads to a higher marginal utility of profit. The first-order condition for optimal hedging is now shown in Equation 27.18:

$$\text{E}\left[U_1(\tilde{\pi}, \tilde{s})(\tilde{g} - g_f)\right] = 0. \tag{27.18}$$

Using the covariance operator, regression dependence, and unbiasedness of the credit derivatives with the underlying reference entity $\tilde{g}$, Equation 27.19 emerges:

$$\text{cov}\left[U_1(\tilde{\pi}, \tilde{s}), \tilde{g}\right] = 0, \tag{27.19}$$

where end-of-period profit is $\tilde{\pi} = \tilde{g}(H - \beta(1 + r_L^*)L) - (\alpha + \tilde{\varepsilon})(1+r_L^*)L + (r_L^* - r_C)L - g_f H$.

The following claim can be made that a beta-hedge is no longer optimal should the banking firm's objective function depend on the state of the business cycle of the economy.

Proposition 4. Assume an unbiased credit derivative, regression dependence between credit risk $\tilde{\theta}$ and the underlying $\tilde{g}$, and state-dependent utility with $U_{12}(\tilde{\pi}, \tilde{s}) < 0$. The bank chooses to hedge more (less) of its credit risk exposure compared to the beta-hedge rule, if credit risk is negatively (positively) correlated with the state variable $\tilde{s}$.

Suppose the economy is in a recession (i.e., the realization of $\tilde{s}$ is low). This state corresponds to a high realization of credit risk $\tilde{\theta}$. In this case of a negative correlation Proposition 4 indicates that the bank hedges more. This proposition is driven by the fact that the marginal utility of profit is high when the state variable takes a low value. Briys and Schlesinger (1993) affirm this insight and show that state dependency of preferences systematically affects optimal hedging.

Having analyzed some economic basics of risk management with credit derivatives at given prices, a more sophisticated view of the risk-sharing market is now introduced. Information on the state of the loan market influences the price of credit derivatives.

Credit Risk, Credit Derivatives, and Market Transparency

The uncertainty faced by a bank may not be the same across time. Traditionally, researchers have analyzed this by considering changes of the distribution of risk in the form of mean-preserving spreads or first-order stochastic dominance (Wong 1997; Eeckhoudt, Gollier, and Schlesinger 2005; Pausch and Welzel 2013). A more recent approach developed in Broll, Eckwert, and Eickhoff (2012) links the change in risk to the availability of publicly observable information. Following this latter approach, this section proposes an information-based concept of uncertainty and, in this setting, revisits the link among credit risk, the use of credit derivatives, and optimal bank behavior.

Suppose that a signal in the economy influences the uncertainty under which asset and liability choices of a bank are taken. A public information system conveys signals about the return distribution of a bank's loans. If this information system is more precise, the random return of an aggregate loan portfolio can be assessed more accurately reducing the uncertainty faced by the bank. The bank updates its beliefs in a Bayesian manner, and the loan market is considered more transparent, if the signal conveys more reliable information.

Assuming that a credit derivative enables the bank to partially or fully hedge the return risk of its loan portfolio, an exogenous reduction of uncertainty (e.g., through a mean-preserving spread or first-order stochastic dominance) is not equivalent to a decline of uncertainty due to a more precise public information system. In fact, an increased reliability of the signals may alter the terms of trade on the market for credit derivatives and thus affect the bank's portfolio and hedging decision. Standard models of banking ignore this interaction and therefore do not necessarily capture the impact of information-induced changes of uncertainty on optimal bank behavior. Higher transparency in the loan market always raises expected bank profits, but may lead to a higher or lower expected loan volume. Moreover, unless risk aversion is very low, economic well-being of the bank is not necessarily positively related to transparency. In fact, if the bank is strongly risk-averse, more transparency may well lead to less expected utility.

THE MODEL

This section considers a representative bank under perfect competition. At the beginning of the period the bank is endowed with a given equity capital K and issues deposits D. Net returns r_D and r_K again are given. The bank uses equity and deposits to extend loans L to customers. As borrowers face uncertainty such as unemployment or risky investment projects, they will not always pay back loans including interest in full. This section does not explicitly model the loan repayment mechanism. Instead, the implied risk for the bank by a random variable is captured in the net return on loans $\tilde{r}$ with a (prior) probability density function $f(\tilde{r})$. This return rate captures both the interest on loans and the credit risk.

The bank chooses deposit and loan volumes D and L after observing the realization of a publicly observable random information signal $\tilde{y}$ with relevance for loan repayments. This signal, which may be released by the central bank, government, or some economic forecasting or rating institution, is correlated with the random return on loans and thus contains information about $\tilde{r}$. From the perspective of the bank, the return rate on its loan portfolio after receiving the realization y is a random variable with density $v(r|y)$.

Let r_f be the price of the credit derivative determined at the beginning of the period. A perfect hedge instrument is assumed (i.e., no basis risk exists). The bank exchanges a fixed payment $r_f H$ against a stochastic payment $\tilde{r}H$. Note again that the volume H of hedging contracts is not constrained and can have a positive or negative sign. The credit derivative market is assumed to be unbiased, as shown in Equation 27.20:

$$r_f(y) = \mathrm{E}\left(\tilde{r}\,|y\right). \tag{27.20}$$

The price of the credit derivative depends on the signal via the posterior probabilities $v(r|y)$. Moreover, r_f is linear in the posterior probabilities. The bank's random end-of-period profit $\tilde{\pi}$ is given by Equation 27.21:

$$\tilde{\pi} = (1 + \tilde{r})L - (1 + r_D)D - (1 + r_K)K - C(L) + \left(r_f(y) - \tilde{r}\right)H. \tag{27.21}$$

The operating cost function $C(L)$ for loans is a strictly increasing and convex function. To keep the exposition simple, deposits are assumed to only cause fixed costs, which are normalized to zero, and capital regulation is omitted. The bank's asset and liability portfolio has to satisfy the balance sheet constraint $L = K + D$, which is solved for D and substituted into the profit function Equation 27.21. Preferences of the bank's owners are described by an increasing and strictly concave utility function $U(\tilde{\pi})$. At the beginning of the period the bank chooses a loan volume and a hedging position to maximize expected utility of its random profit as illustrated in Equation 27.22:

$$\max_{L,H} \mathrm{E} \left[U \left(\tilde{\pi} \, \big| y \right) \right]. \tag{27.22}$$

Equation 27.23 characterizes the solution to the optimization problem:

$$r_f(y) - r_D = C'\left(L^*\right) \tag{27.23}$$
$$H^* = L^*.$$

The first-order condition implies that the bank chooses a strictly positive loan volume, if and only if the price in the market for the credit derivative is uniformly larger than the interest on deposits (i.e., $r_f(y) > r_D$). From Equation 27.23, the bank chooses to fully hedge its loan portfolio and ends up with end-of-period profit, $\pi^* = (r_f(y) - r_D)L^* - (r_K - r_D)K - C\left(L^*\right)$, which is non-stochastic. Furthermore, the bank's optimal loan volume, L^*, is uniquely determined by equating the earnings from the margin, or spread, $r_f(y) - r_D$, to the marginal cost of managing the loans, $C'\left(L^*\right)$.

This establishes for the model the validity of the separation and full-hedge properties (see Proposition 1). Again asset and liability decisions of the bank, which now operates under perfect competition, are independent of attitudes toward risk. Moreover, all risk will be fully hedged if the credit derivative market is unbiased.

H^*, L^*, and π^* all depend on the publicly observable signal y through the forward rate $r_f(y)$. Before analyzing the resulting economic consequences of a more informative signal, the next section presents the notion of transparency, which is based on the signal's informativeness.

TRANSPARENCY IN THE MARKET FOR BANK LOANS

This section develops the transparency of the loan market with the informativeness of y. The informativeness of the signal, in turn, depends on the underlying information (Blackwell 1953). An information system, denoted by γ, specifies for each state of nature, r, a conditional probability density function over the set of signals $\gamma \left(y \, | r \right)$. The positive real number $\gamma \left(y \, | r \right)$ defines the conditional probability that the signal y will be observed, if the true return is r. $\gamma \left(y \, | r \right)$ is common knowledge. Using the Bayes rule, the bank revises its assessment of probabilities and maximizes expected utility on the basis of the updated beliefs. Under the Bayes rule, the density function for the updated posterior distribution is shown in Equation 27.24:

$$v \left(r \, | y \right) = \frac{\gamma \left(y \, | r \right) f(r)}{v(y)}. \tag{27.24}$$

Let γ^1 and γ^2 be two information systems. Information system γ^1 is called more informative than γ^2, if γ^2 can be obtained from γ^1 through a process of randomization. A signal y^1 from information system γ^1 is randomly transformed into a new signal y^2 in the system γ^2. The information system γ^2 can be interpreted as being obtained from the γ^1 by adding random noise. Therefore, the signals from information system γ^2 convey no information about the realization of $\tilde{r}$ that is not also conveyed by the signals under γ^1.

The notion of loan market transparency is based on the information content of the signal. The loan market is said to be more transparent if it operates under a more informative information system and, in this sense, the signals are less noisy.

Kihlstrom (1984) derives a property of information systems that can be used in this analysis: Higher transparency (weakly) raises the expectation of any convex function of posterior beliefs. This property will be used in providing some of the main results in this section.

ECONOMIC IMPLICATIONS OF HIGHER TRANSPARENCY IN THE LOAN MARKET

This section analyzes how transparency in the loan market is related to the bank's optimal loan portfolio, its ex ante expected profits, and ex ante expected utility. The key variable of interest for this comparative static exercise is r_f since the behavior of the bank depends on the information signal only via the price of the credit derivative. Differentiating Equation 27.23 with respect to r_f yields the following claim.

Proposition 5. Let $\bar{L}$ be the expected volume of bank loans before the signal y can be observed. More transparency in the loan market leads to a higher (lower) expected volume of bank loans $\bar{L}$, if the marginal cost function $C'(L)$ is concave (convex).

The intuition for the result in Proposition 5 is as follows. A higher price of the credit derivative raises the spread in the loan market which makes lending more profitable for the bank. Accordingly, the bank responds by expanding its loan portfolio. Observe that the bank's profit is higher for y' than for y, if and only if $r_f(y') > r_f(y)$. Thus, the signal y' is "better" than signal y, if and only if it corresponds to a higher forward rate. The previous section highlighted that the bank expands its loan portfolio if the forward rate increases. Hence, the loan volume is larger for good signals than for bad signals.

With more transparency, a good signal becomes even better because now it is more reliable. Consequently, the loan volume increases. For the same reason, a bad signal becomes even worse in a more transparent loan market and the loan volume declines. If the marginal cost of managing the loans is increasing at a decreasing (an increasing) rate, the transparency-induced expansion of the bank's loan portfolio for good signals is larger (smaller) than the transparency-induced contraction of the loan portfolio for bad signals. As such, the ex ante expected loan volume goes up (down) if the marginal cost function is concave (convex).

The next proposition claims that ex ante expected bank profits are higher, when the loan market is more transparent.

Proposition 6. Let $\bar{\pi}$ be the bank's expected profit before the signal y has been observed. More transparency in the loan market leads to a higher expected bank profit $\bar{\pi}$.

An increase in r_f has a first-order effect on the bank's maximum profit. Since the bank extends more loans when r_f increases, this first-order effect on $\pi(r_f)$ becomes stronger for a higher r_f. As a result, the bank's profit function is convex in the price of the credit derivative and, hence, the bank benefits in terms of ex ante expected profits from more loan market transparency.

EXPECTED UTILITY AND MARKET TRANSPARENCY

Since transparency of the loan market has been shown to affect the portfolio decision of the bank, it also has an impact on its expected utility ex ante (i.e., before a signal has been received). One might expect that lower credit risk due to more market transparency would benefit the bank. However, the literature shows that this is not necessarily the case (Hirshleifer 1971; Eckwert and Zilcha 2001; Schlee 2001). The reason for this ambiguity is that in economic settings where agents can share risks, more transparency typically affects the risk allocation and, thereby, economic well-being.

With more market transparency, from an ex ante perspective the derivative price becomes riskier as it reacts more sensitively to random signal changes. Through this mechanism higher transparency imposes welfare costs on the risk-averse bank. The literature refers to this effect as the *Hirshleifer effect*. The (negative) Hirshleifer effect is caused by a deterioration of the risk allocation, and this effect is more important, if risk aversion is higher. Conversely, the greater informational content of the signal permits the bank to better predict the future state of the economy that may result in welfare gains. This is the so-called the *Blackwell effect*. The total impact of higher transparency in the loan market on the bank's expected utility consists of these two opposing effects.

Proposition 7. More transparency in the loan market raises expected utility, if the bank is risk neutral or if its risk aversion is sufficiently small. For high risk aversion, the bank's expected utility may decline with higher loan market transparency.

The economic intuition is as follows. While more market transparency reduces the uncertainty at the time the signal can be observed, from an ex ante point of view, less risk can be shared through trading on the credit derivative market. Thus, even though the risk allocation is conditionally more efficient given the signal realizations, higher transparency makes risk allocation less efficient from an ex ante perspective. This Hirshleifer effect reduces expected utility and may dominate the Blackwell effect if the bank is highly risk averse.

Further Aspects from the Economics of Credit Derivatives

Having presented insights into the workings and the role of credit derivatives for banks in the previous sections, this section discusses selected issues and open questions from the economic literature on credit derivatives. Credit derivatives are approached from the perspective of the microeconomic theory of financial intermediation and we do not deal with pricing of credit derivatives, which is an important issue in finance.

Two strands exist in the microeconomic theory of financial intermediation in general and of banking in particular: the industrial organization approach and the information economics approach (Freixas and Rochet 2008). The former is supplemented by risk and risk preferences and therefore is used for this analysis. The framework used can be applied to other forms of protection against credit risk than the CDS modeled here. Broll, Schweimayer, and Welzel (2004) analyze the effect of a credit derivative paying a fixed pre-determined amount of money in case of a credit event. They also show how a macro derivative, which may be based on an index aggregating some macroeconomic variables, can be used to hedge credit risk. Determining which derivative offers the highest hedging effectiveness is an empirical question. Also, macro derivatives can be an attractive way to at least insure against systematic risk, especially when the unsystematic risk of a loan because of asymmetric information between buyers and sellers of credit risk may be difficult to insure.

The industrial economics approach also allows analyzing the interaction among credit risk, use of credit protection, and capital regulation in banking. Pausch and Welzel (2013) show how banks react to an increase in credit risk in the presence of capital regulation and CDS markets. They find for the substitution approach included in the Basel II and Basel III Accords that the tendency to react with an over- or under-hedge to a biased CDS market will be lower than without regulation. The regulatory rules with respect to credit derivatives therefore contribute to strengthen bank stability.

Although interesting insights arise from this approach, important issues still should be analyzed. Since banks dominate both the demand and the supply side in CDS markets and these markets are highly concentrated, an oligopoly model with endogenous determination of the CDS price would be needed to move beyond the limits of focusing on single banks and toward a general equilibrium framework.

In the aftermath of the financial crisis of 2007–2008, some blamed the use of credit derivatives for contributing to the crisis. Similarly, in the sovereign debt crisis in the European Union (EU) since 2010, some observers point to an alleged role of CDS on sovereign debt. Authors such as Ayadi and Behr (2009) call for more regulation and less self-regulation of derivatives markets. The question of whether credit derivatives stabilize or destabilize individual banks and the banking system as a whole has long been discussed. At first glance, financial innovations that permit the transfer of previously non-tradable risks and a more efficient risk allocation look favorable. They offer new opportunities for diversification and can increase liquidity. However, a bank can spare regulatory capital and thereby create a higher loan volume by selling credit risk.

Instefjord (2005) is the first to show a potentially destabilizing effect arising from the incentive to take on additional risks. If the underlying loan market is too elastic, the innovation of credit derivatives can destabilize banks by inducing them to act more aggressively in the loan market (Wagner 2007; Heyde and Neyer 2010). However, empirical evidence from Hirtle (2009) suggests that the impact of credit derivatives on loan volumes is small and interacts with other forms of hedging available to banks.

Allen and Carletti (2006) provide a richer model to analyze the impact of credit derivatives on stability of the banking system. They start from the stylized fact that banks, while being major players on both the demand and the supply side of CDS markets, are net buyers of protection whereas insurance companies are net sellers. By modeling a banking and an insurance sector, they show the role of idiosyncratic liquidity risk in the banking industry for the impact of credit risk transfer on stability.

Contagion from the insurance to the banking industry can now occur. Atkeson, Eisfeldt, and Weill (2012) explicitly deal with the highly concentrated structure of CDS markets with a small number of large banks acting as counterparties to a majority of transactions. In a search and matching framework, they show that this market structure, while offering more efficient ex post risk allocation, is subject to systemic risk.

Several recent papers examine the network character of derivatives markets. Duffie and Zhu (2011), for example, look at the efficiency of central clearing of CDS deals and find that central counterparties will not necessarily reduce counterparty risk as Cecchetti, Gyntelberg, and Hollanders (2009) had claimed. Eichengreen, Mody, Nedeljkovic, and Samo (2012) conclude from an analysis of CDS spreads that credit derivatives contributed to infect European banks with problems in the U.S. market for subprime loans.

Credit derivatives alter the balance of power in the contractual relationship between creditor and debtor. A creditor insured through a credit derivative will be less accommodating in a debt renegotiation. A CDS then serves as a commitment device and creditors will have an incentive to over-insure (Bolton and Oehmke 2011). Such an "empty creditor" who holds contractual control rights, but no longer faces credit risk, may even have an incentive to tolerate the credit event (on these corporate finance issues see Arping 2012).

The empty creditor problem differs from the issue of a "naked" CDS. An investor buying a CDS without holding the underlying reference asset (i.e., getting insurance without having a reason to be insured), holds a purely speculative position in a so-called naked CDS. In the sovereign debt crisis in the Euro area since 2010, some observers saw naked sovereign CDS protection as exacerbating the crisis (e.g., by driving CDS prices up to levels not based on economic fundamentals and at the same time creating negative signals for the underlying market in sovereign bonds). In late 2012, the EU felt compelled to ban naked sovereign CDS protection. A recent study by the International Monetary Fund (2013), however, finds no support for such a ban of naked protection. Cont (2010) also concludes that the lack of central clearing and supervision of protection sellers can be detrimental to financial stability.

Using the industrial economics approach comes at the cost of ignoring problems of asymmetric information. The analogy between credit derivatives and insurance suggests the presence of adverse selection and moral hazard. Banks applying the originate-to-distribute (OTD) business model by selling credit risk have a lower incentive to screen loan applications and to monitor debtors. Even worse, a bank can use insider information on the creditor-debtor relationship when buying protection against credit risk. The use of credit derivatives by banks is limited because adverse selection and moral hazard problems make the credit derivatives markets illiquid for the typical credit risks of commercial banks. The informational advantage of the seller of risk that is implicit in the relationship with the debtor creates a barrier to this kind of transferring credit risk.

Minton, Stulz, and Williamson (2009) maintain that these information problems are so severe that banks use credit derivatives predominantly for dealing and only to a very small extent for hedging. Acharya and Johnson (2007) conclude that there is private information of banks buying credit risk insurance, but they find no evidence that this kind of insider trading in CDS markets is directly harmful.

Research on credit derivatives also explicitly considers asymmetric information. Duffee and Zhou (2001) conclude that the kind of asymmetric information matters for the desirability of credit derivatives markets. Nicolò and Pelizzon (2006, 2008) combine asymmetric information and capital regulation in an adverse selection framework. They find that high quality banks can use credit derivatives as signaling devices. Parlour and Plantin (2008) analyze the links between credit derivatives and relationship banking. They find no clear-cut answer to the question of whether credit derivatives are socially beneficial in the presence of relationship banking. Morrison (2005) focuses on the frequent case that borrowers are not informed about the fact that their loan serves as a reference asset for a credit derivative. The bank's selling of the credit risk can destroy the signaling value of the loan for the borrower.

Research on credit derivatives intensified after the banking and financial crisis in the last decade. The focus shifted to some extent away from pricing issues to such topics as stability effects, regulatory consequences, or implications for corporate finance. This is likely to remain an active field in the future.

Summary and Conclusions

This chapter presented stylized facts from the markets for credit derivatives and insights from the literature on the economics of these financial contracts that have gained importance since the 1990s and played a role in the recent banking and financial crisis. Because banks are the most active participants in credit derivatives markets, the chapter reviews the decision problem of a bank acting as financial intermediary between private savers and investors. The bank sells deposits to savers, extends risky loans to investors, and engages in trade on a credit derivative market. The chapter initially assumed the distribution of non-performing loans was given and followed by deriving conclusions relevant to the banking industry and beyond. Next, the chapter clarified the role of basis risk for the optimal hedge ratio and for hedging effectiveness. Then the chapter modeled the return uncertainty of the bank loans through an information system that conveys signals about the unknown loan returns. The degree of transparency in the sense of the informativeness of the information system not only determines the uncertainty under which the bank chooses its deposit-loan portfolio but also may affect the terms of trade on the market for credit derivatives. This information-induced interaction adds a new dimension to the bank's decision problem. The analysis shows that the impact of higher transparency on the behavior of the bank is largely independent of the bank's risk-averse preferences. In particular, more transparency always raises expected profits; and the impact on the expected loan volume can be characterized solely in terms of the curvature of marginal loan management costs. Yet, because the precision of the signals affects the terms of risk-sharing, the consequences for economic welfare are ambiguous. Depending on the bank's attitudes toward risk, economic welfare may increase or decline with higher transparency.

The findings may be considered relevant for the regulation of the banking industry. In fact, to the extent that a bank's accounting information contains forward-looking information about loan returns, the model could shed some light on the channels through which stricter regulatory requirements for the disclosure of balance sheet items in the banking sector affect loan volumes, profits, and economic welfare. Due to the model's simplicity, however, these implications should be handled with care. A framework with a richer set of interactions among financial institutions, private investors/savers, and risk-sharing arrangements might yield further insights into the role of transparency in the banking sector for loan volumes and hedging activities with credit derivatives.

The economic literature on credit derivatives has been growing in scale and scope, especially after the financial crisis of 2007–2008. A much better understanding now exists of the effects of credit derivatives and of the necessity of more transparency in these previously opaque and still highly concentrated markets. Credit derivatives are not bad per se, as some observers wanted to conclude from the banking and financial crisis, but they are financial contracts needing further research and some regulatory attention.

Acknowledgments

We are indebted to the editors, especially Greg Filbeck, for helpful comments and meticulous editing.

Discussion Questions

1. Describe credit default swaps and their benefits for risk management in banking and finance.
2. With basis risk and unbiased futures markets, the optimal hedge with credit derivatives is a fixed proportion of the exposure. Discuss why this result is important for risk management in banking and finance.
3. Discuss how hedge performance can be measured.
4. Discuss why the use of credit derivatives by banks may be limited.
5. Explain why a banking firm might consider the business cycle of the economy when devising its optimal hedging strategy with credit derivatives.
6. Market transparency in the credit market may be related to the bank's optimal loan and hedging transactions. Lower credit risk could be due to more market transparency and lead to a higher loan volume. Explain why this is not necessarily the case.

References

Acharya, Viral V., and Timothy C. Johnson. 2007. "Insider Trading in Credit Derivatives." *Journal of Financial Economics* 84:1, 110–141.
Allen, Franklin, and Elena Carletti. 2006. "Credit Risk Transfer and Contagion." *Journal of Monetary Economics* 53:1, 89–111.
Arping, Stefan. 2012. "Credit Protection and Lending Relationships." Discussion Paper TI 2012–2142, University of Amsterdam, Tinbergen Institute.

Atkeson, Andrew G., Andrea L. Eisfeldt, and Pierre-Olivier Weill. 2012. "Liquidity and Fragility in OTC Credit Derivatives Markets." Working Paper, Department of Economics, University of California, Los Angeles.

Ayadi, Rym, and Patrick Behr. 2009. "On the Necessity to Regulate Credit Derivatives Markets." *Journal of Banking Regulation* 10:3, 179–201.

Bank for International Settlements. 2013. *Statistical Release: OTC Derivatives Statistics at End-December 2012*. Basel: Bank for International Settlements.

Benninga, Simon, Rafael Eldor, and Itzhak Zilcha. 1983. "Optimal Hedging in the Futures Market under Price Uncertainty." *Economics Letters* 13:2/3, 141–145.

Berkshire Hathaway Inc. 2003. *Berkshire Hathaway Annual Report 2002*. Omaha, NE: Berkshire Hathaway Inc.

Blackwell, David. 1953. "Equivalent Comparisons of Experiments." *Annals of Mathematical Statistics* 24:2, 265–272.

Bolton, Patrick, and Martin Oehmke. 2011. "Credit Default Swaps and the Empty Creditor Problem." *Review of Financial Studies* 24:8, 2617–2655.

Briys, Eric, and Harris Schlesinger. 1993. "Optimal Hedging when Preferences Are State Dependent." *Journal of Futures Markets* 13:5, 441–451.

Broll, Udo, and Kit Pong Wong. 2013. "The Firm under Uncertainty: Real and Financial Decisions." *Decisions in Economics and Finance* 36:2, 125–136.

Broll, Udo, Bernhard Eckwert, and Andreas Eickhoff. 2012. "Financial Intermediation and Endogenous Risk in the Banking Sector." *Economic Modeling* 29:5, 1618–1622.

Broll, Udo, Gerhard Schweimayer, and Peter Welzel. 2004. "Managing Credit Risk with Credit and Macro Derivatives." *Schmalenbach Business Review* 56:4, 360–378.

Cecchetti, Stephen, Jacob Gyntelberg, and Mark Hollanders. 2009. "Central Counterparties for Over-the-Counter Derivatives." *BIS Quarterly Review*, September, 45–58.

Cont, Rama. 2010. "Credit Default Swaps and Financial Stability." *Financial Stability Review*, Banque de France, Paris, 14, 35–43.

D'Arcy, Stephen P., James McNichols, and Xinyan Zhao. 2009. *A Primer on Credit Derivatives*. Schaumburg, IL: Society of Actuaries.

Duffee, Gregory R., and Chunsheng Zhou. 2001. "Credit Derivatives in Banking: Useful Tools for Managing Risk?" *Journal of Monetary Economics* 48:1, 25–54.

Duffie, Darrell. 2008. "Innovations in Credit Risk Transfer: Implications for Financial Stability." BIS Working Papers, No. 255, Bank for International Settlements.

Duffie, Darrell, and Haoxiang Zhu. 2011. "Does a Central Clearing Counterparty Reduce Counterparty Risk?" *Review of Asset Pricing Studies* 1:1, 74–95.

Eckwert, Bernhard, and Itzhak Zilcha. 2001. "The Value of Information in Production Economies." *Journal of Economic Theory* 100:1, 172–186.

Ederington, Louis H. 1979. "The Hedging Performance of the New Futures Markets." *Journal of Finance* 34:1, 157–170.

Eeckhoudt, Louis, Christian Gollier, and Harris Schlesinger. 2005. *Economic and Financial Decisions under Risk*. Princeton, NJ: Princeton University Press.

Eichengreen, Barry, Ashoka Mody, Milan Nedeljkovic, and Lucio Sarno. 2012. "How the Subprime Crisis Went Global: Evidence from Bank Credit Default Spreads." *Journal of International Money and Finance* 31:5, 1299–1318.

European Central Bank. 2009. *Credit Default Swaps and Counterparty Risk*. Frankfurt: European Central Bank.

Franke, Guenter, Harris Schlesinger, and Richard C. Stapleton. 2011. "Risk Taking with Additive and Multiplicative Background Risks." *Journal of Economic Theory* 146:4, 1547–1568.

Freixas, Xavier, and Jean-Charles Rochet. 2008. *Microeconomics of Banking*, 2nd Edition. Cambridge, MA: MIT Press.

Froot, Kenneth A., and Jeremy C. Stein. 1998. "Risk Management, Capital Budgeting, and Capital Structure for Financial Institutions: An Integrated Approach." *Journal of Financial Economics* 47:1, 55–82.

Froot, Kenneth A., David S. Scharfstein, and Jeremy C. Stein. 1993. "Risk Management: Coordinating Corporate Investment and Financing Policies." *Journal of Finance* 48:5, 1629–1658.

Helm, Robert W., David M. Geffen, and Stephanie A. Capistron. 2009. "Mutual Funds' Use of Credit Default Swaps-Part I." *Investment Lawyer* 16:12, 3–9.

Heyde, Frank, and Ulrike Neyer. 2010. "Credit Default Swaps and the Stability of the Banking Sector." *International Review of Finance* 10:1, 27–61.

Hirshleifer, Jack. 1971. "The Private and Social Value of Information and the Reward to Incentive Activity." *American Economic Review* 61:4, 561–574.

Hirtle, Beverly. 2009. "Credit Derivatives and Bank Credit Supply." *Journal of Financial Intermediation* 18:2, 125–150.

Instefjord, Norvald. 2005. "Risk and Hedging: Do Credit Derivatives Increase Bank Risk?" *Journal of Banking and Finance* 29:2, 333–345.

International Monetary Fund. 2013. *Global Financial Stability Report*. Washington, DC: International Monetary Fund.

Kihlstrom, Richard E. 1984. "A Bayesian Exposition of Blackwell's Theorem on the Comparison of Experiments." In Marcel Boyer and Richard E. Kihlstrom, eds., >*Bayesian Models of Economic Theory*>, 13–31. New York: Elsevier.

Minton, Bernadette A., René Stulz, andRohan Williamson. 2009. "How Much Do Banks Use Credit Derivatives to Hedge Loans?" *Journal of Financial Services Research* 35:1, 1–31.

Morrison, Alan D. 2005. "Credit Derivatives, Disintermediation, and Investment Decisions." *Journal of Business* 78:2, 621–648.

Nicolò, Antonio, and Loriana Pelizzon. 2006. "Credit Derivatives: Capital Requirements and Strategic Contracting." EFMA 2004 Basel Meetings. Available at SSRN: http://ssrn.com/abstract=498584.

Nicolò, Antonio, and Loriana Pelizzon. 2008. "Credit Derivatives, Capital Requirements and Opaque OTC Markets." *Journal of Financial Intermediation* 17:4, 444–463.

Parlour, Christine A., and Guillaume Plantin. 2008. "Loan Sales and Relationship Banking." *Journal of Finance*, 63:3, 1291–1314.

Pausch, Thilo, and Peter Welzel. 2013. "Regulation, Credit Risk Transfer with CDS, and Bank Lending." *Credit and Capital Markets* 46:4, 443–469.

Schlee, Edward E. 2001. "The Value of Information in Efficient Risk-Sharing Arrangements." *American Economic Review* 91:3, 509–524.

Soros, George. 2009. "One Way to Stop Bear Raids: Credit Default Swaps Need Much Stricter Regulation." Available at http://online.wsj.com/news/articles/SB123785310594719693.

Wagner, Wolf. 2007. "The Liquidity of Bank Assets and Banking Stability." *Journal of Banking and Finance* 31:1, 121–139.

Wong, Kit Pong. 1997. "On the Determinants of Bank Interest Margins under Credit and Interest Rate Risks." *Journal of Banking and Finance* 21:2, 251–271.

28

Foreign Exchange Derivatives in Frontier Markets

OTHMANE BOUKRAMI

Senior Vice President, The Currency Exchange Fund

BERT VAN LIER

Deputy CEO, Chief Investment Officer, The Currency Exchange Fund

Introduction

Frontier markets can be defined as developing countries with relatively undeveloped debt and equity markets. Equity market capitalization is typically low, less than 30 percent of gross domestic production (GDP), and corporate bond markets are immature with limited primary issuances and nonexistent secondary trading. Loans to small and medium-size companies represent merely one-tenth of the size of the economy.

Capital markets have a central role in supporting sustainable development globally by creating and expanding finance accessibility to companies and individuals. During the last few decades, capital markets in emerging countries deepened and secondary markets emerged. For frontier market countries, capital markets are still under developed or nonexistent. Capital markets development includes a comprehensive restructuring program. Decision-makers need to remain attentive to financial markets expanding beyond the regulatory capital on which they are built. As the financial crisis of 2007–2008 demonstrated, an inherent risk exists of markets continuing to grow and attract liquidity, even to the point that the real and financial economies become disconnected, effectively creating a bubble with all the associated risks.

The growth of emerging capital markets is in line with growth levels observed in developed countries, but liquidity in these markets still lags behind. Although emerging economies are probably healthier without the surplus in liquidity that some of the most developed capital markets have experienced, markets should have more depth and scope to become a major source of funds for those emerging countries experiencing regular and substantial growth in their economies.

Capital markets development is a prerequisite for the emergence of a derivatives market. As the name indicates, a *financial derivative* is a contract that derives its value from the performance of underlying entities such as an asset, index, or interest rate. A derivative transaction is priced using the market price of a single or a number of other tradable instruments. Hence, derivative securities allow the buyer to gain exposure to underlying instruments in a single contract and without the need to mobilize large resources. If used rationally as a risk management tool, the derivatives market is important to emerging and frontier markets development because it allows effectively hedging different financial risks.

The existence of a liquid government bond market and a short-term interest-rate-tradable benchmark are important requirements for creating a cross-currency derivatives market. In advanced economies, interest rate differentials are used as a proxy for pricing exchange rate risk. Market makers can offset their exposure through a foreign exchange (FX) spot transaction and two money market operations of borrowing and lending in each currency of the FX derivative transaction. This opportunity is possible when no capital controls exist on trading these currencies or limitations on dealing in the money market of each currency.

In frontier markets, capital controls are often in place and access to the domestic money market is restricted to residents only. These constraints limit hedging opportunities, which are a condition to offshore market makers who want to take part in the FX derivatives market. The lack of possibilities to offset risk generally means that entering these markets is a non-starter for international commercial banks despite the rapid growth prospects in these economies. In such a situation, the first institution evaluating and pricing such risks and willing to take positions without any exit or hedging opportunities would serve as a market creator, enabling others to follow.

Because FX derivatives products are still underdeveloped in frontier markets, the purpose of this chapter is to focus on the recommended steps needed to develop such products. The possible large derivative usage for speculative purposes could defeat the original economic development goal and severely affect local economies. This chapter does not suggest fully removing capital controls. FX derivatives growth pace should be monitored and non-speculative financial institutions offering hedging products to commercial entities operating onshore should have less stringent capital controls and be granted access to the onshore money market. Such conditions would allow the financial institutions offering financial risk intermediation to continue offsetting local entrepreneurs' risk, which would eventually allow better utilization of local companies' capital. Commercial banks could start offering FX derivative transactions in the offshore market, which is not subject to local central banks' regulations. The process of pricing currency derivatives transactions in an environment without tradable benchmarks and limited hedging opportunities will be illustrated by using interest rate proxies.

This chapter is organized into five sections. The first section summarizes the theoretical background on FX forward pricing. The second section focuses on the development of capital markets in general and a liquid local government bond yield curve in particular. The third section describes the relevance of an offshore market for commercial banks wanting to start offering exchange rate derivatives in frontier currencies. The fourth section shows an illustrative historical back-testing simulation. In this simulation FX forwards are priced by using interest rates and inflation rates as proxies for the cost of funds in frontier currencies. The final section provides a summary and conclusions.

Theoretical Background

A fundamental difference between a spot and forward market is timing associated with the transaction. In the FX spot market, the two counterparties of a transaction offer to exchange currencies in a relatively short-term period. A forward transaction allows individuals or companies to organize their buying or selling of foreign currency in advance in order to make an international payment in the future.

Empirical studies both support and oppose the expectations hypothesis (EH) and the unbiased expectation hypothesis (UEH). The EH assumes that the shape of the yield curve fully represents market participants' expectations of future short-term interest rates. Macauley (1938), Hickman (1942), and Culbertson (1975) reject this pure form of expectations. The UEH claims that the forward rate is a full reflection of all available information about the exchange rate expectations (Chiang 1986). The hypothesis assumes that markets are efficient and that the current spot and interest rate carry reflect all information. The *interest rate carry* is defined as the spread between the interest rates of the two currencies priced in the forward.

According to Fama (1984), a forward rate could be interpreted as the sum of the predicted future spot rate and a premium. More precisely, Fama demonstrates that the forward foreign exchange rate observed for a pair of currencies at time $t + 1$ is the determined market certainty equivalent of the expected exchange rate spot at time $T + 1$. His research is related to the changes of both the premium and the predicted components of forwards rates. Assuming a full efficiency of the FX forward market, Fama finds evidence that both parameters of forward rates fluctuate through time. The study offers two important conclusions: (1) changes in the premiums drive most of the change in forward rates and (2) a negative correlation exists between the expected future spot rate components of forward rates and the premium. Fama also finds that the one-month forward rate correctly predicts the spot rate one month ahead, but finds limited evidence that the same conclusion could be drawn for the two- to five-month forwards.

In order to test this hypothesis in other markets, a conventional ordinary least squares (OLS) regression method could be applied as long as the data considered are stationary. The dependent and independent variables would be the spot rate and the forward rate, respectively.

The previous studies use tradable and liquid currencies with observable forward rates. These data are often nonexistent in frontier markets. Therefore, the purpose of this chapter is not to test the validity of the UEH for frontier market currencies, as a regression cannot be performed due to the lack of data. Instead, the chapter demonstrates how to calculate the cost of forwards in selected frontier market currencies and subsequently test whether the interest rate parity principle used to define the carry in setting the forward rate is a good prediction of the future spot rate. The currencies considered as well as the output of the simulation are presented after a more in-depth capital market review in frontier markets.

Capital Markets Development

Even before the financial crisis of 2007–2008 and the economic recession that followed, the developing markets grew much faster than the developed markets. According to the United Nations (2011), frontier and emerging economies drove more than half of the global economic growth since the third quarter of 2009. The rise of emerging countries such as China, Russia, Brazil, and India, which are now among the world's top 10 economies, explains this trend. This serious imbalance in growth since the financial crisis fueled a rapid recovery in both direct and portfolio investment into emerging markets often to above pre-crisis levels. An increasing number of foreign investors sought to benefit from the wealth creation in these new markets and diversify their portfolios away from developed economies. Figure 28.1 shows the Proportion of domestic government securities held by foreigners. In advanced economies such as France and Australia, foreign investors hold more than 50 percent of marketable debts. By contrast, in emerging economies such as Brazil, Thailand or Philippines, the share of foreign investors in domestic debts is less than 30 percent. This percentage is relatively small compared to that of economies with developed capital markets but foreign investors' interest in emerging and frontier markets is still growing.

Sarkissian and Schill (2009) demonstrate that information benefits and often substantial savings may result from emerging markets firms raising funds locally or at least in a regional financial center. In emerging and frontier markets, offshore investors are unlikely to tap into the potential of firms if they do not understand the local markets. Capital controls, taxes, nonexistent benchmarks, as well as the instable regulatory

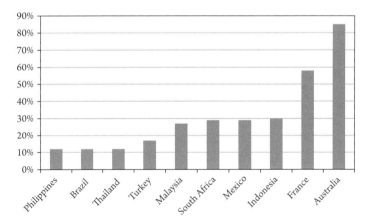

Figure 28.1 PROPORTION OF DOMESTIC GOVERNMENT SECURITIES HELD BY FOREIGNERS INVESTORS.   This figure shows the Proportion of domestic government securities held by foreigners in 11 countries. In advanced economies such as France and Australia, foreign investors hold more than 50 percent of government debt. However, in emerging economies such as Brazil, Thailand, or Philippines, the foreign investors' share in domestic debt is less than 25 percent. This percentage is relatively small compared to that of economies with developed capital markets, but foreign investors' interest in emerging and frontier markets is still growing. Source: Foreign Investment in Local Currency Bonds, The World Bank, December 2012.

framework, are some of the factors that deter foreign investors from investing in the domestic capital markets in frontier economies.

Frontier markets lag emerging markets in many areas and much more so than emerging markets lag developed markets. One main difference is the level of development of non-banking financial services. Other differences concern the progress made in the general business environment and the emergence of the banking sector. Stability in the financial sector is a necessary factor in capital markets development and depends on a complex set of macroeconomic conditions. Emerging markets have a much more stable financial sector than the frontier ones.

Most frontier currencies are so-called *managed floating currencies* with capital controls imposed to residents and nonresidents due to the scarcity of reserve currencies. Currencies are often only convertible for current account transactions. International-trade-focused entrepreneurs with valid underlying commercial operations have access to the purchase of hard currencies to pay their imports. Supporting documentation is often required as proof of the commercial transaction. Foreign investors, who originally converted hard currencies into local currencies to make their initial investment, have the right to buy dollars or other reserve currencies to repatriate their dividends or capital gains.

Many countries impose conditions on nonresidents who want to participate in the local money and/or capital markets to avoid speculative positioning. Regulators often require a minimum security holding period for foreign investors. Additionally, the size of bond markets in frontier economies is not only small compared to GDP but also insignificant overall, as the size of many emerging economies is immaterial compared to foreign investors' investment capacity. Even when offshore investors have a few investment opportunities in frontier countries' government and corporate bonds, the high taxation rate is another obstacle to investing. Further, regulatory frameworks are often perceived as unstable, as central banks and regulators frequently revise investment laws. Short-term needs to either attract foreign investors or prevent them from accessing local markets, depending on the potential impact such investments would have on the exchange rate, often drive changes.

Another constraining factor for investors is the illiquidity of the local securities markets. Many frontier economies have established primary government issuance programs. Yet, extremely few transactions occur in the secondary market, making such markets particularly illiquid. The total liquidity of a market is not the only objective. Hearn, Piesse, and Strange (2010) find that for smaller emerging markets companies, investors require a spread that is higher than would be justified by their risk. Demarigny (2010) shows that large capitalization companies benefit most from available liquidity. This finding implies that policy makers should guarantee that capital markets are not exclusively the domain of large corporations.

Secondary markets provide an exit for investors and an opportunity for valuation and price discovery. The role of liquidity providers is important because they use their expertise and information to benefit from any arbitrage opportunities. Once a liquid sovereign yield curve is developed, it can be used both as a reference for the onshore cost of money and as a proxy for exchange rate risk derivatives. Developing countries gain from such capital market regulatory and accessibility reforms. The effect depends on the markets' ability to generate more investments and on the productivity of these investments. Allowing foreign investors to access local capital markets increases competition among market participants and generally drives bond yields or equities' returns down, partly because of increased liquidity.

In many frontier market economies, liquidity premiums implied in government securities are large. These premiums are substantially reduced when foreign investors take part in the onshore market. Nigeria joined the JP Morgan local currency bond index in 2012. Nigerian government bond yields fell around 300 basis points within a few weeks after JP Morgan announced the country inclusion. Other factors besides an adjustment of the liquidity premiums may have led to this yield decrease. Investors (passively) tracking the index had to build up long positions immediately after the introduction in the index and this temporarily higher demand might have exaggerated the fall in yields.

Mihaljek and Packer (2010) conclude that derivative markets are still moderately small in emerging economies. With a turnover of only 6 percent of GDP, these markets are about one-sixth of the size of their counterparts in advanced economies. According to the Association of Chartered Certified Accountants (2012), the size of the derivatives market in the emerging world has grown fourfold in the period 2000–2010. Trading volume in domestic derivatives markets increased the most in export-driven economies such as Brazil, Hong Kong, Korea, and Singapore where foreign exchange risk is imminent. Growth in interest rate derivatives lags growth in FX derivatives.

Emerging economies such as Brazil, Indonesia, South Africa, and the Philippines have well-established capital markets. Pricing foreign exchange derivatives depends on the availability of tradable money market instruments. In the larger emerging markets, local currency yield curves are available. Thus, liquid and traded fixed income instruments constitute reliable proxies for exchange rate risk. Because many emerging market countries attract foreign investors' attention, international banks and financial institutions have created offshore markets to let those investors take exposure to these currencies in spite of capital controls imposed by local regulators onshore. The offshore markets are highly correlated with the onshore markets in normal circumstances. This relationship cannot be observed in frontier markets because liquid yield curves are unavailable and offshore markets do not exist.

The Offshore Market as a Starting Point

The financial crisis of 2007–2008 emphasized a possible benefit of the internationalization of emerging market currencies. Baba and Packer (2009) and Hui, Genberg, and Chung (2009) highlight that as banks scraped for emergency liquidity, funding markets in dollar and FX swap markets decreased in 2008. As McGuire and von Peter (2009) note, the resulting "dollar shortage" made international trade vulnerable. As a response, many central banks in the emerging world found themselves in the unfamiliar situation of lending dollars to local banks and funding exports. The risk of excessively relying on one reserve currency in payments and international trade became clear.

Some policy makers in emerging markets worry about the response strategy to the economic crisis in the countries where reserve currencies are printed (He and McCauley 2010). Central bank balance sheet enlargement with the fiscal expansion in the world's major reserve currencies raises concerns whether those currencies are still reliable and able to keep their value. Regardless of whether these concerns are legitimate, a shift to a situation where countries from the emerging world are creditors to other developing economies (e.g., the Central Bank of China holding its reserves partly in Indonesian rupiah and Brazilian real) could offer benefits to the countries in internationalizing their currencies while keeping a certain control. Policy makers in emerging markets are worried about the potential risks that arise if they allow their currencies to become internationally accessible. The internationalization of domestic currencies poses risks to monetary and financial stability due to speculative positions that are not trade or capital driven. As a reference point, the Eurodollar market has been well established for years. Historically, the Eurodollar market was the first offshore currency market. It was created after World War II as the quantity of U.S. dollars outside the United States increased dramatically as a consequence of both the Marshall Plan and imports into the United States, which had become the largest consumer market after the World War II.

A large portion of trading in international currencies is still taking place offshore. When non-U.S. residents use the U.S. dollar for making investment and settling transactions, they do not necessary transact through commercial banks and financial markets based in the United States. They usually transact in global financial centers such as the Eurodollar market. In reality, some could argue that, without the existence of the offshore markets, the U.S. dollar may not have reached the leading position it currently has in global trade and payments. Residents outside the United States prefer doing business in dollars offshore. They have a tendency to deposit U.S. dollars in offshore financial institutions and buy U.S. dollar debt issued by non-U.S. residents.

Many emerging and frontier market countries have lower credit ratings than the minimum rating acceptable by foreign institutional investors. Offshore markets can be an alternative route in buying emerging market exposure without having exposure to the country credit risk. Concerns about operational risk concentrations in one country also drive the separation of currency risk from country risk. One of the parameters in choosing between onshore and offshore markets is the differential in yields. Kreicher (1982) finds that through the existence of the dollar market outside the United States (Eurodollar), investors are eager to invest in a financial institution based in London or another center outside the United States if they benefit from higher yields. McCauley and Seth (1992) show that superior yields on dollars placed outside the United States reflected the deposit insurance and domestic reserve requirements' cost for most of the 1980s. U.S. savers paid the cost of the reserve requirement imposed by the Federal Reserve (Fed) and deposit insurance "taxes" on their deposits while offshore depositors did not. The second regulatory reason for holding dollars offshore mostly disappeared in December 27, 1990, when the Fed reduced the reserve ratio on non-personal time deposits and eurocurrency liabilities to zero (Board of Governors of the Federal Reserve System 2013). Despite what the cost of regulation has done to limit the growth of the Eurodollar deposit market, the offshore market has not closed down. This survival indicates that the higher yields observed in the offshore market previously was not the only factor behind investors' interests. The accounting standards, regulatory environment, time zone of the offshore markets' location, and language put them in a more convenient situation than the onshore markets for some investors and fund raisers.

The offshore markets' development in a specific currency poses certain challenges to regulators who are responsible for assuring monetary stability onshore. The presence of an offshore market increases the difficulty of defining and monitoring the monetary mass, hence money supply, in that currency. Similarly, measuring and controlling bank credit in case no barriers exist between the offshore and onshore markets could be a major challenge if an offshore market develops in a given currency. This chapter does not investigate this latter topic because most frontier economies have capital controls in place.

The consequences of offshore transactions for the spot exchange rate depend on the balance between short and long positions in the currency in offshore markets. Capital controls may put constraints on offshore market participants' ability in taking either long or short positions. In this framework, speculative positions in a currency could intensify the pressure on the exchange rate because those bets will be placed in the off-shore, non-deliverable exchange markets. These pressures would become more urgent if the onshore and offshore foreign exchange markets become more integrated. Under more liberalized capital account regimes and over the longer term, the effect on the exchange rate would be contingent mainly on the level of local interest rates compared to international levels. Lower interest rates would lead the currency to become a bor-rower's currency and its usage offshore causing downward pressure on the exchange rate. Similarly, higher interest rates would lead to placing the currency as an investor's currency and therefore investors could use the offshore markets to enter long positions and potentially exert upward pressure on its exchange rate.

As Figure 28.2 shows, the offshore implied interest rates for Chinese renminbi were above the onshore money market rates for many years. This situation reversed

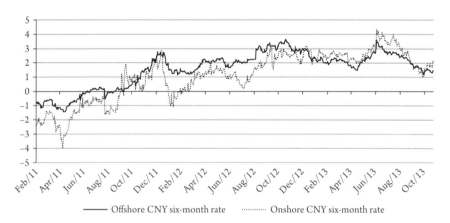

Figure 28.2 THE ONSHORE VS. THE OFFSHORE SIX-MONTH CNY RATE.   This figure shows the historical level of the six-month offshore and onshore Chinese renminbi's interest rates. For almost the entire period since February 2011, the offshore rate was higher than the onshore equivalent. However, since December 2012, this situation reversed due to the prevailing macroeconomic, political, and foreign exchange circumstances such as current account surpluses and the international pressure for a quicker Chinese currency appreciation pace. Source: DLM Finance 2013.

more recently, despite the still existing capital controls in place. This reversal can be attributed to the prevailing macroeconomic, political, and foreign exchange circumstances, such as current account surpluses and the international pressure for a quicker appreciation pace.

Multinational corporations having access both to the domestic FX market, through their branch inside a country, and to the international FX markets when the parent company is offshore based can benefit from possible arbitrage opportunities arising between offshore and onshore markets. As a result, buying or selling pressure could be transferred from the offshore non-deliverable market to the onshore market. If foreign investors, such as corporations with global presence, want to take long positions in the currency, they can facilitate this by keeping earnings in local currency within the country; whereas, these earnings would otherwise have been transferred as dividends in a foreign currency. These long cash positions in the local currency could be profitably covered through the short sale of the currency in the non-deliverable market. Accordingly, demand for dollars on the part of the corporations would be smaller than it would have been otherwise.

In countries where a central bank targets a money market rate, the offshore markets' impact on onshore interest rates should be considered because the offshore curve is a more reliable source of exchange rate risk. Therefore, if the spread increase between the offshore and onshore yields is unjustified by changes in capital controls, investment regulation, or taxation, the central bank's monetary policy could be perceived as ineffective, too generous, or too conservative, which could result in the short-term policy rate being an unreliable reference.

The emerging world counts active non-deliverable offshore markets. The non-deliverable forward foreign exchange market serves as an alternative for the local money market and the non-deliverable interest rate swap market serves as an alternative for the local fixed income market (He and McCauley 2010). Due to capital controls, the yield curves constructed offshore are quite separate from their onshore equivalents. Although opportunities for arbitrage will exist between them, such transactions are difficult to execute and have insufficient weight to force the two yield curves to converge. When such currencies are under appreciation pressure, the offshore yield curves tend to be below their onshore equivalents. Conversely, offshore yields that are much higher than domestic ones could be a bigger worry for the domestic authorities. This is because the premiums above onshore yields, which are demanded by informed foreign investors, can signal a risk of currency depreciation that is higher than what is priced in the onshore curve. Figures 28.3 and 28.4 show the historical onshore and offshore three-year cross-currency swap levels of the Indonesian rupiah and India rupee versus the U.S. dollar. As can be observed, the offshore implied yields were consistently lower than the onshore ones. This condition is mainly due to the capital controls imposed in Indonesia and India.

In the cases of Indonesia and India, the offshore cost of funds was always lower than their onshore counterparts in normal market circumstances, reflecting the cost of regulation applicable only to onshore investments. During crisis times such as the financial crisis of 2007–2008, the offshore market traded above the onshore indicating the faster responsiveness of the offshore market to the crisis and investors' flexibility to liquidate their positions quickly.

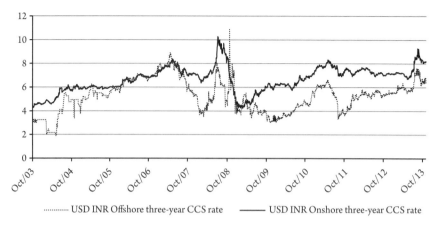

.... USD INR Offshore three-year CCS rate   ——— USD INR Onshore three-year CCS rate

Figure 28.3 THE ONSHORE VS. THE OFFSHORE THREE-YEAR INDIAN RUPEES
CROSS-CURRENCY RATES VS. THE U.S. DOLLAR.   This figure shows the historical
onshore and offshore Indian rupee three-year cross-currency rate vs. the U.S. dollar over
the past decade. The figure shows that the offshore cost of funds was lower than the
onshore rate for almost the entire period. This relationship is explained by the cost of
regulation applicable only to onshore investments. However, during crisis times, such as
the financial crisis of 2007–2008, the offshore market traded above the onshore one
indicating the faster responsiveness of the offshore market to the crisis and investors'
flexibility to liquidate their positions quickly.   Source: DLM Finance 2013.

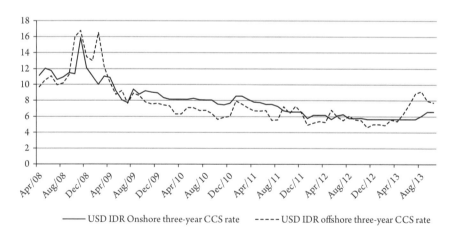

——— USD IDR Onshore three-year CCS rate   - - - - USD IDR offshore three-year CCS rate

Figure 28.4 THE ONSHORE VS. THE OFFSHORE THREE-YEAR INDONESIAN RUPIAH
CROSS-CURRENCY RATES VS. THE U.S. DOLLAR.   This figure shows historical U.S.
dollar vs. Indonesian rupiah onshore and offshore cross-currency three-year tenor swaps
over the past five years. The figure shows that the offshore cost of funds was lower than the
onshore rate for almost the entire period. However, during crisis times, such as the financial
crisis of 2007–2008, the offshore market traded above the onshore indicating the larger
investors' flexibility in liquidating their positions.   Source: DLM Finance 2013.

Pricing Versus Existing Proxies in Selected Currencies

Because most frontier markets do not have developed onshore foreign exchange derivatives or an existing offshore market, analyzing where exchange rate risk should be priced is challenging. As a first attempt, the standard interest rate parity principle will be applied. For this purpose, assume the portfolio includes the following frontier currencies: the Kazakhstan tenge, Nigerian naira, Kenyan shilling, Ugandan shilling, Tanzanian shilling, Zambian kwacha, Ghanaian cedi and Sri Lanka rupee. The period of analysis extends from June 1996 to September 2013 in order to include as many economic cycles as possible. Given the limited capital markets development in many of these countries, few liquid interest rate benchmarks are available. The analysis uses 182-day Treasury bill rates for Ghana, Nigeria, Tanzania, Uganda, and Zambia and six-month interbank deposit rates for Kazakhstan and Sri Lanka. These rates serve as proxies for the costs of local currency funds.

In this simulation, a long local currency book is considered, as hard currencies are usually rare in these countries. This situation is the main historical reason for introducing capital controls. A market is usually created by offering first the buy side and then market makers find innovative solutions to offset their risk. The buy side in this case would allow multinational corporations that are active in these markets to hedge their exchange rate risk.

After building a long local currency portfolio, market makers could then search off-setting opportunities through stimulating offshore investors' interest to go long these currencies.

Mihaljek and Packer (2010) show that the U.S. dollar is still the most frequently used global currency in over-the-counter (OTC) emerging markets derivatives. In 2010, the U.S. dollar was the reference currency in more than 95 percent of transactions in emerging markets, which confirms the current position of the dollar as the international financial transactions leading currency in addition to its leading role in international trade and finance (Goldberg 2010). Even for Eastern and Central European currencies, whose economies have strong links with the euro area, the reference currency for exchange rate derivatives transactions is the dollar, which is used more frequently than the euro. The dollar supremacy is much larger in emerging market currencies trading than elsewhere. Globally, 85 percent of the transactions are dollar denominated. For these reasons, the simulation is performed using the U.S. dollar as a base currency. The historical simulation consists of synthetically calculating six-month foreign exchange forwards in every currency versus the U.S. dollar (USD) for the past 17 years, without any adjustment to the local currency benchmark, hence the premium is ignored. Equation 28.1 illustrates the covered interested rate parity principle in which the foreign exchange forward (FX forward) is priced by multiplying the current exchange rate spot (spot) by the frontier currency interest rate (interest rate lcy) and divided by the cost of the base currency interest rate (interest rate USD). The interest rate in each currency is halved as the forward is computed for a six-month period.

FX forward = Spot * (1 + interest rate lcy/2) / (1 + interest rate USD/2).   (28.1)

On the value date of the FX forward, the predicted spot rate through the forward is compared to the FX spot of the same date. This assumption allows assessment of whether the exchange rate risk is quantified correctly in the forward. In a second phase, an equally weighted average FX forward rate is calculated for the seven currencies under consideration (the portfolio). The same comparison is done to the average spot of the portfolio.

Several observations emerge from the outcome of the analysis. First, over a long period (17 years), the predicted FX spot rate through the forward on a portfolio level, priced using interest rate proxies, is on average aligned to the market spot exchange rate. Second, in crisis times (i.e., post-Lehman in 2008 and post-euro crisis in 2012), a substantial deviation exists between the predicted spot in the FX forward and the actual spot market.

Figure 28.5 shows the result of the back-testing analysis of comparing the portfolio average spot to the proxy average foreign exchange forward for the same spot date. This allows assessment of whether the forwards priced with the defined interest rate proxies were good predictions of the actual spot rate.

Over a long period of analysis (17 years), the predicted portfolio spot exchange rate through the forward calculated by the interest rate carry principle is highly correlated with the actual portfolio spot rate. The correlation between the two variables is higher than 0.98. However, if a shorter period is considered, deviations between the spot and the implied spot through the forward can be high.

If banks had a portfolio of diversified and long positions of short-term forwards (six months in this example), the deviation between the carry and the spot movement over a six-month period can reach 15 percent with an equal distribution between the downside and upside. Indeed, in August 2000 and February 2009, the forward priced six months

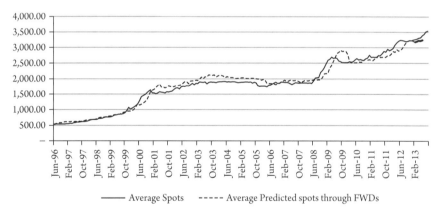

Figure 28.5 THE PORTFOLIO OF CURRENCIES AVERAGE SPOT VS. THE PREDICTED AVERAGE SPOT IN THE FORWARDS: LOCAL INTEREST RATES AS PROXIES.   This figure shows the result of a back-testing analysis of comparing the average spot of a portfolio composed of seven currencies to the proxy average foreign exchange forward for the same spot date. This comparison allows assessing whether the six-month forwards priced with defined interest rate proxies, such as the interbank rate and Treasury-bills rate, were accurately predicting the actual spot rate. The back-testing analysis was done using data for the past 17 years and the currencies chosen in the portfolio are: the Kazakhstan tenge, Nigerian naira, Kenyan shilling, Ugandan shilling, Tanzanian shilling, Zambian kwacha, Ghanaian cedi, and Sri Lanka rupee.   Source: DLM Finance 2013.

earlier was 16 percent lower than the actual spot on these dates. Conversely, in May 2001 and September 2009, the interest rate carry priced in the forward was 15 percent higher than the realized spots. A gap of less than a year exists between the misalignment of the forwards and the spot on each of the highest and lowest points.

Two factors can drive this result. First, interest rate benchmarks reacted post-depreciation of the spot rate. Hence, the benchmark does not price the exchange rate risk that materialized in high depreciation. Therefore, increased inflation post-depreciation could drive the interest rate benchmark resulting in higher forwards compared to the spot after the occurrence of a high depreciation. Second, an overreaction of the spot market could occur due to major and unpredictable events that are not priced in the interest rate benchmark. This is also frequent in developed currencies. The overreaction of the spot is nullified a few months later. This second factor is less probable because frontier market currencies are trade flow driven and not capital driven. Due to capital controls, speculative positions driving the exchange rate spot up or down should be limited.

In another attempt to highlight the outcome of this historical simulation, Figure 28.6 shows the cumulated portfolio return of equally weighted long positions in each of the frontier market currencies analyzed. The internal rate of return (IRR) of the portfolio of diversified long local currencies exposure was 2.39 percent over the 17-year period. The cumulative return was always positive over the entire period. Changing the start date of building a long and diversified local currency portfolio position from January 1996 results in a slightly negative IRR over a one-year period, as highlighted in Figure 28.6 between August 1999 and August 2000 and between May 2008 and January 2009. Thus, a portfolio of diversified long frontier market currencies generates a positive

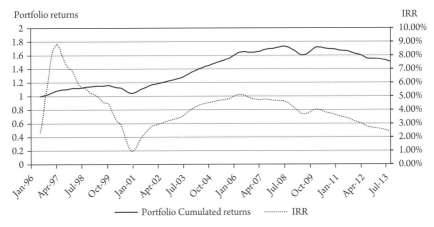

Figure 28.6 THE DIVERSIFIED PORTFOLIO CUMULATED RETURN (100 AS A BASIS) AND IRR: LOCAL INTEREST RATES AS PROXIES.   This figure shows the cumulated portfolio return (left scale) and internal rate of return (IRR) (right scale) of equally weighted long positions in eight currencies (i.e., the Kazakhstan tenge, Nigerian naira, Kenyan shilling, Ugandan shilling, Tanzanian shilling, Zambian kwacha, Ghanaian cedi, and Sri Lanka rupee) vs. the U.S. dollar. The IRR of the portfolio of diversified long local currencies exposure was 2.39 percent over the 17-year period. Source: DLM Finance 2013.

return over the long term. This return is relatively small given the high cost of capital for holding such currencies in banks' balance sheets. Using shorter periods makes the risk of false forward predictability of the spot, using the defined benchmarks, higher. The non-stationary state of data makes any general conclusions from the above analysis only valid over a long-term horizon and should not be used for short-term positioning. The risk for banks taking unhedged open long local currencies short-term positions, even in a diversified portfolio, is substantial. Consequently, the creation of such a forward market on an unhedged basis would be reliant on clients' flows continuity.

The local currency benchmarks used in this section are illiquid and not linked to existing derivatives. In a second attempt, the analysis replaces short-term interest rate benchmarks with yearly inflation rates. If the interest rate parity theory holds, inflation differential translates in an equivalent exchange rate depreciation or appreciation. The hypothesis is made that U.S. LIBOR is a market rate and therefore should be used as a sole cost of USD funds and not replaced by the USD inflation rate. This relationship is highlighted in Figure 28.7, which compares the historical performance of the selected portfolio of currencies average spot rate to the average portfolio forward priced six-month earlier. Inflation is used as interest rate proxies for each frontier currency in the portfolio.

Figure 28.7 shows that when using inflation as a proxy of local cost of funds, the correlation between the market spot and the predicted spot through synthetic forwards in the portfolio was above 0.98. However, as Figure 28.8 shows, using inflation rates as proxies consistently underestimates the exchange rate risk. The IRR of the portfolio over the period of analysis is –3.2 percent, so the portfolio lost more than

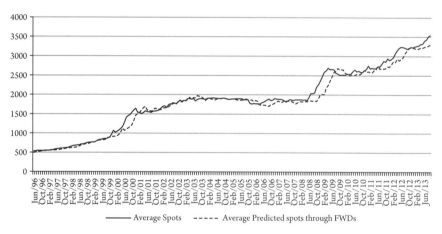

———— Average Spots   - - - - - Average Predicted spots through FWDs

Figure 28.7 The Portfolio of Currencies Average Spot vs. the Predicted Average Spot in the Forwards: Inflation Rates as Proxies.   This figure shows the result of a back-testing analysis of comparing the average spot of a portfolio composed of eight currencies (i.e., the Kazakhstan tenge, Nigerian naira, Kenyan shilling, Ugandan shilling, Tanzanian shilling, Zambian kwacha, Ghanaian cedi and Sri Lanka rupee) to the portfolio's inflation-proxy average foreign exchange forwards for the same spot value date. This allows assessment of whether inflation rates were good proxies for pricing FX forwards rates hence accurately predicting the actual spot rate. Source: DLM Finance 2013.

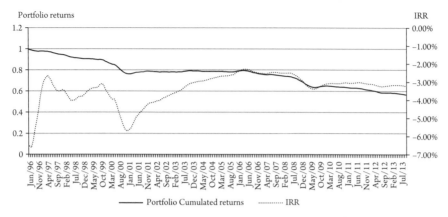

Figure 28.8 THE DIVERSIFIED PORTFOLIO CUMULATED RETURN (100 AS A BASIS) AND IRR: INFLATION RATES AS PROXIES. This figure summarizes the cumulated portfolio return (left scale) and internal rate of return (IRR) (right scale) of an equally weighted portfolio of long positions in eight currencies (i.e., the Kazakhstan tenge, Nigerian naira, Kenyan shilling, Ugandan shilling, Tanzanian shilling, Zambian kwacha, Ghanaian cedi, and Sri Lanka rupee) vs. the U.S. dollar. The IRR of the portfolio of diversified long local currencies exposure was a negative 3.2 percent over the 17-year period while the portfolio lost more than 40 percent of its value over the entire period. Using inflation rates as sole proxies consistently underestimates the exchange rate risk over a long period of time. Source: DLM Finance 2013.

40 percent of its value over the entire period. The spot predicted through the forward has generally been lower than the actual spot exchange rate. Because this difference is statistically significant, inflation rates are not considered reliable proxies for exchange rate risk in frontier currencies. A premium over inflation could have been considered in order to compensate for the consistent underperformance of the predicted FX spot rates through the forwards compared to the actual spot rates. Still, this is not an option because the misalignment is neither stable over time nor normally distributed. Although short-term interest rates in these frontier currencies are illiquid and could be politically manipulated, these interest rate benchmarks are good proxies for exchange rate risk and include information about future FX performance that inflation rates do not capture.

Summary and Conclusions

Currency derivatives in frontier markets are underdeveloped because of capital controls, a lack of offsetting hedging opportunities, and the nonexistence of offshore markets. Capital market development is a prerequisite for the emergence of a yield curve that can be reliably used as a proxy for exchange rate risk quantification. Capital controls should not be a hurdle for commercial banks in promoting and creating an offshore market for frontier currencies that attract investors' interest. However, the lack of hedging opportunities of banks' frontier markets currencies exposure and the disequilibrium between offer and demand for such currencies increase the difficulty for market makers who want to start such portfolios because pricing discovery can only be made through the usage of proxies.

This chapter uses two types of proxies for pricing exchange rate derivatives in selected frontier market currencies: short-term interest rates and inflation rates. Although local interest rate benchmarks are illiquid and infrequently traded, they represent a much better proxy for exchange rate risk than inflation rates in the selected currencies. Local currency benchmarks include financial information that is not captured in inflation differentials. Additionally, banks using such interest rate proxies in order to start a long and diversified frontier market currencies book are expected to make a slightly positive return over the long term as long as demand for such currencies hedging is persistent. This would guarantee continuous flows. This return is in addition to the bid-ask spreads usually priced in derivatives transactions. Misalignment between the spot predicted through the forward and the actual FX spot rate can be substantial over shorter periods, which is why hedge providers can face considerable losses when they do not roll over their positions.

Disclaimer

Past performance is not a guarantee or a reliable indicator of future results. All investments contain risk and may lose value. This material contains the current opinions of the authors but not necessarily those of The Currency Exchange Fund and such opinions are subject to change without notice. This material has been distributed for informational purposes only and should not be considered as investment advice or a recommendation of any particular security, strategy, or investment product. Statements concerning financial market trends are based on current market conditions, which will fluctuate. Information contained herein has been obtained from sources believed to be reliable, but not guaranteed.

Discussion Questions

1. Discuss capital controls that could be beneficial to frontier and emerging economies.
2. Assume an offshore FX derivative market is unavailable for Dominican Republic Peso (DOP) and a corporation approaches a commercial bank offshore to sell its DOP revenues and buy USD. Determine the price of a one-year USD DOP FX non-deliverable forward (NDF) under the following assumptions:
   - The withholding tax on investing in investments in DOP fixed income instruments is 10 percent.
   - The current one-year Dominican Republic treasury bills yield at 9.5 percent.
   - The one-year USD dollar rate of 0.40 percent.
   - The same convention applies to DOP and USD rates.
3. Discuss why the existence of a well-developed capital market is considered a perquisite or at least a crucial parameter for the development of a derivative market.
4. Summarize some of the factors driving differences between offshore and onshore yield curves.

References

Association of Chartered Certified Accountants. 2012. "The Rise of Capital Markets in Emerging and Frontier Economies Global Economic Conditions Survey Report," March. Available at www.accaglobal.com/content/dam/acca/global/PDF-technical/global-economy/pol-tp-rcm.pdf.

Baba, Naohiko, and Frank Packer. 2009. "From Turmoil to Crisis: Dislocations in the FX Swap Market Before and After the Failure of Lehman Brothers." Working Paper, Bank of International Settlements. Available at http://www.bis.org/publ/work285.pdf.

Board of Governors of the Federal Reserve System. 2013. "Reserve Requirements." Available at http://www.federalreserve.gov/monetarypolicy/reservereq.htm.

Chiang, Thomas C. 1986. "On the Predictors of the Future Spot Rates—A Multi-Currency Analysis." *Financial Review* 21:1, 69–83.

Culbertson, James S. 1975. "The Term Structure of Interest Rates." *Quarterly Journal of Economics* 71:4, 485–517.

Demarigny, Fabrice. 2010. "An EU-Listing Small Business Act—Establishing a Proportionate Regulatory and Financial Environment for Small and Medium-sized Issuers Listed in Europe." French Ministry of Economy, Industry and Employment. Available at http://www.mazars.com/content/download/37683/867875/version/2/SBA-smiles-english.pdf.

DLM Finance. 2013. Available at http://www.dlmfinance.com/services.

Fama, Eugene F. 1984. "Forward and Spot Exchange Rates." *Journal of Monetary Economics* 14:3, 319–338.

Goldberg, Linda S. 2010. "Is the International Role of the Dollar Changing?" *Current Issues in Economics and Finance*, Federal Bank of New York, 16:1. Available at http://www.google.fr/url?sa=t&rct=j&q=&esrc=s&frm=1&source=web&cd=1&cad=rja&ved=0CCkQFjAA&url=http%3A%2F%2Fwww.newyorkfed.org%2Fresearch%2Fcurrent_issues%2Fci16-1.pdf&ei=1gi3UsrxEu3Y0QXYgoCADw&usg=AFQjCNFf9g0SvwePn9qErAZ5YhJLwB-uTw.

He, Dong, and Robert McCauley. 2010. "Offshore Markets for the Domestic Currency: Monetary and Financial Stability Issues." Working Paper 320, Bank of International Settlements.

Hearn, Bruce, Jenifer Piesse, and Roger Strange. 2010. "Market Liquidity and Stock Price Premia in Emerging Markets: The Implications for Foreign Investment." *International Business Review* 19:5, 489–501.

Hickman, W. Braddock. 1942. "The Term Structure of Interest Rates: An Explanatory Analysis." *National Bureau of Economic Research*, mimeo.

Hui, Cho-Hoi, Hans Genberg, and Tsz-kin Chung. 2009. "Funding Liquidity Risk and Deviations from Interest-rate Parity during the Financial Crisis of 2007–2009." Working Paper, Hong Kong Monetary Authority.

Kreicher, John. 1982. "Eurodollar Arbitrage." *Federal Reserve Bank of New York. Quarterly Review* 7:2, 10–22.

Macauley, Frederick R. 1938. "Some Theoretical Problems Suggested by the Movements of Interest Rates, Bond Yields and Stock Prices in the United States since 1859." *National Bureau of Economic Research*. New York: Columbia University Press.

McCauley, Robert, and Rama Seth. 1992. "Foreign Bank Credit to U.S. Corporations: The Implications of Offshore Loans." *Federal Reserve Bank of New York. Quarterly Review* 17:1, 52–65. Available at http://www.ny.frb.org/research/quarterly_review/1992v17/v17n1article4.html.

McGuire, Patrick, and Goetz von Peter. 2009. "The US Dollar Shortage in Global Banking." *BIS Quarterly Review*, March, 47–63. Available at http://www.bis.org/publ/qtrpdf/r_qt0903f.pdf.

Sarkissian, Sergei, and Michael J. Schill. 2009. "Are There Permanent Valuation Gains to Overseas Listing?" *Review of Financial Studies* 22:1, 371–412.

Sienaert, Alex. 2012. "Foreign Investment in Local Currency Bonds. Considerations for Emerging Market Public Debt Managers". The World Bank policy research working paper 6284. Available at http://elibrary.worldbank.org/doi/pdf/10.1596/1813-9450-6284.

United Nations. 2011. "World Economic Situation and Prospects 2011." Available at http://www.un.org/en/development/desa/policy/wesp/wesp_current/2011wesp.pdf.

Part Six

GOING FORWARD

29

Risk Management and Financial Disasters

Head of Risk Appetite Portfolio Decisioning, Credit Risk, Royal Bank of Scotland

Introduction

Financial crises have been recurring phenomena in financial markets. This chapter reviews the literature and the history on financial crises and systemic risk. It then addresses the question of whether crises are avoidable and predictable with a specific focus on how financial institutions can mitigate their impact.

The structure of a crisis can be divided into two phases: (1) a run-up phase, in which bubbles and imbalances form, and (2) a crisis phase, during which risk that has built up in the background materializes and the crisis erupts. During the run-up phase, markets experience asset price bubbles and imbalances form. These imbalances typically build up slowly in the background and volatility is low. Initially, imbalances that ultimately lead to a financial crisis are often hard to detect. For example, at first, a boom in asset prices can often be rationalized by appealing to some form of innovation. This innovation could be technological change (e.g., railroads, telegraphs, and the Internet), financial liberalization (e.g., the removal of regulation), or financial innovation (e.g., securitization). However, as the bubble gains momentum, market participants realize that the fundamental improvements that may have warranted an initial increase in asset prices cannot keep up with ever-increasing valuations.

The run-up phase often causes incentive distortions for agents in the economy. These incentive distortions can either be the consequence of rational behavior or caused by behavioral belief distortions. Rational distortions occur when agents in the economy rationally respond to the incentives they face during the run-up phase. These distortions include moral hazard problems that arise from expected bailouts or policies. They also include over-leveraging or over-investment that results from potential fire-sale externalities. Such externalities can arise when individual households or firms experience decreases in asset prices in their decision-making process while not internalizing that their joint investment decision determines the size of the crash.

Belief distortions occur because insufficient data may not exist to establish the formation of a bubble. For example, in the absence of previous nationwide decline in nominal house prices, agents may predict that house prices will also not decline (or decline only marginally) in the future. Alternatively, belief distortions may be based on the "this-time-is-different" rationale. While the asset price boom observed may be out of line with historical data, agents may choose to ignore such patterns by arguing that something is fundamentally different this time around. That is, cautionary signals from history are inapplicable.

The ideal breeding ground for the run-up phase is an environment of low volatility. Usually, during such times, financing is easy to obtain. Speculators can increase their leverage, lowering the return differential between risky and less risky securities. The resulting leverage and maturity mismatch may be excessive because each speculator does not internalize the externalities he causes on the financial system. Brunnermeier and Oehmke (2012) contend that financial stability is a public good. Because everyone benefits from it, a trader may have insufficient incentives to contribute to it and this is why strong regulation and control are needed.

After the gradual build-up of a bubble and the associated imbalances, the crisis phase starts when a trigger event leads to the bursting of the bubble. This sudden transition has sometimes been referred to as a "Minsky moment" (Minsky 1992). The Minsky moment can occur long after most market participants are aware or at least suspicious that a bubble has developed. Overall, the main problem is not the price correction per se, but that the necessary correction often occurs only very late, after extensive increases in risk and large imbalances. The trigger event that catalyzes the crisis does not have to be an event of singular major economic significance. However, because of amplification effects, even small trigger events can lead to major financial crises and recessions.

During the crisis phase, amplification mechanisms play a major role. Amplification mechanisms both increase the magnitude of the correction in the part of the economy that a bubble affects and spread the effects to other parts of the economy. Amplification mechanisms that arise during financial crises can either be direct (caused by contractual links) or indirect (caused by spillovers or externalities that are due to common exposures or the endogenous response of various market participants). Amplifications can be distinguished based on whether credit fueled the imbalances that formed during the run-up or bubble phase. The bursting of credit bubbles leads to more de-leveraging and stronger amplification mechanisms.

While financial crises often erupt suddenly, recovery from crises often takes a long time. This pattern occurs because the negative shock caused by the bursting of the bubble leads to persistent adverse effects and deep and drawn-out recessions. Even after policy responses, such as a recapitalization of the banking system, recovery is typically slow because balance sheets of other agents might still be impaired.

As discussed further in the section on systemic risk, a poor regulatory framework based on the belief that banks could be trusted to regulate themselves serves as a main source of crises. Regulators across the world need to efficiently and consistently monitor the risk management functions of most financial institutions to make sure they are applying the appropriate methods and tools to mitigate risks. At the same time, risk management at most banking institutions needs to make sure that the basic rules for a safe business are followed (i.e., avoid strong concentrations and minimize volatility of returns).

The second part of this chapter provides a discussion and analysis of the main reasons behind the failure of risk management during the financial crisis of 2007–2008 with the aim of offering a view on how they can be solved or improved going forward to ensure a more sound financial system. In particular, the chapter explores such topics as the lack of a defined capital allocation strategy, disaggregated vision of risks, and inappropriate risk governance structure.

Most banks grow their lending portfolios based on market demand without a clear capital allocation strategy. Regulatory pressures such as the recent changes to the Basel II Accord and a greater focus on corporate governance have been a stimulus for many changes in the industry including the recognition of the need to articulate risk appetite more clearly. Risk appetite translates risk metrics and methods into business decisions, reporting, and day-to-day business discussions. It sets the boundaries that form a dynamic link among strategy, target setting, and risk management.

Articulating risk appetite is a complex task that requires the balancing of many views. Some elements can be quantified, but ultimately it is a question of judgment. A bank with a well-defined risk appetite framework will provide internal senior management and external stakeholders with a clear picture of where the bank currently stands and how it wants to grow in terms of concentration and expected returns of its assets.

Although many institutions, particularly the large national and international financial institutions, have already adopted enterprise risk management (ERM) approaches, others are still using more reactive methods of risk monitoring and detection. Typically, these methods are the traditional silo approaches to risk management and are rapidly becoming insufficient in preventing increasingly diversified risks, especially credit, market, and operational risks. Silo-based approaches are reactive and their functions segregated; each silo has its own tools and applications to assist with specific management and reporting requirements. Problems arise because these independent systems do not communicate with one another and risk aggregation across business lines is poor.

A silo view of risks is still a common practice at most banks, which does not allow senior management to have a full picture of risk concentrations and correlations. Similar assets, or assets with a high correlation between them, can reside in different books (e.g., banking or trading book) or off-balance and their risk may never be aggregated causing a substantial understatement of the capital needed.

Last, the current risk governance structure in place at most banks still presents several elements that could be improved to ensure a more effective control of risk. This topic is closely related to the previous ones. Only a clear, well-organized risk structure can provide enterprise-wide risk measures and aggregate risks appropriately before reporting them to the chief risk officer (CRO) and ultimately to the board of directors.

The risk function reporting lines have been undervalued for a long time in the incorrect belief that a good risk manager could influence business decisions providing a good set of analyses even without having clear authority. The financial crisis of 2007–2008 shows that this assumption was untrue and provides an example of what can happen when the role of risk management is underestimated within a financial organization.

After the financial crisis of 2007–2008, financial institutions have reconsidered all methods and processes related to measuring and managing credit and other risks in the belief that these measures did not work as expected. Regulators are leading this review. New rules are being imposed and tougher controls are being applied with the aim of trying to avoid or mitigate another possible financial crisis.

This chapter provides an analysis and discussion of risk management as well as several proposals on how the financial industry should evolve. Several aspects are discussed in terms of how to improve the measurement of risk and provide a quantitative metric that summarizes different risk types such as credit, market, and operational risk. ERM and economic capital (EC) are older concepts finally getting more attention. However, having the best tools to measure and aggregate different risks will be insufficient to reduce the damages of financial crises in the future. Risk management and governance are also key elements to address.

The ability to quantitatively assess risk and take appropriate, timely actions together with the power to enforce these actions will be the main drivers of a new risk management function. New risk management leaders will need to have a strong analytical background and the ability to drive banking strategies. Ultimately, risk management has the opportunity to redefine itself as the main driver of financial institutions' profitability (Aebi, Sabato, and Schmid 2011).

The remainder of the chapter is organized in the following manner. The next section analyzes a brief history of the most important financial disasters and the associated systemic risk. Then, the following section provides a discussion of the most important topics currently under scrutiny with regards to risk management evolution and mitigation of the potential effects of future crises (i.e., capital allocation, ERM, and risk governance). The last section presents conclusions.

Financial Disasters and Systemic Risk

The literature on financial disasters and systemic risk grew tremendously in the past few years. The financial crisis of 2007–2008 reignited a new interest in understanding how asset price bubbles and imbalances form and later erupt into a crisis where money and credit fluctuations may play a fundamental role in the amplification and propagation of the shock. Given the substantial social cost of these crises, regulators and supervisory authorities across the globe have shifted their focus to developing measures of systemic risk that could serve as early-warning signals for policy makers.

This section provides a discussion of some noteworthy financial crises and examines recurring themes and common patterns. It also defines systemic risk and evaluates the recent developments for assessing its measurement.

A BRIEF HISTORY OF FINANCIAL DISASTERS

Historically, bubbles, crashes, and financial disasters have occurred with surprising regularity. This section provides a brief summary of the most relevant crisis episodes and examines their causes and consequences. Many authors provide further details on these episodes including Kindleberger (1978), Shiller (2000), Allen and Gale (2007), and Reinhart and Rogoff (2009).

Although each boom and crisis has its own peculiarities, several recurring themes and common patterns emerge. In particular, a crash generally follows a period of booming asset prices. This crash usually initiates various amplification mechanisms, which often lead to large reductions in economic activity that could be sharp and persistent.

Perhaps the best-documented early examples of asset price bubbles and following crises are the Dutch tulip mania (1634–1637), Mississippi bubble (1719–1720), and South Sea bubble (1720). Each of these episodes involved spectacular rises in the prices of certain assets (i.e., the price of tulips, shares in the Mississippi Company, and shares in the South Sea Company, respectively), followed by sharp declines in the prices of these assets (Neal 1990, 2012; Garber 2000).

When bubbles are fueled by credit, their amplification mechanism is much stronger and the de-leveraging phase tends to affect more the overall economy compared to non-credit bubbles due to the banking sector also being hit. During the nineteenth century, credit fueled the first examples of crises resulting in serious repercussions on the banking systems. In particular, major banking crises occurred in 1837 and 1857 in the United States before the creation of a national banking system in 1863–65. After its creation, banking panics still reoccurred in varied forms in 1873, 1884, 1893, 1907, and 1914 and bubbles before the Civil War or bubbles in railroad bonds after the Civil War preceded many of these crises. Sharp drops in the stock market accompanied most of these financial crises. As banks reduced margin lending, large reductions in real activity occurred (Allen and Gale 2007). The panic of 1907 ultimately led to the creation of the Federal Reserve System in 1914.

During the 1920s, the United States saw a large stock market boom, particularly between 1927and 1929, followed by the famous stock market crash of 1929 and the Great Depression. Although the real estate price boom of the 1920s often receives less emphasis in analyses of the main causes of the Great Depression, a similarity in magnitude exists to the boom and bust cycle in real estate prices associated with the financial crisis of 2007–2008 (White 2009). The stock market bubble that preceded the Great Depression was caused in part by the generous credit financing allowing speculators to buy stocks on margin. The trigger event that led to the bursting of the bubble was when the Federal Reserve started tightening monetary policy in February 1928 followed by the interest rate increase in July 1929. The impact on the banking system was huge and spread quickly across the globe generating a banking panic, several bank failures, and a prolonged recession. Since the Great Depression, banking panics have become rare in the United States, mostly because of the creation of the Federal Reserve System in 1914 and the introduction of deposit insurance as part of the Glass-Steagall Act of 1933. However, these regulatory acts did not prevent the financial crisis of 2007–2008.

Many South American countries experienced severe financial crisis throughout the 1970s and 1980s. During this period, the indebtedness of these countries soared (Kindleberger 1978). However, the sharp increase in U.S. interest rates led to a devaluation of South American currencies and drastically increased the real debt burden from dollar-denominated debt in those countries. In 1982, Mexico declared it would no longer be able to service its debt. Ultimately, the South American debt crises led to the Brady Plan in 1989 (Sturzenegger and Zettelmeyer 2006).

Japan also suffered a major financial crisis in the early 1990s. Similarly to what led to the Great Depression in the United States, a boom in both real estate and the Japanese stock market preceded the Japanese crisis. The losses from this crisis weighed on Japanese banks and the Japanese economy for years, leading to the "lost decade" of the 1990s and continuing slow growth in Japan during the 2000s. The Japanese example illustrates the problems bubbles pose for central banks. Worried about the bubble in real estate and stock prices, the Bank of Japan started raising the official discount rate in May 1989, eventually increasing it from 2.5 percent to 6.0 percent. The Bank of Japan also limited the growth rate of lending to the real estate industry such that it could not exceed the growth rate of total lending ("total volume control") and forced all banks to report lending to the construction industry and nonbank financial industry. Both of these interventions forced the real estate sector to de-lever, driving down prices. Many real estate firms went bankrupt, leading to fire sales in real estate. Since real estate was the primary collateral for many industries, overall lending declined, pushing down collateral value even further. Ultimately, the decrease in real estate prices led to a debt overhang problem for the entire Japanese banking sector, crippling the Japanese economy for decades (Hoshi and Kashyap 2004).

In 1997 and 1998, the focus fell on East Asian countries and Russia. After large equity and real estate booms in East Asia, a run on Thailand's currency led to a reversal of international capital flows to the entire region, triggering a financial crisis that quickly spread to other East Asian countries, such as Indonesia and Korea (Radelet, Sachs, Cooper, and Bosworth 1998). In August 1998, Russia declared a moratorium on its ruble-denominated debt and devalued its currency. Among other things, a decrease in oil prices led to a worsening of Russia's fiscal situation, leading to rising debt to gross domestic product (GDP) ratios, fiscal deficits, and rising interest rates. Ultimately, Russia opted not to defend its exchange rate peg and devalued its currency, declaring at the same time a moratorium on its ruble-denominated debt.

Moving into the twenty-first century, one of the most severe crises started in Argentina. In January 2002, Argentina suspended the peso's peg to the dollar. Within a few days, the peso lost much of its value. The crisis led to a severe decrease in GDP and a spike in inflation. Ultimately, Argentina defaulted on its debts. The Argentinean default led to at least four large debt restructurings. Sturzenegger and Zettelmeyer (2006) provide detailed summaries of the Argentinean crisis and other recent sovereign debt crises.

Recently, the bursting of the U.S. housing bubble and the associated financial market turmoil of 2007 and 2008 led to the most severe financial crisis since the Great Depression (Brunnermeier 2009). The financial crisis of 2007–2008 almost brought down the world's financial system. The subsequent credit crunch turned what was already a nasty downturn into the worst recession in 80 years. Massive monetary and fiscal stimulus prevented a severe depression, but the recovery remained slow compared with previous postwar upturns. As of late 2013, GDP is still below its pre-crisis peak in many rich countries, especially in Europe, where the financial crisis has evolved into the euro crisis.

The crisis had multiple causes. One of the most obvious causes is a lack of appropriate risk management at most financial institutions across the globe. The years before the crisis saw a flood of irresponsible mortgage lending in America. Loans were granted without a proper risk assessment to almost all customers that would apply for them, including the so-called "subprime" borrowers with poor credit histories. Low interest rates and generous lending criteria made large sums of money available to most customers independently from their ability to repay (i.e., affordability) in the short term and even less in the long term. Minimum or no stress was applied to interest rates to check if the same customers who were borrowing at such low interest rates could repay when interest rates would rise. The percentage of the value of the property that could be covered with a mortgage (i.e., loan-to-value) grew exponentially to levels even above 100 percent.

Financial engineers at the big banks turned these risky mortgages into supposedly low-risk securities by putting large numbers of them together in pools. Pooling works when the risks of each loan are uncorrelated. The big banks argued that the property markets in different American cities would rise and fall independently of one another, but this argument proved incorrect. Mortgages are highly correlated as are all assets using real estate as collateral. Moreover, unemployment and house prices are extremely correlated with the quality of any mortgage portfolio: if these go up, the quality of the portfolio will quickly deteriorate. Although this relationship was well known, most financial institutions chose to ignore it.

Starting in 2006, America suffered a sharp decrease in housing prices nationwide. Originators used the pooled mortgages to back securities known as collateralized debt obligations (CDOs), which were sliced into tranches by degree of exposure to default. Investors bought the safer tranches because they trusted the triple-A credit ratings assigned by agencies such as Moody's and Standard & Poor's. This was another mistake. The agencies were far too generous in their assessments of these assets. Low interest rates created an incentive for banks, hedge funds, and other investors to hunt for riskier assets that offered higher returns. Low rates enabled such outfits to borrow and use the extra cash to amplify their investments on the assumption that the returns would exceed the cost of borrowing. The low volatility increased the temptation to "leverage" in this way.

The turning of the U.S. housing market was the trigger event that started the crisis exposing fragilities in the financial system. Pooling and other clever financial engineering did not provide investors with the promised protection. Mortgage-backed securities (MBS) slumped in value, if they could be valued at all. Supposedly safe CDOs turned out to be worthless, despite the ratings agencies' seal of approval. Selling suspect assets at almost any price or using them as collateral for the short-term funding that was essential to many banks became difficult.

Trust, the key element of all financial systems, began to dissolve in 2007, a year before Lehman's bankruptcy, as banks started questioning the viability of their counterparties. Market participants and others became aware that the whole system was built on extremely weak foundations: banks had allowed their balance-sheets to grow quickly, but set aside too little capital to absorb unexpected losses.

Central bankers and other regulators bear responsibility too for not only mishandling the crisis but also failing both to keep economic imbalances in check and to exercise proper oversight of financial institutions. The regulators' most dramatic decision was to let Lehman Brothers go bankrupt. This multiplied the panic in markets.

Moreover, Europe also had its own internal imbalances that proved just as dramatic as those in the United States and China. Southern European economies racked up huge current-account deficits in the first decade of the euro while countries in northern Europe ran offsetting surpluses. Credit flows from the euro-zone core to the overheated housing markets of countries such as Spain and Ireland financed the imbalances. The euro crisis has in this respect been a continuation of the financial crisis by other means, as markets have agonized over the weaknesses of European banks loaded with bad debts following property busts.

Central bankers insist that tempering the housing and credit boom through higher interest rates would have been difficult. Perhaps so, but they had other regulatory tools at their disposal, such as lowering maximum loan-to-value ratios for mortgages, or demanding that banks should set aside more capital. Low capital ratios proved the biggest shortcoming. In 2004, the Basel II Accord replaced the original 1988 Basel I Accord focusing on techniques that allowed banks and supervisors to properly evaluate the various risks that banks face (Basel Committee for Banking Supervision 1988, 2004, 2006, 2008). Because credit risk modeling contributes broadly to the internal risk assessment process of an institution, regulators have enforced more strict rules about model development, implementation, and validation to be followed by banks that want to use their internal models in order to estimate capital requirements (Altman and Sabato 2005, 2007). But these rules did not define capital strictly enough, which let banks smuggle in forms of debt that did not have the same loss-absorbing capacity as equity.

Under pressure from shareholders to increase returns, banks operated with minimal equity, leaving them vulnerable if things went wrong. From the mid-1990s, regulators increasingly allowed banks to use their own internal models to assess risk—in effect setting their own capital requirements. Predictably, banks judged their assets to be safer, allowing balance-sheets to balloon without a commensurate rise in capital. The Basel committee also did not make any rules regarding the share of a bank's assets that should be liquid. It also failed to set up a mechanism to allow a big international bank to go bust without causing the rest of the system to seize up.

All the shortcomings of the minimum capital requirements rules are now being regulated and this will possibly help to mitigate the effects of future financial crises. Even the concept of risk weight that is the foundation of the Basel II accord is being seriously questioned by regulators. Questions remain whether the new capital rules (i.e., the Basel III Accord) will be sufficient to provide markets with more trust in the soundness of the financial system and to what extent they will not penalize lending in a period of capital shortage.

DEFINING AND MITIGATING SYSTEMIC RISK

Governments and international organizations worry increasingly about systemic risk. Widespread confusion exists about the causes, definition, and uncertainty about how to control systemic risk. Academics historically have tended to think of systemic risk primarily in terms of financial institutions. However, with the growth of disintermediation, in which companies can access capital-market funding without going through banks or other intermediary institutions, greater focus has been devoted to financial markets and the relationship between markets and institutions. In general, some contend that systemic risk results from market participants following their own self-interest due to lack of sufficient incentive to limit risk-taking in order to reduce the systemic danger to others. Therefore, some believe regulation plays a fundamental role in reducing systemic risk.

No widely accepted uniform definition of systemic risk is available. Anabtawi and Schwarcz (2011) define systemic risk as the probability that cumulative losses will occur from an event that ignites a series of successive losses along a chain of financial institutions or markets comprising a system. Yet, others including Kaufman (1996) and Acharya (2009) define systemic risk as the potential for a modest economic shock to induce substantial volatility in asset prices, substantial reductions in corporate liquidity, potential bankruptcies, and efficiency losses. Kaufman and Scott (2003) define systematic risk as the risk of collapse of an entire financial system or market serious enough to quite probably have large adverse effects on the real economy. The *real economy* refers to the goods, services, and resources aspects of the economy as opposed to financial markets. In particular, systemic risk involves a potential cascading failure in a system or market due to inter-linkages and interdependencies.

Given the lack of consistency around the definition of systemic risk, a relevant question is whether regulatory solutions would be appropriate to mitigate it. A large part of the existing literature contends that no individual market participant has sufficient incentive, absent regulation, to limit risk taking in order to reduce the systemic danger to other participants and third parties. For example, Bexley, James, and Haberman (2011) consider proprietary trading by banking entities, generally the trading of financial instruments for a banking entity's own account, to have played a critical role in the financial crisis of 2007–2008. These sentiments parallel arguments that the practices of banks and their securities affiliates in the 1920s were partly responsible for the stock market crash of 1929 and the subsequent Great Depression. At the heart of these assertions is the issue of whether combining the businesses of commercial banking and investment banking increases systemic risk.

The Banking Act of 1933 (Glass-Steagall Act) contained provisions that prohibit commercial banks from underwriting, promoting, or selling securities directly or through an affiliated brokerage firm, effectively erecting a wall between commercial banking and investment banking. That wall was gradually weakened and picked apart over the course of the next 60 years or so, finally coming down with the Financial Services Modernization Act of 1999 (Gramm-Leach-Bliley Act), which repealed the last remaining restrictions of the Glass-Steagall Act's wall. The Dodd-Frank Wall Street Reform and Consumer Protection Act (Dodd-Frank Act) of 2010 (2010) reintroduces portions of Glass-Steagall's wall. In particular, the *Volcker rule*, contained in the Dodd-Frank Act, restricts "banking entities" from both engaging in proprietary trading and sponsoring, acquiring, or retaining certain ownership interests in a hedge or private equity fund.

One of the policy justifications for these restrictions is that the prohibited activities increase systemic risk. The implicit contentions in this justification are that if the prohibited activities are too risky they could affect a bank's liquidity, causing the banking entity to be unwilling or unable to extend credit to qualified borrowers or to fail, disrupting credit channels. Similarly, some fear that banking entities may also fail from exposure to failing hedge or private equity funds, further disrupting credit channels.

If the conflicts of interest are the main harm legislators are trying to address, considering other solutions such as additional disclosures and regulations that protect the public from such conflicts may make sense. If, however, systemic risk is truly what the world is trying to address and mitigate, the proposed regulation may be ineffective on its own if the financial institutions are not forced to embed appropriate methodologies and tools to manage risk and design effective growth strategies.

Another important issue that regulators have tried to address in the aim of mitigating systemic risk is reducing inter-linkages among financial institutions (i.e., network risk) by forcing them to use central counterparties (CCPs) and clearing houses. A CCP stands between over-the-counter (OTC) derivatives counterparties, insulating them from each other's default. Effective clearing mitigates systemic risk by lowering the risk that defaults propagate from counterparty to counterparty. Duffie and Zhu (2010) demonstrate that using CCPs can help to mitigate systemic risk. However, some concerns remain around the CCP's ability to sustain defaults of multiple counterparties and what would happen to the system if one of those CCP defaults.

Managing Risk: Lesson Learned

Risk management is a science that is continuously evolving. Even assuming that risk has been measured correctly, managing it appropriately requires much experience and knowledge. Moreover, the governance structure of financial institutions needs to allow risk managers to enforce their decisions and strategies. This section provides a discussion of the most advanced risk management techniques together with a brief analysis of what should be the most appropriate risk governance structure to help mitigate the effects of the next financial crisis.

CAPITAL ALLOCATION STRATEGY

Portfolio selection strategies have been a major topic in the literature during the last 60 years and especially after Markowitz (1952). However, few studies analyze how to apply these strategies to financial institutions. This situation may seem strange considering that financial organizations are among the main investors in the financial markets, but reasons stem from several peculiarities that may have distracted the attention from them.

First, capital tended to be cheap and easy to raise. This opportunity created the belief that every deal that looked profitable could be done by letting market demand drive asset growth. Second, many viewed banking organizations as having a social function of providing funds to companies in order to start or grow their business and to consumers in order to buy homes or goods. Although this social function was prevalent as a capital allocation strategy, shareholders, especially since the 1990s, tended to view banks as a profit-making institution. Thus, to please shareholders and to outperform peers, banking chief executive officers (CEOs) aggressively invested in complex assets mixing their traditional lending culture with a more speculative equity one (Blundell-Wignal, Atkinson, and Lee 2008).

The business model for financial institutions moved toward an equity culture with a focus on faster share price growth and earnings expansion during the 1990s. The previous model, based on balance sheets and old-fashioned spreads on loans, was not conducive to financial institutions becoming "growth stocks." So, the strategy switched more toward an activity-based framework on trading income and fees via securitization. This change enabled financial institutions to grow earnings while at the same time economizing on capital by gaming the Basel Accord system.

In implementing this cultural change, most financial institutions focused mainly on the expected return side of their investment omitting the risk side. Concentrations in highly correlated assets increased markedly without any consideration of the volatility of their losses. Portfolio diversification became a purely theoretical and easily sacrificed concept to allow the market share to grow. Pricing was mainly set to be competitive in the market and not to guarantee an appropriate return.

Ultimately, the most recent financial crisis provides financial institutions with the right incentives to correct the shortfalls mentioned previously. Yet, to achieve this, having a well-defined and fully embedded risk appetite strategy is essential to ensure that accepted risks and rewards are aligned with shareholders' expectations.

In his seminal study, Markowitz (1952) explains how to build the most efficient investment portfolio to find the right balance between expected returns and volatility of losses. He demonstrates that diversification is the best tool to reduce the risk of the entire portfolio.

The risk function of a financial institution cannot define a risk appetite framework by itself, but needs the help of the business (sales) department to model the expected returns. Articulating a consistent and effective risk appetite framework requires joining the efforts of those involved in risk management with others in business through a top-down approach. Ultimately, the board of directors, interpreting shareholders views, needs to steer the way forward in terms of acceptable risks and required returns. Then, following these guidelines, the risk and the business functions can define risk appetite at different levels such as the group, divisional, and portfolio level.

A good risk appetite framework should consist of two parts. The first part presents a picture of the current situation by clarifying how capital is currently allocated among portfolios and identifying the main concentrations and portfolios that are below the expected minimum return. Clarifying this picture also requires defining the required metrics.

Credit risk is conventionally defined using the concepts of expected loss (EL) and unexpected loss (UL). The customer-level risk metrics (i.e., the probability of default (PD), loss given default (LGD), and exposure at default (EAD)) are used as inputs to calculate both values. Because expected loss can be anticipated, it should be regarded as a cost of doing business and not as a financial risk. Obviously, credit losses are not constant across the economic cycle due to substantial volatility (unexpected loss) associated with the level of expected loss. Credit portfolio models are designed to quantify this volatility. Two factors drive the volatility of portfolio losses: correlation and concentration.

Correlation is mainly an exogenous factor that depends on the customer type, geography, and macroeconomic factors. By contrast, concentration is (or should be) the result of conscious decisions of financial institutions' senior management through a well-defined risk appetite framework as discussed in the next section. However, optimal concentration limits cannot be defined without an appropriate measure of capital/risk concentration such as EC and correlations are the most important input for EC.

In order to calculate regulatory capital (RC) (e.g., the Basel II Internal Rating Based Approach), correlations are also used, but these correlations are given by the regulator (e.g., Bank for International Settlements) and are equal for all banks. Moreover, these correlations cover only intra-product ones and not inter-products correlations (e.g., correlations between defaults in different products). This difference is a very strong assumption that fully excludes diversification benefits.

Accurately modeling portfolio credit risk first requires measuring the correlation between exposures. Complexity arises in calculating credit risk correlations directly. The simplest solution is to use aggregate time series to infer credit risk correlation. A more attractive possibility is to use a causative default model that takes more observable financial quantities as inputs and then transforms them into a default probability (Merton 1974). This solution is the most applied for corporate exposures. For retail exposures, correlations are best measured using factor models in the same way that an equity beta is estimated. Factor models usually produce better prospective correlation estimates than direct observation and have the additional benefit, if macroeconomic factors are chosen, of enabling intuitive stress testing and scenario analysis of the credit portfolio.

Measuring concentration using the exposure balance of a portfolio, RC or EC, can make a huge difference in the results of the analysis and on the required actions. Regulators have slowly started to realize this benefit. Consequently, they are now forcing financial institutions to develop and implement sophisticated internal EC models subject to regulatory validation. EC is calculated from the tails of the credit risk distribution by determining the probability that a reduction in portfolio value exceeds a critical value (e.g., 99.95 percent). Thanks to the correlation structures included in its estimation, EC allows large, well-diversified banks to take full advantage of asset diversification. This opportunity is increasingly important in times when the RC ratio is rising as is the case with the new Basel III Accord. Moreover, EC allows banks to include all risks types (e.g., liquidity risk, pension risk, and business risk) and not just credit, market, and operational risk.

Following the guidelines of the board of directors in terms of expected return and volatility of losses, EC can be used to determine the maximum amount of losses under stress that the institution would be willing to accept and design the target portfolio. The minimum expected return and the maximum acceptable risk help to define the *risk capacity* (or risk tolerance) while the desired expected return and the desired acceptable risk determine the bank's *risk appetite*.

Distinguishing risk capacity and risk appetite is important under several aspects. First, these two concepts differ substantially. Hence, confusing them could likely lead to generating uncertainty around what is possible and what is desired. Second, each concept has a specific time horizon. While risk capacity is a long-term statement, risk appetite should change frequently adapting to the market and economic situation.

The risk appetite framework should describe how the capital allocation strategy should change when portfolios end up in the different areas described by the defined limits, but it should not set the specific concentration limits for each product, portfolio, country, or sector. These limits should be set in a limit concentration framework using a top-down approach. Separating the risk appetite framework from the concentration framework is important mainly from the implementation point of view. Concentrations are more difficult to influence and slower to change than the parameters that influence expected returns and volatility of losses.

Once the risk appetite framework is fully embedded, it forces debate and helps ensure that risks are made explicit. To change behaviors in relation to risk, interventions through additional training or changing personnel may be needed. Yet, in most organizations, the tone set by senior management tends to have the greatest impact. Risk appetite is not only a framework but also a deep cultural change that will ensure financial institutions are more solid in the future.

ENTERPRISE RISK MANAGEMENT

Financial institutions and the academic world have extensively discussed ERM for the last 10 years. The numerous papers and books written on this topic provide clear guidelines and theoretical background to support this fundamental change in risk management (Doherty 2000; D'Arcy 2001; Lam 2003; Olson and Wu 2008). Today, few financial institutions have tried to implement ERM and even fewer have been successful in embedding it in their management culture.

The ERM concept is relatively simple. Risks that may affect the value of an organization are of a different nature and their sum does not give the total risk. Several correlations and covariance should be considered when different risks are aggregated. ERM is a rigorous approach to assessing and addressing the risks from all sources that threaten the achievement of an organization's strategic objectives. A well-implemented ERM approach should be able to provide a comprehensive and coherent view of the risks that an institution is facing allowing senior management to focus on the full picture and not on the single "silo."

The first step in operationalizing ERM is to identify the risks to which a firm is exposed. A common approach is to identify the types of risks to be measured. Many firms have gone beyond measuring market, credit, and operational risks. In particular, in recent years, firms have also attempted to measure liquidity, reputation, tax, pension, and strategic risks.

Organizations that have grown through acquisitions or without centralized information technology (IT) departments typically face the problem that they have some systems that are incompatible. Firms need to be able to aggregate common risks across all of their businesses to analyze and manage those risks effectively. The goal is to capture and quantify all risks employing a consistent approach and then aggregate individual risk exposures across the entire organization as well as analyzing the aggregate risk profile considering risk correlations.

Ideally, a good ERM framework should be able to summarize all risks into one metric: the optimal level of available capital. A firm that practices ERM may therefore have an amount of capital that substantially exceeds its regulatory requirements because it maximizes shareholder wealth by doing so. In this case, the regulatory requirements are not binding and would not affect the firm's decisions. The firm could be in a more difficult situation if its required RC exceeds the amount of capital it should hold to maximize shareholder wealth. RC for banks is generally defined in terms of regulatory accounting. For ERM, banks should focus on EC. An exclusive focus on RC is likely to be mistaken because it does not reflect correctly the buffer stock of equity available.

In summary, how to aggregate different risks remains the main challenge for all firms willing to implement an ERM approach and for financial institutions in particular. Often, IT systems are still unable to dialogue between them and the methodologies used to evaluate risks are so different that reconciling them in one single number is almost impossible. Ignoring these main issues by providing ERM reports that address risks "by silos" is useless and dangerous. Some time may be needed to build the right infrastructure to implement an ERM framework, but financial institutions should be convinced that this is the best way to avoid mistakes that could potentially threaten their existence.

RISK GOVERNANCE STRUCTURE

The lack of an appropriate risk governance structure would dissolve any benefit generated by a first-class risk management team. Before the financial crisis of 2007–2008, the role of risk management was extremely marginal at most institutions, leaving the ability of influencing business decisions to the persuasive skills of each risk manager and not to his authority.

The role and importance of the chief risk officer (CRO) and risk governance in the financial industry have been highlighted in newspapers and various reports (Brancato et al. 2006), as well as in practitioner-oriented studies (Banham 2000). Yet, the academic literature has largely neglected these areas so far.

A few recent academic studies (Erkens, Hung, and Matos 2010; Minton, Taillard, and Williamson 2010; Beltratti and Stulz 2012; Fahlenbrach and Stulz 2011) address some other aspects of corporate governance in banks such as board characteristics and CEO pay structure. However, the literature on corporate governance and the valuation effect of corporate governance in financial firms is still very limited. Moreover, financial institutions have their particularities such as higher opaqueness as well as heavy regulation and government intervention (Levine 2004), which require a distinct analysis of corporate governance issues. Adams and Mehran (2003) and Macey and O'Hara (2003) highlight the importance of taking differences in governance between banking and non-banking firms into consideration.

In particular, in most financial institutions, the CRO is still not on the board and the risk managers in the divisions have often only dotted reporting lines to him and solid ones to business heads. This means that risk managers can discuss issues with the bank's CRO, but their boss, the one who will assess their performance and set their objectives, is the head of business whose objectives usually conflict with the ones of risk. This kind of risk structure has clearly proved to be inappropriate because it precludes the possibility for risk to influence strategic decisions when needed. The independence of the risk function must be ensured and supervisory authorities need to continuously monitor this to avoid allowing financial institutions to focus again on short-term speculative investments to generate unsustainable results (Aebi et al. 2011).

Yet, empowering risk management and ensuring its independence will not solve all problems if the quality of the function does not improve accordingly. Senior management needs to drive the improvement toward a more effective and efficient role of risk, increasing substantially its involvement in daily decisions and ensuring the stability and soundness of the overall process. The board needs to pay more attention to risk in general, approving and monitoring the respect of the risk appetite framework through a good ERM reporting.

Summary and Conclusions

The topics covered in this chapter build upon the experience of the past financial crises to determine what factors can help to mitigate their impact on the economy in the future. Much work has been done and quite often in the right direction, but a new era has just started. Regulation is identified as a key element to reduce systemic risk, but improving risk management and control at financial institutions will need to be developed in parallel to reach the expected benefits.

Beyond the immediate pressures of global markets, more demanding customers, and dramatic industry change is a growing recognition that financial institutions have an opportunity to drive competitive advantage from their risk management capabilities, enabling long-term profitable growth and sustained future profitability. These changes mean that risk management at the top-performing organizations is now more closely integrated with strategic planning and is conducted proactively, with an eye on how such capabilities might help a company move into new markets faster or pursue other evolving growth strategies. At its best, risk management is a matter of balance between a company's appetite for risks and its ability to manage them.

Methodologies and tools applied to measure risks have evolved tremendously during the last 20 years. Credit and market risk have led the evolution and have now reached a more advanced status. At present, the focus is moving toward operational and the other "minor" risk types. Also, risk aggregation is the next challenge for most financial organizations.

In terms of risk management, three main topics have emerged after the financial crisis of 2007–2008: (1) capital allocation, (2) ERM, and (3) risk governance structure. Risk management is now a priority at most financial and non-financial companies that are investing substantially in systems and people. This is a great opportunity for risk management to finally find the appropriate leading role in the changing financial culture and help governments and regulators in mitigating the impact of the next financial crises.

Disclaimer

The material and the opinions presented and expressed in this chapter are those of the author and do not necessarily reflect views of Royal Bank of Scotland.

Discussion Questions

1. Discuss the two phases in which crises are usually divided.
2. Define systemic risk and explain how it can be mitigated.
3. Discuss the difference between economic capital and regulatory capital.
4. Define the "Minsky moment" and discuss how this is important to identify crises.
5. Discuss the main objective of ERM.
6. Define risk appetite and discuss why financial institutions should focus on it.

References

Acharya, Viral V. 2009. "A Theory of Systemic Risk and Design of Prudential Bank Regulation." *Journal of Financial Stability* 5:3, 224–255.

Adams, René, and Hamid Mehran. 2003. "Is Corporate Governance Different for Bank Holding Companies?" *Federal Reserve Bank of New York Economic Policy Review* 91, 123–142.

Aebi, Vincent, Gabriele Sabato, and Markus Schmid. 2011. "Risk Management, Corporate Governance, and Bank Performance in the Financial Crisis." *Journal of Banking & Finance,* 36:12, 3213–3226.

Allen, Franklin, and Douglas Gale. 2007. *Understanding Financial Crises,* Clarendon Lectures in Finance. Oxford: Oxford University Press.

Altman, Edward I., and Gabriele Sabato. 2005. "Effects of the New Basel Capital Accord on Bank Capital Requirements for SMEs." *Journal of Financial Services Research* 28:1/3, 15–42.

Altman, Edward I., and Gabriele Sabato. 2007. "Modeling Credit Risk for SMEs: Evidence from the US Market." *ABACUS* 43:3, 332–357.

Anabtawi, Iman, and Steven L. Schwarcz. 2011. "Regulating Systemic Risk: Towards an Analytical Framework." *Notre Dame Law Review* 86:4, 1349–1353.

Banham, Russ. 2000. "Top Cops of Risk." *CFO* 16:10, 91–98.

Banking (Glass-Steagall) Act. 1933. Pub. L. No. 73-66, §§ 16, 20, 21, 32, 48 Stat. 162, 184–185, 188–189, 194.

Basel Committee on Banking Supervision. 1988. "International Convergence of Capital Measurement and Capital Standards." Basel: Bank for International Settlements.

Basel Committee on Banking Supervision. 2004. "International Convergence of Capital Measurement and Capital Standards: A Revised Framework." Basel: Bank for International Settlements.

Basel Committee on Banking Supervision. 2006. "International Convergence of Capital Measurement and Capital Standards: A Revised Framework." Basel: Bank for International Settlements.

Basel Committee on Banking Supervision. 2008. "Principles for Sound Liquidity Risk Management and Supervision." Basel: Bank for International Settlements.

Beltratti, Andrea, and René M. Stulz. 2012. "The Credit Crisis around the Globe: Why Did Some Banks Perform Better during the Credit Crisis?" *Journal of Financial Economics,* 105:1, 1–17.

Bexley, James, Joe James, and James Haberman. 2011. "The Financial Crisis and Its Issues," *Research in Business and Economics Journal* 3, 1–7. Available at http://www.aabri.com/manuscripts/10500.pdf.

Blundell-Wignall, Adrian, Paul Atkinson, and Se Hoon Lee. 2008. "The Current Financial Crisis: Causes and Policy Issues." *OECD Financial Market Trends* 95:2, 1–21.

Brancato, Carolyn, Matteo Tonello, Ellen Hexter, and Katharine R. Newman. 2006. "The Role of U.S. Corporate Boards in Enterprise Risk Management." New York: Conference Board.

Brunnermeier, Markus K. 2009. "Deciphering the Liquidity and Credit Crunch 2007–2008." *Journal of Economic Perspectives* 23:1, 77–100.

Brunnermeier, Markus K., and Martin Oehmke. 2012. "Bubbles, Financial Crises, and Systemic Risk". *Handbook of the Economics of Finance* 2:B, 1221–1288.

D'Arcy, Stephen. 2001. "Enterprise Risk Management." *Journal of Risk Management of Korea* 12:1, 23–37.

Dodd–Frank Wall Street Reform and Consumer Protection Act of 2010. Pub. L. 111–203, 124 Stat. 1376. 2010. Available at http://www.gpo.gov/fdsys/pkg/PLAW-111publ203/content-detail.html.

Doherty, Neil. 2000. *Integrated Risk Management.* New York: McGraw-Hill.

Duffie, Darrel, and Haoxiang Zhu. 2010. "Does a Central Clearing Counterparty Reduce Counterparty Risk?" *Review of Asset Pricing Studies* 1:1, 74–95.

Erkens, David, Mingy Hung, and Pedro Matos. 2010. "Corporate Governance in the 2007–2008 Financial Crisis: Evidence from Financial Institutions Worldwide." Working Paper, European Corporate Governance Institute.

Fahlenbrach, Rudiger, and René M. Stulz. 2011. "Bank CEO Incentives and the Credit Crisis." *Journal of Financial Economics* 99:1, 11–26.

Financial Services Modernization (Gramm-Leach-Blilely) Act. 1999. Pub. L. No. 106–102, Stat. 1338, 1341.

Garber, Peter M. 2000. *Famous First Bubbles: The Fundamentals of Early Manias.* Cambridge, MA: MIT Press.

Hoshi, Takeo, and Anil K. Kashyap. 2004. "Japan's Financial Crisis and Economic Stagnation." *Journal of Economic Perspectives* 18:1, 3–26.

Kaufman, George G. 1996. "Bank Failures, Systemic Risk, and Bank Regulation." *Cato Journal* 16:1, 17–45.

Kaufman, George G., and Kenneth E. Scott. 2003. "What Is Systemic Risk, and Do Bank Regulators Retard or Contribute to It?" *The Independent Review* 7:3, 371–391.

Kindleberger, Charles P. 1978. *Manias, Panics, and Crashes: A History of Financial Crises.* New York: John Wiley & Sons.

Lam, James. 2003. *Enterprise Risk Management: From Incentives to Control.* New York: John Wiley and Sons.

Levine, Ross. 2004. "The Corporate Governance of Banks: A Concise Discussion of Concepts and Evidence." Working Paper, World Bank Policy Research Working Paper 3404.

Macey, Jonathan R., and Maureen O'Hara. 2003. "The Corporate Governance of Banks." *Federal Reserve Bank of New York Economic Policy Review* 9:1, 91–107.

Markowitz, Harry. 1952. "Portfolio Selection." *Journal of Finance* 7:1, 77–91.

Merton, Robert C. 1974. "On the Pricing of Corporate Debt: The Risk Structure of Interest Rates" *Journal of Finance* 29:2, 449–470.

Minsky, Hyman. 1992. "The Financial Instability Hypothesis." Working Paper No. 74. May. Annandale-on-Hudson, NY: The Levy Economics Institute.

Minton, Bernardette A., Jerome Taillard, and Rohan G. Williamson. 2010. "Do Independence and Financial Expertise of the Board Matter for Risk Taking and Performance?" Working Paper, Fisher College of Business, Ohio State University.

Neal, Larry. 1990. *The Rise of Financial Capitalism.* Cambridge: Cambridge University Press.

Neal, Larry. 2012. *I Am Not Master of Events: Speculations of John Law and Lord Londonderry in the Mississippi and South Sea Bubbles.* London: Yale University Press.

Olson, David L., and Desheng Wu, eds. 2008. *New Frontiers in Enterprise Risk Management.* Berlin: Springer.

Radelet, Steven, Jeffrey D. Sachs, Richard N. Cooper, and Barry P. Bosworth. 1998. "The East Asian Financial Crisis: Diagnosis, Remedies, Prospects." *Brookings Papers on Economic Activity* 1, 1–90.

Reinhart, Carmen M., and Kenneth S. Rogoff. 2009. *This Time is Different: Eight Centuries of Financial Folly.* Princeton: Princeton University Press.

Shiller, Robert J. 2000. *Irrational Exuberance.* Princeton: Princeton University Press.

Sturzenegger, Federico, and Jeromin Zettelmeyer. 2006. *Debt Defaults and Lessons from a Decade of Crises.* Cambridge, MA: MIT Press.

White, Eugene N. 2009. "Lessons from the Great American Real Estate Boom and Bust of the 1920s." NBER Working Paper 15573.

30

The Future of Risk Management

HUNTER M. HOLZHAUER

Assistant Professor of Finance, University of Tennessee Chattanooga

Introduction

Bernstein (1996, p. 1) notes, "The revolutionary idea that defines the boundary between modern times and the past is the mastery of risk: the notion that the future is more than a whim of the gods and that men and women are not passive before nature." Bernstein's view is certainly appropriate considering the dramatic changes that have occurred recently involving risk management.

The years following the 2008 recession, which technically lasted 18 months from December 2007 to June 2009 (National Bureau of Economic Research 2010), have proven challenging for many risk managers. Since the fall of both Lehman Brothers and Washington Mutual in 2008, several other notable risk management failures followed. For example, in the wake of the recession, the markets witnessed the 2009 bankruptcies of Thornburg Mortgage and two automobile industry titans, General Motors and Chrysler (Howe 2011). More recently, two high-profile failures of risk management include MF Global and JP Morgan. The 2011 bankruptcy and liquidation of MF Global was the result of over-aggressive trading strategies that cost their customers more than $1.5 billion. In the case of JP Morgan, risk management oversights in the infamous 2012 "London whale" scandal cost the company more than $6 billion in losses and almost another $1 billion in fines. The name "London whale" is actually the nickname of London trader Bruno Iksil, who accumulated outsized positions in the currency default swap market. Much like the collapse of MF Global, the "London whale" scandal gave rise to a number of investigations into the efficiency of risk management systems. Both of these recent risk management failures are even more surprising in that the 2008 recession had forced most firms to focus additional attention toward risk management (Hopkins 2013).

The need for better risk management is growing because new risks are on the horizon. The markets are becoming increasingly volatile due to sovereign debt crises in several areas of the world, political instability in the Middle East, new emerging markets supplying the demand for commodities, and the anticipation of stricter regulations (Professional Risk Managers' International Association 2012). Thus, risk management will need to shift from reactive to proactive. This chapter attempts to cover many of the issues and trends shaping the future of risk management.

The remainder of the chapter contains seven sections. The first section discusses professional organizations for risk management. Next, the chapter focuses on regulatory risk followed by sections on multi-asset class investing, risk measures, and innovations in risk management markets and services. The next to last section provides a wish list for risk managers. The final section offers a summary and conclusions.

Professional Organizations for Risk Management

Chance (2003, p. 569) defines risk management as follows:

> Risk management is the process of identifying the level of risk that an entity wants, measuring the level of risk that an entity currently has, taking actions that bring the actual level of risk to the desired level of risk, and monitoring the new actual level of risk so that it continues to be aligned with the desired level of risk. The process is continuous and may require alterations in any of these activities to reflect new policies, preferences, and information.

Risk management can be easily defined as common business sense. However, to fully understand the complexity of risk management, risk managers must know all of the risks within a firm and how to effectively use modern tools to manage those risks. Two professional organizations are currently devoted to developing risk management. The Global Association of Risk Professionals (GARP) (http://www.garp.com) and the Professional Risk Managers' International Association (PRMIA) (http://www.prmia.org) provide risk managers with a wide range of resources designed to promote and enhance the field of risk management.

In fact, several surveys referenced in this chapter came directly from the resource links on the PRMIA website. For example, the Professional Risk Managers' International Association (2013) involves 375 respondents from primarily Europe, North America, and the Asia Pacific. The respondents represent a diverse range of market segments including both asset/wealth managers (26 percent) and consultants (18 percent). The vast majority of respondents are buy-side regulators and investors. These buy-side firms, which are fiduciary firms focused on managing assets usually for clients, represent various sizes from below $10 billion to more than $100 billion and include private banks, insurance firms, hedge funds, mutual funds, endowments, and sovereign wealth funds. The Professional Risk Managers' International Association (2012) report serves as a reference point for the subsequent Professional Risk Managers' International Association (2013) survey. The summaries of respondents in both surveys are very similar.

According to Professional Risk Managers' International Association (2013), the top three concerns in 2013 for risk managers in buy-side firms involve regulatory risk, liquidity risk, and counterparty risk. The latter two are types of financial risks and are therefore discussed in previous chapters focusing on liquidity risk and credit risk. In contrast, regulatory risk is a type of nonfinancial risk (Chance 2003). Yet, regulatory risk is perhaps an even more important risk for risk managers because of the rapidly changing legal landscape. Thus, the following section explores regulatory risk in detail.

Regulatory Risk

According to Lindo and Rahl (2009), the Federation of European Risk Management Associations (2012), and the Professional Risk Managers' International Association (2012, 2013), regulatory risk is currently the top concern of risk managers due to uncertainty and complexity surrounding recent and upcoming regulations. In fact, the Professional Risk Managers' International Association (2012) reports that almost 90 percent of respondents believe that regulation will have an impact on shaping their risk management practices in the near future. This concern is appropriate given that regulatory risk arises from changes in laws and regulations that can materially affect a security, firm, industry, or market. Thus, regulation is a source of uncertainty. Even unregulated markets such as over-the-counter (OTC) derivatives are subjected to the risk that they will become regulated (Chance 2003). Regulatory changes often reduce the desirability of certain investments, increase operational costs for businesses, and alter the competitive landscape for specific sectors or even the markets as a whole.

Regulations and their costs are a major concern for top management. In a global survey of about 400 executives across 10 major industries, Culp (2011) finds that two of the top three future challenges for risk management listed by executives are reducing costs (47 percent) and implementing regulatory demands (41 percent). Further, more executives (53 percent) listed risk managers as "critical" for managing regulatory compliance than any other purpose within a firm.

According to the Professional Risk Managers' International Association (2012), the perceived impact of regulations is especially prevalent among risk managers for insurance companies (100 percent) and private banks (96 percent). Insurance companies, similar to asset managers and hedge fund managers, face increasingly strict regulations regarding their risk management practices. The percentage for private banks appears high given that they have been subject to the "know your customer/client" (KYC) rule as required by the USA Patriot Act of 2001. However, private banks face a more rigorous interpretation of the KYC rule. Financial Industry Regulatory Authority (FINRA) (2011) recently issued a regulatory notice outlining consolidated guidelines for the KYC rule in order to strengthen investor protection and promote fair dealing with customers in a clearer and more ethical manner.

INCREASED REGULATION

The KYC rule is only one of many regulations that affects or will soon affect risk management practices. Ahuja and Thomas (2013) and Bernanke (2013) discuss many of these regulations. A list of recent and upcoming domestic and international regulations including the approximate year the regulation was or will be enacted follows:

- **Undertakings for Collective Investment in Transferable Securities III (UCITS III) (2001).** UCITS III is a set of European Union (EU) directives aimed to deregulate the EU financial market. Specifically, this directive removes investment barriers that protected local asset managers and allows collective investment schemes to operate freely throughout the EU. Sender (2011) lists several potential non-financial risk exposures from UCITS including liquidity risk, counterparty risk, compliance risk, misinformation risk, and other non-financial risks in the investment industry.

- **Sarbanes-Oxley Act (2002).** The Sarbanes-Oxley Act is a federal law in the United States created to protect investors by reforming accounting practices for publicly traded companies (Kimmel, Weygandt, and Kieso 2011).
- **Basel II (2004).** Basel II is the second Basel Accord. The Basel Accords are a series of recommendations by the Basel Committee on Banking Supervision regarding banking laws and regulations. Basel II specifically focuses on developing a global standard for capital requirements for the banking industry (Bank of International Settlements 2005).
- **Market in Financial Instruments Directive I (MiFID I) (2008).** MiFID is an EU law aimed at increasing investor protection and competition in the EU financial services markets. The law essentially outlines uniform regulations for investment services in all member states (European Union Parliament 2008).
- **Dodd-Frank Act (2010).** In the United States, the Dodd-Frank Act created wide-sweeping changes to the financial services industry as a response to the recent 2008 recession. Specifically, the act consolidated regulatory agencies and created a new oversight council to evaluate systemic risk. The act also demanded increased transparency of the derivatives market, the bankruptcy process, and credit rating agencies (Paletta and Luchhetti 2010). President Obama later added the Volcker Rule, which is discussed later in this chapter (Volcker 2010).
- **Foreign Account Tax Compliance Act (FATCA) (2010).** In the United States, the Foreign Account Tax Compliance Act was created to increase federal tax revenue by mitigating offshore tax evasion. The law establishes mandatory Internal Revenue Service (IRS) reporting guidelines for foreign investment accounts by both the domestic investor and the foreign financial institution (United States Treasury 2012).
- **European Market Infrastructure Regulation (EMIR) (2012).** EMIR was designed to stabilize the over-the-counter (OTC) derivative markets in the European Union. For example, the regulation introduces both reporting and clearing obligations for the OTC derivatives market (European Union Parliament 2012).
- **Alternative Investment Fund Managers Directive (AIFMD) (2013).** The AIFMD regulates hedge funds and alternative investment funds in the European Union in a manner more similar to traditional mutual funds and pension funds. In other words, the purpose of this regulation is to close the gap in the regulatory differences for hedge funds and alternative investment funds by increasing transparency and independent risk management functions (European Securities and Markets Authority 2013).
- **Retail Distribution Review (RDR) (2013).** The Financial Conduct Authority (FCA) designed the RDR to raise professional standards in the financial services industry, especially in terms of retirement and investment planning advice (Financial Conduct Authority 2013).
- **Solvency II (2014).** The Solvency II focuses on creating uniformity in the EU insurance industry with regards to capital requirements. The aim is to increase consumer

protection by reducing the risk of insolvency (European Union Parliament 2009). The European Commission has recently recommended delaying the application date for this regulation from 2014 to 2016 (Barnier 2013).

- **Capital Requirements Directive IV (CRD IV) (2014)**. CRD IV helps to implement the Basel III Accord through a legislative package that covers several rules for the banking and investment industries. The focus of this package is to improve the management of capital, liquidity, counterparty risk, and corporate governance. The legislation also requires firms to report financial information such as certain investment holdings, especially any large exposures (European Union Commission 2013).
- **Market in Financial Instruments Directive II (MiFID II) (2014 or 2015)**. MiFID II updates and builds upon the reforms of its predecessor, MiFID I, which focuses on creating harmonized investment regulations throughout the European Union that protect investors and increase competition (BlackRock 2012).
- **Basel III (2018)**. Basel III, like its predecessor Basel II, focuses on creating an international standard for capital requirements for the banking industry. Basel III also recommends voluntary standards for stress testing and market liquidity risk. The primary purpose of this accord is to increase bank liquidity and decrease bank leverage (Bank of International Settlements 2010).

The specifics of these regulations are outside the scope of this chapter. However, of the regulations listed previously, the Professional Risk Managers' International Association (2012) reports that, in the near term, the Dodd-Frank Act is likely to have the biggest impact on risk management and reporting practices, especially for asset managers, investment banks, and private banks. The Dodd-Frank Act is followed closely by Solvency II, which will have the strongest impact on insurance companies and hedge funds. For example, under Solvency II, hedge funds that provide a basic level of transparency for their holdings face a 49 percent capital charge. For those hedge funds that hold completely opaque assets, regulators may impose a 100 percent capital charge. This punitive capital treatment for hedge funds will have a large influence on investment inflow for this industry (Devasabai 2012). Two other key regulations listed by respondents include two broad-sweeping directives in the European Union, UCITS III and AIFMD. The remaining regulations are local regulations such as the Swiss Collective Investment Schemes Act, Germany's Bafin, the National Association of Insurance Commissioners' Own Risk and Solvency Assessment (2013), and the Securities and Exchange Commission's (SEC) Form PF in the United States. Form PF (private fund) is a new SEC rule requiring private fund advisers to report regulatory assets under management to the Financial Stability Oversight Council (FSOC), an organization established under Dodd-Frank in order to monitor risks within the financial sector. In the long-term, Basel III will help to shape future risk management practices.

Many of these regulations can change quickly. Some recent regulations, such as the KYC rule and the Basel Accords, are updated periodically. A few regulations contain innovative features that allow the regulations to adapt to current market conditions. For example, the Dodd-Frank Act includes mechanisms to permit the FSOC to designate systemically important financial institutions (SIFIs), market utilities, and specific activities for additional oversight if the FSOC determines an extreme vulnerability within the financial system (Bernanke 2013).

As expected, many risk managers view these regulatory changes as an expensive endeavor. From a cost perspective, nearly half of the buy-side firms surveyed by the Professional Risk Managers' International Association (2013) expect that recent financial regulations will increase their overall costs. On the positive side, increased regulatory costs and uncertainty have also made many buy-side firms more risk aware. This awareness may provide the incentive needed for improving old or creating new risk management techniques (Professional Risk Managers' International Association 2013).

DECREASED DEREGULATION

Many once considered deregulation as one of the main driving forces of risk management practices (Alexander 2005). Because deregulation often either mitigates or completely negates previous regulation, it usually reduces or eliminates government control over a specific industry. The major selling point for deregulation is to increase efficiency or competition. In fact, notions of deregulation as a movement to decrease government (or ruler) intervention into private business go back into antiquity. Yet, probably the best known period with respect to deregulation harkens back to laissez-faire (broadly translated as "let them do as they will") liberalism in France in the early nineteenth century. The most recent deregulation movement in the United States gained momentum in the 1970s based on theories outlined by several prominent, free-market economists (Hayek 1945; Friedman 1962; Mises 1978). Deregulation eventually lost momentum in the early 2000s.

One specific deregulation act that was notable for financial markets was the Gramm-Leach-Bliley (GLB) Act (1999), which repealed key parts of the Glass-Steagall Act (Banking Act) (1933). The GLB Act removed barriers to competition among traditional banks, investment banks, and insurance companies. The GLB Act even allowed some firms to participate in all three markets, which quickly blurred the lines between three previously distinct industries. In hindsight, critics often blame deregulation, especially the GLB Act and the Commodity Futures Modernization Act (CFMA) (2000), for creating the 2008 recession. Yet, Gramm (2009) contends that no evidence has ever linked the GLB Act or the CFMA to the financial crisis. Gramm also claims that recent deregulation in the financial markets has been greatly exaggerated. For example, he states that the GLB Act did not deregulate anything. The GLB Act actually established the Federal Reserve (Fed) as a "super regulator" in charge of supervising all Financial Services Holding Companies.

Impact aside, history does at least show that regulation and deregulation are somewhat cyclical within financial markets. This cyclical nature of regulation relates to political cycles as much as economic cycles. Indeed, the only effective technique for managing regulatory risk may be attempting to influence politicians and regulators (Chance 2003). Thus, lobbying efforts aside, risk managers should prepare for increased regulation in the short term and potential deregulation in the long term. The depth of this preparation depends on the firm's particular tolerance to regulatory risk.

SYSTEMIC RISK

According to Rebonato (2007), regulators and risk managers are both concerned with reducing risk but they should approach risk management, especially systemic risk, in different ways. He asserts that individual firms pay too much attention to rare catastrophic events. This assertion has much support. For example, Sornette (2003) makes a detailed case that financial crashes are outliers and should be treated as such by firm risk managers. Greenspan (1998) also offers a similar sentiment by stating that the management of systemic risk, especially catastrophic systemic risk, is primarily the responsibility of the central banks. Hence, private banks should not be required to safeguard capital for the possibility of a financial crash. In other words, central banks offer private banks a form of systemic risk insurance that should allow private banks to focus on managing other types of risk.

Recent history does not support the assertions made by Greenspan (1998), Sornette (2003), and Rebonato (2007). In the aftermath of the financial crisis of 2007–2008, both central banks and individual banks called for additional regulation and systemic risk measures. In fact, Bernanke (2013) asked whether central banks or private banks could even identify systemic risks in advance of a major financial crisis. This assertion is a fair point considering that the Fed as well as most prominent economists and investment firms failed to predict the 2008 recession. Although identifying systemic risk is difficult, Bernanke concedes that specific vulnerabilities could be mitigated by increasing requirements for capital and liquidity.

Bernanke's call for increased regulation echoes the sentiments of former Federal Reserve Chairman Paul Volcker. Volcker, also the recent chairman of President Obama's Economic Recovery Advisory Board from February 2009 until January 2011, proposed a well-known regulation in the Dodd-Frank Act referred to as the Volcker Rule. The Volcker Rule basically restricts U.S. banks from speculative investing that does not directly benefit their customers. In his reasoning for this regulation, Volcker (2010) asserts that a healthy commercial banking system is essential to the stability of the entire financial system. He also claims that high-risk speculative investing produces unacceptable levels of systemic risk and that speculators played a key role in the financial recession of 2008. Investor sentiment after the recent recession appears to agree, at least for the moment, with Volcker and public officials touting more regulation. Over time, a different light might be shed on the recent recession.

Multi-Asset Class Investing

According to the Professional Risk Managers' International Association (2012, 2013), multi-asset class investing is becoming increasingly important to avoid some of the volatility in equity markets. The days of single-asset class investing, particularly in equities may have ended. This change is not surprising given that realized equity volatility has been trending higher for several years. In fact, the volatility for the S&P 500 index has doubled from about 10 percent half a century ago to about 20 percent in 2013 (Ploutos 2012). Although most risk managers know that the Chicago Board Options Exchange (CBOE) Volatility Index (VIX) has tracked volatility since the early 1990s (Whaley 1993), tracking volatility at the individual stock level has become a recent trend. In 2011, the CBOE created volatility index values for five active optionable equities: Amazon.com (AMZN), Apple (AAPL), Goldman Sachs (GS), Google (GOOG), and IBM (IBM) (Schaeffer 2011). This trend is not surprising given that the volatility for specific stocks has increased even more dramatically than index volatility, especially when measured at intraday frequency. For example, Alexander (2005) reports that the five-year average volatility of IBM almost doubled between 1990 and 2005, far outpacing the volatility growth for the S&P 500 index.

To avoid volatility, risk managers are increasingly using asset class diversification to shift weight away from equity markets and toward multi-class investing strategies. According to the Professional Risk Managers' International Association (2012, 2013), 45 percent (49 percent for 2012) of risk managers report that multi-asset class coverage was very important, 35 percent (32 percent for 2012) indicate that it is important, and 15 percent (same for 2012) state that it is moderately important. Thus, only 5 percent (4 percent for 2012) report that multi-class investing is unimportant. According to those surveyed, the fastest growing asset classes are commodities including energy, fixed income, infrastructure, structured products, and equity. Although equity is in fifth place, 46 percent of the respondents do not expect a decline in the growth prospects for this asset class. In order of ranking, other investment classes include private equity, real estate, event-driven instruments, asset-backed securities, credit derivatives, foreign exchange, and interest rate swaps (Professional Risk Managers' International Association 2013).

From a risk management perspective, this trend toward multi-class investing is noteworthy because the initial design of many risk management systems focused only on managing equity investment risk. Hence, less than half of respondents indicate that their firms are adequately managing their multi-asset class risk. This may result from many firms not being technologically equipped to obtain a complete view of risk across multiple asset classes. This lack of integration may soon change. The majority (77 percent) of risk managers report that they are planning to change their risk management system in 2013 with 25 percent planning to integrate risk systems, 21 percent intending to review their risk systems, and 15 percent planning to consolidate their risk systems (Professional Risk Managers' International Association 2013).

Risk Measures

Another key trend for risk management will be the creation of a proven success measure. Successful risk measurement should not be simply defined as an absence of losses. Success also includes avoiding or mitigating financial crises, issues with regulators, and communication problems with other decision makers in the firm. These challenges mirror the sentiments of risk managers calling for better integration of risk into investment decisions, better methods for complying with regulations, and a better risk culture within their firm (Professional Risk Managers' International Association 2013).

Currently, buy-side firms use a wide range of risk measures including stress testing, value-at-risk (VaR), volatility, counterparty risk, historical scenarios, concentrations by sector/currency/country, credit risk, liquidity risk, standard deviation, risk attribution, tracking error, and expected shortfall. In Asia and Europe, the top three measures are

VaR, stress testing, and volatility. These rankings are similar in North America with one notable exception. U.S. and Canadian firms are far less reliant on VaR, which ranks as only the fourth most commonly used risk measure. This point is noteworthy from an integration perspective because VaR is not as useful for investment and asset allocation decisions as the top three North American risk measures: stress testing, volatility, and concentrations by sector, currency, or country. Thus, finding that a lower percentage of North American firms have separate risk and investment teams than European firms and Asian firms is not surprising. Focusing less on VaR risk measures may be one reason that North America is leading the way in the global trend for better integration (Professional Risk Managers' International Association 2013).

Culp, Ebersbach, and Mouille (2012) report other global trends in risk management where North American firms can improve such as risk management spending and enterprise risk management. According to Culp (2011), 90 percent of Latin American firms have planned for significant or moderate increases in their risk management budgets compared to only 82 percent of North American and Asian-Pacific firms. Additionally, almost all (99 percent) Latin American firms studied have existing enterprise risk management (ERM) programs in place compared to only 60 percent of North American firms and 52 percent of European firms. *Enterprise risk management* refers to a centralized or firm-wide risk management practice (Chance 2003). Thus, Latin American firms appear to be doing a better job of focusing on the overall risk management picture.

A CLOSER LOOK AT VAR

U.S. firms are moving away from VaR and toward stress testing for several reasons. On the surface, VaR is a widely accepted risk measure that many risk managers prefer because it is simple and easy to understand. Although VaR gives the minimum (or maximum) expected loss for a given portfolio, probability, and time horizon, it is associated with many problems. For example, the accuracy of VaR relies heavily on the accuracy of the probability and time horizon assumptions. Thus, VaR can be difficult to validate because it can offer a wide array of values. VaR often ignores positive scenarios and overemphasizes negative scenarios. Even with negative scenarios, VaR often mitigates or does not consider the probability of extremely poor returns. VaR can also be difficult to calculate for large firms with many different risk exposures (Chance 2003).

According to Rebonato (2007), one of the more discrete problems with VaR is that it lacks subadditivity. That is, a risk manager can increase total VaR by combining two different portfolios. This property of VaR runs contrary to standard notions of diversification and risk. Although problematic, Rebonato contends that risk managers can mitigate this issue by applying conditional expected shortfall. Conditional expected shortfall is useful in that it measures the average of the losses past a desired percentile.

A CLOSER LOOK AT STRESS TESTING

Kilpatrick (2007, p. 1615) reports that Warren Buffet made the following comments during the 1997 Berkshire Hathaway Annual Meeting,

If you understood a business perfectly and the future of the business, you would need very little in the way of a margin of safety. So, the more vulnerable the business is, assuming you still want to invest in it, the larger margin of safety you'd need. If you're driving a truck across a bridge that says it holds 10,000 pounds and you've got a 9,800 pound vehicle, if the bridge is six inches above the crevice it covers, you may feel okay, but if it's over the Grand Canyon, you may feel you want a little larger margin of safety.

Stress testing involves creating a hypothetical scenario that includes a specific set of highly adverse financial or economic assumptions such as a deep recession. Different firm stakeholders usually project expected revenues, losses, and capital and publicly disclose the results. At the time of this writing, aftershocks of the 2008 recession still affect the markets. As a result, stress testing is now the most common risk management method for risk managers in buy-side firms in North America (Professional Risk Managers' International Association 2013). According to the Professional Risk Managers' International Association (2012), 90 percent of respondents to its survey believe that stress testing is or will soon be very important, especially among insurance companies, investment banks, and private banks. Even the Fed has jumped on the stress testing bandwagon. For example, Bernanke (2013) finds stress testing to be an important method for managing systemic risk and a valuable source of supplementary information for the Fed, especially for SIFIs. The chapter mentioned SIFIs earlier regarding the Dodd-Frank Act, which charges the Fed with monitoring standard indicators such as regulatory capital, leverage, and funding mix. Bernanke states that several of these measures such as regulatory capital ratios tend to be backward looking, which is disadvantageous for anticipating changes in firm conditions. Thus, the Fed has placed special emphasis on forward looking approaches such as stress testing.

Stress testing analysis by the Fed for assessing SIFIs such as large bank holding companies has increased dramatically since 2009. Bernanke (2013) outlines three specific benefits of stress testing over other standard risk management methods. First, stress testing provides measures of capital that are more forward looking regarding future adequacy and are more robust to adverse developments such as global financial instability than other measures. Second, stress testing offers a way of assessing vulnerabilities on a micro level such as firm-wide risk and on a macro level such as industry-wide or market-wide risk. Third, stress testing provides critical information that can be disclosed to the public to increase investor confidence and help firms better manage their risk exposures. Consequently, stress testing is likely to play a vital role in the future of risk management.

NEW RISK MANAGEMENT METHODS

New risk management tools such as network analysis are also likely to emerge. *Network analysis* is a risk management method combining research in engineering, communications, and neuroscience to identify critical links between firms and market activities that could potentially destabilize the system. This analysis may also measure firm distress and help predict how shock effects may spread throughout the financial system. For example, the Fed and potentially other concerned public and private entities may soon use network analysis to help monitor the interconnectedness between financial institutions and markets. One way to measure interconnectedness is by analyzing common holdings of assets and exposures of firms to their counterparties (Bernanke 2013).

Another new risk management tool is risk parity, which first gained attention in the United States and is now spreading to Europe. Risk parity is an approach to investment portfolio management that focuses on allocating risk rather than allocating capital. Risk parity claims that when asset allocations are adjusted to the same risk level, risk parity portfolios can achieve a higher risk-adjusted return than traditional asset allocation portfolios. Yet, risk parity has plenty of skeptics. For example, Mariathasan (2011) contends that risk parity is a useful concept but it is awkward in practice. He concludes that risk parity may have some value as a benchmark, but no theoretical rationale exists for the strategy. Unless future research helps validate this strategy, risk parity may be reduced to a clever marketing slogan for over-weighted fixed-income portfolios.

Innovation in Risk Management Markets and Services

Li (2003) outlines several future trends for financial risk management that still ring true a decade after publishing his original predictions. Li predicts that new instruments and markets will continue to emerge and create value for risk managers. Recent financial engineering has led to the development of several products that increase investment options and solve risk management problems. Exchange-traded funds (ETFs) are a good example of low cost index funds that provide quick diversification and can be leveraged for both speculative and hedging strategies.

DERIVATIVE SECURITIES

Derivative securities are another prime example of a market that has been evolving for decades in unpredicted ways. A *derivative security* is one whose price is dependent upon or derived from one or more underlying assets. The most common underlying assets include stocks, bonds, commodities, currencies, interest rates, and market indexes. Early in the 1980s, derivatives represented an intellectual term reserved almost exclusively for the vocabulary of sophisticated investors. In the mid-1990s, the connotation of the word derivatives became more negative and risky after several prominent loss events connected with Gibson Greetings, Metallgesellschaft, Proctor & Gamble, Orange County California, Barings, Sumitomo Corp, and Long-Term Capital Management (Smithson 1988; Hyman 2006). Even prominent investors such as Warren Buffett expressed concern about the potential danger of derivatives. Buffett (2002, p. 15), who views derivatives as time bombs for both the parties involved and the overall economy, goes so far as to state that "derivatives are financial weapons of mass destruction." Yet, a large percentage of investors are apparently not heeding Buffett's warning. According to the Bank of International Settlements (2012), the notional principal of global OTC derivatives has grown by nearly 650 percent from $100 trillion in 2001 to $648 trillion a decade later. The increased popularity of derivatives has firmly rooted the term into the normal lexicon of mainstream investors, most of whom are risk-averse or have risk-averse clients. Derivatives are now classified as a word associated with safety instead of risk. In the future, derivatives may become more associated with risk aversion and seen primarily as a tool for risk management.

Derivatives markets frequently add new tools to the risk manager's toolbox. Some recent exchange-traded and OTC derivatives include futures, forwards, swaps, and options on catastrophe insurance, credit, commodity indexes, debt and other financial instruments in emerging economies, real estate, and even utilities such as electricity and gas (Smithson 1998). One relatively recent and innovative derivative market favored by the utility industry is using weather derivatives to hedge weather risks. Perez-Gonzalez and Yun (2013), who study weather derivatives for gas and electricity utilities, show that active risk management policies lead to an increase in firm value.

Other research suggests that many derivative products can increase firm value, especially when hedging against risks unique to a firm or industry. For example, researchers report similar increases in firm value for hedging strategies for exchange rate exposure using foreign currency derivatives (Allayannis and Weston 2001; Bartram, Brown, and Minton 2010) and for hedging strategies for jet fuel exposure in the airline industry (Carter, Rogers, and Simkins 2006; Carter, Rogers, Simkins, and Treanor 2013). Not all derivative products have the same value. Jin and Jorion (2006) study hedging strategies for U.S. oil and gas producers and find that hedging does not significantly affect firm value. Thus, as risk management research continues to shed light on the risk management policies that most affect firm value, new products and markets will emerge.

TECHNOLOGICAL ADVANCES

Li (2003) predicts an increasing demand for better risk management practices as markets become more efficient due to technology advances. For example, Culp (2011) lists data management in terms of availability, consistency, and organization as one of the top five future challenges for risk management. His study reports that 90 percent of executives are either currently implementing (49 percent) or plan to soon implement (41 percent) changes to their data management process. Technology will play a role in improving the data management process. According to the Professional Risk Managers' International Association (2012), risk technology offers several contributions to risk management in the near future including more flexible risk reporting, faster risk reporting, extended asset coverage, and more timely market data.

Potential users are unlikely to quickly embrace all technological advances. For example, as the Professional Risk Managers' International Association (2012) reports, despite the recent popularity of cloud computing, buy-side institutions continue to have concerns over software service and browser-based solutions. Specifically, less than one-third of these institutions prefer hosted and application service provider (ASP) software solutions over locally installed software solutions. Large firms ($1 billion or more in assets under management) are twice as likely to prefer hosted and ASP software solutions compared with small firms ($500 million or less in assets under management). Additionally, hedge funds are more inclined to pursue this technology compared to private banks and investment banks.

The major reasons for preferring ASP technology include reducing costs, no maintenance, and following IT policy. The two primary reasons for preferring locally installed solutions, which are both related to security, are security concerns and local storage of confidential information. A smaller percentage of respondents are concerned about the speed and accuracy of data processing with outsourced technology. For example, some respondents express having difficulty understanding what software the ASP is actually running and what modeling assumptions are made. Some risk managers may have difficulty approving a software system that gives them less control. Consequently, risk management may lag somewhat behind technology until the technology offers a proven advantage. As technology evolves, best practices will also evolve as risk managers learn to efficiently and effectively use new technology.

A Wish List for Risk Managers

As for other risk management trends, if risk managers could make one positive change for risk management, those at buy-side firms would either opt to create a better risk culture or create better integration of risk into the investment process (Professional Risk Managers' International Association 2013).

BETTER RISK CULTURE

The need for a better risk culture ranks higher than all of the other wish list items for risk managers (Professional Risk Managers' International Association 2012, 2013). The importance of improving risk culture is also listed as one of the eight trends by Culp et al. (2012) that will shape the future of financial risk management. *Risk culture* is the established guidelines and expectations for appropriate risk taking and decision making for the entire firm. According to Lindo and Rahl (2009), 85 percent of their survey respondents report having a credit risk officer (CRO) or the functional equivalent of a CRO within their firm. Culp (2011) reports that 86 percent of responding firms have a CRO, a senior executive that serves as the CRO, or a manager that performs a similar role. Lindo and Rahl also find that a large percentage of financial institutions do not currently value risk appetite statements. For example, the highest financial institution group with a current risk appetite statement is banks/investment banks with 58 percent. Also, the highest financial institution group considering creating such a statement in the future is insurance companies at only 37 percent.

Recent survey results by the Professional Risk Managers' International Association (2013) provide evidence that not all employees understand their roles in managing risk. Specifically, about 70 percent of responding firms report that risk management is an entirely separate function from the investment team. This percentage is much higher for Asian firms (80 percent) compared to European firms (73 percent) and North American firms (60 percent). Recent reports predict that this percentage may be decreasing.

In light of the financial crisis of 2007–2008, Culp et al. (2012) report that another upcoming trend is for the CRO and the chief financial officer (CFO) to increasingly collaborate and align risk and finance goals. Lindo and Rahl (2009) echo this trend and state that 70 percent of CROs report directly to the CEO, 14 percent to the CFO, and 16 percent to the Chairman of the Board. The Professional Risk Managers' International Association (2012) also reports that the board or internal management currently produce more than half (54 percent) of risk data. Fund managers and investors are also end consumers for risk data. Regulators produce only a small fraction of risk data. According to Culp (2011), nearly half of the responding executives believe that risk management is a critical driver for enabling long-term profitable growth and sustaining future profitability. Thus, the importance of risk as a primary business driver has increased (Professional Risk Managers' International Association 2013).

INTEGRATED RISK MANAGEMENT

The move toward integrated risk management includes providing an aggregate view of the different types of risk across the many different strategic areas of a firm. For instance, the Federation of European Risk Management Associations (FERMA) (2012) lists six categories for strategically integrating risk management decisions: (1) major projects, (2) strategic planning, (3) investment, (4) contracts/bids, (5) acquisitions/transfers, and (6) budgeting. Culp (2011) includes many of these same categories in the 11 areas that involve the risk function in essential decision-making processes. Some of these areas include: defining health, safety, and environmental controls; defining insurance requirements; setting objectives and incentives; aiding in outsourcing and multi-sourcing decisions; aiding in the performance management process; and aiding in procurement.

With so many decision-making areas, risk management integration is easier said than done. Alexander (2005) states that properly integrating risk systems is a top agenda item for evolving risk management. Yet, implementing an integrated risk management system is one of the most difficult challenges facing financial risk managers given the growing trend toward more complex financial markets. The complexity of financial markets has created several other trends such as increasing reliance on technologically sophisticated systems for analyzing additional countries and risk factors. This increased reliance on technology has substantially increased the costs of information technology, which has created demand for more collaboration among competitors and peers to create tangible cost reductions. Many firms also want to consolidate technology requirements such as data warehousing. In other words, integration is challenging because firms must create efficient risk management systems that effectively monitor many scenarios based on several different markets and several different risks (Culp et al. 2012).

Analyzing multiple risk factors has not always been the standard for risk management. For example, Alexander (2005) reports that financial econometric research focuses primarily on assessing market and credit risk while largely ignoring other easily quantifiable risks such as operational, business, and systemic risks. Lindo and Rahl (2009) report similar findings. Specifically, the authors survey 121 financial institutions and show that most risk managers communicate to their boards about market and credit risk, but a far lower percentage of risk managers report on liquidity risk, operational risk, and counterparty risk. Culp (2011) also reports that at least 70 percent currently measure business risks, market risks, credit risks, and regulatory risks. Beyond these risks, the majority of responding companies measure operational risks, legal risks, liquidity risks, strategic risks, reputational risks, and emerging risks. Only 43 percent of participants report measuring political risks.

Although financial risk management is evolving quickly, a strong need exists to report and integrate more risk measures into the decision-making process. The Professional Risk Managers' International Association (2013) reports that 42 percent of the responding firms currently have mechanisms such as a dashboard for all risk measures to allow their board or CRO to keep tabs on firm-wide risk. Not surprisingly, a risk dashboard and better insight into firm-wide risk by the board or CRO ranked third and fourth, respectively, on PRMIA's respondents' wish lists. Other items on the risk managers' wish lists include: extended asset coverage; better defined risk tolerances; easier, more flexible, and faster risk reporting methods; and more timely market data.

Summary and Conclusions

Although the purpose of risk management is simply to manage risk, the usefulness of this definition depends on how the role of risk management is viewed. According to the Professional Risk Managers' International Association (2013), the primary uses of risk management are for monitoring key risk indicators, reporting to the board/management, and dealing with regulatory compliance/reporting. These three drivers of risk management are not surprising given the economic challenges of operating in a post-recession environment that includes several recent regulation changes. Other reasons for risk management focus on investment decision making such as portfolio construction, tactical asset allocation, and shaping investment strategy. The remaining reasons for risk management include client reporting and investor reporting. The vast majority of respondents also view risk management as essential for raising assets. The Professional Risk Managers' International Association (2012) reports a similar percentage, which suggests a constant, long-term trend of vitality for current risk management practices. Finally, nearly 90 percent of respondents view risk management as central to maintaining a firm's financial health and see the role of risk management increasing in the near future. Culp (2011) echoes this finding and reports that 98 percent of the responding executives view risk management as a higher priority than they did in 2009.

The road to acceptance for many risk managers has been a long and sometimes lonely journey. Recent changes including the 2008 recession, increased regulations, and improved technology have helped steer many business decisions toward risk management. Culp (2011) reports that more than 80 percent of the responding executives surveyed consider risk management as essential for dealing with marketplace volatility. Moreover, 86 percent of these executives identify risk managers as the drivers that help their firms effectively navigate the increasing volatility of the economic and financial environment. Thus, risk managers appear to be finally getting acknowledged for the value they add to the investment decision process. Culp (2011, p. 5) notes "a clear maturation of risk management capabilities across all industries—a rapid march up the business value chain and the development of governance and organizational structures that give risk a voice at the executive table." Risk management systems are also gaining acceptance due to better public and private research.

In conclusion, the future road for financial risk management will most likely be a continuation of the present path. Risk managers are facing a rapidly changing digital economy. New risk management products and markets spawn even newer innovations, which make the pace and magnitude of potential shocks (or crashes) very difficult to predict. Risk management can bring great advances when used properly, but risk management tools must be properly controlled to avoid disaster. Risk management practices will also need to evolve and adapt to keep pace. Hence, the best risk managers are likely to be those who can make decisions at an accelerated pace and under difficult conditions. In the future, drivers of business decisions will need to be more proactive rather than reactive. Thus, reliable risk management practices will be essential for navigating future risks. Specifically, risk managers need to focus on the unique possibilities facing their firms and develop effective mechanisms to monitor and integrate all potential risks.

Discussion Questions

1. Define regulatory risk and identify five major regulations that are likely to have the largest impact on the future of risk management.
2. Define the two most common risk measures in terms of global use and describe differences between these measures including limitations and benefits.
3. Indicate whether derivatives are a risky or safe risk management tool and provide evidence that derivatives add value to a firm.
4. Discuss the unique characteristics of two risk management objectives on risk manager's wish lists.

References

Ahuja, Vivek, and David Thomas. 2013. "Financial Regulation: The Year Ahead." *Wall Street Journal.* Available at http://blogs.wsj.com/source/2013/01/07/financial-regulation-the-year-ahead/.

Alexander, Carol. 2005. "The Present and Future of Financial Risk Management." *Journal of Financial Econometrics* 3:1, 3–25.

Allayannis, George, and James P. Weston. 2001. "The Use of Foreign Currency Derivatives and Firm Market Value." *Review of Financial Studies* 14:1, 243–276.

Bank of International Settlements. 2005. "International Convergence of Capital Measurement and Capital Standards: A Revised Framework." Available at http://www.bis.org/publ/bcbs118.pdf.

Bank of International Settlements. 2010. "Group of Governors and Heads of Supervision Announce Higher Global Minimum Capital Standards." Available at http://www.bis.org/press/p100912.pdf.

Bank of international Settlements. 2012. "Statistical Release: OTC Derivatives Statistics at End-December 2011." Available at http://www.bis.org/publ/otc_hy1205.pdf.

Barnier, Michel. 2013. "Statement by Commissioner Michel Barnier on the Application Date of Solvency II." Press Release on 02/10/2013 by the European Commission. Available at http://europa.eu/rapid/press-release_MEMO-13-841_en.htm?locale=en.

Bartram, Söhnke M., Gregory W. Brown, and Bernadette A. Minton. 2010. "Resolving the Exposure Puzzle: The Many Facets of Exchange Rate Exposure." *Journal of Financial Economics* 95:2, 148–173.

Bernanke, Ben S. 2013. "Monitoring the Financial System." Board of Governors of the Federal Reserve System Speech at the 49th Annual Conference on Bank Structure and Competition, Chicago. Available at http://www.federalreserve.gov/newsevents/speech/bernanke20130510a.htm.

Bernstein, Peter L. 1996. *Against the Gods*. New York: John Wiley & Sons.

BlackRock. 2012. "Update on the Regulatory Developments in Europe: An Overview and Analysis." BlackRock's *ViewPoint*. Available at https://www2.blackrock.com/webcore/litService/search/getDocument.seam?venue=PUB_IND&source=GLOBAL&contentId=1111166579.

Buffett, Warren. 2002. "Berkshire Hathaway Inc. 2002 Annual Report." Available at http://www.berkshirehathaway.com/2002ar/2002ar.pdf.

Carter, David A., Daniel A. Rogers, and Betty J. Simkins. 2006. "Does Hedging Affect Firm Value? Evidence from the U.S. Airline Industry." *Financial Management* 35:1, 53–86.

Carter, David A., Daniel A. Rogers, Betty J. Simkins, and Stephen D. Treanor. 2013. "Does Operational and Financial Hedging Reduce Exposure? Evidence from the U.S. Airline Industry." Working Paper, California State University.

Chance, Don M. 2003. *Analysis of Derivatives for the CFA® Program*. Baltimore, MD: United Book Press, Inc.

Culp, Steve. 2011. "Report on the Accenture 2011 Global Risk Management Study: Risk Management as a Source of Competitive Advantage and High Performance." Available at http://www.accenture.com/SiteCollectionDocuments/PDF/Accenture-Global-Risk-Management-Study-2011.pdf.

Culp, Steve, Karsten Ebersbach, and Christophe Mouille. 2012. "Eight New Risk Management Trends: Businesses Are Beginning to Tie Risk Management to Business Outcomes and Tangible Savings." *Sascom Magazine*. Available at http://www.sas.com/news/sascom/risk-management-trends.html.

Devasabai, Kris. 2012. "Hedge Fund Industry Seeks Solutions to Solvency II Challenges." *Hedge Funds Review*. Available at http://www.risk.net/hedge-funds-review/feature/2248181/hedge-fund-industry-seeks-solutions-solvency-ii-challenges.

European Securities and Markets Authority. 2013. "Final Report: Guidelines on Key Concepts of the AIFMD." Available at http://www.esma.europa.eu/system/files/2013-600_final_report_on_guidelines_on_key_concepts_of_the_aifmd_0.pdf.

European Union Commission. 2013. "Capital Requirements - CRD IV/CRR—Frequently Asked Questions." European Commission - MEMO/13/690 16/07/2013. Available at http://europa.eu/rapid/press-release_MEMO-13-690_en.htm.

European Union Parliament. 2008. "Directive 2008/10/EC of the European Parliament and of the Council." *Official Journal of the European Union*. Available at http://eur-lex.europa.eu/LexUriServ/LexUriServ.do?uri=OJ:L:2008:076:0033:0036:EN:PDF.

European Union Parliament. 2009. "Directive 2009/138/EC of the European Parliament and of the Council." *Official Journal of the European Union*. Available at http://eur-lex.europa.eu/LexUriServ/LexUriServ.do?uri=OJ:L:2009:335:0001:0155:en:PDF.

European Union Parliament. 2012. "Regulation (EU) No 648/2012 of the European Parliament and of the Council." *Official Journal of the European Union*. Available at http://eur-lex.europa.eu/LexUriServ/LexUriServ.do?uri=OJ:L:2012:201:0001:0059:EN:PDF.

Federation of European Risk Management Associations. 2012. "FERMA Risk Management Benchmarking Survey 2012, 6th Edition." Available at http://www.ey.com/Publication/vwLUAssets/FERMA_European_Risk_Management_Benchmarking_Survey_2012/$FILE/Etude percent20Ferma percent202012_VF.pdf.

Financial Conduct Authority. 2013. "Retail Distribution Review (RDR)." Available at http://www.fca.org.uk/firms/firm-types/sole-advisers/rdr.

Financial Industry Regulatory Authority. 2011. "Regulatory Notice: Know Your Customer and Suitability." Available at http://www.finra.org/web/groups/industry/@ip/@reg/@notice/documents/notices/p122778.pdf.

Friedman, Milton. 1962. *Capitalism and Freedom*. Chicago: University of Chicago Press.

Gramm, Phil. 2009. "Deregulation and the Financial Panic: Loose Money and Politicized Mortgages Are the Real Villains." *Wall Street Journal.* Available at http://online.wsj.com/article/SB123509667125829243.html.

Greenspan, Alan. 1998. "Understanding Today's International Monetary System." Board of Governors of the Federal Reserve System Speech at the 34th Annual Conference on Bank Structure and Competition, Chicago. Available at http://www.federalreserve.gov/boarddocs/speeches/1998/19980507.htm.

Hayek, Freidrich A. 1945. "The Use of Knowledge in Society." *American Economic Review* 35:4, 519–530.

Hopkins, Alex. 2013. "'London Whale' Scandal Costs JPMorgan Nearly $1B: CEO Dimon Says Lessons Learned from Loose Trading." *Washington Times.* Available at http://www.washingtontimes.com/news/2013/sep/19/london-whale-scandal-costs-jpmorgan-nearly-1b/.

Howe, Alex. 2011. "The 11 Largest Bankruptcies in American History." *Business Insider.* Available at http://www.businessinsider.com/largest-bankruptcies-in-american-history-2011-11?op=1.

Hyman, Michael. 2006. *New Ways for Managing Global Financial Risks: The Next Generation.* Hoboken, NJ: John Wiley & Sons.

Jin, Yanbo, and Philippe Jorion. 2006. "Firm Value and Hedging: Evidence from U.S. Oil and Gas Producers." *Journal of Finance* 61:2, 893–919.

Kilpatrick, Andrew. 2007. *Permanent Value: The Story of Warren Buffett*, Volume 2. Birmingham, AL: Andy Kilpatrick Publishing Empire.

Kimmel, Paul, Jerry Weygandt, and Donald Kieso. 2011. *Financial Accounting: Tools for Business Decision Making*, 6th Edition. Hoboken, NJ: John Wiley & Sons.

Li, Steven. 2003. "Future Trends and Challenges of Financial Risk Management in the Digital Economy." *Managerial Finance* 29:5/6, 111–125.

Lindo, Steve, and Leslie Rahl. 2009. "Risk Governance: A Benchmarking Survey." *Capital Market Risk Advisors.* Available at http://www.prmia.org/sites/default/files/references/Risk_Governance_Survey_Report.pdf.

Mariathasan, Joseph. 2011. "Risk Parity: Nice Idea, Awkward Reality." *Investment & Pensions Europe.* Available at http://www.ipe.com/magazine/risk-parity-nice-idea-awkward-reality_40026.php?categoryid=19950.

Mises, Ludwig von. 1978. *The Clash of Group Interests and Other Essays.* New York: The Center for Libertarian Studies.

National Association of Insurance Commissioners. 2013. *NAIC Own Risk and Solvency Assessment (ORSA) Guidance Manual.* Available at http://www.naic.org/documents/committees_e_orsa_wg_related_docs_guidance_manual_2013.pdf.

National Bureau of Economic Research. 2010. "Business Cycle Dating Committee, National Bureau of Economic Research." Available at http://www.nber.org/cycles/sept2010.html.

Paletta, Damian, and Aaron Lucchetti. 2010. "Law Remakes U.S. Financial Landscape." *Wall Street Journal.* Available at http://online.wsj.com/news/articles/SB10001424052748704682604575369030061839958.

Perez-Gonzalez, Francisco, and Hayong Yun. 2013. "Risk Management and Firm Value: Evidence from Weather Derivatives." *Journal of Finance* 68:5, 2143–2176.

Ploutos (pseudonym). 2012. "Are Stock Markets Becoming More Volatile?" *Seeking Alpha.* Available at http://seekingalpha.com/article/580701-are-stock-markets-becoming-more-volatile.

Professional Risk Managers' International Association. 2012. "2012 Buy-side Market Risk Management Trends." *Sungard Survey.* Available at: http://www.prmia.org/sites/default/files/references/Sungard-2012BuySideTrends.pdf.

Professional Risk Managers' International Association. 2013. "2013 Buy-Side Market Risk Management Trends." *Sungard Survey.* Available at: http://www.prmia.org/sites/default/files/references/Sungard-BuySideTrends2013.pdf.

Rebonato, Riccardo. 2007. *Plight of the Fortune Tellers: Why We Need to Manage Financial Risk Differently*. Princeton, NJ: Princeton University Press.

Schaeffer, Bernie. 2011. "The Coming of Volatility Gauges for Individual Stocks." *Barron's*. Available at http://online.barrons.com/article/SB5000142405297020455550457607589009725863 6.html.

Sender, Samuel. 2011. "Action Needed to Shield Investors from UCITS Risk." *Financial Times*. Available at http://www.ft.com/intl/cms/s/0/e20bc0d6-5859-11e0-9b8a-00144feab49a.html#axzz2kHMYcDUu.

Smithson, Charles W. 1998. *Managing Financial Risk*. New York: McGraw-Hill, Inc.

Sornette, 2003. *Why Stock Markets Crash? Critical Events in Complex Financial Systems*. Princeton, NJ: Princeton University Press.

United States Treasury. 2012. "Treasury and IRS Issue Proposed Regulations under the Foreign Account Tax Compliance Act to Improve Offshore Tax Compliance and Reduce Burden." Press Release on 02/08/2012 by the U.S. Department of the Treasury. Available at http://www.treasury.gov/press-center/press-releases/Pages/tg1412.aspx.

Volcker, Paul. 2010. "How to Reform Our Financial System." *The New York Times*. Available at http://www.nytimes.com/2010/01/31/opinion/31volcker.html?pagewanted=all&_r=0.

Whaley, Robert E. 1993. "Derivatives on Market Volatility: Hedging Tools Long Overdue." *Journal of Derivatives* 1:1, 71–84.

Discussion Questions and Answers

Chapter 2 Measuring and Managing Risk

1. Discuss the uses and limitations of the standard deviation (volatility) as a risk measure.

    The standard deviation is a widespread measure of variability in statistics. It is used in many models in finance (here often applied to log-returns) such as in Roy's safety first rule, the capital asset pricing model (CAPM), the Sharpe ratio, and the Black-Scholes formula. However, the standard deviation weights the positive and negative deviations from the expectation equally and therefore is inconsistent with utility theory. This measure is also sensitive to outliers and may underweight small deviations (e.g., compared to the linear-quadratic measure).

2. Discuss the advantages and disadvantages of VaR as risk measure.

    Value-at-risk (VaR) is easy to calculate and to explain. The Basel Accords and other regulatory frameworks use VaR as a risk measure. VaR is not convex leading to the paradox that portfolio diversification may result in higher risk, which is contrary to intuition and common sense.

3. Explain why basing risk management on the profit-and-loss distribution is reasonable.

    Basing risk management on the profit-and-lost distribution forces the risk manager to carefully identify risk factors and to estimate their impact on the profit-and loss function, which leads to a better understanding of business risks and chances. A profit-and-loss distribution expresses all adverse or favorable out-comes and the related likelihoods, so no important scenario is missing. This permits comparing figures calculated from loss distributions of different types of portfolios.

4. Discuss the different roles of a risk measure in the context of financial optimization.

    A risk measure serves different roles in the context of financial optimization. It can be in the objective function to minimize risk, but subject to a desired return. A risk measure can also represent a constraint. In this setting, the total return is maximized instead.

5. Identify the drawbacks of the described profit-and-loss distributional approach.

    The described profit-and-loss distributional approach works only if reasonable estimations for the joint distribution of risk factors are available. Here, estimations could originate from statistical models, expert opinion, or other sources. If the resulting models are questionable, model risk becomes a critical issue. Although an enhanced approach is still based on the profit-and-loss distribution, the models must be extended to take into account model ambiguity.

Chapter 3 How Risk Management Adds Value

1. How does hedging differ from insurance?

    Firms hedge in response to market/price risks such as interest rate, foreign currency, or commodity price risks affecting all firms that are directly or indirectly exposed to these risks. They purchase insurance to reduce or eliminate the impact of firm-specific risks such as damage to assets, legal liability, worker injury, employee benefits, and reputational loss.

2. Why does hedging create value only if the firm's cost structure is convex in the hedgeable risk?

    When the value of risk exposure is positive, value is added to the firm and a firm should not hedge. When the value of risk exposure is negative, firm value is destroyed and thus a firm should hedge. A negative value of risk exposure occurs when firm revenues are concave in risk factor price and costs are convex in risk factor price, and therefore hedging in this situation would create value for the firm.

3. Explain whether financial risk management allows a better assessment of managerial quality.

    Assessing managerial performance or quality is a difficult task to accomplish, given the information asymmetry between the managers and the shareholders. Most often, companies use market-based performance measures such as stock prices, which provide an incentive for managers to maximize shareholder value. These measures are imperfect because they expose managers to market risk that they cannot control. If the firm hedged its market risk, stock price would be a cleaner measure of managerial performance. However, this is complicated by the cost of hedging, which makes full hedging unlikely, as well as by the type of compensation that a manager receives.

4. Discuss the following assertion. Entering into a financial derivative position creates no value directly and destroys value in the short run. Thus, the only reason that non-financial firms use such instruments is to speculate.

    Entering a financial derivative contract at the fair market price creates no value to the firm directly because the purchase price reflects the average of the possible value at maturity. In fact, such a contract destroys value in the short run because of transactions costs when entering such transactions. Even considering any direct net costs of using financial derivatives, the value to the firm could be positive in the medium and long run under several conditions: (1) if the derivative position is negatively correlated with the firm's cash flows; (2) if its total cost function is convex in the hedged risk; and (3) if it reduces the expected amount of taxes that the firm will pay. Another possibility is that hedging reduces the cost of coordinating managerial activities in the firm. By reducing those costs, firm value increases as a consequence of hedging, despite the failure of hedging to create value.

Chapter 4 Accounting and Risk Management

1. Given that accounting is backwards looking, explain why accounting accruals are informative about the future.

    Accounting statements should be prepared such that current earnings help investors better predict future cash flows from the operations of the firm. Accounting standards allow some flexibility to managers who prepare the financial statements that auditors review. Managers may use the flexibility within accounting standards to better signal the business model of their firm or to conceal information such as delaying the revelation of unfavorable news. Notwithstanding that the latter scenario is typically associated with lower quality earnings, restatements, or even accounting scandals, empirical research supports that current accounting earnings are better than current cash flows at predicting future cash flows.

2. Given that investors appear to process accounting information imperfectly, discuss one price anomaly and how investors may profit from using this anomaly.

    Post-earnings announcement drift is the phenomenon that the stock market is inefficient at processing earnings news, which in turn leads to a predictable stock return pattern concentrated around the subsequent quarters' earnings announcement. Predictability of future stock returns based on past public information runs counter to the semi-strong form of market efficiency.

3. List several useful variables in predicting large corporate frauds and discuss the implications for investment decisions.

    The Beneish model of predicting large corporate fraud relies on the following eight variables: (1) increasing days sales receivable, (2) decreasing gross margins, (3) increasing fractions of "other" assets, (4) high sales growth, (5) decreasing depreciation rates, (6) increasing selling, general, and administrative (SG&A) expenses, (7) high leverage, and (8) high accruals relative to total assets. For portfolio investment decisions, applying a threshold of predicted values at which one no longer invests in a stock avoids the negative stock return effect if a fraud is discovered.

4. Identify the conditions under which forecasting of firm-specific volatility may or may not be valuable for investment decisions.

    If firm-specific risk is diversifiable and not priced, then information about firm-specific information is not relevant or valuable for portfolio investment decisions. If instead, the market prices idiosyncratic risk, then better information about firm-specific volatility becomes valuable.

5. Practitioners have used and disclosed VaR since the 1990s. The Basel Committee on Banking Supervision has proposed replacing VaR with a different one-sided risk measure called expected shortfall, which represents the average VaR among all sufficiently unfavorable outcomes. Discuss how this will change the reporting of risks under *FRR 48*.

FRR 48 allows three risk disclosure formats: VaR, sensitivity, or tabular. If expected shortfall (ES) replaces VaR in the regulation of banks, then banks would be expected to initiate voluntary disclosures of ES as Barclays has done. Further, the SEC would be expected to replace the requirement of disclosure of VaR and to require or permit the disclosure of ES.

6. Before January 1, 2005, Norwegian Telenor ASA prepared its financial statements according to Norwegian Generally Accepted Accounting Principles (N GAAP). Starting in 2005, Telenor ASA used International Financial Reporting Standards (IFRS). Telenor also provided reconciliation to U.S. GAAP. Telenor has a defined benefit pension plan and therefore needs to assume a discount rate to determine its pension benefit obligations.

   At the end of 2005, the same discount rate is used for both IFRS and US GAAP. At the end of 2004, a lower discount rate is used under IFRS than for US GAAP. For US GAAP the discount rate included an assumed risk premium for corporate rate bonds over the Norwegian government bond rate. At the end of 2005, assume that the more conservative government bond rate could also be used as the discount rate for US GAAP. Application of a more conservative approach to determining the US GAAP discount rate is regarded as a change in an estimate (Telenor 2005).

Year	Accounting Standard	Discount Rate Assumed to Determine Pension Obligations
2002	N GAAP	6.5
2003	N GAAP	5.7
2004	N GAAP	5.0
2004	US GAAP	5.0
2004	IFRS	4.5*
2005	IFRS	3.9
2005	US GAAP	3.9

*As stated in the 2005 financial statements.

Discuss the effect of lower assumed discount rates on the pension obligations and whether Telenor should apply different discount rates when reporting 2004 fiscal year performance under IFRS and U.S. GAAP.

The effect of a lower discount rate on obligations is to decrease the present value of the pension obligations. Although assumed or estimated discount rates can vary over time as market conditions change, they should not differ between accounting standards applied by a given firm at any given point in time.

Chapter 5 Market Risk

1. Explain how demographic shifts might change the aggregate supply of the willingness to bear risk and affect asset prices.

As the population ages, the supply of risk-bearing services will likely shrink. Absent a corresponding decrease in the total amount of risk to be borne by investors, this decrease in supply will probably lead to an increase in discount rates for risky assets. To the extent that this relationship is true, stock prices would fall. A change in the supply of the willingness to bear risk does not signal a profit opportunity. Specifically, it does not mean that investors can expect to make a profit by selling shares before the demographic shift begins, continues, or accelerates. Rather, rational investors will anticipate these trends so that prices will fall in advance of the shifts themselves. This expectation is similar to the well-known January effect, which, according to Wall Street professionals, now begins before Thanksgiving.

2. Identify the tasks that gain importance for investment advisors and portfolio managers if apparent excess returns turn out to have their origin in previously unknown systematic risk factors.

Tailoring portfolios to match risk preferences will become more important in the future resulting in more difficulty in achieving diversification. Even now, astute investors hedge their investment income by investing less in their employer's stock. In a world with many more systematic risk factors, individual investors will be able to bear some sources better than others. These investors should tailor their portfolios to take larger positions in those sources and smaller ones in assets carrying risks that are more dangerous to them than they are to the representative or marginal investor.

3. Discuss whether constructing a well-diversified portfolio is possible that completely hedges all market risks including beta, value, and size risks. Indicate whether such portfolios would be characterized by a zero alpha.

Investors can potentially hedge beta-risk by choosing assets and their weights so that the fund beta is near zero, possibly with a long-short portfolio. That is, given a long (i.e., positive) position of an asset with positive beta in the fund, either a short (i.e., negative) position of an asset with a positive beta or a long position of an asset with negative beta may be considered for the fund. However, negating the size and value risks would mean investing in growth stocks with large capitalization. One dilemma is that investors may be unable to find a well-diversified set of assets in the latter category in a way to hedge the beta risk simultaneously. If investors form such a portfolio, the fund return may become well-below expectations, possibly indicating an alpha near zero.

4. Explain how the state of the economy might affect market risk and what caution an investment advisor might give to a potential client on the risk exposure of a portfolio.

Market risk, whether exhibited in a strong or weak economy, affects asset returns due to the expected co-movement of prices, measured by asset covariance with the market. Such covariances are time-varying and economic state-dependent. Consequently, a portfolio constructed with asset betas computed under the assumption that the market is in a stationary state could possibly subject the fund to an elevated market risk exposure should the economic state change. Still, asset betas computed conditionally on the economic state might allow the advisor to recommend rebalancing of the portfolio in such a way to mitigate over-exposure to market risk in an ex-ante manner.

Chapter 6 Credit Risk Measurement and Management

1. Explain the difference between "point-in-time" and "through-the-cycle" credit risk indicators.

    Point-in-time and through-the-cycle credit risk indicators differ in several ways. Point-in-time indicators are more dependent on current economic environment, often are output of quantitative models (e.g., a logit model with macroeconomic variables and Merton models), and focus on shorter term default prediction (one to three years). By contrast, through-the-cycle indicators are stable, long-term historic average estimation of risk, and are typically measures produced by credit rating agencies.

2. Explain a methodology that can be used to build a transition matrix from a history of 25 years of rating information and whether this matrix can be used to derive default probabilities for longer horizons.

    The cohort approach is a methodology that can be used to build a transition matrix using 25 years of rating information. Using this approach involves counting the number of transitions in every year and dividing by the total number of firms in an initial rating at the beginning of the year. The average transition matrix is then computed. This matrix can be used to derive default probabilities for longer horizons. Using the Markov assumption permits estimating longer term migration matrices $TM_T = (TM_1)^T$. The last column of this matrix reveals the T-year probabilities of default.

3. Define VaR and discuss how this measure is used in practice.

    Value-at-risk (VaR) is a frequently used tail risk measure and defined by the following equation: $VaR_\alpha(L) = min_l (P(L \leq l) \geq \alpha$ where L denotes the portfolio loss, and alpha is a confidence level. More specifically, the realization of loss l that would not be exceeded with a probability of $1 - \alpha$ is called the VaR at confidence level α.

4. Identify the key inputs to a credit portfolio simulation model and three practical areas of usage for such models.

    The key inputs to a credit portfolio simulation model are probabilities of default (PD), loss given default (LGD), and correlation. Such models can be used for risk measurement (e.g., VaR and ES), structuring and securitization (e.g., estimating tranche loss probability), and input to risk-adjusted return on capital measurement and therefore risk-based pricing.

5. Explain one main difference between the Merton model and a statistical credit scoring model such as the linear logit model for estimating probabilities of default.

    Because the Merton model requires equity market information, it is suitable mostly for large-cap companies. This model does not necessarily require historic default data for calibration. By contrast, regression requires default information and is more suitable for a wide range of asset classes and problems.

Chapter 7 Operational Risk

1. List and discuss three pillars of the Basel II Accord framework.

    Three pillars of the Basel II Accord framework are: (1) minimum capital requirements, which can be calculated using the basic indicator, standardized or advanced measurement approaches; (2) supervisory review process, which involves supervision of bank's systems and capital adequacy by regulators; and (3) market discipline, which involves public disclosure of risk measures and risk management information.

2. List two methods for calculating operational risk capital and discuss the differences.

    Two conceptual approaches for calculating operational risk capital are top-down and bottom-up approaches. Under the top-down approach, estimating a firm's operational risk is based on macro data such as gross income or analyzing overall company losses. Under the bottom-up approach, the risks are quantified at the local level (process level, event types, business units, or business line/event type risk cells) and aggregated to find the risk for the whole firm. For example, the basic indicator approach is a top-down method and the loss distribution approach, which quantifies the frequency and severity in each risk cell, is bottom-up method.

3. Identify and discuss issues with using VaR and ES for measuring operational risk.

    VaR may fail the diversification property (i.e., VaR of the sum of risks may be larger than the sum of the VaRs of these risks). This situation is often the case for heavy tailed distributions. ES always satisfies the diversification property, but it may not exist for very heavy-tailed distributions with an infinite mean. Also, ES can be highly sensitive to the tail parameter for heavy tailed distributions, which is an unpleasant property for capital.

4. Discuss the need to combine internal data with external data and scenario analysis for estimating operational risk.

    The data sets for low-frequency/high-impact risks that have the largest contribution to capital are very small. The intention of using several data sources is to develop a model based on the largest possible data set to increase the accuracy and stability of the capital estimate. Also, historical data are backward looking, while scenario analysis is forward looking.

Chapter 8 Liquidity Risk

1. Define liquidity as related to finance.

    Liquidity consists of two different but related parts: asset/market liquidity and funding liquidity. Market liquidity is the ease with which an asset or a security is traded. Funding liquidity denotes the ease with which traders can get funding. Liquidity is not a one-dimensional concept but has components related to depth, resilience, immediacy, tightness, or breadth.

2. Discuss how funding liquidity and market liquidity are linked.

    Although the liquidity provided by traders to the market depends on their ability to get funding, their capital and margin requirements (i.e., funding) also depend on the asset's market liquidity. When margins are destabilizing, such as during a financial crisis, market liquidity and funding liquidity can be mutually reinforcing and cause liquidity spirals. Liquidity risk becomes extremely important to parties who currently hold or are about to hold an asset and affects their ability to trade.

3. Discuss why measuring liquidity is difficult.

Liquidity is a multidimensional concept with no unique and widely accepted definition. Thus, devising a single measure that is capable of capturing the various aspects of liquidity is difficult.

4. Identify the most reliable illiquidity measures among those used in empirical studies and justify why this is the case.

Recent studies suggest that the Amihud (2002) measure seems to be the most appropriate for measuring illiquidity within-country analysis. Goyenko, Holden, and Trzcinka (2009) demonstrate that Amihud's measure is a good proxy for price impact. Dick-Hielsen, Feldhütter, and Lando (2009) reach a similar conclusion in the context of bonds spreads. For cross-country analysis, Lesmond (2005) finds that price-based liquidity measures proposed by Roll (1984) and Lesmond, Ogden, and Trzcinka (1999) outperform volume-based liquidity measures.

Chapter 9 Country Risk

1. Analysts often argue that a country cannot default on its local currency bonds because it has the power to print more currency to pay off its debt. Explain why this argument is incorrect.

Although the statement that a country cannot default on its local currency bonds because it has the power to print more currency to pay off its debt is technically true, companies have to make trade-offs. Although printing currency to pay off debt may stave off default, it comes at the cost of debasing the currency. Countries that have weighed these costs sometimes find that the latter is higher than the former, which explains why local currency defaults exist.

2. Discuss whether sovereign ratings are good measures of sovereign default risk.

Over long periods, sovereign ratings are correlated with sovereign default risk. The problems with ratings are twofold. First, sovereign ratings are lagging indicators of default risk, with ratings changes often lagging markets by six months or more. Second, the potential for bias in ratings coming from ratings agencies feeling under pressure from clients such as the rated entities, investors, and portfolio managers, sometimes overstates ratings.

3. The sovereign default spread for a government can be estimated from sovereign bonds in U.S. dollars or the sovereign CDS market. Explain why the two approaches discussed in this chapter may result in different answers.

The sovereign bond market and the sovereign CDS market often attract different investor clienteles. In recent years, speculators have found making their plays on the CDS market easier. This change makes CDS spreads more sensitive to news stories and rumors and thus more volatile. Additionally, sovereign CDS markets provide insurance with a catch: the seller of the insurance may be subject to default risk, making CDS spreads higher than they should be.

4. Given that country equity risk is diversifiable to global investors, discuss whether it should be included in the price.

Some but not all country risk is diversifiable. In fact, as investors and companies have globalized, the correlation across markets has increased. In simple terms, a market risk factor seems to cut across emerging markets, with global shocks being felt across markets, with small shocks in developed markets translating into larger shocks in emerging markets. That, in turn, implies that a premium for emerging market risk should be built into the cost of equity, even for globally diversified investors, and hence into the price.

5. ERPs in emerging markets converged toward ERPs in developed markets between 2008 and 2012. Explain reasons for this trend.

    One reason for the convergence of ERPs in emerging markets toward ERPs in developed markets was the maturation of many emerging markets including their governments, economies, and investors. However, a more important reason was the financial crisis of 2007–2008 made developed markets in the United States and Western Europe more risky. As investors demanded larger ERPs in the latter markets to compensate for the higher risk, the ERPs converged across emerging and developed markets.

6. Discuss whether analysts should use models that assume U.S. companies are not exposed to emerging market risk.

    Analysts should not use models that assume U.S. companies are not exposed to emerging market risk. As U.S. companies increasingly expand into emerging markets for growth, analysts should factor in not only the higher growth from these markets into their cash flow estimations but also the higher risk into the cost of equity/capital.

7. All companies in an emerging market are not equally exposed to the risk in that emerging market. Identify several factors that explain differences in country risk exposure across companies and discuss how to measure that risk exposure.

    Several factors help to explain differences in country risk exposure across companies. One factor is where the company obtains its revenues, with those companies that obtain their revenues in other countries being less exposed to country risk. Another factor is the location of the company's production facilities, with companies that have their operations entirely in the emerging market more exposed than companies with operations spread across many countries.

Chapter 10 Systemic Risk

1. Discuss how systemic risk differs from systematic risk.

    Although both systemic and systematic risk capture the risk of widespread losses affecting the market as a whole, the key difference between the two concepts is systemic risk spreads the losses from one market participant to another (e.g., from one bank to another bank) in a domino effect. The losses inflicted on one market participant affect other market participants, (e.g., a bank will sell assets in response to being forced to repay deposits). This sale reduces market prices and imposes losses on other banks holding the same assets. In contrast, in cases of systematic risk, the direct cause of the losses is identical (e.g., a loss in confidence in the market) and is not the result of a domino effect. Therefore, the impact of the event is simultaneous on all market participants.

2. Give some examples of how sources of systemic risk are connected.

   As an example of how sources of systemic risk are connected, consider a bank facing a bank run. In order to meet its obligations to depositors, a bank is required to sell assets quickly. This action will reduce the value of all such assets, including those held by other banks, imposing losses on them. These losses might be large enough for some banks to fail. Any failing bank having taken interbank loans will now impose losses on their lenders, who in turn might be unable to cover their losses and fail. Any observer of such events unfolding will be reluctant to lend banks money for longer periods of times but rather would provide short-term funds only in order to be able to withdraw money quickly if losses seem imminent, or not provide funds to the bank at all, causing a funding squeeze. Hence, a systemic event includes one that started as a bank run, then resulted in market risk in combination with asset correlation to credit risk contagion including funding liquidity risk.

3. Discuss the problem of assessing systemic risk when only the risk of individual banks can be determined.

   The risks of individual banks do not easily aggregate to become a measure of systemic risk. Unlike in much of risk management, determining a correlation between different risks (here banks) to obtain the portfolio risk (here the banking system) is difficult. The different sources of systemic risk and different mechanism any losses can propagate make such an approach nearly impossible.

4. Regulators can only constrain the behavior of individual banks through incentives such as capital and liquidity requirements but they cannot affect systemic risk directly. Identify the problems that such a regulatory approach might cause in effectively regulating systemic risk.

   The best option would be to be able to regulate systemic risk directly such as by directing banks to invest into different assets and thus minimizing the risks arising from asset correlation. As this situation is impossible in a market economy, regulators can only attempt to provide incentives that direct the behavior of banks to obtain the desired outcome. The problem is that the behavior of all banks together affects systemic risk. The impact of a single bank's behavior depends on the behavior of all other banks. Coordinating such a complex situation without revealing detailed information on the behavior of other banks is challenging and unwanted side effects seem inevitable.

Chapter 11 Behavioral Risk

1. Discuss the importance of framing or mental accounting from a behavioral risk perspective and its relationship to Benartzi and Thaler's explanation of the equity premium puzzle.

   Mental accounting describes the process in which people code and evaluate economic outcomes. The way economic agents subjectively perceive reality is the crux of behavioral finance. The judgment process of how individuals collect information involves the assessment of consequences or outcomes and this influences the final investment decision. The framing process is a key aspect of prospect theory and relates to such behavioral risks as representativeness, availability, and anchoring.

The framing process of how individuals might derive utility from realized gains and losses rather than terminal wealth explains several market anomalies including the low average return of volatile stocks, which is inconsistent with the conventional notion of risk.

Mental accounting plays a crucial role in explaining the equity premium puzzle of Benartzi and Thaler (1995). It relates to the evaluation period by investors, or more precisely, to the moment when investors set the reference point against which they derive their prospect/loss aversion preferences. The authors find that an evaluation period of about one year makes investors, with prospect theory preferences, indifferent between holding all their assets in stocks or bonds. Increasing the evaluation period or equivalently changing the framing process affects the equity premium. Benartzi and Thaler conclude that fighting the temptation to not evaluate the portfolio frequently may change the allocation of bonds and stocks and may substantially increase returns.

2. Explain whether the absence of an arbitrage opportunity necessarily implies that markets are efficient.

The issue of whether the absence of an arbitrage opportunity necessarily implies that markets are efficient refers to an important debate between classical finance theorists and behaviorists involving the efficient market hypothesis. Classical finance theorists maintain that actual prices reflect fundamental values because otherwise this situation would create systematic arbitrage opportunities for market participants, which contradicts empirical evidence. By contrast, behaviorists contend that mispricing does not imply systematically arbitrage opportunities. They claim that if market participants detect mispricing, arbitrage opportunities are typically restricted because of the presence of a fundamental risk associated with the possibility of taking advantage of such mispricing. This particular risk refers to noise trader risk. Behaviorists assert that the presence of irrational traders makes the possibility of taking advantage of mispricing very risky and costly, specifically for short horizon investors. In certain circumstances, recent research shows that rational traders should behave irrationally in order to cope with noise trader risk.

3. Explain the implications of familiarity bias for asset allocation.

Familiarity bias in asset allocation decisions implies that individuals tend to invest in stocks they know, which leads to under-diversified portfolios. For example, such investors may lack geographical diversification, a phenomenon called *local bias* in which individuals hold a disproportional share of stocks from their region. At an international level, investors often hold a disproportionate share of stocks of companies from their home country. Thus, they exhibit a *home bias*. If they invest in countries with which they are familiar, this exhibits so-called *foreign bias*.

Apart from a geographical under-diversification, investors also exhibit a tendency toward investing in projects based on technology with which they are familiar, which is called *disciplinary bias*. When individuals learn about an investment project, they initially focus on information in their area of expertise and then confirm their focal hypothesis with the information from other sources.

4. Explain how pareidolia and apophenia can be observed in financial markets.

Hume and McFadden (1999) recognize the human tendency to see patterns in randomly generated data. Humans see faces in the moon, armies in the clouds, and Christ in pancakes or snow. Given that individuals have a tendency to reject randomness when they mistakenly see recognizable patterns, they systematically underestimate the probability that such patterns can occur by chance. In financial markets, the observation of return streaks, which can be seen as price momentum or price reversal, and trading on past observations goes against the weak form efficiency of capital markets. Nevertheless, many trading strategies are based on recognizable stock price and stock return patterns. These patterns are the domain of application of technical analysis. Technical analysts base their trading strategies on apophenia. The profitability of technical analysis rests on the analysts' ability to infer the investors' behavior and anticipation from past price movements.

5. One well-established bias in decision-making is overconfidence, i.e. people's tendency to overestimate their abilities and chances of success. Explain how the anchoring heuristic is related to an agent's overconfident behavior and illustrate how overconfidence affects trading behavior.

When people are asked to estimate a confidence interval for some random variable, they tend to anchor on their best estimate of that variable. They then typically assess the confidence interval to be much smaller than it actually is, hence overestimating the quality of their estimate. The anchoring heuristic is thus one explanation of overconfident behavior. Investors that are overly confident in their abilities tend to purchase risky stocks because they are confident they will be able to profit from the upside potential instead of suffering losses in case their predictions are wrong. They also tend to under-diversify their portfolios because they are confident that their investment strategy will result in favorable outcomes. Neglecting the need for hedging would also reduce the upside potential of their portfolios.

Chapter 12 Governance Risk

1. Discuss the role of the board in an organization.

Boards set the direction for an organization. Although they do not necessarily set the strategy themselves, boards choose the general direction. Boards are tasked to set the organizational tone, which implies defining or affecting the culture of the organization including the risk appetite. In many governance environments, the board is also in charge of selecting and nominating the chief executive officer (CEO) and possibly the CEO's team. Some exceptions include state-owned enterprises where the government often directly makes the nomination. Boards also supervise the performance of the management team and specifically that of the CEO. Finally, boards support the management team to achieve success such as by helping with business relationships or by giving authority to the CEO within the organization. Thus, the board's ultimate responsibility is to ensure the organization's success.

2. Discuss the factors making a board effective or ineffective.

No simple metrics of board effectiveness exist. From a theoretical perspective, governance is a complex area that draws on many different fields in the social sciences. A good approach to assess effectiveness is to follow a specific set of indicators such as the four pillars of effectiveness. The first pillar concerns the individual characteristics of the board members. Many dimensions exist within this pillar including knowledge, competency, dedication, and personality. The second pillar addresses information issues that have been at the heart of many crises. Boards often do not get sufficiently involved in information design and information architecture. The third pillar concerns structures and processes. As boards become more sophisticated, they need to be more refined in their processes (e.g., board nominations) as well as their structures (e.g., committee structures). The fourth pillar is group dynamics. Information on all four pillars typically transpires to the public. Deeper company knowledge can help investors understand and pinpoint areas of strength and weakness.

3. Identify and explain conditions in which boards experience failure.
   Boards typically fail in four areas:

   - Risk assessment and management. This failure occurred during the financial crisis of 2007–2008 as many boards did not have the qualifications required to understand the sophisticated collateralized products used by their institutions, despite a large proportion of profits coming from these activities.
   - Strategy. Boards are particularly concerned with long-term, fundamental strategic issues rather than operational ones. Long-term strategic problems can be considered the responsibility of the board rather than top executives. A decision by a bank of pursuing investment banking rather than commercial or private banking would also be a board responsibility.
   - CEO nomination and supervision. Nomination of a new CEO is a complex and demanding undertaking that requires defining what the organization needs to achieve and what skills and personality traits are required to do so. A sophisticated CEO nomination process is important for organizational success.
   - Integrity. The lack of integrity is widespread. Sometimes, it consists of illegal or illegitimate undertakings as was the case at Olympus in Japan where some board members had a company that was receiving transaction fees on deals approved by the board (i.e., themselves). More often, integrity may simply be that a board member does not operate in the organization's best interests because of conflicts of interest or other activities.

4. Identify and explain positive signals of effective governance.
   One positive signal of effective governance includes board transparency about its practices such as board nomination, board tenure, board member performance, and evaluation processes. Another signal involves committee structures that are pertinent to the specifics of the organization. The presence of creative personalities on the board along with highly technical ones can be a strong indication of productive diversity. Also, the personality of the board chair as a powerful, discrete, well connected individual who leaves front page presence to the CEO but is clearly influential can be a good signal. A final positive signal of effective governance is the ability to identify positive signals and check the completeness of the governance system along the four pillars of board effectiveness to avoid blind-spots.

Chapter 13 Inflation Risk

1. Explain why an inflationary scenario can be expected after three decades of moderate price changes

   The expectation of higher inflation in coming years is based on expansive global monetary policies. To avoid economic collapse, central banks flooded markets with money. In order to save their banks and to stimulate their economies, governments of the Western industrialized countries accumulated high levels of debt. The ways to reduce the debt levels are based on austerity measures or inflating the debt away. Some countries implemented austerity measures, which are highly unpopular and usually result in protests against the government. A politically less painful approach would be to allow increased inflation to proportionately reduce the debt.

2. Discuss how central banks strategies toward inflationary concerns developed since the 1970s.

   In the 2010s, central banks generally acted more independently than they did in the 1970s. Now, they have formal mandates to fight inflation. Their statistical toolkits are better developed and inflation expectations are better anchored than previously. Central banks are more credible today and have enhanced the way they communicate.

3. Discuss how standard investment instruments perform in an inflationary scenario and the difficulty in using these instruments as an inflation hedge.

   Over horizons of 10 years and more, equities provide inflation protection. Over shorter time horizons, equities tend to be negatively correlated with inflation. Studies show that equities tend to suffer in times of high inflation. In times of rising inflation and increasing interest rates, nominal bonds with a fixed coupon lose value. In contrast, inflation-linked bonds can be a good hedge against inflation. However, changes in the reference index can occur, and the suitability of the basket of goods underlying the index used to measure inflation can be insufficient. Also, inflation-linked bonds do not provide leverage and are not apt to protect other parts of the portfolio against inflation. Silver has dual usage in industry and as a store of value. Although both gold and silver can serve as long-term hedges against inflation, both are volatile and timing of entry and exit proves challenging. Physical, exchange-traded funds or futures commodity investments are exposed to various costs and operational challenges. Such challenges include the cost of rolling forward contracts and carry costs of storage, insurance, and financing. Timber serves as an inflation hedge assuming that investors have sufficient resources and knowledge to handle these types of investments. Real estate can work well as an inflation hedge when investors place attention on the selection process and invest directly instead of through real estate investment trusts. Real estate is very sensitive to changing interest rates and economic growth. Inflexibility to respond to these factors puts investors at the mercy of these variables as inflation reaches different phases.

4. Discuss why and how investors can use trend-following strategies as a hedge against inflation.

   Trend-following strategies can capture major trends that tend to occur during inflationary dislocations across all asset classes. The strategy is dynamic and can respond to the changing magnitude of price changes in different phases of inflationary development. The ability to time long and short position exposures allows trend followers to profit from price changes to the upside and downside. Additionally, these strategies assume positions between different geographic interest rates and currencies to profit from relative changes in these spread values. The added value comes from the ability to actively change risk exposures in the direction of price developments in an effort to protect against unexpected developments.

Chapter 14 Risk Aggregation and Capital Management

1. Define risk aggregation and discuss its importance.

    Risk aggregation describes the total risk of a portfolio or a group of portfolios that may be segregated based on business lines or risk factor types. Aggregating risk is important because it offers a perspective into the residual risks remaining after netting opposite risks and an understanding of the diversification benefits in the correlated aggregation process. This understanding enables banks to control risk and limit it to the specified risk appetite, ensure capital adequacy, and make informed decisions on such matters as pricing products and services.

2. Explain the structural approach used to measure credit risk.

    The credit risk structural approach is based on Merton's (1974) asset value model. Under this approach, an asset's value is forecasted based on its relationship with systematic and idiosyncratic risk factors. The asset value correlation between different borrowers is observed from the correlation between the systematic risk factors. Correlated asset values are converted to transitioned ratings at the measurement horizon, assets are marked-to-market with the applicable credit spreads, and portfolio value at risk is estimated.

3. Explain the approaches used to measure market risk.

    Market risk measures the risk of a change in the market values of financial instruments at a 99 percent confidence level over a 10-day holding period. Market risk may be aggregated using various approaches such as the variance-covariance approach, historical simulation, and Monte Carlo simulation. The variance-covariance approach is an analytical approach that assumes risk factors have multivariate normal distributions. This approach is useful if the risk-return payoffs of instruments in a portfolio are linear so that the assumption of linear correlation holds true. The historical simulation approach does not assume any distributional assumption on the risk factor. It uses a historical data set of risk factor (asset return) changes and uses these changes to simulate the risk factor values going forward. This approach naturally incorporates the correlation in risk factors as it is based on the actual values. Monte Carlo simulation re-prices a position using thousands of market states obtained from a stochastic risk factor model in order to compute VaR. For example, a one-factor short-rate model can be used to simulate yields in case of a fixed income portfolio.

4. List various measures used in reporting total risk and discuss their relative strengths and weaknesses.

Two methods of measuring and reporting total risk are value-at-risk (VaR) or expected shortfall (ES). Although VaR is not a coherent measure of risk due to its lack of subadditivity, ES is perfectly coherent. When VaR or ES are based on a normal distribution, they are not useful for measuring risk if asset returns are known to have fat tails. VaR or ES alone may not serve to describe the tail risk. VaR and ES calculations based on extreme value theory (EVT) are enhanced to include tail curve fitting done using a generalized Pareto distribution (GPD).

5. List various approaches for risk aggregation and discuss pros and cons of each.

The two main approaches for risk aggregation are the top-down approach and the bottom-up approach. Either of these approaches may be used based on what provides reliable estimates given the type of portfolios held by a bank. The top-down approach combines individual marginal distribution of the individual risk types by way of dependency modeling either with a copula that allows modeling of dependency or using a simple correlation matrix that does not model dependency but allows only linear interaction. The top-down approach assumes that risk portfolios can be segregated based on the risk factors. The bottom-up approach comes from a practical perspective that portfolios cannot be neatly bifurcated as sensitive to either credit or market risk. Therefore, risk aggregation under this approach basically involves modeling market and credit risk jointly to measure the risk of any portfolio.

Chapter 15 Value-at-Risk and Other Risk Measures

1. Explain the circumstances under which VaR would be a "good" risk measure.

Only under very stringent assumptions can VaR serve as a "good" risk measure. In particular, the profit and loss distribution must exhibit an elliptical distribution. Whenever extreme events are possible or risks may be highly dependent, VaR fails as a risk measure.

2. Discuss VaR's advantages and disadvantages.

A major advantage of VaR lies in its simplicity. VaR is just the quantile of the profit and loss distribution. It is also intuitive and can be easily communicated. Furthermore, its calculation, at least in the one-dimensional case, is straightforward. These advantages are the main cause for its popularity in the financial industry. However, VaR has some serious disadvantages. In particular, it neglects all the information below the quantile level of the profit and loss distribution. This part of the loss distribution should be a key concern to any risk manager.

3. Explain what a "good" risk measure should be and relate it to the coherency axioms.

A "good" risk measure should address four axioms. The first axiom is subadditivity. Subadditivity means that the risk of two portfolios should be less than or equal to adding the risk of two separate portfolios. This property formalizes the principle of diversification. The second axiom is homogeneity, which means that doubling the size of a portfolio would double the risk. The third axiom is monotonicity. That is, if portfolio A always has better values than portfolio B under all scenarios, then *B* should be less risky than *A*. The final axiom is translation invariance, which quantifies the impact of adding cash to the portfolio, which acts like insurance. Hence, the risk is reduced by adding cash. Although these axioms are merely a convention, they are motivated by the fact that all these properties are the ones investors expect to hold for a risk measure.

4. Discuss the weighting schemes of VaR, ES, and a spectral risk measure and relate these weighting schemes to the "utility" function of the risk manager.

   The weighting of VaR corresponds to the Dirac delta function that puts infinite mass to the quantile of the profit and loss distribution. All realizations above and below the quantile obtain zero weights and hence do not provide any information to the risk manager using VaR. Such weighting does not make sense from a decision-theoretic perspective. A more sensible choice for a weighting would be to put equal weights to all the losses below the quantile level. This weighting corresponds to using expected shortfall and can be interpreted as an optimal choice for a "risk-neutral" risk manager. A "risk-averse" risk manager would put increasing weights with increasing losses. Such a weighting scheme is propagated by spectral risk measures. Furthermore, spectral risk measures put a weight on the whole distribution. Hence, all quantiles are well-defined and all the information from the profit and loss distribution is used.

5. Identify the potential disadvantages of spectral risk measures.

   Estimates of spectral risk measures become more volatile when the probability of infrequent and large losses is high. Although they are theoretically sound risk measures and preferable to VaR, the standard errors of their estimates are by a multiple larger than the standard errors of the VaR estimates. Although neglecting the severity of losses in the tail of the distribution results in a theoretically flawed risk measure, using spectral measures comes at a cost of making backtesting much more difficult.

6. Discuss the potential dangers of regulating financial markets using VaR and other risk measures.

   Regulating financial markets by using market-based risk measures such as VaR and ES may cause adverse feedback effects. These adverse effects do not necessarily arise from the non-coherency of risk measures such as VaR. Instead, the feedback effects are caused by the market dependency of these risk measures. This dependency may also generate adverse incentives and agency problems. Hence, studying the effect of regulation with a general equilibrium framework is important to understanding its impact on the stability of the financial system.

Chapter 16 Stress Testing

1. Assume that the interest rate sensitivities of a financial institution's assets and liabilities are perfectly matched. Discuss whether the institution has a zero interest rate risk.

   Due to the perfect match between the interest rate sensitivity of its assets and that of its liabilities, the institution has zero direct interest rate risk. However, it may have nonzero indirect interest rate risk if changes in the interest rate affect its borrowers' creditworthiness and ability to repay. In other words, despite being shielded from direct interest rate risk, the institution is still exposed to the indirect effects of interest rate movements via credit risk.

2. Discuss whether the following statement is correct: For direct foreign exchange risk calculations, off-balance sheet positions need to be excluded from the net open position.

   The statement that off-balance sheet positions need to be excluded from the net open position for direct foreign exchange risk calculations is incorrect. The input data should reflect not only assets and liabilities but also off-balance sheet positions. The net open positions in foreign currency should reflect the delta equivalents of foreign exchange options.

3. Identify which type of foreign exchange solvency risk is larger for most banks—direct or indirect—and explain why.

   Indirect foreign exchange risk is often more important than indirect foreign exchange risk. While banks' direct foreign exchange risk is typically closely monitored and regulated by measures such as limits on banks' net open positions, their indirect foreign exchange risk often receives much less scrutiny. This situation emerges in part because monitoring indirect foreign exchange risk properly requires comprehensive knowledge of the foreign exchange exposures of bank's corporate and household counterparts. Such information that is not always available to banks' risk managers and supervisors. The indirect foreign exchange risk can become sizeable during prolonged periods of exchange rate stability (e.g., in countries with closely managed exchange rate pegs). Such periods of stability can lull banks' counterparts into a false sense of security and into accepting sizeable foreign exchange exposures and thus saddling the banks with indirect foreign exchange risk.

4. Discuss the differences between a "pure" and "macro" interbank contagion test.

   The main difference between the "pure" and the "macro" contagion stress tests is that the "pure" contagion test assumes a failure occurring in a bank for an internal reason such as fraudulent behavior within the bank. It does not distinguish the relative likelihood of the failure of various banks. In contrast, the "macro" contagion test analyzes situations when all banks are weakened at the same time by a common external (typically macroeconomic) shock, which affects each bank differently depending on its exposures to the various risk factors, and makes some banks fail.

   Another difference is that while the "macro" contagion test is a single test for the system as a whole, the "pure" contagion test is a series of separate stress tests, showing for each bank what would be the direct impact of its failure on the capital of each of the other banks. In other words, the "pure" contagion stress test provides a measure of systemic importance of individual banks: the bigger the decline in the system's capital or capital adequacy ratio, the more systemically important the bank whose default is assumed.

5. Discuss whether the following statement is correct: The "worst-case approach" to stress testing allows for creating more stressful scenarios than the "threshold approach."

   The statement that the "worst-case approach" to stress testing allows for creating more stressful scenarios than the "threshold approach" is incorrect. The two approaches are essentially equivalent ways of analyzing the same issue (i.e., robustness of a bank or banking system). Any scenario generated under the "worst-case approach" can also be arrived at by selecting an appropriate threshold under the "threshold approach."

Chapter 17 Risk Management and Regulation

1. Discuss the nature of financial intermediation.

    Financial intermediaries act as a conduit between savings-surplus and savings-deficit units in an economy. They reconcile the conflicting needs of the parties concerned by time or maturity, size, and risk transformation while reducing information search costs and transactions costs. The typical example is provided by a bank or thrift association receiving small amounts of savings lodged in a savings account, which can be withdrawn on demand and transformed into larger, longer term loans and mortgages. Intermediaries have standardized loan evaluation procedures enabling them to cut the costs of credit evaluation and lower the cost (margin or spread) between the payments to depositors and the interest rate charged on longer term loans.

2. Discuss the securitization process.

    Mortgage loans can remain on the books of a financial intermediary financed by deposits. They can also be pooled and repackaged and sold to wholesale investors who want to purchase the yield on mortgage loans. Rating agencies assess these mortgages when they are repackaged. Repackaged mortgage form the basis of the collateralized debt obligations (CDOs) and mortgage-backed securities (MBSs) that were stumbling blocks in the financial crisis of 2007–2008. Nothing is inherently wrong with creating CDOs or MBSs. However, if the repackaging is done in a complex manner such as repackaging CDOs and selling them into further tranches, the problem of assessing the risk of the package at a time when housing prices are falling can become very complex and difficult. This situation can result in an information asymmetry problem.

3. Identify several factors that drive financial innovation.

    Financial innovation may be driven by technical or economic changes such as the development of the Internet or by regulatory restrictions, in what is termed regulatory arbitrage. Such innovation is usually intended to reduce costs, increase the convenience to investors, and make markets more complete in some sense. Examples of financial innovation include home banking or stock trading over the Internet. Because physical location is no longer an issue, this enhances the ability to immediately transact.

4. Define regulatory arbitrage.

    Regulatory arbitrage refers to financial schemes or arrangements that are driven by a desire to avoid or profit from regulatory differences under different national authorities. An example includes back-to-back loans.

5. Discuss the primary objectives of the Basel Accords.

    The Basel I Accord focused mainly on ensuring that banks had sufficient risk capital with a concentration on credit risk and risk-weighted assets. The Basel II Accord expanded the scope to include operational risk and market risk. In response to the global financial crisis, the Basel III Accord further broadened the mandate to include liquidity requirements, leverage ratios, and a concern with the monitoring of systemic risk.

Chapter 18 Risk Budgeting

1. Discuss the importance of measuring risk in a way that is consistent with the criterion used for asset allocation.

    If the utility function maximized in the asset allocation process and the statistic used to measure portfolio risk differ, the portfolio that is achieved by managing risk may eventually diverge from the optimal portfolio constructed by maximizing the utility function used in asset allocation. This scenario might occur if an investor builds a portfolio based on minimizing downside risk but manages risk using the standard deviation as a risk measure. In this case, an investor may add bonds to a portfolio in an attempt to reduce standard deviation. However, the bond returns may be insufficient to meet the relevant downside risk target, resulting in a portfolio that is suboptimal.

2. Discuss why VaR is not a coherent risk measure and why having coherence risk measures is important.

    VaR is not a coherent risk measure because it only represents a "worst outcome." A portfolio manager can more easily obtain the worst outcome when that portfolio is diversified. Intuitively, a better chance exists for something to "go wrong" when a portfolio has more components. Coherence is an important property of risk measures because most utility functions based on which portfolios are constructed use downside risk and standard deviation. This framework is consistent with the idea of diversification. A good risk measure should also be consistent with this idea.

3. Discuss why dollar weights differ from risk weights in a portfolio.

    Individual risks of components and correlations between components are determinants of the risk contributions of these assets to overall portfolio risk. For example, for an asset with considerable stand-alone risk, adding only a few assets to the portfolio could result in disproportionately increasing the risk. The following equation illustrates the risk decomposition of the portfolio in which the w reflects portfolio weights for a portfolio with n assets.

$$\rho(w_1, \ldots, w_N) = w_1 \frac{\partial \rho}{\partial w_1} + \ldots + w_N \frac{\partial \rho}{\partial w_N}.$$

The relative risk contribution of a component is determined both by the component's weight in the portfolio and the marginal risks, $\partial \rho / \partial w_n$. The marginal risk represents the rate at which the total portfolio risk changes as the weight of the n-th component changes. Thus, that risky component's contribution to overall portfolio risk can be high even when its dollar weight is small.

4. Some contend that the method used to compound returns is important but others argue that compounding, high (low) returns always leads to high (low) returns. Thus, the method is irrelevant as long as it is used consistently. Critique the validity of this argument.

High returns remain high regardless of how they are compounded, but the risk may compound in a different manner depending on the method used for compounding returns. In turn, this may cause the risk-reward ratios to evolve differently depending on which type of compounding formula is used. For example, if risk increases faster when using geometric compounding, then risk-reward ratios become smaller as the holding period increases. Whether investors are properly compensated for the risk taken depends on the method used in compounding the returns.

5. Explain the difference between VaR and CVaR.

VaR only expresses a threshold level for how bad the returns can be but offers no indication about what is happening below that value. By contrast, the CVaR is an average of all the values that are smaller than or equal to the VaR. Therefore, CVaR offers a more complete picture of what is happening in the left tail of the return distribution. Unlike VaR, CVaR is a coherent risk measure.

6. Maximum drawdowns become more severe as more data become available. Discuss whether this statement implies that risk increases over time.

The statement that maximum drawdowns become more severe as more data become available does not mean that risk increases over time. Instead, it implies that more realistic estimates of the maximum drawdown have been taken, which for a continuous, normal distribution should be equal to minus infinity in theory.

Chapter 19 Risk-Adjusted Performance Measurement

1. Stochastic dominance implies that if the same return can be obtained with two different investments, X and Y, yet the likelihood of a return exceeding a threshold α is greater for X, investors will prefer X over Y. Strict dominance occurs if $P_X (R > \alpha) > P_Y (R > \alpha)$ and weak dominance if $P_X (R > \alpha) \geq P_Y (R > \alpha)$ for any α. Provide an example showing that the Sharpe ratio does not respect weak dominance.

Stochastic dominance only considers the likelihood of returns being higher or lower than a threshold, without taking their variability into account. The Sharpe ratio, however, considers both returns that exceed the risk-free return (numerator) and variability (denominator). Therefore, the likelihood of higher than risk-free returns can be greater for a specific asset, while the mean divided by the standard deviation can be lower. The following table provides an example.

Probability	Excess Return X (%)	Excess Return Y (%)
0.1	30	50
0.8	20	20
0.1	−30	−30

In this case, an investor would choose asset Y based on stochastic dominance because the expected return for asset Y (18 percent) is higher than for asset X (16 percent). Yet, calculating the Sharpe ratio produces a different result with asset X having a higher Sharpe ratio than asset Y, 1.02 and 0.98, respectively.

	Asset X	Asset Y
Expected return	16.00%	18.00%
Standard deviation	15.62%	18.33%
Sharpe ratio	1.02	0.98

The investor would choose asset X because of the higher Sharpe ratio. Thus, neither the Sharpe ratio nor other RAPMs respect the property of stochastic dominance.

2. Discuss countering views as to whether a higher or lower negative Sharpe ratio is better.

Assume two assets in which A presents a 10 percent negative excess return and B a 5 percent negative excess return. If they both have the same level of risk as measured by the standard deviation, an investor will prefer asset B because its negative return is smaller. For a 10 percent standard deviation for each asset, the Sharpe ratio for asset A is –1.0, but it is –0.5 for asset B. Assume that both assets have an 8 percent negative excess return, but the standard deviations of 10 percent and 20 percent, respectively. Asset B would have a higher risk despite have a higher Sharpe ratio: –0.4 for asset B and –0.8 for asset A. Some investors would justify the choice of a higher Sharpe ratio by claiming that having a negative return is a better outcome than having inconsistently negative returns (i.e., higher standard deviation) rather than consistently negative returns (lower standard deviation).

3. Relative to the Kappa index, considerable debate exists about which order and threshold values are best for ranking funds. Indicate what the following options imply: (a) a higher Kappa order and (b) a high threshold value relative to a value equal to the risk-free value.

According to the Kappa index, a more risk-averse investor will be more sensitive to the asymmetry or excess kurtosis of downside returns. A highly risk-averse investor would choose a high order for the Kappa index (3 or 4) than a less risk-averse investor because the index determines how strongly negative deviations from threshold are weighted. The threshold values are less clear. Some suggest using the risk-free values, but others justify using a higher value because investors should be indifferent to above-threshold returns.

4. Discuss the advantages and disadvantages of using VaR as a risk measurement.

The main advantages of using VaR are related to its definition. Because VaR measures maximum potential loss, investors can use it with the desired confidence level and time period. VaR also distinguishes between upside and downside risk. Yet, VaR has several disadvantages. The measure does not consider exceptional events (i.e., extreme values) and can produce different results depending on the model used. VaR fails to control the risk of large losses with a small probability and does not meet the subadditivity condition.

5. Discuss the consequences of using drawdown to evaluate a manager's ability.

   Drawdown measures the magnitude of the loss incurred by a client who invested with the manager in the past. Drawdown is sensitive to the length of the time series. Drawdown will be greater the longer the time series, and longer time series are more sensitive to obtaining greater drawdown values. In general, surviving managers show a greater ability to overcome adversities, so drawdown is a less direct measure of a manager's quality than could initially be assumed.

Chapter 20 Risk Attribution Analysis

1. Discuss why considering performance attribution alone can be misleading in evaluating portfolio performance. Identify what the process lacks to be consistent with financial theory.

   The method of performance attribution exhibits an intrinsic weakness in that it does account for risk. Thus, performance attribution penalizes some optimal choices of the fund manager. Consider a rational portfolio manager with perfect knowledge of the expectations and the variances of the returns of all the assets, as well as the correlation between the different assets' returns. Because the distribution of the returns is supposed to be multivariate normal, it assumes that the manager anticipates it perfectly. Then, the portfolio manager has to find the portfolio with minimum tracking error variance for a given expected total return relative to the benchmark. Although the manager selected the portfolio in an optimal manner with optimal information, the performance attribution (alone) will be negative in some attributes. Although these results seem paradoxical, the attribution of performance is incomplete because it neglected risk. Also, a well-known fact is that each optimal decision that contributes negatively to the outperformance can be interpreted in terms of relative risk reduction.

2. Discuss why risk attribution is defined by tracking error volatility decomposition and not by volatility decomposition.

   A measure is needed for the effect on portfolio risk both for the decision to over or under weight each asset class in the benchmark and for stock selection inside each asset class. Moreover, this measure needs to be consistent with the portfolio management context, namely a benchmarked portfolio. A natural candidate should be relative risk as measured by tracking error volatility.

3. Discuss the different decompositions of the standard deviation of the tracking error. A first decomposition relies on the covariance:

$$T = \tfrac{1}{T} \left[Cov(AA, S) + Cov(SE, S) + Cov(I, S) \right]$$

$$T = \tfrac{1}{T} \left[Cov\left(\sum_{i=1}^{n} \left(w_{pi} - w_{bi} \right) \left(R_{bi} - R_b \right), S \right) + Cov\left(\sum_{i=1}^{n} w_{bi} \left(R_{pi} - R_{bi} \right), S \right) \right.$$
$$\left. + Cov\left(\sum_{i=1}^{n} \left(w_{pi} - w_{bi} \right) \left(R_{pi} - R_{bi} \right), S \right) \right]$$

where $S = R_P - R_b$ is the total value added by the portfolio managers. AA is the asset allocation effect. SE is the selection effect and I represents the interaction term. This decomposition does not introduce stand-alone risk of the relative return of asset class i.

A second decomposition uses the relationship between covariance and correlation and thus introduces stand-alone risk of the relative return of asset class i:

$$T = \sum_{i=1}^{n} \left[\left(w_{pi} - w_{bi}\right) \sigma \left(R_{bi} - R_b\right) \rho\left(AA_i, S\right) + w_{bi}\sigma \left(R_{pi} - R_{bi}\right) \rho\left(SE_i, S\right) + \left(w_{pi} - w_{bi}\right) \sigma \left(R_{pi} - R_{bi}\right) \rho\left(I_i, S\right) \right]$$

4. Discuss why risk attribution applied to Markowitz efficient portfolios does not lead to perfect consistency with performance attribution.

    Instead of a tracking-error variance (TEV) efficient portfolio, if a mean/variance efficient frontier portfolio is analyzed some inconsistencies between performance attribution and risk attribution remain. For example, this indicates that some optimal choices (asset allocation or stock selection) can lead to both underperformance and a positive contribution to relative risk. This situation occurs because mean/variance portfolio optimization is not the correct method in a framework of portfolio optimization with a benchmark.

5. Discuss an issue arising when undertaking risk-adjusted performance attribution.

    Risk-adjusted performance attribution analysis introduces the stand-alone information ratio of the decision, component information ratio, and contribution of the component (asset allocation or stock selection) to the information ratio of the portfolio. Various conflicts exist between some of the three terms of the decomposition.

Chapter 21 Risk and Mortgage-Backed Securities in a Time of Transition

1. Discuss borrower and property characteristics that lenders should consider in qualifying someone for a mortgage.

    To qualify someone for a mortgage, lenders should document and verify a borrower's income, employment, other debt, financial assets, and credit score as well as the value of the property through an appraisal. Lenders should also determine whether the property will be owner-occupied or be an investment or a second home.

2. Describe differences between the CFPB's ability to repay standards and the "affordability products" originated in the subprime market.

    The ability to repay standards requires lenders to verify borrower income, employment, debt, and property value. The standards require a maximum debt-to-income (DTI) ratio of 43 percent or a ratio consistent with the standards of the government-sponsored enterprise (GSE) or the Federal House Administration (FHA). If the mortgage carries a variable rate, the borrower is qualified based on a reasonable projection of interest payments over the first five years of the mortgage.

Lenders did not verify the stated income or no-documentation loans and debt-to-income (DTI) ratios used in the affordability products in the subprime market. They used interest only loans to reduce DTI ratios. Lenders qualified borrowers based on an initial "teaser" rate that generally underestimated the borrower's ability to repay.

3. Discuss how the over valuation of properties contributed to the housing bubble associated with the financial crisis of 2007–2008 and how CRAs are now attempting to determine sustainable home prices.

Inflated home values misrepresented true loan-to-value (LTV) ratios and presented borrowers as having equity in their properties that did not exist. Using such inflated values allowed borrowers whose monthly payments had increased or whose income had fallen to refinance at a lower initial rate and monthly payment. Credit rating agencies (CRAs) are now computing "sustainable" home prices based on unemployment rates, income, rental prices, population, housing starts, and mortgage rates.

4. Describe the difference between a loan issued under the ATR standard and one that is classified as a Qualified Mortgage.

The ability to repay (ATR) standard requires the originator to make a reasonable and good faith effort to verify the borrower's ability to repay. No limits on points and fees exist. Additionally, features such as interest only are allowed and the term need not be 30 years. Regulatory penalties exist for noncompliance as well as a borrower's right to recover fees and charges, and an extended window to bring suit alleging violations. Borrowers can use the failure to meet the standard as a defense in foreclosure proceedings.

A Qualified Mortgage (QM) is a regularly amortized, 30-year loan underwritten to standards enumerated in the ATR Rule, with limited points and fees and a maximum DTI ratio. For an adjustable rate mortgage (ARM), a borrower is qualified on the highest rate that may apply over the first five years of the loan. A loan is also QM if qualified under GSE or FHA mortgage programs. A QM offers a safe harbor and a rebuttable presumption for the lender and securitizer.

Chapter 22 Credit Value Adjustment

1. Using the Merton (1974) model, describe how credit risk embedded in corporate debt can be understood as an option.

Merton's (1974) insight is to recognize that one can replicate corporate debt with a combination of default-free debt and a short position in a put option on the value of the firm's assets. Should the firm's assets exceed the value of the debt obligation, the firm's owners (stockholders) can pledge the assets to obtain further debt financing. This assumption insures that the firm's owners are capable of repaying the debt obligation. Because the value of assets exceeds the value of the debt, the residual is the value of the equity holdings that the firm's owners will act to retain. When the value of assets is less than the firm's debt obligation, the residual amount is negative. This scenario implies that repaying the debt will require the firm's owners to increase their equity position in the firm. Alternatively, they can default on their debt obligation. Hence, the put option is the right to hand over the firm's assets to the bondholders in exchange for the bondholders relinquishing their claims on the firm's owners.

2. Summarize three measures that the ISDA undertook to mitigate the credit risk inherent in OTC derivatives.

   Three measures taken by the International Swap Dealers' Association (ISDA) to mitigate the credit risk inherent in OTC derivatives are:

   • Standardizing OTC interest-rate and foreign-exchange swap contracts to avoid misunderstandings that might lead to default.
   • Creating netting rules that eliminate cherry picking. Cherry picking occurs when defaulting counterparties collect on contracts on which they are owed while defaulting on contracts on which they are obligated to pay out.
   • Establishing collateral protocols that give some ability to equalize credit risk between counterparties.

3. List and describe the three components of a unilateral CVA.

   The three components of a unilateral CVA are:

   • Probability of default: The likelihood that default will occur.
   • Exposure: The amount of loss from the contract should default occur.
   • Loss given default. The loss amount incurred as a general claimant on the assets of the defaulting counterparty.

4. Using a vanilla interest-rate swap, describe the determinants of CVA for both counterparties.

   Each party to the contract of a vanilla interest-rate swap will assign a probability of default to its counterparty. Both will determine a loss given default amount. Finally, each party will determine its cost to replace the contract given that its counterparty has defaulted.

5. Describe the circumstances leading to including CVA in the Basel III Accord and how the CVA requirement might be expected to alleviate future problems.

   The financial crisis of 2007–2008 revealed a substantial amount of previously unrecognized credit risk. Before that crisis, the credit value adjustment (CVA) amounts were immaterial and rarely appeared on financial statements. On recognizing the extent of credit risk, financial regulators have heightened standards for determining CVA and are imposing capital requirements on CVA variability. To the extent that CVA accurately measures this source of risk, the additional capital requirements should lessen bank failures.

Chapter 23 Risk Management and Hedge Funds

1. List and explain several examples of hedge fund downside and drawdown risk measures.

   Downside risk measures weigh the negative returns more heavily than traditional measures and also allow for non-normal return distributions. Downside risk measures generally ignore returns above a certain target rate and only consider those below the target. If the target rate is set equal to the average historical return, downside risk is also called semi-deviation.

Drawdown is the (percentage) decline in net asset value (NAV) from the highest historical return level or the peak-to-valley rate of return. It comes in at least three different types: worst, average, and current drawdown. The worst drawdown measures the worst peak to valley drawdown. The average downturn is the average continuous negative return over an investment period. The current drawdown is computed as the average return from the most recent peak. Related to the drawdown and downside risk measures is the average recovery time (ART), which is found as the average time in a recovery from the low point of the drawdown to a new peak.

2. Discuss the advantages of risk-adjusted returns relative to absolute return measures. In particular, compare and contrast the Sharpe ratio with the Sortino, Sterling, and Calmar ratios.

   An absolute risk measure is risk without a specific context and simply measures the probability of a certain outcome (i.e., return) occurring. Relative risk measures the difference between two different risk levels. The Sharpe ratio measures the excess return per unit of volatility (as measured by the standard deviation) of a fund. In contrast to the Sharpe ratio, the Calmar ratio is a statistic that combines a fund's return with the drawdown risk to enable investors to see the potential opportunity gain versus opportunity loss of investing with a particular manager. It is calculated by dividing a fund's compound annualized rate of return over a certain period (say three years) by the fund's maximum drawdown. The lower this ratio is, the worse the investment performed over the specified time period. Unlike the Sharpe ratio, the Sortino ratio measures the incremental return over a minimum acceptable return (MAR) adjusted by the downside deviation below this MAR. The Sortino ratio can accommodate different degrees of target returns as well as different downside deviations for different minimum acceptable rates. The Sterling ratio is computed by dividing the average annual rate of return for the past three calendar years to the average of the maximum annual drawdown in each of those three years plus 10 percent.

3. Discuss the nonlinear payoff structure of hedge fund returns and provide an example of how hedge fund returns need to be adjusted for risk in this case.

   The non-linear payoff structure of hedge fund returns displays option-like patterns such as those typical of lookback straddles or those resembling the payoff from selling uncovered index put options. Similarly, nonlinear payoff structures include lookback straddles on interest rates and equity and out-of-the-money index put options. Therefore, the ability of a fund manager to generate alpha rests with his ability to produce returns in excess to those of a passive strategy that simply mimic the systematic risk factors of the benchmark. Risk-adjusted measures in this context are proxied by appraisal ratios that are obtained by dividing the fund alphas over the standard deviation of alphas. The appraisal ratio provides a measure of performance reasonably robust to the lookback bias frequently encountered when ranking managers by performance.

4. Discuss the possible types and the importance of operational risks for managing hedge fund risks. Provide an example of how to quantify operational risks in the hedge fund context.

   According to the Basel II Accord stipulations, *operational risk* is the risk of direct or indirect losses due to failed internal processes, people, or systems or even due to external events. One possible operational risk variable is simply an indicator variable that is one if the fund has external relationships conflicts of interest. Such conflicts of interest include whether the fund recommends securities in which a related party has an ownership interest, if the company buys and sells between itself and the clients, or if the fund uses external research from the same broker that executes its trades.

   Combining these observed variables to form a single construct of operational risk by defining a linear combination that maximizes the correlation with the cross-section of Form ADV disclosures results in the so-called ω-score. Regressing fund returns on the operational risk ω-score shows that operational risk has a negative and significant impact on fund performance, other things equal. Previous research shows that operational risk as measured by the ω-score is even more significant than financial risk in explaining fund failure.

Chapter 24 Options

1. Distinguish between a call option and a put option.

   A call option gives the owner the right, but not the obligation, to buy a specified quantity of an asset from the option seller (writer) at the exercise price specified in the option contract for a given time period. If the buyer chooses to exercise the option, the seller is obligated to sell the asset at the exercise price.

   A put option gives the owner the right, but not the obligation to sell a specified quantity of an asset to the option seller (writer) at the exercise price specified in the option contract for a given time period. If the buyer chooses to exercise the option, the seller is obligated to buy the asset at the exercise prices.

2. Explain how exchange-traded options differ from OTC options.

   Exchange-traded options are standardized, regulated, and backed by a clearinghouse. Over-the-counter (OTC) options are customized, largely unregulated, and have counterparty risk.

3. Define the separation and full-hedging theorems.

   The separation theorem states that the firm's production decision depends neither on the risk attitude of the firm nor on the incidence of the output price uncertainty. The full-hedging theorem states that the firm should completely eliminate its output price risk exposure by adopting a full-hedge should the commodity futures market be unbiased.

4. Explain why the separation and full-hedging theorems hold in the context of the competitive firm under output price uncertainty.

   In the context of the competitive firm under output price uncertainty, the firm could have completely eliminated its output price risk exposure had it chosen a full-hedge (i.e., $X = Q$) within its own discretion. That is, the degree of output price risk exposure to be assumed by the firm should be totally unrelated to its production decision. The firm as such chooses the optimal output level that maximizes $E(\tilde{P})Q - C(Q)$, which gives rise to the usual optimality condition that the marginal cost of production is equated to the expected output price. Hence, the separation and full-hedging theorems hold.

5. Identify possible reasons that support the hedging role of options.

   Possible reasons supporting the hedging role of options include export flexibility, production flexibility, multiplicative interaction of hedgeable and nonhedgeable risks, delivery risk, liquidity risk, and cross-hedging.

6. When the multiplicative revenue shock prevails, the competitive firm optimally uses options for hedging purposes. Identify the key factors that drive the firm to include options in its optimal hedge position.

   When the multiplicative revenue shock prevails, the competitive firm is driven by the correlation motive and the precautionary motive to opt for an option position.

Chapter 25 Futures

1. Comment on the validity of the following statement. "A naive ratio of one is completely useless for hedging. Either find the optimal hedge ratio or don't hedge at all."

   This statement is incorrect. Often the optimal hedge ratio is very close to one. Thus, in many circumstances, even using a hedge ratio of one is sufficient to reduce the risk.

2. Discuss whether hedging is useless in markets where the commodity is not storable given the lack of a relationship tying the futures price to the spot price.

   Although the no-arbitrage relationship is difficult to establish in the absence of storage, this does not mean that the market is inefficient. For example, evidence shows that efficiency exists in the weather derivatives market.

3. Discuss whether an airline company can hedge its oil demand given that jet oil futures do not trade with sufficient liquidity on the exchanges.

   Although jet fuel futures are not very liquid, airlines can cross-hedge with crude oil and other oil contracts that are correlated with jet fuel oil by estimating an optimal hedge ratio. For small companies, even jet fuel futures might be sufficient for hedging.

4. Describe how hedgers can use weather futures and commodity futures to hedge both price and quantity risk simultaneously.

   Although determining the actual mathematical relationships between the appropriate number of weather futures and commodity futures to hedge can be complex, the concept is simple. A hedger could use crude oil prices or heating oil prices to hedge the actual price risk of the demand for heating oil in a particular city. The hedger could use weather futures to hedge the quantity demanded risk. This arrangement requires the hedger to estimate the relationship between typical demand and weather to find a mapping of that relationship. It also requires the user to separate the effect of general heating oil prices from a particular city's demand. Finally, the hedger might have to estimate a simultaneous regression of quantity and price as they endogenously influence each other.

5. Explain why some hedging techniques might be superior to others.

    The general rule is to always estimate an optimal hedge to make sure that the hedging instrument does not have any complicated features. However, when hedging with a commodity on the underlying instruments, a hedge ratio of one with near-term futures contracts usually works sufficiently well. However, the optimal hedge ratio will usually be superior to a hedge ratio of one. If the hedge ratio is equal to one, then the optimal hedge ratio will be close to one. However, in cases when it does not equal one, using the estimated optimal hedge ratio will be important. Thus, the optimal hedge ratio will be superior to simple general assumptions such as a hedge ratio is equal to one.

Chapter 26 Swaps

1. Mowal Plc. is offered a bank loan at a fixed rate of 6 percent or a floating rate of LIBOR + 0.5 percent. Sika Ltd. can borrow at a floating rate of LIBOR + 0.25 percent or a fixed rate of 5.25 percent.
   - Determine the individual benefits of both companies entering into an interest rate swap contract.

    Sika Ltd. has the advantage in both the fixed market (an advantage of 0.75 percent = 6 percent − 5.25 percent), and the floating market (an advantage of 0.25 percent = (LIBOR + 0.5 percent) − (LIBOR + 0.25 percent)). The net difference between the two is 0.5 percent (= 0.75 percent − 0.25 percent). If the two firms decide to enter a swap agreement, then they will exchange the following interest rates:

    Mowal borrows at a floating rate of LIBOR + 0.5 percent and pays 5.25 percent to Sika. Sika borrows at fixed rate of 5.25 percent and pays LIBOR to Mowal.

    Splitting the benefit of 0.5 percent between the two companies is a matter of negotiation. One possible solution of this negotiation is to split the benefit equally so each firm receives 0.5 percent/2 = 0.25 percent. This exchange would result into the following net cash flows:

    Mowal: − (LIBOR + 0.5 percent) − 5.25 percent + LIBOR = 5.75 percent

    Sika: − 5.25 percent − LIBOR + 5.25 percent = LIBOR

    Both companies will pay cash flows computed with the interest rates they originally prefer. Each will also benefit from lower interest rates by 0.25 percent relative to not entering the swap agreement.

   - Assuming that a financial intermediary makes this arrangement and charges a fee of 0.25 percent, explain the benefit for the two companies.

    If the financial intermediary charges 0.25 percent, a profit will still exist for the companies to use a swap instead of not entering into a swap agreement. One possible solution would be the following:

    Mowal borrows at the floating rate of LIBOR + 0.5 percent and pays the bank 5.375 percent.

    Sika borrows at fixed rate of 5.25 percent and pays the bank LIBOR.

    A financial intermediary pays LIBOR to Mowal and 5.125 percent to Sika and receives LIBOR from Sika and 5.375 percent from Mowal.

This would result in the following net cash flows:

Mowal: $-$ (LIBOR + 0.5 percent) $-$ 5.375 percent + LIBOR = 5.875 percent

Sika: $-$LIBOR $-$5.25 percent + 5.125 percent = LIBOR + 0.125 percent

Bank: + LIBOR $-$ LIBOR + 5.375 percent $-$ 5.125 percent = 0.25 percent

2. Discuss the main benefits of entering into a swap contract involving a financial intermediary.

Companies do not swap both interest payments but one party makes a net payment representing the difference (i.e., one counterparty pays the net proceeds to the other counterparty). Swaps enable locking cash flows for longer periods and different delivery dates than other derivative products such as forwards. Also, swaps do not require constant monitoring. In this way, using swaps enables firms to exploit small inefficiencies in the capital markets, especially when their creditworthiness reflected typically in their credit ratings varies across each type of loan. The main disadvantage of these contracts is the counterparty default risk and the fact that the pricing of this risk is done at the initial agreement and cannot be reviewed during the life of the swap contract.

3. Explain how an interest rate swap works.

Both financial and non-financial firms widely use interest rate swaps to maximize value for both parties of a swap deal by exploiting a notion called comparative advantage. Respective parties are usually arranging an interest rate swap agreement through a financial institution acting as an intermediary and providing temporary "warehousing." Interest rate swaps involve "swapping" cash flows, specifically interest rate payments, computed based on a notional value of debt between two parties. The cash flows are usually denominated in the same currency and the swap contract explicitly states the dates on which the cash flows are due to be exchanged.

4. Al Maya Plc. can borrow capital at a fixed rate of 8.5 percent or a floating rate of LIBOR + 0.5 percent. Dil Plc. has been offered a fixed rate of 7.75 percent and a floating rate of LIBOR + 0.25 percent. A financial institution has agreed to act as an intermediary for a swap between the two parties at a fee of 0.10 percent for each party. Assuming the two companies share the benefits of the swap equally, demonstrate how a swap contract can reduce the cost of borrowing to each company.

The Borrowing Conditions	Fixed	Floating	Benefit to Share
Al Maya Plc.	8.50%	LIBOR + 0.50%	
Dil Plc.	7.75%	LIBOR + 0.25%	
Difference	0.75%	0.25%	0.50%
Less: Commission to bank			0.20%
(0.10% each)			
Net benefit to be shared equally			0.30%

Dil enjoys a borrowing comparative advantage relative to Al Maya. This advantage is witnessed on both borrowing alternatives, either at a floating or a fixed rate. The benefit to share is 0.50 percent (0.75 percent $-$ 0.25 percent). If both companies use a bank to warehouse the swap deal, the bank would charge 0.2 percent, which means each company would have to pay the bank 0.1 percent on the notional amount of the swap on a yearly basis.

The Swap	Al Maya	Dil
Al Maya borrows externally at a floating rate	− (LIBOR + 0.5%)	
Dil borrows externally at a fixed rate		−7.75%
Swap		
Al Maya lends at a floating rate to Dil and receives	LIBOR	−LIBOR
Dil lends at a fixed rate to Al Maya and receives	−7.75%	7.75%
Actual cost after entering the swap	−8.25%	−LIBOR
Bank charges	−0.10%	−0.10%
Net cost after entering swap via a bank	8.35%	−(LIBOR + 0.10%)
Cost without entering swap	8.50%	−(LIBOR + 0.25%)
Benefit from the swap	0.15%	0.15%

Both companies have reduced their cost of borrowing by 0.15 percent after paying the bank's commission (0.25 percent if not using a bank). If the notional amount of the swap was $100 million and the maturity of both debts was seven years, then each company would save $1.05 million. The bank would receive $1.4 million over the deal period for warehousing the swap. The borrowing cost reduction for the better company (Dil) implies that it will be exposed to increasing credit risk as Al Maya has a higher risk profile.

5. Discuss the effects of using a swap on a firm's risk exposure.

A strand of the literature defends the view that interest rate derivatives and swaps in particularly reduce a bank's risk. For example, Allayannis and Ofek (2001) and Makar and Huffman (2001) show that using currency derivatives reduces the exchange rate exposure firms face. Brewer, Jackson, and Moser (1996) find that greater use of derivatives is associated with lower risk exposures. Choi and Elyasiani (1997) stress the relative influence of risk reduction involving exchange rates compared to the reduction in interest rate risk. Chaudhry and Reichert (1999) contend that using interest rate swaps decreases the systemic or non-systemic risk of commercial banks holding large assets.

Another group of researchers such as Gorton and Rosen (1995) suggest that in most cases using interest rate swaps leads to higher interest rate risk exposure. A third group of researchers supports the argument of the non-existing relationship between banks risk and the use of derivatives. These scholars suggest that banks use derivatives to be involved as an intermediary in a financial transaction and to generate profit from the transactions and intermediation fees. Hentschel and Kothari (2001), who find no statistically or economically significant association of these risk measures with derivatives use, conclude that for most firms even large derivative positions typically have a small effect on risk exposures. Thus, defining the impact of swaps on a firm's risk profile is an issue of ongoing debate and has not currently been explicitly defined.

Chapter 27 Credit Derivatives

1. Describe credit default swaps and their benefits for risk management in banking and finance.

    A credit default swap (CDS) is basically insurance against losses incurred by banks in the event that a borrower defaults on its debt obligations. The protection buyer pays a premium to the protection seller in exchange for a payment if the loan defaults. In the event of default, the buyer of the CDS receives compensation and the seller of the CDS takes possession of the defaulted loan. A CDS offers risk-sharing opportunities and eases the task of transferring risk. A CDS also involves low transaction costs in managing a hedged position.

2. With basis risk and unbiased futures markets, the optimal hedge with credit derivatives is a fixed proportion of the exposure. Discuss why this result is important for risk management in banking and finance.

    This result holds for all risk-averse financial and non-financial firms or institutions, irrespective of the underlying preferences and the joint probability distributions between the futures price and the spot price. No need exists to know the exact form of the risk preferences or the probability distributions involved: The optimal hedge policy is always a beta-hedge. Even pure risk minimizers want to hedge a fixed proportion of their exposure under these circumstances. Furthermore, the hedge ratio beta can be empirically estimated and be used to find a proper hedge instrument.

3. Discuss how hedge performance can be measured.

    The risk-reducing quality of a financial hedging instrument can be evaluated using the concept of hedging effectiveness. An index of hedging effectiveness is defined as one minus the ratio of the variance of profits with hedging, over the variance of profits without hedging. If a perfectly correlated financial hedging instrument is available, the index is equal to one. The presence of basis risk leads to a less than perfect hedge and thus the index of hedging effectiveness is less than one. Consequently the index is equal to the coefficient of determination between the change in the cash price and the change in the futures price.

4. Discuss why the use of credit derivatives by banks may be limited.

    Moral hazard and adverse selection problems make the market for credit derivatives illiquid. The lack of liquidity of the credit derivatives market for typical credit risks explains to some extent the limited use of credit derivatives for hedging loans.

5. Explain why a banking firm might consider the business cycle of the economy when devising its optimal hedging strategy with credit derivatives.

    Suppose that each state of nature yields both a profit level and a set of business opportunities in the economy. If utility is a function of profit only, the utility function will differ in each state of the economy, reflecting different business opportunities. Because preferences are state dependent, they systematically affect the optimal hedge ratio.

6. Market transparency in the credit market may be related to the bank's optimal loan and hedging transactions. Lower credit risk could be due to more market transparency and lead to a higher loan volume. Explain why this is not necessarily the case.

   The credit market tends to be more transparent if it is endowed with a more reliable information system about the risky loans. The model incorporates risk-sharing markets. That is, financial and non-financial institutions have access to a credit derivatives market in which they can hedge the risk of their loan portfolios conditional on the realization of the public signal. Higher market transparency in the financial market raises expected bank profits, but may lead to a higher or lower expected loan volume. With more transparency, a good signal becomes even better. Consequently, the loan volume of the bank increases. A bad signal becomes even worse in a more transparent credit market, and thus the loan supply of the bank declines. If the marginal cost of managing loans is increasing (concave), the transparency-induced expansion of the bank's portfolio of loans for good signals is larger than the information-induced contraction of the loan portfolio for bad signals. Therefore, the ex-ante expected loan volume goes up (down) if the marginal cost function is concave (convex).

Chapter 28 Foreign Exchange Derivatives in Frontier Markets

1. Discuss capital controls that could be beneficial to frontier and emerging economies.

   The International Monetary Fund (IMF) used to be the strongest supporter of dropping all capital controls and letting currencies float freely. On December 3, 2012, the IMF changed its position and dropped its opposition to capital controls. The IMF now views direct capital controls are acceptable to bring down market volatility caused by strong cross-border capital flows. The IMF's new position supports a temporarily and transparent usage of capital controls. The IMF still believes free movement of capital is beneficial, but acknowledges it could destabilize economies with underdeveloped financial systems. Before implementing capital controls, the IMF argues that other measures to limit rapid capital inflows have be implemented such as tightening fiscal policy, cutting interest rates, and letting the exchange rate fluctuate.

   Countries could largely benefit from free capital flows. The financial sector gains competitiveness due to capital inflow. On a global scale, capital flows tend to accomplish a better capital allocation that leads to higher growth rates and smooth adjustment of economic imbalances between countries. Important risks are also linked to capital flows. Flows can be volatile and can be substantial relative to the size of a country's financial markets or economy. This can lead to credit or asset prices inflation or deflation and can make countries more vulnerable to contagion from global instability.

2. Assume an offshore FX derivative market is unavailable for the Dominican Republic Peso (DOP) and a corporation approaches a commercial bank offshore to sell its

DOP revenues and buy USD. Determine the price of a one-year USD DOP FX non-deliverable forward (NDF) under the following assumptions:

- The withholding tax on investing in investments in DOP fixed income instruments is 10 percent.
- The yield of the current one-year Dominican Republic treasury bills is 9.50 percent.
- The one-year USD dollar rate is 0.40 percent.
- The same convention applies to DOP and USD rates.

If a market does not exist, pricing offshore NDFs will be based on arbitrage-free opportunities. Therefore, if a financial institution based offshore wants to replicate the carry priced in an FX derivative, it could do so by accessing onshore capital markets, assuming domestic financial regulation allows nonresidents to access local markets and make investments in the domestic currency. The local government bond curve is usually considered to be the local risk-free curve. The opportunity cost of replicating such a DOP investment would be the net return of the investment in pesos for a period of two years. Nonresidents usually have direct access to USD liquidity. The one-year USD rate of 0.40 percent serves as the cost of funding. The nonresident exchanges its dollars for pesos at the spot rate and invests the pesos for one-year before buying the USD back. The peso investment in one-year Treasury bills would generate a yield of 9.50 percent minus the withholding taxes of 10 percent that have to be paid on such investments. The true return of the investment in DOP is then 8.55 percent. The net yearly return of such investment would be 8.55 percent – 0.40 percent = 8.15 percent. This serves as the fair level of the yearly carry priced in the offshore non-deliverable forward.

Besides the simplified structure, two additional parameters must be considered. First, the Dominican bonds, which are used as a proxy for investments in the peso, exposes the holder of such instrument to the government default risk even if considered as the least risky investment domestically. This credit risk exposure is not translated in the pricing of the NDF because the latter does not embed a credit default risk but rather a counterparty risk that should be collateralized. Second, holding frontier currencies and fixed income instruments in a financial institution's balance sheet requires a substantial capital requirement. In an NDF, capital is required for the currency exposure only. In case of full investment in DOP domestically, capital is kept aside for the currency exposure as well as for the credit risk embedded in the domestic bonds and bills. Convertibility and local regulatory risks can have a substantial impact on domestic investments hence all these parameters will be included while fine-tuning proxy pricing.

3. Discuss why the existence of a well-developed capital market is considered a perquisite or at least a crucial parameter for the development of a derivative market.

A derivative is a contract that derives its value from the performance of the underlying instrument such as an asset, index, or interest rate. A derivative transaction is therefore priced using the market price of a single or a number of other tradable instruments. A well-established and liquid capital market where the underlying instruments are regularly and fairly priced allows a rational pricing of the derivative contract. If financial instruments are illiquid and rarely traded in existing capital markets, the derivative based on such instruments will most probably be illiquid and reflects some of the large risk premiums embedded in the underlying assets. Therefore, derivative market development is tightly linked to the derivative price makers' capacity to hedge their risks in the markets where exchange rate, interest rate, index or asset of the derivative are priced.

4. Summarize some of the factors driving differences between offshore and onshore yield curves.

Several factors lead to a difference between the offshore and onshore yield curves. First, capital controls imposed domestically prevent investors from buying reserve currencies such as the U.S. dollar for the purpose of capital transfer. Because the offshore market is not subject to such capital controls, lower yields are observed in these markets compared to the ones in the onshore and regulated markets in normal market circumstances. In crises times, given the high flexibility offered by offshore markets, yields tend to react much faster to negative news. Thus, interest rate volatility can be much higher compared to onshore rates volatility. Another factor making offshore yields differ from the onshore rates is the withholding tax applicable to onshore money market and bond investments. Many regulators impose taxes on returns from domestic investments while offshore markets are not subject to these financial obligations, usually resulting in lower yield. Another factor contributing to the misalignment between the onshore and offshore curves is the reserve requirement. Foreign investors are often required to hold unremunerated reserves requirements for investing in the onshore bond market. This situation leads to a lower net investment return. Offshore markets are not subject to this requirement hence yields are priced at a discount compared to the onshore ones. Finally, a central bank in a closed economy has more power to influence the local curve by adjusting the monetary policy rate and/or change the liquidity of the market.

Chapter 29 Risk Management and Financial Disasters

1. Discuss the two phases in which crises are usually divided.

The majority of the literature agrees in dividing crises into two phases: the run-up phase and the crisis phase. The structure of a crisis can be divided into a run-up phase, in which bubbles and imbalances form, and a crisis phase, during which risk that has built up in the background materializes and the crisis erupts. During the run-up phase, asset price bubbles and imbalances form. These imbalances typically build up slowly in the background and volatility is low. The public typically realizes that a bubble has formed when it is too late and that a small, insignificant event may work as a trigger of the crisis phase and generate panic directly proportional to the size of the bubble.

2. Define systemic risk and explain how it can be mitigated.

No widely accepted uniform definition of systemic risk is available. Some define systemic risk as the probability that cumulative losses will occur from an event that ignites a series of successive losses along a chain of financial institutions or markets comprising a system. Others define systemic risk as the potential for a modest economic shock to induce substantial volatility in asset prices, substantial reductions in corporate liquidity, potential bankruptcies, and efficiency losses. Still others define it as the risk of collapse of an entire financial system or market serious enough to quite probably have large adverse effects on the real economy. Regulation plays a fundamental role in mitigating systemic risk and regulators have released several new rules after the financial crisis of 2007–2008. However, improvements in the risk management function at most financial institutions are also needed.

3. Discuss the difference between economic capital and regulatory capital.

Correlation is mainly an exogenous factor that depends on the customer type, geography, and macroeconomic factors. Concentration is or should be the result of conscious decisions of financial institutions' senior management through a well-defined risk appetite framework. Optimal concentration limits cannot be defined without an appropriate measure of capital/risk concentration such as economic capital (EC), and correlations are the most important input for EC. Calculating regulatory capital (RC) (e.g., the Basel II Internal Rating Based Approach) requires using correlations, which are given by the regulator (e.g., Bank for International Settlements) and are equal for all banks.

4. Define the "Minsky moment" and discuss how this is important to identify crises.

The crisis phase starts when, after the gradual build-up of a bubble and the associated imbalances, a trigger event leads to the bursting of the bubble. Some refer to this sudden transition as a "Minsky moment." A Minsky moment can occur long after most market participants are aware, or at least suspicious, that a bubble has built up in the background.

5. Discuss the main objective of ERM.

Ideally, a good enterprise risk management (ERM) framework should be able to summarize all risks into one metric: the optimal level of available capital. The goal is to capture and quantify all risks employing a consistent approach and then aggregate individual risk exposures across the entire organization as well as analyzing the aggregate risk profile considering risk correlations.

6. Define risk appetite and discuss why financial institutions should focus on it.

Risk appetite translates risk metrics and methods into business decisions, reporting, and day-to-day business discussions. Risk appetite sets the boundaries forming a dynamic link among strategy, target setting, and risk management. As the primary concern of banks is risk management, the risk appetite helps the board of directors in designing the future growth strategy of the bank and ensuring strategic choice, not market demand, drives asset growth. Profitability and volatility of the assets are key inputs needed to define an effective risk appetite framework.

Chapter 30 The Future of Risk Management

1. Define regulatory risk and identify five major regulations that are likely to have the largest impact on the future of risk management.

    Regulatory risk arises from changes in laws and regulations that can materially affect a security, firm, industry, or market. Regulation is a source of uncertainty. Regulations that will most likely affect risk management practices in the near term include the Dodd-Frank Act, especially for asset managers, investment banks, and private banks. Solvency II will have the strongest impact on insurance companies and hedge funds. Two other key regulations affecting the European Union are UCITS III and AIFMD. Finally, the Basel III Accord will influence future risk management practices.

2. Define the two most common risk measures in terms of global use and describe differences between these measures including limitations and benefits.

    The two most common risk measures are VaR and stress testing. VaR gives the minimum or maximum expected loss for a given portfolio, probability, and time horizon. Stress testing involves creating a hypothetical scenario that includes a specific set of highly adverse financial or economic assumptions such as a deep recession. VaR is more commonly used in Asia and Europe than stress testing whereas the opposite occurs in North America. From an integration perspective, VaR is limited regarding investment decisions and asset allocation choices. These limitations may be a reason U.S. firms do not rely as heavily on VaR. The accuracy of VaR relies heavily on the accuracy of probability and time horizon assumptions. Thus, VAR can be difficult to validate because it can offer a wide array of values. VaR can also ignore positive scenarios and overemphasize negative scenarios. Even with negative scenarios, VaR often mitigates or does not consider the probability of extremely poor returns. VaR also lacks subadditivity. Consequently, a risk manager can increase total VaR by combining two different portfolios. This property of VaR is inconsistent with standard notions of diversification and risk.

    Unlike VaR, all assumptions for stress testing and the results are publicly disclosed. Stress testing is also an important method for managing systemic risk and a valuable source of supplementary information for insurance companies, investment banks, private banks, and even the Federal Reserve. Stress testing has three major benefits over other standard risk management methods. First, stress testing provides measures of capital that are more forward looking regarding future adequacy and are more robust to adverse developments such as global financial instability. Second, stress testing can be used to assess vulnerabilities on a micro level such as firm-wide risk and on a macro level such as industry-wide or market-wide risk. Third, stress testing provides critical information that can be disclosed to the public to increase investor confidence and to help firms better manage their risk exposures. Thus, stress testing is likely to play a vital role in the future of risk management.

3. Indicate whether derivatives are a risky or safe risk management tool and provide evidence that derivatives add value to a firm.

    Although derivative securities are safe risk management tools for competent and informed risk managers, they can be very dangerous if used carelessly. In the mid-1990s, derivatives garnered a risky connotation after several prominent losses due to their improper use. Even prominent investors such as Warren Buffett expressed concern about the potential danger of derivatives. Most current risk managers and investors use derivatives to manage risk and see the instruments as safe. The derivatives markets grew nearly 650 percent between 2001 and 2011 and are frequently adding new tools to the risk manager's toolbox.

From a value-added perspective, much research indicates that derivative products can increase the risk-adjusted returns of portfolios, especially when hedging against risks unique to a firm or industry. For example, research suggests that derivative hedging strategies have been effective in the utilities industry to reduce weather exposure, in the foreign currency market to reduce foreign exchange rate risk, and in the airline industry to reduce jet fuel exposure. However, some industries such as the U.S. oil and gas industry have been unable to substantially affect firm value by hedging risk with derivatives. Thus, derivatives can add value to a firm, but do not guarantee such an increase in value.

4. Discuss the unique characteristics of two risk management objectives on risk managers' wish lists.

Risk managers want to create a better risk culture and to create better integration of risk into the investment process. Creating a better risk culture involves establishing guidelines and expectations for appropriate risk taking and decision making for the entire firm. This is important to risk managers because evidence suggests that not all employees understand their roles in managing risk. Moreover, the risk management team and investment team often operate as separate divisions of the firm. Thus, creating a better risk culture allows risk managers to have a larger impact on important decisions within the firm.

The move toward integrated risk management includes providing an aggregate view of the different types of risk across the many different strategic areas of a firm. Yet, implementing an integrated risk management system is one of the most difficult challenges facing risk managers given the growing trend toward more complex financial markets. Integration is challenging because firms must create efficient risk management systems that effectively monitor many scenarios based on several different markets and several different risks.

Index